# THE
# LAW OF CORPORATE
# INSOLVENCY IN
# SCOTLAND

# THE
# LAW OF CORPORATE
# INSOLVENCY IN
# SCOTLAND

**John B St Clair** BA(Oxon), LLB (Glasgow), Advocate

*and*

**J E Drummond Young** QC, BA (Cantab),
LLB (Edinburgh), LLM (Harvard)

*Consultants: Dorman, Jeffrey & Co,*
*Solicitors in Glasgow and Edinburgh*

Second Edition

Edinburgh
Butterworths
1992

| | |
|---|---|
| United Kingdom | Butterworth & Co (Publishers) Ltd, 4 Hill Street, EDINBURGH EH2 3JZ, 88 Kingsway, LONDON WC2B 6AB |
| Australia | Butterworths Pty Ltd, SYDNEY, MELBOURNE, BRISBANE, ADELAIDE, PERTH, CANBERRA and HOBART |
| Belgium | Butterworth & Co (Publishers) Ltd, BRUSSELS |
| Canada | Butterworths Canada Ltd, TORONTO and VANCOUVER |
| Ireland | Butterworth (Ireland) Ltd, DUBLIN |
| Malaysia | Malayan Law Journal Sdn Bhd, KUALA LUMPUR |
| New Zealand | Butterworths of New Zealand Ltd, WELLINGTON and AUCKLAND |
| Puerto Rico | Equity de Puerto Rico, Inc, HATO REY |
| Singapore | Butterworth & Co (Asia) Pte Ltd, SINGAPORE |
| USA | Butterworth Legal Publishers, ST PAUL, Minnesota; SEATTLE, Washington; BOSTON, Massachusetts; AUSTIN, Texas and D & S Publishers, CLEARWATER, Florida |

A CIP Catalogue record for this book is available from the British Library.

ISBN 0 406 00910 4

Typeset by Phoenix Photosetting, Chatham, Kent
Printed and bound in Great Britain by Mackays of Chatham PLC, Chatham, Kent

# Preface

We have attempted in this book to write a comprehensive and up-to-date account of the law of corporate insolvency in Scotland. Since the publication of the first edition of the work there have been a large number of legal cases in this field, some of which have radically altered previous accepted understanding of the law, as well as statutory changes, such as the Companies Act 1989, which, when fully enacted, will be of wide-reaching significance.

Given the importance of these changes in the law, we were persuaded to undertake a second edition of our book. We also took the opportunity to expand it to include new material on debt subordination, securitisation, powers of attorney, security law generally, and finally a long chapter on the international dimensions of corporate insolvency – an important and fast evolving field, but not one, so far as we are aware, previously covered in Scotland. We have found the writing of the book exceedingly difficult and taxing, not least by the fact that the material is often to be found in diverse and abstruse locations, or in certain important instances, not reported at all. We have been given much help and encouragement, and must thank above all Dorman Jeffrey & Co, Solicitors, for acting as consultants throughout, and in particular Ian Cuthbertson, a registered insolvency practitioner and the partner leading their insolvency department. At all levels they have made a significant contribution – both in suggestions and criticisms, and in advising on how appreciated our efforts would be by those who have to operate in this complicated field.

The law is stated at 1 September 1992.

JOHN B ST CLAIR
JAMES DRUMMOND YOUNG

# Contents

# Abbreviations

Because this book contains references to cases decided in several jurisdictions, the authors list here the abbreviations used. This is followed by references to the major sources referred to.

REPORTS

| | |
|---|---|
| AC (preceded by date) | Law Reports, Appeal Cases, House of Lords and Privy Council |
| ACLC | Australian Law Cases 1982– |
| ACLR | Australian Current Law Review 1969–1971 |
| ACLR | Australian Company Law Reports 1974– |
| | Loose-leaf pages located in Paterson, W and Ednie, H, Australian Company Law Service, 2 edn, Bulletin volume, then from 1982 contained in booklets. Reprinted in bound volumes. |
| ALR | Australian Law Reports 1973– |
| All ER (preceded by date) | All England Law Reports, 1936–(current) (eg [1936] 2 All ER) |
| All ER Rep | All England Law Reports Reprint, 36 vols, 1843–1935 |
| App Cas | Law Reports, Appeal Cases, House of Lords, 15 vols, 1875–1890) |
| B & CR (preceded by date) | Reports of Bankruptcy and Companies Winding up Cases, 20 vols, 1918–1941 (eg [1918–1919] B & Cr) |
| B & S | Best and Smith's Reports, Queen's Bench, 10 vols, 1861–1870 |
| BCC | British Company Law Cases |
| BCLC | Butterworths Company Law Cases |
| Bankr & Ins R | Bankruptcy and Insolvency Reports, 2 vols, 1853–1855 |
| CB(NS) | Common Bench Reports, New Series, 20 vols, 1856–1865 |
| CLY (preceded by date) | Current Law Year Book, 1947–(current) |
| CMLR (preceded by date) | Common Market Law Reports, 1962–(current) (eg [1962] CMLR) |
| Ch (preceded by date) | Law Reports, Chancery Division, since 1890 (eg [1891] 1 Ch) |
| Ch App | Law Reports, Chancery Appeals, 10 vols, 1865–1875 |
| Ch D | Law Reports, Chancery Division, 45 vols, 1875–1890 |
| D | Dunlop, Court of Session Cases (Scotland), 2nd Series, 24 vols, 1838–1862 |
| DLR | Dominion Law Reports (Canada), 1912–1955 |
| DLR (2d) | Dominion Law Reports, Second Series (Canada), 1956–1968 |
| DLR (3d) | Dominion Law Reports, Third Series (Canada), 1969–1984 |
| DLR (4th) | Dominion Law Reports, Fourth Series (Canada), 1984–(current) |
| ECR (preceded by date) | European Court Reports |
| EG | Estates Gazette, 1858–(current) |
| EGLR | Estates Gazette Law Reports 1985–(current) |
| Eq Rep | Equity Reports, 3 vols, 1853–1855 |
| F | Fraser, Court of Session Cases (Scotland), 5th series, 8 vols, 1898–1906 |
| FTLR | Financial Times Law Reports |
| Gl & J | Glyn and Jameson's Reports, Bankruptcy, 2 vols, 1819–1828 |
| GWD | Green's Weekly Digest |
| HLC | Clark's Reports, House of Lords, 11 vols, 1847–1866 |
| HKLR | Hong Kong Law Reports |
| IR (preceded by date) | Irish Reports, since 1893 (eg [1894] 1 IR) |
| KB (preceded by date) | Law Reports, King's Bench Division, 53 vols, 1901–1952 (eg [1901] 2 KB) |
| LJ Ch | Law Journal, Chancery, 1931–1946 |
| LJKB or QB | Law Journal, King's Bench or Queen's Bench, 1831–1946 |
| LJPC | Law Journal, Privy Council, 1865–1946 |

| | |
|---|---|
| LJR (preceded by date) | Law Journal Reports, 1947–1949 (eg [1947] LJR) |
| Lloyd's MCLQ | Lloyd's Maritime and Commercial Law Quarterly |
| LR Eq | Law Reports, Equity Cases, 20 vols, 1965–1875 |
| M | Macpherson, Court of Session (Scotland), 3rd series, 11 vols, 1862–1873 |
| Macq | Macqueen's Scotch Appeals, House of Lords, 4 vols, 1849–1865 |
| Mor | Morison's Dictionary of Decisions, Court of Session (Scotland), 43 vols, 1532–1808 |
| NLJ | New Law Journal, 1965–(current) |
| OB & F | Ollivier Bell and Fitzgerald's Reports (New Zealand), 1 vol, 1878–1880 |
| QB | Queen's Bench Reports (Adolphus and Ellis, New Series), 18 vols, 1841–1852 |
| QB (preceded by date) | Law Reports, Queen's Bench Division, 1891–1900; and since 1952 (eg [1891] 1 QB) |
| QBD | Law Reports, Queen's Bench Division, 25 vols, 1875–1890 |
| OJ | Official Journal of the European Communities |
| OJLS | Oxford Journal of Legal Studies |
| Qd R | Queensland Reports, 1958–(current) |
| R | Rettie, Court of Session Cases (Scotland), 4th series, 25 vols, 1872–1898 |
| S | Shaw, Court of Session Cases (Scotland), 1st series, 16 vols, 1821–1838 |
| SC (preceded by date) | Court of Session Cases (Scotland), since 1906 (eg 1906 SC) |
| SC (HL) (preceded by date) | Court of Session Cases (Scotland) (House of Lords), since 1906 (eg 1906 SC (HL)) |
| SCLR | Scottish Civil Law Reports |
| SLT | Scots Law Times, 1893–(current) |
| TLR | The Times Law Reports, 71 vols, 1884–1950 |
| TLR (preceded by date) | The Times Law Reports, 1951–1952 (eg [1951] 1 TLR) |
| UCR | Upper Canada Reports, King's Bench, 6 vols, 1831–1844; Queen's Bench, 46 vols, 1844–1881; Common Pleas, 32 vols, 1850–1882 |
| WLR | Weekly Law Reports |
| WN (preceded by date) | Law Reports Weekly Notes, 1866–1952 (eg [1866] WN) |

## SOURCES

| | |
|---|---|
| Anton | *Private International Law*, by A E Anton, 2nd edn, Edinburgh, 1991 |
| Bell, *Comm.* | *Commentaries on the Law of Scotland and the Principles of Mercantile Jurisprudence*, by G J Bell, 7th edn, by John McLaren, 2 vols, Edinburgh, 1870–71 |
| Bell, *Prin* | *Principles of the Law of Scotland*, by G J Bell, 10th edn, by W Guthrie, Edinburgh, 1899 |
| Dicey and Morris | *The Conflict of Laws*, by A V Dicey, 11th edn, by Lawrence Collins and others, London, 1987 |
| Erskine | *An Institute of the Law of Scotland*, by John Erskine, 8th edn, by J B Nicholson, 2 vols, Edinburgh, 1870 |
| Erskine, *Prin.* | *Principles of the Law of Scotland*, by John Erskine, 21st edn, by Sir John Rankine, Edinburgh, 1991 |
| Gloag | *Law of Contract*, by W M Gloag, 2nd edn, Edinburgh, 1929 |
| Gloag & Irvine | *Law of Rights in Security*, by W M Gloag and J M Irvine, Edinburgh, 1897 |
| Goudy, *Bankruptcy* | *A Treatise on the Law of Bankruptcy in Scotland*, by H Goudy, 4th edn, Edinburgh, 1914 |
| McBryde | *The Law of Contract in Scotland*, by William W McBryde, Edinburgh, 1987 |
| Stair | *The Institutions of the Law of Scotland*, by Viscount Stair, 2nd edn, 1693, reprinted, edited by D M Walker, Edinburgh and Glasgow, 1981 |
| Graham Stewart | *Law of Diligence*, by J Graham Stewart, Edinburgh, 1898 |
| Wilson | *The Scottish Law of Debt*, 2nd edn, by Professor W A Wilson, Edinburgh, 1991 |

# Table of statutes

# Table of orders, rules and regulations

# Table of cases

PAGE

Chapter 1

# Historical background and theory

## Introduction

With the coming into force of the Insolvency Act 1986 and attendant legislation, the law relating to the insolvency of companies in Scotland was radically
reformed. This legislation was the most significant change in the field since
the Companies Act 1856 allowed limited liability to joint stock companies in
Scotland. The new law came into force on 29 December 1986, and tried to
give a clear statutory framework. However, the new law cannot in any sense
be said to provide a comprehensive legal code. The new law has to draw on
decisions of the Scottish courts going back centuries.

A feature of the new law is that, to a minor extent, it applies only to
windings up which have commenced after 29 December 1986[1]. This means
that windings up started before 29 December 1986, and in certain aspects
before 1 April 1986, are still largely to be conducted under the old procedures,
and subject to the old law even where it has been repealed. The effect is that
for some years to come, the old and the new law will be operating in tandem.
Accordingly, this book will try to describe both the old and the new law.
Because, however, the new law has largely displaced the old in practice, the
new law is given primary place and the old law is commented on by footnotes
or briefly in text, if that does not interrupt it.

The scheme of this Chapter is:

(a)  in Part I to give a brief history of corporate insolvency law in Scotland
     bringing out some of the most important historical differences between
     Scottish and English law;
(b)  in Part II to look at the legal and economic thinking behind the current
     reforms;
(c)  in Part III to give a brief chart of the new legislation, with commence-
     ment dates and important repeals and show how the legal jigsaw fits
     together; and
(d)  in Part IV to give some comments on the workings of the new legislation.

## I. HISTORY OF CORPORATE INSOLVENCY LAW IN SCOTLAND

### Early history

Until the nineteenth century Companies Acts, there were two ways by which
companies were brought into existence – (a) by Act of the Scottish and then

1  See Insolvency Act 1986, Sch 11, para 4(1).

the United Kingdom Parliament or by Royal Charter (or its equivalent, *viz.* Letters Patent from the Sovereign); and (b) by private association. There was no procedure for the registration of companies, which is the modern procedure.

## (1) *Act of Parliament and Royal Charter*

Until the growth of trade in the eighteenth century, most commercial activity was carried on by individual merchants or by partnerships. There were however certain areas of national concern where the investment of a large amount of capital was necessary, such as foreign trade and banking. When companies were set up for these purposes they were usually incorporated either under Act of Parliament or under Royal Charter. Transferability and transmissibility of the shares (ie they could be sold or bequeathed) were accepted necessary conditions of their corporate personality. As regards limitation of liability – at all events after 1707 – it was not even thought competent for the Crown to incorporate by charter except with limited liability since a charter providing for unlimited liability would have been *ultra vires* of the royal prerogative without the consent of Parliament. Companies incorporated by Act of Parliament or Royal Charter were also usually given a legally enforceable monopoly, which was seen as a necessary protection for the shareholders.

The Darien Company and the Bank of Scotland, for example, were incorporated by Acts of the Scots Parliament in 1695. The Darien was incorporated for the purpose of trading with Africa and the Indies and setting up a Scottish colony in Panama. It has been estimated that as much as one-third of Scottish savings were invested in it. Its total failure, including 2,000 lives lost, was a national disaster and convinced many of the economic necessity of a merger of Scotland and England[1]. The Bank of Scotland, on the other hand, has survived to this day. The Royal Bank of Scotland had an Act of Incorporation in 1719 followed by a Royal Charter in 1727, and also still survives as an independent company. Both these banks had transferability, transmissibility and limited liability from the beginning, although without statutory monopoly.

## (2) *Voluntary associations*

Appreciation of the advantages attaching to trading as joint stock companies, with official management and interests freely transferable, as exemplified by the statutory and chartered corporations, led to attempts in England and Scotland to achieve the same results by voluntary association – with differing results in the two Kingdoms.

---

1 In 1707 one of the last acts of the Scottish Parliament, as it sat on to wind up its affairs after the Treaty of Union with England, was to recommend William Paterson to Queen Anne for his 'good service' in helping to draft the trade and finance articles of the Treaty of Union and calculate the Equivalent. Paterson was the founder of the Bank of England – adopted by the English Parliament in 1694 – and inventor of the English national debt. He was also architect of the Darien scheme. The Equivalent was a key financial inducement in the Treaty – £398,085 10s. – which was to be paid by England to Scotland as a one-off capital compensation payment for the part of the Scottish revenue to be appropriated to service the English national debt. First priority claim on the Equivalent after currency adjustment was payment in full of the £250,000 invested in the Darien Company with accrued interest at five per cent.

English law recognised no half-way house between full incorporation under statute or charter and a loose association of individuals. There was no such thing in England as the legal personality of a partnership, as distinct from its component members[1] let alone a non-statutory joint stock company with limited liability. Even holding an organisation out to be a company was illegal, and a creditor could immediately go against any member of the partnership or association for debt and without first constituting the debt against the partnership.

In Scotland, in contrast, where a partnership had legal personality, a debt had to be first constituted against the partnership, and if the partnership's assets could not satisfy the debt, the creditor could then go against the partners.

The fact that in England joint stock companies were not recognised in law, like the chartered companies with limited liability, meant that subscribers to shares in unincorporated joint stock companies became immediately liable for the total debts of these companies. Despite their illegality and unlimited liability in England, however, there was a rush of joint stock companies and a mania of speculation, fraudulent prospectuses and crashed companies at the beginning of the eighteenth century. This led to the Bubble Act 1720. Its preamble described what had been going on: 'Whereas in many cases, undertakers or subscribers have presumed to act as if they were corporate bodies, and have pretended to make their shares transferable or assignable without legal authority, either by Act of Parliament, or Charter from the Crown.' It enacted that all such undertakings or attempts were to be deemed 'illegal' and 'void', and put down as 'common and public nuisances'.

Although the Bubble Act extended to Scotland, joint stock companies continued to flourish. The Act seems to have been pled only twice in the Scottish courts. In the case of the 'Masons of Lanark'[2] it was pled, but the court disposed of the questions raised without reference to the Act. In *MacAndrew v Robertson*[3], it was held that the Act did not apply to a company – although it was managed by directors and had shares which were transferable on certain conditions.

Both the Royal Bank of Scotland and the British Linen Company, which was incorporated by letters patent in 1746, seem to have been preceded by some form of joint stock company. Probably the fact that a partnership had legal personality in Scotland served as a useful model for the development by the common law of the legal personality of the joint stock company. The Act of 1825[4], which coincided with the virtual repeal of the Bubble Act[5] in that year, vouched for their success. It stated that the practice had prevailed in Scotland of instituting societies having joint stocks with shares either transferable or conditionally transferable for the 'purpose of carrying on banking and other commercial concerns, many of which had transacted business for a number of years, to the great advantage of that country'. (A parliamentary return printed in the following year lists no fewer than 32 unchartered Scottish banks.) Joint stock companies, engaged in activities other than banking, were also common.

1 See Sir William Holdsworth, *History of English Law* (3rd edn), vols 8 and 15.
2 (1730) Mor 14555.
3 (1828) 6 S 950.
4 6 Geo 4 c 131.
5 6 Geo 4 c 91.

## *Arran Fishing Company* and *Douglas Bank* cases

### *Arran Fishing Company case*

A good example of the typical Scottish joint stock company of the period was probably the Arran Fishing Company whose affairs were brought out in the case of *Stevenson & Co v MacNair* in 1757[1]. The Arran Fishing Company had been formed by 40 people in order to advance the fishing trade at the mouth of the Clyde and in the Western Isles. Each subscriber paid £50 making a total stock of £2,000. The trade was to be carried on by directors mentioned in the deed of association, with one clause giving the directors the power 'to give such orders and directions concerning the stock and employment of the whole of the company's affairs as to them should seem meet which should be binding on the partners to the extent of their respective subscriptions until such orders or directions should be altered by general meeting . . . provided, nevertheless, that nothing herein contained shall be understood to import a power to the directors to compel any partner or subscriber to pay or contribute any more money to the stock than the sum by him subscribed'.

In the case, the pursuers, Stevenson and Company of the Rope Work at Port Glasgow who had supplied £72 worth of ropes, brought a case, not against the company or the partners in general, but against two or three partners who were monied men, 'being advised that each and all of the partners were liable conjunctly and severally'. The defence was: (1) that all the partners, or at least the directors representing the partners, should have been called as defenders; and (2) that the directors could not, by contracting debt, subject to liability any of the partners beyond the funds severally subscribed by them; and that the defenders, having paid into the company the whole sum subscribed by them, were not further liable.

The court waived giving judgment on the second defence but upheld the defenders on the first defence on the grounds that all parties having an interest were not called into the field, or in the words of the Lord President, 'that in all societies, there is no bringing the partners into Court without calling either the managers or the whole partners'. The second defence in relation to the limiting of liability came up in front of the court again a month later. The Lord Ordinary did not uphold the second defence but found the defenders liable, conjunctly and severally. The Whole Court, however, unanimously altered the Lord Ordinary's judgment and, according to Kames, sustained the defence upon the following grounds:

'There is an obvious difference between the present case and that of a company trading without reference to a stock. In the latter case, each partner must be liable in solidum for the company's debts, for there is nothing here to limit the credit, and if the partner be liable at all, he must be liable in solidum. In the present case, the managers are liable for the debts they contract, and each partner is liable to make good his subscription. But upon what medium can he be made further liable? Not upon the common law, for he has neither contracted the debt nor given authority to contract beyond his stock. The very meaning of confining the trade by a joint stock is that each should be liable for his subscription and no further . . . with respect to equity, Grotius justly observes (1.2,c ii s 13) "that it is not expedient to make partners further liable, because it would deter everyone from entering into a trading company". To show the inexpediency and even absurdity of making each

1 Mor 14560 and 14467; Kam Sel No 135; 5 Brown Sup 340; and Bell's *Commentaries*, ii, 517 and 518.

partner liable for the whole debts of a company, having a joint stock, consider only the Whale Fishing Company composed of a vast number of partners for the subscription of £35 each. According to the interlocutor pronounced by the Lord Ordinary, any one partner loaded with the whole debts of the company might be crushed to atoms in a moment.'

For many years, the *Arran Fishing Company* case was regarded as fixing the law in favour of limited liability in the case of joint stock companies. Professor Bell, in his treatment of joint stock companies in the *Commentaries*, accepted the view as sound in law[1]. Adam Smith, writing 20 years later, regarded each partner 'being bound only for his share', as one of the characteristic features of the joint stock company in Scotland[2].

### Douglas Bank case

The judgment in the Arran Fishing Company case, however, was not followed when the question came before the court again in 1778 by the failure of the Douglas Bank[3]. The matter was complicated by the fact that the question was at the instance of the company, which called upon certain members to furnish contributions for the liquidation of the banking indebtedness of the concern in excess of their subscription; that the company, while trading indifferently as the 'Douglas Bank' and the 'Ayr Bank' was really carried on under the social name of 'Douglas, Heron and Company'; and that it was possible to regard the provision in the deed as to contribution of a certain amount of capital as merely providing for the original contribution of the partners and not as the subscription of a certain defined amount to the stock. The *Arran Fishing Company* case does not seem to have been considered by the court which held the partners, who were sued personally, jointly and severally liable to pay the further sums called for by the company.

### Pressure for reform

From the date of the *Douglas Bank* case until 1856 the fact of unlimited liability of members of joint stock companies seems to have been accepted as a matter of course. Each shareholder was liable for the whole debts of a company. Sir Walter Scott was ruined by the failure of Ballantynes' in 1825. The Mercantile Law Commission in their report in 1854 accepted unlimited liability as a fact without question[4]. The growing necessities, however, of a rapidly developing trade and the example of foreign nations at length created a pressure in favour of reform and the introduction of limited liability in the modern sense, although the Mercantile Law Commission in 1854 recommended against its introduction. The matter came to Parliament as a Bill for Limitation of Liability and was passed by large majorities in 1855. Limited liability did not extend to Scotland until the following year.

### Limited Liability Act of 1855

The Limited Liability Act passed on 18 August 1855[5], introduced limited liability by the very simple measure of limiting the liability of a shareholder

1 Bell (5th edn, 1826), ii, 628.
2 *Wealth of Nations*, Book V, chap i, pt 3; (Bohn's edn), ii, 261.
3 Douglas, Heron & Co v Alexander Hair (1778) Mor 14605.
4 1854 Report, Lord Curriehill's Memorandum, p 11 of app.
5 18 & 19 Vict c 133.

upon execution against him (in default of the company) to the portion of his shares not paid up, and providing that execution should only issue against a shareholder by leave of the court in which action or proceeding had been brought[1]. Lord Palmerston said in discussing the measure in Committee:

'My own opinion is – and no one denies it – that these Bills are of the utmost interest and importance . . . I will say in a few words that I consider that this contest lies between the few and the many. It is just one of those instances in which, I won't say the prejudices, but in which the opinions of the few are to be set against the interests of the great bulk of the community. There is nothing, I am persuaded, that would tend more to the general advantage of the public and the setting free of capitals, as these Bills propose to do, that they may be turned to profitable employment. The present law prevents that being done. There is consequently a great quantity of small capital locked up which if these Bills were passed might be employed for the benefit of those who possess them, and also for the advantage of the community at large.'[2]

The Bill as originally drafted applied only to companies having a nominal capital of £50,000 divided into shares of a nominal value of not less than £25 each. The capital requirement was reduced when the Bill passed into law. The main ground of opposition to limited liability was that it would be a 'rogues' charter', enabling Victorian 'bandit' firms to defraud creditors. The original high capital requirement had been an attempt to deny the privilege of limited liability to the small business sector, where the fraudulent abuse of limited liability at the expense of creditors was most to be expected, and indeed has been prevalent, until the present day. However, the counter-argument that this restriction would make the privilege of limited liability even worse – a rich man's charter – won the day.

### Companies Acts 1856 and 1862/winding up

The principle of limited liability was extended to Scotland by the Companies Act 1856[3] which first introduced companies constituted in the modern manner by memorandum and articles of association. However, it was the Companies Act 1862 which really laid down the foundations upon which all modern legislation relating to companies has been built. It introduced the concept of the company with limited liability available upon complying with the statutory formality of registration. It also provided a modern régime for dealing with a company which became insolvent. Briefly it provided:

(1)   a company might be wound up voluntarily whenever the members had resolved that the company could not, by reason of its liabilities, continue in business and that it was advisable to wind up. The liquidator in such a voluntary winding up was appointed by the members and its proceedings were conducted without any representation on the part of the creditors (a distinction was not made, nor was it to be made for another 67 years until the 1929 Act, between the concept of the members' (solvent) liquidation and the creditors' (insolvent) liquidation);

(2)   if the company had resolved to be wound up voluntarily, the court might

---

1  s 8.
2  *Hansard*, Vol 139, ser 3, cols 1389, 1390.
3  19 & 20 Vict c 47.

make an order directing that the voluntary winding up should continue, 'but subject to such supervision of the Court, and with such liberty for creditors, contributories, or others to apply to the Court, and generally upon such terms and subject to such conditions as the Court thinks just';

(3)   a company might be wound up by the court in certain circumstances, such as the company was 'unable to pay its debts'; a company was 'deemed to be unable to pay its debts' in three particular cases:

(a)  whenever a creditor served on the company at its registered office a written demand requiring the company to pay any sum due, and the company had, for the space of three weeks, 'neglected to pay such sum, or to secure or compound for the same to the reasonable satisfaction of the creditor';

(b)  whenever an execution on a judgment obtained by a creditor against the company had been returned unsatisfied in whole or in part;

(c)  whenever it was proved to the satisfaction of the court that the company was unable to pay its debts.

Where the company was wound up by the court, the person appointed to assist the court and to administer the proceedings, was called an 'official liquidator'. There was also power, where an order for the winding up of a company subject to supervision of the court was subsequently superseded by an order directing the company to be wound up compulsorily, to appoint the voluntary liquidator to be official liquidator.

Not all companies registered with limited liability. Apart from the chartered banks which had limited liability, the other banks[1] took the view that unlimited liability was good for public confidence. The City of Glasgow Bank was in that position when it collapsed in 1878. Its liabilities stood at £12,400,000[2] with assets of £7,200,000. Advances stood at 132.7 per cent of deposits. The shareholders, in addition to the loss of their paid up capital, had to find another £4,400,000. Calls totalling £2,750 per shareholder were made. Only 254 of the 1,819 shareholders avoided bankruptcy, although depositors were eventually paid. All the directors were charged in the High Court in Edinburgh – a Glasgow jury being thought too biased – of fraudulently uttering false balance sheets. They were all found guilty and imprisoned.

It is still not compulsory for companies to register with limited liability; unlimited liability companies are still registered notwithstanding the City of Glasgow Bank disaster. There is provision in Part V of the Insolvency Act 1986 for the winding up of unregistered companies and in terms of section 226(2) of that Act, a contributory is liable for all the debts of the company including winding-up expenses.

---

1  Like Lloyd's of London today, or the bodies who control the provision of accounting and legal services and deny their members the full benefits of incorporation with limited liability which those providing banking services enjoy. Lloyd's is now reviewing its unlimited liability in the face of staggering underwriting losses, spread unevenly among its members. In the case of the leading accounting firms and legal firms, which are structured so that the partners are not only more numerous, but collectively more highly paid than the boards of any UK listed company, it is thought that the risks of unlimited liability are becoming too great. The exposure of Price Waterhouse, Ernst and Young and Allen and Overy arising out of the collapse of BCCI runs potentially to thousands of millions of dollars.

2  These figures should be multiplied by about 30 times to achieve today's values.

## Floating charges and receivers

The Scottish common law never managed to invent a 'floating charge'. A floating charge is a legal instrument which gives security over corporeal moveable property (ie physical assets). In common law this is contrary to the principle of Scottish law that security over such property cannot be created without delivery of the property. The floating charge came to Scotland from England where it was devised by the Court of Chancery in the 1860s. Its three principal characteristics were as follows:

(1) it is a charge on a class of assets of a company specified in the charge both present and future;
(2) those assets are of a kind which, in the ordinary course of business of a company, would be changing from time to time; and
(3) it is contemplated that, until some step is taken by or on behalf of those interested in the charge, the company may carry on its business in the ordinary way, and dispose of all or any of those assets in the ordinary course of business.

The floating charge as devised by the English Court of Chancery was, therefore, an equitable charge on present and future assets. It was quickly adopted by the English financial community because it gave an easy security upon the entire undertaking of the borrowing company, thus conferring maximum security upon the lender, while at the same time permitting the borrowing company complete freedom to deal with and dispose of its assets in the ordinary course of business.

Recognition of the usefulness of the floating charge as a financial instrument led to it being introduced to Scotland by statute, by the Companies (Floating Charges) (Scotland) Act 1961. Soon, however, it was recognised that the reform introduced by floating charges would not succeed unless the English idea of receivership, a mechanism for enforcing a security, was also transplanted.[1] Scotland had no institution of a receiver or any office of 'official receiver'. Without the appointment of a 'receiver', the only way the holder of a floating charge could enforce his security was to petition for the winding up of the company. Receivers were accordingly introduced to Scotland by the Companies (Floating Charges and Receivers) (Scotland) Act 1972. There is still no office of 'official receiver' in Scotland.

English and Scottish law prohibiting corporate bodies from acting as receivers is not changed by the new legislation[2], although this prohibition has come in for serious criticism[3]. Scottish law also still prohibits a partnership being appointed as a receiver[4], which cannot arise in England where a firm or partnership is not held to have legal personality.

1 See Scottish Law Commission Report, Cmnd 4336 (1970), para 38.
2 Insolvency Act 1986, ss 30 and 51.
3 See Gower, *Principles of Modern Company Law* (4th edn, 1979), p 488.
4 Insolvency Act 1986, s 51(3).

# II. THINKING BEHIND REFORM OF LAW

## Background to insolvency law reform

The need for law reform had been recognised for many years. The Scottish Law Commission published major reports in recent years dealing with the Scottish law of insolvency[1].

In England an advisory committee was appointed in 1973 under Sir Kenneth Cork to report on the implications of the draft EEC Bankruptcy Convention. This committee reported in 1976[2]. The committee highlighted the need for reform of the domestic insolvency laws. Subsequently the Secretary of State for Trade and Industry announced the setting up of a review committee in October 1976 on insolvency law and practice[3]. The committee again was established in January 1977, again under the chairmanship of Sir Kenneth Cork. Its remit was nothing short of a total review of all aspects of personal and corporate insolvency. Its terms of reference were:

(1)  to review the law and practice relating to insolvency, bankruptcy, liquidation and receivership in England and Wales and to consider what reforms were necessary or desirable;
(2)  to examine the possibility of formulating a comprehensive insolvency system and the extent to which existing procedures might, with advantage, be harmonised and integrated;
(3)  to suggest possible less formal procedures as alternatives to bankruptcy and company winding-up proceedings in appropriate circumstances; and
(4)  to make recommendations.

The committee considered representations from Scottish bodies and issued their final report in June 1982[4].

## Recommendations of Scottish Law Commission

The Scottish Law Commission dealt mostly with personal insolvency. Where they dealt with corporate insolvency, such as in their recommendations with regard to (a) gratuitous alienations and (b) unfair preferences, the recommendations have largely been acted upon. A further main recommendation, that, where possible, the law in relation to bankruptcy and liquidation should be harmonised, has also been followed to a large extent. Examples of the harmonisation are:

(1)  **Unfair preferences** – harmonised by section 36 of the Bankruptcy (Scotland) Act 1985 and section 243 of the Insolvency Act 1986.

(2)  **Gratuitous alienations** – harmonised by section 34 of the Bankruptcy (Scotland) Act 1985 and section 242 of the Insolvency Act 1986.

---

1 Memorandum No 16 on *Insolvency, Bankruptcy and Liquidation in Scotland* in 1971; and *Report on Bankruptcy and Related Aspects of Insolvency and Liquidation* in 1982 (Scot Law Com No 68).
2 Cmnd 6602.
3 *Hansard*, HC Deb Vol 918, (Oct 1976), written answer no 20.
4 Cmnd 8558.

(3) **Effects of diligence** – harmonised by section 37(1)–(6) of the Bankruptcy (Scotland) Act 1985 and section 185(1)(a) of the Insolvency Act 1986.

(4) **Management and realisation of assets** – harmonised by section 39(3), (4), (7) and (8) of the Bankruptcy (Scotland) Act 1985 and section 185(1)(b) of the Insolvency Act 1986.

(5) **Preferential debts** – broadly harmonised by Schedule 6 to the Insolvency Act 1986 which lists the preferential debts in winding up and Schedule 3 to the Bankruptcy (Scotland) Act of 1985 which lists preferential debts in bankruptcy.

(6) **Criminal offence in relation to producing false claims or evidence** – section 22(5) and (10) of the Bankruptcy (Scotland) Act 1985.

(7) **Further evidence in relation to claims** – section 48(5), (6) and (8), together with sections 44(2) and (3) and 47(1) as applied by those sections of the Bankruptcy (Scotland) Act 1985.

(8) **Adjudication of claims** – section 49 of the Bankruptcy (Scotland) Act 1985.

(9) **Entitlement to vote and draw dividend** – section 50 of the Bankruptcy (Scotland) Act 1985.

(10) **Liabilities and rights of co-obligants** – section 60 of the Bankruptcy (Scotland) Act 1985.

(11) **Determination of amount of creditor's claim** – Schedule 1, except paras 2, 4, and 6, to the Bankruptcy (Scotland) Act 1985.

All applied to liquidations by rule 4.16 of the Insolvency (Scotland) Rules 1986

(12) **Accounting periods, taxation of accounts, unclaimed dividends** – sections 52, 53, and 58 of the Bankruptcy (Scotland) Act 1985 applied to liquidations by rule 4.68 of the Insolvency (Scotland) Rules 1986.

Against this harmonisation of the statutory provisions in relation to personal and corporate insolvency, it must be remembered that there is an important difference between the objectives of the personal and corporate insolvency laws. In the case of the individual insolvent, society is primarily concerned to relieve him from the harassment of his creditors and enable him to regain financial stability with a fresh start, whereas in the case of an insolvent company, the objective is the dissolution of the company after its assets have been used to pay off its creditors and shareholders. Society has no interest in the preservation or rehabilitation of the company as such, though it may have a legitimate concern for the preservation of the commercial enterprise[1]. Despite the different objectives of the two branches of insolvency law, however, and the different procedures, the principles of law are often indistinguishable in relation to the actings of the insolvent person or insolvent

---

1 See Cork Report, Cmnd 8558, Chap 4.

company prior to formal proceedings[1]. This will be apparent from the number of cases which will be cited, which the courts have used almost interchangeably as authority for insolvency law principles common to both branches of the law.

## Cork Committee recommendations

The Cork Committee Report contained 'numerous recommendations, and many of them radical and far reaching', to use its own words. Its most radical recommendations were:

### (1) *10 per cent fund*

The Cork Committee pointed out that there was widespread dissatisfaction with the way that holders of floating charges were often in a position to attach for the holder of the floating charge the whole assets of a company, leaving no surplus funds for ordinary creditors. This also deterred ordinary creditors from participating in the winding up. The committee accordingly recommended that a fund equal to 10 per cent of the net realisations of assets subject to a floating charge should be made available for distribution among the ordinary creditors. This recommendation was not accepted by the Government or passed by Parliament.

### (2) *Crown preference*

The Cork Committee approved the comments of Lord Anderson in the Scottish case of *Admiralty v Blair's Trustee* in 1916 SC at page 248. Lord Anderson had expressed the view that it was unjust that the Crown should have preference in insolvency for its debts at the expense of the individual creditor. Lord Anderson rejected the principle of Crown preference for the following reasons:

'In the first place, because the principle is inequitable. In the case of *Palmer* Lord Macnaughten justifies the doctrine on the ground that its assertion results in the benefit of the general community (that is, the general body of taxpayers) although at the expense of the individual. I should have thought this was a reason for condemning the principle. Why should individuals be made to suffer for the general good, especially in a case like the present, where the general is infinitesimal but the individual loss substantial? In the second place, this alleged prerogative is hostile to the general policy of the Bankruptcy Acts, which aim at equal treatment of all creditors in the matter of the distribution of the estates of a bankrupt.'

The Cork Committee proposed the abolition of Crown preference in relation to unpaid tax. The Government resisted efforts to cut down the Crown's privileged position as a preferential creditor for unpaid tax, but Parliament overrode the Government's proposals and amended the Bill so as to eliminate Crown preference in respect of taxes assessed upon the company directly as taxpayer to the Inland Revenue[2]. The Cork Committee also proposed the abolition of VAT preference, which the Scottish Law Commission had also

---

1 See *Bank of Scotland v Liqrs of Hutchison, Main & Co Ltd* 1914 SC (HL) 1 at 3.
2 See Insolvency Act 1986, Sch 6.

proposed in its recommendations in relation to bankruptcy (see para 15.8 of the 1982 Report). This recommendation was not accepted but Parliament again overrode the Government and reduced the preferential treatment of VAT to that attributable within a six-month period as opposed to a 12-month period for other debts due to Customs and Excise.

### (3) *Local rates*

Both the Cork Committee and the Scottish Law Commission recommended the abolition of preference for local rates. This was rejected by the Government but passed by Parliament[1].

### (4) *Company administrators*

The Cork Committee was of the view that, where there was no floating charge giving a receiver power to take charge of an ailing company, in a significant number of cases companies have been forced into liquidation, and potentially viable businesses capable of being rescued have been closed down for want of a floating charge under which a receiver and manager could have been appointed. Accordingly the Cork Committee proposed a new insolvency procedure known as 'administration order procedure' which would enable the management of a failed or failing company to be placed under the control of an administrator for a period of time with a view to securing the survival of as much of the company as could be saved, or alternatively, the most orderly and advantageous realisation of its assets as could be achieved.

This recommendation contained in Chap 9 of the Cork Report was accepted by the Government and is now made law in sections 8–27 of the Insolvency Act 1986.

### (5) *Voluntary arrangements*

The Cork Committee was of the view that the arrangements available whereby a company would be able to effect an arrangement with its creditors were defective. The system was cumbersome and it was difficult to get the requisite majorities of votes of the creditors in order to bind them all. The Cork Committee proposed a procedure whereby a company would be able to effect formal and binding arrangements with its creditors subject only to a majority vote of the creditors without any need for any sanction of the court. This proposal, contained in Chap 7 of the Cork Report, was accepted in part by the Government and is now made law by sections 1–7 of the Insolvency Act 1986.

### (6) *Delinquent directors*

The Cork Committee was concerned at the fraud and other abuses widespread on company insolvency by directors, managers and liquidators, and made recommendations in this regard including the disqualification of delinquent directors and their being made personally liable for the debts of insolvent companies under certain circumstances. These proposals, contained in Chap

---

1 See Insolvency Act 1986, Sch 6.

45 of the report, were adopted by the Government with modification and are now made law in the Company Directors Disqualification Act 1986.

### (7) Insolvency practitioners

The Cork Committee thought that there should be public control of who could act as insolvency practitioners and that they should have professional qualifications and experience as a condition of being allowed to act. The detailed proposals contained in Chap 15 of the report were largely adopted by the government with only members of recognised bodies, or specially authorised persons, now allowed to act as insolvency practitioners in terms of sections 388 to 394 of the Insolvency Act 1986.

## III. THE CURRENT LEGISLATION

### Statutes

#### (1) Insolvency Act 1985 and Insolvency Act 1986

The new legislation on insolvency was introduced in a rolling programme. As far as corporate insolvency was concerned, the main statute was the Insolvency Act 1985 passed on 30 October 1985. It was, however, subject to five commencement orders (SIs 1986/185, 463, 840 and 1924). Most of that Act is now consolidated into the Insolvency Act 1986.

The Insolvency Act 1986, contains most of the new law in relation to corporate insolvency in Scotland. It had a slightly unusual procedure for its commencement. In terms of section 443 of the Insolvency Act 1986, the Insolvency Act 1986 was to come into force on the day appointed under section 236(2) of the Insolvency Act 1985 for the coming into force of Part III of the Insolvency Act 1985. The fifth commencement order under the Insolvency Act 1985 brought into force Part III of the Insolvency Act 1985 on 29 December 1986. This had the effect of simultaneously bringing into force the Insolvency Act 1986 which repealed the Insolvency Act 1985.

#### (2) Company Directors Disqualification Act 1986

On the same date as the coming into force of the Insolvency Act 1986, came into force the Company Directors Disqualification Act 1986, which largely consolidated into a separate statute provisions relating to directors previously in the Companies Act 1985 and the Insolvency Act 1985. Certain of the previous statutory provisions were brought into force on 28 April 1986. The Act itself was not retrospective.

#### (3) Bankruptcy (Scotland) Act 1985

The third statute which touched on corporate insolvency in Scotland in the rolling programme was the Bankruptcy (Scotland) Act 1985. In terms of paragraphs 19–22 of Schedule 7 it amended the Companies Act 1985, in particular by the introduction of two new sections, namely section 615A dealing with gratuitous alienations and section 615B dealing with unfair preferences. These provisions were to be common to individual bankruptcy and corporate insolvency. Those sections of the Companies Act 1985 were repealed by the Insolvency Act 1986 and corresponding provisions consolidated into the Insolvency Act 1986 by sections 242 dealing with gratuitous alienations in Scotland and 243 dealing with unfair preferences in Scotland. Some of the provisions in that Act in relation to a trustee in bankruptcy are made applicable to a liquidator by section 169 of the Insolvency Act 1986 and by the Insolvency (Scotland) Rules 1986.

### (4) *Companies Act 1989*

This makes transactions on a recognised stock exchange immune from some of the normal insolvency law workings. It is an example of computerised dealing being impossible under the usual régime and the realities of commerce forcing a major derogation from normal legal rules.

## Rules

### (1) *The Insolvency (Scotland) Rules 1986 (SI 1986/1915)*

These rules came into force on the same date as the Insolvency Act 1986, namely 29 December 1986. They were made under section 411 of the Insolvency Act 1986 and must be read in conjunction with the Insolvency Act 1986. They apply only to insolvency proceedings after 29 December 1986.

### (2) *The Receivers (Scotland) Regulations 1986 (SI 1986/1917)*

These Regulations came into force on 29 December 1986 and were passed in exercise of powers given to the Secretary of State in terms of the Insolvency Act 1986. These regulations have to be read alongside the Insolvency Act 1986 in relation to the law as to receivers in Scotland. They only apply to receiverships after 29 December 1986.

### (3) *The Insurance Companies (Winding Up) (Scotland) Rules 1986 (SI 1986/1918)*

These regulations came into force on 29 December 1986 and were made under section 411 of the Insolvency Act 1986 and section 59 of the Insurance Companies Act 1982. These rules apply in relation to an insurance company which the courts in Scotland have jurisdiction to wind up (rule 3(1)). They only apply to windings up commenced after 29 December 1986.

### (4) *The Insolvent Companies (Reports on Conduct of Directors) (No 2) (Scotland) Rules 1986 (SI 1986/1916)*

These rules, which came into force on 29 December 1986, have to be read with the Company Directors Disqualification Act 1986. They are not retrospective.

### (5) *The Insolvency (Scotland) Amendment Rules 1987 (SI 1987/1921)*

These came into force on 11 January 1988. They do not iron out all the problems.

## Acts of Sederunt

(1) *Act of Sederunt (Sheriff Court Company Insolvency Rules) 1986 (SI 1986/2297)*

This Act of Sederunt came into force on 29 December 1986 and deals with the procedure in relation to company insolvency in the sheriff court. It repealed the previous Rules but the previous Rules are to apply to windings up commenced before 29 December 1986.

(2) *Act of Sederunt (Rules of Court Amendment No 11) (Companies) 1986 (SI 1986/2298)*

This Act of Sederunt came into force on 29 December 1986. It deals with the procedure in relation to winding up in the Court of Session. It repeals the previous rules but the previous rules are to apply to windings up commenced before 29 December 1986.

(3) *Act of Sederunt (Company Directors Disqualification) 1986 (SI 1986/2296)*

This Act of Sederunt sets out further procedure in relation to disqualification orders in terms of the Company Directors Disqualification Act 1986. It is not retrospective.

# IV. OPERATION OF NEW LEGISLATION

## Working of the new legislation

Since the coming into force of the Insolvency Act 1986 and attendant legislation, there has been a pronounced upturn in insolvency activity in the United Kingdom economy. It is difficult to appraise, other than from anecdotal evidence, how effective the legislation has been in its objectives, and how efficient it has been in achieving those objectives. Although the Department of Trade and Industry has set up an insolvency service, which collates insolvency statistics from different parts of the United Kingdom, these statistics are insufficient to get a clear picture of what is happening from year to year. Although the absolute figures for liquidations, receiverships and administrations are obtainable, these can be misleading for two reasons:

(1)   One Maxwell style corporate collapse is equivalent in its knock-on effect on the economy to many minnows going under. The statistics published by the Department of Trade and Industry through returns made to it by Companies House, do not give an indication either of the size of the companies which have gone into liquidation, receivership or administration, or the size of the deficit. Also no statistics are published for companies which have effectively suffered the same fate as winding up, namely being struck off the register. These are liquidations in all but name and their non-inclusion in the official figures underestimates the number of corporate insolvencies; and

(2)   There are no published figures for the fees charged by insolvency

practitioners to handle liquidations, receiverships and administrations. It is not possible to gauge what percentage on a sliding scale, of an insolvent company's assets are applied in satisfaction of the insolvency practitioners' remuneration, ie go in the transaction costs of the insolvency. It is not possible to assess the costs creditors are paying in reduction in amount of dividend for equitable distribution.

It would appear from the statistics for administrations, that both in England and Scotland they have not proved particularly popular. It is thought that there are two reasons for this. The first is that, except in exceptional circumstances, a bank having a debenture with a floating charge over the assets of a company, is much more likely to want to keep control of the procedure through the receivership mechanism, and secondly that the fact that an administration takes the management of a company effectively out of the hands of the directors, means that directors are reluctant to propose this machinery.

The other main observation, which has been subject to much comment both by the banks and by the judiciary in England is the escalating level of fees charged by the large accountancy firms in the case of corporate insolvency. While it is understandable that the persons concerned require a high level of expertise especially dealing with large cross-border insolvencies, like BCCI, Polly-Peck and Maxwell, the fees have been very large indeed. Although there has been a commitment by the Government to competitive tendering in the provision of services generally, the increasing concentration of the big accountancy firms has narrowed choice. Secondly, especially given the role of the banks in sponsoring persons to be liquidators and receivers, there is no real competitive market for the provision of the services. Though the banks would perhaps be expected to try to get the best price possible from insolvency practitioners, the depletion of the company's assets in insolvency practitioner expenses, often does not fall on the banks, if their loans are covered by the assets subject to the floating charge.

# Chapter 2

# Various legal regimes on insolvency

## Introduction

If a company becomes insolvent in Scotland, or runs into severe financial difficulties, it can be placed under three separate and distinct legal régimes, the major effect of which is to wrest control of the company from its board of directors and pass it to a liquidator, administrator or receiver. Because these régimes often overlap, and an administration order is a comparatively recently introduced régime, it is proposed in this chapter briefly to explain what the key features of these régimes are, who the leading personnel involved are, and how the régimes may overlap.

The three régimes are:

(1) winding up;
(2) administration; and
(3) receivership.

In addition, a voluntary arrangement may be entered into between a company and its creditors; such an arrangement can precede any of those régimes, or can be entered into during winding up, administration or receivership.

## Winding up

A company in financial trouble may be wound up or liquidated – the two terms are used interchangeably. Winding up is the most final and drastic of the three legal régimes – it being the machinery by which a company incorporated under the Companies Acts is terminated[1]. Termination of the company's existence is effected at the stage of its dissolution under section 205(1)(a) and (2) of the Insolvency Act 1986.

There are *two* modes of winding up:

(1) voluntary winding up; and
(2) compulsory winding up by the court.

### (1) *Voluntary winding up*

This first mode of winding up is far more common than compulsory winding up. It may be conducted without any recourse to the court.

---

1 *Princess of Reuss v Bos* (1871) LR 5 HL 176, 193; the only other method of termination is removal of a defunct company from the register under the Companies Act 1985, s 652.

*Members' voluntary winding up.*    If the company is solvent, what happens is that the members of the company resolve to wind up the company. A liquidator is then appointed by the members. The company's assets are then realised by the liquidator, its creditors paid off, and any surplus paid to shareholders. This is known as a members' voluntary winding up.

There are many reasons why members might wish to wind up a company, eg the company has only short-term objects which have been fulfilled, like the holding of an exhibition in a particular year[1], or the company does not look like having a viable future, because it cannot by reason of its liabilities continue in business and therefore it is advisable to wind it up[2]. Alternatively the company for a variety of reasons, eg the company's money could better be invested elsewhere, may not want to stay in business and resolves by a special resolution[3] that it be wound up voluntarily[4]. Apart from reconstructions and amalgamations, the most common reason for members winding up voluntarily is that the company is making losses and does not appear to have a viable future.

*Creditors' voluntary winding up.*    A second type of voluntary winding up is a 'creditors' voluntary winding up'. This again is a winding up without the involvement of the court. Because the company is insolvent, the members meet and resolve to have the company wound up. Again, as in a members' voluntary winding up, a liquidator is appointed (by the creditors), assets are realised by him and distributed to the creditors. The key difference between a members' and a creditors' voluntary winding up is the solvency of the company[5]. When the company is insolvent effective charge of the company's affairs passes from the members to the creditors.

There are situations where a members' voluntary winding up (commencing as apparently solvent) emerges as an insolvent winding up. In that case a members' voluntary winding up by legal process converts to a creditors' voluntary winding up[6].

## (2) *Compulsory winding up*

This type of winding up takes place by an application petitioning the court to wind the company up[7] presented by either the company or the directors or by any creditor or creditors, contributory or contributories, or by all or any of those parties together or separately. The Insolvency Act 1986 lists the various grounds on which the court may wind up a company[8]. In relation to insolvency, the most usual ground is that contained in section 122(1)(e) of the Insolvency Act 1986, namely that 'the company is unable to pay its debts'. A

---

1  *Drysdale and Gilmour, Petrs v Liqr of International Exhibition of Electrical Engineering and Inventions* (1890) 18 R 98.
2  *Wilson v McGenn & Co* (1876) 3 R 474.
3  Where the company is for a limited duration an ordinary resolution is sufficient (Insolvency Act 1986, s 84(1)(a)); where the company resolves to wind up by reason of its liabilities an extraordinary resolution is required (Insolvency Act 1986, s 84(1)(c)); otherwise a special resolution is required: s 84(1)(b)).
4  The three types of case listed above are the three cases under the Insolvency Act 1986, s 84 which entitle a company to have a members' winding up.
5  Insolvency Act 1986, s 90.
6  Ibid, s 96.
7  Ibid, s 124(1).
8  Ibid, s 122(1).

voluntary winding up may be made compulsory by a petition to the court[1] under certain circumstances (see page 88).

In both voluntary and compulsory windings up a liquidator is appointed to administer and manage the company during the period he is realising its assets. In the case of a members' and a creditors' voluntary winding up, the appointment of the liquidator is a private matter of the members and/or creditors. In the case of a winding up by the court, a liquidator is appointed by the court but if members and creditors nominate someone, that person becomes the liquidator[2], the creditors' nomination being the dominant one.

During the period between the presentation of the winding-up petition and the appointment by the court of the liquidator at the stage it grants a winding up order[3], the court may appoint a 'provisional liquidator'[4]. The provisional liquidator has the functions which the court decides to confer on him[5]. In the case of a voluntary winding up there is no provisional liquidator.

### Administration order

At any time prior to winding-up proceedings, the court may appoint an administrator. The office of administrator was the creation of the Insolvency Act 1985 (now consolidated in the Insolvency Act 1986). This was a new type of legal régime, suggested by the Cork Committee. The régime allows the court to appoint an officer to administer the company in order to try to set its affairs in order, or to realise its assets in a more advantageous way for its creditors than if the company went into immediate liquidation. The appointment of an administrator is sometimes described as affording a breathing space to the company, because it gives it a moratorium on payment of its debts. Hence unlike liquidation, which is a 'terminal ward', administration may be just a 'sick ward', depending on the patient. During the administration although debts may not be enforced against the company (or a winding-up order made against the company without the leave of the court), there is no authorisation to the company to postpone payment of its debts or to have a discharge from its liabilities.

Usually, if there is an administration order, the company will not be subject to any other legal régime, e g liquidation or receivership. There is an exception of a technical nature in that an administrator may be appointed even if the company is in administrative receivership, but the two régimes may not operate simultaneously (see page 108). It is however only a temporary overlap until it is resolved which régime should rightfully be in place.

There is a further proviso which is really a question of wording. Previously in Scotland there was only one class of receiver. However the Insolvency Act 1985 introduced two classes of so called 'receiver' depending on the extent of the company's property covered by a floating charge held by the person appointing the receiver. Where a receiver is now appointed by the holder of a floating charge in a case where the whole (or substantially the whole) of the company's property is attached by the floating charge, then he is known as 'an

1 Ibid, s 116.
2 Ibid, s 139(3).
3 Ibid, s 138(1).
4 Ibid, s 135(1).
5 Ibid, s 135(4).

administrative receiver'[1]. In any other case he will be known simply as a 'receiver'. The distinction is important in relation to administrations, in that a 'receiver', ie the minor actor, may exercise his powers alongside an administrator but an administrative receiver, ie the major actor, may not[2]. The distinction may however be academic in this context because even the 'receiver' must vacate office if required to do so by the administrator[3].

## Receivership

Receivers are a creation of the Companies (Floating Charges and Receivers) (Scotland) Act 1972. Prior to that date, if the holder of a floating charge (ie a type of security not attached to specific assets of a company) wished to enforce his security in the event of a default by the company in paying its debts under a debenture, the holder of the debenture which created the floating charge had no machinery for enforcing the floating charge other than petitioning the court for the liquidation of the company. This differed from all types of securities in Scotland. For example the holder of a security over heritable property can realise the heritable property in the event of default on the instrument creating the security, without recourse to the court[4]. Those having security over physical moveable property have normally possession of the moveable property and can usually enforce their security by selling the property without recourse to the court. Similarly if debts or receivables or other rights (trade marks, patents, etc) are to be used as security they would normally have to be assigned first to the security holder 'in security', and in the event of default, the security holder collects the assigned debts, or keeps the trademark, etc, without recourse to the court or any other party.

Since 1972, the holder of a floating charge may enforce the floating charge by appointing a receiver over the company. Although the receiver has general duties to the company and its creditors, he is primarily the appointee of the holder of the floating charge and answerable to him. His primary duty is to realise the assets of the company covered by the floating charge in order to satisfy the debts secured by the floating charge. Accordingly receivership is not really a statutory legal régime quite in the same sense that liquidation or administration is. It is much more a private matter.

The law generally does not stop holders of securities enforcing their securities because a winding up supervenes. Hence 'administrative receivers' and 'receivers' appointed by the holders of floating charges are entitled to exercise their powers although the company is being wound up. The effect is that a company is often 'in receivership' and 'in liquidation' at the same time.

1 Insolvency Act 1986, s 251.
2 Ibid, s 11(1).
3 Ibid, s 11(2).
4 Conveyancing and Feudal Reform (Scotland) Act 1970, ss 19–27.

# Chapter 3

# Insolvent liquidations

## Introduction

There are procedural differences between the way a creditors' voluntary winding up and a winding up by the court are conducted. However it is thought by the authors that the general law in relation to insolvent liquidations in Scotland forms a unity (as opposed to two systems that share features), and that the reader will understand the general law better if the general law is given primary place. The procedural differences are brought out in the text, but given secondary place.

The chapter is divided into *six* parts:

Part I       describes the legal effects of winding up;
Part II      describes the appointment, removal, resignation and release of the liquidator;
Part III     describes the title, status and functions of the liquidator;
Part IV      describes the duties and powers of the liquidator;
Part V       describes the back-up powers of the court, which the liquidator may call to assistance; and
Part VI      describes the various stages in the liquidation not already covered.

The areas of trusts, the nature of a security, retention of title, mandates and powers of attorney, proof and ranking of claims, subordinated debt agreements, set-off, liquidation committees and remuneration of the liquidator are dealt with in Chapters 9–15, 18 and 19.

## I. LEGAL EFFECTS OF WINDING UP

### Date of commencement of winding up

Winding up commences at the time of the passing of the resolution for winding up[1], or in the case of a winding up by the court (where there has been no resolution for winding up), at the time of the presentation of the petition to the court for winding up[2]. When an order for winding up is made on more than one petition, the order and therefore the commencement of the winding up dates from the earliest[3].

1 Insolvency Act 1986, ss 86 and 129(1).
2 Ibid, s 129(2).
3 *Re Filby Bros (Provender) Ltd* [1958] 2 All ER 458, 460.

### Effect of winding up on carrying on of business

The resolution for a creditors' voluntary winding up or a winding-up order does not affect the corporate state and corporate powers of the company, which continue until the company is dissolved[1]. However, articles of association which are inconsistent with the winding-up provisions of the statutes cease to operate; for example an article restricting the right of the company to make calls[2], or an article giving rights inconsistent with the reconstruction facility now contained in section 110 of the Insolvency Act 1986[3].

When winding up commences, the company must cease to carry on its business[4] in the case of a creditors' voluntary winding up, except that the company may carry on its business so far as the carrying on of the business may be required for a beneficial winding up[5]. There is no statutory right of a company being compulsorily wound up to carry on its business, even if required for its beneficial winding up. However, the court or the liquidation committee has the discretion to sanction the company to carry on the business of the company so far as may be necessary for its beneficial winding up[6]. Because winding up is deemed to commence from the date of the presentation of the petition, a company in provisional liquidation could not carry on business without the sanction of the court or the liquidation committee. In relation to the powers of a provisional liquidator, it is suggested that the high-water mark of a provisional liquidator's powers would be if he had the same powers as the liquidator[7].

In order to satisfy the test whether the carrying on of the business is 'necessary' or 'required' for the beneficial winding up, the question is not one of preferred options, but rather whether there is a 'mercantile necessity' that its business is carried on; which would not include carrying on business with the hope that prospects might improve, or be determined by whether a majority of creditors is in favour or not[8]. However where the liquidator has the requisite authority, it is sufficient that he bona fide and reasonably believes that the carrying on of the business is necessary for the beneficial winding up of the company[9]. The liquidator must not carry on business with a view to reconstructing the company[10], although he may in order to sell it as a going concern. He does not have the powers of an administrator or Scottish receiver given in Schedules 1 and 2 to the Insolvency Act 1986 to set up subsidiaries and hive down the business to them, which is a form of reconstruction. It will often be a difficult matter to determine whether the carrying on of the business is necessary. There will often be no guarantee that the proposal will be beneficial, but rather it will be a question of assessing whether the prospects of success with their beneficial results make the proposal a business necessity. For example authority was granted to a liquidator to carry on the business, when the

---

1 Insolvency Act 1986, s 87(2) and *Smith v Lord Advocate* 1978 SC 259 at 271.
2 *Newton v Anglo-Australian Investment Co's Debenture-holders* [1895] AC 244.
3 *Payne v Cork* [1900] 1 Ch 308.
4 Insolvency Act 1986, s 87(1).
5 Ibid, s 87(1).
6 Ibid, s 167(1)(a) and Sch 4, para 5.
7 See *Re ABC Coupler and Engineering Co Ltd (No 3)* [1970] 1 WLR 702.
8 *Liquidator of Burntisland Oil Co Ltd v Dawson* (1892) 20 R 180.
9 *Re Great Eastern Electric Co Ltd* [1941] 1 Ch 241.
10 *Re Wreck Recovery Co* (1880) 15 Ch D 353.

property of a company in liquidation consisted of a hall, let for public enter-
tainments, and it was expedient to delay its sale until the time of the year when
such property could be sold to best advantage[1]. Because, however, the corporate state and powers continue, a business could not be continued which was
*ultra vires* the objects of the company. Hence a limited duration company
could not be carried on in business beyond its set span. The advice, in doubt,
should be to ask the court even if the liquidation committee approves.

### Effect of winding up on receiver carrying on business

A receiver may carry on the business attached by a floating charge[2]. He is personally liable on contracts entered into by him or contracts of employment
adopted by him[3]. Until a resolution to wind up or a winding-up order is made,
the receiver may carry on the business of the company in the name of the company (all commercial documentation must give notification that the company
is in receivership)[4].

The law governing the receiver's rights to carry on the business after a
winding up is not easily understandable. At best the liquidator may only carry
on business for the 'beneficial winding up' of the company. The logical presumption would therefore suggest that, if the company in liquidation is
restricted in carrying on its business, its deemed agent, 'a receiver', would
also be restricted. Statute, nevertheless, appears to have cut across the logical
presumption. By statute a floating charge attaches the company's assets on
crystallisation at winding up[5], and if a receiver is appointed he has the power
to carry on the business of the company which is covered by the floating
charge[6]. He may enforce the security and exercise all the powers listed in
Schedule 2 to the Insolvency Act 1986[7], provided they are not inconsistent
with the terms of the floating charge, and in this his rights take precedence to
those of the liquidator[8]. The holder of the floating charge however is under no
obligation to appoint a receiver and he can leave it to the liquidator to secure
his rights[9].

### Effect of winding up on company's property

Unlike vesting in a bankruptcy, the company's property does not vest in the
liquidator by statute. He takes no new or independent title to the property
unlike a trustee in bankruptcy[10], although an order may be sought, vesting the
property of the company in the liquidator[11].

---

1 *Liquidator of Victoria Public Buildings Co* (1893) 30 SLR 386.
2 Insolvency Act 1986, s 55(2), Sch 2, para 14.
3 Ibid, s 57(2).
4 Ibid, s 64(1).
5 Companies Act 1985, s 463.
6 Insolvency Act 1986, s 55(2), Sch 2, para 14.
7 Ibid, s 55(2).
8 *Manley, Petr*, 1985 SLT 42.
9 *Libertas-Kommerz GmbH Appellants* 1978 SLT 222.
10 *Gray's Trs v Benhar Coal Co Ltd* (1881) 9 R 225; *Clark v West Calder Oil Co* (1882) 9 R 1017;
   *Queensland Mercantile and Agency Co Ltd v Australasian Investment Co Ltd* (1888) 15 R 935 at 939.
11 The power to vest the property in the liquidator in a winding up by the court may be sought under
   s 145 of the Insolvency Act 1986; the power to vest in the liquidator could be sought under s 112(2)
   of the Insolvency Act 1986 in the case of a creditors' voluntary winding up. The authors know of
   no case in which these provisions have been used in Scotland.

### Effect of winding up on directors' powers

In a creditors' voluntary winding up, all the powers of the directors in relation to the business ceases on the appointment of a liquidator, except so far as the liquidation committee (or, if there is no such committee, the creditors) sanctions their continuance[1]. Similarly in a compulsory winding up the directors' powers to act on behalf of the company cease on a winding-up order[2], or on the appointment of a provisional liquidator if there is an appointment of a provisional liquidator prior to the winding up order[3]. Unlike the position in a creditors' voluntary winding up, there is no power in a compulsory winding up for the directors' powers to be continued[4]. It is thought that the appointment of a liquidator or the making of a winding-up order does not cause the directors to cease to hold office[5], and they will continue to be directors unless and until they formally resign. The directors retain certain residuary powers including the right to appeal against a winding-up order[6], and have certain duties imposed upon them in relation to the winding up[7]. The directors will also still exercise powers they may have vested in them as trustees of the company's pension scheme[8].

In relation to creditors' windings up commenced after 29 December 1986[9], the powers of directors are severely limited between the date of the commencement of the winding up (ie the date of passing of the resolution to wind up), where no liquidator has been appointed or nominated, until the nomination or appointment of the liquidator. In terms of section 114 of the Insolvency Act 1986 (acting partly on the recommendations of the Cork Committee), statute has intervened to regulate the conduct of the company's affairs in this period and restrict the former unfettered powers of the directors to act during this period since unscrupulous behaviour had not been uncommon. (Indeed the Cork Committee had gone so far as to recommend that a provisional liquidator should take over immediately upon the passing of the resolution of the board of directors; entailing that the directors find a qualified person willing to act as a provisional liquidator before the passing of the resolution.) In terms of section 114(2) of the Insolvency Act 1986, the powers of the directors may not be exercised during that period except for the purposes of summoning the creditors' meeting and making out the Statement of Affairs in terms of sections 98 and 99 of the Insolvency Act 1986. The directors are, however, allowed to dispose of perishable goods and other goods, where the value is likely to diminish if they are not immediately disposed of[10]. They may also do other things which are necessary for the protection of the company's assets[11].

---

1 Insolvency Act 1986, s 103.
2 *Fowler v Broad's Patent Night Light Co* [1893] 1 Ch 724.
3 *Re Mawcon Ltd* [1969] 1 WLR 78 at 82.
4 *Re Farrow's Bank Ltd* [1921] 2 Ch 164.
5 *Madrid Bank Ltd v Bayley* (1866) LR 2 QB 37.
6 *Re Union Accident Insurance Co Ltd* [1972] 1 All ER 1105 at 1113, per Plowman J. In saying that the directors had the residuary power to appeal against a winding-up order, he added that a good test of the extent of directors' residuary powers was to inquire whether the power which the board is said to have lost is one which can be said to have been assumed by the liquidator.
7 Production of a statement of affairs under s 99(1) of the Insolvency Act 1986 in the case of a creditors' voluntary winding up and under s 131(3) in the case of a compulsory winding up.
8 *Smith, etc, Petrs* 1969 SLT (Notes) 94.
9 See the Insolvency Act 1986, Sch 11, para 4.
10 Ibid, s 114(3)(a).
11 Ibid, s 114(3)(b).

The present linguistic formula, 'to do all such things as may be necessary for the protection of the company's assets', does not specify what precisely this power means, and is very difficult to construe. It is not clear whether this means 'doing everything necessary to ensure that the balance sheet is in the healthiest possible state at the date of the appointment of the liquidator' or is specifically confined to doing things analogous to 'disposing of perishable goods and other goods the value of which is likely to diminish'. It is suggested that this power must be read narrowly. Otherwise, it totally detracts from the purpose of the section. Accordingly, it is suggested that it means 'to take what legal steps are necessary or other immediate measures necessary to preserve assets', and has nothing to do with trading – which would also involve liabilities – or any other type of conduct involving the carrying on of the business[1].

### Effect of winding up on contracts other than employment contracts

Apart from contracts of employment which are in a special category (see infra), or unless there is an express term of the contract that a liquidation should constitute an event of default or breach, contracts are not terminated by liquidation.

The liquidator has the option of adopting[2] any contract beneficial to the company (independently of his decision in respect of any other contract), or of terminating it and allowing a ranking for damages[3]. It is necessary for the liquidator to intimate within a reasonable time (which depends on the nature of the contract) whether he intends to adopt the contract; otherwise he will be held to have abandoned the intention to proceed with it[4]. It will be a question of circumstance what the period will be during which the intention must be made clear. There is no statutory grace period[5]. If the company through the liquidator decides to occupy a property beneficially after the winding up, rates will be payable as an expense of the winding up[6]. Utilities may not now refuse to supply services to a company in liquidation until paid arrears (although they may require the liquidator to guarantee payment in respect of services to the company in liquidation)[7].

Building and engineering contracts frequently make express provision for forfeiture of materials and plant in the event of failure by the contractor to implement the contract, or even for the deemed vesting of plant and materials in the employer as soon as they are delivered to site[8]. The validity of such clauses must be determined by the general principles of Scots law relating to the transfer of moveable property; for this purpose, the underlying commercial reality of the clause must be examined carefully. It is thought that clauses

---

1 It is to be noted that a similar provision in the Bankruptcy (Scotland) Act 1985, s 39(6) is concerned with the preservation of the market value of assets.
2 'Adopt' means to refrain from repudiating; per MacPherson J *Re Diesel's & Components Pty Ltd* (1985) 9 ACLR at 827.
3 *Gray's Trs v Benhar Coal Co* (1881) 9 R 225; *Commercial Bank of Scotland v Pattison's Trs* (1891) 18 R 476; *Asphaltic Limestone Concrete Co Ltd v Glasgow Corporation* 1907 SC 463; *Clyde Marine Insurance Co v Renwick* 1974 SC 113; *Turnbull v Liquidator of Scottish County Investment Co* 1939 SC 5; *Smith v Lord Advocate* 1978 SC 259.
4 *Crown Estate Commissioners v Liquidators of Highland Engineering Ltd* 1975 SLT 58.
5 Insolvency Act 1986, ss 19(5) and 57(5) provide for a statutory grace period of 14 days in employment contracts in administrations and receiverships.
6 *Re National Arms Ammunition Co* (1885) 28 Ch D 474; *Re Blazer Fire Lighter Ltd* [1895] 1 Ch 402.
7 Insolvency Act 1986, s 233.
8 See ICE Conditions of Contract (1973 edn), cll 53, 54.

which purport to vest plant in the employer are invalid, on the basis that the commercial reality of such a clause can only be security; possession of the contractor's plant will not normally be transferred from the contractor to the employer, and thus the security will be invalid. Clauses which purport to vest materials on site in the employer are likely to be valid, since transfer of property in the materials accords with the commercial reality of a building contract; there seems to be no reason why the general rules applicable to sale of goods should not apply to such cases. It has been held in England that, if a building contract is terminated owing to the insolvency of the contractor, a clause purporting to forfeit materials and plant is invalid in a question with the liquidator[1]. It is thought that the same reasoning should apply in Scotland.

The liquidator may not adopt contracts which are not in the interests of the creditors and members, where these contracts are not legally enforceable but binding only in honour[2]. If, however, the liquidator had the authority to carry on the business of the company, it might be argued that the honouring of non-legally enforceable obligations was a legitimate aspect of the carrying on of the business[2]. The liquidator may ratify, on behalf of the company as agent of the company, acts which are invalid, which the company in general meeting could have ratified[3].

### Effect of winding up on contracts of employment

The law in this important area in Scotland is not wholly satisfactory or settled. It appears inconsistent and has grown up piecemeal. The common law in relation to bankruptcy has had to be grafted on to the statutory codes in the Employment Acts. English cases predating the major Employment Acts are cited. When the common law was developing over the last century employees did not have by statute the accumulated entitlements they now have. The legal effect of a winding-up order, or winding up, was not judicially considered in depth in any reported case until 1978, when the First Division (the Scottish appeal court) in the leading case of *Smith v Lord Advocate*[4] looked at the effects of liquidation[5]. The case however was concerned with whether there was a change of employer on the appointment of a liquidator. Having decided that there was not, the court went on to hold that there was continuous employment as far as redundancy payments were concerned from the date of the company's employment of the employees initially until eventual dismissal by the liquidator on the grounds of redundancy. The court did not have to decide the legal effect of a winding-up order on contracts of employment. It was argued by the present Lord Mackay of Clashfern for the Lord Advocate that a winding-up order acts as 'constructive notice' of termination but does not itself terminate the contract. This legal expression was used by

---

1 *Ex p Baxter* (1884) 26 Ch D 510. On the matters discussed in this paragraph, see Chap 11.
2 *Clyde Marine Insurance Co v Renwick* 1924 SC 113.
3 *Alexander Ward and Co Ltd v Sam Yang Navigation Co Ltd* 1975 SC (HL) 27.
4 1978 SC 259.
5 The liquidation in question was the liquidation of Upper Clyde Shipbuilders Ltd. That liquidation was important politically in leading to the Heath Administration's change of policy in the face of rising unemployment. It was also important legally in that the Government showed that it did not regard itself as constitutionally bound to underwrite the debts of a limited company in public ownership in the same way as it constitutionally underwrote the debts of nationalised industries, although not necessarily certain statutory bodies in public ownership, eg Mersey Docks Board.

Lord Stormonth Darling in the case of *Day v Tait*[1] in holding that where an employer acts in a particular way (such as in that case going into insolvent liquidation) he can be held to have committed a breach of contract sufficiently serious in employment law to amount to constructive notice of termination, entitling the employee no longer to be bound by the contract and to claim damages. The breach consists in saying to the employee that he cannot rely on having a job and on his wages being paid. This principle in *Day v Tait* was accepted by Lord Cameron in his judgment when he said: 'there is no doubt that the effect of a winding-up order on contracts of employment is one of dismissal without notice and therefore constitutes a breach of contract which entitles the dismissed employee to damages for that breach[2]'. That view was consistent with the present Lord Mackay's argument provided dismissal is read to mean 'constructive dismissal'. However, Lord Cameron went on to say: 'It is of course true that a winding-up order does not automatically terminate contractual liabilities of a company in liquidation other than in contracts of employment, but I think it can properly be said that it would be plainly inequitable that an insolvent company should be in a position to require its servants to continue to work for it when it has publicly announced that it cannot pay its debts as they accrue.' That statement of Lord Cameron suggests automatic termination, which is inconsisent with 'breach' and with the employee having the right not to be bound. It is suggested by the authors, following *Day v Tait* (supra), that a winding-up order amounts to repudiatory breach entitling the employee to affirm the contract or to treat it as discharged. If he elects to treat the contract as discharged he must do so within a reasonable period[3]. There is no statutory grace period of 14 days in employment contracts as provided for in administrations and receiverships by sections 19(5) and 57(5) of the Insolvency Act 1986. Otherwise the contract of employment continues. The slightly slack use by high judicial authorities of the expression 'termination of a contract' in cases of breach was criticised in the House of Lords 18 months later in the case of *Photo Production Ltd v Securicor Transport Ltd*[4], by both Lords Wilberforce and Diplock. In particular Lord Wilberforce said: 'the well accepted principle of law, stated by the highest modern authority that when in the context of breach of contract one speaks of "termination" what is meant is no more than the innocent party or, in some cases, both parties, are excused from further performance'.

Accordingly it is suggested that the correct Scottish law is that a winding-up order acts as constructive notice of dismissal, which entitles the employee, if he so elects, to be no longer bound by the contract and claim damages. Otherwise the contract continues, and the liquidator may then adopt it, or repudiate it, i e by actual notice of dismissal.

It is difficult to assess whether the appointment of a provisional liquidator has the same effect. On the one hand a prima facie case may have been made out that the company is insolvent and the company, except with the sanction of the court, ceases to carry on business (which could mean no work being provided). On the other hand the appointment of a provisional liquidator should not affect the rights of third parties[5]. It is suggested that provisional

1 (1900) 8 SLT 40.
2 *Smith v Lord Advocate* 1978 SC 259 at 280.
3 *Crown Estate Commissioners v Liquidators of Highland Engineering Ltd* 1975 SLT 58.
4 [1980] 1 All ER 556.
5 *Re London Dry Docks Corpn* (1888) 29 Ch D 306 at 314.

liquidation does not have the same effect if it is 'provisional' in so far as the provisional liquidator carries on the business. Otherwise it may have the same effect.

In relation to voluntary windings up the law perhaps depends on the type of winding up. In England, the mere fact of a voluntary winding up has been held not to operate as dismissal[1] but a voluntary winding up coupled with the sale of the company's business has been held to operate as a dismissal[2]. For the purpose of determining in a voluntary liquidation whether there has been dismissal the following facts have been held to be relevant in England: whether the company is solvent or insolvent[3]; whether the company has previously intimated to the relevant employee that his employment is likely to terminate on liquidation[4]; whether the liquidation involves the immediate cessation of the company's business and whether the employee's continuation in office is inconsistent with the role of the liquidator, eg the case of the managing director[5]. The Scottish cases of *Day v Tait*, supra and *Smith v Lord Advocate*, supra suggest that the insolvency of the company is the key aspect; which is consistent with the underlying reasoning running through the English cases namely, 'Can the employee rely on having a job and being paid his wages?' Accordingly a resolution for a creditors' voluntary winding up has probably the same effect as a winding-up order on employment contracts. It acts as constructive notice of termination entitling the employee to claim damages because, to use Lord Cameron's words, it has 'publicly announced that the company cannot pay its debts as they accrue' (including wages).

## Effect of winding-up on pending actions

At any time after the presentation of a winding-up petition, and before a winding-up order has been made, if there is any action or proceeding against the company pending, the company or any creditor or contributory may apply to the court having jurisdiction to wind up the company to restrain the proceedings, and the court has then a discretion to stay, sist or restrain the proceedings on such terms as it thinks fit[6]. If however the action or proceeding against the company is in the High Court or the Court of Appeal in England and Wales or Northern Ireland, the application has to be made to the court in which the action or proceeding is pending[7]. If, after a winding-up petition has been presented, but before a winding-up order has been made, a provisional liquidator is appointed, no action or proceeding may be proceeded with or commenced against the company or its property except by leave of the court and subject to such terms as the court may impose[8]. This rule applies also from the time that a winding-up order is made[8]. Leave of the court is not required to counter-claim against a company in liquidation if the counter-

1 *Midland Counties District Bank v Attwood* [1905] 1 Ch 357.
2 *Reigate v Union Manufacturing Co* [1918] 1 KB 592.
3 *Gerard v Worth of Paris* [1936] 2 All ER 1905; *Fowler v Commercial Timber* [1930] 2 KB 1; *Reigate v Union Manufacturing Co* [1918] 1 KB 592.
4 *Reigate v Union Manufacturing Co*, supra.
5 *Fowler v Commercial Timber Co* [1930] 2 KB 1 at 16; see for partnerships: *Briggs v Oates* [1990] ICR 473.
6 Insolvency Act 1986, s 126(1)(b).
7 Ibid, s 126(1)(a).
8 Ibid, s 130(2).

claim is for less than the amount sued for by the company[1]. In the case of a company registered under section 680 of the Companies Act, no action or proceeding may be commenced or proceeded with against the company or its property and any contributory of the company, in respect of any debt of the company, except by leave of the court, and subject to such terms as the court may impose[2]. Where a petition or application for leave to proceed with an action or proceeding against a company which has been wound up is unopposed and is granted by the court, the cost of the petition or application must, unless the court otherwise directs, be added to the amount of the petitioner's or applicant's claim against the company[3]. These provisions do not affect any action taken by an investment exchange or clearing house recognised under the Financial Servces Act 1986 for the purposes of its default proceedings[4]. If property (other than land) is held by recognised investment exchange or recognised clearing house as margin in relation to market contracts, or is subject to a market charge, no diligence or execution or other legal process for the enforcement of any judgment or order may be commenced or continued without the consent of the investment exchange or clearing house in question (in the case of property provided as cover for margin) or of the person in whose favour the charge was granted (in the case of a market charge)[5].

In order to avoid loss to parties who deal with the company after it has gone into liquidation, section 188 of the Insolvency Act 1986 imposes a requirement that every invoice, order for goods or business letter issued by or on behalf of the company or the liquidator after the winding-up order has been made must contain a statement that the company is in liquidation. A criminal penalty in the form of a fine is imposed upon the company and any of its officers, or the liquidator, who knowingly and wilfully authorise or permit default in respect of this requirement.

### Effect of winding up in relation to stamp duty

In the case of a winding-up by the court, or of a creditors' voluntary winding up of a company registered in Scotland, various documents are by statute exempt from stamp duty. They include conveyances relating solely to property which forms part of the company's assets but only property which, after the execution of the conveyance, remains the company's property for the benefit of its creditors[6].

### Effect of winding up on dispositions of property

Section 127 of the Insolvency Act 1986 provides that in a winding up by the court, any disposition of the company's property, and any transfer of shares, or alteration in the status of the company's members, made after the commencement of the winding up is, unless the court otherwise orders, void. Because winding up is deemed to commence on the presentation of the petition on which the winding-up order was made, unless the company was already in voluntary liquidation at the time of the petition, in which case the winding up

1 *G & A Hotels Ltd v THB Marketing Services Ltd* 1983 SLT 497.
2 Insolvency Act 1986, s 130(3).
3 Ibid, s 199.
4 Companies Act 1989, s 161(4).
5 Ibid, s 180(1).
6 Insolvency Act 1986, s 190.

is deemed to commence on the passing of the resolution for voluntary winding up[1], dispositions of the company's property are blocked from the date of the presentation of the petition. The purpose of the provision being backdated, is to prevent the dissipation of the company's assets while the hearing of the petition is pending. The provision catches all dispositions, whether preferences or bona fide business transactions. Except where there is a provisional liquidator, who has been given powers by the court, it is important that the company obtain authority from the court to enable it to continue trading while there is a hearing of the petition. After a liquidator is appointed, he is given powers under section 167 of the Insolvency Act 1986 which would appear to remove the need for separate permission under section 127 of that Act. It is also thought that a receiver in Scotland would not need to make an application under the section[2]. Property comprised in a standard security may be sold by the holder of the security following the procedures laid down in the Conveyancing and Feudal Reform (Scotland) Act 1970[3]. In the case of an insolvent company it is necessary for the applicant to satisfy the court that the proposed transaction would be beneficial to the company[4]. A shareholder may make an application[5]. The granting of a floating charge has been held in Scotland to be a disposition of the company's property for the purposes of the predecessor of section 127 of the Insolvency Act 1986[6]. In such a situation the disposition would be void, but it may be validated[7]. It has been held in England that a disposition in implementation of a contract would not require leave under section 127 of the Insolvency Act 1986[8]. It is thought that a right of set-off would not be covered by section 127. Similarly assets held by a company are not its property to the extent of any security interest it has given over them in favour of a creditor. The principles upon which a court would grant applications for the validation of dispositions is discussed in detail in the English case of *Re Gray's Inn Construction Co Ltd*[9].

# II. APPOINTMENT, REMOVAL, RESIGNATION AND RELEASE OF LIQUIDATORS

## Presentation of petition

Where a company is insolvent, a winding-up petition is usually presented by:

(a)    the company[10];

1 Insolvency Act 1986, s 129.
2 *Manley* 1985 SLT 42.
3 Conveyancing and Feudal Reform (Scotland) Act 1970, s 24(1).
4 *Re AI Levy (Holdings) Ltd* [1964] Ch 19, [1963] 2 All ER 556; *Re Burton and Deakin Ltd* [1977] 1 All ER 631; and *Re Webb Electrical Ltd* [1988] BCLC 382, 4 BCC 230.
5 *Re Argentum Reductions (UK) Ltd* [1975] 1 All ER 608.
6 *Site Preparations Ltd v Buchan Developments Co Ltd* 1983 SLT 317.
7 *Re Park Ward & Co Ltd* [1926] Ch 828.
8 *Re French's (Wine Bar)* [1987] BCLC 499.
9 [1980] 1 All ER 814; for what is a company's property, see chapter 9; R M Goode, *Legal Problems of Credit and Security* (2nd edn, 1988) p 35.
10 Insolvency Act 1986, s 124(1). Where the company has already gone into voluntary liquidation, it is competent for the liquidator to present the petition. Cf *Re Zoedone Co* [1884] 53 LJ Ch 465. Where the company is in administration, or if an administrative receiver has been appointed, the office holder is entitled to present a petition for the winding-up of a company in terms of para 21 of Sch 1 to the Insolvency Act 1986.

(b) the directors[1];
(c) a creditor or creditors (including any contingent or prospective creditor or creditors)[2]; and
(d) a contributory or contributories[2].

## Petition by the directors

In *Re Instrumentation Electrical Services Ltd*[3] it had been suggested that a winding-up petition had to be supported by all the directors. This is probably not the case given the judgment in *Re Equiticorp International plc*, which concerned the same position in relation to the presenting of a winding-up petition, and it was held that it was sufficient that the petition had been approved by a resolution of the directors[4].

## Petition by creditor or creditors

A petition may be presented by a contingent or prospective creditor[5]. 'Contingent creditor' means a creditor in respect of a debt which will only become due in an event which may or may not occur, and 'prospective creditor', means a creditor in respect of a debt which will certainly become due in the future, either on some date which has already been determined or some date determinable by reference to future events[6]. If there is a genuine doubt that there is a bona fide dispute, the court would normally sist the petition to allow the petitioners to constitute their debt[7]. Where a petitioner is found not to be entitled to present the petition, the court may sist as petitioner in the place of the original petitioner any other creditor or contributory who is entitled, in the opinion of the court, to present a petition[8]. If the alleged contingent debt is disputed by the company in good faith, the petition would normally be dismissed[9].

## Petition by a contributory

The right of a contributory to petition for a winding up is limited in that, except where the ground of the petition is that the number of members is reduced below two, the shares in respect of which the petitioner is a contributory, or some of them, must either have been originally allotted to the petitioner, or have been held by him, and registered in his name, for at least six months during the eighteen months before the commencement of the

---

1 Insolvency Act 1986, s 124(1). Cf *Re Emmadart Ltd* [1979] Ch 540, which held that the directors were not entitled to present a petition in the name of the company without the sanction of a general meeting. The need for the sanction of a general meeting is no longer necessary in terms of the Insolvency Act 1986, s 124(1).
2 Insolvency Act 1986, s 124(1).
3 [1988] BCLC 550, 4 BCC 301.
4 [1989] BCLC 599, [1989] 1 WLR 1010.
5 Insolvency Act 1986, s 124(1).
6 *Walter L Jacob & Co Ltd v Financial Intermediaries, Managers and Brokers Regulatory Association* 1988 SCLR 184, Sh Ct; *Stonegate Securities Ltd v Gregory* [1980] Ch 576.
7 *Landauer & Co v WH Alexander & Co Ltd* 1919 SC 492.
8 Rule of Court 218c (substituted by AS (Rules of Court Amendment No 11) (Companies) 1986, SI 1986/2298); AS (Sheriff Court Company Insolvency Rules) 1986, SI 1986/2297, r 21.
9 *Re Fitness Centre (South East) Ltd* [1986] BCLC 518; *Re a Company (No 003028 of 1987)* [1988] BCLC 282, 3 BCC 575.

winding up, or have devolved on the petitioner through the death of a former holder[1]. This provision is designed to prevent an outsider from acquiring shares simply in order to have the company wound up by the court. The expression 'contributory' includes an allottee whose name does not appear on the register, but if there is a genuine dispute as to the validity of the allotment, the petitioner must first establish the validity of the allotment before proceeding with the petition[2]. If a petitioner is found not entitled to present a petition (and in certain other circumstances specified in Rules of Court), the court may sist as petitioner in place of the original petitioner, any creditor or contributory whom the court is of the opinion is entitled to present a petition[3]. In addition to the above restrictions, a contributory whose shares are fully paid up will not be permitted to proceed with a petition unless he can show that he has a tangible interest in the relief sought. This would normally mean that there were assets available for distribution to the shareholders. In the case of *Re Commercial and Industrial Insulations Ltd*[4] Hoffmann J stated the principle:

'The rule in the case of a contributory's petition is that no order may be made for a winding-up unless the contributory has shown what Jessel MR in *Re Rica Gold Washing Co* [1879] 11 Ch D 36 at 43 called "a tangible interest". That usually means that there will be a surplus for distribution on a winding-up, although that is not the only instance of a tangible interest and other examples were given by Oliver J in *Re Chesterfield Catering Co Ltd* [1976] 3 All ER 294, [1977] Ch 373. In this case, however, it does not appear to me that the evidence shows that in his capacity as a contributory the petitioner would have any tangible interest in the event of a winding-up.

It was argued that there is an exception to this rule in a case in which the petitioner's inability to prove his tangible interest is due to the company's own default in providing him with information to which as a member he is entitled. The way in which that proposition is put by Oliver J in the *Re Chesterfield Catering Co Ltd* case is that the petition will not in that event be regarded as demurrable[5] on the ground of the petitioner's lack of *locus standi*. This, if I may say so, seems to me to be commonsense, because it would obviously be unjust to the petitioner to have his petition struck out *in limine* because he was unable to allege a surplus on a winding-up on account of wrongfully being deprived of access to the necessary information.

The position is, I think, different once the petition has come to be heard. By that time the petitioner will have been able to take advantage of procedural mechanisms available for obtaining information needed to support his case.'[6]

It has been suggested that such a shareholder will not therefore be able to petition for winding up on the ground that the company is unable to pay its debts, unless his shares are partly paid up and his financial interest lies in procuring that the company's affairs are wound up before his liability to contribute is increased by further losses. In cases where the company may have claims against directors and others under sections 211, 213, and 214 of the Insolvency Act 1986, the company may nevertheless be unable to pay its debts but the contributor would have a right to petition for its winding up on

---

1 Insolvency Act 1986, s 124(2).
2 *Re J N 2 Ltd* [1977] 3 All ER 1104, [1978] 1 WLR 183.
3 Rule of Court 218c.
4 [1986] BCLC 191.
5 Demurrable means 'dismissible'.
6 See also *Re Martin Coulter Enterprises Ltd* [1988] BCLC 12, 4 BCC 212.

the ground of inability to pay debts because this type of action would give him a financial interest. This is especially the case where there is potentially a claim under section 214 against directors and others for wrongful trading. Of course in such a situation he would be entitled to bring an action on the 'just and equitable' ground also, but the 'unable to pay its debts' ground might be simpler for him to prove. In doubt the petition should list both grounds, especially because it would be easier relevantly to aver material in a 'just and equitable' ground which could enable the petitioner to recover documents.

## Appointment of liquidators

### (1) *Creditors' voluntary winding up*

The creditors and members at their respective meetings in a creditors' voluntary winding up may each nominate a liquidator, but the nomination of the creditors will prevail, subject only to a successful application to the court by any director, member or creditor within seven days after the date of the nomination challenging the appointment[1]. (See also page 76 for a case of a members' voluntary winding up converted to a creditors' voluntary winding up.) On a successful challenge the court may then appoint the members' nominee jointly, or replace the creditors' nominee with some other person[2]. During the interval between the members' nomination and the creditors', the members' nominee's powers are restricted (see page 49).

### (2) *Compulsory winding up*

The procedure is similar in a winding-up by the court except that the court appoints a liquidator (to be known as an interim liquidator) when it makes a winding-up order[3]. The interim liquidator then summons meetings of members and creditors, for the purpose of choosing the liquidator[4]. These meetings are known respectively as 'the first meeting of contributories' and 'the first meeting of creditors', and jointly as 'the first meeting in the liquidation', and any such meetings of creditors or contributories must be summoned for a date not later than 42 days after the date of the winding-up order, unless approved by the court[5]. The meetings (with creditors' having precedence) then choose the liquidator[6]. As in the case of creditors' voluntary windings up, there is a right of challenge in court within seven days of nomination, by creditors and contributories, where meetings are held and different persons are nominated[7]. The directors do not have the right of challenge since their powers cease on the winding-up order[8].

1 Insolvency Act 1986, s 100(3).
2 Ibid, s 100(3).
3 Ibid, s 138(1) and (2).
4 Ibid, s 138(3) and (4).
5 Rule 4.12(2) and (2A) of the Insolvency (Scotland) Rules 1986 as amended by paragraph 14 of the Schedule to the Insolvency (Scotland) Amendment Rules 1987.
6 Insolvency Act 1986, s 139(3).
7 Ibid, s 139(4).
8 Ibid, s 103.

## Grounds of challenge to appointment of liquidators

There are various grounds of challenge open when a decision of the meetings are challenged under sections 100(3) and 139(4) of the Insolvency Act 1986. In practice now, however, the latitude of discretion in appointments is circumscribed by the fact that liquidators must be qualified 'insolvency practitioners'[1] and challenges are likely to be less frequent. Where a firm of insolvency practitioners is appointed liquidator, or provisional liquidator, it is important to check that there is not a conflict of interest within the firm, although it has been held that there was no conflict of interest in the case of a firm of insolvency practitioners who had been appointed to act as provisional liquidators of one company, the associates of whose controlling shareholder controlled other companies in respect of which the same firm had been appointed in England as receivers by the court[2].

Although it is not illegal to appoint a liquidator who is not resident in Scotland, he must normally be resident in Scotland unless there are strong grounds for departing from that practice[3]. However, persons resident in England have been appointed liquidators where there was a strong reason, for example, to enable contracts beneficial to the company to be continued[4]. A former director may also be appointed liquidator but probably only where he is not the sole liquidator[4]. This is because the court attaches particular importance to the office holder being independent and being seen to be independent of the persons he may have to investigate. In *Re Corbenstoke Ltd (No 2)*[5], Harman J discussed the possibility of a director acting as a liquidator. He observed:

'In my view, it is most unlikely that a director could ever be a proper liquidator of a company. I do not say it is totally impossible, but it must be a matter of the rarest occurrence because inevitably a director will have responsibility for the affairs of the company even if, as is said to be the case, this company were a non-trading company operating through a web of subsidiaries and sub-subsidiaries. In such a case the liquidator is bound to investigate the attitudes and actions of the director in controlling the subsidiaries of the company, and it cannot be right that the same person should both be liquidator and director.'

Any objection to an appointment should be of 'a tangible and definite nature'[6]. Normally the wishes of the creditors will be followed but this is not binding, so that in the case of *Matthew Wishart, Petitioner*[7] both the company and the creditors sought a joint liquidator in addition to the then current liquidator, but the court refused because of the small size of the company, seeing no reason 'why there should be two horses in a one horse concern'. The court will appoint an additional liquidator or additional liquidators in matters of complexity[8]. Where joint liquidators are appointed, the appointment or nomination must contain a clear indication whether the joint office holders

---

1 Insolvency Act 1986, ss 388 and 390.
2 *Re Arrows Ltd* [1992] BCC 121.
3 *Barberton Development Syndicate Ltd* (1898) 24 R 654.
4 *Liquidators of Bruce Peebles & Co Ltd v Shiells* 1908 SC 692.
5 (1989) 5 BCC 767, [1990] BCLC 60.
6 *Anderson & Sons v Broughty Ferry Picture House* 1917 SC 622.
7 1908 SC 690.
8 *Liquidator of Ecuadorian Association v Fox* (1906) 14 SLT 47.

must act together, or whether one or more can do any act on their own authority[1]. Following the policy, however, of trying to give effect to the wishes of the creditors in appointing liquidators, the court has confirmed the appointment of an auditor as liquidator because he was knowledgeable of the affairs of the company and has replaced a managing director as liquidator with a neutral liquidator, where the other liquidator was also well versed in the affairs of the company[2].

It is thought that these decisions would not be followed today and that the court would require a much greater degree of independence. In the Australian case of *Re Capital Management Securities Ltd*[3] the court refused leave for an auditor to act as liquidator. McLelland J stated:

'Mere grounds of convenience and the improbability of any wrong-doing having occurred which may be discovered by a liquidator seem to me to be elements which are likely to be present in many cases, and are not the kind of matters which should induce the Court to depart from the legislative policy that normally a liquidator should be, and be seen to be, entirely independent of the pre-liquidation activities of the company.'

In another Australian case, *Attalex Pty Ltd v Brian Cassiday Electrical Industries Pty Ltd*[4] the court ordered the appointment of an independent liquidator where there were good balance of convenience arguments in favour of the appointment of the same person who had already acted as provisional liquidator. What swayed the court was the fact that a partner of the provisional liquidator had advised in relation to the affairs of the company and a possible scheme of arrangement in connection with which the company had commenced the winding-up proceedings. There was no adverse reflection either on the partner or the provisional liquidator. However, McLelland J observed:

'The question at issue really amounts to how much weight should be given in the circumstances to a liquidator's being seen to be completely detached from those associated with the company whose conduct he will be under an obligation to investigate.'

This stricter modern approach is also taken in relation to conflicting interests and duties of liquidators. There is a specific need to avoid conflicting duties and interests. The case of *Re Corbenstoke Ltd (No 2)*[5], gives a good illustration of the type of conflicts of interest and duty which can arise. That was an application for the removal of a liquidator. The liquidator was also acting as trustee in bankruptcy for an individual's estate. The statement of affairs of the bankrupt had claimed ownership of 99 per cent of the share capital issued by the company. In order to protect that interest the liquidator had appointed himself as a director of the company and had held that office for a few weeks. For a short period he had even been the sole director of the company. In the capacity as trustee in bankruptcy he then claimed to be a creditor of the company by virtue of subrogation following discharge of

1 Insolvency Act 1986, s 231.
2 *Argylls v Ritchie & Whiteman* 1914 SC 915.
3 [1986] 4 ACLC 157.
4 [1984] 2 ACLC 654.
5 (1989) 5 BCC 767, [1990] BCLC 60.

guarantee liabilities. As a result of his activities in relation to another company, the liquidator was also a debtor of Corbenstoke Ltd. In commenting on the affidavit in support of the application for removal Harman J observed:

'The affidavit goes on to set out the grounds for removing [the liquidator] as liquidator; first, that he was a director of the company before it went into liquidation; secondly, that he claimed to be a creditor; thirdly, that he appears to be a debtor; and fourthly – a quite separate matter – grounds of his previous conduct.

As counsel puts the matter to me, there are really two separate categories of grounds: first, that [the liquidator] is in a position where his duty, and not necessarily his interest, but his other duty in a different capacity, are in inevitable conflict. So far as it is alleged that he is a debtor of the company, it is also a matter where his duty as liquidator and his personal interest as debtor must be in conflict. It is the oldest rule of all in equity that a man should not place himself in a position where his duty and his interest conflict, without the fullest disclosure of the conflict and the approval of his continuing to hold that position despite the conflict. It is a proposition which applies across many fields to anyone holding a fiduciary office. Here the office of liquidator is well set out by Swinfen Eady J in *Re Charterland Goldfields Ltd* (1909) 26 TLR 132, and it is plain that a liquidator, although not strictly speaking a trustee, is nonetheless a fiduciary, holding an office with statutory duties analogous to the duties of a trustee to his beneficiaries being the duties of a liquidator to his creditors.'

A particular problem in relation to conflict of duty arises where an insolvency practitioner deals with the liquidation of a group of companies. That this is an appropriate course in the right circumstances is recognised in the Secretary of State's 'code of conduct' in relation to insolvency practitioners. It states:

'. . . In certain circumstances there will be an advantage, seen and agreed by creditors, for all the companies in a group, or otherwise associated, to be administered by one insolvency practitioner; but such prospect of economy should not hold sway where there is any suggestion that the affairs of individual companies within such a "group" have been dealt with oppressively to the advantage of others.'

Although there are statements suggesting a very strict test[1], the Court of Appeal in England in *Re Esal (Commodities) Ltd*[2], suggested that provided insolvency practitioners behaved sensibly such appointments were not to be ruled out. Dillon LJ stated:

'Of course there are possible conflicts of interest. It is unnecessary to go into them in detail, but one of the more obvious is that in an insolvency situation the subsidiary will have its own creditors whose claims will have to be met. Sometimes the creditor will include the parent company or the subsidiary next up the line. Sometimes the interests of the parent company or subsidiary next up the line will merely be an interest as shareholder which ranks behind the creditors of the subsidiary. But these sorts of potential conflicts do not in practice give rise to any serious difficulty because they are well known to the experienced insolvency practitioners.'

---

1  See comments of Harman J in *Re Corbenstoke Ltd (No 2)* (Supra); *Re P Turner (Wilsden) Ltd* [1987] BCLC 149; *Re Bi-Print Ltd* [1989] 2 Insolvency Intelligence 76; *Re GK Pty Ltd* [1983] 1 ACLC 848.
2  (1988) 4 BCC 475, [1989] BCLC 59.

## Provisional liquidators

### (1) *Appointment*

The court has power to appoint a 'provisional' liquidator at any time before the first appointment of a liquidator[1]. This applies in a winding up by the court only[2]. (The 'provisional' liquidator should not be confused with the 'interim' liquidator which is the name given to the liquidator appointed by the court in a winding up when the winding-up order is given[3]. He is called an 'interim' liquidator to cover a situation where, after the meetings of the company's contributories and creditors, somebody different from the interim liquidator is selected to be liquidator, and who then replaces the interim liquidator as liquidator[4].) The petition for winding up usually contains an application for the appointment of a provisional liquidator. The application for the appointment of a provisional liquidator may be made by the petitioner in the winding up or by a creditor of the company, or by a contributory or by the company itself or by any person who would be entitled to present a petition for the winding up[5]. It is usual practice for the application to be granted, unless the petition is opposed on grounds which appear substantial. The appointment of a provisional liquidator is not a first step in the winding up of the company, but rather a holding operation pending the decision whether or not to wind up[6]. In considering whether to make an appointment the court is primarily concerned to maintain the status quo in the affairs of the company and to avoid prejudice to parties[7]. In an English case it was stated[8]: 'Now the provisional liquidator's appointment is not only provisional, but contingent in this sense, that it operates to protect the property for an equal distribution only in the event of an order for compulsory winding up being made; and if no such order is made, then his appointment ought not to interfere with the rights of third persons.'

### (2) *Powers and duties of provisional liquidators*

Subsections 135(4) and (5) of the Insolvency Act 1986 merely state that the provisional liquidator shall carry out such functions as the court may confer on him, and that the powers of the provisional liquidator may be limited by the order appointing him. How the second provision should be properly interpreted has been the subject of some discussion in Scotland[9]. The better view is that express powers should be sought[10]. He has the statutory power to require a statement of affairs to be produced[11]. (See Chapter 17 on accounting law and practice.) Also, because winding up commences at the presentation

1 Insolvency Act 1986, s 135(3).
2 Ibid, s 135(1).
3 Ibid, s 138(2).
4 Ibid, s 139(3).
5 Insolvency (Scotland) Rules 1986, r 4.1.
6 *Teague, Petr*, 1985 SLT 469.
7 *Levy v Napier* 1962 SLT 264.
8 *Re Dry Docks Corporation of London* (1888) 39 Ch D 306 at 314, per Fry LJ on appeal.
9 See McBryde, 'The Powers of Provisional Liquidators', 1977 SLT (News) 145.
10 *Lochore and Capledraw Cannel Coal Co Ltd* (1889) 16 R 556; *Wilsons (Glasgow and Trinidad) Ltd (in Liquidation)* 1912 2 SLT 330; *Drummond Wood Ltd*, 7 December 1971, unreported.
11 Insolvency Act 1986, s 131(1).

cf the petition[1], and he has been appointed liquidator provisionally[2], he has in principle the normal powers of a liquidator in a compulsory winding up. However the view that the provisional liquidator's powers are restricted and that express powers should be sought, is now given extra backing by the new section 135(4) which requires him to have express 'functions' conferred by the court. What powers he should have will depend on what functions are conferred, ie which will be necessary for the carrying out of the functions. It is the usual practice to ask in the winding-up petition for the powers in Part II of Schedule 4 to the 1986 Act, but others may be added as appropriate.

The provisional liquidator has a duty to notify his appointment to the Registrar of Companies, to the company, and to any receiver that there is over any part of the property of the company[3]. He is also under a duty to advertise his appointment according to any directions laid down by the court[4]. His main duty, however, as stated above, is to preserve the status quo and to avoid prejudice to the parties. He is not really there therefore to 'liquidate' the company as a liquidator proper, and perhaps would be better named a 'caretaker'. One could not after all talk about a 'provisional executioner'.

As in the case of a winding-up order, where there has been an order to appoint a provisional liquidator, no action or proceeding may be proceeded with or commenced against the company or its property, except by leave of the court and subject to what terms the court may impose[5]. (See also pages 22, 24, and 25 for effect of appointment of provisional liquidator on directors' powers, carrying on of business and contracts of employment.)

### (3) *Remuneration of provisional liquidators*

The remuneration of the provisional liquidator is fixed by the court[6]. If a winding-up order is not made, his remuneration is to be paid out of the assets of the company, and where a winding-up order is made as an expense of the liquidation[7]. If no winding-up order is made he may retain out of the company's property such sums or property as are or may be required for meeting his remuneration and expenses[8].

### (4) *Release of provisional liquidator*

The provisional liquidator gets his release (for release see page 41) on an application by him to the court from such time as the court may determine[9].

## Appointment of special manager

The liquidator may now apply to the court for the appointment of a 'special manager' under section 177 of the Insolvency Act 1986, when it appears to

1 Insolvency Act 1986, s 129(2).
2 Ibid, s 135(1).
3 Insolvency (Scotland) Rules 1986, r 4.2(1).
4 Ibid, r 4.2(2).
5 Insolvency Act 1986, s 130(2).
6 Insolvency (Scotland) Rules 1986, r 4.5(1).
7 Ibid, r 4.5(3).
8 Ibid, r 4.5(3a) and (4) as inserted by paragraph 10 of the Schedule to the Insolvency (Scotland) Amendment Rules 1987.
9 Insolvency Act 1986, s 174(5).

him that the nature of the company's business or property, or the interests of the company's creditors or contributories or members generally, require the appointment of another person to manage the company's business or property, and the special manager may be granted any of the powers of a liquidator. This is a recently introduced procedure in Scotland, and is likely to be used only in the case of large or complicated companies. The liquidator must support any application for a special manager with a report giving the reasons for the appointment and include the estimate of the value of the assets in respect of which the special manager is to be appointed. The special manager's appointment must be for a specific duration, or until a certain occurrence, or be made subject to renewal. His remuneration, and what his areas of competence are, are to be fixed by the court[1]. There is no requirement for the special manager to be a 'qualified insolvency practitioner'. The traditional way the court met the need for special managers was by the appointment of joint liquidators from persons knowledgeable in a business. Because, however, liquidators now must be 'qualified insolvency practitioners' it is no longer open to the court or creditors to appoint an expert in the field who is not qualified as an insolvency practitioner. A key difference in the new system, however, is that only the liquidator may make the application under section 177 of the Insolvency Act 1986 whereas, in relation to the appointment of liquidators, creditors and contributories may.

**Removal of liquidator**

The liquidator may be removed on an application to the court or by the resolution of the creditors.

(1) *Application to court*

In terms of section 108 of the Insolvency Act 1986, the court may on cause shown remove a liquidator and appoint another. This power is additional to the power to remove on a successful challenge made within seven days of nomination (see page 33). Where a person has refused to act as a liquidator, he is not held to have been validly appointed and an action of removal is not necessary[2]. Even if a majority of creditors wants a liquidator removed, 'cause' must be shown[3]. Misconduct does not need to be established, but it is necessary to show that it is in the best interests of the liquidation[4]. Conflict of interest is a reason for the removal of a liquidator[5]. The appointment of a receiver as liquidator has been successfully challenged[6]. It is generally undesirable that the same person should be both receiver and liquidator.

The Insolvency Act 1986 makes the appointment of a liquidator a matter for the members and creditors if they so choose[7]. Accordingly the former discretion of the court in deciding who was to be liquidator in a compulsory

1 Insolvency (Scotland) Rules 1986, r 4.69.
2 *Charles, Petr* 1963 SC 1.
3 *Ker, Petr* (1897) 5 SLT 126.
4 *McKnight & Co v Montgomery Ltd* (1892) 19 R 501; *Gaunt's Exrs v Liqrs of Mancha Syndicate Capital Ltd* (1907) 14 SLT 675.
5 *Monkland Iron Co v Dun* (1886) 14 R 242; *Lysons v Liquidator of the Miraflores Gold Syndicate* (1895) 22 R 605.
6 *Re Karamelli & Barnett Ltd* [1917] 1 Ch 203.
7 Insolvency Act 1986, ss 100(2) and 139(3).

winding up is effectively gone. However it will still be open to any director, member or creditor in a voluntary winding up, or any member or creditor in a compulsory winding up, to appeal against the exercise of the court's discretion where they have judicially challenged an appointment within seven days under sections 100(3) and 139(4) of the Insolvency Act 1986. However, where a judge has exercised his discretion in appointing or confirming a liquidator with the material facts before him, the decision will not be reviewable, unless it can be shown that there are circumstances affecting the personal character or honesty of the liquidator or that there was something improper in the appointment[1]. If a judge has removed a liquidator, and an appeal is taken against the interlocutor removing him, that interlocutor is suspended and the liquidator may still act[2]. Although there are provisions in terms of section 162(2) and (3) of the Insolvency Act 1986 for certain orders made by the Vacation Judge[3] to be given effect until the Inner House (Appeal Court) has disposed of the matter, the position in Levy, Petitioner[4] is the more usual position. Accordingly, where an unsuitable liquidator is using the appeal process to delay loss of powers, the position is not wholly satisfactory.

## (2) Creditors' resolution

A liquidator may be removed (but not a provisional liquidator[5]) by resolution of the creditors at a meeting of creditors specially summoned for that purpose under section 171(2)(b) of the Insolvency Act 1986 (in the case of a creditors' winding up), and under section 172(2) of the Insolvency Act 1986 (in the case of a winding up by the court). A meeting must be summoned by the liquidator for this purpose, if he is requested to do so by creditors representing not less than one quarter in value of the creditors[6]. In the case of a liquidator who has been appointed by the court under section 108 of the Insolvency Act 1986 in a creditors' voluntary winding up (ie on a vacancy or after a successful removal application), there is a requisite percentage required of at least half in value for summoning a meeting for the removal of the liquidator[7]. The requisite majority to remove is a majority in value of creditors voting[8].

## Resignation of liquidator

### (1) Resignation of liquidator

The liquidator may resign only because of ill health or because a joint liquidator is no longer required, or because he intends to cease practising as an insolvency practitioner, or there has been some conflict of interest or change of personal circumstances which precludes or makes impracticable by him the further discharge by him of the duties of the liquidator[9]. If a liquidator resigns, in a creditors' voluntary winding up, the creditors may fill the

---

1 Steel Scaffolding Co v Buckleys Ltd 1935 SC 617.
2 Levy, Petr 1938 SC 46.
3 Those listed in the Insolvency Act 1986, Sch 3, Pt II.
4 1938 SC 46.
5 Insolvency Act 1986, s 172(2).
6 Insolvency (Scotland) Rules 1986, r 4.23(1).
7 Insolvency Act 1986, s 171(3)(b).
8 Insolvency (Scotland) Rules 1986, r 7.12(1).
9 Ibid, r 4.28(3).

vacancy[1]. In a compulsory winding up by the court, the court fills the vacancy[2]. Before resigning his office, the liquidator must call a meeting of the creditors for the purpose of receiving his resignation. The notice summoning the meeting must draw attention to the law in relation to his being granted a 'release'[3] (see infra). The notice must also be accompanied by an account of the liquidator's administration of the winding up, including a summary of his receipts and payments[4]. The meeting may accept the liquidator's resignation. If it is accepted, it is effective from the date that the creditors' meeting determine[5]. If the resignation is accepted, the liquidator must then send a notice of his resignation to the registrar of companies on a Form 4.16 (Scot) and also to the court in a compulsory winding up on a Form 4.15 (Scot)[6]. If the liquidator's resignation is not accepted, the court may, on the liquidator's application, make an order giving him leave to resign[7].

## (2) *Vacation of office*

If the liquidator does not resign, he 'vacates' office after the final meeting of creditors as soon as he has sent notice to the Registrar of Companies on a Form 4.26 (Scot), and also to the court in a compulsory winding up[8]. Where a liquidator vacates office, by for example, automatically vacating office through loss of his practising certificate, he still has sufficient interest to apply to the court under section 108(1) of the Insolvency Act 1986 to have some other person including a colleague appointed in his stead[9].

## Release of liquidator

A release is a 'discharge' which discharges the liquidator from all liability in respect of both his acts and omissions in the winding up[10]. He is still, however, potentially liable under section 212 of the Insolvency Act 1986[11]. The procedure is for the liquidator, on resignation, removal, or vacation of office, first to seek a release from the creditors and, if he is not granted release by the creditors, to apply to the Accountant of Court for his discharge using a Form 4.12 (Scot)[12]. The procedure works as follows:

## (1) *Removal*

When creditors' meetings are summoned for the purpose of removing a liquidator, the notice summoning the meeting must draw attention to section

1 Insolvency Act 1986, s 104.
2 Ibid, s 108(1).
3 Insolvency (Scotland) Rules 1986, r 4.28(2).
4 Ibid, r 4.28(2).
5 Ibid, r 4.29(2) and (7); see also r 4.29(6) as inserted by para 20 of the Schedule to the Insolvency (Scotland) Amendment Rules 1987.
6 Insolvency Act 1986, ss 171(6) and 172(6); Insolvency (Scotland) Rules 1986, r 4.29.
7 Ibid, r 4.30.
8 Insolvency Act 1986, ss 171(6) and 172(8).
9 *Re AJ Adams (Builders) Ltd* [1991] BCC 62.
10 Insolvency Act 1986, ss 173(4) and 174(6).
11 Summary remedy against delinquent directors, liquidators, etc, see chapter 7.
12 Insolvency (Scotland) Amendment Rules 1987, r 4.29(4) applying r 4.25(2) and (3); r 4.25(2) and (3); r 4.31(6) as also applied to creditors' voluntary windings up applying r 4.25(2) and (3) of the Insolvency (Scotland) Rules 1986; Insolvency Act 1986, s 173(2)(b) and s 174(4)(b).

174 of the Insolvency Act 1986, which entitles the meetings summoned for that purpose either to resolve against or for the liquidator's 'release'[1]. If the creditors do not resolve to 'release' the liquidator he is not released unless he applies to the Accountant of Court and the Accountant of Court gives him a release.

## (2) *Resignation*

The notice summoning the meeting to consider a liquidator's resignation must refer to the discretion of creditors in giving a release in the same way as a notice summoning a meeting for his removal[2]. It may either resolve against or for his release and if he is not granted a release, he is not released unless the Accountant of Court grants it.

## (3) *Winding up*

The final statutory meeting in a compulsory winding up and in a creditors' winding up may also release or resolve against releasing the liquidator. There is no provision in the legislation however for the notice summoning the final meeting to draw this to the attention of the creditors.

# III. TITLE, STATUS AND FUNCTIONS OF LIQUIDATOR

## Title of liquidator

The liquidator of a company in Scotland should be styled 'the liquidator', formerly called 'the official liquidator'[3]. The liquidator must be an individual[4].

## Liquidator required to be insolvency practitioner

The liquidator must be a 'qualified insolvency practitioner'[5] as defined by section 390(2) of the Insolvency Act 1986. A provisional liquidator also must be a 'qualified insolvency practitioner', as must an administrator, administrative receiver, and a supervisor under a voluntary arrangement[6]. In order to qualify as an insolvency practitioner an individual must be authorised to do so by virtue of membership of a duly recognised professional body and be permitted so to act by the rules of that body, or hold authorisations so to act granted by the Secretary of State or another competent authority[7]. The Secretary of State may declare a body to be a recognised professional body for the purpose of the recognition of insolvency practitioners if it is a body which regulates the practice of a profession and maintains and enforces rules for

1 Insolvency (Scotland) Rules 1986, r 4.23; Insolvency Act 1986, s 174(4)(a) and (b).
2 Insolvency (Scotland) Rules 1986, r 4.28(2).
3 Insolvency Act 1986, s 163(a).
4 Ibid, s 390(1).
5 Ibid, s 230(3).
6 Ibid, s 388(1).
7 Ibid, s 390(2)(a) and (b).

securing that such of its members as are permitted by or under the rules to act as insolvency practitioners, are fit and proper persons so to act, and meet acceptable requirements as to education and practical training and experience[1]. The Insolvency Practitioners Regulations 1990[2] lay down certain prescribed requirements in relation to the practical training and experience that the recognised professional bodies will be expected to demand of their members. Given the different legal practice in Scotland, the Law Society of Scotland does not require any particular number of cases to be handled or hours spent on insolvency business in any particular period prior to the time of application for a certificate. The recognised professional bodies at present are the Law Society of Scotland, the Institute of Chartered Accountants of Scotland, the Insolvency Practitioners Association, the Law Society, the Institute of Chartered Accountants in England and Wales, the Institute of Chartered Accountants in Ireland and the Chartered Association of Certified Accountants[3]. In addition a practitioner may apply direct to the Secretary of State or, in relation to a case of any description specified in directions given by the Secretary of State, to the body or person so specified in relation to cases of that description, for an authorisation under section 392 of the Insolvency Act 1986. The Secretary of State or body concerned is referred to as the 'competent authority'. The application must be made in such manner as the competent authority may direct and must contain or be accompanied by such information as the authority may reasonably require and must be accompanied by a prescribed fee. Authorisations are granted subject to a maximum duration of three years[4]. There is also a procedure for an appeal to the Insolvency Practitioners' Tribunal under section 397 of the Insolvency Act 1986.

Nobody other than insolvency practitioners is allowed to act as liquidator, as well as be a liquidator. The requirement of entrusting the insolvency procedures to qualified insolvency practitioners was affirmed by Hoffmann J in the English case of *Re Ipcon Fashions Ltd*[5]. That case was concerned with an application under section 6 of the Company Directors Disqualification Act 1986, in which it was sought to disqualify a director on the ground of unfitness. The director had stated before the official receiver's examiner that, at a time when the company was already insolvent, he had decided to 'wind down the company's affairs with a view to paying all creditors'. Hoffmann J observed that:

'[The director] suggested that he was in effect acting as a liquidator at lower rates than a professional liquidator would have charged. But the law, for good reason, requires a liquidator to be an independent and qualified insolvency practitioner and I do not think [the director] was entitled to take into his own hands the liquidation of an insolvent company.'

*Making over of assets to employees*

It was formerly the case that a company might be prevented from making *ex gratia* payments to employees after the cessation or sale of its trade on the

1 Insolvency Act 1986, s 391(1) and (2).
2 SI 1990/439.
3 Insolvency Practitioners (Recognised Professional Bodies) Order 1986, SI 1986/1764.
4 Insolvency Practitioners Regulations 1990, reg 10.
5 (1989) 5 BCC 773.

ground that such payments were not for the benefit of the company and hence were *ultra vires* or, more strictly, an abuse of power[1]. The position was changed by the Companies Act 1980 the provisions of which have now been re-enacted in section 187 of the Insolvency Act 1986 and section 719 of the Companies Act 1985. Section 719 of the Companies Act 1985 empowers a company to make provision for the benefit of its employees or former employees of the company or its subsidiaries in connection with the cessation of the whole or part of the undertaking of the company or a subsidiary, or its transfer to any other person[2], whether or not the exercise is in the best interests of the company[3]. The section provides that, on the winding up of a company, whether by the court or voluntarily, the liquidator may make any payment which, before the commencement of the winding up, the company decided to make under section 719 of the Companies Act 1985. In addition, the power to make provision for employees or former employees conferred by section 719 may be exercised by the liquidator after the commencement of winding-up provided that:

(1)   the company's liabilities have first been fully satisfied and provision has been made for the expenses of the winding-up;
(2)   the exercise of the power has been sanctioned by the appropriate resolution of the company; and
(3)   any other requirement applicable to the exercise of the power by the company has been met.

The required resolution referred to in (2) above is an ordinary resolution of the company, or, if a memorandum or articles require the exercise of the powers to be sanctioned by a resolution requiring more than a simple majority, with the sanction of a resolution of that description[4]. These provisions will only be relevant in a case where there is supervening solvency in the liquidation.

## Status of liquidator

Lord Fraser stated that the exact status of the liquidator was in some doubt[5]. In most liquidations the question of the status of the liquidator is of academic interest only but it can be important in some contexts such as in taxation questions, standards of care and probity, etc.

### (1) *Agent of creditors/members*

The liquidator has been described as an agent of the creditors but is so only in the sense that he represents the creditors through the company[6]; he is not the agent of the members, so that in the case of an overpayment by the liquidator

---

1 *Gibson's Executor v Gibson* 1978 SC 197, 1980 SLT 2, applying *Parke v Daily News Ltd* [1962] Ch 927 [1962] 2 All ER 929.
2 Companies Act 1985, s 719(1).
3 Ibid, s 719(2).
4 Companies Act 1985, s 719(3)(a), (c).
5 *Taylor v Wilson's Trs* 1974 SLT 298.
6 *Waterhouse v Jamieson* (1870) 8 M (HL) 88.

to members through an error in law the liquidator could not rely on any agency to seek return of the money[1].

## (2) *Trustee of creditors*

The liquidator has been described as a trustee for the creditors. Thus Lord Selborne said: 'The hand which receives the calls necessarily receives them as a statutory trustee for the equal and rateable payment of all the creditors'[2]. It cannot be inferred from that decision that all the results follow which would follow if the liquidator were a trustee in the full sense; although relying on the trustee concept, he has been held bound to disclose to the general body of creditors a report he had obtained on the possibility of an application under section 322(1) of the Companies Act 1948[3], and it has been confirmed by the House of Lords that, in the context of a taxing statute, when a company enters insolvent liquidation it ceases to be the 'beneficial' owner of its assets[4].

## (3) *Agent and administrator of company*

The liquidator is primarily the agent and administrator of the company[5]. As agent he acts as an administrator[6]. Lord President Emslie described the multifaceted nature of the liquidator's status in the case of *Smith v Lord Advocate*[7]:

'I have not forgotten either that, in the particular circumstances of the many cases cited by counsel for the liquidator, a liquidator has been described in many ways, e g a paid agent for the Court, an Officer of the Court, an agent or administrator for the creditors and contributories. None of these cases decides, however, that he may not in, for example, the matter of completion of a company contract, be regarded as acting as a manager, for and on behalf of the company itself. The liquidator is an official with many characteristics and he may, in certain circumstances, quite properly attract one or more of the descriptions which have been applied to him. There is nevertheless nothing inconsistent between his answering to such descriptions in appropriate circumstances and his possession of the character of manager and administrator of the company's affairs, and of a person acting for and on behalf of the company in the matter of the completion of company contracts. In such circumstances he may also, at the same time, have the character of a person with certain statutory obligations of a fiduciary character, or of an officer of the Court or, indeed, of an administrator or agent for the benefit of creditors and contributories.'

## (4) *Fiduciary status*

A liquidator, as Lord Emslie stated, occupies a fiduciary position[8]. He must not make a secret profit[9], or allow conflicts of interest to continue. Any transaction entered into by an associate may be set aside by the court at the

---

1 *Taylor v Wilson's Trs* 1975 SC 146.
2 *Re Black & Co's Case* (1872) 8 Ch App 254 at 262 (CA).
3 *Liqr of Upper Clyde Shipbuilders* 1975 SLT 38; the law is changed in emphasis by r 7.27 of the Insolvency (Scotland) Rules 1986.
4 *Ayerst v C & K (Construction) Ltd* [1975] 3 WLR 16 (HL).
5 Insolvency Act 1986, ss 165(3), 167(1) and Sch 4.
6 *Smith v Lord Advocate* 1978 SC 259.
7 1978 SC 259 at 273.
8 See also *Lamey v Winram* 1987 SLT 635.
9 *Silkstone and Haigh Moor Coal Co v Edey* [1900] 1 Ch 167.

instance of any interested party and the liquidator ordered by the court to compensate the company for any loss occasioned. Such transaction may not be set aside if sanctioned by the court or if it is shown to the court's satisfaction that the transaction was for value *and* that it was entered into by the liquidator without knowing or having any reason to suppose that the person concerned was an associate[1]. The same type of action for misfeasance, breach of trust, etc, may be brought against him as against a director under section 212 of the Insolvency Act 1986, and he can be ordered to pay an appropriate sum to the company's assets. An action seeking such an order may be brought by a creditor or contributory[2] except that a contributory needs leave of the court but need not benefit from any order the court might grant[3].

## (5) *Officer of court*

Liquidators in a compulsory winding up are also 'officers of the court'[4] and can be appointed by the court in a creditors' winding up. This jurisdiction may have implications in relation to judicial review in Scotland (see page 49).

## (6) *Liquidator's standard of care*

The liquidator must exercise a degree of care and skill appropriate to the circumstances; so that, for example, although he is not an insurer he must show the degree of skill appropriate to the task he has assumed, and by assuming, held himself out as possessing[5]. When, however, he does a specific act after seeking and obtaining the approval of the court he cannot be held liable in negligence[6]. Also the option which the liquidator now has of applying to the court to appoint a 'special manager', means that he can avoid getting into the hot water of taking on responsibilities beyond him. This option, it is thought, will impose a duty to exercise such care in the appointment of a special manager in a situation that every reasonable liquidator would apply.

## (7) *Personal liability of liquidator on contracts*

The liquidator does not incur personal liability when entering into contracts on behalf of the company[7]. He may engage on behalf of the company and warrant that the company's assets are sufficient to cover the contract, but does not need to do this[8]. He should be able to avoid personal liability not only by changing all commercial documentation to show that the company is in liquidation (as required under section 188 of the Insolvency Act 1986), but also by signing as 'liquidator' of the particular company. Where the liquidator

---

1 Insolvency (Scotland) Rules 1986, r 4.38.
2 Insolvency Act 1986, s 212(3).
3 Ibid, s 212(4).
4 *Millar* (1890) 18 R 179.
5 *Re Home and Colonial Insurance Co* [1930] 1 Ch 102, 125 and 133.
6 *Highland Engineering Ltd v Anderson* 1979 SLT 122.
7 *County Council of Lanarkshire v Brown* (1905) 12 SLT 700.
8 See *Smith v Lord Advocate* 1978 SC 259.

grants a disposition, he incurs liability in practice by granting certain warranties[1]. In litigation expenses have been awarded against liquidators on the ground that liquidators of a company (like trustees who defend actions in a representative capacity) personally warrant the sufficiency of the funds in their hands, and are personally liable for expenses[2]. A company when it litigates may be asked to find caution for expenses in terms of section 726(2) of the Companies Act 1985, but because a liquidator is personally liable, caution will not be required if there is no suggestion that he would be unable to honour the obligation[3]. The liquidator has a right of relief out of the funds[4] except where the funds are insufficient, or the action is caused by his personal blameworthiness and the decree finds him personally liable[5].

Those who contract with a liquidator acting for and on behalf of a company in the carrying on of a company's business are entitled to full satisfaction before any question of the ranking of the creditors at the date of the winding up comes to be decided[6].

**Functions of liquidator**

The Insolvency Act 1986 uses several expressions to denote the functions of a liquidator in an insolvent liquidation. For example:

(a) the liquidator in a creditors' voluntary winding up is described by section 100(1) as: 'liquidator for the purpose of winding up the company's affairs and distributing its assets';

(b) section 130(4) states: 'An order for winding up a company operates in favour of all the creditors and all of the contributories of the company as if made on the joint petition of a creditor and contributory'; and

(c) section 143(1) states: 'The functions of a liquidator of a company which is being wound up by the court are to secure that the assets of the company are got in, realised and distributed to the company's creditors, and, if there is a surplus, to the persons entitled to it'.

Legal cases make quite clear what these expressions taken together mean. Liquidators are administrators of the company's assets with the management of the company vesting in them[7]. 'They are administrators for the purpose of dividing the estate among the creditors of the company, and if there is any balance, for dividing it among the contributories. But if the estate is insolvent, then the sole purpose for which the liquidators administer is to distribute it amongst the various creditors of the company according to their rights as creditors[8].'

---

1 *Liqr of Style & Mantle Ltd v Price's Tailors Ltd* 1934 SC 548.
2 *Sinclair v Thurso Pavement Syndicate* (1903) 11 SLT 364; *Liquidator of the Consolidated Copper Co of Canada v Peddie* (1877) 5 R 393; *Aitken* (1898) 5 SLT 374.
3 *Stewart v Steel* 1987 SLT (Sh Ct) 60.
4 *Smith v Lord Advocate* 1978 SC 259 at 273, per Lord President Emslie.
5 *Kilmarnock Theatre Co v Buchanan* 1911 SC 607; and *Liquidator of the Nairn Public Hall Co Ltd* 1946 SC 395.
6 *Smith v Lord Advocate*, supra at 273, per Lord Emslie; Insolvency (Scotland) Rules 1986, r 4.67(1)(a).
7 *Smith v Lord Advocate* 1978 SC 259.
8 *Clark v West Calder Oil Co* (1882) 9 R 1017; see Lord President Inglis at 1025 and Lord Shand at 1030.

*Caution*

Section 390(3)(b) of the Insolvency Act 1986 and Regulations 11 and 12 of the Insolvency Practitioners Regulations 1990 (SI 1990/439) require an insolvency practitioner to have a bond of caution which complies with the requirements in Part I of Schedule 2 to the Regulations. Such caution must be for at least £250,000, and a certificate of specific penalty must be obtained in respect of each company in liquidation, subject to the exceptions in regulation 13 (where a provisional liquidator or liquidator in a voluntary winding up or administrator becomes liquidator in a winding up by the court). Registration in the sederunt book of the liquidation and with the Registrar of Companies is required by regulation 15. A person who appoints an insolvency practitioner to any office must satisfy himself that the person appointed has caution, in terms of rule 7.28(1) of the Insolvency (Scotland) Ruless 1986. The liquidation committee is, in any event, under a duty to review the amount of caution from time to time, in terms of rule 7.28(2). Rule 7.28(3) provides that the expense of caution is an expense of the liquidation. Rules 4.3 and 4.4 make specific provision for caution of a provisional liquidator, and for his failure to find or maintain caution.

# IV. DUTIES AND POWERS OF THE LIQUIDATOR

## DUTIES OF LIQUIDATOR

(1) **Duty to take control of the company's assets**, which will involve examining persons who have been involved with the company, including examination of witnesses and obtaining orders, where necessary, for the company's property in the wrong hands to be delivered back;

(2) **Duty to make out a list of the company's creditors and contributories**, which is to enable the liquidator to assess the liabilities of the company and to pay debts owed to creditors as far as the company's assets allow, and to pay the contributories if there is any surplus, the contributories also being creditors (although subordinated creditors) of the company;

(3) **Duty to realise the assets of the company**, i e to 'liquidate' the assets of the company in order to pay the creditors and contributories. Included among assets will not only be the fixed assets, current assets, e g receivables, stock, etc, but any uncalled capital of the company, i e claims against contributories where they become liable as debtors of the company for issued but not fully paid up shares;

(4) **Duty to discharge the debts of the company according to law**, which involves paying the creditors their debts or a part of their debts as 'dividends' out of the assets of the company in accordance with the 'ranking' rules laid down by law; and

(5) **Duty to pay any surplus after payment of the creditors of the company to the contributories in their capacity as subordinated creditors of the company.**

# POWERS OF LIQUIDATOR

Liquidators are given by law a formidable battery of powers to enable them to perform the duties given to them by law. Although liquidators appointed in a creditors' voluntary winding up are not 'officers of the court' – if the liquidator is appointed by the creditors and not by the court, all liquidators have powers which go beyond the powers which a company itself if not in liquidation or any other private organisation would have. They can require evidence in relation to claims. They are entitled to access to documents relating to the business in the hands of third parties. They can require delivery of title deeds of the company even if they are subject to a lien. They 'adjudicate' claims. They must be drawn from a pool of authorised 'insolvency practitioners'. This jurisdiction will make them subject to judicial review in Scotland where no appeal is available.

Liquidators have *two* classes of powers:

(1) **Ordinary powers**, by which is meant powers which all liquidators have for which no further authority is necessary before they use them.

(2) **Extraordinary powers**, by which is meant those special powers which liquidators obtain only with the sanction of the court or the liquidation committee (for liquidation committee see page 371) or sometimes only with the sanction of the court. Sanction may be granted retrospectively[1].

There is no difference between the 'ordinary powers' and the 'extraordinary powers' exercisable by the liquidator in an insolvent liquidation whether it is a creditors' voluntary winding up or a compulsory winding up, except in relation to two of the powers listed as 'ordinary powers' (nos. (n) and (o) and marked by asterisks**), which require sanction in the case of compulsory winding up, and certain powers (no. (k)) which are exercised by the liquidator in a creditors' winding up but by the court in a compulsory winding up. In a creditors' voluntary winding up none of the powers may be exercised by the liquidator if he has been appointed by the members, except with the sanction of the court, prior to the creditors confirming the liquidator at their meeting, except the taking custody and control of property, disposing of perishable goods and protecting assets[2].

## (1) Ordinary powers of a liquidator

### (a) *Sale of assets*

The liquidator has the power, without the sanction of the court or the liquidation committee, to sell any of the company's property by public auction or private contract, with power to transfer the whole of it to any person or to sell the same in parcels[3].

This power, with power to execute deeds includes the power to sell in any fashion any of the company's property – heritable or moveable – with power to convey heritage. A disposition is given in the name of the company with the

---

1 *Re Associated Travel Leisure and Services Ltd* [1978] 2 All ER 273.
2 Insolvency Act 1986, s 166(2).
3 Ibid, ss 165 and 167 and Sch 4, para 6.

consent of the liquidator. seal and signed by the liquidator before two witnesses. (For the liquidator's personal liability on a disposition see page 47.) The liquidator may not sell a lease which contains a covenant against assignation without the landlord's consent. He may accept consideration for a sale other than cash[1].

The liquidator is entitled to sell heritable property, even if there is a security over the heritable property, if he is able to obtain a price high enough to discharge every security over the property[2].

Where the liquidator has intimated to the secured creditor that he intends to sell, the creditor is precluded from taking any steps to enforce his security; but equally where a creditor has intimated to the liquidator that the creditor intends to commence the procedure for sale of that part of the property covered by his security, the liquidator may not commence the procedure for the sale of that part secured by the creditor[3]. If there is any failure to comply with any requirement in relation to the procedure described above, the validity of the title of any purchaser of the heritable property shall not be challengeable on that ground[4]. If there is any doubt as to the propriety of a sale, such as in relation to a member of the liquidation committee, the liquidator should seek the sanction of the court[5] (see also under 'Fiduciary Status', supra).

(b) *Execution of deeds*

The liquidator has the power, without the sanction of the court or the liquidation committee, to do all acts and execute, in the name and on behalf of the company, all deeds, receipts and other documents and for that purpose to use, when necessary, the company's seal[6]. (If there are joint liquidators the need for counter-signature will depend on determination at appointment[7].)

(c) *Claiming in bankruptcy*

The liquidator has the power, without the sanction of the court or the liquidation committee, to prove, rank and claim in the bankruptcy, insolvency or sequestration of any contributory for any balance against his estate, and to receive dividends in the bankruptcy, insolvency or sequestration in respect of that balance, as a separate debt due from the bankrupt or insolvent, and rateably with the other separate creditors[8].

---

1 *Agra and Masterman's Bank* (1866) LR 12 Eq 509.
2 Insolvency (Scotland) Rules 1986, r 4.22(1) as amended by paragraph 18 of the Schedule to the Insolvency (Scotland) Amendment Rules 1987.
3 Insolvency Act 1986, s 169(2); and Bankruptcy (Scotland) Act 1985, s 39(4) as applied to liquidations by r 4.22(1) of the Insolvency (Scotland) Rules 1986 amended as above, but subject to the modifications in r 4.16(2) and any other necessary modifications.
4 Insolvency Act 1986, s 169(2); and Bankruptcy (Scotland) Act 1985, s 39(7) as applied to liquidations by r 4.22(1) of the Insolvency (Scotland) Rules 1986 amended as above, but subject to the modifications in r 4.16(2) and any other necessary modifications.
5 *Dowling v Lord Advocate* 1963 SLT 28.
6 Insolvency Act 1986, ss 165, 167, Sch 4, para 7.
7 Ibid, s 231.
8 Ibid, ss 165 and 167 and Sch 4, para 8.

## (d) *Drawing of bills*

The liquidator has the power, without the sanction of the court or the liquidation committee, to draw, accept, make and indorse any bill of exchange or promissory note in the name and on behalf of the company, with the same effect with respect to the company's liability as if the bill or note had been drawn, accepted, made or indorsed by or on behalf of the company in the course of its business[1]. The liquidator must be careful to state on any bill: 'For and on behalf of [name of company] [signature] liquidator'. He may be personally liable if he merely signs '[signature] liquidator'[2].

## (e) *Mortgaging assets*

The liquidator has the power, without the sanction of the court or the liquidation committee, to raise on the security of the assets of the company any money requisite[3]. The liquidator may not grant a security in priority to any existing secured creditors except with consent or if they are personally barred[4]. Obligations incurred have priority (even if not secured) out of the assets of the company[5].

## (f) *Acting as executor to a contributor*

The liquidator has the power, without the sanction of the court or liquidation committee, to take out in his official name confirmation or letters of administration to any deceased contributory and to do in his official name any other act necessary for obtaining payment of any money due from a contributory or his estate which cannot conveniently be done in the name of the company. In all such cases the money due is deemed, for the purpose of enabling the liquidator to take out the confirmation or letters of administration or recover the money, to be due to the liquidator himself[6].

## (g) *Appointment of agent*

The liquidator has the power, without the sanction of the court or liquidation committee, to appoint an agent to do any business which the liquidator is unable to do himself[7]. He must exercise his discretion personally[8], and in Australia was held not entitled to appoint an agent to effect a compromise of a debt owing to the company[9], or to give a general authority to his accountants to act as his agents for the purposes of the liquidation and all accounting matters[10]. He may employ a solicitor and pay for legal services but they may

---

1 Ibid, ss 165 and 167 and Sch 4, para 9.
2 See the Bills of Exchange Act 1882, s 26(1); *cf. Hutcheson & Co v Eaton & Son* (1884) 13 QBD 861.
3 Insolvency Act 1986, ss 165, 167, Sch 4, para 10.
4 *Re Regent's Canal Ironworks Co, ex p Grissell* (1875) 3 Ch D 411.
5 Insolvency Act 1986, s 115.
6 Ibid, ss 165 and 167 and Sch 4, para 11.
7 Ibid, ss 165 and 167 and Sch 4, para 12.
8 *The Scotch Granite Co* (1868) 17 LT 533.
9 *Rendall v Conroy* (1897) 8 QLJ 89.
10 *The Timberland LHS* (1979) ACLR 259.

not be paid for before taxation by the auditor[1], and in the case of a compulsory winding up the liquidator must give notice to the liquidation committee that he is employing a solicitor[2]. Law agents must not do any of the liquidator's job and may only be employed specially where legal work is necessary[3], and the liquidator's fee will be reduced by the court if a law agent has done the liquidator's work[4].

(h) *Power to require evidence from persons in relation to claims*

The liquidator has the power, without the sanction of the court or the liquidation committee, to require any creditor who has submitted a claim to produce further evidence, or require any other person who he believes can produce evidence, to produce the evidence. If they fail to comply, or delay, he may apply to the court for an order for private examination before the court. The court may make an order requiring the creditor or any other person to attend for private examination before it on a date at least eight and not more than 16 days after the order, at a time specified in the order, and the examination should be on oath. The liquidator may have a solicitor or advocate to represent him or he may appear himself[5].

(i) *Power of access to documents in the hands of third parties*

The liquidator is entitled, without the sanction of the court or liquidation committee, to access to all the documents relating to the assets of the business or financial affairs of the company sent by or on behalf of the company to a third party and which are in that third party's hands. He is entitled to make copies of these documents. If the liquidator meets with obstruction he may apply to the court for an order ordering any person to cease obstructing him[6]. It is easier in court to get a negative interim interdict order than an interim positive order so that mechanically an order forbidding persons 'obstructing' would be easier to obtain than an order for access.

(j) *Power to require delivery of title deeds of company*

The liquidator may, without the sanction of the court or the liquidation committee, require to have delivered to him any title deed or other document of the company even where there is a right of lien claimed over the title deed or document. The title deed holder keeps any preference as holder of the lien[7].

---

1 Insolvency Act 1986, s 169(2) and Bankruptcy (Scotland) Act 1985, s 53(2) as applied to liquidations by r 4.68(1) of the Insolvency (Scotland) Rules 1986.
2 Insolvency Act 1986, s 167(2)(b).
3 *Leith and East Coast Steam Shipping Co (in Liquidation)* 1911 SLT 371.
4 *AB & Co Ltd (in Liquidation)* 1929 SLT 24.
5 Insolvency Act 1986, s 169(2) and Bankruptcy (Scotland) Act 1985, ss 48(5), (6) and (8), 44(2), (3) and 47(1) as applied to liquidations by r 4.16(1) of the Insolvency (Scotland) Rules 1986.
6 Insolvency (Scotland) Rules 1986, r 4.22(2) and (3) as inserted by para 18 of the Schedule to the Insolvency (Scotland) Amendment Rules 1987.
7 Insolvency (Scotland) Rules 1986, r 4.22(4) as inserted by para 18 of the Schedule to the Insolvency (Scotland) Amendment Rules 1987.

### (k) *Settling list of contributions, making calls*

In a creditors' voluntary winding up, the liquidator has the power (without the sanction of the court or the liquidation committee) and the duty to settle the list of contributories, make calls, and summon general meetings of the company and pay the company's debts and adjust the rights of the contributories among themelves[1]. In a winding up by the court, the court settles the list of contributories[2], makes calls[3], adjusts rights[4], and causes assets to be realised and debts discharged[5]. In a creditors' voluntary winding up the powers may only be exercised with the sanction of the court prior to the first creditor's meeting[6].

### (l) *Adjudication of claims*

The liquidator has power, without the sanction of the court or liquidation committee, to adjudicate on claims, but the adjudication may be appealed by any claimant or by any creditor[7]. The determining of the amount of a claim is governed by paragraphs 1, 3 and 5 of Schedule 1 to the Bankruptcy (Scotland) Act 1985[8].

### (m) *Payment of dividends*

The liquidator has the power, without the sanction of the court or liquidation committee (and the duty, if the funds of the company's estate are sufficient after making allowance for future contingencies), to pay a dividend out of the estate of the company to the creditors in respect of each 26-week accounting period[9]. If the liquidator is not ready to pay a dividend in respect of an accounting period, or he considers it would be inappropriate to pay a dividend because the expense of doing so would be disproportionate to the amount of the dividend, he may postpone the payment to a date which must be not later than the time for making of the dividend in respect of the next accounting period[10]. Where the liquidator considers that it would be expedient he is entitled to shorten the accounting period, with the consent of the liquidation committee, to end on the date agreed, and the next accounting period should run from the end of that shortened period[11]. Where an appeal is taken against the acceptance or rejection of a creditor's claim, the liquidator has power to set aside an amount sufficient to cover the claim if the determination on appeal

---

1 Insolvency Act 1986, s 165(4) and (5).
2 Ibid, s 148(1).
3 Ibid, s 150(1).
4 Ibid, s 154.
5 Ibid, s 148(1).
6 Ibid, s 166(2).
7 Ibid, s 169(2); and Bankruptcy (Scotland) Act 1985, s 49, as applied to liquidations by r 4.16(1) of the Insolvency (Scotland) Rules 1986.
8 Insolvency (Scotland) Rules 1986, r 4.16(1).
9 Insolvency Act 1986, s 169(2) and Bankruptcy (Scotland) Act 1985, s 52(3) as applied to liquidations by r 4.68(1) of the Insolvency (Scotland) Rules 1986.
10 Insolvency Act 1986, s 169(2) and Bankruptcy (Scotland) Act 1985, s 52(2) as applied to liquidations by r 4.68(1) of the Insolvency (Scotland) Rules 1986.
11 Insolvency Act 1986, s 169(2) and Bankruptcy (Scotland) Act 1985, s 52(6) as applied to liquidations by r 4.68(1) of the Insolvency (Scotland) Rules 1986.

was that the claim should be accepted[1]. Where late claims are put in for dividends, the liquidator has power to pay dividends to which a creditor would have been entitled[2]. The liquidator is not entitled to pay a dividend to the creditors until his accounts are audited, his outlays and remuneration fixed and a scheme of division prepared. This will usually mean that payment of the dividend will be eight weeks after the end of the accounting period, but this period is postponed if the liquidator or any creditor appeals against a determination by the liquidation committee or court determining the amount of outlays and remuneration payable to the liquidator; in which case the dividend may not be paid until the appeal is determined[3]. Where a creditor's claim is adjusted upwards or downwards, the liquidator may adjust any dividend upwards or downwards, or require the creditor to repay any part of any dividend already paid[4].

Unclaimed dividends and unapplied or undistributable balances must be lodged by the liquidator in a Scottish bank on deposit receipt in the name of the Accountant of Court and the deposit receipt sent to the Accountant of Court[5]. Any person producing evidence of his right may apply to the Accountant of Court to receive a dividend from the money so deposited if the application is made not later than seven years after the date of the deposit[6].

(n) *Power to engage in legal proceedings*★★

The liquidator in a creditors' voluntary winding up (but not in a winding up by the court) may, without the sanction of the court or liquidation committee, bring or defend any action or other legal proceedings in the name and on behalf of the company[7].

Unless proceedings are under section 145(2) of the Insolvency Act 1986, under which the liquidator may sue in his own name after an order has been made under section 145(1) of the Insolvency Act 1986 vesting property in him personally (a virtual dead letter), a liquidator sues in the name of the company[8]. If sanction is not obtained from the court or liquidation committee the competency of the action is not affected[9]. Before an action has been raised by a third party, a liquidator is entitled to ask the court in a compulsory winding up (as an officer of the court) for himself to be substituted for the original pursuer where the pursuer was a trustee in bankruptcy[10].

1 Insolvency Act 1986, s 169(2) and Bankruptcy (Scotland) Act 1985, s 52(7) as applied to liquidations by r 4.68(1) and (2) of the Insolvency (Scotland) Rules 1986.
2 Insolvency Act 1986, s 169(2) and Bankruptcy (Scotland) Act 1985, s 52(9) as applied to liquidations by r 4.68(1) of the Insolvency (Scotland) Rules 1986.
3 Insolvency Act 1986, s 169(2) and Bankruptcy (Scotland) Act 1985, s 52 as applied to liquidations by r 4.68 of the Insolvency (Scotland) Rules 1986.
4 Insolvency Act 1986, s 169(2) and Bankruptcy (Scotland) Act 1985, s 53(9) as applied to liquidations by r 4.68(1) of the Insolvency (Scotland) Rules 1986.
5 Insolvency Act 1986, s 193(2).
6 Bankruptcy (Scotland) Act 1985, s 58(1) as applied to liquidation by r 4.68(1) of the Insolvency (Scotland) Rules 1986.
7 Insolvency Act 1986, ss 165, 167, Sch 4, para 4.
8 *Munro v Hutchison* (1896) 3 SLT 268.
9 *Stewart v Gardner, etc* 1933 SLT (Sh Ct) 11.
10 *Millar* (1890) 18 R 179.

(o) *Carrying on business*★★

The liquidator has the power, in a creditors' voluntary winding up, to carry on the business of the company so far as may be necessary for its beneficial winding up[1]. In the case of a compulsory winding up the liquidator only has the power to carry on the business of the company so far as may be necessary for its beneficial winding up with the sanction of the court or the liquidation committee[2].

(p) *Ancillary powers*

The liquidator has the power, without the sanction of the court or the liquidation committee, to do all other things as may be necessary for winding up the company's affairs and distributing its assets in addition to the powers listed[3].

## (2) Extraordinary powers of a liquidator

The liquidator of a company has the following extraordinary powers, ie powers only exercisable with the sanction of the court or the liquidation committee, or sometimes only with the sanction of the court:

(a) *Distribution of estate*

The liquidator is entitled to pay the expenses of the liquidation as defined in rule 4.67 at any time, and the preferred debts at any time but only with the consent of the liquidation committee or the court[4].

(b) *Shortening of accounting period*

As referred to at page 53 supra, where the liquidator considers that it would be expedient, he is entitled to shorten the accounting period, with the consent of the liquidation committee, to end on the date agreed and the next accounting period should run from the end of that shortened period[5].

(c) *Payment of a class of creditors in full*

The liquidator has the power, with the sanction of the court or the liquidation committee, to pay any class of creditors in full[6].

(d) *Compromises and arrangements with creditors*

The liquidator has the power, with the sanction of the court or the liquidation committee, to make any compromise or arrangement with creditors or

1 Insolvency Act 1986, s 165, Sch 4, para 5.
2 Ibid, s 167 and Sch 4, para 5.
3 Ibid, ss 165 and 167 and Sch 4, para 13.
4 Ibid, s 169(2) and Bankruptcy (Scotland) Act 1985, s 52(4) as applied to liquidations by r 4.68(1) and (2) of the Insolvency (Scotland) Rules 1986.
5 Insolvency Act 1986, s 169(2) and Bankruptcy (Scotland) Act 1985, s 52(6) as applied to liquidations by r 4.68(1) of the Insolvency (Scotland) Rules 1986.
6 Insolvency Act 1986, ss 165, 167 and Bankruptcy (Scotland) Act 1985, s 52(6) and Sch 4, para 1.

persons claiming to be creditors, or having or alleging themselves to have any claim (present or future, certain or contingent, ascertained or sounding only in damages) against the company, or whereby the company may be rendered liable[1].

### (e) *Compromises with debtors*

The liquidator has the power, with the sanction of the court or the liquidation committee to compromise, on such terms as may be agreed:

(i)   all calls and liabilities to calls, all debts and liabilities capable of resulting in debts, and all claims (present or future, certain or contingent, ascertained or sounding only in damages) subsisting or supposed to subsist between the company and the contributory or alleged contributory or other debtor or person apprehending liability to the company; and

(ii)  all questions in any way relating to or affecting the assets or the winding up of the company, and take any security for the discharge of any such call, debt, liability or claim and give a complete discharge in respect thereof[2].

A compromise entered into with one contributory does not discharge his transferor from liability as another contributory. They do not stand to each other in the relation of principal and guarantor[3]. The liquidator cannot be forced to compromise a call[4], and a discharge got by designedly false statements or intentional misrepresentations may be reduced (legally quashed) by the court[5]. The fact that the liquidator may compromise debts and liabilities of the company with the sanction of the liquidation committee is a very strong reason for having a liquidation committee. Otherwise the valuable right to compromise would require the sanction of the court.

Section 65(1) of the Bankruptcy (Scotland) Act 1985 states:

'(1) The permanent trustee may (but if there are commissioners only with the consent of the commissioners, the creditors or the court)—

(a)   refer to arbitration any claim or question of whatever nature which may arise in the course of the sequestration; or

(b)   make a compromise with regard to any claim of whatever nature made against or on behalf of the sequestrated estate

and the decree arbitral or compromise shall be binding on the creditors and the debtor.'

Given the terms of section 65(1) of the Bankruptcy (Scotland) Act 1985 and the powers of the liquidator referred to above, it is competent in Scotland if the liquidator in a liquidation, or liquidator in liquidations agrees, and the trustee in a sequestration agrees, that the court or the liquidation committee and commissioners in the sequestration sanction that the liquidation or liquidations and the sequestration proceed jointly to the effect that a single scheme of division should be prepared. This would normally be sought where

---

1 Insolvency Act 1986, ss 165 and 167 and Sch 4, para 2.
2 Ibid, ss 165 and 167 and Sch 4, para 3.
3 *Nevill's Case* (1870) 6 Ch App 43; *Hudson's Case* (1871) LR Eq 1.
4 *Tennent v City of Glasgow Bank* (1879) 6 R 972.
5 *Liquidators of City of Glasgow Bank v Assets Co* (1883) 10 R 676 at 678.

the assets in a liquidation and personal assets were so intermingled that this would be the most expeditious solution[1].

(e) *Sales for shares*

The liquidator has the power, with the sanction of the court or the liquidation committee, to sell or transfer the whole or part of the company's business or property in return for shares, policies or other interests in the company to which the business is being transferred[2]. This power is expressly written into the Insolvency Act 1986 in the case of a creditors' voluntary winding-up[3]. The liquidator probably also has this power with the sanction of the court in a compulsory winding-up[4].

# V. BACK-UP POWERS OF THE COURT

The court has the following powers in both compulsory windings up and creditors' voluntary windings up. Usually the court is given the powers in a compulsory winding up but it may exercise these powers in a creditors' voluntary winding up on the application of the liquidator or any contributory or creditor under section 112(1) of the Insolvency Act 1986 provided it is convinced that the exercise of the power is just and beneficial.

### Public examination of officers in a compulsory winding up

The liquidator in a compulsory winding up[5] may apply at any time to the court for the public examination of any person who has been an officer of the company, or has acted as liquidator or administrator or receiver of its property, or has been concerned with its promotion, formation or its management. In addition the liquidator, if requested by creditors representing one-half in value of the company's liabilities, or by the contributories representing three-quarters in value, is under a duty to make an application to the court[6]. When the liquidator makes the application, it is mandatory for the court to direct that a public examination of the person to whom the application relates takes place[7].

This obligation on the court to grant an order for a public examination when the liquidator makes an application, is to be contrasted to an application for a private examination, where the court has discretion whether to grant it.

---

1 *Peter Cranbourne Taylor, the Official Liquidator of George Morris (Hotels) Ltd and Others*, Note in the liquidation of, Court of Session 5 June 1991 per Lord Osborne, unreported, affirming *Juba Property Company Ltd*, Note in, 17 January 1978 per Lord Kincraig.
2 Insolvency Act 1986, s 110(1) and (2).
3 Ibid, s 110(1).
4 Ibid, s 167(1)(b) and Sch 4, para 13; see *Re Agra and Masterman's Bank* (1866) LR 12 Eq 509, n. and *Re Cambrian Mining Co* (1882) LT 114. It is suggested that Lord Romilly was wrong in the case of *Re London and Exchange Bank* (1867) 16 LT 340 to suggest that this type of sale could not be effected in a compulsory liquidation. It cannot be intended that the court has less power than liquidators.
5 Insolvency Act 1986, s 133(1).
6 Ibid, s 133(2).
7 Ibid, s 133(3).

A further distinction between a 'public examination' and a 'private examination' is that an order for a public examination may be made on the persons whether or not they are British subjects and whether or not they are within the jurisdiction of the Scottish court whereas a private examination is thought to be competent only where the person to be examined is subject to the jurisdiction of the Scottish court. In *Seagull Manufacturing Co Ltd*[1] Mummery J explained the reasoning behind his decision as follows:

'The provisions for private examinations are different from the provisions of section 133 in two important respects. First, the power of the court to summon persons to appear before it for private examination extends to a very much wider class of persons than the court's power in the case of a public examination. The power to summon for a private examination applies not only to any officer of the company (or to the bankrupt) but also to any person who may have in his possession any property of the company (or of the bankrupt) or who may be indebted to the company (or the bankrupt). It even extends to any person who may be able to give information to the court concerning the company (or the bankrupt) and the relevant dealings, affairs and property.

As was observed by Dillon LJ in *In re Tucker* [1990] Ch 148, 156G, if the words "any person" are given their natural meaning in the private examination provisions they "cover any person of any nationality in any part of the world". The very width of the class of person specified in the private examination provisions in the bankruptcy legislation was an important factor leading the court to the conclusion that the relevant class of persons must be limited by the territoriality principle and therefore confined to persons in England at the relevant time who could be served with a summons of the English court in England.

By way of contrast, the power of the court to order public examination under section 133 is confined to a restricted class of persons who have voluntarily concerned themselves in a specified capacity in the affairs of the company which is being wound up, ie as officer, liquidator, administrator, receiver or manager, or as participant in the promotion, formation or management of the company.

The second important difference between the provisions for public examination and for private examination is that the latter contain express provisions (namely section 237(3) in the case of a company and section 367(3) in the case of a bankrupt) which, in the words of Dillon LJ in *In re Tucker*, "conclusively" and "inevitably" connote that if the person in question is not in England he is not liable to be brought before the English court. By way of contrast, such a provision is conspicuously absent from both section 133 and the provisions for its enforcement in section 134.'

After there has been an order made for a public examination, the court must appoint the day for the public examination and make a direction that the person named in the application must attend on that day and be publicly examined as to the promotion, formation or management of the company or as to the conduct of its business and affairs or his conduct of dealings in relation to the company[2]. At the public examination questions may be asked by the liquidator, any special manager, any creditor who has submitted a claim in the winding up, and any contributory of the company[3]. Unless the court has made an order differently, the liquidator must give at least 14 days notice of the time and place of the examination to those who are entitled to ask questions as described above, and he may, if he thinks fit, advertise the public examination in newspapers circulating in the area of the principal place of

1 [1991] WLR 307.
2 Insolvency Act 1986, s 133(3).
3 Ibid, s 133(4).

business of the company[1]. It is important however that no advertisement must appear in a newspaper before at least seven days have elapsed from the date when the person to be examined was served with the order of the court[2]. This provision allows the person to be examined the opportunity to appeal against an order, although it is difficult to see what grounds are open because it is mandatory once the application is made. An appeal would have the effect of postponing the evil day of the examination because the appeal would recall the order. Alternatively, at the stage at which the application is made, it might be open to the person whose examination was sought to seek reduction of the application and interim suspension of it. A possible ground of challenge, for example, could be that this was improper persecution. Although the Cork Committee[3] suggested that one of the justifying reasons in favour of public examination was for it to act as a sanction or deterrent, this was not written into the legislation. Accordingly it could be argued that a liquidator was misdirecting himself if the application is not for a liquidation purpose, but is extraneous to the beneficial winding up, ie it is aimed *only* at punishing directors by putting them in a public pillory.

Those creditors or contributories requesting the liquidator to ask the court for a public examination (where he has not of his own initiative asked for the public examination) must give a list to the liquidator of all the creditors or contributories wanting the public examination and specify the name of the person to be examined and what relationship he had to the company and the reasons why his examination is requested[4]. They must also deposit with the liquidator such sum as the liquidator may determine to be appropriate by way of the expenses of the hearing of a public examination[5]. When a liquidator gets a request to make an application to the court for a public examination, he must make the application within 28 days of receiving the request or apply to the court for an order relieving him of the obligation to make the application if he is of the opinion that the request is an unreasonable one in the circumstances[6]. The liquidator may make an application for an order relieving him of the obligation to apply *ex parte*[7]. If the court makes an order relieving him of the liability to make an application, he must give notice of the order straight away to the requisitionists who have asked him to make the application[8]. Alternatively, if the court does not relieve him of the liability to make the application, he must make the application forthwith on the conclusion of the hearing of the application for a relieving order.

The legislation does not lay down rules in Scotland as to how the public examination should be conducted. The legislation allows questioners to ask questions in relation to the dealings with the company with which the person to be examined was concerned[9]. The court may make an order directing what questions might be put to the person to be examined to keep the questions within the scope of what are lawful questions in the circumstances of the

1 Insolvency (Scotland) Rules 1986, r 4.74.
2 Ibid, r 4.74.
3 Cork Committee Report, paras 653–657.
4 Insolvency (Scotland) Rules 1986, r 4.75.
5 Ibid, r 4.75(3).
6 Ibid, r 4.74(5).
7 Ibid, r 4.75(6).
8 Ibid, r 4.75(6).
9 Insolvency Act 1986, s 133(3).

case[1]. There is authority that the proper conduct of a public examination in an individual sequestration is for the trustee to question the bankrupt, and creditors can then ask any questions which they think necessary to supplement the trustee's questions but may not cross-examine the bankrupt on claims of other creditors[2]. However, it is suggested that the public examination of an officer of a company is so wide-ranging in its scope that it is not possible to lay down rules in advance for how an examination should be conducted. It is suggested that apart from the restrictions mentioned above, there should be no restriction on the questions or number of questions which those attending may ask or on the duration of the public examination. It is suggested that questions to the person to be examined are directed through the chairman. The Insolvency Act 1986 and the Insolvency (Scotland) Rules 1986 do not seem to impose any duty on the person to be examined to answer questions[3]. One of the aims of the public examination will of course, incidentally, have been obtained even if no questions are answered. It will still have acted as a public pillory to assuage public anger. The issue of whether questions must be answered, and if so on what basis, is not thought to be closed by the absence of a specific duty in terms of the Insolvency (Scotland) Rules 1986 but may be inferred by implication from the terms of section 47(3) of the Bankruptcy (Scotland) Act 1985. This issue is discussed fully on pages 64–69 in relation to the answering of questions in both a public and private examination.

### Power to order private examination in a compulsory winding up

The court may, on the application of the liquidator, summon to appear before it any officer of the company, any person known or suspected to have in his possession any property of the company or supposed to be indebted to the company, or any person whom the court thinks capable of giving information concerning the promotion, formation, business, dealings, affairs or property of the company[4]. The court may require any of these people to submit an affidavit to the court containing an account of their dealings with the company or to produce any books, papers or other records in their possession or under their control relating to the company or generally about their dealings with the company[5]. The court has power to issue a warrant for the arrest of someone who fails to appear in front of it without reasonable cause or looks like absconding and for the seizure of any books, records, money or goods in that person's possession, and the person may be kept in custody[6]. If it appears to the court that any person has in his possession any property of the company,

---

1 *Jacks' Tr v Jacks' Trs* 1910 SC 34.
2 *Delvoitte v Baillie's Trs* (1887) 5 R 143 at 144.
3 See, in contrast, the Bankruptcy (Scotland) Act 1985, s 47(3) which states, 'the debtor or the relevant person shall be required to answer any questions relating to the debtor's assets, his dealings with them or his conduct in relation to his business or financial affairs and shall not be excused from answering any such questions on the ground that the answer may incriminate or tend to incriminate him or on the ground of confidentiality'; the Bankruptcy (Scotland) Act 1856, s 91 which states: 'the bankrupt and such other persons shall answer all questions relating to the affairs of the bankrupt', and the English rule which states: 'The examinee shall at the hearing be examined on oath; and he shall answer all such questions as the court may put, or allow to be put to him', r 4.215 of the Insolvency Rules 1986.
4 Insolvency Act 1986, s 236(2).
5 Ibid, s 236(3).
6 Ibid, s 236(4), (5) and (6).

the court may, on the application of the liquidator, order that person to deliver the property to the liquidator, or, if it appears to the court that the person is indebted to the company the court may order the person to pay the money to the liquidator[1]. The court is unlikely, unless there has been a miscarriage of justice, to upset on appeal an order to appear in front of the court for examination[2], or unless the application is oppressive[3]. An order for a private examination may be obtained by the liquidator, a creditor or contributory but the court has a discretion whether to make the order or not although weight will be given to the views of the liquidator who is closely acquainted with the company's affairs[4]. Strangers to the company may be examined if they are capable of giving useful information and this includes those with information coming into existence after the company ceased active trading, although the court may refuse disclosure of privileged materials[5]. An order authorising messengers-at-arms to search for and recover books, and if necessary to open lockfast places, is competent[6].

The procedure in Scotland involves the citation of the individual concerned to appear for examination on oath before the insolvency judge[7]. He may be required to bring all documents in his custody as specified in the note for such examination. He may be represented by counsel and re-examined by him to explain his evidence but his counsel may not attend when other witnesses are examined[8]. It is a private examination. Rule 9.4 of the Insolvency Rules 1986 lays down the procedure for a private examination of the officer of a company in England, including the requirement that he must answer the questions. As in the case of a public examination of an officer of the company etc, there is no statutory provision in Scotland in relation to whether the person being privately examined must answer questions, and if so on what basis. This issue is discussed more fully on pages 64–69.

## Public and private examination in a creditors' voluntary winding up

### (a) *Public examination*

Although the Insolvency Act 1986 does not give the liquidator in a creditors' voluntary winding up any express power to apply to the court for a public examination which the court must grant, he has the power, as does any contributory or creditor, to apply to the court to exercise all or any of the powers which the court might exercise if the company were being wound up by the court[9]. The object of that section is to leave the company, its contributories and creditors, if possible, to settle their affairs without coming to the court for a compulsory order, but to provide them under this section with the means of access to the court in the voluntary winding up, just as in a compulsory winding up[10]. The court has discountenanced any distinction between the jurisdiction in a voluntary winding up and a winding up under a

1 Ibid, s 237(1) and (2).
2 Re Joseph Hargreaves [1900] 1 Ch 347.
3 Heiron's Case (1880) 15 Ch D 139.
4 Re Maville Hose [1939] Ch 32.
5 Re Highgate Traders Ltd [1984] BCLC 151.
6 Kerr v Hughes 1970 SC 380.
7 Ibid; Welch 1930 SN 112.
8 Liquidators of Larkhall Collieries (1905) 13 SLT 752.
9 Insolvency Act 1986, s 112(1).
10 Rance's Case (1870) 6 Ch App 104, 115.

compulsory order[1]. In the case of a compulsory winding up, the court has the power to order a public examination and has no discretion in the matter if there is an application from a liquidator. It is thought that the application by the liquidator in a compulsory liquidation is a formal requirement in relation to the court exercising its jurisdiction. The application is not a condition precedent for the existence of the jurisdiction. Accordingly, it is thought that an application may also be made in a creditors' voluntary winding up. However, unlike the case of an application under section 133(2) of the Insolvency Act 1986, the granting of the application is not mandatory, but rather the court must be satisfied that the exercise of the power will be 'just and beneficial'[2]. In a creditors' voluntary winding up, because the liquidator is not bound by the statutory obligation to make an application for a public examination when requested by the liquidation committee, as a compulsory liquidator is, it will be a matter for the liquidator's discretion whether he makes an application under section 112(1) for an order that a person be publicly examined[3].

(b) *Private examination*

It is thought that the liquidator in a creditors' voluntary winding up may apply for an order under section 112 of the Insolvency Act 1986 for a private examination of an officer of the company etc on the same arguments as above in relation to a public examination. This proposition has been affirmed recently in England by the Court of Appeal in *Re Bishopsgate Investment Management Ltd (in prov liq) v Maxwell*[4]. In the words of Dillon LJ:

'It should be noted, however, that though s 270 of the 1948 Act and its predecessors applied in terms only in winding up by the court and only on provision of a further report by the Official Receiver, it was held by Wynn-Parry J in *Re Campbell Coverings Ltd (No 2)* [1954] 1 All ER 222, [1954] Ch 225, following a suggestion of Evershed MR in *Re Campbell Coverings Ltd* [1953] 2 All ER 74 at 78, [1953] Ch 488 at 497, with which Denning LJ had concurred, that public examination was available in a voluntary liquidation because s 307 of the 1948 Act enabled the court, on the application of the liquidator or any contributory or creditor of a company in voluntary liquidation, to exercise all or any of the powers which the court might exercise if the company were being wound up by the court. Section 112 of the Insolvency Act 1986 is in the same terms as s 307.'[5]

Accordingly sections 133 and 236 should be seen as covering both compulsory and voluntary insolvent windings up.

**Exercise of the court's discretion in ordering a private examination**

It has been noted above that where there is an application for an order under section 133 of the Insolvency Act 1986, it is mandatory that the court make such an order. Where a liquidator is requested by one-half, in value, of the

---

1 *Black and Co's Case* (1872) 8 Ch App 254.
2 Insolvency Act 1986, s 112(2); see *Re Gold Co* (1879) 12 Ch D 77 and *Heiron's Case* (1880) 15 Ch D 139.
3 Schedule 1 to the Insolvency (Scotland) Rules 1986 states that Chap 11 does not apply in a creditors' winding up but relates only to an order under s 133(4), not under s 112 of the Insolvency Act 1986.
4 [1992] 2 All ER 856.
5 Ibid at 870.

company's creditors, or three-quarters, in value, of the company's contributories, the liquidator shall make an application unless the court directs otherwise. Accordingly in that situation the court has a discretion as to whether to veto an application for a public examination. In contrast there is always a discretion where there is an application for a private examination under section 236 of the Insolvency Act 1986. Section 236 entitles administrators and administrative receivers equally with liquidators to seek a private examination involving the production of documents and oral examination. In the recent case of *Cloverbay Limited (Joint Administrators) v Bank of Credit and Commerce International SA*[1], the English Court of Appeal reviewed the previous authorities on the court's exercise of discretion. In the course of his judgment Sir Nicholas Browne-Wilkinson V-C, set out how the court should exercise its discretion in relation to both the production of documents, and oral examination:

'The words of the statute do not fetter the courts' discretion in any way. Circumstances may vary infinitely. It is clear that in exercising the discretion the court has to balance the requirements of the liquidator against any possible oppression to the person to be examined. Such balancing depends on the relationship between the importance to the liquidator of obtaining the information on the one hand and the degree of oppression to the person sought to be examined on the other. If the information required is fundamental to any assessment of whether or not there is a cause of action and the degree of oppression is small (for example in the case of ordering premature discovery of documents) the balance will manifestly come down in favour of making the order. Conversely, if the liquidator is seeking merely to dot the i's and cross the t's of a fairly clear claim by examining the proposed defendant to discover his defence, the balance would come down against making the order. Of course, few cases will be so clear: it will be for the judge in each case to reach his own conclusion.

That said there are a number of points which in my judgment should be borne in mind in exercising the discretion. First, the reason for the inquisitorial jurisdiction contained in s 236 is that a liquidator or administrator comes into the company with no previous knowledge and frequently finds that the company's records are missing or defective. The purpose of s 236 is to enable him to get sufficient information to reconstitute the state of knowledge that the company should possess. In my judgment its purpose is not to put the company in a better position than it would have enjoyed if liquidation or administration had not supervened. In many cases an order under s 236 may have *the result* that the company is in such improved position e g an order for discovery of documents made against a third party in order to reconstitute the company's own trading records may disclose the existence of claims which would otherwise remain hidden. But that is *the result* of the order not *the purpose* for which it is made.

Second, as a corollary to the first point, I do not think that the test of absolute "need" as opposed to a reasonable requirement for the information is a workable or appropriate test. . .

Third, in my judgment the case for making an order against an officer or former officer of the company will usually be stronger than it would be against a third party. Officers owe the company fiduciary duties and will often be in possession of information to which the company is entitled under the general law. Their special position as officers of the company is emphasised by s 235 of the Act, which imposes on them a statutory obligation to assist the liquidator or administrator. The enforcement of these duties owed by its officers to the company may require an order under s 236 even though it exposes such officers to the risk of personal liability. No such considerations apply when an order is sought against a third party. He owes no duty to the company. In an otherwise proper case he may be required to disclose documents or answer questions so as to provide the liquidator with information

1 [1991] BCLC 135.

necessary to carry out his functions even though this may have unfortunate repercussions for him. But he owes no general duty to give such information (apart from an order under s 236) and if by giving the information he risks exposing himself to liability this involves an element of oppression. That is not to say that an order cannot or should not be made against a third party. But it should be borne in mind that the degree of possible oppression is greater in his case.

Fourth, although the section treats the production of documents and the oral examination of witnesses together, an order for oral examination is much more likely to be oppressive than an order for the production of documents. An order for the production of documents involves only advancing the time of discovery if an action ensues: the liquidator is getting no more than any other litigant would get, save that he is getting it earlier. But oral examination provides the opportunity for pre-trial depositions which the liquidator would never otherwise be entitled to: the person examined has to answer on oath and his answers can both provide evidence in support of a subsequent claim brought by the liquidator and also form the basis of later cross-examination. In my judgment this greater risk of oppression when examination of witnesses is ordered calls for a more careful approach to such orders than to order for the disclosure of documents.

In *Re J T Rhodes Limited* [1987] BCLC 77 Hoffmann J suggested that the time may have come to reconsider whether oral examination is oppressive even if it does involve the risks which I have mentioned. He pointed to the change in attitudes since Victorian times and to the growth of investigatory powers such as those given to inspectors appointed by the Department of Trade and Industry. Those remarks were made in the context of a case where oral examination was sought of the "moving light" and *de facto* director of the company; I have already said that in my view the fiduciary duties owed to the company by such a person may well justify a more stringent approach. But for myself I am unable to accept, in the absence of specific statutory authority, that it is not oppressive to require someone suspected of wrongdoing to prove the case against himself on oath before any proceedings are brought. In the exercise of its discretion, the court may consider that the legitimate requirements of the liquidator outweigh such oppression; but it remains oppressive.'

Until the passing of the Insolvency Act 1986, it had been thought that a contributory had *locus standi* to ask the court for an examination under the statutory predecessors of sections 133 and 236 of the Insolvency Act 1986[1]. However the terms of sections 133 and 236 of the Insolvency Act 1986 would seem to preclude anyone other than an office holder making the application.

### Power to order company officer to attend meetings

The court has power to order any officer of the company to attend any meeting of creditors or contributories or liquidation committee for the purpose of giving information as to the trade, dealings, affairs or property of the company[2]. The court may control what questions are to be asked at such a public examination[3].

*Possible divergence of approach to the answering of questions at a public and private examination between England and Scotland*

Although the liquidator in England and Scotland relies on the same statutory provisions to hold a public or private examination of an officer of a company

---

1 *Re Silkstone & Dodworth Coal and Iron Co, Whitworth's Case* [1881] 19 Ch D 118; *Re Embassy Art Products Ltd* [1988] BCLC 1.
2 Insolvency Act 1986, s 157.
3 *London and Globe Finance Corporation v Basil Montgomery* (1902) 18 TLR 661.

there would appear to be an important difference in approach between England and Scotland as to whether the officer must answer questions ie whether all questions must be answered—

(1) unconditionally; or
(2) unconditionally subject to certain immunities; or
(3) conditionally.

At a public examination of an officer of a company, in terms of rule 4.215(1) of the Insolvency Rules 1986, in England:

'The examinee shall at the hearing be examined on oath; and he shall answer all such questions as the court may put, or allow to be put, to him.'

There is no corresponding rule in England covering a private examination. However, in the recent case of *Re Bishopsgate Investment Management Ltd* and *Mirror Group Newspapers Plc* and *Mirror Group Newspapers Ltd v Maxwell*[1] the Court of Appeal held that the provision in relation to a public examination was also applicable to a private examination in England. They held this to be the case for two main reasons:

(a) it would be anomalous if a witness had to answer questions unconditionally at a public examination and not at a private examination when it was always open, provided fraud was alleged, to seek a public examination instead of a private examination. Also the matters able to be examined at a public and private examination were the same; and
(b) the bankruptcy provisions relating to individuals contained in sections 366 and 367 of the Insolvency Act 1986 in relation to a private examination in England have to be read with the corresponding statutory provisions in relation to private examination of an officer of a company. Parliament would not have intended there to be a difference of approach under two such similar régimes contained in the one Act. For example the procedure in rule 4.215 1(1) of the Insolvency Rules 1986 relating to a public examination of an officer of a company had its exact counterpart in rule 6.175 in relation to the public examination of a bankrupt. Also, the similarities, *mutatis mutandis*, between sections 236 and 237 and sections 366 and 367, which are concerned with private examination in individual insolvency, are obvious. It could not have been the intention of Parliament that the privilege against self-incrimination should be available in one case, and not in the other. The clear reading of the intent behind sections 366 and 367 was that the bankrupt could not rely on the privilege against self-incrimination so as to refuse to answer questions put to him in his bankruptcy. It was illogical that the directors of a company should be entitled to rely on an alleged privilege against self-incrimination in a private examination under section 236, if the individual insolvent was not entitled to do so on a private examination under section 366.

1 [1992] 2 All ER 856.

The English position, therefore, in light of the *Bishopsgate Investment Management Ltd* case[1] is that a debtor or officer of a company must answer questions unconditionally and without any immunity in public examinations and private examinations.

In Scotland, by contrast, the provisions relating to the public and private examination of a bankrupt are contained in sections 44, 45 and 47 of the separate Bankruptcy (Scotland) Act 1985. In the case of both a public and private examination in terms of section 47(3):

'The debtor or a relevant person shall be required to answer any question relating to the debtor's assets, his dealings with them or his conduct in relation to the business or financial affairs and shall not be excused from answering any such question on the ground that the answer may incriminate or tend to incriminate him or on the ground of confidentiality:

Provided that—

(a) a statement made by the debtor or a relevant person in answer to such a question shall not be admissible in evidence in any subsequent criminal proceedings against the person making the statement, except where the proceedings are in respect of a charge of perjury relating to the statement;

(b) a person subject to examination shall not be required to disclose any information which he has received from a person who is not called for examination if the information is confidential between them.'

There is no corresponding provision in the Insolvency Act 1986 determining whether the officer of a company must answer a question, and if so whether conditionally, or unconditionally with a certain immunity as in the case of section 47(3) of the Bankruptcy (Scotland) Act 1985 in relation to the public and private examination of a bankrupt.

*Interpretation of sections 133 and 236 in Scotland*

The decision of the Court of Appeal in the *Bishopsgate Investment Management Ltd* case[1] raises difficult questions of interpretation of sections 133 and 236 of the Insolvency Act 1986 as they apply to Scotland.

The first problem is whether the approach contained in section 47(3) of the Bankruptcy (Scotland) Act 1985 should be applied to public and private examinations of officers of a company under the Insolvency Act 1986. In favour of this approach are the following two arguments:

(1) Section 169(2) of the Insolvency Act 1986 gives the liquidator in a winding-up in Scotland (subject to the rules) the same powers as a trustee on a bankrupt estate. That section is critical to the implementation of a major part of the Insolvency Act 1986 as it relates to Scotland. The Insolvency Act 1986 makes use of that provision on a great number of occasions to determine a liquidator's powers in Scotland. Accordingly it is clear that no extraordinary divergence of approach would be being taken if the applying of the relevant powers contained in the Bankruptcy (Scotland) Act 1985 approach were adopted; and

(2) The Court of Appeal has stated that the English bankruptcy provisions

---

1 [1992] 2 All ER 856.

contained in the Insolvency Act 1986 should be read together with the provisions in relation to the examination of officers of a company. Accordingly it would make sense for the provisions in the Bankruptcy (Scotland) Act 1985 to be read as applying to public and private examinations in a winding up. Although the Bankruptcy (Scotland) Act 1985 is a separate statute covering bankruptcy in Scotland, whereas the corresponding provisions in England are contained in the Insolvency Act 1986, the two statutes must be read together given the terms of section 169 as regards to both the general approach, as well as individual instances of implementation.

Against the above approach are the following arguments:

(a) it is not clear that the requirement of the debtor in section 47(3) of the Bankruptcy (Scotland) Act 1985 is a 'power' of the trustee as required by section 169(2) of the Insolvency Act 1986;

(b) also the proviso that a statement may not be admissible in evidence in any subsequent criminal proceedings in terms of section 47(3)(a) of the Bankruptcy (Scotland) Act 1985 is difficult to describe as a 'power' of the trustee. It is more a restriction on the use of evidence by other parties in criminal proceedings; and

(c) both section 133 of the Insolvency Act 1986 which deals with a public examination, and sections 236 and 237 which deal with a private examination, have been held in the *Bishopsgate* case[1] to embody in themselves the powers of the liquidator. Indeed in the *Bishopsgate Investment Management Ltd* case[2] Lord Justice Dillon states:

'In his judgment in *Re British and Commonwealth Holdings Plc*, Woolf LJ referred on page 1 to Part VI of the 1986 Act as having conferred upon the Court a remarkable armoury of summary weapons with which to assist "office holders". He then referred to provisions in *sections 234 to 237*, and continued on *page 3*:

"The nature and range of these summary powers make clear the importance that Parliament attached to administrators and other office holders being able to perform their functions in an effective and expeditious manner. They illustrate that in relation to a company in liquidation or administration, a liquidator or administrator is intended to be in quite a different position from that of the directors of a company which is not an administration. The Court has to use these powers to enable administrators to perform their function in this way, and must not use its discretion to frustrate the intent which can be discerned from Part VI of the Act that office holders should be supported by these powers."

I respectfully agree, subject to the point to which Woolf LJ next refers, that the possibly oppressive effect upon those against whom the orders are made must not be ignored.'[2]

It is difficult to contemplate that Parliament would legislate for sections 234 to 237 to embody a complete armoury of powers in England but not to be exhaustive in Scotland.

---

1 [1992] 2 All ER 856.
2 Ibid at 875–876, per Dillon LJ.

*Problems in implementation of the Insolvency Act 1986, ss 133 and 236 if the Bankruptcy (Scotland) Act 1985, s 47 is applied*

If the provisions in relation to the conduct of an examination contained in section 47 of the Bankruptcy (Scotland) Act 1985 are applied in the case of liquidations, the following problems arise:

(1)  The régime with regard to the requirement of an officer of a company to answer questions is circumscribed in Scotland by the provision in relation to the inadmissibility of statements in subsequent criminal proceedings and the non-requirement of disclosure of confidential information. This means that the régime in Scotland is different from the régime in England. It is normally the policy of Parliament that company matters as far as possible should be the same on both sides of the border;

(2)  The Insolvency Act 1986, section 426 deals with co-operation between courts in different parts of the United Kingdom exercising jurisdiction in relation to insolvency. In terms of section 426(1):

'An order made by a court in any part of the United Kingdom in the exercise of jurisdiction in relation to insolvency law shall be enforced in any other part of the United Kingdom as if it were made by a court exercising the corresponding jurisdiction in that other part.'

This provision however is qualified to a certain extent in that in terms of section 426(5):

'. . . a request made to a court in any part of the United Kingdom by a court in any other part of the United Kingdom or in a relevant country or territory is authority for the court to which the request is made to apply, in relation to any matters specified in the request, the insolvency law which is applicable by either court in relation to comparable matters falling within its jurisdiction.
    In exercising its discretion under this subsection, a court shall have regard in particular to the rules of private international law.'

Although, superficially, this would appear to be a case where the court could apply the Scottish rule in relation to a request by an English court to have a person examined in Scotland, it is totally unsatisfactory because the Scottish court would not be in a position, nor would the English court, to make a statement made in Scotland inadmissible in a subsequent prosecution in England, if it is being made under English law. The Scottish court might refuse the request as being in terms of Scots private international law against public policy. Secondly a request by a Scottish court to the English court could not guarantee the inadmissibility of statements made as far as a possible English prosecution were concerned if the order for examination were under Scots law (see chapter 20) for a recent case; and

(3)  The provision in the Bankruptcy (Scotland) Act 1985, section 47(3) that a statement made by the debtor shall not be admissible in evidence in any subsequent criminal proceedings, was recommended by the Scottish Law Commission in its Report on Bankruptcy. It followed a recommendation in the Blagden Report on Bankruptcy in Ireland. In the Irish Report no formal recommendation was made to this effect but their draft Bill contained a similar provision. It is slightly paradoxical that it was

Scotland which followed the Irish provision rather than England. The provision itself does not offer any immunity from prosecution in relation to evidence gathered flowing from information obtained in the statement. It is the person's barest possible protection and essentially offers protection from the person's statement being used as the only basis of a prosecution[1].

This of course is not open in Scotland where corroboration by other evidence would be required, whereas in England the statement itself would be sufficient in law for a conviction. Accordingly it would have been more appropriate that such a provision had been introduced in England rather than in Scotland.

*Confidentiality restriction in the Bankruptcy (Scotland) Act 1985, section 47(3)(b)*

There is a problem in how to interpret the word 'confidential' in section 47(3)(b) of the Bankruptcy (Scotland) Act 1985. In the draft Bill as proposed by the Scottish Law Commission the corresponding provision to section 47(3)(b) of the Bankruptcy (Scotland) Act 1985 was clause 44 (3)(b) which read:

'Any person subject to examination shall not be required to disclose any matter which is privileged between himself and any other person, not being a person called for examination.'

The corresponding provision in section 47(3)(b) reads:

'A person subject to examination shall not be required to disclose any information which he has received from a person who is not called for examination if the information is confidential between them.'

The question is whether 'confidential' is to be construed as confidential in the widest sense or 'privileged'. The problem is that what is now known as 'privilege' was until fairly recently referred to as 'confidentiality'[2].

The better view is that 'confidential' is much wider than 'privileged'. The Scottish Law Commission used the more modern word 'privileged'. There was a deliberate change from the unambiguous 'privileged' to the apparently wider word 'confidential'.

### Confidential in relation to directors of companies

If section 47(3)(b) of the Bankruptcy (Scotland) Act 1985 is applied to companies by implication or by section 169(2) of the Insolvency Act 1986, and the powers of a trustee are circumscribed by the provisions contained in section 47, then directors of a company will be covered by the proviso in section 47(3)(b). The question then is whether a director could invoke this protection in relation to his fiduciary duty of confidentiality to the company.

---

1 See paras 200–250 of Criminal Law Revision Committee Eighth Report for discussion.
2 Supra.

This has been rejected in the *Bishopsgate* case[1] but only on the basis that that was not the common law. The position might have been very different if there had been an express protection as in Scotland. Directors etc have a statutory duty under section 235 of the Insolvency Act 1986 to assist a liquidation. There is also a general public duty of those closely involved in the company's affairs to co-operate with and provide information to a liquidator[2]. The first problem is that the Scottish provision is directed at persons who are natural persons. The qualification 'who is not called for examination' is directed in the Bankruptcy (Scotland) Act 1985 to a natural person. A company cannot be called for examination. However the provision does not expressly exclude non-natural persons who have information confidential to them and the person subject to the examination. Accordingly the expression 'who is not called for examination' could mean 'who has not been called for examination for many reasons including that it is not legally possible to call the person for examination because the person is not a natural person'. If the provision is read to include a director's duty of confidentiality to the company, the question is whether a director of a company in liquidation may invoke the protection of the provision. This matter has not been decided in Scotland. If it is a private examination there is an argument that the liquidator is now the agent of the company and he would be requiring another agent of the company namely a 'director' to confide to him matters which were confidential and would remain confidential in the same way as a principal authorised one agent to give information to another agent. This however is not the whole story because both at a public and a private examination creditors may put questions to the officers. It is by no means clear that a director would not be breaching a duty of confidentiality if creditors were made aware of matters confidential to the company. In England the problem does not arise because there is not a provision similar to that in Scotland. However once the provision is expressly stated, the position is not clear. It might be argued that there would be no point in the examination of officers of a company if they could invoke the fiduciary duty of confidentiality. That argument would entail that all questions were concerned with matters which were confidential. It is not clear that that would be the case. It is thought by the authors that this important issue should be clarified by legislation.

### Power to order arrest of a contributory

The court has the power to arrest a contributory who appears about to abscond[3].

### Power to order inspection of books by creditors

The court may at any time give creditors and contributories the right to inspect the company's books and papers[4]. This facility is not open to persons other than creditors and contributories. A stranger to the company may not obtain an order to inspect the register of members after commencement of the

---

1 See Walker & Walker, *Law of Evidence in Scotland* (Hodge, 1964) Chapter XXXI and Field, *The Law of Evidence in Scotland* (W Green, 1988) p 248.
2 The *JT Rhodes* [1987] BCLC 77.
3 Insolvency Act 1986, s 158.
4 Ibid, s 155(1).

winding up[1]. These books of the company are not to be confused with the sederunt book of the liquidation. The power to allow inspection of the company's books under section 155 should be exercised for the benefit of those interested in the liquidation, and not to assist actions by individual shareholders against directors[2], or to assist creditors in obtaining information to pursue a scheme to terminate the liquidation and reconstruct the company[3].

## Power of rescission of contracts by the court

The court may, on the application of a person who is either benefited or burdened by a contract with the company in liquidation, make an order rescinding the contract on such terms as to payment by or to either party of damages for the non-performance of the contract, or otherwise as the court thinks just[4]. If damages are payable under an order to the person, they rank as a debt in the winding up[5]. Where there are several unconnected contracts between some person and the company, it does not follow that, because one or more may be rescinded, all of them will be rescinded[6].

This provision has been extended to Scotland for the first time by the Insolvency Act 1986. The statutory code of disclaimer in England has not been introduced to Scotland. The Scottish Law Commission was of the opinion that the existing Scottish common law has much the same effect as the statute law in England and there had been no complaints[7]. The provision however would allow the rescission of a contract where, for example, a liquidator had inadvertently adopted a contract by not repudiating it within the time that a court would have thought reasonable.

The Companies Act 1989 excludes these rights of rescission arising under the Insolvency Act 1986 and the common law from application to certain contracts of person engaged in financial markets. It provides that section 186 of the Insolvency Act 1986 and the rule of law in Scotland corresponding to section 178 of the Insolvency Act 1986 (Disclaimer of Unprofitable Contracts and Onerous Property in England and Wales) do not apply to a market contract or a contract effected by a recognised investment exchange or clearing house for the purpose of realising property provided as a margin in relation to market contracts[8]. It also provides that where action has been taken by a recognised investment exchange or clearing house against a company under its default rules, a liquidator of that company is bound by any market contract or other such contract as mentioned above notwithstanding the rule of law in liquidations corresponding to the provisions in section 42 of the Bankruptcy (Scotland) Act 1985 concerning deemed refusal to adopt contracts (section 164(2)) of the Companies Act 1989[9].

---

1 *Re Ken Coalfields Syndicate Ltd* [1890] 1 QB 754.
2 *Re North Brazilian Sugar Factories* (1887) 37 Ch D 84.
3 *Halden v Liquidator of Scottish Heritable Security Co Ltd* (1887) 14 R 633.
4 Insolvency Act 1986, s 186(1).
5 Ibid, s 186(2).
6 *Re Castle* [1917] 2 KB 725.
7 Scottish Law Commission Memorandum no 16, p 146.
8 Companies Act 1989, s 164(1).
9 'Recognised' means recognised under the Financial Services Act 1986.

## Power to order delivery of property to liquidator

Where *any* person has in his possession or control any property, books, papers or records to which the company appears to be entitled, the court may require that person to pay, deliver, convey, surrender or transfer the property, books, papers or records to the provisional liquidator or liquidator[1]. This is an important reform in the law open only in liquidations commenced after 29 December 1986[2]. Previously the power was available only against a contributory, trustee, receiver, banker, agent or officer of the company[3]. This provision would apply to property which the company was entitled to have conveyed to it under contract and the policy of the section is that, in the winding up of insolvent companies, the representative of the creditors is to be put into immediate possession of the property to which the company has a substantial right[4]. Where the liquidator seizes or disposes of any property which is not the property of the company, and at the time of seizure or disposal believes, and has 'reasonable grounds' for believing that he is entitled to seize or dispose of that property, the liquidator is not liable except where loss is caused by the liquidator's negligence[5]. 'Reasonable grounds for believing' would cover general reasonable grounds and where a court order had been made[6]. Where property has been seized or disposed of, the liquidator has a lien on the property, or the proceeds of its sale, for expenses which would be incurred in connection with the seizure or disposal[7].

## Appointment of special manager

In the case of a provisional liquidation or a liquidation, the court has the power, on the application of the liquidator, to appoint a special manager[8].

## Rectification of the register

The court has power, in a compulsory winding up, to rectify the register of members of the company[9]. The liquidator, or any contributory or creditor, may apply to the court to have the register rectified in a voluntary winding up[10]; the power is that given by section 359 of the Companies Act 1985 which continues after a winding up.

## Power of court to cure defects in procedure

In all windings up, of all types, and in administrations and receiverships the court now has a broad power to remedy and cure defects. This power now does not need to be exercised through the equitable jurisdiction of the Court

---

1 Insolvency Act 1986, s 234(2).
2 Ibid, Sch 11, para 4(2).
3 Companies Act 1985, s 551.
4 *Dunlop v Donald* (1893) 21 R 125 at 133.
5 Insolvency Act 1986, s 234(3), (4)(a).
6 Ibid, s 234(3)(b).
7 Ibid, s 234(4)(b).
8 Ibid, s 177.
9 Ibid, s 148(1).
10 Ibid, s 112(1).

of Session but may be exercised by a judge, either in the Court of Session or in the sheriff court, who is dealing with the insolvency proceedings. This power is in addition to the equitable jurisdiction of the Court of Session which can be a call of last resort[1].

### General power to determine questions

There is a general power of the court to determine any question in a voluntary liquidation given by section 112 of the Insolvency Act 1986 which invokes the powers exercisable by the court in a winding-up by the court[2]. In the case of *Leith and East Coast Steam Shipping Co (in Liquidation)*[3], Lord Johnston speaking for the First Division stated: 'I think expense could often be saved by liquidators requesting the Lord Ordinary to grant them an interview to arrange matters incidental to the liquidation, without presenting formal notes.'

# VI. STAGES IN INSOLVENT LIQUIDATIONS

### Differences between voluntary and compulsory winding up

A voluntary winding up commences by a different procedure from a compulsory winding up. Briefly, in a creditors' voluntary winding up, or a members' voluntary winding up converted to a creditors' voluntary winding up, the liquidation is a non-judicial affair. It is largely in the hands of the members, creditors and their nominee, the liquidator. It is initiated by the board of directors calling a meeting of the members of the company at which a resolution is proposed to wind up the company. If this is passed, a creditors' meeting is called at which the creditors have the right to nominate a liquidator. In contrast, a compulsory winding up is initiated by a petition to the court asking the court compulsorily to wind up a company. Thereafter the court appoints a liquidator, who barring challenges, is the choice of the creditors if they so choose. From the stage of the appointment of the liquidator, the procedure in a creditors' voluntary winding up and a liquidation by the court is very similar. The main differences are that:

(1)   as already described in Part IV a liquidator in a creditors' voluntary winding up and a liquidator in a compulsory winding up have slightly different powers;
(2)   certain functions in a voluntary winding up are carried out by the liquidator whereas in a compulsory winding up they are legally done by the court (although in fact the court is really making the orders on the initiative of the liquidator). These functions are to settle the list of contributories[4], to make calls[5], to adjust rights between contributories[6], and cause assets to be realised and debts discharged[7];

1 The power is given by r 7.32(1) of the Insolvency (Scotland) Rules 1986, applying the Bankruptcy (Scotland) Act 1985, s 63 to insolvency proceedings.
2 *Black & Co's Case* (1872) 8 Ch App 254.
3 1911 1 SLT 371 at 373.
4 Insolvency Act 1986, s 148(1).
5 Ibid, s 150(1).
6 Ibid, s 154.
7 Ibid, s 148(1).

(3) there are different reporting requirements in the two types of liquidation. In a liquidation by the court, the liquidator has to report to the court;

(4) only registered companies may be voluntarily wound up, whereas a whole range of types of company may be wound up by the court; and

(5) a creditors' voluntary winding up may proceed if the directors are unable to make a statement of solvency in relation to the company, or in a members' voluntary winding up the liquidator finds that the company is insolvent, whereas in a compulsory winding up the legal position is much more complex. There are other grounds for winding up a company by the court (some of which directly relate to solvency, others indirectly and others not at all).

Because most of the differences in the two types of liquidation are at the initial stage it is proposed to treat separately the initial stage of a creditors' voluntary winding up and the initial stage of a compulsory winding up but thereafter to treat the two together.

# 1. COMMENCEMENT OF CREDITORS' VOLUNTARY WINDING UP

**Directors' duties**

The first steps in putting a company into creditors' voluntary liquidation are taken by the directors. Under normal procedure they do the following:

(1) Call a meeting of the company, ie the members, for the purpose of:
   – putting the company into liquidation;
   – nominating a liquidator; and
   – nominating the members' appointees on the liquidation committee[1].
(2) Call a meeting of the creditors for the purpose of:
   – nominating a liquidator[2]; and
   – nominating the creditors' representatives on the liquidation committee[3].
(3) Prepare a statement of the company's affairs for laying before the creditors' meeting[4].
(4) Appoint one of their members to preside at the creditors' meeting[5], although the proceedings are not invalidated if no director attends[6].

**Meeting of members**

The business of the meeting of members is as follows:

---

1 Insolvency Act 1986, ss 98(1)(a), 100(1) and 101(2).
2 Ibid, s 100(1).
3 Ibid, s 101(1).
4 Ibid, s 99(1).
5 Ibid, s 99(1)(c).
6 *The Salcombe Hotel Development Co Ltd* [1991] BCLC 44.

(1)   It passes either a special resolution that the company be wound up voluntarily[1]; or an extraordinary resolution to the effect that the company cannot, by reason of its liabilities, continue in business, and that it is advisable to wind it up[2].
(2)   It nominates, by ordinary resolution, the liquidator[3]. As has been seen, if the meeting of creditors nominates a different person as liquidator, the creditors' nomination will prevail (see page 33).
(3)   In addition the meeting may nominate up to five persons to act on the liquidation committee appointed by the creditors[4]. (See chapter 18.)

## The creditors' meeting

The company has a duty to do the following:

(1)   it must summon a meeting of its creditors for a day not later than the 14th day after the day on which there is to be held the company meeting at which the resolution for a voluntary winding up is to be proposed;
(2)   it must have the notices of the creditors' meeting sent by post to the creditors not less than seven days before the day on which that meeting is to be held; and
(3)   it must have notice of the creditors' meeting advertised once in the *Edinburgh Gazette* and once in at least two newspapers circulating in the relevant locality (that is to say the locality in which the company's principal place of business in Great Britain was situated in the six months immediately preceding the day on which the notices are sent summoning the meeting of the company)[5]. (For styles see Appendix VIII.)

## Business of creditors' meeting

At the creditors' meeting the following business is conducted:

(1)   *Statement of affairs* – the directors of the company are obliged to make out a statement of affairs (see Appendix III) and lay the statement of affairs before the creditors' meeting.
(2)   *Nomination of liquidator* – the creditors may nominate a person to be liquidator for the purpose of winding up the company's affairs and distributing its assets[6].
(3)   *Liquidation committee* – the creditors at the first meeting or at any subsequent meeting may, if they think fit, appoint a liquidation committee of not more than five persons[7].

---

1 Insolvency Act 1986, s 84(1)(b).
2 Ibid, s 84(1)(c).
3 Ibid, s 100(1).
4 Ibid, s 101(2).
5 Ibid, s 98(1).
6 Ibid, s 100(1).
7 Ibid, s 101(1).

The chairman of the meeting is one of the directors who must be appointed by the directors to attend the meeting and to preside at it[1].

## Members' voluntary winding up converted to creditors' voluntary winding up

The Insolvency Act 1986 makes an important change in the law in relation to voluntary windings up where there is insolvency. Under the law applicable to windings up commenced before 29 December 1986, one had an insolvent voluntary winding up in two sets of circumstances:

(a)   *a creditors' voluntary winding up* (as described above);
(b)   *a members' voluntary winding up*, with the liquidator finding supervening insolvency.

In the second set of circumstances where there was a members' voluntary winding up and the liquidator formed the opinion that the company would not be able to pay its debts in full, he was obliged to summon a meeting of the creditors and lay before the meeting a statement of the company's assets and liabilities[2]. If the winding up continued for more than one year, the liquidator had to summon a general meeting of the company and a meeting of the creditors at the end of the first year from the commencement of the winding up, and of each succeeding year, or at the first convenient date within three months from the end of the year (or a longer period allowed by the Secretary of State) and lay before the meetings an account of his acts and dealings and of the conduct of the winding up during the preceding year[3]. He also had to call a final meeting of the company and its creditors[4].

Although the liquidator had the obligation under the law applicable to windings up commenced before 29 December 1986, to summon these creditors' meetings '*as if*', in terms of section 586, of the Companies Act 1985, the members' voluntary winding up were a creditors' voluntary winding up, the winding up legally stayed a members' voluntary winding up. Accordingly the power of appointing a liquidator and fixing his remuneration remained with the members[5]. Also there was no statutory authority to enable the appointment of a committee of inspection[6].

## Law applicable to windings up commenced after 29 December 1986

The Insolvency Act 1986 brings the law up-to-date and makes it more rational. A voluntary winding up under the supervision of the court in terms of section 606 of the Companies Act 1985 is abolished[7]. Where there now is a members' voluntary winding up and the liquidator forms the opinion that the company is insolvent, then the members' voluntary winding up is converted

1 Insolvency Act 1986, s 99(1)(c).
2 Companies Act 1985, s 583(1).
3 Ibid, ss 594 and 586.
4 Ibid, ss 595 and 586.
5 Ibid, ss 579 and 580.
6 Ibid, ss 487 and 590.
7 Although this procedure is technically competent in relation to voluntary windings up started before 29 December 1986, it was virtually extinct as a procedure and as far back as 1962 the Jenkins Committee had recommended its abolition.

to a creditors' voluntary winding up[1]. The creditors may now appoint the liquidator[2], with the right for a director, member or creditor to apply to the court in relation to who should be liquidator, where there are different nominations[3]. These creditors may also now appoint a liquidation committee[4]. The above results are clear when sections 96, 97(2) and 102 of the Insolvency Act 1986 are read together, although the logic and the English are convoluted.

The only differences now between a creditors' voluntary winding up and a members' voluntary winding up which has been converted into a creditors' voluntary winding up are:

## (1) Meeting of creditors

In the case of a converted winding up the liquidator summons a meeting of the creditors which is to be not later than 28 days after the day he formed the opinion that the company was insolvent[5]. In the case of a creditors' voluntary winding up, the company summons a meeting of its creditors, which should be not later than 14 days after the day on which was held the company meeting at which voluntary winding up was proposed[6].

## (2) Statement of affairs

In a converted winding up the liquidator makes out a statement of affairs, lays the statement before the creditors' meeting and attends and presides at the meeting[7]. In a creditors' voluntary winding up the directors make out a statement of affairs, have the statement of affairs laid before the creditors' meeting and appoint one of their number to preside at the meeting[8]. In a converted voluntary winding up, the statement of affairs is to be verified by affidavit of the liquidator[9], whereas in a creditors' voluntary winding up the statement of affairs is verified by affidavit of some or all of the directors[10].

## (3) Information to creditors

In the case of a converted winding up, the liquidator must furnish the creditors, free of charge, with information concerning the affairs of the company as they may reasonably require[11]. In a creditors' voluntary winding up, the notice sent to the creditors must state *either* the name and address of a person qualified to act as an insolvency practitioner who in the period up to the date of the meeting can give them information as to the company's affairs that they may reasonably require *or* allow them an inspection of the creditors'

---

1 Insolvency Act 1986, s 96.
2 Ibid, s 100(1) and (2).
3 Ibid, s 100(3).
4 Ibid, s 101(1).
5 Ibid, s 95(2)(a).
6 Ibid, s 98(1)(a).
7 Ibid, s 95(3).
8 Ibid, s 99(1).
9 Ibid, s 95(4).
10 Ibid, s 99(2).
11 Ibid, s 95(2)(d).

list in a place within the locality of the company's principal place of business on two business days prior to the day of the creditors' meeting[1].

# 2. COMMENCEMENT OF COMPULSORY LIQUIDATION

The Scottish courts have a wide jurisdiction in both:

**(1)   The types of company which may be wound up;** and
**(2)   The grounds of winding up.**

### (1) Types of company which may be wound up

(a) *Registered companies*

Any company registered in Scotland may be wound up[2]. The Court of Session has jurisdiction to wind up any company registered in Scotland and certain unregistered companies (see chapter 20). The sheriff court has jurisdiction concurrently with the Court of Session to wind up any company whose registered office is situated within the sheriffdom, provided that the company's share capital paid up or credited as paid up does not exceed £120,000[3]. The sheriff court may not wind up a company limited by guarantee or an unlimited company[4].

(b) *Unregistered companies*

Unregistered companies, as defined by section 220 of the Insolvency Act 1986, may be wound up. That includes any association and any company. The essential feature of a company is that there are mutual obligations or liabilities among the membership[5]. Railway companies incorporated by Act of Parliament are excluded[6] whether they are dissolved or have ceased to carry on business (section 221(5)(a)). Included in the category of unregistered companies have been trustee savings banks, building societies not registered under the building societies legislation[7], life assurance companies[8], friendly societies[9], companies incorporated by Royal Charter[10], companies incorporated

---

1 Insolvency Act 1986, s 98(2).
2 Ibid, s 120(1); for the definition of company see the Insolvency Act 1986, s 251 and the Companies Act 1985, s 735.
3 Insolvency Act 1986, s 120(3).
4 *Pearce, Petitioner* 1991 SCLR 861. There would seem to be no good reason why the Sheriff Court should not be given jurisdiction in the case of companies limited by guarantee, subject to an amount of the guarantee, preferably the same amount as the paid up share capital limit.
5 *Caledonian Employees Benevolent Society* 1928 SC 633.
6 Insolvency Act 1986, s 220(1)(a).
7 *Smith's Trs v Irvine and Fullerton Property and Investment Building Society* (1903) 6 F 99; *Re Ilfracombe Permanent Mutual Benefit Building Society* [1901] 1 Ch 102.
8 *Re Great Britain Mutual Life Assurance Society* (1880) 16 Ch D 246.
9 *Canavan, Petrs* 1929 SLT 636.
10 *Re Oriental Bank Corporation* (1884) 54 LJ Ch 481.

by Special Act[1] and foreign companies having assets and liabilities in Scotland[2].

### (c) *Companies incorporated under certain statutes*

Companies and organisations incorporated under certain Acts may be wound up, eg building societies under sections 88–90 of the Building Societies Act 1986, industrial and provident societies under section 55 of the Industrial and Provident Societies Act 1965, but not trade unions[3].

### (d) *Insurance companies*

Insurance companies carrying on business within the United Kingdom may be wound up[4].

### (e) *Foreign companies carrying on business in Scotland*

Companies incorporated outside Great Britain carrying on business in Scotland may be wound up even if wound up under an order of a foreign court[5].

## (2) Grounds for a compulsory winding up

The Scottish courts have *five* main grounds for winding up registered and unregistered companies. They are:

(a)  technical reasons;
(b)  just and equitable grounds;
(c)  special resolution;
(d)  insolvency; and
(e)  prejudice to a floating charge.

The first three grounds are dealt with very briefly by way of elucidation because they do not relate to insolvency.

### (a) *Technical reasons*

In the case of registered companies, they may be wound up for technical reasons, such as, in the case of a public limited company, that it has not been issued with a certificate under section 117 of the Companies Act 1985 (public company share capital requirements)[6], or that it has not commenced its

---

1 *Re South London Fish Market Co* (1888) 39 Ch D 324; *Re Bradford Navigation Co* (1870) LR 10 Eq 331.
2 *Marshall* (1895) 22 R 697.
3 See the Trade Union and Labour Relations Act 1974, ss 2, 3.
4 Insurance Companies Act 1982, ss 53, 54 and 55 (see chapter 19).
5 Insolvency Act 1986, s 225; *Re Compania Merabello San Nicolas SA* [1973] Ch 75; *Re Allobrogia Steamship Corporation* [1982] Ch 43; for cases on Russian banks which were dissolved by Soviet decrees in the Russian Revolution, see Buckley on the *Companies Acts* (14th edn), p 852.
6 Insolvency Act 1986, s 122(1)(b).

business within a year from its incorporation or suspends its business for a whole year[1], or that the number of its members is reduced below two[2].

### (b) *Just and equitable*

In the case of registered and unregistered companies the court may wind up the company if the court is of the opinion that it is just and equitable that the company should be wound up[3]. The expression 'just and equitable' covers an unrestricted number of circumstances[4]. Winding-up orders have been made on the grounds that the substratum of the company had gone (the substratum is the main object for which the company is formed)[5], that the company was a bubble[6] and that there was complete deadlock[7]. The 'just and equitable' ground has relevance in relation to the law of insolvency only in a situation where a business is unsuccessful and, although not yet insolvent, would become insolvent. A winding-up order on 'just and equitable' grounds may be granted where the requisite majority for a special resolution for voluntary winding up is not obtainable[8].

### (c) *Special resolution to wind up*

The company may be wound up compulsorily if it passes a special resolution resolving that the company be wound up by the court[9]. This is not common, because it is more likely that a company will be wound up voluntarily than that a special resolution seeking compulsory winding up will be passed, but it is used from time to time.

### (d) *Insolvency*

Both registered[10] and unregistered[11] companies may be compulsorily wound up if they are unable to pay their debts. This is the most common basis for compulsory winding up.

There are *four* statutory provisions under which a creditor or member may legally prove that the company is unable to pay its debts.

*Creditor's demand notice.*    First, a company is deemed to be unable to pay its debts if a creditor (by assignation or otherwise) to whom the company is indebted in a sum exceeding £750·00 then due has served on the company, by leaving at the company's registered office, a written demand (using Form 4.1 (Scot) (see Appendix I)) requiring the company to pay the sum so due and the company has for three weeks thereafter neglected to pay the sum or to secure

---

1 Insolvency Act 1986, s 122(1)(d).
2 Ibid, s 122(1)(e).
3 Ibid, ss 122(1)(g) and 221(5)(c).
4 *Ebrahami v Westbourne Galleries Ltd* [1973] AC 360, per Lord Wilberforce at 379.
5 *Re Suburban Hotel Co* (1867) 2 Ch App 737, approved in *Galbraith v Merito Shipping Co* 1947 SC 466.
6 *Re London and County Coal Co* (1867) LR 3 Eq 355.
7 *Re Expanded Plugs Ltd* [1965] 1 WLR 514.
8 *Pirie v Stewart* (1904) 6 F 847.
9 Insolvency Act 1986, s 122(1)(a).
10 Ibid, s 122(1)(f).
11 Ibid, s 221(5)(b).

or compound for it to the reasonable satisfaction of the creditor[1]. A winding-up order may be resisted if the company finds caution for the amount of the claim on the basis that the debt is disputed[2]. Alternatively the amount of the claim may be consigned to court[3]. It is a defence to a winding-up petition that the debt is secured in the hands of the creditor[4]. The procedure envisages the creditor being able to point to a debt of a specified sum that cannot be seriously questioned as to its existence or quantum[5]. The debt must be 'then due', which means 'presently payable'[6]. The formal demand it is thought may not be made by fax although the position in England may be different[7]. The period of omission to pay the money demanded is probably 21 clear days from the date of service[8]. If a sum larger than the sum due is demanded, this may not imply a demand for the lesser sum. In *Re A Company*[9], Nourse J described a demand as 'a solemn document with potentially serious consequences'. He said that in that case 'the discrepancy between the figures of £161,000 and £83,000 is so enormous that I am by no means certain that the telex-demand for £160,000 could be relied on as a statutory demand for the lesser sum'.

The statutory demand must be delivered at the debtor company's registered office by a person duly authorised by the creditor to do so[10].

It is normal practice to have the statutory demand delivered by an officer of the court, but this is not necessary in Scotland[11].

*Expiry of charge.* A second mode of proof of 'inability to pay debts' is if the *induciae* of a charge (the time limit on the statutory demand notice) for payment on an extract decree or an extract registered bond, or an extract registered protest, have expired without payment being made[12]. There is no financial limit on this provision[13].

*Unable to pay debts as they fall due.* A third method of proof is to prove to the satisfaction of the court that the company is unable to pay its debts as they fall due[14]. This may be demonstrated in a number of ways, eg a company

---

1 Ibid, s 123(1)(a) and s 222(1); in the case of an unregistered company the letter should be left at its principal place of business, or by delivering to the secretary or some director, manager or principal officer of the company or otherwise as the court might direct.
2 *Pollok v Gaeta Pioneer Mining Co Ltd* 1907 SC 182.
3 *Cunninghame v Walkinshaw Oil Co* (1886) 14 R 87.
4 *Commercial Bank of Scotland Ltd v Lanark Oil Co Ltd* (1886) 14 R 147.
5 *Re a Company (No 003729 of 1982)* [1984] BCLC 323.
6 *Re Bryant Investment Co Ltd* [1974] 2 All ER 683.
7 Insolvency Rules 1986 (England) rr 4.5 and 4.6; *Re a Company* [1985] BCLC 37. The demand must nevertheless be in the form prescribed, ie Form 4.1 (Scot): see s 123(1)(a) and r 7.30.
8 This seems the case from the wording of Form 4.1 (Scot) and s 123(1)(a) of the Insolvency Act 1986 which supersedes the case of *Neil McLeod and Sons, Petrs* 1967 SLT 46.
9 [1985] BCLC 37 at 41 and 43.
10 Rule 7.21(3) of the Insolvency (Scotland) Rules 1986; *Craig v Iona Hotels Ltd* 1988 SCLR 130, Sh Ct: see in contrast *Re A Company (Number 008790 of 1990)* [1991] BCLC 561, where a demand was sent by registered post and delivery was not disputed at the registered office and it was held that that was sufficient for the purposes of the section.
11 *Lord Advocate v Blairwest Investment Ltd* 1989 SCLR 352, 1989 SLT (Sh Ct) 97: *Lord Advocate v Traprain Ltd* 1989 SLT (Sh Ct) 99.
12 Insolvency Act 1986, ss 123(1)(c), 224(1)(b).
13 *Speirs & Co v Central Building Co Ltd* 1911 SC 330.
14 Insolvency Act 1986, ss 123(1)(e), 224(1)(d).

dishonouring acceptances[1], or the company has admitted that it has no assets[2], or no good defence to an action has been put forward[3].

As noted above in the case of *Pollok v Gaeta Pioneer Mining Co Ltd*[4], a winding-up petition will be refused if the debt is disputed. In the case of *Blue Star Security Services (Scotland) Ltd v Drake & Scull (Scotland) Ltd*[5], a creditor petitioned for the winding-up of a debtor, claiming that invoices in respect of security services remained unpaid. The sheriff refused warrant to cite on the ground that, the debtor company having a claim against the creditor in respect of items stolen from their premises, there was insufficient evidence that the debt was undisputed and therefore that the debtor company was unable or unwilling to pay. On appeal, it was held by the Sheriff Principal that the correspondence indicated the debtor's continuing failure to pay despite pressure from the creditor. Accordingly the debtor's claim did not, strictly speaking, bring the creditor's debt into dispute, and in any event not to more than the value of the debtor's claim, which the creditor had excluded in his petition from the amount said to be due[6]. It has been held in England that, where a cheque in payment of a debt has been dishonoured, and the cheque has been re-presented, the creditor is not allowed to petition for winding up of the debtor company if he has first re-presented the cheque. In the case of *Re A Company (No 001259 of 1991), ex Parte Medialite Ltd*[7] Harman J held that the re-presenting of a cheque amounted to a suspension of a presenter's right to sue. While the cheque was in the clearing it had to constitute a conditional payment which, if the cheque is honoured, would amount to a payment as from the date of presentation. The inability to pay debts is not related to the solvency of the company. Where a creditor's debt is clearly established, the creditor has a right to present a winding up petition even though it appears that the company is solvent because the persistent non-payment of the debt suggests that the company is unable to pay its debts[8].

Although the serving of a statutory demand is a useful ground whereby an unpaid creditor who may have no detailed knowledge of the debtor company's financial state of affairs, can force the company either to settle the debt in question or, be deemed to be 'unable to pay its debts' so that it may be wound up on the creditor's petition, the drawback of a statutory demand is that the debtor company has three weeks from the date of the service of the demand in which it can comply with it. During that intervening period, the assets remaining to the company may be dissipated in a final attempt by the

---

1 *Re Globe New Patent Iron and Steel Co* (1875) LR 20 Eq 337; *Gandy*, 1912 2 SLT 276.
2 *Re Flagstaff Silver Mining Co of Utah* (1875) LR 20 Eq 268.
3 *Stephen v Scottish Banking Co* (1884) 21 SLR 764.
4 1907 SC 182.
5 1992 GWD 15–844.
6 See in England the case of *Re FSA Business Software Ltd* [1990] BCLC 825, in which the Chancery Division held that where there was a counterclaim in respect of the debt on which a winding-up petition was founded, the court had a discretion to be exercised on all the facts to dismiss the petition or make a winding-up order. In that case, on the facts, failure to make a winding-up order would mean that the petitioning company would be kept out of its money to which it was undoubtedly entitled for a long period of time and the debtor company might eventually fail in its counterclaim. In addition the debtor company would have 7 days in which to pay the petitioning creditor's debt were a winding-up order made, and accordingly in the light of those considerations, it was proper that a winding-up order be made.
7 [1991] BCLC 594.
8 *Re Globe New Patent Iron & Steel Co* (1875) LR 20 Eq 337; *Cornhill Insurance Improvement Services Ltd* [1986] BCLC 26.

directors to keep the company in business, and by the holders of floating charges who may take steps to crystallise their floating charges and secure assets solely for the payment of their debts. A final drawback is that, if the company eventually is put into liquidation, the commencement of the winding up is deemed to be at the date of the presentation of the winding-up petition, and not at the date of the service of the statutory demand[1]. Hence the petition of the creditor founding on the statutory demand may be too late to achieve his object.

These considerations have suggested to creditors to refrain from using the statutory demand method and to seek the more direct route using section 123(1)(e) of the Insolvency Act 1986, whereby the mere fact of a company having failed to pay a debt as and when it was due is treated by the court as a sufficient indication that the company is unable to pay its debts. All the creditor has to do is to present a winding-up petition averring that the company is indebted to the petitioner for an amount which is more than the minimum amount which would have entitled the creditor to serve the statutory demand; that the debtor company has not suggested in any way that the debt is disputed; and that the company is accordingly unable to pay its debts and the winding-up petition should be granted. The propriety of this approach has been approved in England by the Court of Appeal in the case of *Taylors Industrial Flooring Ltd v M & H Plant Hire (Manchester) Ltd*[2]. In that case Taylors were indebted to the company for an aggregate amount of almost £10,000 which was owing at the date when the winding-up petition was presented. It was averred that the company had been given full notice of the debt, and that the company had given no notification of any dispute in connection with the invoices. The court held that there was no requirement that a creditor must serve a statutory demand before presenting a winding-up petition, and that if a debt is due from a company and it is not disputed, the failure of the debtor company to pay is evidence of an inability on the part of the company to pay its debts. Dillon LJ, who gave the leading judgment, was careful to confirm that where a company disputes a debt it must establish a substantial ground for doing so in order to avoid the winding-up petition being successful. Further endorsing what Dillon LJ said and almost encouraging this ground of winding up, Staughton LJ stated:

'I entirely agree with everything that has been said by Dillon LJ. Many people today seem to think that they are lawfully entitled to delay paying their debts when they fall due or beyond the agreed period of credit, if there is one. Alternatively they may think that no remedy is in practice available to the creditor if they do delay payment. There is a greater degree of truth in the second belief than the first. Legal remedies are in themselves slow and expensive. A creditor will often tolerate late payment, rather than incur further expense. But this can cause great hardship to honest traders, particularly those engaged in small businesses recently started. Anything which the law can do to discourage such behaviour in my view should be done.

In my judgment M & H Plant Hire (Manchester) Ltd had allowed quite enough gratuitous time for payment to the company when they presented their petition. Indeed, they would have been justified, like Lord Clive, in being astonished at their own moderation.'

---

1 Insolvency Act 1986, s 129(2).
2 [1990] BCLC 216.

In determining whether a company is unable to pay its debts, only debts which are due and payable are to be taken into account. Existing debts payable in the future, prospective debts and contingent liabilities must be ignored. In the case of *Re European Life Assurance Co*[1], a petition sought the winding up of an insurance company under section 80 of the Companies Act 1862 on the ground of its inability to pay its debts. It was not disputed that the company was paying its debts as they fell due but it was argued that this was achieved only by using current premium income to pay past liabilities and that the company would be unable to meet substantial future claims. The contention was rejected. Sir W M James V-C stated:

'I take it that the court has nothing whatever to do with any question of future liabilities, that it has nothing whatever to do with the question of the probability whether any business which the company may carry on tomorrow or hereafter will be profitable or unprofitable. That is a matter for those who may choose to be the customers of the company and for the shareholders to consider. I have to look at the case simply with reference to the solvency or insolvency of the company, and in doing that I have to deal with the company exactly as it stood on the date to which the evidence relates – viz., the 31st of December, 1868 which I assume to represent substantially the state in which the company stands now. I must take it as if all the business which the company ever intended to do was then done, as if its business were confined to its existing contracts, and as if it did not mean to enter into one single fresh contract or do anything more.'

Debts even if they are technically due, may be ignored where there is no evidence that the creditors are requiring repayment[2]. If that were not the case, most banks would be insolvent, because they operate on the basis that at any particular time not all the depositors would demand repayment. Even if it is proved that the company is unable to pay its debts, it is thought that in Scotland the court has a discretion whether to grant the winding-up order. Outside factors, such as the prospect of additional finance for the company which has a deficiency of assets may be taken into account when the judge is exercising his discretion as to whether to grant a winding-up petition[3].

*Balance sheet test.*    A fourth mode of proof of inability to pay its debts is if it is proved to the satisfaction of the court that the value of the company's assets is less than the amount of its liabilities, taking into account its contingent and prospective liabilities[4]. The law underwent a major reform with the Insolvency Act 1986. Previously the appropriate section read 'if it is proved to the satisfaction of the court that the company is unable to pay its debts, and, in determining whether a company is unable to pay its debts, the court shall take into account the contingent and prospective liabilities of the company'[5]. That provision was interpreted in England to mean 'unable to pay debts in full as they fell due', which is the third statutory mode of proof now. In Scotland, however, the courts on occasion ordered winding up on the basis of a company's balance sheet alone, where it disclosed large deficiencies of both total assets and current assets. The case of *Re A Company (No 007694 of*

---

1 (1869) LR 9 Eq 122.
2 *Re Capital Annuities Ltd* [1978] 3 All ER 704.
3 *Byblos Bank SAL v Al-Khudhairy* (1986) 2 BCC 99 at 549, per Nicholls LJ.
4 Insolvency Act 1986, ss 123(2), 224(2).
5 Companies Act 1948, s 223(d) and Companies Act 1985, s 518(1)(e).

*1983)*[1] decided the interpretation of the previous wording in England, but its detailed analysis elucidates how the present wording should be read. Winding up was sought on the ground *inter alia* that when contingent and prospective liabilities of the company were taken into account it was insolvent in balance sheet terms. Nourse J stated:

'In the present case I have come to the conclusion that the test has not quite been satisfied on the facts which are before me. Although the company has ever since March 1982 been paying the petitioner only at the last possible moment, I think that, on the evidence, the company is just able to pay its debts as they fall due. If, on the other hand, the company pursued the same course of conduct any longer, it might very well be that the court would take the opposite view.

That is the first part of section 233(b). That is not an end of the matter, because I must now consider the second part, which required me to take into account the contingent and prospective liabilities of the company. Counsel for the petitioner submits, correctly, that every time the company borrows money from somebody else to pay off the petitioner or the supporting creditor, or whoever, that borrowing increases its prospective liabilities, because it incurs a further debt prospectively due to the lender. Counsel says that if I take into account the contingent and prospective liabilities of the company, it is clearly insolvent in balance sheet terms. So indeed it is if I treat the loans made by the associated companies as loans which are currently repayable. However what I am required to do is to "take into account" the contingent and prospective liabilities. That cannot mean that I must simply add them up and strike a balance against assets. In regard to prospective liabilities I must principally consider whether, and if so when, they are likely to become present liabilities. As to that, I have evidence from a director of the company, to the effect that there is no question of those loans being withdrawn. He has exhibited four loan agreements under which the loans are expressed not to be repayable until 30th June 1985. He adds that, although all of them bear interest, interest has so far been waived by the lenders and that they intend to continue to waive it. It seems to me, on the basis of that evidence, that if I take account of the prospective liabilities, I must approach the company's financial position on the footing that those loans will not be called in until 30th June 1985, and possibly until later.

In those circumstances, I am in the end satisfied that the petitioner has not established that the company is unable to pay its debts even taking into account its contingent and prospective liabilities.'

The yardstick is now radically different. It is no longer necessary to prove to the satisfaction of the court that the company is unable to pay its debts which is a *cash flow* or *liquidity* test. It is *deemed* unable to pay its debts provided the statutory test is satisfied. The test is whether the value of the company's assets is less than the amount of its liabilities. That *is* a *balance sheet* test.

*Contingent liabilities*

There is a problem in determining the level of a provision for a contingent liability. One approach is to argue that if there is more than a 50/50 chance of the contingency occurring, there should be a provision for the full amount of the liability discounted to take account of its futurity. Following this approach, a contingent liability with an 80 per cent chance of accrual would not be discounted for the 20 per cent chance that it would not accrue, whilst a liability with a 50 per cent chance of accrual would be discarded altogether. Another method is to value the contingent liability at the percentage of the

1 [1986] BCLC 261.

likelihood of its occurrence, so that where there was an 80 per cent likelihood of the liability occurring, the provision would be 80 per cent of the full liability discounted to reflect its present value. Following the latter approach, a contingent liability with a 10 per cent chance of accrual would be estimated at the present value of 10 per cent of the full liability. The prevailing accounting practice is to value the contingency in full (less any discount for futurity) if it will probably occur and is capable of valuation and disregard it altogether in other cases[1]. It is thought that the second approach should be the legal approach. The cost of removing a contingent liability from a balance sheet will be roughly the amount of the contingent liability divided by the chances of it occurring. By that formula it would cost roughly £20 to remove from any balance sheet a contingent debt of £100 where there was a one in five chance of the debt being payable.

*Liabilities to be taken into account*

The Insolvency Act 1986 employs two distinct formulations as to the liabilities to be taken into account in applying the balance sheet test:

(1)  *All liabilities, taking into account contingent and prospective liabilities*
     This is the formulation used in the provisions relating to winding up[2], administration[3], in England the avoidance of challengeable transactions[4] and in Scotland gratuitous alienations[5]. However, the expenses of a winding-up are not included.
(2)  *Debts and other liabilities and expenses of winding up*
     This is the definition of 'insolvent liquidation' which relates to wrongful trading[6] and the disqualification of directors[7]. It includes contingent or prospective liabilities[8].

It is thought that normal accounting practice will be followed in 'taking into account' contingent and prospective liabilities on the balance sheet, ie a provision if prudence requires it for a contingent liability, and, perhaps, under certain circumstances, long term non-interest bearing loans discounted to reflect the net present liability.

*Valuation of assets on a 'going concern basis'*

Although the provisions of section 123 of the Insolvency Act 1986 are consistent with section 214 of that Act, apart from the inclusion in section 214 of expenses of the winding up as a liability to be taken into account, it is not clear on what basis assets should be valued, ie whether on a 'break up' basis or on a 'going concern' basis. It is thought that they should be valued on a 'break up' basis for the purposes of section 214 (see page 190). For the purposes of that

---

1  SSAP No 18.
2  Insolvency Act 1986, s 123(2).
3  Ibid, s 8(1).
4  Ibid, ss 240(2), 245(4), applying s 123.
5  Ibid, s 142(4)(a) read with s 382(3).
6  Ibid, s 214(6).
7  Company Directors Disqualification Act 1986.
8  Insolvency Act 1986, s 382(3).

section the director is to look to see what the position would be in a liquidation and to assess what the balance sheet would be. For the purposes of that section, going into a non-insolvent liquidation would not constitute 'wrongful trading'. For the purposes of section 123 of the Insolvency Act 1986, the balance sheet is to be struck at the date of the hearing of the petition. That is not a prospective test. The question is what the value of the company's assets is as at that date, which is before the company has gone into liquidation, and on the basis of the balance sheet struck at that date, the decision is made whether the company should go into liquidation. SSAP No 17 on *Accounting for Post Balance Sheet Events* distinguishes 'adjusting events' from 'non-adjusting events'. Paragraph 8 of SSAP No 17 provides:

'Some events occurring after the balance sheet date, such as a deterioration in the operating results and in the financial position, may indicate a need to consider whether it is appropriate to use the going concern concept in the preparation of financial statements. Consequently these may fall to be treated as adjusting events.'

Paragraph 22 of the Appendix to SSAP No 17 makes it clear that this adjustment is to be made whether the application of the going concern basis becomes inappropriate as a result of events which provide additional evidence of conditions existing at the balance sheet date or solely as a result of post balance sheet date events not related to such conditions. Because the balance is struck at the date of the hearing of the petition, there can be no question of post balance sheet events requiring the adjustment. It might be argued that the bringing of the petition itself, could adversely affect the status of the company and hence introduce a distress element in the sale of its assets, even if the company did not go into liquidation. While this might be the case, where there were a number of winding-up petitions brought, and the company lost credibility in the market place, it is thought that a court would reject this argument. The first ground for rejection would be that the dismissal of the petition on the basis that the company was solvent, should restore the credit-worthiness and status of the company. Secondly, it would be inequitable if a winding-up petition itself was allowed to interfere with what is meant to be an objective test. If the court had to hold hearings on the adverse effect of the winding-up petition on the status of the company, these hearings would further undermine the company's status.

The thinking of section 123 is consistent with the 'wrongful trading' provisions of section 214 of the Insolvency Act 1986, under which directors may be personally liable where they do not take all reasonable steps to minimise the potential loss to a company's creditors when there is no reasonable prospect that the company will avoid going into insolvent liquidation, i e into liquidation when its assets are insufficient for the payment of its debts and other liabilities and the expenses of the winding up. One route, under the 'wrongful trading' provision, by which a director avoids liability is by minimising the loss to creditors through ceasing to trade and liquidating the company. The alternative method, is that new equity is put into the company to cover its debts. The threat of a winding-up order may be what Parliament had in mind as a way of compelling shareholders and backers of companies to ensure that companies are properly capitalised.

(e) *Prejudice to floating chargeholder*

In Scotland a company which the Court of Session has jurisdiction to wind up may be wound up by the court if there was a floating charge over property comprised in the company's property and undertaking, and the court is satisfied that the security of the creditor entitled to the benefit of the floating charge is in jeopardy[1]. A creditor's security is deemed by law to be in jeopardy if the court is satisfied that events have occurred or are about to occur which render it unreasonable in the creditor's interests that the company should retain power to dispose of the property which is subject to the floating charge[2]. This provision has survived from the period when a floating charge holder could not appoint a receiver in Scotland.

## 3. CREDITORS' VOLUNTARY WINDING UP MADE COMPULSORY WINDING UP

The fact that a creditors' voluntary winding up has commenced does not bar a creditor or contributory applying to the court to have the company compulsorily wound up, although, in the case of an application to the court by a contributory, the court would have to be satisfied that the rights of the contributories would be prejudiced by a voluntary winding up[3].

In deciding the matter, the court may have regard to the wishes of the creditors or contributories and, if it thinks fit, summon meetings of the creditors or contributories to ascertain their wishes, and in assessing these wishes regard, in the case of the creditors, is had to the value of the creditors' debt and, in the case of the contributories, regard is had to the number of votes conferred on each contributory by the Companies Act or the Articles[4]. Where there is a creditors' petition, the wishes of the company or its members will not result in the petition being refused[5]. Where creditors differ as to whether there should be a compulsory winding up, the court will normally have regard to the wishes of the majority in value of the creditors[6]. Even if the creditors in favour of a continuation of the voluntary liquidation are a minority in value, the court may refuse a compulsory order if there appears to be no advantage to creditors in making one[7], such as if the voluntary liquidation was almost completed and a compulsory order would only add to the expense.

As in deciding on schemes of arrangement, the court must have regard to the general principles of fairness and commercial morality. The court may also take into account not only the value of the debts but the possible or probable motive of creditors in making their choice. Thus creditors who are also shareholders or connected with the former management may have less weight given to their view than those who have no interest except in their capacity as creditors. In the case of *Re Palmer Marine Surveys*[8], Hoffman J, using these principles, held that 'a judicial exercise of discretion should not

---

1 Insolvency Act 1986, ss 122(2), 221(7).
2 Ibid, ss 122(2) and 221(7).
3 Ibid, s 116.
4 Ibid, s 195.
5 *MacDonnell's Trs v Oregonian Railway Co* (1884) 11 R 912.
6 *Pattisons Ltd v Kinnear* (1899) 1 F 551; *Elsmie and Son v Tomatin Spey District Distillery* (1906) 8 F 434.
7 *Re Medisco Equipment Ltd* [1983] BCLC 305.
8 [1986] BCLC 111.

leave substantial independent creditors with a strong and legitimate sense of grievance'[1].

# 4. STOPPING LIQUIDATION PROCEEDINGS ONCE COMMENCED

The court may, at any time after an order for winding up, make an order sisting the proceedings either altogether or for a limited time, if it is proved to the satisfaction of the court that all proceedings in the winding up ought to be sisted[2]. The liquidator or any contributory or creditor may make a similar application in the case of a voluntary winding up[3]. The sist will not be granted if this will have the effect of benefiting the directors but not the creditors[4]. Also a sist will not normally be granted in the absence of firm and acceptable proposals for satisfying all creditors and in the absence of consent from, or arrangements binding, the liquidator and all members[5]. The criteria for what are acceptable proposals are strict. In the case of *Re Lowston Ltd*[6], Harman J stated the level of detailed assurances that a court would require before it allowed a stay of proceedings. He stated:

'In my view, the test I have to apply is still that laid down by the first Buckley J in *Re Telescriptor Syndicate Limited* [1903] 2 Ch 174 that the court has to be satisfied that it is right to stay the winding-up proceedings, and, if there be matters as to which the court has doubts, it should not so stay. Megarry J was of the same view in *Re Calgary & Edmonton Land Co Ltd* [1975] 1 All ER 1046, [1975] 1 WLR 355. I have to be satisfied that it is proper to allow this company with this history to re-emerge back as an unencumbered company able to trade and carry on business.

In my view, the fact that there is a claimant who has a disputed debt against it does not in any way mean that the present winding up ought to remain on foot. The winding-up order was made upon a basis which has proved to have been false. . . . It may turn out to be correct but that will require substantial litigation. . . . In those circumstances it seems to me I must look at the history of this company and see whether there are any shady practices or unattractive incidents which would disable the applicants from having the company restored to their hands. In the *Telescriptor* case there were dealings which were of an extremely curious nature which led Buckley J, . . . to refuse to restore the company to the register in that state.

The position today is quite different. I am offered . . . undertakings by both applicants who are creditors and contributories that they will procure that the company will file all necessary statutory accounts and returns within 3 months of the making of this order and will submit them to the relevant inspector of taxes. That means inevitably that a whole series of procedural steps which appear to have been omitted, such as the fixing of an accounting reference date, the appointment of auditors, the preparation of accounts, the audit of the accounts, etc, will all have to be conducted and, since the undertakings are given by the two applicants personally, they will be personally at risk if they are not complied with, which may involve them in financing those matters.'

---

1 See also Hoffmann J's remarks in *Re Lowestoft Traffic Services Ltd* [1986] BCLC 81.
2 Insolvency Act 1986, s 147(1).
3 Insolvency Act 1986, s 112(1).
4 *Re F Burrows (Leeds) (in Liquidation)* (1982) 126 SJ 227.
5 *Re Calgary & Edmonton Land Co Ltd* [1975] 1 WLR 355.
6 [1991] BCLC 570.

The court was also offered assurances that the creditor undertook to be postponed to other creditors, which gave proper protection for present and putative future creditors of the company.

# 5. SETTLING OF LIST OF CONTRIBUTORIES

## Procedure

In a creditors' voluntary winding up the liquidator settles the list of contributories[1], and in a winding up by the court this is done by the court[2]. What hapens is the list is prepared by the liquidator and submitted to the court by way of a note in the petition. The court will normally order intimation to all persons on the list allowing seven days (eight days in the sheriff court) for answers to be lodged. The list is then settled by the court after disposing of any objections which may be lodged. If it appears to the court or to the liquidator that there is no uncalled capital or that there is to be no surplus for members, the liquidator or the court may dispense with the settling of the list of contributories[3]. The sort of case in which the court could properly dispense with the settlement of a list of contributories is likely, in an insolvent liquidation, to be a case where there is a small number of shareholders and the company is clearly insolvent, when it is possible to establish that the position is perfectly clear without going through the rules relating to the settlement of the list. In the case of a large company with a large number of shares widely held by a large number of shareholders, the settlement of the list should not be dispensed with[4].

## Definition of 'contributory'

Contributories are members or former members of the company who are:

(1)    as *debtors* of the company, liable for 'debts' of the company. 'Debts' in the case of a company registered with limited liability entails liability to the amount of any unpaid capital on their shares[5]. 'Debts' in the case of a company not registered with limited liability entails liability for all the debts of the company including the expenses of the winding up[6]. 'Debts' in the case of a company limited by guarantee entails liability of the contributory to the extent of his guarantee unless the company has a share capital in which case the member would be liable for the amount of his non-paid up share capital[7]; and

(2)    as *creditors* of the company, entitled, in an insolvent liquidation, to share in any surplus which turns out to be available to shareholders after the payment of other creditors.

---

1 Insolvency Act 1986, s 165(4).
2 Ibid, s 148(1).
3 Ibid, ss 148(2) and 165(4)(a).
4 *Re Paragon Holdings Ltd* [1961] 2 All ER 41.
5 Insolvency Act 1986, s 74(1), (2)(d).
6 Ibid, ss 74(1) and 226.
7 Ibid, s 74(3).

The liability of past members is restricted to those who have been members within one year from the commencement of the winding up, and only then when existing members are unable to pay the debts due by them. A past member is not liable to contribute in respect of any debt or liability of the company contracted after he has ceased to be a member[1]. It is perhaps thought unfair that past members should be liable, but the thinking is clear that if one assigns or transfers an onerous obligation, there should be some residual surety that the assignor is good for his money – at least for a year – although strictly the relationship is not that of surety but a primary obligation.

In terms of section 74(2)(f) of the Insolvency Act 1986, where a company is being wound up, a sum due to any member of the company (in his character of a member) by way of dividends, profits or otherwise is deemed to be a debt of the company, payable to that member in a case of competition between himself and any other creditor not a member of the company, but any such sum may be taken into account for the purpose of the final adjustment of the rights of the contributories among themselves. It has been held in Scotland that dividends declared but unpaid may be converted into loans. In the case of *Liquidator of Wilsons (Glasgow and Trinidad Ltd) v Wilson's Trs*[2] the court considered section 123(1)(vii) of the Companies (Consolidation) Act 1908, which was the statutory predecessor of section 74(2)(f) of the Insolvency Act 1986. In that case a member of the company, Mr Wilson, maintained with the company a 'cash account current' which at its inception recorded the purchase price paid by the company for the purchase of a business and, as well, the issues of shares in the company to Mr Wilson. Thereafter for some years there were various debts and credits in the account of a miscellaneous nature including dividends carried to the credit of the account on Wilson's instructions. Balances were regularly struck and interest was paid. The company had the benefit of the balances for the purposes of its business. The ultimate balance was, in the liquidator's view, made up of unpaid dividends. In rejecting the liquidator's contention, Lord Cullen stated:

'On a consideration of the nature of the account and the dealings with it I am unable to agree with the liquidator's view. The account extends over a considerable period of years. It is a miscellaneous account. To Mr Wilson's credit there were carried not only dividends payable by the company but also dividends received by him from other companies and miscellaneous receipts. On the other side there were debited a series of miscellaneous payments made from it on Mr Wilson's behalf. On credit balances interest at 6 per cent was allowed and credited by the company to Mr Wilson. In short, the company would seem, *quoad* this account, to have acted as bankers for Mr Wilson. It is conceded that if the company had paid over such dividends to Mr Wilson and he had immediately paid the same back in order that it should be credited to him in the account current the view taken by the liquidators would not have applied. I do not think that the absence of this circuity of dealing should affect the result. The account current, as is conceded, was a *bona fide* account, and not a mere makeshift resorted to in order to obviate actual payment of the company dividends to Mr Wilson. The true view in law, as it seems to me, is that when sums payable as dividends to Mr Wilson were credited to the account current they did not thereafter retain the character of unpaid dividends, but were sums of money lent by Mr Wilson to the company, bearing interest at 6 per cent, while not drawn out on his behalf.'

1 Ibid, s 74(2).
2 1915 1 SLT 424.

In that case there was no suggestion that any express or implied agreement had to be shown in order to effect a change in the character of debt. The judge appears to have been influenced by such considerations as – (a) the account was a miscellaneous account extending over many years; (b) interest was payable on the recurring balances; (c) its inception was due to the purchase price of the business being carried there; (d) the company acted in the way of a banker; (e) the account was not constituted to obviate the actual payment of dividends. A recent English case of *Re L B Holliday & Co*[1], which seems to tighten the test and to get out of the grip of section 74(2)(f), requires that the claimant must show that the unpaid dividends were (a) the subject of some agreement express or implied between the claimant and the company or (b) the company must, with the passage of time, be taken necessarily to be in the same position as if the dividends had in fact been paid and then paid back to the company as a loan, in other words recognition necessarily of a loan situation[2].

## Forfeiture of shares

If shares have been forfeited within a year before the winding up, or if the shares have been transferred within the year and forfeited, the shareholder is still liable as a past member[3]. Where shares have been forfeited more than one year before the winding up, the former owner is not liable as a contributory even where the articles provide that their member remains 'liable to pay to the company all calls owing on such shares at the time of such forfeiture, though he may be sued for the calls even after the expiry of one year from the forfeiture'[4].

## A and B classes of contributories

The practice in preparing the list is to have an A list of contributories who are present members and primarily liable, and a B list of contributories who are the past members who have ceased to be members within a year preceding the winding up. The list must contain a statement of the name and address of, and the number of shares and extent of interest to be attributed to, each contributory, the amount called up, and the amount paid up in respect of such shares or interest, and distinguish between the several classes of contributories[5]. It is competent to settle the A and B lists separately[6].

### Representative and unrepresentative contributories

When settling the list of contributories, the court or the liquidator must distinguish between persons who are contributories in their own right and

1 [1986] BCLC 227.
2 See also *Re Rural & Veterinary Requisites Ltd* (1978) 3 ACLR 597; *Re Harry Simpson & Co Pty Ltd* (1963) 81 WN (Pt 1) (NSW) 207; and *Re Associated Electronics Services Pty Ltd* [1965] Qd R 36.
3 *Re Blakely Ordnance Co, Creyke's Case* (1869) 5 Ch App 63; *Re Accidental & Marine Insurance Corporation, Bridger's Case and Neill's Case* (1869) 5 Ch App 266.
4 *Re Blakeley Ordnance Co, Needham's Case* (1867) LR 4 Eq 135; *Ladies' Dress Association Ltd v Pulbrook* [1900] 2 QB 376.
5 Rules of the Court of Session, r 211(1)(a).
6 *Liquidator of Caledonian Heritable Security Co Ltd* (1882) 9 R 1130.

persons who are contributories as being representatives of or liable for the debts of others[1].

### (a) Trustees in bankruptcy

When a contributory becomes bankrupt either before or after he has been placed on the list, his trustee in bankruptcy represents him for all purposes of the winding up and is a contributory[2]. There may be proved against the bankruptcy estate the estimated value of his liability to future calls as well as calls already made[3]. The discharge of the bankrupt frees him entirely from liability to calls made after its date[4].

### (b) Executors

If a contributory dies either before or after he has been placed on the list of contributories, his personal representatives, and the heirs and legatees of heritage of his heritable estate in Scotland, are liable to contribute to the assets of the company in discharge of his liability[5]. Where executors themselves apply for shares, they are personally liable as contributories, but where the executors are holders of a deceased member's shares they are liable only to the amount of the estate and not personally liable unless they have acted in some way which shows that they are to be treated as members[6]. They have two options with different legal effects. They may have the shares transferred into their own names and become members of the company, or, if they do not wish to have the shares transferred into their own names, they have a reasonable time to sell the shares and to produce a purchaser who will take the transfer of them[6]. The question will be whether the placing of their names on the register was authorised by the executors, but personal liability will not be inferred from the mere form of entries in the company's ledger and dividends received by him[7].

### (c) Trustees

Notice of trust may be entered on the register but, unlike executors who are generally not personally liable as contributories, trustees are personally liable, with a right of indemnity against the trust estate. The law was laid down by Lord Chancellor Cairns in one of four cases taken by trustees to the House of Lords arising out of the collapse of the City of Glasgow Bank (see chapter 1). Lord Cairns stated:

'On the whole, my Lords, I am of the opinion that the decision of the Court of Session now under appeal is correct, and I must move your Lordships to dismiss the appeal. It is difficult to use words which will adequately express the sympathy I feel for those who have been overwhelmed in the disaster of the City of Glasgow Bank; and that sympathy is peculiarly due to those who, without any possibility of benefit to themselves, and probably

---

1 Insolvency Act 1986, s 148(3).
2 Ibid, s 82.
3 Ibid, s 82(4).
4 *Cresswell Ranch and Cattle Co v Balfour Melville* (1901) 29 SLR 841.
5 Insolvency Act 1986, s 81(1).
6 *Buchan v City of Glasgow Bank* (1879) 6 R (HL) 44.
7 Ibid, per Lord Selborne at 49.

without any trust estate behind them sufficient to indemnify them, have become subject to loss or ruin by entering, for the advantage of others, into a partnership attended with risks of which they probably were forgetful or which they did not fully realise.'[1]

The trustee whose name is on the register, and who resigns office but does not intimate the resignation to the company, remains liable as a contributory[2]. Assumed trustees are liable where new certificates have been issued and their names are on the register though their names had not been entered in the 'stock ledger'[3]. The trustee's name may not be removed from the register if, before the date of the winding up, the company had become hopelessly insolvent[4].

# 6. RECTIFICATION OF REGISTER

The liquidator may apply to the court to have the register rectified as may any contributory or aggrieved person[5]. This right is important mainly in the case of unlimited companies or where there are partly-paid shares, as in recent privatisations. Transfers after the commencement of a winding up are void, except on the sanction of the court, in a compulsory winding up[6]. In a voluntary winding up a transfer may be made with the sanction of the liquidator[7]. The power of rectification may be retrospective to a date before the liquidation so as to allow the transferee the right of a dissentient[8].

Until the register is rectified the liquidator is bound to enter on the A list the name of every person who is on the register of members[9]. There are several grounds on which persons may ask the liquidator to apply to the court for rectification of the register, or, if the liquidator is unwilling, apply themselves.

## (a) Unnecessary delay

If shares have been sold and a transfer has been presented for registration but owing to the delay of the company the transfer has not been registered, the register will be rectified in favour of the transferor[10]. The test is whether the name of any person is, without sufficient cause, entered in or omitted from a company's register of members, or whether default has been made or unnecessary delay taken place in entering on the register the fact of any person having ceased to be a member[11]. The shareholder is not entitled on the eve of liquidation to insist on registration; the directors ought to refuse registration if the facts are such that the rights of creditors have intervened although a

---

1 *Muir v City of Glasgow Bank* (1879) 6 R (HL) 21 at 27, reaffirming the Lord Justice-Clerk who observed: 'It is now well settled that in this or any like company no one can become a partner with a limited liability, or with any other liabilities than such as are borne in common by all the partners'.
2 *Kerr v City of Glasgow Bank* (1879) 6 R (HL) 52.
3 *Bell v City of Glasgow Bank* (1879) 6 R (HL) 55.
4 *Mitchell v City of Glasgow Bank* (1879) 6 R (HL) 60.
5 Companies Act 1985, s 359; Insolvency Act 1986, ss 148(1) and 112(1).
6 Insolvency Act 1986, s 127.
7 Ibid, s 88.
8 *Re Sussex Brick Co* [1904] 1 Ch 598.
9 *Reese River Silver Mining Co v Smith* (1869) LR 4 (HL) 64.
10 *Dodds v Cosmopolitan Insurance Corporation* 1915 SC 992.
11 Companies Act 1985, s 359(1).

winding up has not commenced[1]. The transfer ought to be confirmed by the directors at the first meeting at which, in the ordinary course of business, it can be confirmed, and thereupon registered. If not so confirmed, there is 'unnecessary delay'[2]. Though transferors know that the company is on the eve of winding up voluntarily, this will not prevent their validly transferring their shares[3].

## (b) Default of company

What amounts to default on the part of the company is a matter of circumstances. For example, if before the winding up the transfer duly executed has been left for registration, and the directors have neglected to approve or disapprove of it, and if there is no reason why they should have disapproved, the court will rectify the register[4]. If the reason for the non-registration is the default of the company, the court will not rectify on the application of the liquidator, whatever may be the right of the transferor to rectification. The liquidator represents only the company, to whose default the error is owing – and the contributories have no interest except through the company, and the creditors have no right in equity against the person who has never been held out to them[5]. Conversely, however, if a shareholder has sold his shares, he is not relieved from being a contributory if, owing either to his own neglect or that of his transferee, or if, in fact, owing to any cause except the neglect of the company, his transferee's name has not been substituted for his at the date of the winding up. Only if the omission to substitute the name of the transferee is owing entirely to the neglect and default of the company will the register be rectified[6]. The default by the company will not however be sufficient in itself to have a name removed from the register. The court's power is discretionary and regard must be had to the 'justice of the case'[7]. Accordingly, where there is a dispute between two individuals as to who should be registered as a member of the company, then a default of the company takes second place to the merits of their competing claims[8]. Where a formal requirement in relation to a transfer has not been met, such as if the articles require that the transfer be executed by both transferor and transferee, the court will not interfere if that formal requirement has not been met and as a result the transfer has not been reflected in the register[9]. If, however, the transfer is void by, for example, being *ultra vires* of the company, the court may reduce (quash) the transfer and rectify the register to put the transferor back on the register even if there is a delay of several years[10].

## (c) Misrepresentation and fraud

A transfer which has been executed before insolvency may not be reduced on

---

1 *Nelson Mitchell v City of Glasgow Bank* (1879) 6 R (HL) 66.
2 *Re Joint Stock Discount Co, Nation's Case* (1866) LR 3 Eq 77.
3 *McLintock v Campbell* 1916 SC 966; *Re Taurine Co* (1883) 25 Ch D 118.
4 *Hill's Case* (1867) 4 Ch App 769, n.
5 *Sichell's Case* (1867) 3 Ch App 119.
6 *Marshall v Glamorgan Iron and Coal Co* (1868) LR 7 Eq 129 at 137, per Giffard V-C.
7 *Sichell's Case*, supra, at 122.
8 *Howe v City of Glasgow Bank* (1879) 6 R 1194.
9 *Marino's Case* (1867) 2 Ch App 596.
10 *General Property Investment Co and Liqr v Matheson's Trs* (1888) 16 R 282.

the grounds of fraudulent misrepresentation inducing purchase of the shares and the register rectified if the entry on the register is prior to insolvency[1]. If, however, it can be shown that the alleged member has never agreed to become a shareholder and accordingly any contract was void, it is immaterial that the name is on the register at the commencement of insolvency[2]. If, before the insolvency of the company, the shareholder has stopped all connection with the company and has commenced proceedings to have his name removed from the register, and to rescind the contract, he will be entitled to relief, although between the date of bringing his action and the judgment of the court upon it, an order has been obtained to wind up the company[3]. He will not be able to claim damages but only be entitled to rank as a creditor for money paid to the company[4]. The fact that a shareholder may only rank for his money subscribed on shares allotted and registered may not in normal circumstances be of much help. However, where there are likely calls on insolvency, it is critical that the member is quick off the mark in bringing his action for rescission of the contract on the ground of fraud or misrepresentation. The case of *Tennent v City of Glasgow Bank*[5] puts the critical date back to the date of the stoppage of the bank and a notice of a meeting to propose a resolution to wind up. It is unclear whether after the commencement of a receivership or an administration order it would be too late to bring an action of rescission. It is suggested that a receivership does not have this effect but that an administration order, where it is clear that the company is going to go into liquidation, would have that effect.

# 7. MAKING CALLS

In a creditors' voluntary winding up, the liquidator makes calls[6]. In a winding up by the court, the call is made by the court[7]. This is done by the liquidator applying to the court by way of a note, stating the proposed amount of call and the reasons for making it.

The call may be made at any time either before or after the court or the liquidator has ascertained the sufficiency of the company's assets, and calls may be made on all or any of the contributories who are on the list of contributories to the extent of their liability. The liability extends to the satisfying of the company's debts and liabilities, the expenses of winding up, and the liability for the adjustment of the rights of the contributories among themselves[8]. Terms varying liability cannot be implied into a company's articles of association based on extrinsic evidence linked to surrounding circumstances, and a member therefore cannot be forced by such an implication to contribute sums to a company over and above the amounts he has subscribed for[9].

The liability of a contributory is a debt due as from 'the time when his

---

1 *Tennent v City of Glasgow Bank* (1879) 6 R (HL) 69.
2 *Gorrissen's Case* (1873) 8 Ch App 507.
3 *Smith's Case* (1867) LR 2 Ch 604.
4 *Houldsworth v City of Glasgow Bank* (1880) 7 R (HL) 53.
5 (1879) 6 R (HL) 69.
6 Insolvency Act 1986, s 165(4)(b).
7 Ibid, s 150(1).
8 Ibid, ss 150(1) and 165(4)(b).
9 *Bratton Seymour Service Company Ltd v Oxborough, The Times*, 2 March 1992.

liability commenced', but payable only when a call is made. Prescription can accordingly operate to extinguish liability five years after the date of the call[1]. Also, if a call has been made by the directors and it has prescribed, the liquidator or court cannot make the call for the same money. The court or liquidator may recover interest on calls at the rate of 5 per cent[2]. If, however, the liquidator is repeating calls made before by the directors, he may demand payment of a higher rate of interest if it is provided for in the articles of association of the company[3]. The call, if and when the liquidator determines to make it, will be made by an instrument in writing under his hand, and notice of the making of the call is sent to the contributories. He may call a meeting first before making the calls, to consider the matter and invite the members to attend. In the case of a compulsory winding up, the call is effectively a decree by the court. The procedure is first to make calls on those on the A list, and if these calls are not sufficient to satisfy the debts, to make a call on those on the B list.

Calls should be made *pari passu*, there being an implied condition of equality among shareholders in a company[4].

Where calls are not answered it is open to the liquidator under section 161 of the Insolvency Act 1986 in the case of a compulsory winding up, or in terms of section 112(2) of the Insolvency Act 1986 in the case of a voluntary winding up, to produce a list certified by him of the names of the contributories liable in payment of any calls and the court may forthwith pronounce a decree against these contributories for payment of the sums certified, and the liquidator may enforce these calls by summary diligence. Where a company has been wound up, all books and papers of the company and of the liquidator are, as between the contributories, *prima facie* evidence of the truth of all matters purporting to be recorded[5].

# 8. ADJUSTMENT OF RIGHTS

Where the assets turn out to be sufficient to pay off creditors and pay the costs of the winding up, before any payment by way of a distribution may be made to members, the surplus funds must be first applied to adjusting the rights of the contributories among themselves. This is mandatory in a compulsory and a voluntary winding up. In the case of a compulsory winding up, it is effected by the court[6], and in a voluntary winding up it is done by the liquidator[7]. Accordingly, unless the articles provide otherwise[8], where shares are unequally paid up an adjustment must be made between the contributories, or if the surplus assets are not sufficient to make the adjustment, a further call must be made to allow this if there is still uncalled share capital[9].

---

1 Prescription and Limitation (Scotland) Act 1973, s 6, Sch 1.
2 Insolvency Act 1986, ss 161, 165(4)(b).
3 *Liqrs of Benhar Coal Co Ltd* (1882) 9 R 763.
4 *British and American Trustee and Finance Corporation Ltd v Couper* [1894] AC 399.
5 Insolvency Act 1986, s 191.
6 Ibid, s 154.
7 Ibid, s 165(5).
8 *Ex p Maude* (1870) LR 6 Ch App 51.
9 See *Re Phoenix Oil and Transport Co Ltd* [1958] Ch 560 for the meaning of 'adjustment'.

# 9. TAKING CONTROL OF ASSETS

## Custody and control of assets

The liquidator, as soon as he is able after his appointment, must take possession of all the assets of the company and any property, books, papers or records in the possession or control of the company or to which the company appears to be entitled[1]. In the case of a creditors' voluntary winding up, there is also statutory power under which a liquidator proposed at a members' meeting may exercise the power to take custody and control of the property of the company prior to his appointment by the creditors' meeting[2]. Only companies registered under the Companies Acts may be wound up voluntarily[3] but some unregistered companies may register and then wind up voluntarily[4].

# 10. KEEPING RECORDS

## Sederunt book

The liquidator must maintain a 'sederunt' book during his term of office for the purpose of providing an accurate record of the liquidation process and in particular he must make up and maintain an inventory and valuation of the assets which he must retain in the sederunt book[5]. By 'maintain' is perhaps suggested that the valuations must be kept up to date but such expense is not usually justified and it is not the practice. Rule 7.33(1) of the Insolvency (Scotland) Rules 1986 as amended by Article 51 of the Schedule to the Insolvency (Scotland) Amendment Rules 1987 makes it mandatory for each insolvency practitioner to maintain a sederunt book in which must be recorded everything that is required to be recorded by any provision of the Insolvency Act 1986 or the Insolvency (Scotland) Rules 1986. There is no prescribed form for the 'sederunt' book. The expression can mean a loose leaf lever-arch file on a retrieval system if it can be reproduced in legible form. All minutes of meetings, resolutions, notices, interlocutors, accounts, schemes of division, compromises, schemes of arrangement and voluntary arrangements must be kept in it. The sederunt book must be made available for inspection at all reasonable hours by any interested person.

## Access to records

Certain documentation may be withheld from interested parties in terms of rule 7.27 of the Insolvency (Scotland) Rules 1986 as amended by Article 50 of the Schedule to the Insolvency (Scotland) Amendment Rules 1987. If the liquidator considers that it should be treated as confidential, or that it is of

---

1 Insolvency (Scotland) Rules 1986, r 4.22, inserted by para 18 of the Schedule to the Insolvency (Scotland) Amendment Rules 1987.
2 Insolvency Act 1986, s 166(3).
3 Ibid, s 221(4).
4 *Southall v British Mutual Life Assurance Society* (1871) LR 6 Ch 614.
5 Insolvency (Scotland) Rules 1986, r 4.22(1)(b), inserted by para 18 of the Schedule to the Insolvency (Scotland) Amendment Rules 1987.

such a nature that its disclosure would be calculated to be injurious to the interests of the company's creditors or its members or the contributories in its winding up, he is entitled to decline to allow the record to be inspected by a person who would otherwise be an interested party. Members of the liquidation committee may be refused access, but on refusal any person who is interested may seek an order from the court allowing them inspection of the record[1].

# 11. ANNUAL AND FINAL MEETINGS

## (a) First meeting

The interim liquidator must summon a first meeting of creditors and contributories primarily to appoint a liquidator in terms of section 138 of the Insolvency Act 1986. Similarly in a creditors' voluntary winding up, the company summons a first meeting of creditors in terms of section 98 of the Insolvency Act 1986 primarily to nominate a liquidator.

## (b) Annual meetings

After the first meetings mentioned above, the liquidator, in both a voluntary winding up and a compulsory winding up must summon a meeting of the creditors in each year during which the liquidation is in force, and has the discretion to summon a meeting of the creditors or the contributories at any time for the purpose of ascertaining their wishes in all matters relating to the liquidation[2]. In a creditors' voluntary winding up he must summon a general meeting of the company and a meeting of creditors at the end of the first year from the commencement of the winding up, and of each succeeding year or at the first convenient date within three months from the end of the year or such longer period as the Secretary of State may allow[3]. The liquidator must lay before each of the meetings an account of his acts and dealings and of the conduct of the winding up during the preceding year[4]. These provisions in relation to annual meetings are not new in relation to creditors' voluntary windings up[5]. The duty of the liquidator, in a compulsory winding up, to call an annual meeting of creditors (but not a general meeting of the company as in a creditors' voluntary winding up) is new and does not apply to compulsory windings up commenced prior to 29 December 1986.

## Final meeting

In both a creditors' voluntary winding up and a compulsory winding up, the liquidator shall summon a final meeting of the creditors[6]. In a compulsory winding up the liquidator summons the meeting 'if it appears to him that the

1 Ibid, r 7.27(3).
2 Ibid, r 4.23.
3 Insolvency Act 1986, s 105(1).
4 Ibid, s 105(2).
5 Companies Act 1985, s 595.
6 Insolvency Act 1986, ss 106, 146.

winding up is for practical purposes complete"[1]. In a creditors' voluntary winding up, the liquidator summons meetings of the company and of the creditors as soon as the company's affairs are fully wound up and he has made up an account of the winding up, showing how it has been conducted and how the company's property has been disposed of[2]. In a final meeting of creditors in a compulsory winding up the creditors receive the liquidator's report of the winding up, and determine whether the liquidator should have his release. In a creditors' voluntary winding up the creditors receive an 'account' as well as a report.

The law has not, for practical purposes, changed in relation to a creditors' voluntary winding up, but in relation to windings up commenced after 29 December 1986 it has changed in relation to compulsory windings up. Formerly there was no duty to summon a final meeting of creditors in a compulsory winding-up. Previously the company was dissolved by the liquidator making an application to the court[3]. This is no longer the case. There is no need to have a final meeting or annual meeting where an early dissolution is sought by the liquidator under section 202 or 112 of the Insolvency Act 1986.

# 12. DISSOLUTION OF THE COMPANY AND STRIKING OFF REGISTER

## (a) Dissolution of the company

In a creditors' voluntary winding up, within one week from the date of the final meeting at which the liquidator's final account was presented to creditors, he must send a copy of the account to the Registrar of Companies and make a return to him[4]. The Registrar, on receiving the account and return, must forthwith register them, and on the expiration of three months from the registration of the return the company is deemed to be dissolved[5]. However the court may, on the application of the liquidator or any other person who appears to the court to be interested, make an order deferring the date at which the dissolution of the company is to take effect[6].

The procedure in a compulsory winding up is similar. The liquidator has to send a notice to the court and to the Registrar of Companies (Form 4.17 (Scot)) that the meeting has been held and of the decisions (if any) of the meeting[7]. The registrar must register the notice forthwith on receipt and at the end of three months, beginning with the day of the registration of the notice, the company is dissolved[8]. Again, as in a voluntary winding up, the court may, on application of any person who appears to have any interest, defer the dissolution of the company for such period as the court thinks fit[9].

---

1 Insolvency Act 1986, s 146(1).
2 Ibid, s 106(1).
3 Companies Act 1985, s 568(1).
4 Insolvency Act 1986, s 106(3); this should be done on a form 4.26 (Scot) (App. VII).
5 Ibid, s 201(2).
6 Ibid, s 201(3).
7 Ibid, s 172(8).
8 Ibid, s 205(2).
9 Ibid, s 205(5).

## (b) Early dissolution of company

In a compulsory winding up and in a creditors' voluntary winding up, if after the first statutory meeting it appears to the liquidator that the realisable assets of the company are insufficient to cover the expenses of the winding up, he may apply to the court for an order that the company be dissolved[1]. Where the liquidator makes the application, if the court is satisfied that the realisable assets of the company are insufficient to cover the expenses of the winding up and it appears to the court appropriate to do so, the court shall make an order that the company be dissolved[2]. The liquidator must then forward to the registrar within 14 days of the date of the order a copy of the order. The registrar must register it forthwith and at the end of a period of three months beginning from the day of the registration of the order, the company is dissolved[3]. As in the usual dissolution, the court may defer the dissolution on the application of any person who appears to the court to have an interest[4].

## (c) Effect of dissolution of company

When a company is dissolved, all property and rights vested in or held in trust for the company immediately before its dissolution are deemed to be '*bona vacantia*' (unowned goods) and belong to the Crown[5]. That does not include property held by the company on trust[5]. When a company is dissolved, the court has no longer any jurisdiction to reach it, for there is no company[6], because there are no officers or other agents who can be served with notices or writs on behalf of the company.

## (d) Power to declare dissolution void

Where a company has been dissolved, the liquidator or any other person appearing to the court to be interested, may apply to the court for an order declaring the dissolution void[7]. Before the coming into force of the amending provisions of the Companies Act 1989[8] it had been necessary in terms of the statute that the application be made within two years of the date of dissolution although the Scottish courts had granted an order under that section ten years after dissolution in exercise of its *nobile officium*[9]. In an English case, *Bradley v Eagle Star Insurance Co Ltd*[10], a former employee of a company which had been dissolved raised proceedings against insurers under the Third Parties (Rights against Insurers) Act 1930 in which it was claimed that the plaintiff had suffered a disability by reason of her employment by the company. Under that Act, if a winding-up order is made in respect of a company and the company is insured against liabilities to third parties, any rights of the company against the insurer, whether arising before or after that event, are

1 Insolvency Act 1986, ss 112(1) and 204(2); for discussion of the jurisdiction under s 112. see p 62.
2 Ibid, s 204(3).
3 Ibid, s 204(4).
4 Ibid, s 204(5).
5 Companies Act 1985, s 654(1).
6 *Re Westbourne Grove Drapery Co* (1879) 39 LT 30.
7 Companies Act 1985, s 651; *Liqr of McCall & Stephen* 1920 SLT 26.
8 Companies Act 1989, s 141.
9 *Collins Brothers & Co Ltd* 1916 SC 620.
10 [1989] AC 957, [1989] 1 All ER 961 (HL).

transferred to the third party[1]. Because in the *Bradley* Case the company had been dissolved before the existence and amount of the company's liability had been established, it was held by the House of Lords that the employee's claim could not succeed because no right of the company against the insurers capable of being transferred to the employee had arisen at the time of dissolution. Because the dissolution of the company had occurred more than two years previously, the company could not be restored to the register for the purpose of the employee's claim against the company being established, and therefore the plaintiff was left without a remedy. Because of this decision, section 651 of the Companies Act 1985 was amended to provide that an application for the purpose of bringing proceedings against the company for damages in respect of personal injuries or under the Fatal Accidents Act 1976 or the Damages (Scotland) Act 1976 may be made at any time, provided that it appears to the court that those proceedings will not be time-barred[2]. In terms of section 651(5) of the Companies Act 1985:

'"Personal injuries" includes any disease and any impairment of a person's physical or mental condition.'

It has been held in England that the court may take into account any power that the court in those proceedings has to extend the prescriptive period which would otherwise apply[3]. On the making of an order the court may direct that the period between the dissolution of the company and the making of the order is not to count for the purposes of statutory prescription or limitation[4]. The time limits under section 651, apart from the above exception are:

(a)    The company must not have been dissolved more than two years from the date of the application, and

(b)    an application under the exception is not competent over twenty years from the date of the dissolution[5].

In any event the order of the court may be made after the expiry of the two year period, provided the application is made within the two years[6].

If property has gone to the Crown as *bona vacantia*, it must account to the company for the proceeds after the dissolution has been declared void[7]. The effect of an order declaring a dissolution void is that all consequences flowing from such dissolution are themselves voided[8]. The main object of the provision allowing the declaration of a dissolution void is to enable assets which subsequently come to light to be distributed properly. If facts come to light which would require the dissolution being declared void, an application to the court should be made as soon as possible after these facts come to light[9].

1  Third Parties (Rights against Insurers) Act 1930, s 1(1).
2  Companies Act 1985, s 651(5), (added by the Companies Act 1989, s 141(3)).
3  *Re Workvale Ltd* [1992] 1 WLR 416.
4  Companies Act 1985, s 651(6) as amended.
5  Companies Act 1985, s 651(4) as added and Companies Act 1989, s 141(4).
6  *Dowling Petr*, 1960 SLT (Notes) 76.
7  Companies Act 1985, s 655(2).
8  Ibid, s 651(2); *Re C W Dickson* [1947] Ch 251; *Champdany Jute Co Ltd* 1924 SC 209.
9  *Re Thompson and Riches Ltd* [1981] 1 WLR 682.

### (e) Striking off Register

Companies which are not carrying on business or have minimal assets are often disposed of without a winding up, under the provisions of section 652 of the Companies Act 1985. Under that provision, where the Registrar has reasonable cause to believe that a company is not carrying on business or in operation, he may send to the company a letter of inquiry. If he does not within a month receive an answer, he is, within 14 days, to send a second letter by registered post and if to this he does not receive a reply that the company is carrying on business, or receives a reply stating that the company is not carrying on business or in operation, he may publish in the *Gazette* and send to the company by post a notice that, at the expiration of three months, the name of the company will be struck off the register and the company dissolved. The notice may be addressed to the company at its registered office, or, if no office has been registered, to the care of some officer of the company, or if there is no officer of the company whose name and address are known to the Registrar, to each of the persons who subscribe to the memorandum at the addresses mentioned on it. At the expiry of the period mentioned in the notice, the name is struck off and the company dissolved. However, the liability of every director, managing officer and member is continuous, and may be enforced as if the company had not been dissolved.

Also where a company is being wound up, if the Registrar has reasonable cause to believe that no liquidator is acting, or that the affairs of the company are fully wound up, and the proper returns have not been made by the liquidator for six months and the Registrar has published in the *Gazette* and sent to the company, or to the liquidator at his last known place of business, a notice, the company's name may be struck off the Register with the same result.

The main difference between the company being dissolved in this manner and through a winding-up is that the liabilities mentioned above continue. Further, any company, member, or creditor aggrieved by the proceeding may within 20 years from the publication of the notice in the *Gazette* apply to the court in which the company is liable to be wound up, and the court, if satisfied that the company was carrying on business or in operation when struck off, or that it is just to do so, may order its restoration to the Register and, on an office copy of the order being delivered to the Registrar, it is deemed to have continued in existence as if its name had never been struck off[1].

---

1 Companies Act 1985, s 653(3).

# Chapter 4

# Administrations

## Introduction

Several countries have legal procedures aimed at achieving the rehabilitation of companies which have run into financial difficulties, but which might have a reasonable prospect of recovery if afforded a type of moratorium from their creditors, or an opportunity to enter into a scheme of arrangement with their creditors or to try to reconstruct their affairs (eg South Africa and Australia)[1]. The United States has a fully developed system for corporate reorganisation in Chapter XI of the Bankruptcy Code, under which such famous names as Pan Am and Texaco have filed for protection from their creditors[2]. The introduction of such a similar régime on insolvency was one of the main recommendations of the Cork Committee as discussed in Chapter 1. Usually the court is given power to appoint an officer to regulate the company's affairs although in the United States existing management remains in control. In the United Kingdom now an officer is appointed.

Section 8 of the Insolvency Act 1986 gives power to the court[3] to make an administration order, ie an order that during the time while the order is in force, the affairs, business and property of the company shall be managed by an officer known as an 'administrator', appointed by the court, who must be an 'insolvency practitioner'[4]. The main effect of an administration order is that while it is in force, creditors may not enforce their claims against the company. The company has a moratorium from action by its creditors, although the debts themselves are not affected. The other main effect is that the ultimate enforcement measure open to a creditor – getting a winding-up order – is barred.

## Powers of administrators

The administrator has the power, when the administration order is made, to do everything necessary for the management of the company's affairs and in addition is given a wide list of specific powers in Schedule 1 to the Insolvency

---

1 See Fore, *Principles of Company Law* (3rd edn), pp 550–555.
2 See Rosenburg and M. Lurey, Collier, *Lending Institutions and the Bankruptcy Code* (1986).
3 Court of Session (or sheriff court concurrently if the paid-up share capital is under £120,000) – Insolvency Act 1986, ss 120 and 251 and Companies Act 1985, s 744. The sheriff may not put into administration companies limited by guarantee or unlimited companies: see *Pearce, Petitioner* 1991 SCLR 861. There is no good reason why the sheriff court should not be given jurisdiction in the case of companies limited by guarantee, subject to the amount of the guarantee.
4 Insolvency Act 1986, s 230. If the appointed person is unqualified, the appointment will be valid, but the court should replace him. See *Garden Mews – St Leonards Ltd v Butler Pollway Ltd* [1985] 9 ACLR 117).

Act 1986[1]. These powers are the same powers as an English administrative receiver has[2], including the power to present or defend a winding-up petition (a power unlikely to be used in practice). The administrator has no greater powers than the company itself has in its memorandum, with the result that the administrator has no power to do acts which are *ultra vires* of the company. Although section 4 of the Companies Act 1985 allows a company to change its objects, it allows the change only in certain limited ways, and these do not include a power to change its objects to carry on some business other than its then authorised business. A company may be able to change its objects within the course of an administration subject to that proviso[3]. Persons dealing with the administrator in good faith and for value do not need to inquire whether the administrator is acting within his powers.[4]

The main restriction on the administrator's powers is that until the date of the approval of his proposals, he must manage in accordance with the directions given by the court[5], and from then on must manage in accordance with the proposals, or revised proposals[6]. There is also an important restriction on how the administrator may deal with property which is subject to a charge or security.

The administrator also has powers under sections 133, 134, 236 and 237 of the Insolvency Act 1986 to apply to the court for an order for public and private examination of directors etc of the company and production of documents (see chapter 3).

## Charged or secured property

Section 15 of the Insolvency Act 1986 gives the administrator power to dispose of, or exercise his powers in relation to, charged property. The Insolvency Act 1986 divides charged property into two categories: (1) property subject to a floating charge; and (2) property subject to any other security.

### (1) *Property subject to a floating charge*

The administrator may, without the sanction of the court, dispose of, or exercise his powers in relation to, any property of the company subject to a floating charge, as if it were not subject to a floating charge[7]. When the administrator disposal of property, the holder of the floating charge maintains the same security over the proceeds of the sale of the property disposed of as he had over the disposal of property[8]. Hence, cash received from a sale, or goods bought in, remain secured by the floating charge. Although a floating charge which has crystallised acts in Scotland as an assignation in security of company debts to the holder of the floating charge, the section is quite clear that these assets

---

1 Insolvency Act 1986, s 14(1).
2 Ibid, s 42(1).
3 *Re Home Treat Limited* [1991] BCLC 705.
4 Ibid, s 14(6): see in contrast s 35(2) of the Companies Act 1985 where there is a presumption of good faith.
5 Insolvency Act 1986, s 17(2)(a).
6 Ibid, s 17(2)(b).
7 Ibid, s 15(1) and (3).
8 Ibid, s 15(4).

are to be treated as if they were not subject to a security (ie had not been assigned) and hence able to be collected in for the running of the business.

Effectively, because an administrator may 'exercise his powers in relation to the property', this means that the company's cash or other assets may thus be used to buy goods and services, and the business may be conducted as if the floating charge had not crystallised. Although the holder of the floating charge has his priority maintained, his fear of course will be that his position may be worsened if the effect of the administration order is the net outflow of funds from the business. The conflict is unlikely to arise if the floating charge holder has been quick off the mark, because an administration order will not be granted if an administrative receiver has been appointed[1] subject to an exception mentioned at page 108. This of course would not be the situation with a non-administrative receiver, because that type of appointment does not preclude an administration order.

At any time after the granting of the administration order including the period prior to the approval of his proposals, when the administrator must manage the property according to the direction of the court[2], a creditor who feels the business is being managed in a manner 'unfairly prejudicial' to him may apply to the court for an order to protect his interests[3]. He can ask for an order which could stop the disponing of property subject to the floating charge, or the administrator exercising his powers in relation to charged property (a course which might dissipate the assets)[4]. The concept 'unfair prejudice' is discussed in chapter 6. General protection under section 27 is discussed later in this chapter.

## (2)   *Property subject to securities other than a floating charge*

The administrator may dispose of other charged property, with the permission of the court, free from any security, and sell goods in the possession of the company which are under hire purchase agreements, chattel-leasing agreements, conditional sale agreements, as if all rights of the owner under the agreements were vested in the company[5]. This is a radical statutory intervention in this area. The court must first be satisfied that the sale would be likely to promote one or more of the proposals specified in the administration order[5]. The net proceeds are to be applied first towards discharging the sums secured by the securities[6]. If the sums realised are less than could be realised in the open market, any deficiency is to be made up[7]. It can be assumed that unless the company is in a position to make up this deficiency, the court would not lift the security. There is no provision for how a claim for the deficiency would rank if its being met was not a condition of the lifting of the security.

In Scotland, where secured property is disposed of, the person to whom it is

1 Insolvency Act 1986, s 9(3).
2 Ibid, s 17(2)(a).
3 Ibid, s 27(1).
4 Ibid, s 27(6).
5 Ibid, s 15(2).
6 Ibid, s 15(5).
7 Ibid, s 15(5)(b).

disposed ('the disponee') must be granted an appropriate document of transfer[1], and in the case where assets subject to a security are disposed of, the disponee gets a title free of liabilities to third parties[2].

## Circumstances in which the court may make an administration order

An administration order may not be made if there is already (1) an administrative receivership; or (2) winding up; or (3) the company is an insurance company as defined in the Insurance Companies Act 1982. Interim administrators are competent in Scotland[3]. Also a court will refuse to accede to a petition to have a company placed in administration where the petition is opposed by the company's creditors and there are grounds for investigating the reason why the company became insolvent. In those circumstances the appropriate course is compulsory liquidation[4].

### (1) *Administrative receivership*

An administrator may not be appointed if the holder of a floating charge has appointed an administrative receiver unless the court is satisfied[5] either that the appointer has consented or that, if the administration order were made, the charge or security by virtue of which the receiver was appointed would be liable to be released or discharged as an unfair transaction, being a gratuitous alienation or unfair preference under section 242 or 243 of the Insolvency Act 1986, or would be avoided under section 245 of the Insolvency Act 1986. Where the floating charge's validity, or that of the appointment is in doubt, the court may still hear the petition and grant an interim order[6]. It is suggested that where the validity of a floating charge is challenged, the fact that an administrative receivership bars the making of an administration order would on the balance of convenience make the court more likely to grant an interdict stopping the holder of the floating charge making an appointment. On the strict wording of section 9(3)(*b*), floating charges may only be challenged under sections 242, 243 and 245 of the Insolvency Act 1986 after an administration order has been made, or the company has been placed in liquidation; strictly speaking this means that, at the date when a petition is heard for an administration order, the court could not at that stage decide whether a floating charge was open to challenge under these sections. Nevertheless, in spite of the wording of section 9(3)(*a*), it is thought that the court would determine the question of the validity of the floating charge before making an administration order.

It has been held in England[7] that a petition for an administration order will be dismissed where the court is satisfied that there is an administrative receiver in post appointed under a debenture containing a valid floating charge. The court will not look behind a floating charge or disregard it simply because it may have been demanded by a bank to forestall the possibility of an administation order. A floating charge by its very nature was capable of covering

1 Ibid, s 16(1).
2 Ibid, s 16(2).
3 Interim orders may be made (ibid, s 9(4)) and an interim administrator may be appointed: *Air Ecosse Ltd v Civil Aviation Authority* 1987 SLT 751; *Avenel Hotel Ltd*, March 1987, unreported.
4 *Re Arrows Limited (No 3)* [1992] BCC 131.
5 Insolvency Act 1986, s 9(3).
6 Ibid, s 9(4). It is thought that the Insolvency Act 1986, s 244 may also be relevant to floating charges.
7 *Re Croftbell Limited* [1990] BCC 781.

*acquirenda* and it was therefore immaterial that at the date that the floating charge was granted there were little or no assets to be secured by the charge. A charge created merely for its function of being able to block the appointment of an administrator has become known as a 'lightweight floating charge'.[1] The holder of a floating charge is not entitled to block the making of an administration order, he is the only person entitled to notice of a petition for an administration order. Also the administrator has a duty to carry out proposals which aim to achieve the purpose of his appointment. Because he has a potentially unlimited tenure, his appointment removes two key rights from the chargee, namely, the ability to control the timing and conduct of the realisation of his security. The result may be that the property has depreciated when the administrator leaves office. Further the administrator may not even sell the property at all, or for some time. For these various reasons, a first mortgagee may insist that he takes a first floating charge over the company's undertaking, even although he has a specific security fully securing his exposure. Another reason for taking lightweight floating charges is the powers given to a receiver. Under section 61 of the Insolvency Act 1986 '(1) Where the receiver sells or disposes, or is desirous of selling or disposing, of any property or interest in property of the company which is subject to the floating charge by virtue of which the receiver was appointed and which is –

(a) subject to any security or interest of, or burden or encumbrance in favour of, a creditor the ranking of which is prior to, or *pari passu* with, or postponed to the floating charge, or
(b) property or an interest in property affected or attached by effectual diligence executed by any person,

and the receiver is unable to obtain the consent of such creditor or, as the case may be, such person to such a sale or disposal, the receiver may apply to the court for authority to sell or dispose of the property or interest in property free of such security, interest, burden, encumbrance or diligence.' Thus a lender with only a fixed charge may find that another lender has this potential ability to dispose of property subject to his security. In the event he will lose control over the timing and conduct of realisation of his security.

## (2) *Winding up*

An administration order may not be made in respect of a company after it has gone into liquidation[2].

## (3) *Insurance companies and companies not registered under the Companies Acts*

Banks which are or have been authorised institutions in terms of the Banking Act 1987 may now be placed in administration but an administration order may not be made where the company is an insurance company within the meaning of the Insurance Companies Act 1982[3], or a company which is not

1 See Oditah: 'Lightweight Floating Charges' Journal of Business Law [1991] 49.
2 Insolvency Act 1986, s 8(4). A winding-up order is required before the company has 'gone into liquidation', notwithstanding the terms of section 129(2): see section 247(2): *Avenel Hotel Ltd*, 1987, unreported.
3 Insolvency Act 1986, s 8(4); Banks (Administration Proceedings) Order 1989.

formed and registered under the Companies Act 1985 or certain of the earlier Companies Acts[1].

## Reasons justifying appointment of an administrator

An administrator may be appointed only where *two* conditions are met:

(1) that the court is satisfied that the company is or is likely to become unable to pay its debts[2]; and
(2) that the court considers that the making of such an order would be *likely* to achieve any one or more specified purposes.

## Definition of 'likely to achieve'

Before going on to discuss the purposes which a court has to be satisfied are likely to be achieved, it should be noted that the construction of the word '*likely*' in section 8 of the Insolvency Act 1986 is unsurprisingly contentious and controversial. Its construction is the main area of focus of any court contemplating administration proceedings. The reported case law so far is English. In the early case of *Re Consumer and Industrial Press*[3], Peter Gibson J adopted a restrictive interpretation in holding that an administration order would only be granted if it was more probable than not that it would achieve its aim. He stated:

'As I read s 8 the court must be satisfied on the evidence put before it that at least one of the purposes in s 8(3) is likely to be achieved if it is to make an administration order. That does not mean that it is merely possible that such purpose will be achieved; the evidence must go further than that to enable the court to hold that the purpose in question will more probably than not be achieved. Further, the court has to specify in the order the purpose which it is satisfied will be achieved. It is not a question of being satisfied that one purpose is likely to be achieved, and then adding in the order one or more of the other purposes which might perhaps be achieved, but in respect of which the evidence is less compelling.'

By contrast in *Re Harris Simons Construction Limited*[4], Hoffmann J held that it sufficed that there was a real prospect that one or more of the stated purposes

---

1 Companies Act 1985, s 735 (applied by the Insolvency Act 1986, s 251).
2 Insolvency Act 1986, s 8(1); 'unable to pay its debts' is defined by s 123; the word 'satisfied' in section 8(1)(a) of the Insolvency Act 1986, in contrast to 'considers' in section 8(1)(b) of the Insolvency Act 1986 suggests that a higher threshold of persuasion is needed for the former than for the latter.
   See *Re Harris Simons Construction Ltd* [1989] 5 BCC 11 at 13, per Hoffmann J, dealing with the degree of likelihood required by s 8(1)(b); and *Re Imperial Motors (UK) Ltd* [1990] BCLC 29 in which Hoffmann J held that on the facts of that case the company was not unable to pay its debts within the meaning of section 123 of the Insolvency Act 1986 by being insolvent in the sense that its liabilities exceeded its assets. It was however insolvent within the meaning of section 123(1)(e) of the Insolvency Act 1986 as it could not pay its debts as they fell due. In determining whether or not to make an administration order he had to balance the interests of the petitioning creditor company in achieving a more advantageous realisation of the company's assets on the one hand and on the other hand the interests of the company, its shareholders and management in not having the business of the company taken out of their hands. Because the interests of the petitioning creditor appeared to be adequately secured therefore the risk to them in not making the order was not great, it was not appropriate to make an order.
3 [1988] BCLC 177.
4 [1989] 5 BCC 11.

would be achieved, even if not as high on the probability scale as a figure in excess of 50 per cent. The same approach was adopted by Vinelott J in *Re Primlaks (UK) Limited*[1] (referred to with approval by R M Goode in: *Principles in Incorporate Insolvency*). It would appear that in England the approach of Hoffmann J is now the accepted position. It was followed by Harman J in *Re Rowbotham Baxter Ltd*[2] and by Peter Gibson J in *Re S C L Building Services Limited*[3] in which he stated:

'The court has jurisdiction under s 8(1) to make an administration order if (a) it is satisfied that the company is or is likely to become unable to pay its debts, and (b) it considers that the making of an order under the section would be likely to achieve one or more of the s 8(3) purposes. If the court has jurisdiction through the satisfaction of those conditions, then the court may make an administration order in relation to the company. The meaning of the words 'is likely' in s 8(1)(b) has given rise to difficulties. In *Re Consumer & Industrial Press Limited* [1988] BCLC 177 at 178 I expressed the view that the evidence must enable the court to hold that the purpose in question will more probably than not be achieved. I do not recall that the meaning of the words in questions was the subject of extensive argument, but I believe that I had particularly in mind (1) the use of the words 'is likely' both in s 8(1)(a) as well as in s 8(1)(b), (2) what might be thought to be the obvious meaning of the words in s 8(1)(a), and (3) the *prima facie* improbability that the same words would have a different meaning in the same subsection. Harman J in *Re Manlon Trading Limited* [1988] 4 BCC 455 appears to have followed my approach, but Hoffmann J in *Re Harris Simons Construction Limited* [1989] BCLC 202, [1989] 1 WLC 368 took a different view, and very recently Vinelott J in *Re Primlaks (UK) Limited* [1989] BCLC 734 agreed with Hoffmann J, both those judges adopting the test that there must be a real prospect. As Hoffmann J rightly said, the Companies Court judges are still feeling their way with this legislation, but given the views that my brethren have expressed in these last two cases after full consideration of my earlier view, in the interests of certainty I am content to apply that real prospect test without saying anything more on the point, particularly as I do not believe that on the facts of the present case it makes any difference which test is used.'

In applying the above test perhaps the most crucial piece of evidence is the report of the independent person prepared under rule 2.2 of the Insolvency (Scotland) Rules 1986. Although this report is not a mandatory statutory requirement it is clear that in practice the courts will not accede to the petition unless a favourable report is produced[4].

## Purposes specified

The purposes specified referred to above as those which the court must be satisfied are likely to be achieved are:

(a)   the survival of the company, and the whole or any part of its undertaking, as a going concern;

(b)   the approval of a composition in satisfaction of the company's debts or a scheme of arrangement under Part I of the Act (see Voluntary Arrangements);

(c)   the sanctioning under section 425 of the Companies Act 1985 of a

---

1 [1989] 5 BCC 510.
2 [1990] BCLC 397.
3 [1990] BCLC 98.
4 See Vinelott J in *Re Primlaks (UK) Limited* [1989] BCLC 734.

compromise or arrangement between the company and its creditors and/or members (see under Voluntary Arrangements); and

(d) a more advantageous realisation of the company's assets than would be effected on a winding up.

The order must specify the purpose(s) for whose achievement it has been made[1].

There are therefore four purposes which individually or together with one or more others may justify an administration order. These purposes, as drafted, are complex and difficult to interpret without close analysis. The middle two purposes, namely 'arrangements with creditors', are examined first, because the other two purposes really dovetail with them.

### Arrangements with creditors and shareholders

In the case of arrangements under Part 1 of the Insolvency Act 1986 and section 425 of the Companies Act 1985 the meaning is clear. The achievement of one of these schemes is a justifying purpose of an administration order. The arrangement does not have to achieve any broader purpose such as a better deal for creditors or the survival of the company. However, it is likely that an arrangement will ensure the survival of the company at least in the short term. Otherwise there would be little point in making such an arrangement. What an administration order therefore does, by providing a moratorium against enforcement of claims by creditors, is to give the company a breathing space to put together a deal with its creditors and members. It is important to realise, however, that before granting an administration order the court must be satisfied that the company is not merely proposing an arrangement under Part 1 of the Insolvency Act 1986 and/or under section 425 of the Companies Act 1985, but that any arrangement is going to be attained, i e approved by the requisite creditor majority. The court must be satisfied that the survival package is likely to get the necessary approvals.

Although there is no broader objective written into these purposes, and they can stand separately, it is clear that creditors are unlikely to go along with an arrangement unless they are convinced that the deal they get through a voluntary arrangement under Part 1 of the Insolvency Act 1986 or an arrangement under section 425 of the Companies Act 1985 is a better deal than they would get in a winding up.

The types of deal which can be expected, depending on the circumstances and the persons involved, to appeal to members and creditors are variations of the following:

(1) a rescheduling of debts so that they are paid in full with interest in the future when the company is strong enough to do this;

(2) a composition by which the creditors waive part of the debts due to them (this could be coupled with a rescheduling). This type of arrangement may well appeal to creditors because a suitable voluntary arrangement could have the effect of preserving the company as a going concern. Trade creditors, unlike personal creditors, often have an interest in trying to ensure that the company, with which they trade, continues as a

---

1 Insolvency Act 1986, s 8(3).

going concern and thus keeps them in business, rather than going into liquidation;

(3) the exchange of 'debt' for 'equity'. This is a method by which financial pressure is taken off a company but the creditors get a stake in the company, and can look to the realisation of the stake in future as a way of being paid.

A good example of the last type of deal is to be found in the case of *Gillies v Dawson*[1]. In that case the court sanctioned a scheme of arrangement to convert secured debt and ordinary debt into preference shares. It was argued for the petitioning creditors of a mineral oil company in liquidation that:

'unless the scheme of arrangement went through, there would be no alternative but a forced sale of the works. It was highly improbable, however, in view of the then depressed condition of the mineral oil trade that the works would be sold as a going concern, and the only alternative to the proposed scheme was the sale of the works at their breaking-up value. Such a sale would realise very little for the creditors as in addition to the smallness of the price to be received for the works, the sale of the property belonging to the company, and forming one of its most important assets, would be entirely lost so far as the present creditors were concerned . . . if the scheme were carried through, the creditors believed that the company's works and property might yet turn out to be very valuable.'

A minority could, of course, object to certain debt/equity deals or arrangements as being 'unfairly prejudicial' where, for example, the owners of the company vote to convert their own loans to the company into equity – loans which were equity in all but name anyway – and use their voting power to bring the other creditors into such an arrangement.

(4) a deal by which all the creditors agree to waive part of their debts and postpone the payment of the debts in return for an injection of new money into the company. This way the creditors have the chance of getting more money back than on a liquidation (subject to the performance of the company), and the injector of capital gets this accommodation with the creditors in return for his placing his capital at risk. In this way the creditors are betting on the future performance of the company. This type of deal, of course, would depend on the creditors being convinced by the corporate plan. Although creditors have to go along with an arrangement approved by the requisite majority, an arrangement cannot be used to foist new positive obligations on creditors, eg to supply goods or lend money to the company, as opposed to the imposition of restrictions on the exercise of existing rights. The rights of gas, electricity, water and telephone utilities are somewhat circumscribed by statute in this context, in so far as they may not make it a condition of supply that outstanding debts are first paid[2].

Accordingly, any company trying to convince the court that an administration order was justified on the basis of the likelihood of the company getting an arrangement with its creditors and/or members as outlined above has to examine closely the type of arrangement which it has in mind and its attractive features to creditors. The company will often be well advised to have a major

---

1 (1893) 20 R 1119.
2 Insolvency Act 1986, s 233.

creditor alongside approving the arrangement at the time of the application for the administration order, and perhaps have some informal positive soundings available for the court in relation to the proposed arrangements[1]. In addition, rule 2.1 of the Insolvency (Scotland) Rules 1986 allows an expert report on the company in support of the petition to be prepared, explaining why an administration order would be expedient. The report must, in terms of rule 10(1)(h) of the Act of Sederunt[2], be lodged with the petition, or an explanation must be given as to why no such report has been prepared. It may be prepared by a person with adequate knowledge of the company, who may be the proposed administrator. The obvious persons to do the report would be the company's auditors or merchant bank. As a practical matter, the solicitors acting for the petitioners should always check that the person who prepares the report does in fact have an adequate knowledge of the company, independently of the directors. He should have verified the information being put to the court.

## Survival of the company, and the whole or any part of its undertaking, as a going concern

The first justifying purpose has two components. The company must survive *and* the whole or any part of its undertaking must survive. This is more restrictive than the Cork Committee had in mind. The Cork Committee was concerned to salvage viable parts of businesses as going concerns to preserve employment and prevent the dissipation of economic assets and collections of skills. Its formula was 'rehabilitating the company or preserving all or part of its business as a going concern'. The present formula does not cater for having as a sole objective the hiving-off from the company of the whole or part of its undertaking as a going concern if the company itself does not survive as a going concern. Those putting forward a proposal along the second lines would have to rely on the fourth purpose, namely that 'there would be a more advantageous realisation of the company's assets'.

It is often the case that, if an undertaking can be kept as a going concern, it will fetch more in the market. However, it may need financing until it is sold and purchasers may exact a price for the taking over. Because the transferor company's liabilities under the employees' contracts of employment are taken over by the transferee company in terms of regulation 5(1) of the Transfer of Undertakings (Protection of Employment) Regulations 1981, transferee companies have to assess this commitment financially and reflect it in any purchase price, especially if the employees have large accumulated entitlements.

Finally, there may be a possible interpretation difficulty in the first purpose, if it is interpreted to permit the possibility of hive-off. It could be argued that both the company and the undertaking must survive as 'a' (ie 'one') going concern. The authors, however, read 'a going concern' to include 'going concerns'[3].

---

1 *Re SCL Building Services Ltd* [1990] BCC 98 at 101; *Re Land & Property Trust Co plc (No 2)* [1991] BCLC 849.
2 Act of Sederunt (Sheriff Court Company Insolvency Rules) 1986, SI 1986/2297.
3 Interpretation Act 1978, s 6: 'In any Act, unless the contrary intention appears, – . . . (c) words in the singular include the plural.'

## A more advantageous realisation of the company's assets than would be effected on a winding up

The main advantages the administrator has in comparison with the liquidator in seeking a more advantageous realisation of the company's assets are:

(1) the fact that he can exercise his powers in relation to the company's assets as if any floating charge still floated; and
(2) the fact that the company can trade, without diligence being permitted – eg arrestment of receivables, etc.

Utilising these advantages, the administrator in the right circumstances may be likely to realise the company's assets better than a liquidator. The achievement of this purpose happens really in only two distinct sets of circumstances:

(a) the company survives, because the administrator is able to sell off assets in a less hurried way than a liquidator and thus realises a better price and enables the company to overcome a cash-flow problem. Originally the survival of the company might not have been thought achievable;
(b) the administrator, at a better price than a liquidator for the same reasons as in (a), realises all the company's assets, and then applies for a discharge of the administration order under section 18(1) of the Insolvency Act 1986. There is then an application for a winding-up order and winding up follows directly upon the administration. The fact that a two-stage exercise is envisaged is indicated by section 140 of the Insolvency Act 1986 which makes provision for the administrator to be made the liquidator where a winding-up order follows immediately upon the discharge of an administration order. It would accordingly appear that in relation to this (realisation of assets) purpose it is not the administrator's duty to distribute assets through initiating voluntary arrangements unless one of the purposes of the administration order is the achievement of a voluntary arrangement. The purpose of 'a more advantageous realisation of assets' only covers the ingathering stage, not the distribution stage. Accordingly, unless a purpose is specified, enabling a voluntary arrangement, this would not be part of the administrator's duties. The administrator gathers in assets and then leaves distribution to the liquidator.

### Administration procedure – petition for an administration order

Section 9(1) of the Insolvency Act 1986 lists the persons who are entitled to present a petition for an administration order. These are: the company itself or the directors; or a creditor or creditors (including any contingent or prospective creditor or creditors); or all or any of those parties acting together or separately.

A company has a sufficient interest to give it standing to present a petition to be wound up under section 124 of the Insolvency Act 1986. The company has an interest, quite apart from the members as contributories who would have no interest in a company that is wholly insolvent, in having its affairs properly conducted and adequately wound up and in satisfying its duty to pay its debts, or at least, to have them met *pari passu* out of its assets when it is wholly insolvent. By the same token, because of the close similarities between a winding-up under section 124 and a petition for an administration order under section 9 of the Insolvency Act 1986, a company has sufficient interest to present a petition for an administration order[1].

In relation to the directors, the Act requires the directors to act collectively in presenting a petition for an administration order. The use in section 9(1) of the Insolvency Act 1986 of the expression 'the directors' and the lack of any alternative reference to 'director' in the singular form, means that an individual director, or indeed a group of directors forming a minority on the board may not present a petition for an administration order[2]. A petition can be presented by the company but it is of course necessary for the company to approve or ratify the presentation of the petition in general meeting unless the directors are empowered by the articles to present the petition in the company's name. Where a creditor is bringing a petition, the court will not entertain the petition if the debt is disputed. Where the administration order is sought by secured creditors, their interests are weighed lighter than those of unsecured creditors, since the unsecured creditors have more to lose[3].

In addition to the persons listed in section 9(1) of the Insolvency Act 1986, certain other persons may petition where the company is a person authorised to carry on investment business under the Financial Services Act 1986[4].

**Effect of presentation of petition**

When a petition for an administration order is presented, either by the company or the directors, or by a creditor or creditors, then until either the administration order is made, or the petition is dismissed, the company has *three* far reaching protections:

(1)  no resolution may be passed or order made for the winding-up of the company;
(2)  no steps may be taken to enforce any charge on or security over the company's property or to repossess goods in the company's possession under any hire-purchase agreement, conditional sale agreement, chattel leasing agreement and retention of title agreement except with the leave of the court; and
(3)  no other proceedings, including debt-enforcement proceedings (called 'diligence' in Scotland) and no execution or other legal process may be taken except with the leave of the court[5]. Nevertheless, the expression 'no other legal proceedings' is confined to proceedings such as proceedings by a creditor to recover a debt, and does not extend to such matters as proceedings before the Civil Aviation Authority to revoke an air transport licence[6].

1  *Re Land and Property Trust Co plc* [1991] BCLC 845.
2  *Re Instrumentation Electrical Services Limited* [1988] 4 BCC 301, as interpreted in *Re Equiticorp International plc* [1989] 5 BCC 599.
3  *Re Consumer & Industrial Press Limited* [1988] 4 BCC 68; *Re Imperial Motors (UK) Limited* [1989] 5 BCC 214.
4  Financial Services Act 1986, s 74; see also Banks (Administration Proceedings) Order 1989 for banks.
5  Insolvency Act 1986, s 10(1).
6  *Air Ecosse Ltd v Civil Aviation Authority* 1987 SLT 751. The case deals with s 11(3)(d), and holds that that paragraph must be construed *ejusdem generis* with (confined to the categories outlined in) s 11(3)(a)–(c).

There is a qualification in that, if the petition is presented at a time when there is an administrative receiver, the restrictions do not operate unless and until the appointer consents to the making of the administration order[1]. In other words, the effect of the presentation of the petition is to give the company protection from any type of legal process by its creditors, the most drastic of which would be a winding-up order. The assets may not be attached. These provisions are now examined.

### No resolution for winding up or winding-up order

This is an absolute prohibition, although there is no bar on the presentation of a winding-up petition[2]. Once a petition for an administration order has been presented the court will accede to an application to restrain advertisement of the winding-up petition until the administration petition has been heard, since the administration process has priority over all other processes. The reason is that it is contrary to the whole essence of the administration petition that anything be done during the pendency of such a petition to continue with legal proceedings and to do anything which may be seen in public to damage the company, such as the advertisement of a winding-up petition. The reason that a winding-up petition is allowed to be presented during the hearing of the administration petition is because of all the many important consequences that follow from the date of presentation of a winding-up petition[3].

### No enforcement of a security or repossession of goods

In terms of section 248(b)(ii) of the Insolvency Act 1986 a 'security' means in relation to Scotland 'any security (whether heritable or moveable), any floating charge and any right of lien or preference and any right of retention (other than a right of compensation or set-off)[4].

### No other legal process

The provisions in sections 10(1) and 11(3) of the Insolvency Act 1986 which provide for far-reaching protection of the company from creditor action where there is an administration order application pending or an administration order in force respectively, are the core provisions of the administration order procedure. A series of cases in the English and Scottish courts have now established a more or less settled corpus of law on the subject. First, it is only 'enforcement' of the security that is prohibited. A secured creditor is entitled to take possession of his security or realise it if (a) he obtains the company's consent, given through the administrator, or if there is an interim administrator appointed under section 9(4) of the Insolvency Act 1986, the interim administrator; or (b) with the leave of the court. If neither of these consents is

---

1 Insolvency Act 1986, s 10(3).
2 Ibid, s 10(2)(a).
3 *Re Manlon Trading Limited* [1988] 4 BCC 455; *Re a Company (No 001992 of 1988)* [1989] BCLC 9; and *Re a Company (No 001448 of 1989)* [1989] BCLC 715.
4 Not covered is a 'market charge' which is defined as a charge in favour of a recognised investment exchange or recognised clearing house for the purpose of securing liabilities under contracts entered into by a member of the exchange or clearing house under its rules: sections 173(1) (amended by the Financial Markets and Insolvency Regulations 1991, SI 1991/800, reg 9); section 175(1)(a) and section 190(1) of the Companies Act 1989.

granted, a person having a lien over goods is not entitled to retain them. In the case of *Re Sabre International Products Ltd*[1], Harman J held that 'enforcing a lien' is merely holding on to the goods if there has been a demand from an administrator for them to be delivered to him. The term 'security' as used in sections 10, 11 and 248 of the Insolvency Act 1986 is wide enough to cover a right of re-entry conferred on a landlord by the terms of a lease and therefore a landlord would be precluded from exercising his right of re-entry without the consent of the administrator or the court[2]. However, where a company has assigned receivables to a third party in security of obligations of the company to the third party, the third party does not have a security or charge over the receivables, and is entitled to payment of the receivables[3]. The expression 'no other proceedings' in section 10(1)(c) and section 11(3)(d) is confined to proceedings such as proceedings by a creditor to recover a debt, but would not extend to administrative procedures such as applications by a Chief Constable for suspension of a public house licence or other administrative constraints which might otherwise affect a company such as the exercise of its functions by a civil aviation authority in determining whether a company was fit to operate aircraft and had the requisite financial resources to carry on business to a requisite statutory standard[4]. *Air Ecosse*, supra, dealt with section 11(3)(d) and holds that that paragraph must be construed *ejusdem generis* with (confined to the categories outlined in) s 11(3)(a)–(c). An application to a court for an extension of time in which to register a charge by a company does not constitute proceedings 'against the company or its property'[5]. A statutory right to detain an aircraft under section 88 of the Civil Aviation Act 1982 in security of landing fees and dues, constitutes a passive right, even if there is not actual security until the aircraft is detained, and would require the leave of the court before it could be lawfully exercised[6].

The problem in relation to the rights of security holders and those wanting to enforce liens or take other proceedings is how to balance their interests against the interests of the company and other creditors. Certain guidelines were issued by Sir Nicholas Browne-Wilkinson V-C in the case of *Bristol Airport plc*[7]. These guidelines were referred to with approval and much expanded in the English Appeal Court in the case of *Atlantic Computer Systems plc (No 1)*[8]. In that case the company in administration carried on the business of leasing computer equipment to end users, for which purpose it needed to borrow funds to finance the purchase of the equipment which it then leased out. Two funders were the Norwich Union Group and the Allied Irish Group. There were two methods by which the funders provided finance. The first was for the funder to supply the equipment to the company under a hire-purchase agreement and the second was for the funder to lease the equipment to the company, in each case the company subletting the equipment to the end users. An administration order was made in relation to the company for the

1 [1991] BCLC 470.
2 *Exchange Travel Agency Limited v Triton Property Trust plc* [1991] BCLC 396.
3 *Re Atlantic Computer Systems plc* [1991] BCLC 606 at 629 in which the Court of Appeal held that the assignee of the benefit of sub-leases of computing equipment in security of payments due by the assignor to the assignee under the head lease, is entitled to enforce that type of security.
4 *Air Ecosse Limited v Civil Aviation Authority*, 1987 SLT 751.
5 *Re Barrow Borough Transport Limited* [1990] Ch 227, 5 BCC 646.
6 *Bristol Airport plc and Another v Powdrill and Others* [1990] BCLC 585.
7 *Supra.*
8 [1991] BCLC 606.

purpose of achieving a more advantageous realisation of the company's assets. After administrators had been appointed, rental payments from the end users were paid to the administrators. During their appointment the administrators did not pay any monies which were due to the funders. The administrators declined to consent to the funders exercising their rights to terminate the head leases.

Two of the funders applied to the court to decide whether the equipment leased to end users constituted 'goods in the company's possession under any hire-purchase agreement'. If they were such, the next question was whether the court would grant leave under section 11(3)(c) of the Insolvency Act 1986, entitling the funders to enforce their security. In the court of First Instance Ferris J held that the equipment was not in the possession of the company for the purposes of section 11(3)(c) of the Insolvency Act 1986[1]. If however leave to bring an action had been needed, the case for granting it would be very strong and to the extent that property of the funders was being used in the company's business while the administration order was in force, the funders would be entitled as 'expenses of the administration' to receive the payments provided for in their agreements with the company.

The Court of Appeal discussed the differences between a liquidation and an administration. Briefly an administration was intended to be an interim and temporary régime. Whether or not those with proprietary rights against the company should be allowed to enforce those rights against the company depended on all the circumstances of the case, and it would be inappropriate to adopt the inflexible rule for winding up that if land or goods in the company's possession under an existing lease or hire-purchase agreement were used for the purposes of the administration, the continuing rent or hire charges should automatically be treated as expenses of the administration. This was backed up by the terms of section 19(5) of the Insolvency Act 1986, in terms of which there is no automatic priority on third parties whose contracts with the company are adopted by the administrator, except in the case of contracts of employment. Secondly the equipment being leased, as far as between the company and the funders, remained in the possession of the company. Therefore the funders needed the consent of the court, or the administrators, to remove the equipment. At the end of a long and complicated judgment, the court laid down certain guidelines for future reference which state in detail the principles which courts must follow when making decisions in this complicated area of administration law. They have become known as the 'the Atlantic Computer Guidelines'.

## The Atlantic Computer guidelines

Nicholls LJ ended the opinion of the Appeal Court as follows:

'There is one final matter to which we now turn. In the course of argument we were invited to give guidance on the principles to be applied on applications for the grant of leave under s 11. It is an invitation to which we are reluctant to accede, for several reasons: first, Parliament has left at large the discretion given to the court, and it is not for us to cut down that discretion or, as it was put in argument, to confine it within a straitjacket. However

---

1 *Re Atlantic Computer Systems plc (Nos 1 and 2)* [1990] BCLC 729.

much we emphasise that any observations are only guidelines, there is a danger that they may be treated as something more. Secondly, s 11(3)(c) and (d) applies to a very wide range of steps and proceedings, and the circumstances in which leave is sought will vary almost infinitely. Thirdly, it is the judges who sit in the Companies Court who have practical experience of the difficulties arising in the working out of this new jurisdiction, not the members of this court.

However, we have already drawn attention to the important role of the administrator in this field. He should respond speedily and responsibly to applications for consent under s 11. Parliament envisaged that in the first place s 11 matters should be dealt with by him. It is to be hoped, in the interests of all concerned, that applications to the court will become the exception rather than the rule. But we recognise that for this to be so, authorised insolvency practitioners and their legal advisors need more guidance than is available at present on what, in general, is the approach of the court on leave applications. We feel bound, therefore, to make some general observations regarding cases where leave is sought to exercise existing proprietary rights, including security rights, against a company in administration:

(1) It is in every case for the person who seeks leave to make out a case for him to be given leave.

(2) The prohibition in s 11(3)(c) and (d) is intended to assist the company, under the management of the administrator, to achieve the purpose for which the administration order was made. If granting leave to a lessor of land or the hirer of goods (a 'lessor') to exercise his proprietary rights and repossess his lands or goods is unlikely to impede the achievement of that purpose, leave should normally be given.

(3) In other cases when a lessor seeks possession the court has to carry out a balancing exercise, balancing the legitimate interests of the lessor and the legitimate interests of the other creditors of the company (see Peter Gibson J in *Royal Trust Bank v Buchler* [1989] BCLC 130 at 135).

The metaphor employed here, for want of a better, is that of scales and weights. Lord Wilberforce adverted to the limitations of this metaphor in *Science Research Council v Nassé, BL Cars Limited (formerly Leyland Cars) v Vyas* [1979] 3 All ER 673 at 681 [1980] AC 1028 at 1067. It must be kept in mind that the exercise under s 11 is not a mechanical one; each case calls for an exercise in judicial judgment, in which the court seeks to give effect to the purpose of the statutory provisions, having regard to the parties' interests and all the circumstances of the case. As already noted, the purpose of the prohibition is to enable or assist the company to achieve the object for which the administration order was made. The purpose of the power to give leave is to enable the court to relax the prohibition where it would be inequitable for the prohibition to apply.

(4) In carrying out the balancing exercise great importance, or weight, is normally given to the proprietary interests of the lessor. Sir Nicholas Browne-Wilkinson V-C observed in *Bristol Airport plc v Powdrill* [1990] BCLC 585 at 602, [1990] 2 All ER 493 at 507 that, so far as possible, the administration procedure should not be used to prejudice those who were secured creditors when the administration order was made in lieu of a winding-up order. The same is true regarding the proprietary interest of a lessor. The underlying principle here is that an administration for the benefit of unsecured creditors should not be conducted at the expense of those who have proprietary rights which they are seeking to exercise, save to the extent that this may be unavoidable and even then this will usually be acceptable only to a strictly limited extent.

(5) Thus it will normally be a sufficient ground for the grant of leave if significant loss would be caused to the lessor by a refusal. For this purpose loss comprises any kind of financial loss, direct or indirect, including loss by reason of delay, and may extend to loss which is not financial. But if substantially greater loss would be caused to others by the grant of leave, or loss which is out of all proportion to the benefit which leave would confer on the lessor, that may outweigh the loss of the lessor caused by the refusal.

Our formulation was criticised in the course of the argument, and we certainly do not claim for it the status of a rule in those terms. At present we say only that it appears to us the nearest we can get to a formulation of what Parliament had in mind.

(6)   In assessing these respective losses the court will have regard to matters such as: the financial position of the company, its ability to pay the rental arrears and the continuing rentals, the administrator's proposals, the period for which the administration order has already been in force and is expected to remain in force, the effect on the administration if leave were given, the effect on the applicant if leave were refused, the end result sought to be achieved by the administration, the prospects of that result being achieved, and the history of the administration so far.

(7)   In considering these matters it will often be necessary to assess how probable the suggested consequences are. Thus if loss to the applicant is virtually certain if leave is refused, and loss to the others a remote possibility if leave is granted, that will be a powerful factor in favour of granting leave.

(8)   This is not an exhaustive list. For example, the conduct of the parties may also be a material consideration in a particular case, as it was in *Bristol Airport v Powdrill*. There leave was refused on the ground that the applicants had accepted benefits under the administration, and had only sought to enforce their security at a later stage: indeed, they had only acquired their security as a result of the operations of the administrators. It behoves a lessor to make his position clear to the administrator at the outset of the administration and, if it should become necessary, to apply to the court promptly.

(9)   The above considerations may be relevant not only to the decision whether leave should be granted or refused, but also to a decision to impose terms if leave is granted.

(10)   The above considerations will also apply to a decision on whether to impose terms as a condition for refusing leave. Section 11(3)(c) and (d) makes no provision for terms being imposed if leave is refused, but the court has power to achieve that result. It may do so directly, by giving directions to the administrator: for instance, under s 17, or in response to an application by the administrator under s 14(3), or in exercise of its control over an administrator as an officer of the court. Or it may do so indirectly, by ordering that the applicant shall have leave unless the administrator is prepared to take this or that step in the conduct of the administration.

Cases where leave is refused but terms are imposed can be expected to arise frequently. For example, the permanent loss to a lessor flowing from his inability to recover his property will normally be small if the administrator is required to pay the current rent. In most cases this should be possible, since if the administration order has been rightly made the business should generally be sufficiently viable to hold down current outgoings. Such a term may therefore be a normal term to impose.

(11)   The above observations are directed at a case such as the present where a lessor of land or the owner of goods is seeking to repossess his land or goods because of non-payment of rentals. A broadly similar approach will be applicable on many applications to enforce a security: for instance, an application by a mortgagee for possession of land. On such applications an important consideration will often be whether the applicant is fully secured. If he is, delay in enforcement is likely to be less prejudicial than in cases where his security is insufficient.

(12)   In some cases there will be a dispute over the existence, validity or nature of the security which the applicant is seeking leave to enforce. It is not for the court on the leave application to seek to adjudicate upon that issue, unless (as in the present case, on the fixed or floating charge point) the issue raises a short point of law which it is convenient to determine without further ado. Otherwise the court needs to be satisfied only that the applicant has a seriously arguable case.'

## Interim orders

Under section 9(4) of the Insolvency Act 1986, the presentation of a petition allows the court, on hearing the petition, to dismiss it or adjourn the hearing conditionally or unconditionally or make any interim order or any other order that it thinks fit. The court may make an administration order, even prior to the presentation of the petition, if all the supporting evidence convinces the court that an administration order will be made[1]. The court has held that an *interim* administration order may be made under this subsection at a hearing immediately after the presentation of the petition[2]. It should be noted that the form of interlocutor used involves the making of an *interim* administration order. It is thought that such an order is an administration order for all purposes of the Act except that its duration is limited to the period until the full hearing of the petition. The interim order may restrict the exercise by the directors of the company of any of their powers[3]. It is thought that such an interim order would not include the lifting of an inhibition, which is a Scottish order effectively disabling a company granting a clear title to heritable property and therefore frustrating the sale of the property.

In contrast in England the position seems to be that an interim administration order is not competent. In *Re Gallidoro Trawlers Ltd*[4], Harman J following Vinelott J stated:

'It seems to me that the observations of Vinelott J reported in *Re a Company* (No 00175 of 1987) [1987] BCLC 467, are plainly right. The learned judge held firstly that the court was entitled to abridge time for service. Secondly that there is no power to appoint an interim administrator and that the only power in respect of administrators is to appoint an administrator or refuse to do so; finally that under s 9(4) of the 1986 Act, the court having a specific power to make an interim order or other order as it thinks fit, and under s 9(3) of the Act to make orders restricting the exercise of powers, in that case the judge held on that evidence that it was desirable, indeed necessary, to have a manager to cover the interim period.'

## Effect of dismissal of administration petition

If the court decides not to make an administration order, the normal practice will be to dismiss the petition, leaving winding up as the likeliest alternative route for the company to follow. Where an administration order petition has

1 *Re Cavco Floors Limited* ([1990] BCLC 940; see also *Re Chancery plc* [1991] BCLC 712, where Harman J also granted an administration order where there had not been proper formal service, and held the hearing in camera.
2 *Air Ecosse Ltd*, 1987 SLT 751; *Avenel Hotel Ltd*, (1987) (unreported), where the competency of such an appointment was the subject of argument; Lord Davidson held that an *interim* order was competent. It is thought that serious practical difficulties would arise otherwise, as there would be a gap between the presentation of the petition and the making of a full administration order during which the directors would remain in full control. In *Avenel Hotel Ltd*, a provisional liquidator had been appointed, but no winding-up order had been made, when the *interim* administration order was made. The provisional liquidator moved for the recall of the *interim* administration order. Lord Davidson granted the motion. He held that the onus was on the *interim* administrator to justify his appointment, and that the 'stigma' of liquidation was not by itself a sufficient justification for the replacement of a provisonal liquidator by an *interim* administrator. He further held that, because there was no significant difference in the policies advocated by the provisional liquidator and the *interim* administrator (both thought that realisation of the company's assets was essential), the earlier appointment should prevail.
3 Insolvency Act 1986, s 9(5).
4 [1991] BCLC 411.

been presented reasonably and on appropriate professional advice, it has been held that the costs incurred in the administration order application down to the hearing at which it was dismissed, could be treated as allowable costs in the subsequent winding up[1]. The underlying rationale is that it would otherwise be difficult for directors, solicitors or accountants to act in good faith in preparing and presenting an administration order to recover the costs thereby incurred. This would work against the legislative intention which is that the administration course should be adopted wherever practical as the best method of averting a winding up. Harman J held in the case of *Re Land and Property Trust Co (No 3)*[2], that that course had not been followed. He stated:

'I entirely follow that directors who are doing their best to save their companies and who make an ill-advised, as it turns out, presentation of an administration petition, should not normally be penalised by an order to pay costs personally. I do accept that it has to be shown that there are exceptional reasons in the conduct of the matter why the directors personally should be called upon to answer for what are undoubtedly their personal resolutions. . . . But the facts of these petitions do not give any hint that that careful process was here adopted. The main petition, seeking an administration order in respect of the parent company of the group was first presented. There then followed in pell-mell haste these 29 petitions in respect of the subsidiary companies. The petitions existed for only a few days including a weekend, and were abandoned by leading counsel for the companies without any attempt to urge the court to grant the petitions. I can only infer that experienced leading counsel on reading the evidence available in opposition considered, and if he did he was in my judgment correct, that the petitions were all absolutely doomed to failure. The gap of 21 days between the board's resolution and the date of presentation does not seem to have been taken up, at least there is no evidence that it was, by consultation with and consideration of the advice of the proposed administrators.

Thus the costs of the petitions were incurred not in reliance on the reports under r 2.2, although the costs were no doubt largely incurred after the signing of the report, but in pursuance of the directors' resolutions all passed in so short a space of time at noon on 7 January. It was those resolutions which authorised solicitors to incur costs on behalf of the companies. In my judgment I am entitled on the evidence and on the conduct of all these petitions before me to conclude that the directors never properly considered the matter on a basis of whether there was any real risk of flooding the market or any real benefit to be attained by the making of administration orders, and simply embarked on a course of action which had no rational prospect of succeeding in a perhaps desperate attempt to free the companies from the intense pressure by the various creditors.'

First it is clear from this extract from Harman J's judgment that directors of companies could be exposed to the costs of unsuccessful administration order applications, if they are irresponsibly brought. Secondly it is thought that the directors could be personally exposed, if third parties suffer unnecessary losses as a result of the bringing of an administration order application in these circumstances. Thirdly it is thought that solicitors acting for directors contemplating the bringing of an administration order petition are under a duty of care to advise the directors of these risks.

### Effect of administration order

When an administration order is pronounced, the effect is to continue the general moratorium from creditor action in relation to the company's affairs

---

1  *Re Gosscott (Groundworks) Limited* [1988] BCLC 363; see in contrast *Re W F Fearman Ltd (No 2)* (1988) 4 BCC 141.
2  [1991] BCLC 856; this view of Harman J has superseded his previous judgment in *Re W F Fearman Ltd (No 2)*, which is thought wrong.

which commenced with the presentation of the petition (ie no enforcement of a 'security' etc or other legal proceedings). In addition, however, (1) no winding-up petition may be presented[1]; (2) any administrative receiver of the company must vacate office[1]; (3) a receiver of part of the company's property must vacate office if required to by the administrator[2]; and (4) no administrative receiver of the company may be appointed[3].

Once the administrator is appointed, he has the general powers outlined earlier in this chapter. In addition, he has the power to appoint and remove directors[4], and the power to call meetings of members and creditors[5]. This last power means that, although no resolution may be passed while an administration order is in force for the winding-up of the company, the administrator may convene meetings for the purpose of commencing winding up, and time them so that when he has obtained a discharge he is ready to be appointed liquidator (as provided for in section 140(1) of the Insolvency Act 1986). Legal proceedings may be brought against the company only with the leave of the court or the administrator.[6] This would allow for example action under sections 459 to 461 of the Companies Act 1985 (protection of minority interests) although no order could be made for winding up. A petition in respect of prejudicial conduct by the administrator would not require leave[7].

### Effect of administration order on directors

In terms of section 14(4) of the Insolvency Act 1986 all powers of the company and its officers which could be exercised in such a way as to interfere with the exercise by the administrator of his powers cease to be exercisable except with the consent of the administrator, which may be given either generally or in relation to particular cases. The language suggests that the test for the continuance of any power in the directors is not whether a particular exercise of a particular power *would* interfere, but whether any exercise *could* interfere. This suggests that no powers will survive in the directors. It is difficult to believe that the Insolvency Act 1986 intended to stop the directors applying to the court in the name of the company for the discharge of the administrator or of the administration order, or from appealing against the making of the administration order only because the administrator is given statutory powers to bring or defend proceedings in the name of the company. The granting of the directors' parallel powers to bring proceedings in the name of the company could not interfere with his own powers. Provided that the action is in relation to the appointment of an administrator, he is entitled to defend any action or appeal, and none of his duties are interfered with. It is not an interference in power that flows from an action to challenge the appointment, whereas to challenge an act would be. (See discussion of residuary powers of directors (page 24)). There might be a problem, however, of how the directors would fund their legal action. They would probably not be able to use company money unless successful.

1 Insolvency Act 1986, s 11(1).
2 Ibid, s 11(2).
3 Ibid, s 11(3).
4 Ibid, s 14(2)(a).
5 Ibid, s 14(2).
6 Ibid, s 11(3).
7 Ibid, s 27.

## Effect of administration on contracts of employment and other contracts

The effect of an administration order on contracts of employment has not been judicially determined in Scotland. It is one of the most difficult legal problems as far as Scottish law is concerned in the new legislation. It has been assumed in England that an administration order will not act like a winding-up order as far as contracts of employment are concerned[1]. Section 19 of the Insolvency Act 1986 talks of an administrator 'adopting' contracts of employment, which is consistent with the contract of employment continuing, which it would if an employee was entitled to affirm it in the face of a breach of contract by his employer, or if there was no breach and adoption, but not if there was automatic termination. However there is no express statutory provision that the contract will not be terminated as section 57(4) of the Insolvency Act 1986 provides in relation to receivership. It would obviously be more difficult to get administrations off the ground if they have the effect of acting like winding-up orders, ie as constructive notice of dismissal (see page 26) and entitling the employee to damages and statutory entitlements. One of the problems in trying to determine the law in relation to winding up is that the leading case[2] predates the modern statutory entitlements on dismissal on winding up, and certainly does not envisage the peculiar animal of an administration order. In a winding up, the business ceases to be carried on – at least after a short period – and hence the question of the payment to employees of their accumulated entitlements is only a question of timing. The problem with the law on administrations is that, if an administration order acts as, or can act as, constructive notice of dismissal, the potential costs of meeting claims would have to be included in the figures backing up the facts put to the court arguing how one or more of the justifying purposes of an administration order was likely to be achieved.

The approach that is proposed is to try to arrive at a suggested solution by looking at the analogy of an insolvent winding-up, and seeing what areas relevant to employment law administratorship and insolvent winding-up have in common. This paragraph must be read alongside pages 26–28 which deals with this problem in insolvent windings up. The leading case on the effects of winding up in Scotland is the First Division (Scottish Court of Appeal) case of *Smith v Lord Advocate*[3], from which the following five propositions may be derived:

(1) A company in liquidation continues to exist until it has been wound up and there is no basis for the view that a change in its personality occurs when a winding-up order is made. Until it has been wound up, it remains legal owner of all its assets and interests. These interests include rights under contracts entered into but not completed before the date of the winding-up order, and the corollary is that the company is not divested of liabilities under which it has come before that date[4].

(2) The liquidator has the character of manager and of administrator of the

---

1 See Lightman and Moss, *The Law of Receivers of Companies* (1986), para 23–08; this is also suggested for Scotland's position: see *Stair Memorial Encyclopaedia*, vol 4, para 624.
2 *Day v Tait* (1900) 8 SLT 40.
3 *Smith v Lord Advocate* 1978 SC 259.
4 At 271 per Lord President Emslie.

company's affairs, and of a person acting for and on behalf of the company in the matter of the completion of company contracts[1].

(3) A liquidator who employs men to enable the company's business to be carried on can only be properly regarded as employing them for and on behalf of the company[2].

(4) If the liquidator re-engages employees (adopts their contracts of employment) they are treated as continuously employed by the one employer from the dates of their initial engagement by the company before a winding-up order is made down to the dates of their dismissal by the liquidator.

(5) The effect of a winding-up order is to act as a constructive notice of termination. The employer's insolvency is a breach of contract, and the employee is not bound to work for him when he has announced that he will not be able to pay debts (including wages) as they become due. Other contracts are not affected by winding up unless there is an express term to that effect.

It would appear to the authors that in the case of an administration order, conditions (1), (2), (3) and (4) are met. The administrator is the manager of the company[3]. He is deemed to be the agent of the company[4].

To make the analogy complete, so that the effect of an administration order in relation to contracts of employment is the same as that of a winding-up order, condition (5) would have to be fulfilled. The rationale of condition (1) in Scotland is as stated by Lord Cameron in *Smith v Lord Advocate*[5], namely that it would be inequitable that an insolvent company should be in a position to require its servant to continue to work when he cannot rely on his wages being paid[6]. An administration order constitutes 'insolvency' for certain purposes of the Employment Protection (Consolidation) Act 1978[7]. The court grants an administration order if it is satisfied that a company is unable to pay its debts (which is the classical definition of insolvency), or 'is likely to become unable to pay its debts'. The order does not have to specify which of these two components is satisfied. Unlike a winding-up order in an insolvent liquidation, however, which publicly declares that a company is unable to pay its debts, an administration order says one of two things: *either* (a) 'Although the company is unable or unlikely to pay its debts at the moment, the court is convinced that an administration order is likely to enable it to pay its debts' *or* (b) 'The company is unable to pay its debts, but an administration order will achieve a better realisation of assets than immediate winding up'.

It is suggested that the alternative (b) would make an administrative order analogous for employment purposes with insolvent liquidation. The company is saying that it is insolvent and the employee cannot rely on having a job with the company and on his wages being paid.

---

1 At 273 per Lord President Emslie.
2 At 272 per Lord President Emslie.
3 Insolvency Act 1986, s 14(1)(a).
4 Ibid, s 14(5).
5 1978 SC 259 at 281.
6 See *Hoey v McEwan and Auld* (1867) 5 M 814 at 817; *Day v Tait* (1900) 8 SLT 40; *Laing v Gowans* (1902) 10 SLT 461, and in England *Re General Rolling Stock Co* (*Chapman's Case*) (1866) LR 1 Eq 346; *Reid v Explosives Co* (1887) 19 QBD 264; *Measures Bros v Measures* [1910] 2 Ch 248; *Reigate v Union Manufacturing Co* [1918] 1 KB 592.
7 Employment Protection (Consolidation) Act 1978, s 127(2).

Where the administration order specifies one or more of the other purposes, the matter is much less clear. Section 247(1) of the Insolvency Act 1986 does seem to equate administration with insolvency. If the court was only saying that the company was insolvent, it is suggested that that would be analogous to a winding-up order. If, however, it is saying that, notwithstanding the insolvency, it is likely that the employee will have a job and his wages will be paid through the effect and results of the administration order, it is suggested that the employee may not treat an administration order as constructive notice of dismissal, because in that situation the court is saying that it is likely that the employee will have a job and his wages will be paid[1].

In relation to other contracts administration being less far down the line to insolvency than winding up *a fortiori* should not affect other contracts but might have implications for set-off (see Chapter 15).

### Duty of company to produce a statement of affairs

The administrator may require some or all of the following to make and submit a statement of affairs[2]:

(1) existing or past officers of the company;
(2) persons who took part in the company's formation at any time within one year before the date of the administration order;
(3) persons employed under contracts of service or services at the date of the order or within one year before that date who in the administrator's opinion are capable of giving (some of) the information required; and
(4) officers or employees under contracts of service or services (whether present or within the past year) with a company which itself is or was within that year an officer of the company.

These persons are all under a statutory duty to co-operate with the administrator and give such information concerning the company and its promotion, formation, business, dealings, affairs or property as the administrator may reasonably require, and to attend on the administrator at such time as the administrator may reasonably require[3]. Failure to comply with any obligation to co-operate with the administrator renders the person concerned liable on conviction to a fine[4].

### Legal status of administrator

It is thought that the administrator acts in several capacities. He is

(1) an officer of the company;
(2) an agent of the company;
(3) a public office holder; and
(4) an officer of the court.

---

1 *Reigate v Union Manufacturing Co, supra.*
2 Insolvency Act 1986, s 22(3).
3 Ibid, s 235(2).
4 Ibid, s 235(5).

## (1)   *Officer of the company*

The administrator, like a liquidator (but unlike a receiver), is an officer of the company because, like the liquidator, he is the governing body of the company managing its affairs as well as its business and property[1]. As an officer of the company, he is liable in a winding up to misfeasance proceedings[2]. If, in the course of the winding up, it appears that the administrator has misapplied or retained, or become accountable for, any money or other property of the company, or been guilty of misfeasance or breach of any fiduciary or other duty in relation to the company in connection with the carrying out of his duty as an administrator, the court may grant a summary order against him on the application of the liquidator or any creditor or contributory, and the court may examine the conduct of the administrator and compel him (a) to repay, restore or account for the money or property or any part of it, or (b) in the event of misfeasance or breach of fiduciary or other duty, to make payment of whatever sum the court thinks just[3].

As an 'officer of the company' an administrator is entitled to protection under section 727 of the Companies Act 1985. In the case of *Re Home Treat Ltd*, Harman J stated[4]:

'The answer may be that the court can afford protection to the administrators pursuant to s 727 of the 1985 Act. That allows, in proceedings for negligence, default, breach of duty or breach of trust – and this, I think, would be an allegation of default – against an officer of the company or person employed by the company, the court, if it appears that that officer may be liable in respect of the wrong but has acted honestly and reasonably and ought fairly to be excused, to relieve him. Those phrases are, of course, reminiscent of the phrases in s 61 of the Trustee Act 1925.

The question is whether under that power to relieve officers of the company, an administrator can be relieved. I have been shown a decision of Parker J as he then was, later Lord Parker of Waddington, who was a very great authority in all these matters. In *Re X Co Limited* [1907] 2 Ch 92 Parker J held that a liquidator might be given relief on the footing that he is an officer of the company to do a certain act concerned with the memorandum under the Stamp Act 1891. The notes to s 448 of the Companies Act 1948 in *Buckley on the Companies Act* [14 edn 1981] p 892, that section being the direct predecessor of s 727 of the 1985 Act, say "firstly, *semble* a liquidator is an officer within the meaning of this section", and they refer to *Re X Co Limited*, and they go on to say that s 448 extends to a transaction *ultra vires* of the company . . .

It seems to me quite clear that the word "officer", which merely means somebody who holds an office, and an office in relation to the company, can apply to an administrator. That is so although he is also an officer of the court, there being in that context no conflict of duties between his duty as officer of the company and his duty as an officer of the court. In both capacities his duties are to manage the business and property of the company for the better effecting of the purpose for which the court made the order, in the interests of the creditors and it may be eventually of the contributories of the company.

I therefore come, at the end of this somewhat lengthy recitation, to the conclusion that the application under s 727 of the 1985 Act is justified and the administrators ought to be given a direction as set out in the intended application which has been put before me, validating their conduct of the affairs of the company.'

1 Ibid, s 17(2).
2 Ibid, s 212.
3 Ibid, s 212(3).
4 [1991] BCLC 705.

## (2)  *Agent of the company*

The administrator is deemed to be acting as agent of the company[1]. He is not personally liable on any contract entered into or adopted by him in the carrying out of his duties as administrator, except if the contract provides otherwise[2]. This is different to a receiver, who is personally liable on any contract adopted[3]. However, people must be put on notice that the company is subject to an administration order. Every invoice, order for goods and business letter on or in which the company's name appears issued by or on behalf of the administrator or the company must contain the administrator's name and a statement that the affairs, business and property of the company are being managed by the administrator[4]. If this provision is breached without reasonable excuse, the administrator is liable to a fine[5]. The specified documents on which the administrator's details are to be specified are those which will be seen by persons dealing with the company and those supplying it with goods. Accordingly the administrator may expose himself to personal liability for breach of this provision if in ignorance of the administration order persons supply goods to the company not knowing that it is insolvent or likely to become insolvent. Suppliers, including utilities, may insist on personal guarantees from the administrator before the provision of services or goods[6].

## (3)  *Office holder*

The administrator is an office holder. He is vested with special powers and privileges under sections 230 to 246 of the Insolvency Act 1986. He may secure the provision of continued supply by utilities without providing arrears accrued prior to the date of the administration order[6]. He has powers to inquire into the company's dealings[7]. He has power to challenge prior transactions of the company (sections 242, 243, 244 and 245 of the Insolvency Act 1986) and is given special exemption from liability for loss or damage occasioned by his seizure or disposal of property which does not belong to the company[8]. His acts as administrator are also validated even if there has been a defect in his appointment or qualifications[9].

## (4)  *Officer of court*

The administrator like the liquidator appointed on a compulsory liquidation[10] is an officer of the court. This status involves special privileges and responsibilities. He is protected by the law of contempt against any interference with the performance of his duties and has a right of access to the court for directions.

Finally, the administrator owes to the company fiduciary duties to exercise

1 Insolvency Act 1986, s 14(5).
2 Ibid, s 19(5).
3 Ibid, s 57(2).
4 Ibid, s 12(1).
5 Ibid, s 12(2).
6 Ibid, s 233.
7 Ibid, s 236.
8 Ibid, s 234(3) and (4).
9 Ibid, s 232.
10 A liquidator in a voluntary liquidation is not an officer of the court: *Re Bateson (John) & Co* [1985] BCLC 259.

good faith and a duty to exercise the professional skill and care of an insolvency practitioner. He is not allowed to have any conflict of interest between his duty as administrator and any private interest. If the administrator is a solicitor or accountant, he may however be free to employ his own firm to assist in the performance of his duties as administrator[1].

## Administrative duties of administrator

### (1) Taking custody of property

The administrator is under a duty to take into his custody or under his control all the property to which the company is, or appears to be, entitled[2] and may apply to the court for orders for the restoration to the company of assets disposed of for no consideration or inadequate consideration[3], or assets disposed of which create a preference in favour of a creditor to the prejudice of the general body of creditors[4].

### (2) Notification of appointment

The administrator has a formal requirement on the making of the administration order: (1) within 14 days to send an office copy of the order certified by the Clerk of Court to the Registrar of Companies[5] as well as to (a) any person who has appointed an administrative receiver, or has power to do so; (b) an administrative receiver, if appointed; (c) a petitioner in a petition for the winding up of the company, if that petition is pending; (d) any provisional liquidator of the company, if appointed; and (e) the Keeper of the Register of Inhibitions and Adjudications for recording in that register[6]. A notice of the order must forthwith also be sent to the company, and it must be published in terms of rule 2.3 of the Insolvency (Scotland) Rules 1986 by advertising the making of the order once in the *Edinburgh Gazette* and once in a newspaper circulating in the area where the company has its principal place of business or in such newspaper as the administrator thinks most appropriate for ensuring that the order comes to the notice of creditors. Notice must be sent to all the creditors within 28 days of the order at their addresses as far as the administrator is aware of their addresses[7].

### (3) Notification on stationery

In terms of section 12(1) of the Insolvency Act 1986 the administrator must ensure that every invoice, order for goods, or business letter which, at a time when the administration order is in force, is issued by or on behalf of the company or the administrator contains a statement that the affairs, business and property of the company are being managed by the administrator. It must

1 See *Bridal Centre* (1985) 9 ACLR 481.
2 Insolvency Act 1986, s 17.
3 See 'gratuitous alienations,' (Insolvency Act 1986, s 242).
4 See 'unfair preferences,' (Insolvency Act 1986, s 243).
5 Form 2.2 (Scot).
6 Insolvency (Scotland) Rules 1986, r 2.3(3) as amended by article 5 of the Schedule to the Insolvency (Scotland) Amendment Rules 1987.
7 Insolvency Act 1986, s 21(1)(b).

also contain the administrator's name. The need for this formality applies only to documents on which the company's name appears.

## Administrator's proposals

The administrator has a duty within three months (unless the court allows a longer period) to do the following:

(1) to send to the Registrar of Companies and to all creditors (where he knows their addresses) a statement of his proposals for achieving the purpose or purposes specified in the administration order[1];

(2) either to send a copy of the statement of proposals to all members of the company (where he knows their addresses) or publish a notice in the *Edinburgh Gazette* and in the newspaper in which his appointment was advertised stating an address to which members of the company should write for copies of the statement to be sent to them free of charge[2];

(3) to hold a meeting of the company's creditors to be summoned for the purpose on not less than 14 days' notice, and to lay before the meeting a copy of the statement of proposals[3]. The creditors may then approve the proposals at the meeting[4], or only with modifications[5], provided the administrator consents to the modifications. For the conduct of meetings, see Chapter 19.

The administrator has a duty after the meeting considers his proposals to report to the court[6]. If the meeting approves the administrator's proposals, the court has merely to note this fact unless a petition is presented by a creditor or member under section 27 of the Insolvency Act 1986 within 28 days of the approval, challenging the implementation of the proposals[7]. If the meeting does not approve the proposals, the court has to decide what has to be done. It may discharge the administration order or make any other order[8]. If the administrator wants to make substantial revisions to the proposals once they have been adopted, he must go through the same procedure again to obtain the approval of the meeting of creditors, except that he does not have to report the result of the meeting to the court. As in the case of challenges to the original proposals, an aggrieved creditor may petition against any revision[9]. If revisions to the proposals are not substantial, he does not have to make a reference to the court or creditors. This is not expressly stated in the statute, but is inferred by the authors. It would not make sense to have an express power to make substantial revisions but no power to make minor revisions. The legal argument in favour of a latitude would be that the proposals are the 'same' if there are only minor revisals. To avoid any doubt on this point the proposals should have a degree of flexibility written into them. However the administrator's proposals must match the original purposes which were

1 Insolvency Act 1986, s 23(1)(a).
2 Ibid, s 23(2), and Insolvency (Scotland) Rules 1986, r 2.8.
3 Insolvency Act 1986, s 23(1)(b).
4 Ibid, s 24(1).
5 Ibid, s 24(2).
6 Ibid, s 24(4).
7 Ibid, s 27(3).
8 Ibid, s 24(5).
9 Ibid, s 27(3).

expressed in his order of appointment. Proposals which are not within the terms of his remit could not be *intra vires* unless the court first effected a variation of the express terms of his appointment[1]. However it has been held in England that, where the proposals which have been approved by the creditors have become impracticable by for example there not being time to obtain authorisation of revised proposals from creditors, the court has jurisdiction to authorise administrators to enter into an alternative scheme[2].

### Variation or discharge of order

The administrator may apply to the court at any time for a discharge of the administration order or for it to be varied in order to incorporate an additional purpose[3]. He is under a duty to make an application to the court if it appears to him that the purpose or each of the purposes specified in the administration order either has been achieved, or is incapable of achievement[4]. Similarly, he must make an application if a meeting summoned for the purpose requires him to make the application[5]. The court may discharge or vary the administration order or make such other order as it thinks fit[6]. In *Re Charnley Davies Business Services Ltd*[7], the High Court in England exercised its discretion to discharge a series of administration orders although the administrator had not submitted reports to the creditors under section 23 of the Insolvency Act 1986, and appointed the administrator as liquidator in the case.

The court has no jurisdiction under these provisions to make a winding-up order, since that can be effected only by a petition under section 124 of the Insolvency Act 1986[8].

### Remuneration of the administrator

The administrator's remuneration is to be determined from time to time by the creditors' committee or, if there is no creditors' committee by the court, and is to be paid out of the assets of the company as an 'expense of the administration'[9]. His remuneration and any expenses properly incurred by him are to be charged on and paid out of any property of the company which is in his custody or under his control at that time in priority to any floating charge[10]. The basis for determining the amount of the remuneration payable to the administrator may be a commission calculated by reference to the value of the company's property with which he has to deal, but in any event there has to be taken into account the work which, having regard to that value, was reasonably undertaken by him and the extent of his responsibilities in administering the company's assets[11]. The provisions which relate to the

---

1 *Re St Ives Windings* [1987] 3 BCC 634; *Re Sheridan Securities Ltd* [1988] 4 BCC 200.
2 *Re Smallman Construction Ltd* [1989] BCLC 420. See also *Re F M S Financial Management Services Ltd* [1989] 5 BCC 191.
3 Insolvency Act 1986, s 18(1).
4 Ibid, s 18(2)(a).
5 Ibid, s 18(2)(b).
6 Ibid, s 18(3).
7 [1987] 3 BCC 408.
8 *Re Brooke Marine Limited, Re Brooke Yachts Ltd* [1988] BCLC 546.
9 Insolvency (Scotland) Rules 1986, r 2.16.
10 Insolvency Act 1986, s 19(4).
11 Insolvency (Scotland) Rules 1986, r 2.16(2).

determination of the remuneration of an administrator are those which apply to a liquidator and a trustee in bankruptcy[1]. In terms of these, if the administrator seeks remuneration higher than that determined by the creditors' committee he may seek approval for higher remuneration in the first place by resolution of the creditors, and thereafter by application to the court. In contrast to a liquidation, there is no right for creditors representing at least 25 per cent of the creditors by value to apply to the court for reduction of remuneration fixed by the creditors' committee or by resolution of the creditors.

### Creditors' committee

At the meeting which the administrator is required to summon under section 23 of the Insolvency Act 1986 to consider his proposals, the creditors may establish a 'creditors' committee'[2]. If a creditors' committee is established, it may at any time require the administrator to attend before it and furnish it with any information relating to the carrying out by him of his functions as it may reasonably require[3].

The creditors' committee must consist of at least three and not more than five creditors of the company who are elected at the meeting[4]. Any creditor of the company who has lodged a claim is eligible to be a member of the committee so long as his claim has not been rejected for the purpose of his entitlement to vote[5]. A corporate body or a partnership may be a member of the committee. A representative of a corporation must produce to the chairman of the meeting a copy of the resolution from which he derives authority, which must be executed in accordance with the provisions of section 36B(3) of the Companies Act 1985, i e a document subscribed by two persons authorised by the company to subscribe or subscribed by two directors or a director and secretary without witnesses, or (which would be the most obvious way to do it) certified by the secretary or a director of the corporation to be a true copy[6]. The provisions in relation to meetings are to be found in chapter 19. The committee is given the specific power on a vacancy occurring in the office of administrator to apply to the court to fill the vacancy[7]. The committee has no power to convene meetings of creditors and the administrator is not required to summon a meeting if requested by the committee[8]. However, on their advice this would appear the proper thing to do.

### Safeguards for creditors and members

In addition to his obligation to summon meetings to approve his proposals[9] and substantial revisions[10], the administrator is obliged to summon a meeting

1 Insolvency (Scotland) Rules 1986 rr 2.16, 4.32, 4.33, 4.35 and the Bankruptcy (Scotland) Act 1985, s 53.
2 Insolvency Act 1986, s 26.
3 Ibid, s 26(2).
4 Insolvency (Scotland) Rules 1986 r 3.4(1) as applied to administrations.
5 Ibid, r 3.4(2).
6 Ibid, r 3.4(3).
7 Insolvency Act 1986, s 13(3).
8 Ibid, s 26.
9 Ibid, ss 23 and 24.
10 Ibid, s 25.

of the creditors if requested by one-tenth in value of the company's creditors[1], or if directed to do so by the court[1]. There is no obligation to call a meeting of the members unless required to do so by the court[2].

In addition to these safeguards, an aggrieved creditor may (1) apply for the administrator's removal under section 19(1) of the Insolvency Act 1986; (2) petition for a winding-up order with the leave of the court; or (3) petition under section 27 of the Insolvency Act 1986 on the grounds that his interests are being 'unfairly prejudiced'. The first two remedies are likely to be infrequent. Section 19(1) does not lay down the ground on which an administrator may be removed from office. Section 19(2) of the Insolvency Act 1986 makes it compulsory for an administrator to vacate office if he ceases to be qualified as an 'insolvency practitioner'. In addition, rule 2.18(1) of the Insolvency (Scotland) Rules 1986 states that: 'the administrator may give notice of his resignation on grounds of ill health or because – (a) he intends ceasing to be in practice as an insolvency practitioner, or (b) there is some conflict of interest or change of personal circumstances, which precludes or makes impracticable the further discharge by him of the duties of administrator'.

It is suggested that the reasons in rule 2.18(1)(b) above would be the type of grounds on which a creditor could move the court to remove an administrator. It is very unlikely that a creditor would be given leave to petition for a winding-up order if an administration order is in force. The purpose of an administration order is to be an alternative to winding up or to be an ordered stage prior to winding up. Although the court might grant a winding-up order to a member under section 122(1)(g) of the Insolvency Act 1986 on the grounds that it was just and equitable to wind the company up, there would appear to be no reason why a winding-up order should be granted to a creditor. The main safeguard of a member or creditor is to apply to the court under section 27 for an order on the ground: (a) that the company's affairs, business and property are being or have been managed by the administrator in a manner which is, or was, unfairly prejudicial to the interests of its creditors or members generally or of some part of its creditors or members (including at least himself); or (b) that any actual or proposed act or omission of the administrator is or would be so prejudicial. The concept of unfair prejudice is taken from sections 459 to 461 of the Companies Act 1985 (for a discussion of the concept see chapter 6).

After the hearing of the petition, the court may make such order as it thinks fit for giving relief in respect of the matters complained of, or adjourn the hearing or make an interim order or any order it thinks fit. That would include: (a) regulating the future management by the administrator of the company's affairs, business and property; (b) requiring the administrator to refrain from doing or continuing an act complained of by the petitioners or to do an act which the petitioner has complained he has omitted to do; (c) requiring the summoning of a meeting of creditors or members for the purpose of considering such matters as the court might direct; (d) discharge the administration order or making such consequential provisions as the court thinks fit[3].

As in the case of voluntary arrangements generally (see chapter 6), a

---

1 Insolvency Act 1986, s 17(3).
2 Ibid, s 27(4)(c).
3 Ibid, s 27(4).

challenge to the administrator's actings under section 27 of the Insolvency Act 1986 cannot be used to upset a voluntary arrangement if 28 days have elapsed from the approval of the voluntary arrangement[1].

1 Insolvency Act 1986, s 27(3).

Chapter 5

# Receivership

## Introduction

The book *The Law and Practice of Receivership in Scotland* by Greene and Fletcher, the second edition of which was published in June 1992, gives a valuable account of the law relating to receivership in Scotland. The authors in this chapter accordingly give a description and analysis of the law of receivership in Scotland, but do not duplicate the practical aspects of receivership already well covered in the book referred to above. The authors also try to highlight differences between receivership and other legal régimes on insolvency so that receivership can be seen in the general context of insolvency.

This chapter is divided into three parts as follows:

Part I covers the general nature of floating charges, the legal effects of the crystallisation of floating charges, and receivership;

Part II covers the appointment of receivers, joint receivers, the resignation of receivers, the removal of receivers, and the remuneration of receivers; and

Part III covers the duties and powers of receivers.

The changes brought in by the reforms in the law apply only to receivers appointed after 29 December 1986.[1]

## I. NATURE OF FLOATING CHARGE AND EFFECT OF CRYSTALLISATION OF FLOATING CHARGE AND RECEIVERSHIP

### Basis of appointment of receivers

Floating charges are legal instruments which give the holder of the floating charge a security or charge over the assets of a company to the extent described in the charge. In terms of section 51(1) of the Insolvency Act 1986 the holder of a floating charge over all or any part of the property (including uncalled capital) may appoint a receiver under certain defined circumstances. Where the floating charge covers the whole (or substantially the whole) of the company's property, the receiver so appointed is known as an 'administrative receiver'.[2] Where the floating charge does not cover the whole (or substantially the whole) of the company's property, then the receiver is known merely

---

1 Insolvency Act 1986, Sch 11, para 3(1).
2 Ibid, s 251.

as a 'receiver'.[1] A receiver in Scotland may only be appointed by the holder of a 'floating' charge[2]. The floating charge may be created by any incorporated company which the Court of Session has jurisdiction to wind up[3]. Effect will accordingly be given to floating charges by companies which have been incorporated by a private Act of Parliament or by a Royal Charter, or under predecessor legislation to the Companies Act. Also charges granted by companies incorporated in other parts of Great Britain and by foreign companies are given effect to. The recognition in Scotland of a floating charge by a foreign company is not dependent on either the company itself or the charge in question being registrable in Scotland under sections 424 or 691 of the Companies Act. It is necessary only that the company is 'incorporated', i e that it has a separate status as a legal person in its local legal system and that the charge is seen to be of the nature of a 'floating charge'.

Although only holders of 'floating' charges may appoint receivers, an understanding of charges or securities generally is necessary in order to appreciate the legal rights of the holder of the floating charge on the crystallisation of the floating charge by the appointment of a receiver or winding up.

### Fixed and floating charges

Important legal consequences arise from the difference between 'fixed' and 'floating' charges. A fixed security is a security over land and any other type of property of the company which will be effective on the winding up of the company[4]. The statutory definition follows the old legal maxim that bankruptcy is the test of all legal rights. A fixed security therefore gives the holder of the fixed security the effective and almost unqualified right in competition with any other creditors to have the secured assets realised for the benefit of the holder of the security. In contrast where there is a floating charge, although the security has legally the same effect in relation to the assets secured 'as if it were' a fixed security[5], this is subject to a major qualification. Before the security holder is entitled to the proceeds of the sale of an asset secured by a floating charge, the rights of any person who holds a fixed security over the property must be satisfied. Secondly before the holder of the floating charge is entitled to the proceeds of any sale of assets secured by a floating charge, preferential creditors must be paid[6]. Preferential debts are a category of debts as defined by section 386 of and Schedule 6 to the Insolvency Act 1986. They form quite an extensive category of debts (see pages 297–301) and the satisfaction of these debts may not leave any proceeds for the holder of the floating charge.

A second major difference between a fixed charge and a floating charge is that a fixed charge is specific to a particular asset, whereas a floating charge is not specific. In *Re Yorkshire Woolcombers Association*[7], Vaughan-Williams LJ explained the nature of a fixed security:

1 Insolvency Act 1986, s 251.
2 Ibid, s 51(1).
3 Companies Act 1985, s 462(2).
4 Insolvency Act 1986, s 70(1).
5 Companies Act 1985, s 463(2).
6 Insolvency Act 1986, s 59(1).
7 [1903] 2 Ch 284 at 294.

'I do not think that for a "specific security" you need have a security of a subject-matter which is then in existence. I mean by "then" at the time of the execution of the security; but what you do require to make a specific security is that the security whenever it has come into existence, and has been identified or appropriated as a security, shall never thereafter at the wish of the mortgagor cease to be a security. If at the wish of the mortgagor he can dispose of it and prevent it being any longer a security, although something else may be substituted more or less for it, that is not a "specific" security.'

In contrast, a floating charge is not immediately effective or enforceable. Rather it 'floats' over the company's assets, entitling the company to deal with the property in the ordinary course of business. When the floating charge becomes effective, it is said to 'crystallise', which occurs on the winding up of the company or on the appointment of a receiver[1]. It then attaches the property of the company as if it were a fixed security. What assets are then secured depends on the terms of the floating charge[2]. Where the floating charge stipulates that the assets of the company, present and future, are covered by the charge, the charge attaches assets re-acquired after the receiver's appointment, and indeed any property which comes into the company's hands[3].

In the *Yorkshire Woolcombers* case[4], Romer LJ set out three characteristics of a floating charge:

(1)  a charge on a class of assets of a company present and future;
(2)  that class is one which in the ordinary course of business of the company would be changing from time to time; and
(3)  it is contemplated that until some future step is taken by the chargee the company may carry on in its ordinary course of business in respect of the charged assets.

There is now a further qualification to the rights of the holder of a floating charge. An administrator may be appointed when a receiver has been appointed if the receiver is not an 'administrative receiver' or if the 'administrative receiver' has consented to the appointment of an administrator[5]. If an administration order is made, the administrator may require the receiver to vacate office[6], and an administrative receiver must vacate office[7]. Although, during the period in which the administration order is in force, the floating charge is still crystallised and secures the assets,[8], the administrator is allowed to dispose of or deal in the property attached as if the floating charge had not crystallised[9]. This is not the position with fixed securities[10].

The wording of the statute does not limit the appointment of a receiver to floating charges created after the introduction of receivers to Scotland by the Companies (Floating Charges and Receivers) (Scotland Act) 1972. It would

1 Companies Act 1985, s 463(1); Insolvency Act 1986, s 53(7).
2 Companies Act 1985, s 462(1).
3 *Ross v Taylor* 1985 SLT 387.
4 [1903] 2 Ch 284 at 295.
5 Insolvency Act 1986, s 9(3).
6 Ibid, s 11(2).
7 Ibid, s 11(1)(b).
8 Ibid, s 62(6).
9 Ibid, s 15(1).
10 Ibid, s 15(2).

also appear possible to limit the circumstances in which a receiver could be appointed[1]. There would seem no reason in principle why the holder of a floating charge could not have all his rights to appoint a receiver limited by contract, so that the floating charge would crystallise only in the event of a winding up.

**Types of fixed security**

In general, all assets of a company may be made subject to a fixed security in Scotland. In the case of certain assets, however, any security is void unless it is registered by the company. The following fixed securities must be registered:

(1) a charge on land or any interest in land;
(2) a security over the uncalled share capital of a company;
(3) a security over incorporeal (non-physical) moveable property of any of the following categories:
    (a) the book debts of a company;
    (b) calls made but not paid;
    (c) goodwill;
    (d) a patent or a licence under a patent;
    (e) a trademark;
    (f) a copyright or a licence under a copyright; and
(4) a security over a ship or aircraft or any share in a ship[2].

In relation to rights (of which the most valuable in relation to a company are usually receivables or book debts), the mechanism for creating a fixed security is the assignation of the right to the security holder, and, in the case of receivables, intimation to the debtor. This is important in relation to insolvency because the courts have interpreted the crystallisation of the floating charge having effect as if the charge were a fixed charge[3] literally to mean that the holder of the floating charge was to be in the same position as he would have been had he set up the mechanics of a normal fixed charge[4]. The fact that the crystallisation of a floating charge effectively assigns receivables to the holder of the floating charge, is important in relation to set-off (see chapter 15).

**Registration of floating charges/obligations securable**

As in the case of the fixed charges referred to above, a floating charge must be registered in Scotland if it is to have the effect of securing assets[5]. The floating charge may be to secure a debt (ie in an instrument known as a 'debenture'). However, it may also be used to secure other obligations including a guarantee[6]. The attachment of a floating charge on the appointment of a receiver, or

---

1 See the Insolvency Act 1986, s 52(1) which speaks of a receiver being able to be appointed 'in so far as not otherwise provided for by the instrument on the occurrence of any of the following events . . .'
2 Companies Act 1985, s 410(4); see also Companies Act 1989, s 93.
3 Ibid, s 463(1); Insolvency Act 1986, s 53(7).
4 *Forth v Clyde Construction Ltd v Trinity Timber & Plywood Ltd* 1984 SLT 94.
5 Companies Act 1985, s 410(4)(e).
6 Ibid, s 462(1).

in the case of winding up, gives security not only for the principal of the debt or obligation in question but also for both pre- and post- receivership interest until payment of the sum due under the charge[1].

## Crystallisation of floating charges/assets charged

When a floating charge crystallises and attaches on the company going into liquidation, the property which is attached is 'the property then comprised in the company's property and undertaking or, as the case may be, in part of that property and undertaking'[2]. The wording of sections 53(7) and 54(6) of the Insolvency Act 1986 is slightly different. In terms of these sections the property attached is 'the property then subject to the charge'. It is not clear that the different wording has any legal import.

## Acquirenda

Where a floating charge is expressed to relate to the whole assets of the company, present and future, *acquirenda*[3] would appear to be charged on the crystallisation of the floating charge.

In the case of *Ross v Taylor*[4] the Inner House considered the effect of a floating charge which was expressed to relate to the whole assets of a company, present and future, while the instrument was in force. According to Lord President Emslie, the true question was not 'what was the property comprised in the company's property and undertaking on the date of the receiver's appointment?' Rather the question was what property was subject to the charge. Upon a proper construction of the instrument the charge was over the whole of the property of the company existing and from time to time emerging and it followed that under the provisions of that floating charge goods which were reacquired after the receiver's appointment fell under the attachment of the charge. Any property which came into the company's hands after the appointment of the receiver would be attached and available, if need be, for realisation by the receiver. A second question put to the court in *Ross v Taylor*[4] was, if goods did not form part of a company's assets at the date of the appointment of a receiver, on the liquidation of the company would the floating charge re-crystallise to the effect that any acquirenda since the date of the receiver's appointment would fall within the assets covered by the floating charge for distribution purposes in a liquidation? The court answered the question in the affirmative on the grounds that the floating charge, on the commencement of a winding up, attached to the property then comprised in the company's property and undertaking and had effect as if it were a fixed security over the property. The reason for the court arriving at a 'double crystallisation' solution was their strict reading of the wording of section 1(2) of the Companies (Floating Charges and Receivers) (Scotland) Act 1972 which provided that a floating charge 'shall, on the commencement of the winding-up . . . attach to the property then comprised in the company's property and undertaking etc.' On consolidation the terminology was altered and section 463(1) of the Companies Act provided that:

1 Companies Act 1985, s 463(4); *National Commercial Bank of Scotland Ltd v Liquidators of Telford Grier Mackay & Co* 1969 SC 181.
2 Companies Act 1985, s 463(1).
3 *Acquirenda* is a Scots legal dog Latin term meaning assets acquired subsequently.
4 1985 SLT 387.

'On the commencement of the winding-up of a company, a floating charge created by the company attaches to the property then comprised in the company's property and undertaking, etc'.

This wording has been further altered by section 140(1) of the Companies Act 1989 which substitutes for 'on the commencement of the winding-up of a company' the words 'where a company goes into liquidation within the meaning of section 247(2) of the Insolvency Act 1986'. Sections 53(7) and 54(6) of the Insolvency Act 1986 provide that on the appointment of a receiver the charge 'attaches to the property then subject to the charge'.

It is not possible to say whether in future a court, on the new wording, would stick to the concept of 'double attachment'. What is clear however is that future assets of the company are attached.

## Assets of the company

### Consigned funds

It is not clear always what are assets of the company for the purposes of being covered by a Scottish charge. Where funds have been consigned to court to await the result of pending litigation it has been held in Scotland that the funds are not 'property' of a company and hence are not attached by a floating charge[1].

### Trust assets

Where property is held by the company subject to a valid trust in favour of a third party, that property is not attached by the floating charge on the appointment of a receiver[2].

### Unfair preferences and gratuitous alienations

It has been held in England in *Re Yagerphone Ltd*[3] that money recovered from a creditor on the grounds that it had been paid out as a fraudulent preference was not subject to a floating charge over the company's assets as the money at the time that the charge crystallised did not constitute property of the company nor a 'contingent interest'. Following on that reasoning the court also was of the opinion that the right to recover money from a creditor who had been fraudulently preferred was conferred for the purpose of benefiting the general body of creditors and therefore should form part of the general assets of the company for distribution to the general creditors. The Inner House in *Ross v Taylor*[4] said that the English cases of *Re Yagerphone Ltd*[5] and *N W Robbie & Co v Witney Warehouse Co Ltd*[6], did not afford any reliable assistance, but turned upon their own facts and the particular terms of the relevant debentures. It is thought that the reasoning in *Re Yagerphone Ltd* is

---

1 *Hawking v Hafton House Ltd* 1990 SLT 496.
2 *Tay Valley Joinery Ltd v Cf Financial Services Ltd* 1987 SLT 207. (See Chapter 9).
3 [1935] Ch 392.
4 1985 SLT 387.
5 [1935] Ch 392.
6 [1963] 3 All ER 613.

open to challenge. It may be argued, and is thought by the authors, that the right to recover assets paid out as a preference or as a gratuitous alienation is an asset of the company and the fact that the action is one vested *inter alia* in the liquidator[1] is merely one machinery designed to underpin the *pari passu* principle of insolvency law[2]. The reduction of voidable transactions in Scotland is not entirely without retrospective effect, and reduction may have the effect of bringing the relevant asset within the 'assets of the company'[3].

*Misfeasance proceedings*

It is thought that sums recovered under sections 212 of the Insolvency Act 1986 are in a different category from fraudulent preferences and must be covered by an appropriately drafted floating charge[4]. The misfeasance provisions create no new liabilities but merely establish a summary procedure for compelling directors to account for any breach of duty. The right being vindicated is a right which inheres in the company at the time the directors breach their duty. The proceedings are procedural[5].

*Wrongful trading*

The position of sums recovered under the 'wrongful trading' provisions of section 214 of the Insolvency Act 1986, has not yet been decided in Scotland. In England in *Re Produce Marketing Consortium (No 2) Ltd*[6] Knox J considered that factors relevant to the determination of the amount that directors should contribute in a section 214 case were (1) that the warning of the auditors of the dangers of continuing to trade was ignored, and (2) the fact that any contribution would go in the first place to satisfy the claims of the bank as a secured creditor. An implicit assumption of Knox J's decision was that the bank's charge would attach to the contribution the directors were being ordered to make under section 214(1) of the Insolvency Act 1986. The matter does not seem to have been argued. Against the decision of Knox J it may be argued that a section 214 claim is a right vested in the liquidator, and has not, like a section 212 claim, ever inhered in the company. Claims under section 214 arise only when the company goes into liquidation. It is thought that sums recovered under section 214 would go into the general pool of assets available to meet the claims of all creditors and not merely to satisfy the claims of victims of the wrongful trading. If it were only the victims of wrongful trading who were to be benefited by sums recovered under section 214, there would be an incentive on the directors of the company to pay off these creditors in preference to other creditors and thus reduce the extent of their potential liability.

1 See *Willmott v London Celluloid Co* (1886) 31 Ch D 425; affd (1886) 34 Ch D 147.
2 D P Sellar, 1983 SLT 253; see also for an excellent discussion *Oxford Journal of Legal Studies*, vol 10, No 2.
3 In the case of *N A Kratzmann Pty Ltd (No 2) v Tucker* (1970–71) 123 CLR 295, 301–2, the Australian courts were prepared to recognise an exception to the *Yagerphone* rule where specific property which had been the subject of a fraudulent preference is recovered and it was covered by the terms of the charge.
4 *Re Asiatic Electric Co Pty Ltd* (1970) 92 WN (NSW) 361; *Re William C Leitch Bros Ltd* [1932] 2 Ch 71.
5 *Re B Johnson & Co (Builders) Ltd* [1955] Ch 634.
6 [1989] BCLC 520.

*Fraudulent trading*

The arguments relating to an action under section 214, it is thought would also apply to assets under section 213, namely the fraudulent trading provisions. It is a statutory remedy, like a section 214 remedy, and vests only in the liquidator: whereas an action under the misfeasance provisions may be brought by any creditor including the debenture holder; as can an action, both in terms of the statute and at common law, under the statutory and common law gratuitous alienation and unfair preference law.

*Extortionate credit transactions*

Slightly more problematical is the position of sums recovered under the 'extortionate credit transactions' provisions of section 244 of the Insolvency Act 1986. Section 244(2) provides:

'The court may, on the application of the office holder, make an order with respect to the transaction if the transaction is or was extortionate and was entered into in the period of three years ending with the day in which the administration order was made or (as the case may be) the company went into liquidation.'

Section 244(4) provides for the remedy of reduction. This type of order may therefore be obtained by a receiver when the company is in liquidation or by an administrator when the company is in administration. It is thought that sums recovered under the extortionate credit transaction provisions of section 244 would be treated in the same way as sums recovered under the gratuitous alienations and unfair preferences provisions of sections 242 and 243. It is thought that this certainly would be the case if there was an action of reduction and a contract or disposition was reduced. There is very little reason why section 244 was included in the Insolvency Act 1986. It has a good consumer ring about it but it is difficult to see why any action brought under section 244 could not also in essence be brought under statute and at common law as a gratuitous alienation.

It is to be regretted that the insolvency legislation did not deal explicitly with the question in England and Scotland as to how recoveries under sections 212 to 214 and 238 to 244 of the Insolvency Act 1986 should be treated where there is a charge.

## Remedies in England and Scotland

In relation to sections 238 and 242 of the Insolvency Act 1986 which deal with 'transactions at an undervalue' in England and Wales and 'gratuitous alienations' in Scotland, and sections 239 and 243 which deal with 'preferences' in England and Wales and 'unfair preferences' in Scotland, there is a further problem in relation to the types of remedy available. Briefly in terms of section 238(3) and 239(3) of the Insolvency Act 1986 the court in England and Wales will make an order restoring the position to what it would have been had there not been a challengeable transaction. This means that if heritage was bought at an undervalue, the recipient of the alienation is ordered to make up the difference. In Scotland in contrast, in such a situation the transaction has to be reduced, the heritage reverts to the company and the recipient only ranks for the non-gratuitous element; and accordingly invariably gets nothing[1]. Because an action brought under the English sections is likely to lead to a financial order, whereas an order under the Scottish sections could involve reduction of a disposition, it is less likely that the decision in *Yagerphone*[2], which was based on a financial order, will be challenged because it would need to go to the Court of Appeal in England. The difference of procedure in relation to remedies, let alone the uncertainty in relation to the scope of the charge, causes problems in relation to a Scottish charge over English property and an English charge over Scottish property. In terms of section 72(1) of the Insolvency Act 1986:

'(1) A receiver appointed under the law of either part of Great Britain in respect of the whole or any part of any property or undertaking of a company and in consequence of the company having created a charge which, as created, was a floating charge may exercise his powers in the other part of Great Britain so far as their exercise is not inconsistent with the law applicable there.'[3]

Section 426 of the Insolvency Act 1986 provides for cross-border co-operation *inter alia* between Scotland and England and Wales. Section 426(5) provides:

'(5) For the purposes of sub-section (4) a request made to a court in any part of the United Kingdom by a court in any other part of the United Kingdom or in a relevant country or territory is authority for the court to which the request is made to apply, in relation to any matters specified in the request, the insolvency law which is applicable by either court in relation to comparable matters falling within its jurisdiction.
    In exercising its discretion under this subsection, a court shall have regard in particular to the rules of private international law.'

It is thought that if the Scottish and English courts were to adopt different positions as to whether assets recovered under sections 213, 214, 238–244 came within the ambit of a floating charge, the courts in the different jurisdictions would attempt to enforce the foreign courts' ruling in the local jurisdiction. It is difficult to see that these differences in approach would amount to matters of 'public policy'[4]. A difficulty arises however given the terms of section 426(3) and 426(6) of the Insolvency Act 1986. They provide:

'(3) The Secretary of State, with the concurrence in relation to property situated in England and Wales of the Lord Chancellor, may by order make provision for securing that a trustee or assignee under the insolvency law of any part of the United Kingdom has, with such modifications as may be specified in the order, the same rights in relation to any property situated in another part of the United Kingdom as he would have in the corresponding circumstances if he were a trustee or assignee under the insolvency law of that other part . . .'
'(6) Where a person who is a trustee or assignee under the insolvency law of any part of the United Kingdom claims property situated in any other part of the United Kingdom (whether by virtue of an order under subsection (3) or otherwise), the submission of that claim to the court exercising jurisdiction in relation to insolvency law in that other part

---

1 Insolvency Act 1986, ss 242(4), 243(5) and *Short's (Alexander) Trustee v Chung* 1991 SCLR 269.
2 *Re Yagerphone Ltd* [1935] Ch 392.
3 See *Norfolk House plc (in receivership) v Repsol Petroleum* 1992 SLT 235, for working of provision effectively of English charge covering Scottish heritable property, despite floating charge converted to a fixed charge in England.
4 See Chapter 20; *Barclay's Bank plc v Homan* (1992) Independent, 1 September.

shall be treated in the same manner as a request made by a court for the purpose of subsection (4).'

The clear intention of these subsections is to enable courts in different parts of the United Kingdom to enforce their property claims in other parts. This would not cause problems with an English financial order in Scotland arising out of sections 238 and 239 of the Insolvency Act 1986 being enforced in Scotland, but it would cause problems if a request went from a Scottish court to the English court to provide a result equivalent to that achieved by reduction under sections 242(3) and 243(5) of the Insolvency Act 1986 in Scotland. It is thought by the authors that the legislature should look at the harsh working of the reduction provisions in sections 242 and 243 of the Insolvency Act 1986. The fact that they are so different to the procedure in England does not seem to have been commented on at the time of their enactment. The English provisions follow the recommendations in the Cork Report[1].

### Date of commencement of receivership

Receivership commences and the floating charge crystallises on the appointment of a receiver[2]. Receivership is deemed to commence on the day on which, and at the time at which, the instrument of the receiver's appointment is delivered to the receiver[3]. It must be accepted by the receiver by the end of the first business day following that on which the instrument of appointment is received[4].

### Effect of receivership on carrying on of the business

Unlike a winding up, which can be carried on only for the purpose of the beneficial winding up of the company, there is no restriction on the right of the company to carry on business on the appointment of a receiver. Indeed he is given the explicit power 'to carry on the business of the company or any part of it' covered by the charge[5].

Although a receiver is the appointee of the holder of a security, the security holder may not wish to appoint the receiver merely for the purpose of immediately realising assets to honour the debt or other obligation. There are at least three possible purposes in appointing a receiver:

(1)   the receiver may be appointed to act as 'liquidator' and liquidate the assets of the company covered by the floating charge in order immediately to honour the obligation contained in the instrument of the floating charge;
(2)   the receiver may be appointed to carry on the business with a view to selling off parts of the business at a better price than if the business were liquidated straight away (in this way the holder of the floating charge

---

1 Cmnd 8558, Ch 28.
2 Insolvency Act 1986, s 53(7).
3 Ibid, s 53(6)(b).
4 Ibid, s 53(6)(a).
5 Ibid, s 42(1) and Sch 2, para 14.

would at the end of the day have a more valuable realisable asset covered by his security than if the company were liquidated straight away); and
(3)   The receiver may be appointed in order to try to 'turn round' an ailing business.

The third purpose is now subject to two areas of risk. First, a 'company doctor' may now be appointed as an administrative receiver only if he is a 'qualified insolvency practitioner'[1]. The receiver does not have the option, as a liquidator does, to ask the court to appoint a special manager if it appears to him that the nature of the business or property of the company requires the appointment of another person to manage the company's business or property[2]. Secondly, a receiver is personally liable for all the debts of the company incurred after his appointment unless he specifically excludes liability[3]. (Until the receiver is appointed, if the directors of a company took its directions from the holder of a floating charge (often a bank), the holder of the floating charge might be liable for 'wrongful trading' in terms of section 214 of the Insolvency Act 1986, the bank being liable as a 'shadow' director'. This provision does not apply, however, to a receiver or to the holder of the floating charge who directs a receiver[4].

### Effect of receivership on directors' powers

The directors of a company remain in office on receivership. Indeed the Insolvency Act 1986 refers to the current directors of a company being required to make a statement of affairs to the receiver[5]. The extent of the directors' remaining power depends on the scope of the floating charge. If the floating charge covers all the assets and undertaking of the company, present and future, the powers of the directors will be very limited. Where, however, the floating charge only covers a part of the company, the directors may run the rest of the company.

When looking to what powers the directors have, a good test of the extent of the directors' powers is to inquire whether the powers which the board are said to have lost are ones which can be said to have been assumed by the receiver[6]. The general rule is that the appointment of a receiver: 'entirely supersedes the company in the conduct of its business, deprives it of all power to enter into contracts in relation to that business, or to sell, pledge or otherwise dispose of the property put into the possession, or under the control of the receiver and manager. Its powers in these respects are entirely in abeyance'[7]. The board has during the currency of the receivership no powers over assets in the possession or control of the receiver[8]. This however does not preclude the directors from raising actions in connection with the charged

---

1 Ibid, ss 388 and 390.
2 Ibid, s 177(1) and (2).
3 Ibid, s 57(2).
4 'A shadow director' means a person in accordance with whose directions or instructions the directors of the company are accustomed to act: Companies Act 1985, s 741(2).
5 Insolvency Act 1986, s 66(3)(a).
6 *Re Union Accident Insurance Co Ltd* [1972] 1 All ER 1105 at 1113; although that case concerned directors' residuary powers on liquidation, the test, it is suggested, is also a good test on receivership.
7 *Moss Steamship Co v Whinney* [1912] AC 254 at 263, per Lord Atkinson.
8 *Gomba Holdings UK Ltd v Homan; Gomba Holdings UK Ltd v Johnson Matthey Bankers Ltd* [1986] BCLC 331 at 336.

property[1]. In the case of *Newhart Developments Ltd v Co-operative Commercial Bank Ltd*[2], directors were held to have residual powers to bring proceedings against a debenture holder who had appointed the receiver. In that case however, the Court of Appeal had been impressed by two matters. First, it was impressed by the fact that the company had been indemnified by outside sources against all liability not only for its own costs but also for costs which the company might be ordered to pay to the other party. Therefore the bringing of proceedings by the directors in the company's name could not in any circumstances prejudice the property over which the receiver had a charge. The court was also impressed by the fact that the receiver was in an invidious position in deciding whether or not to take proceedings by reason of the fact that he was being invited to sue those who had appointed him. Doubt has been recently thrown on that decision by Sir Nicholas Browne-Wilkinson V-C, in *Tudor Grange Holdings Ltd v Citibank N A*[3] where he stated:

'I have substantial doubts whether the *Newhart* case was correctly decided . . . The decision seems to ignore the difficulty which arises if two different sets of people, the directors and the receivers, who may have widely differing views and interests, both have power to bring proceedings on the same cause of action. . . . Further, the Court of Appeal in the *Newhart* case does not seem to have had its attention drawn to the fact that the embarrassment of the receiver in deciding whether or not to sue can be met by an application to the court for directions as to what course should be taken, an application now envisaged in s 35 of the Insolvency Act 1986.'

Because during receivership, the conduct of the business of the company is taken out of the hands of the directors, the directors' residual powers do not create any duty upon their part to the creditors such as to advise them that their interests could be jeopardised unless they petitioned for the winding-up of the company[4].

A company in receivership may sue a receiver who acts improperly and in breach of his duties to the company. In *Watts v Midland Bank plc*[5] Gibson J stated:

'It is common ground between the parties, and I suggest, common sense, that there must be some redress obtainable by a company in receivership against a receiver who acts improperly and in breach of his duties to the company to the detriment of the company. It is also common ground that the liquidator of a company in receivership can sue the receiver. Why should a company in receivership have to go into liquidation before the receiver could be sued by the company? There is no doubt that a mortgagor can sue a mortgagee improperly exercising a power of sale. Why should not a mortgagor company in receivership sue the receiver appointed by the mortgagee to realise the security so as to repay the mortgagee if the receiver acts improperly and to the detriment of the company?

---

1 *Shanks v Central Regional Council* 1987 SLT 410 per Lord Weir, disapproving of a judgment of Lord Grieve in *Imperial Hotel (Aberdeen) Ltd v Vaux Breweries Ltd* 1978 SC 86.
2 [1978] 2 All ER 896, [1978] QB 814.
3 [1991] BCLC 1009 at 1019.
4 *Re Joshua Shaw & Sons Ltd* [1989] BCLC 362; that case concerned a company which had been in receivership for nine years. The directors had submitted that the company was absolutely solvent. The receivers said that it was unlikely that there would be any money for unsecured creditors. However, after nine years of receivership, there was a surplus of £350,000 available for ordinary creditors. This the court ordered to be paid to the contributories through a voluntary winding-up on the basis that the creditors were time barred. Hoffmann J said that there may be a gap in the law in that the appointment of a receiver does not stop time running for the purposes of limitation.
5 [1986] BCLC 15 at 21.

Of course the court will not allow any interference by the company in receivership with the proper exercise by a receiver of a power of sale, but I can see no reason in principle why the court should not allow the company to sue the receiver in respect of an improper exercise of his powers.'

A decision of a receiver could be challenged on the grounds of bad faith or that it was a decision which no reasonable receiver could have made[1].

### Effect of receivership on contracts other than employment contracts

Unless receivership is an event of default written into a contract, contracts entered into by or on behalf of the company prior to the appointment of a receiver continue in force[2]. This includes contracts of employment. A receiver is not personally liable for contracts which are in force when he is appointed[3]. The receiver is personally liable on any contract entered into by him in the performance of his functions, unless he specifically excludes his personal liability in the contract[4]. The statutory provisions apply to both 'administrative' receivers and ordinary receivers[5].

A receiver becomes liable to pay rates in respect of the period of his occupancy[6].

### Contracts of employment

In this important area, the law has been radically changed by section 57(2) of the Insolvency Act 1986. That provision only covers receiverships commenced after 29 December 1986[7]. The former position was that where a receiver was appointed, and he 'adopted'[8] a contract, the employee had a claim against the company only for his accumulated entitlements and salary. The change in the law was prompted by the English case of *Nicol v Cutts*[9] in which a receiver three weeks after his appointment terminated an employee's contract of service on one month's notice and sold the business of the company as a going concern. The employee claimed from the receiver the amount of his salary in respect of the period after the date of the receiver's appointment. His claim for this sum against the company in its liquidation would have been worthless in view of the company's insolvency. It was argued for the employee 'that an employee, whose service contract is continued by the bank's receiver in order to assist in realising the company's assets to the best advantage should not, *qua* payment of his remuneration for the period of that continuation of his service contract, get nothing (save from the State's Redundancy Fund) and be postponed to the bank getting full payment.' The Court of Appeal were unable to find any legal basis for the employee's claim.

---

1 *Gomba v Holdings UK Ltd v Homan; Gomba Holdings UK Ltd v Johnson Matthews Bankers Ltd* [1986] BCLC 331 at 337.
2 Insolvency Act 1986, s 57(4).
3 Ibid, s 57(4).
4 Ibid, s 57(2).
5 Ibid, s 57(1).
6 *Taggs Island Casino Ltd v Richmond Upon Thames BC* [1967] RA 70; 14 RRC 119.
7 Insolvency Act 1986, Sch 11, para 3.
8 'Adopt' a pre-receivership contract means that he refrains from repudiation: *Re Diesel's and Components Pty Ltd* (1985) 9 ACLR 825 at 827, per McPherson J.
9 [1985] BCLC 322.

The new statutory provision tries to rectify the situation described above but in its turn raises two difficult legal questions:

(1) Can the receiver contract out of the term?
(2) Is the receiver liable for accumulated entitlements?

## (1) *Contracting out*

Section 57(2) of the Insolvency Act 1986 does not provide for the possibility of contracting out. It has been suggested that the mischief aimed at is only that receivers should not encourage expectations of payment and then disappoint, and that it would be easy for the section to be avoided by means of a dismissal and re-engagement by the company, and accordingly contracting out is the better view[1]. However, the section should be read as a whole. It states: 'A receiver (including a receiver whose powers are subsequently suspended under section 56) is personally liable on any contract entered into by him in the performance of his functions, except in so far as the contract otherwise provides, and on any contract of employment adopted by him in the carrying out of those functions.'

It is suggested that the contracting-out provision has been expressly applied only to the first type of contract and its omission with regard to contracts of employment in the same sentence must have significance. It is also consistent with the emphasis against contracting-out provisions in most of the employment protection legislation.

## (2) *Extent of receiver's liability on adoption of contract*

The question is whether the liability of the receiver on the adoption of the contract is the same as the liability of the company, or whether it is limited to the satisfaction of the rights enjoyed by the employee during the period of 'adoption'. The case of *Nicol v Cutts* was concerned with the wages of the employee while employed by the receiver. The new provision is clearly different. There is no new contract or transfer of contract. The receiver 'adopts' the contract on behalf of the company just as a liquidator does[2] and the employee is continuously employed. Hence the receiver must be liable for the continuous employment contract.

## (3) *Dismissal through receivership*

Although the appointment of a receiver does not *per se* act as constructive notice of dismissal, it could if the appointment was inconsistent with the terms of a particular contract of employment, such as a manager[3].

---

1 This is the view taken by Lightman and Moss in *The Law of Receivers of Companies*.
2 *Smith v Lord Advocate* 1978 SC 259 at 272.
3 *Re Mack Trucks (Britain) Ltd* [1987] 1 All ER 977 at 982.

# II. APPOINTMENT, REMOVAL AND RESIGNATION OF RECEIVERS

### Qualifications of receivers

*Appointment of receivers*

Only an individual is qualified to act as an 'administrative receiver'[1], and he must be qualified to act as an insolvency practitioner by virtue of being authorised by a recognised professional body, or by holding an authorisation from those bodies themselves or from the Secretary of State[2]. Disqualified directors, undischarged bankrupts and individuals who have been judicially assessed by reason of mental disorder incapable of managing and administering their own affairs are not eligible to be insolvency practitioners[3].

### Power of holder of floating charge and court to appoint a receiver

The receiver may be appointed by the holder of a floating charge over any part of the property of a company[4], or alternatively a receiver may be appointed by the court on the application of the holder of the floating charge[5]. The authors know of no case where the court has appointed a receiver. There is no power in Scotland as in England[6] for creditors to apply to the court to appoint a receiver in a winding up.

### Circumstances justifying appointment by the holder of a floating charge

Unless section 11(3)(b) of the Insolvency Act 1986 applies, preventing the appointment of an administrative receiver while an administration order is in force, a receiver may be appointed under the following circumstances:

(1)  On the occurrence of circumstances specified in the instrument creating the floating charge as entitling the holder of the floating charge to appoint a receiver, a receiver may be appointed by the holder of the floating charge[7].
(2)  On the occurrence of events laid down by statute, the holder of a floating charge, unless it provides otherwise, may appoint a receiver. The events laid down by statute are:
(a)  the expiry of a period of 21 days after the making of a demand for payment of the whole or any part of the principal sum secured by the charge, without payment having been made;
(b)  the expiry of a period of two months during the whole of which interest due and payable under the charge has been in arrears;
(c)  the making of an order or the passing of a resolution to wind up the company; and

---

1 Insolvency Act 1986, ss 388 and 390(1).
2 Ibid, ss 390, 391 and 392.
3 Ibid, s 390(4).
4 Ibid, s 51(1).
5 Ibid, s 51(2).
6 Ibid, s 32.
7 Ibid, s 52(1).

(d)    the appointment of a receiver by virtue of any other floating charge created by the company[1].

Provided no other receiver has been appointed, the court may appoint a receiver in the same circumstances provided it is satisfied that the position of the holder of the charge is likely to be prejudiced if no appointment of a receiver is made[2]. A debenture holder in exercising a contractual power to appoint a receiver is under no duty to be altruistic to the borrowing company when deciding whether to exercise that power. The only requirement is one of good faith[3].

### Payment on demand

There is a frequent provision in a floating charge that a receiver may be appointed on default by the company to pay on demand what is due. This causes difficulties, because on the one hand justice to the company suggests that the company should be given a reasonable time to pay, whereas on the other hand the lender may legitimately wish to take immediate action to avoid jeopardy to the assets of the company which are secured. 'Once a decision [has] been made by the Bank to call up its money, there must be a risk that delay of any length would enable assets secured by the debenture to disappear or to be seized by other creditors'[4]. Greene and Fletcher suggest that an 'on demand' facility would allow a period of 24 hours from the making of the demand for repayment[5]. However, in England it has been held that an 'on demand debenture' allowed the borrower merely sufficient time during banking hours to collect the money from its bank or some other 'convenient place' to make payment, and the company was not entitled to raise the money either from its bank or elsewhere[6], which was a case concerning the money markets. It is suggested that what the contracting parties have in contemplation is the key aspect. A loan to a crofter in Benbecula may envisage more time on an 'on demand' notice than one to a commodity dealer.

In the case of *Toynar Ltd v Whitbread & Co Ltd*[7] interim suspension of the appointment of receivers was applied for and interim interdict against their continuing to act in that capacity on the ground that the alleged arrears in interest relied on in appointing the receivers was not in fact owed. Although there was an argument that the arrears were not owed, the Inner House upheld the Lord Ordinary's rejection of the application on the ground that the Lord Ordinary had correctly applied the 'balance of convenience' test in

---

1 Insolvency Act 1986, s 52(1).
2 Ibid, s 52(2).
3 *Shamji v Johnson Matthey Bankers* [1991] BCLC 36.
4 *ANZ Banking Group (NZ) Ltd v Gibson* [1981] 2 NZLR 513 at 519 per Holland J.
5 *Greene and Fletcher*, para 1.31.
6 *Titford Property Co Ltd v Cannon Street Acceptances Ltd* (unreported), Goff J, 22 May 1975, referred to in *Williams & Glyns Bank Ltd v Barnes* [1981] Com LR 205 at 210. See also *Bank of Baroda v Penessar* [1987] Ch. 335, where it was held that because a debenture was a commercial matter, a short but adequate period limited to the implementation of the mechanics of payment was to be preferred to the test of a 'reasonable time depending on the circumstances of the case'. The precise form of demand envisaged by the charge must be adhered to: *Elwick Bay Shipping Co Ltd v Royal Bank of Scotland Ltd* 1982 SLT 62.
7 1988 SLT 433.

finding that the holders of the floating charge would be subject to greater prejudice than the petitioners if the interim relief were granted.

## Mode of appointment by holder of charge

The appointment of a receiver by the holder of a floating charge must be made by means of a validly executed instrument in writing, a copy of which must be delivered by or on behalf of the person making the appointment to the Registrar of Companies for registration within seven days of its execution and must be accompanied by a notice.[1]

In the case of a company the position was until recently unclear. In terms of section 53(3)(a) of the Insolvency Act 1986 the instrument of appointment of a receiver is validly executed, if it is executed in accordance with the provisions of section 36 of the Companies Act as if it were a contract. Section 130 of the Companies Act 1989 (which came into force on 31 July 1990[2]) replaced section 36 of the Companies Act 1985 with new sections 36–36B, with sections 36 and 36A applying to England and Wales and section 36B applying to Scotland. Section 36B was criticised after it became effective and was substituted by a new section 36B enacted by section 72(1) of the Law Reform (Miscellaneous Provisions) (Scotland) Act 1990, which became effective on 1 December 1990[3]. That Act is retrospective, as from 31 July 1990 and relates to the execution of any document including an instrument for the appointment of a receiver under the law of Scotland (whether by a Scottish company or otherwise)[4]. The practical effect is that an instrument of appointment of a receiver by a company which is dated on or after 31 July 1990 requires no greater formality than being executed by a single director, the secretary or a duly authorised person, in accordance with the revised section 36B(2). There is no requirement that it should be a probative document.

In terms of section 53(3)(b) of the Insolvency Act 1986[5] an instrument of appointment by any person other than a company had to be executed as an attested deed, which included the signature of two witnesses. The necessity for attestation ceased with the repeal of section 53(3) of the Insolvency Act 1986 on 1 December 1990, and for instruments executed on or after that date the signature by or on behalf of the charge-holder is therefore sufficient.

Although an unregistered floating charge is void, unless already presented for registration[6], it is not thought that mere failure to file the notice with the Registrar would invalidate the appointment of a receiver. Although there is a statutory duty to register the appointment, there is no provision deeming an unregistered appointment void.

1 Insolvency Act 1986, s 53(1).
2 Commencement (No 6) Order and Transitional and Savings Provisions Order 1990, SI 1990/1392.
3 Law Reform (Miscellaneous Provisions) (Scotland) Act 1990 Commencement (No 1) Order 1990, SI 1990/2328.
4 Companies Act 1985, s 36B(1) (substituted by the Law Reform (Miscellaneous Provisions) (Scotland) Act 1990.
5 Repealed.
6 Companies Act 1985, s 410(2); *N V Slavenburg's Bank v Intercontinental National Resources Ltd* [1980] 1 All ER 955.

## Joint receivers, etc

Joint receivers may be appointed[1]. The appointment of any joint receiver has no effect unless the appointment is accepted by all of them[2]. Their appointment as joint receivers is deemed to be made on the day on, and at the time at which, the instrument of appointment is received by the last of them[3]. At the date of the commencement of the joint receivership each joint receiver may docquet receipt of the instrument of appointment[4]. They must both indorse on the instrument of appointment the receipt of the instrument of appointment[5]. It is the joint receiver who last endorses his docquet of acceptance who is required to send a copy of the instrument of appointment to the holder of the floating charge[6]. If there are two or more floating charges, each holder of the floating charge may appoint a receiver, but if one charge has priority to the other, the receiver appointed under that charge shall have the powers given to a receiver to the exclusion of any other receiver[7]. If two or more floating charges rank equally, the receivers appointed under them are deemed to be appointed as 'joint receivers'[8]. Two equally-ranking floating charges would not entail 'joint receivers' unless the assets covered are the same assets. The one floating charge would not have priority to the other floating charge in such a case. If a receiver, under a floating charge that has priority of ranking, is appointed subsequently to another, the powers of the previous receiver are suspended[9]. However, the suspension of the powers of a receiver does not have the effect of requiring him to release any part of the property (including any letters or documents) of the company from his control until he receives from the receiver superseding him a valid indemnity (subject to the limit of the value of such part of the property of the company as is subject to the charge by virtue of which he was appointed) in respect of any expenses, charges and liabilities he may have incurred in the performance of his functions as receiver[10]. The suspension of the powers of a receiver, however, does not cause the floating charge by virtue of which he was appointed to cease to attach to the property to which it attached[11]. Because joint receivers must act together, unless there is provision made in the instrument of appointment[12], in the event of disagreement, the only option is for the holder of the floating charge or a receiver to seek directions from the court using the provisions of section 63 of the Insolvency Act 1986.

## Removal of receiver

A receiver may be removed by the court under section 62(3) of the Insolvency Act 1986. It is suggested that conflict of interest or misconduct would be

---

1 Insolvency Act 1986, s 56(3).
2 Receivers (Scotland) Regulations 1986, reg 5(a).
3 Ibid, reg 5(b).
4 Insolvency Act 1986, s 53(6).
5 Insolvency (Scotland) Rules 1986, r 3.1.
6 Ibid, r 3.1(4).
7 Insolvency Act 1986, s 56(1).
8 Ibid, s 56(2).
9 Ibid, s 56(4).
10 Ibid, s 56(5).
11 Ibid, s 56(6).
12 Ibid, s 56(3).

grounds for removal of a receiver. It is only open to the holder of the floating charge to apply to the court under the statute to remove a receiver. It has been suggested that in certain circumstances the Court of Session exercising its *nobile officium* (equitable jurisdiction) might entertain a petition for removal presented by a person other than the holder of the charge by virtue of which he was appointed, eg a creditor of the company[1].

There is however another remedy open to a creditor in terms of section 62(2) of the Insolvency Act 1986, which states: 'A receiver shall vacate office if he ceases to be qualified to act as an insolvency practitioner in relation to the company'. Although only 'administrative receivers' need to be insolvency practitioners[2], it is thought that the effect of the section is that any receiver (whether he needed to be a 'qualified insolvency practitioner' or not) must vacate office if he ceases to be a qualified insolvency practitioner. Accordingly, if a creditor thinks that a receiver is abusing his position, representations could be made by him to the Secretary of State or to the recognised professional body, laying the evidence before them and requesting them to withdraw their authorisation for the accused receiver to act as an insolvency practitioner[3].

### Resignation of receiver

A receiver may resign his office[4].

Where a receiver resigns or vacates office on completion of the receivership or in consequence of his ceasing to be qualified as an insolvency practitioner, he must give the Registrar of Companies notice to that effect and the Registrar enters the notice in the Register of Charges[5]. He must also give notice of his vacating office to:

(1)   the holder of the floating charge by virtue of which he was appointed;
(2)   the members of the creditors' committee, if any;
(3)   the company or, if it is in liquidation, the liquidator; and
(4)   the holder of any other floating charge and any receiver appointed by him[6].

In the case of a resignation, there must be at least seven days' notice of the resignation[7] and in all other cases the notice must be within 14 days of the vacation of the office[8].

### Remuneration

The remuneration of a receiver is to be determined by agreement between the receiver and the holder of the floating charge by virtue of which he was appointed[9]. If the receiver's remuneration cannot be determined in accord-

1 Palmer's *Company Law* (24th edn), 87.17.
2 Insolvency Act 1986, s 388(1)(a).
3 Ibid, s 393(4).
4 Ibid, s 62(1).
5 Ibid, s 62(5); Form 3 (Scot).
6 Insolvency (Scotland) Rules 1986, r 3.11; Receivers (Scotland) Regulations 1986, reg 6.
7 Receivers (Scotland) Regulations 1986, reg 6.
8 Insolvency (Scotland) Rules 1986, r 3.11.
9 Insolvency Act 1986, s 58(1).

ance with an agreement, or, where it is determined but disputed by the receiver, the holder of any floating charge or fixed security over all or any part of the property of the company, the company itself, or the liquidator of the company, it may be determined by the Auditor of the Court of Session by an application of the receiver or any of these other persons disputing it[1]. The payment to the receiver of his remuneration has priority to the payment of the floating chargeholder[2].

If there is no agreement between the receiver and the holder of the floating charge in terms of which the holder of the floating charge undertakes to pay the remuneration of the receiver, the receiver has to look to the assets of the company for the payment of his remuneration, and in this regard he is similar to the liquidator of a company, in so far, except by express agreement, the creditors who have appointed a liquidator have no liability to pay his remuneration[3]. Unless there is an agreement between the chargeholder and the receiver, the fact that the chargeholder appoints the receiver does not entail that there is an implied obligation on the chargeholder to pay for the services of the receiver[4].

### Publication of receivership

On the appointment of a receiver he must forthwith send to the company and publish notice of his appointment[5]. He must also within 28 days after his appointment, unless the court directs otherwise, send notice of his appointment to all the company's creditors so far as he is aware of their addresses[6].

### Refloating

On the expiry of one month following upon the removal of a receiver or his ceasing to act as a receiver, if no other receiver has been appointed, the floating charge under which he was appointed ceases to attach the property subject to it, and again subsists as a floating charge[7]. It will of course crystallise again on a winding up[8], and there seems no reason why a receiver should not be appointed at a subsequent date if there is a subsequent default.

## III. DUTIES AND POWERS OF A RECEIVER

## A. DUTIES OF RECEIVER

The receiver has certain duties laid on him by statute and certain general duties of care. The general duties of care arise from the statutory duties.

---

1 Insolvency Act 1986, s 58(2).
2 Ibid, s 60(1)(d).
3 *Hill Samuel & Co Ltd v Laing* 1989 SLT 760.
4 Ibid at 761.
5 Insolvency Act 1986, s 65(1)(a); Form 4 (Scot).
6 Ibid, s 65(1)(b).
7 Ibid, s 62(6).
8 Companies Act 1985, s 463(1).

## Statutory duties

(1)  *Payment of floating chargeholder after satisfaction of prior claims*

A receiver has one main statutory duty to perform. He must pay moneys received by him to the holder of the floating charge by virtue of which he was appointed in or towards satisfaction of the debt secured by the floating charge. He must first however pay the following persons:

(a)   the holder of any fixed security which is over property subject to the floating charge and which ranks prior to, or *pari passu* with, the floating charge;
(b)   all persons who have effectually executed diligence on any part of the property which is subject to the charge by virtue of which the receiver is appointed;
(c)   creditors in respect of all liabilities, charges and expenses incurred by or on behalf of the receiver;
(d)   the receiver in respect of his liabilities, expenses and remuneration, and any indemnity to which he is entitled out of the property of the company; and
(e)   the preferential creditors entitled to payment[1].

(2)  *Reporting to creditors and creditors' committee*

A receiver has a statutory duty (within three months or such longer period as the court may allow) after his appointment to send to the Registrar of Companies, to the holder of the floating charge by virtue of which he was appointed and to any trustees for secured creditors of the company and (so far as he is aware of their addresses) to all such creditors a report[2]. The report must detail:

(a)   the events leading up to his appointment, so far as he is aware of them;
(b)   the disposal or proposed disposal by him of any property of the company and the carrying on or proposed carrying on by him of any business of the company;
(c)   the amounts of principal and interest payable to the holder of the floating charge by virtue of which he was appointed and the amounts payable to preferential creditors; and
(d)   the amount (if any) likely to be available for the payment of other creditors[2].

In addition, he must also within three months send a copy of the report (so far as he is aware of their addresses) to all *unsecured* creditors of the company, or publish a notice stating an address to which unsecured creditors of the company should write for copies of the report to be sent to them, which is to be free of charge[3]. He must also summon a meeting of the company's unsecured creditors on not less than 14 days' notice and lay a report before the meeting[3]. Where a meeting of creditors is summoned, the meeting may

1 Insolvency Act 1986, s 60(1).
2 Ibid, s 67(1).
3 Ibid, s 67(2).

establish a 'creditors' committee'[1]. (For role and composition of 'creditors' committee' see chapter 18).

### (3) Keeping records

The receiver must keep a sederunt book as an insolvency practitioner[2].

### (4) Notification on notepaper, etc

All invoices, orders for goods, business letters issued by the company or the receiver or the liquidator must contain a statement that a receiver has been appointed[3].

### (5) Statement of affairs

In terms of section 66(1) of the Insolvency Act 1986, where a receiver is appointed 'he *shall* forthwith require' a statement of affairs from certain designated persons (for details see chapter 17).

This statutory duty extends to all receivers in Scotland but only to administrative receivers in England[4]. This discrepancy is strange and apparently gives the Scottish receiver jurisdiction over the affairs of the company not covered by the floating charge. The rule[5] says: 'where the receiver decides to require from any person a statement of affairs . . ., he shall send a notice' on a Form 3.1 (Scot). Given the statutory duty, the discretionary decision implied by the rule must only be as to who shall be required to make a statement.

## Standard of care

A receiver must exercise his powers without negligence and exercise care in disposing of assets to make sure that they achieve the value which they might reasonably be expected to realise[6]. He must exercise any power of sale bona fide and with regard to the interests of the company and obtain a fair price[7].

## Duty to company and guarantor

The Scottish courts have suggested that the approach to the duties of a receiver and holder of a floating charge should be as close as possible in Scotland and England[8]. The position in English law is now settled. Both the holder of the floating charge and the receiver owe duties of care to the

---

1 Insolvency Act 1986, s 68(1).
2 Insolvency (Scotland) Rules 1986, r 7.33(1).
3 Insolvency Act 1986, s 64(1).
4 Ibid, s 47(1).
5 Insolvency (Scotland) Rules 1986, r 3.2(1).
6 *Forth & Clyde Construction Co Ltd v Trinity Timber & Plywood Co Ltd* 1984 SLT 94 at 97, per Lord President Emslie.
7 *Rimmer v Thomas & Sons Ltd* 1967 SLT 7.
8 See comments of Lord Weir in *Shanks v Central Regional Council* 1987 SLT 410 at 414, and of Lord Grieve in *Imperial Hotel (Aberdeen) Ltd v Vaux Breweries Ltd* 1978 SC 86.

company and any guarantor of the sums secured by the floating charge. In *Standard Chartered Bank Ltd v Walker*[1], Lord Denning MR said:

'We have had much discussion on the law. So far as mortgages are concerned the law is set out in *Cuckmere Brick Co Ltd v Mutual Finance Ltd*[2]. If a mortgagee enters into possession and realises a mortgaged property, it is his duty to use reasonable care to obtain the best possible price which the circumstances of the case permit. He owes this duty not only to himself (to clear off as much of the debt as he can) but also to the mortgagor so as to reduce the balance owing as much as possible, and also to the guarantor so that he is made liable for as little as possible on the guarantee. This duty is only a particular application of the general duty of care to your neighbour which was stated by Lord Atkin in *Donoghue v Stevenson*[3] and applied in many cases since: see *Home Office v Dorset Yacht Co Ltd*[4] and *Anns v Merton London Borough*[5]. The mortgagor and the guarantor are clearly in very close "proximity" to those who conduct the sale. The duty of care is owing to them, if not to the general body of creditors of the mortgagor. There are several dicta to the effect that the mortgagee can choose his own time for the sale, but I do not think this means that he can sell at the worst possible time. It is at least arguable that, in choosing the time, he must exercise a reasonable degree of care.

'So far as the receiver is concerned, the law is well stated by Rigby LJ in *Gosling v Gaskell*[6], a dissenting judgment which was approved by the House of Lords[7]. The receiver is the agent of the company, not of the debenture holder, the bank. He owes a duty to use reasonable care to obtain the best possible price which the circumstances of the case permit. He owes this duty not only to the company (of which he is the agent) to clear off as much of its indebtedness to the bank as possible, but he also owes a duty to the guarantor, because the guarantor is liable only to the same extent as the company. The more the overdraft is reduced, the better for the guarantor. It may be that the receiver can choose the time of sale within a considerable margin, but he should, I think, exercise a reasonable degree of care about it. The debenture holder, the bank, is not responsible for what the receiver does except in so far as it gives him directions or interferes with his conduct of the realisation. If it does so, then it too is under a duty to use reasonable care towards the company and the guarantor.

'If it should appear that the mortgagee or the receiver have not used reasonable care to realise the assets to the best advantage, then the mortgagor, the company, and the guarantor are entitled in equity to an allowance. They should be given credit for the amount which the sale should have realised if reasonable care had been used. Their indebtedness is to be reduced accordingly.'

*Standard Chartered Bank Ltd v Walker* has subsequently been referred to, seemingly with approval, by Lord Ross in *Lord Advocate v Maritime Fruit Carriers Ltd*[8], and the principles which Lord Denning stated have since been reinforced by the Privy Council in 1983 in the case of *Tse Kwong Lam v Wong Chit Sen*[9], and followed in *American Express International Banking Corpn v Hurley*[10]. Unfortunately in the only Scottish case on the subject, *Imperial Hotel (Aberdeen) Ltd v Vaux Breweries Ltd*[11] Lord Grieve followed a much

1 [1982] 3 All ER 938 at 942.
2 [1971] Ch 949.
3 [1932] AC 562.
4 [1970] AC 1004.
5 [1978] AC 728.
6 [1896] 1 QB 669.
7 See [1897] AC 575.
8 1983 SLT 357.
9 [1983] 1 WLR 1349.
10 [1986] BCLC 52.
11 1978 SC 86 at 91.

earlier English case, *Re Johnson & Co (Builders) Ltd*[1], which had been already superseded and discredited by the case of *Cuckmere Brick v Mutual Finance Ltd*[2]. Accordingly, it is suggested (especially since Lord Grieve was trying to follow English authority) that his decision that 'there is no duty on the mortgagee to see that there is as much as possible left over for those interested in the "equity" of the company' was wrongly decided.

## Duty to creditors

### (1)   Preferential creditors

The receiver is under a statutory duty to pay preferential creditors before paying the holder of a floating charge[3]. It is a positive duty, not simply a negative one not to pay the holder of the instrument containing the floating charge without paying the preferential creditors[4]. If the receiver carries on the business in such a way as to dissipate assets which would otherwise be available to pay preferential creditors or accounts to the company or the holder of the instrument containing the floating charge before paying the preferential creditors he will be liable for breach of statutory duty[5]. The statutory duty to pay preferential creditors is imposed by section 59(1) of the Insolvency Act 1986. That section applies only where the company is not being wound up. However, section 60 of the Insolvency Act 1986 lays down that the receiver shall pay monies received by him to the floating chargeholder after satisfaction of the category of creditors including preferential creditors. He then must pay over any surplus to 'the company or its liquidator as the case may be'[6]. This envisages a situation where the receiver makes these distributions although the company is in liquidation. This is in keeping with the Scottish law that a receiver's powers supersede those of a liquidator[7] and that a receiver may be appointed after the commencement of a liquidation[8]. The result is that there is a duty to the preferred creditors by the receiver if he is appointed before or after the company is in liquidation. It is important because if the receiver pays over the money for the liquidator to distribute he could render himself liable to the preferential creditors. This is because the order of priority in distribution by the liquidator is different to the order of priority imposed by statute on the receiver[9]. The liquidator has the expenses of the liquidation as a prior claim to preferential debts. Accordingly the expenses of the liquidation could eat into or use up moneys available to pay preferential creditors. One effect of this is that preferential creditors will have a financial incentive often to persuade the holder of a floating charge to appoint a receiver. If the sums were significant, they might underwrite the receiver's costs. A problem arises, however, where a liquidation has commenced and a receiver is appointed. Liquidation expenses will have been incurred

---

1 [1955] Ch 634.
2 [1971] Ch 949.
3 Insolvency Act 1986, s 59(1).
4 *Westminster Corpn v Haste* [1950] Ch 442.
5 See *IRC v Goldblatt* [1972] Ch 498; and *Westminster Corpn v Haste*, supra.
6 Insolvency Act 1986, s 60(2)(c).
7 *Manley, Petr* 1985 SLT 42.
8 *Libertas-Kommerz GmbH v Johnson* 1977 SC 191.
9 Insolvency (Scotland) Rules 1986, r 4.66.

and it would appear following *Manley, Petitioner*[1], that the liquidator could be at risk for them. Nevertheless, the question of entitlement to such expenses has not been the subject of a judicial decision. Common sense suggests that in Scotland the liquidator should be entitled to his expenses until he hands over to the receiver.

In the English case of *Re First Express Ltd*[2], a company went into liquidation. Shortly afterwards, the bank appointed an administrative receiver under its debenture. The liquidator accounted to the bank – under its fixed charge – for money collected from the company's book debts, but retained a small amount against the liquidation costs. Hoffmann J accepted that there were liquidation costs as to the payment of which the liquidator was entitled to priority and therefore, might retain some of the money collected. The authors cannot see any special provision in the English insolvency rules why that ruling should be applicable only to England.

Administrative receivers often seek an indemnity from a liquidator when they pass funds to the liquidator. Because an administrative receiver is under a statutory duty to pay surplus funds not required for the discharge of his obligations to the company over which he is appointed, which is in liquidation, he is not entitled to an indemnity in respect of the performance of this obligation. If, however, a liquidator for some reason seeks to receive monies earlier than the time when the administrative receiver would normally be in a position to pay over, it is thought that in those situations an indemnity should be demanded.

### (2)   Duty to ordinary creditors

It has been suggested that the receiver owes a duty of care to ordinary creditors[3]. Although the proximity between the receiver and creditors is perhaps closer now that the Insolvency Act 1986 sets up a 'creditors' committee' on receivership, it is suggested that the receiver does not owe a duty of care to creditors merely as creditors. Unless there is a breach of a statutory duty in relation to distribution, creditors' interests are represented and their rights enforced through the company. In *Standard Chartered Bank Ltd v Walker*[4], Lord Denning MR said: 'the mortgagor and the guarantor are clearly in very close "proximity" to those who conduct the sale. The duty of care is owing to them, if not to the general body of creditors of the mortgagor.'

Nevertheless, a receiver may owe a direct duty of care to creditors whose relationship with the company extends beyond that of mere creditors. The rationale of the rule suggested in the last paragraph is that the creditors' claim is in respect of a debt owed by the company, and such a claim should therefore be made through the company. In certain cases, however, the claim in issue does not relate to a debt owed by the company, and the fact that the claimant is a creditor of the company is merely incidental to the claim. For example, a receiver will clearly owe a duty of care to persons who have deposited property with the company; in such cases the duty arises out of their ownership of the property deposited. If the property cannot be retained by the company, the receiver must notify the owners of that fact and must give them a reasonable

1 1985 SLT 42.
2 See *Greene and Fletcher*, para 3.51.
3 [1991] BCC 782.
4 [1982] 3 All ER 938 at 942.

opportunity to remove their property; until it is removed the receiver must continue to look after it. Likewise a receiver owes a duty of care not to prejudice the rights as against third parties of persons dealing with the company. A good example of this is the pension and life assurance entitlement of employees of the company; the receiver clearly owes a duty to preserve that entitlement, by continuing to pay the pensions to the institution providing the pension and life assurance until such time as the employees have had a reasonable opportunity to make alternative arrangements on their own account. This means that employees must be given notice that the receiver is to stop paying the premiums in time for them to take action to preserve their rights. In the case of *Larsen's Executrix v Henderson*[1], the executrix of a deceased employee of a company had sought damages from the receiver appointed to the company for loss allegedly sustained through the termination by the receiver of life insurance provisions effected through the company which it would have been open to the deceased to have continued, despite his fatal illness. The court held that there existed a duty of care on the part of the receiver of a company to employees with rights under a pension scheme not to terminate the pension scheme without first giving an indication that such an event might occur, but that in this particular case the receiver had given adequate notice.

If the receiver has been negligent, the ordinary creditors' rights may be enforced through the company or its liquidator. Alternatively, in the case of an administrative receivership only, the court may, on application of the liquidator, or of any creditor or contributory examine into the misfeasance of an administrative receiver under section 212(1)(b) of the Insolvency Act 1986. This remedy open to a creditor (not just the liquidator) enables the court to order the administrative receiver concerned: (a) to repay, restore or account for moneys, or (b) to contribute a sum to the company's assets by way of compensation in respect of the misfeasance or breach of fiduciary or other duty as the court thinks just[2]. Again here, the emphasis is on the former administrative receiver paying the *company* compensation.

# B. POWERS OF RECEIVER

## Agency of receiver

In Scotland a receiver is deemed to be the agent of a company in relation to such of the property of the company as is attached by the floating charge by virtue of which he was appointed[3]. This is in contrast to England, where only an administrative receiver is deemed to be the company's agent. In England the administrative receiver is only the agent unless and until the company goes into liquidation[4]. There is no corresponding provision in Scotland that the agency of a receiver terminates on liquidation. Because receivers are by statute agents of the company and usually expressly or by implication in terms

1  1990 SLT 498.
2  Insolvency Act 1986, s 212(3).
3  Ibid, s 57(1).
4  Ibid, s 44(1)(a).

of the debenture in which they are appointed, it is thought that they may be held to be 'the occupiers' of premises for the purposes of certain statutes[1].

## Statutory powers of Scottish receiver

All Scottish receivers (not just administrative receivers) have whatever powers are specified in the instrument creating the floating charge in relation to property covered by the floating charge[2]. In addition the receiver has a further set of powers specified by statute, provided they are not inconsistent with any provision of the instrument creating the floating charge, in relation to the property covered by the floating charge[3], but subject to the rights of any person who has effectually executed diligence on all or any part of the property of the company prior to the appointment of the receiver, and subject to the rights of any person who holds over all or any part of the property of the company a fixed security or floating charge which has priority over, or ranks *pari passu* with, the floating charge by virtue of which the receiver was appointed[4]. The statutory powers given by the Insolvency Act 1986 include in addition to minor amendments five new powers which are those listed at the end of the list and starred. These powers are only available to receiverships commenced after 29 December 1986 unless written into the instrument creating the floating charge[5]. The powers are as follows:

### (1) *To take possession of property*

A receiver has the power to take possession of, collect and get in the property from the company or a liquidator or any other person, and for that purpose to take such proceedings as may seem to him expedient[6]. This is the power which enables the receiver to fulfil his main function, which is to realise on behalf of his appointer the assets subject to the floating charge in order to satisfy the claim of the holder of the floating charge. Where a liquidator has been appointed on the winding up of a company, whether this is before or after the receiver's appointment, the liquidator must hand over property covered by the charge to the receiver and his powers are superseded[7]. The provision also allows him to collect debts due to the company by taking proceedings in the name of the company[8].

### (2) *Power to sell property*

The receiver has the power to sell, feu, hire out or otherwise dispose of the property by public roup or private bargain and with or without advertisement[9].

---

1 *Lord Advocate v Aero Technologies Ltd* 1991 SLT 134.
2 Insolvency Act 1986, s 55(1).
3 Ibid, s 55(2).
4 Ibid, s 55(3).
5 Ibid, Sch 11, para 3.
6 Ibid, s 55(2) and Sch 2, para 1.
7 *Manley, Petr* 1985 SLT 42.
8 *McPhail v Lothian Regional Council* 1981 SLT 173; *Forth & Clyde Construction Ltd v Trinity Timber & Plywood Co Ltd* 1984 SLT 94.
9 Insolvency Act 1986, s 55(2) and Sch 2, para 2.

### (3)   *Power to borrow*

The receiver has power to raise or borrow money and grant security for it over the property[1].

### (4)   *Power to appoint solicitor or accountant*

The receiver has the power to appoint a solicitor or accountant or other professionally qualified person to assist him in the performance of his functions[2].

### (5)   *Power to bring or defend legal actions*

The receiver has the power to bring or defend any action or any other legal proceedings in the name and on behalf of the company[3]. Where a receiver brings an action in the name of the company, he acts as agent but does not incur any personal liability, other than in relation to contracts he may enter into by, for example, instructing solicitors or counsel, when he has a right of relief against the property of the company subject to the floating charge[4]. Where a receiver litigates, he is entitled to have his liabilities, expenses and any indemnity to which he is entitled paid out of the property of the company covered by the floating charge before payment of the proceeds of the real-isations of secured assets covered by a floating charge to the holder of a floating charge[5]. Where he litigates, he merely incurs a liability on behalf of the company, and is not personally liable for that liability. In contrast, where a liquidator litigates, he is personally held to warrant the sufficiency of the funds in his hands and is personally liable for expenses[6]. Accordingly, when a company litigates, it will not normally be required to find caution in terms of section 726(2) of the Companies Act 1985 if there is no suggestion that the liquidator, if he is bringing the action, would be unable to honour the obligation[7]. In contrast, because a receiver will not be personally liable, it is suggested that the company will be ordered to find caution to pay the defender's expenses, if it litigates in receivership and there is reason to believe that the company will be unable to pay the defender's expenses[8].

### (6)   *Power to refer to arbitration*

The receiver has power on behalf of the company to refer to arbitration all questions affecting the company[9].

---

1 Insolvency Act 1986, s 55(2) and Sch 2, para 3.
2 Ibid, s 55(2) and Sch 2, para 4.
3 Ibid, s 55(2) and Sch 2, para 5.
4 Ibid, s 57(3).
5 Ibid, ss 60(1)(e) and 57(3).
6 *Sinclair v Thurso Pavement Syndicate* (1903) 11 SLT 364.
7 *Stewart v Steel* 1987 SLT (Sh Ct) 60.
8 Companies Act 1985, s 726(2).
9 Insolvency Act 1986, s 55(2) and Sch 2, para 6.

(7)  *Insurance*

The receiver has power to effect and maintain insurances in respect of the business and property of the company[1]. A receiver will have to be very careful with company insurance policies. In relation to insurance policies entered into prior to the receivership, he will not be personally liable for the premiums. However, if he renews a contract he will be personally liable[2]. Most company policies will cover public liability for which he may not have a concern in their being insured. He should check his exposure before entering into unnecessary policies.

Section 1 of the Third Parties (Rights against Insurers) Act 1930 provides that, where under any contract of insurance a company is insured against liabilities to third parties which it may incur, then in the event of a receiver being appointed, if any such liability is incurred by the insured, the rights of the insured against the insurer under the contract in respect of the liability shall, notwithstanding anything in any Act or rule of law to the contrary, be transferred to and vest in the third party to whom the liability was so incurred. This means that the crystallisation of the floating charge does not attach the insured's rights against the insurance company in such a way that the third party was left merely ranking for a claim.

(8)  *Power to use company's seal*

The receiver has the power to use the company's seal[3].

(9)  *Execution of deeds*

The receiver has the power to do all acts and to execute in the name and on behalf of the company any deed, receipt or other document[4].

(10)  *Negotiable instruments*

The receiver has power to draw, accept, make and endorse any bill of exchange or promissory note in the name and on behalf of the company[5].

(11)  *Agents and employees*

The receiver has power to appoint agents, to do any business which he is unable to do himself, or which can more conveniently be done by an agent, and power to employ and dismiss employees[6]. The receiver has much greater scope to appoint an agent than a liquidator. He may appoint an agent to do any business 'which can more conveniently be done by an agent'. A liquidator does not have this latitude[7].

---

1  Ibid, s 55(2) and Sch 2, para 7.
2  Ibid, s 57(2).
3  Ibid, s 55(2) and Sch 2, para 8.
4  Ibid, s 55(2) and Sch 2, para 9.
5  Ibid, s 55(2) and Sch 2, para 10.
6  Ibid, s 55(2) and Sch 2, para 11.
7  Ibid, ss 165, 167 and Sch 4, para 12.

### (12)   *Work on property*

The receiver has the power to do all such things (including the carrying out of work) as may be necessary for the realisation of the property[1].

### (13)   *Incidental payments*

The receiver has power to make any payment which is necessary or incidental to the performance of his functions[2].

### (14)   *Power to carry on the business of the company*

The receiver has the power to carry on the business of the company or any part of it[3]. There is a change in the law here in relation to receiverships commenced after 29 December 1986. Previously, the receiver had power only to 'carry on the business of the company'.[4] This the authors read to mean that, where a receiver was only appointed by the holder of a floating charge having security over part of a company, the receiver might not have had the statutory power to carry on the business of the company in relation to that part. Normally, however, that power would have been written into the instrument containing the floating charge.

### (15)   *Winding-up petitions*

The receiver has power to present or defend a petition for the winding up of the company[5]. The receiver may wish to petition to wind up the company if there is a surplus on assets after payment of the floating chargeholder but that surplus is insufficient to pay all the ordinary creditors on a winding-up, or if the holder of a floating charge is owed money by the company which is not secured by the floating charge. He would have the same grounds, as agent of the company, in opposing a petition for the winding up of the company as the company itself would have. Where a creditor seeks a winding-up order on the ground that a company is unable to pay its debts, the petition for winding up will not be dismissed unless there are compelling reasons for it[6].

### (16)   *Ranking in debtors' estates*

The receiver has power on behalf of the company to rank and claim in the bankruptcy, insolvency, sequestration or liquidation of debtors of the company, to receive dividends and to accede to trust deeds for creditors of the debtors[7].

---

1 Insolvency Act 1986, s 55(2) and Sch 2, para 12.
2 Ibid, s 55(2) and Sch 2, para 13.
3 Ibid, s 55(2) and Sch 2, para 14.
4 Companies Act 1985, s 471(1)(o).
5 Insolvency Act 1986, s 55(2) and Sch 2, para 21.
6 *Foxhall and Gyle (Nurseries) Ltd, Petrs* 1978 SLT (Notes) 29.
7 Insolvency Act 1986, s 55(2) and Sch 2, para 20.

(17)   *Leases and tenancies*

The receiver has power on behalf of the company to grant or accept a surrender of a lease or tenancy of any of the property, and to take a lease or tenancy of any property required or convenient for the business of the company[1].

(18)   *Uncalled capital*

The receiver has now power to call up any uncalled capital of the company[2]. Prior to the present legislation, it was competent under the law of Scotland to have a floating charge over the uncalled capital of a company[3], but the receiver did not have the power to call up uncalled capital unless this was provided for in the instrument creating the floating charge. Where the company has created reserve liability under section 120 or 124 of the Companies Act 1985, such capital may only be called up by the liquidator.

(19)   *Establishment of subsidiaries*

The receiver now has a statutory power to establish subsidiaries of the company[4]. Again there is no power to establish subsidiaries in a receivership commenced prior to 29 December 1986 unless this is provided for in the instrument creating the floating charge.

(20)   *Power to transfer business to subsidiaries*

The receiver, as in establishing subsidiaries, now has the power to transfer to subsidiaries of the company the business of the company or any part of it and any of the property of the company[5]. That power and the above power are necessary to enable a receiver to hive down businesses of the company into newly established subsidiaries in order to sell them.

(21)   *Compromises and arrangements*

The receiver now has power to make any arrangements or compromise on behalf of the company. It is thought that compromises and arrangements on behalf of the company would be contracts and, accordingly, the receiver would be personally liable on the compromises and arrangements under section 57(2) unless the contract provided otherwise. In such cases part of each creditor's claim against the company is normally compromised. Unless the contract effecting the compromise provides for a discharge of that compromised element, if the company defaults on the compromise contract the creditor can claim the full sum that was originally due to him. In that event, however, he would only rank for that sum in the company's insolvency, and the receiver would merely be liable for the amount due to the creditor under the contract effecting the compromise (see chapter 6).

1  Ibid, s 55(2) and Sch 2, para 15.
2  Ibid, s 55(2) and Sch 2, para 17.
3  Companies Act 1985, s 467.
4  Insolvency Act 1986, s 55(2) and Sch 2, para 18.
5  Ibid, s 55(2) and Sch 2, para 22.

## (22)   *Power to change company's registered office*

The receiver now has power to change the situation of the company's registered office[1]. A company may change the situation of its registered office only in the part of the United Kingdom in which it is registered. If the company wanted to change its registered office to an address outwith Scotland, this would have to be done by a Private Act of Parliament. Accordingly, the receiver as agent of the company could only change the registered office within Scotland.

## (23)   *Disposal of interest in property*

Where a receiver sells or disposes or wishes to sell or dispose of property of the company which is subject to the floating charge by virtue of which he was appointed, and which is subject to the security or interest of a prior *pari passu* or postponed ranking creditor or is property affected by effectual diligence and the receiver cannot obtain the consent of the creditor or the person entitled to the effectual diligence, the receiver may apply to the court for authority to sell or dispose of the property[2]. The court may authorise the sale or disposal of the property or interest in question free of the security, interest, burden, encumbrance or diligence, and on any terms or conditions it thinks fit[3]. However, where there is a fixed security over the property or interest in question which ranks prior to the floating charge, and has not been met or provided for in full, the court will not authorise the sale or disposal of the property or interest in question unless it is satisfied that the sale or disposal would be likely to provide a more advantageous realisation of the company's assets than would otherwise be the case[4]. There is a further condition to an authorisation to sell. In terms of section 61(4) of the Insolvency Act 1986 the authorisation must have as a condition that the net proceeds of the disposal are applied towards discharging the sums secured by the fixed security, and if the net proceeds are less than what is determined by the court to be the net amount which would be realised on a sale of the property or interest on the open market by a willing seller, that deficit has to be made good[5]. There is a similar provision in relation to administrators under section 15(5) of the Insolvency Act 1986.

## (24)   *Incidental powers*

The receiver has the power to do all other things incidental to the exercise of the powers contained in the instrument creating the floating charge and his statutory powers[6].

## (25)   *Exercise of powers in England*

The Scottish receiver may exercise his powers in England in so far as their exercise is not inconsistent with English law[7].

1 Insolvency Act 1986, s 55(2) and Sch 2, para 22.
2 Ibid, s 61(1).
3 Ibid, s 61(2).
4 Ibid, s 61(3).
5 Ibid, s 61(4).
6 Ibid, s 55(2) and Sch 2, para 23.
7 Ibid, s 72(1).

# Chapter 6

# Voluntary arrangements

## Introduction

With the coming into force of sections 1 to 7 (Part I) of the Insolvency Act 1986 and the related rules in Part I of the Insolvency (Scotland) Rules 1986 there are now *three* main procedures under which insolvent companies can come to an arrangement with their creditors and members.

### (1) A 'voluntary arrangement' under Part I of the Insolvency Act 1986

Under the above procedure, which is an innovation of the Insolvency Acts, a company, whether in the course of winding up or not, or subject to an administration order, may effect a 'composition in satisfaction of its debts, or scheme of arrangement of its affairs' which is legally binding on its creditors and/or members, subject to it being approved by three-quarters in value of those voting in the case of a creditors' meeting and a simple majority in value of those voting in the case of a members' meeting[1].

The procedure is open, whether winding up has commenced prior to 29 December 1986 or not, to companies registered under the Companies Acts. 'Companies' (except for the purposes of winding up, when an unregistered company may be wound up) means a registered company in the Insolvency Act 1986[2]. There is a difficulty here in 'company' meaning registered company because the procedure is open to the liquidator of an unregistered company[3]. A solution might be that only when it is being wound up is this type of arrangement open to an unregistered company.

### (2) 'Compromise or arrangement' under section 425 of the Companies Act 1985

This is a procedure by which a company comes to a compromise or arrangement with its creditors, or any class of them, or with its members or any class of them, which is legally binding on all the creditors and/or members. It is available in all windings up, administrations, receiverships and to a company at any time. To be legally binding, there must be approval by a majority in number representing three-quarters in value of the creditors or members voting, as in a voluntary arrangement under section 1 of the Insolvency Act 1986.

---

1 Insolvency (Scotland) Rules 1986, r 7.12.
2 Insolvency Act 1986, s 251, and Companies Act 1985, Pt XXVI.
3 Insolvency Act 1986, s 221(1), read with s 1(3) of the Act.

There must, however, be in addition a sanction by the court of the arrangement[1].

(3) *Compromises by a company at common law, by liquidators under sections 165 and 167 of the Insolvency Act 1986, administrators under section 14 of the Insolvency Act 1986 and receivers under section 55(2) of the Insolvency Act 1986*

These compromises do not go beyond bilateral agreements between the company, liquidators, administrators or receivers and creditors who bind themselves in the agreement. They cannot bind non-acceding parties (see page 176).[2]

## Voluntary arrangements

The Cork Committee criticised[3] the procedure for a compromise or arrangement under section 425 of the Companies Act 1985 as being too slow and complicated in the case of insolvency. It could not be effected in under eight weeks, by which time matters had moved on. The court also had to be closely involved. The committee accordingly suggested the adoption of a similar procedure to that under section 425 but subject only to creditor and shareholder approval without the need for sanction by the court. Its recommendation was adopted. In addition a voluntary arrangement under Part I of the Insolvency Act 1986, and a compromise or arrangement under section 425 of the Companies Act 1985, are now built into the 'administration' régime (also recommended by the Cork Committee), as two of the four legally justifying purposes for which an administration order may be made[4].

### Scope of voluntary arrangements under Part I of the Insolvency Act 1986 and schemes under section 425 of the Companies Act 1985

The wording used in section 1 of the Insolvency Act 1986 and that of section 425 of the Companies Act 1985 are different. In terms of section 1 of the Insolvency Act 1986, a 'voluntary arrangement' is a 'composition in satisfaction of a company's debts or a scheme of arrangement of its affairs'. Section 425 of the Companies Act 1985 talks of a 'compromise or arrangement between a company and its creditors, or any class of them, or between the company and its members, or any class of them'.

An examination of these expressions suggests that the wording should be read as legally synonymous in Scotland.

---

1 Companies Act 1985, s 425(2).
2 In addition to the procedures outlined in paragraph 1 there is, in relation to voluntary windings up commenced before 29 December 1986, whether members' or creditors', a procedure by which a company may enter into an 'arrangement' which is binding on the company if sanctioned by an extraordinary resolution, and binding on the creditors if acceded to by three-fourths of them in number and value (section 601 of the Companies Act 1985, repealed by the Insolvency Act 1985, section 135(3) and Schedule 10, Part II). These majorities are potentially more difficult to obtain than the three-quarters of value only, and only those voting, now required to bind creditors in a scheme under Part 1 of the Insolvency Act 1986. This section is accordingly unlikely to be used, and was described in any event by the Cork Committee as a 'dead letter'.
3 Cork Report, Chap 7, Part II.
4 Insolvency Act 1986, s 8(3).

## Compositions and compromises

In certain English cases, the expression 'compromise' has been discussed[1]. These cases suggest in England that for there to be a compromise there must be some dispute, e g as to the power to enforce rights, or as to what those rights are. In Scotland, 'compromise' in most circumstances means the settlement of a claim where there is a dispute[2]. However, in liquidation the word seems to be stretched to mean a 'composition', which is an agreement by which a creditor accepts a portion of the debts owed to him by the debtor in full discharge of the debtor's obligations[3]. A deal, where the debt has been admitted by the liquidator, and the creditors have agreed to accept a sum of money, has been described as a 'compromise'[4]. In that case, in a sense, however, one could just argue that the liquidator compromised with the creditors on the sum which they could expect to get in a ranking as dividend (illegally compromised by not obtaining sanction of the court), and hence the element of dispute might be held to have persisted. In the case of *City of Glasgow Bank v Geddes' Trustees*[5], however, there was no dispute between the creditors and the liquidator and full payment to the creditors was assured. A composition paying the money up front was referred to as a 'compromise' and the note by the liquidators seeking sanction of the court was brought *inter alia* under the section of the Companies Act 1862 which was the statutory predecessor of section 425 of the Companies Act 1985. Whatever the meaning of 'compromise' – i e whether it covers a composition or not – 'arrangement' will cover a composition.

## Arrangements of affairs under section 1 of the Insolvency Act 1986 and arrangements under section 425 of the Companies Act 1985

The expression 'arrangement of its affairs' used in section 1 of the Insolvency Act 1986 has probably the same scope as an 'arrangement . . . proposed between a company and its creditors, or any class of them, or between the company and its members' used in section 425 of the Companies Act 1985. The expression is in the context of a 'proposal to the company' (i e members) and to its creditors. These are the same parties involved in an 'arrangement' under section 425 of the Companies Act 1985. The wording is broadly similar. Accordingly, it is suggested that section 1 of the Insolvency Act 1986 can be interpreted in the light of interpretation given to section 425 of the Companies Act 1985 and its predecessors.

Section 425 is to be interpreted 'broadly', in Scotland, to cover a wide variety of different types of arrangement[6]. It covers *inter alia* consolidations of shares[7], arrangements with creditors[8], alterations of class rights in

---

1 *Sneath v Valley Gold Ltd* [1893] 1 Ch 477 at 491n.; *Mercantile Investment and General Trust Co v International Co of Mexico* [1893] 1 Ch 484n.; *Mercantile Investment and General Trust Co v River Plate Trust, Loan and Agency Co* [1894] 1 Ch 578.
2 Stair, I, xvii, 2.
3 Bell, *Comm*, ii, 398.
4 *Liqr of R D Simpson Ltd* (1908) 15 SLT 649 and *R D Simpson Ltd and Liqr v Hudson Beare* (1908) 15 SLT 875.
5 (1880) 7 R 731.
6 *Singer Manufacturing Co v Robinow* 1971 SC 11 at 14, per Lord President Clyde.
7 Companies Act 1985, s 425(6).
8 *Shandon Hydropathic Co Ltd, Petrs* 1911 SC 1153.

memoranda of association[1], and schemes by which the holder of the majority of shares acquires the minority on favourable terms[2]. It would not cover arrangements *ultra vires* the company[3] nor where there is another statutory procedure[4].

## Difference between voluntary arrangements under Part I of the Insolvency Act 1986 and compromises and arrangements under section 425 of the Companies Act 1985

There would appear to be no difference in the meaning of the definitions of the two types of 'arrangement' under Part I of the Insolvency Act and section 425 of the Companies Act 1985. There is a difference in their implementation, however. Under Part I of the Insolvency Act, in terms of section 4, unless the person concerned agrees, a secured creditor may not be affected by any proposal and the holder of a preferential debt must be given priority and paid *pari passu* with the other preferential debtors. This restriction gives the secured creditor or preferential creditor an absolute veto. Under section 425, by contrast, provided that the requisite majorities are obtained in the different classes under a section 425 scheme, a dissenting minority can be bound by an arrangement (subject to the sanction of the court)[5]. In determining what is a 'class', it must be confined to those persons whose rights are not so dissimilar as to make it impossible for them to consult together with a view to their common interest, and if there is a different state of facts existing among different creditors which may differently affect their minds and their judgments, they must be divided into different classes[6]. Accordingly it is not just a question of 'secured' and 'unsecured', etc. The underlying interests must be looked at to ensure equity.

The key reason that both types of scheme are justifying purposes for an 'administration order' (although a 'voluntary arrangement' under Part I can be achieved by an easier majority than a section 425 scheme), is that when a section 425 scheme is sanctioned the court may also sanction arrangements external to the company under section 427 of the Companies Act 1985, which effect reconstructions or amalgamations involving other companies. This type of reconstruction involving outside parties is not open in conjunction with voluntary arrangements under Part I of the Insolvency Act 1986.

## Judicial control of voluntary arrangements under Part I of the Insolvency Act 1986

A voluntary arrangement under Part I of the Insolvency Act 1986 legally takes effect subject to approval by a meeting of the company's creditors and a meeting of members (for voting and meetings, see chapter 18), from the date of the approval by the creditors' meetings[7]. Unlike a scheme under

1 *Edinburgh Railway Access and Property Co v Scottish Metropolitan Assurance Co* 1932 SC 2.
2 *Singer Manufacturing Co v Robinow, supra.*
3 See *Re Cooper, Cooper v Johnson* [1902] WN 199; *Re Stephen Walters & Sons* [1926] WN 236; *Re Oceanic Steam Navigation Co* [1939] Ch 41.
4 *Re Guardian Assurance Co* [1917] 1 Ch 431.
5 *La Lainière de Roubaix v Glen Glove Co* 1925 SC 91.
6 *Sovereign Life Assurance Co v Dodd* [1892] 2 QB 573, approved in *La Lainière, supra.*
7 Insolvency Act 1986, s 5(2).

section 425 of the Companies Act 1985 creditors do not have to be divided into classes. After approval, the voluntary arrangement under Part I of the Insolvency Act 1986 may be challenged within 28 days of the report of the approval to the court by any creditor, member or contributory who was entitled to vote at meetings[1]. Although the voluntary arrangement is effective during this period when it is open to challenge, the court is not allowed during that period to discharge the administration order, or sist or stay the winding up[2]. This is an obvious safeguard in case the challenge is successful. Those drafting voluntary arrangements should perhaps make the day on which the proposals are to be implemented (although already binding) at least 28 days after the creditors' meeting, in case during that period they are challenged and have to be unscrambled, or make it 28 days plus any extension of that risk period triggered by legal proceedings. (During the further period in which legal proceedings are being brought challenging the voluntary arrangement, an order discharging an administration, or sisting (granting a stay of) a winding up may not be granted)[3].

### Grounds of legal challenge under section 6 of the Insolvency Act 1986 – and grounds of approval of a scheme under section 425 of the Companies Act 1985

The difference in the judicial control procedure between a 'voluntary arrangement' under Part I of the Insolvency Act 1986 and a 'compromise or arrangement' under section 425 of the Companies Act 1985 is that the first is subject to negative vetting by the court if challenged within 28 days of the meetings, whereas a section 425 'arrangement' requires positive vetting by the court before it is effective.

*(1)   Negative vetting under section 6 of the Insolvency Act 1986*

Voluntary arrangements under Part I of the Insolvency Act 1986 may be challenged in court under section 6 by the liquidator or administrator or any interested member or creditor. They may also be challenged by the 'nominee' (which is the name given by section 1 of the Insolvency Act 1986 to the 'insolvency practitioner' as defined by the Act, who must sponsor a proposal of a voluntary arrangement). The nominee can be the liquidator or administrator himself, if he chooses to sponsor his own proposals, or a qualified third party. Where the directors make proposals (and it is thought that a company in receivership may make proposals – see page 173) they must submit them to an outside insolvency practitioner, to act.

If the above-mentioned parties choose to challenge the arrangements, the grounds of challenge are (a) that the voluntary arrangement 'unfairly prejudices the interests of a creditor, member or contributory of a company', or (b) that there has been a material irregularity at the meetings summoned under section 3 of the Insolvency Act 1986. The expression 'unfairly prejudices' has not been defined in relation to this section. It has been discussed in relation to section 459(1) of the Companies Act 1985 which uses a similar expression in relation to the interests of a member of a company being

---

1 Ibid, s 6(2).
2 Ibid, s 5(4)(a).
3 Ibid, s 5(4)(b).

prejudiced[1]. The key to understanding seems to be that there must not only be prejudice. It must be to the creditor's or member's interest as a creditor or member[2]. In the case of most voluntary arrangements members and creditors have 'prejudice' to their interests in making the arrangement. The arrangement must cause 'unfair' prejudice. Building on the case of *Re Bird Precision Bellows Ltd* the objective must be to avoid what is not considered 'fair and equitable in all the circumstances of the case'[3]. It is suggested that the need for equity and fairness is the overriding objective, and that fairness is amongst members and amongst creditors and between creditors and members. Fairness overrides the question of whether legal rights are being infringed[4]. It is further suggested that, although the wording is different, the common law in relation to the court's grounds for approving a 'compromise or scheme or arrangement' under section 425 should be used to interpret what would be 'unfair prejudice'. It is unlikely that the legislature, having tied these two types of voluntary arrangement together as justifying purposes of an administration order, would have the court use different principles for accepting one and rejecting another. For example, the thinking in having classes based on underlying interests, which is absent in an arrangement of this type, is an expression of an attempt to achieve the equity suggested above (see page 170). 'Unfair prejudice' is also used in section 27(1)(a) of the Insolvency Act 1986 as the ground on which an aggrieved interested party may legally challenge an administrator's management of a company's affairs.

If the court is satisfied in relation to a challenge on the ground of irregularity or unfair prejudice, it may suspend or revoke the approval of the meetings and at its discretion order new meetings to consider revised proposals or make any other order[5]. Except challenged in the above manner, meetings are deemed regularly conducted[6]. If the court refuses the approval but allows further meetings and then is satisfied that no revised proposals are being submitted, it must revoke or suspend the approval[7].

## (2)   *Positive vetting of scheme under section 425 of the Companies Act 1985*

The criteria by which the Scottish courts decide whether to sanction a scheme under section 425 were set down by Lord President Dunedin in the case of *Shandon Hydropathic Co Ltd*[8] as follows:

'What the Court has to do is to see first of all that the statutory provisions have been complied with; and secondly, that the majority has been acting *bona fide*. The Court also has to see that the minority is not being overridden by a majority, having interests of its own clashing with those of the minority whom they seek to coerce. Further than that, the Court has to look at the scheme and see whether it is one as to which persons, acting honestly and viewing the scheme laid before them in the interests of those whom they

---

1 See *Re Bird Precision Bellows Ltd* [1985] BCLC 493, *McGuinness v Bremner plc* 1988 SLT 891 and 898.
2 *Re a Company (No 004475 of 1982)* [1983] Ch 178.
3 [1985] BCLC 493 at 499.
4 *Re a Company (No 008699 of 1985)* (1986) The Times, 18 February, 1986 PCC 296.
5 Insolvency Act 1986, s 6(4).
6 Ibid, s 6(7).
7 Ibid, s 6(5).
8 1911 SC 1153 at 1155, quoting Lindley LJ in *Re Alabama, New Orleans, Texas and Pacific Junction Ry Co* [1891] 1 Ch 213 at 238.

represent, take a view which can be reasonably taken by business men. The Court must look at the scheme and see whether the Act has been complied with, whether the majority are acting *bona fide* and whether they are coercing the minority in order to promote interests adverse to those of the class whom they purport to represent; and then see whether the scheme is a reasonable one, or whether there was any reasonable objection to it, or such an objection to it as that any man might say that he could not approve of it.'

(Lord Dunedin also held that in considering and coming to the conclusion that a scheme was a reasonable one, the court was entitled to take into consideration the fact that the requisite majority of creditors who approved the scheme were businessmen in Glasgow.)

## Procedure for approval – voluntary arrangements under Part I of the Insolvency Act 1986

The nominee, to whom the directors send their proposals, or to whom the administrator or liquidator send their proposals if they are not the nominee, must submit a report to the court within 28 days of being given notice of the proposal stating whether in his opinion meetings of the company and of its creditors should be summoned to consider the proposal and, if he thinks so, give details of the meetings[1]. For the purpose of preparing his report, the nominee, if not the liquidator or administrator, must be sent a copy of the proposals and a 'statement of the company's affairs'[2]. In all cases, meetings of the company's members and creditors must then be summoned[3]. Creditors to be summoned are all those whose claim and address are known to the person summoning the meeting[4]. The meetings must be summoned on at least 14 days' notice[5], and included with the notice summoning the meeting must be a copy of the proposals and a copy of the company's statement of affairs or summary[6]. Details of the contents of all proposals are listed in rule 1.3 of the Insolvency (Scotland) Rules 1986. These include requirements to list *inter alia*:

(1)    a full breakdown of the company's financial affairs;
(2)    the proposed duration of the voluntary arrangement;
(3)    how third-party creditors and creditors who are connected with the company are to be dealt with;
(4)    how prior arrangements which can be struck at legally are to be dealt with;
(5)    what further credit facilities are to be made available to the company; and
(6)    all details in relation to the person who is to act as supervisor of the voluntary arrangement.

These are very detailed rules and should be carefully checked before any proposals are drafted. There are provisions in the Insolvency (Scotland) Rules

---

1 Insolvency Act 1986, s 2.
2 Ibid, s 2(3).
3 Ibid, s 3.
4 Ibid, s 3(3).
5 Insolvency (Scotland) Rules 1986, r 1.11(1).
6 Ibid, r 1.11(2).

1986 for additional disclosure of information if required by the nominee[1]. The meetings to be called of members and creditors, where there is a nominee, shall be not more than 28 days from the date on which he lodged his report in court[2].

After the meetings (for meetings, see chapter 19), a report must be prepared by the person who is chairman of the meetings[3] stating whether the proposal for a voluntary arrangement was approved or rejected and, if approved, with what (if any) modifications, setting out the resolutions which were taken at each meeting, and the decision on each one, and listing the creditors and members of the company (with their respective values) who were present or represented at the meeting, and how they voted on each resolution, and including any other information which is thought appropriate. Although the sanction of the court is not required for a voluntary arrangement, a copy of the chairman's report must be lodged in court[4].

### Procedure for approval of scheme of arrangement under section 425 of the Companies Act 1985

The procedure in a section 425 arrangement is for the liquidator, or administrator, or any member or creditor, or the company (ie through the directors) to petition the court[5]. It is thought that the receiver may petition the court. Only the company is given a statutory right under section 425 of the Companies Act 1985 as only the directors have a statutory right under section 1 of the Insolvency Act 1986 to put forward proposals. The holder of a floating charge however could petition as a creditor. Where the petition is for sanction of an arrangement between a company and its members, the practice is to omit from the petition any reference to the meeting of the members of the company, and to ask only for an order for separate meetings of special classes of shareholders[6]. Where the arrangement is between the company and its creditors, an order for separate meetings of different classes of creditors is sought[7]. Where the creditors are not involved it is unnecessary to call a creditors' meeting[8]. The first order of the court will be an order for intimation and for summoning the necessary meetings in the manner the court prescribes[9]. The court may then appoint a reporter.

The meetings will ordinarily be summoned not only by individual notices to the shareholders and others concerned, but also by advertisement in newspapers[10]. If the notice is sent to the creditors or members, there must also be sent a statement explaining the effect of the compromise or arrangement, and notice given by the advertisements must also contain this statement.

1 Insolvency (Scotland) Rules 1986, r 1.6.
2 Ibid, r 1.9(1).
3 Ibid, r 1.17.
4 Ibid, r 1.17(3).
5 Companies Act 1985, s 425(1).
6 *Cayzer, Irvine & Co, Petrs* 1963 SC 25.
7 *Tritonia* 1948 SN 11.
8 *Clydesdale Bank, Petrs* 1950 SC 30.
9 Companies Act 1985, s 425.
10 *Merchiston Castle School* 1946 SC 23.

These requirements are essential[1] and if they are not met the meetings have to be reconvened[2].

When the compromise or arrangement under section 425 is duly passed at the meeting, it is submitted to the court, answers are allowed, and a remit is made to the reporter if ordered in the first order. The reporter acts very much like the 'insolvency practitioner' in relation to a voluntary arrangement under Part I of the Insolvency Act 1986.

### Effect of voluntary arrangements under Part I of the Insolvency Act 1986 and schemes of arrangement under section 425 of the Companies Act 1985

An approved voluntary arrangement under Part I of the Insolvency Act 1986 takes legal effect as if made at the creditors' meeting and binds every person who in accordance with the rules had notice of and was entitled to vote at that meeting (whether or not he was present or represented at the meeting), as if he were a party to the voluntary arrangement[3]. Similarly where an order is made sanctioning a scheme under section 425 of the Companies Act 1985 it becomes binding (subject to registration under subsection (3) of that section). These arrangements do not operate as an agreement between the parties affected but have a statutory force. One set of legal obligations is substituted for another by statute (known legally as 'statutory novation'). Consequently the discharge under a scheme of one of several debtors who are jointly and severally liable does not discharge the others[4] unless there is an express provision in the scheme to that effect[5]. It is also not legal for a company, which has become bound by a scheme approved or sanctioned, to vary the scheme by agreement with the other parties affected[6]. If the parties wish to do that they have to petition for another scheme.

### Implementation of voluntary arrangements under Part I of the Insolvency Act 1986

Section 1(2) of the Insolvency Act 1986 stipulates that the 'nominee' shall act as trustee or otherwise supervise the implementation of a voluntary arrangement. He is to be known as the supervisor[7]. The Insolvency (Scotland) Rules 1986 give details on the procedure in relation to the supervisor's duties[8]. It would appear now that all the company's assets may be handed over to trustees for the benefit of all its creditors. This used to be void under section 615 of the Companies Act 1985, which has now been repealed. Section 7(3) of the Insolvency Act 1986 gives any of the company's creditors, or any other person who is dissatisfied by any act, omission or decision of the supervisor, the power to apply to the court for a court order in relation to the supervisor's

---

1 Companies Act 1985, s 426.
2 *Rankin and Blackmore* 1950 SC 218, applied in *Scott & Co* 1950 SC 507; *Coltness Iron Co* 1951 SC 476; *City Property Investment Trust Corp* 1951 SC 507, followed in *Scottish Eastern Investment Trust* 1966 SLT 285; *Second Scottish Investment Trust* 1962 SLT 392.
3 Insolvency Act 1986, s 5(2).
4 *Re Garner's Motors* [1937] Ch 594.
5 *Shaw v Royce Ltd* [1911] Ch 138.
6 *Srimati Premil Devi v People's Bank of Northern India* [1938] 4 All ER 337.
7 Insolvency Act 1986, s 7(2).
8 Insolvency (Scotland) Rules 1986, First Pt, Chap 6.

dealings. It is thought that the court would not interfere with the supervisor's conduct of the arrangement unless he acted contrary to the voluntary arrangement or purported to exercise powers beyond those implied to him as supervisor, or acted unreasonably.

### Compromises, arrangements and compositions at common law

Compromises, arrangements and compositions at common law (ie non-statutory agreements, unlike agreements under Part I of the Insolvency Act 1986 which are made legally binding by statute) may be made by a company which is insolvent (although it would have to be careful that there was no fraudulent preference), or by a company under an administration order or by a company in liquidation with the sanction of the court or by a company in receivership[1]. All the statutes do is to give the company in liquidation, etc, the same power of compromise both with creditors and debtors as an individual would have[2]. These types of common law arrangements are likely to be less common now in view of the voluntary arrangements which can be effected under Part I of the Insolvency Act 1986. However they are still an option, and may be used where requisite majorities are difficult to get or would be inconvenient to get. The power however should not be used to effect the sort of compromise or arrangement contemplated in Part I of the Insolvency Act 1986 or under section 425 of the Companies Act 1985[3], eg distributing assets of the company otherwise than strictly in accordance with the rights of creditors in the liquidation.

Composition contracts or compromise contracts are purely contractual and hence only binding on the contracting parties. Where the sanction of the court is required, there is no legally binding agreement until the sanction is obtained[4], and the court will not give a general power to compromise[5]. If the court has given its sanction without having a material fact disclosed the court will grant reduction of the decree sanctioning the compromise[6]. The terms of the contract vary as well as the number of acceding parties. It may be made a condition of the contract that there must be agreement of all the creditors[7]. A trust deed is sometimes granted to secure payment of the composition[8]. A composition agreement does not imply that a debtor has been given a discharge, although that can be agreed[9]. Non-acceding creditors are not bound by a non-statutory agreement, although they may by their actings be barred from claiming that they are not bound[10]. Whether a composition agreement gives a discharge depends on the terms of the agreement and subsequent actings[11]. Accession to a composition agreement may be proved by any form of writing – a signature is sufficient[12].

---

1 Insolvency Act 1986, ss 14, 55(2), 165 and 167.
2 *Re Albert Life Assurance Co* (1871) LR 6 Ch 381.
3 *Re Trix Ltd* [1970] 3 All ER 397.
4 *Reid & Laidlaw v Reid* (1905) 7 F 457.
5 *Pattisons Ltd, Liqr of* (1899) 6 SLT 372; *Bennett & Co, Liqr of* (1906) 13 SLT 718.
6 *Henderson & Co v Stewart* (1894) 22 R 154.
7 *Brown v M'Intyre* (1830) 8 S 847.
8 *Miller v Downie* (1876) 3 R 548.
9 *Ogilvie & Son v Taylor* (1887) 14 R 399.
10 *Weighton v Cuthbert & Sons* (1906) 14 SLT 251.
11 *Campbell & Co v Scott's Trs* 1913 1 SLT 149; *Craig v Somerville* (1894) 2 SLT 139 and 243.
12 *Henry v Strachan & Spence* (1897) 24 R 1045.

If the debtor under a composition agreement defaults, the other party to the contract can sue for the whole amount of his debt[1]. In this way, a non-statutory composition or compromise agreement differs radically from a statutory compromise agreement where the fact of statutory novation means that default does not allow one to sue for the previous debt. Where there is a composition in satisfaction of debts, it is important in relation to securities whether the composition is with the company in winding up or not. If there is no liquidation, the creditors are entitled to a composition on the full amount of their debts without deduction of any security they have[2]. Where there is a winding-up, securities must be deducted before a ranking is admitted[3]. Where a creditor grants a discharge to the debtor under a composition contract, the guarantor of any debt is thereby freed, unless the consent, express or implied, of the guarantor to remaining bound has been obtained, or unless the guarantor has failed to pay the debt and claim against the debtor when called upon by the creditor to do so, or unless the contract expressly reserves the right to go against the guarantor[4]. The corollary of course is that where no discharge is granted or implied the guarantor remains bound.

## Compromises and the Unfair Contract Terms Act 1977

In terms of section 15(1) of the Unfair Contract Terms Act 1977, the provisions of that Act did not affect the validity of any discharge or indemnity given by a person in consideration of the receipt by him of compensation in settlement of any claim which he has. The position in the rest of the United Kingdom has not been altogether clear except when the discharges related to awards of compensation made for pneumoconiosis contracted in the coal industry[5]. In the English case of *Tudor Grange v City Bank*[6], it was argued that the English section 10 of the Unfair Contract Terms Act 1977 could render unenforceable a discharge between two parties which had the effect of depriving a third party of their rights. It was held that the Unfair Contract Terms Act dealt solely with exemption clauses in the strict sense (ie clauses in a contract modifying prospective liability) and did not affect retrospective compromises of existing claims. Section 10 dealt only with attempts to evade the Act's provisions by the introduction of such an exemption clause into a contract with a third party, and that view as to the English position was consistent with the construction of section 23 of the Act, which had similar application to Scottish law. Section 15(3)(a)(ii) disapplies the Unfair Contract Terms Act 1977 to any contract to the extent that the contract 'relates to the formation, constitution or dissolution of any body corporate or unincorporated association or partnership'. It is thought that that clause and the general import of the Scottish provision would mean that shareholder agreements, share option schemes and such contracts would not be covered by the Act,

1 *Alexander and Austine v Yuille* (1873) 1 R 185; *Woods Parker and Co v Ainslie* (1860) 22 D 723.
2 *McBride v Stevenson* (1884) 11 R 702.
3 Bankruptcy (Scotland) Act 1985, Sch 1, para 5, as applied by Insolvency (Scotland) Rules 1986, r 4.16(1).
4 Bell, *Comm*, i. 376; Goudy on *Bankruptcy*, p 494; *Smith v Ogilvie* (1821) 1 S 159 (NE 152); affirmed (1825) 1 W and S 315; *Flemming v Wilson* (1823) 2 S 336 (NE 296); *Morton's Trs v Robertson's JF* (1892) 20 R 72.
5 Unfair Contract Terms Act 1977, Sch 1, para 5.
6 [1991] BCLC 1009.

it having been held in England that a director who was arguably wrongfully dismissed by his company was precluded from taking advantage of the benefit of a share option agreement which had been drafted in such a way as to disentitle any director who ceased to hold office 'for any reason whatsoever', in that such a clause was not prohibited by section 3 of the Unfair Contract Terms Act 1977 in that it was included in a contract for securities, specifically excluded from the operation of the Act by Schedule 1, para 1(e)[1].

1 *Micklefield v S A C Technology Ltd* [1990] 1 WLR 1002.

# Chapter 7

# Directors' liabilities on insolvency

## Introduction

Limited liability was introduced by statute over a century ago to encourage the taking of risks with capital. It has always however been recognised that there are attendant risks of creditors and companies being defrauded or abused. The opposition last century to 'limited liability' was largely on that ground (see page 6). The Cork Committee concluded in the 1970s that the law was totally inadequate in dealing with problems of fraud both by liquidators and by delinquent directors. The committee stated:

'We believe that this is an urgent problem which demands immediate attention, before the law falls into even greater disrespect and contempt. An entirely fresh approach is now required. The nature of the problem is vividly illustrated by the following extracts from written evidence submitted by a Divisional Consumer Protection Officer of the South Yorkshire County Council:

'"The doctrine of limited liability may have its good points, but it also leads to some indifference and lack of concern when company officials know that if the company goes down, they will not have a financial liability . . . There are many fraudulent practices concerned with the formation and liquidation of companies. Companies are formed, debts run up, the assets milked and the company put into liquidation. Immediately a new company is formed and the process is repeated ad infinitum. Associated with the basic fraud is the practice of new companies buying the remaining stock of the old company (from the liquidator) at give away prices, taking on the premises complete with fittings which are unpaid for, again at nominal prices."'

The Cork Committee had two main proposals for change in the law to meet the problems in relation to directors:

(1) The introduction of a new concept of 'wrongful trading', so that those concerned in the management of a company's affairs would be made liable for the financial consequences of their wrongful or reckless conduct ('wrongful trading');
(2) The disqualification of delinquent directors, and their being made personally liable for the debts of their companies in certain defined circumstances ('disqualification procedure').

### (1) *Wrongful trading*

The concept of 'wrongful trading' is now contained in section 214 of the Insolvency Act 1986. The provision applies only to a company in a creditors' winding-up or a winding-up by the court. Briefly, what the new law does is significantly widen directors' exposure to action by a liquidator in relation to how they conducted the affairs of the company when they ran it. Any action under the section has to be brought by the liquidator. No action may be brought by a creditor or contributory under this section. A full discussion of the new law is to be found at pages 87–194.

## (2) Disqualification procedure

Sections 8 and 10 of the Company Directors Disqualification Act 1986 give two new grounds for making a disqualification order on a director, which are additional to the previously existing grounds which were contained in sections 295 to 302 of and Schedule 12 to the Companies Act 1985, now largely consolidated into the Company Directors Disqualification Act 1986. (The legal framework for making and registering disqualification orders, which was also contained in the Companies Act 1985, is continued in the Company Directors Disqualification Act 1986.) The two additional grounds for making a disqualification order are:

(a)   being held responsible as a director for a company's 'wrongful' or 'fraudulent' trading[1]; and
(b)   'unfitness' found following an investigation of a company's affairs on the order of the Secretary of State for Trade and Industry[2].

**Continuity, overlap and change in old and new law**

There is a significant continuity and overlap in the previous and present law. For example, directors' liability for negligence generally and their liability for breach of duty are not changed by the reforms except in relation to action brought under statute by a liquidator. (There is thus no change in the type of action a company in receivership, or the administrator of a company can bring against directors.) Secondly, an action (formerly under section 631 (now repealed) of the Companies Act 1985) ('misfeasance') may still be brought by the liquidator or a creditor or contributory under section 212 of the Insolvency Act 1986. The liability extends beyond directors, liquidators, officers of the company and other persons variously involved with the company's affairs to administrators and administrative receivers[3]. Action for fraudulent trading under section 213 of the Insolvency Act 1986 re-enacts section 630 of the Companies Act 1985 except that action may only be brought by the liquidator and not by a creditor or contributory.

The type of action open to a liquidator under the 'wrongful trading' provision of section 214 of the Insolvency Act 1986 is in contrast a radical addition to the previously existing law. It is however best understood by looking at the general law in relation to the duties of directors and seeing how wrongful trading goes beyond them and also how action based on it by a liquidator is a parallel remedy to action based on the 'fraudulent trading' provision of section 213 of the Insolvency Act 1986.

Accordingly, it is proposed to deal with:

---

1 Company Directors Disqualification Act 1986, s 10.
2 Ibid, s 8.
3 Insolvency Act 1986, s 212.

(a) negligence and breach of duty of directors;
(b) misfeasance action under section 212 of the Insolvency Act 1986; and
(c) fraudulent trading action under section 213 of the Insolvency Act 1986,

before moving on to 'wrongful trading' and the other major elements of the reforms.

### Negligence and breach of duty

The duties of a director to a company, until the reforming legislation, were those set out by Romer J in *Re City Equitable Fire Insurance Co*[1] where he stated:

'In order, therefore, to ascertain the duties that a person appointed to the board of an established company undertakes to perform, it is necessary to consider not only the nature of the company's business, but also the manner in which the work of the company is in fact distributed between the directors and the other officials of the company, provided always that this distribution is a reasonable one in the circumstances, and is not inconsistent with any express provisions of the articles of association. In discharging the duties of his position thus ascertained a director must, of course, act honestly, but he must also exercise some degree of both skill and diligence. To the question of what is the particular degree of skill and diligence required of him, the authorities do not, I think, give any very clear answer. It has been laid down that so long as a director acts honestly, he cannot be made responsible in damages unless guilty of gross or culpable negligence in a business sense. But as pointed out by Neville J in *Re Brazilian Rubber Plantations and Estates Limited*,[2] one cannot say whether a man has been guilty of negligence, gross or otherwise, unless one can determine what is the extent of the duty which he is alleged to have neglected. For myself, I confess to feeling some difficulty in understanding the difference between negligence and gross negligence, except in so far as the expressions are used for the purpose of drawing a distinction between the duty that is owed in one case and the duty that is owed in another. . . .

'There are, in addition, one or two other general propositions that seem to be warranted by the reported cases: (1) A director need not exhibit in the performance of his duties a greater degree of skill than may reasonably be expected from a person of his knowledge and experience. A director of a life insurance company, for instance, does not guarantee that he has the skill of an actuary or of a physician. In the words of Lindley MR: "If directors act within their powers, if they act with such care as is reasonably to be expected from them, having regard to their knowledge and experience, and if they act honestly for the benefit of the company they represent, they discharge both their equitable as well as their legal duty to the company"[3]. It is perhaps only another way of stating the same proposition to say that directors are not liable for mere errors of judgment; (2) A director is not bound to give continuous attention to the affairs of his company. His duties are of an intermittent nature to be performed at periodical board meetings; and at meetings of any committee of the board upon which he happens to be placed. He is not, however, bound to attend at all such meetings, though he ought to attend whenever in the circumstances, he is reasonably able to do so. (3) In respect of all duties that, having regard to the exigencies of the business, and the articles of association, may properly be left to some other official, a director is, in the absence of grounds for suspicion, justified in trusting that official to perform such duties honestly.'

---

1 [1925] Ch 407 at 427; see also *Norman v Theodore Goddard (a firm)* [1991] BCLC 1028 in which Hoffmann J cites this judgment, and states that that standard is that now stated in section 214(4) of the Insolvency Act 1986 and that directors may trust others until there is a reason to distrust them.
2 [1911] 1 Ch 425.
3 *Lagunas Nitrate Co v Lagunas Syndicate* [1899] 2 Ch 392 at 435.

The level of diligence and skill, as will be noted, up until the reforming legislation, required of directors, would be the reasonable care which an ordinary man might be expected to take, in the circumstances, on his own behalf, but not without the need to exhibit a greater degree of skill than could reasonably be expected from a person of his knowledge and experience. The duties of a director whether executive or non-executive were considered to be the same, and a non-executive director could not plead that he did not have any duties to perform[1]. However, the responsibility of a person who nominates directors to the board of directors of a particular company which subsequently becomes insolvent relates only to the question of negligence in the making of the initial appointment. The person nominating is not responsible for the acts and defaults of those nominees whilst acting as company directors. Such responsibility lies at the door of the company for which they are acting as directors[2].

Romer J did not set an absolute standard for a director's duty of diligence. He quoted with approbation Lord Macnaghten's judgment in *Dovey v Cory*[3]: 'I do not think it desirable for any tribunal to do that which Parliament has abstained from doing – that is to formulate precise rules for the guidance or embarrassment of businessmen in the conduct of business affairs.'

The problem with Romer J's definition and that running through other attempts at definitions is that a director is not thought to be like a professional man with professional skills. He can be anybody off the street, and the thinking is that one cannot legally require of him anything more than one could expect from the man off the street. Hence 'errors of judgment' are acceptable. If there is to be a basis of fault it has to go beyond errors of judgment, and be something like 'gross negligence'. Gross negligence, or something similar, is the traditional test in Scotland[4]. The law in this area really is not formed with a modern economy in mind, requiring as it does only a level of skill to be expected of the particular individual – not of a person filling a particular job, however responsible the job. Not surprisingly in view of the exceptionally low level of skill legally required of them, there are few reported cases in England or Scotland of directors being sued for negligence, although quite a number on breach of trust, or breach of contract.

In addition to the duty of diligence as described in the *City Equitable* case, directors are also trustees for the company, in that they must act in good faith for the benefit of the general body of members[5].

If directors are negligent or in breach of these duties as detailed above, they may be sued by the company[6]. The action will be open to an insolvent company, an insolvent company in receivership and an insolvent company under

---

1 *Dorchester Finance Co Ltd v Stebbing* ([1989] BCLC 498.
2 *Kuwait Asia Bank EC v National Mutual Life Nominees Ltd* [1990] 3 WLR 297.
3 [1901] AC 479.
4 *Lees v Tod* (1882) 9 R 807 at 833, per Lord Deas; *Thompson v J Barke & Co (Caterers) Ltd* 1975 SLT 67. The concept of 'gross negligence' is almost unknown elsewhere in the law of Scotland and is not known in the law of professional negligence (*Hunter v Hanley* 1955 SC 200). It is still applicable to trustees, who, like directors, can be anyone 'off the street'. If there were a professional standard required, people might be reluctant to accept the responsibility.
5 *Re City Equitable Fire Insurance Co* [1925] Ch 407; *Harris v Harris (A) Ltd* 1936 SC 183; *Selangor United Rubber Estates v Cradock* [1968] 2 All ER 1073.
6 *Western Bank v Baird's Trs* (1872) 11 M 96; *Industrial Development Consultants Ltd v Cooley* [1972] 2 All ER 162.

an administration order. If the company is in liquidation, the action should be brought under section 212 of the Insolvency Act 1986.

In exceptional circumstances directors may be sued directly by third parties, where for example the directors effectively 'are the company' by being owners and directors.[1] The company may have a right of action against a negligent director in addition to a claim for any breach of an employment contract it might have with him.

Section 310 of the Companies Act 1985 makes void any article of association of a company or contract with the company or other provision providing indemnity to the director for negligence. There are, however, policies of negligence insurance available to directors, but it is unsettled whether the company may pay the premiums.

## Action under section 212 of the Insolvency Act 1986 ('misfeasance action')

The liquidator has a right to apply to the court asking the court to examine into the conduct of a director if it appears that the director has misapplied or retained or become liable or accountable for any money or property of the company, or been guilty of misfeasance or breach of trust in relation to the company, and the court may then compel a delinquent director to repay or restore any money which he has misapplied or retained or become liable or accountable for to the company or to contribute to the company's assets an appropriate sum by way of compensation[2]. The section also permits the court to enforce the company's right at the initiative of a creditor or a contributory.

An action under this section or its statutory predecessors going back to the Companies Act 1862 has been traditionally known in England, but not in Scotland as a 'misfeasance action', initiated by a 'misfeasance summons'. Misfeasance however is only one of the grounds of action, and the slightly exotic word 'misfeasance' is used as shorthand for a basketful of grounds including misfeasance. In fact a 'misfeasance action' does not create any additional grounds of action to those listed above. It is a procedural matter only. The statute merely provides a summary method of enforcing the liabilities that might have been enforced by the company itself or by its liquidator by means of an ordinary action, including new rights created by the winding up[3]. Action may also be taken under this section against other persons connected with the formation, promotion or running of the company in addition to directors, and also against liquidators, administrative receivers and administrators[4].

In the case of *Farquhar v McCalls*[5], the court had ordered an examination into the conduct of two directors of a company proceeding on an application by a creditor in the liquidation of *Ardtalla Yachts Ltd* which sought to compel them to contribute sums to the company's assets by way of compensation in respect of misfeasance or breach of fiduciary or other duty. The court had held that in the liquidation, the court had first to be satisfied that there was a *prima*

---

1 *Brenes & Co v Downie* 1914 SC 97 at 104.
2 Insolvency Act 1986, s 212.
3 Buckley, *Companies Acts* (14th edn), vol I, p 773.
4 This only applies after 28 April 1986.
5 10 April 1991, Oban Sh Ct, Unreported. See also *Blin v Johnstone* 1988 SLT 335 and *Gray v Davidson* 1991 SCLR 38, Sh Ct.

*facie* case against the directors before an examination was ordered. At the *prima facie* stage ex parte statements and affidavits were sufficient to substantiate the Note in the liquidation. In that case the court held that the sale by a company of its business and assets without consideration for a goodwill element amounted to a breach of fiduciary duties. There had also been a breach of fiduciary duty by putting into liquidation a viable company which could have traded out of a short-term liability.

For there to be an action under section 212 of the Insolvency Act 1986, it is necessary that loss is shown to have been borne by the company. It is not sufficient that there has been misappropriation of funds if the funds have been paid back[1]. If a company is solvent and likely to remain so, it is open to its members to ratify what would otherwise have been a breach of duty by directors provided that the conduct to be ratified was not itself unlawful or a fraud in the company or its creditors[2]. In that case the liquidator would have no cause of action to pursue in the company's name[3]. If however a transaction is likely to cause loss to creditors because the company is insolvent a purported approval or ratification by the members of a breach of duty by the directors causing loss to the company will be ineffective[4].

Most of the cases in England brought under this section, or its statutory predecessors, have involved breach of trust or breach of other duties or improper or *ultra vires* actions, eg payment of dividends out of capital[5]; the making of secret profits by a promoter[6]. In Scotland procuring the payment of private claims to directors after a winding-up petition was caught[7]. The substantive law in Scotland appears from the interchangeability of authorities cited in court to be the same as in England[8].

There are not provisions within section 212 itself, nor in Schedule 9 to the Insolvency Act 1985, nor in Schedule 11 to the Insolvency Act 1986 (which contain transitional provisions relating to the implementation of the two Acts) to limit the effects of the section to acts of misfeasance or breaches of duty which occur after the section has been brought into force. Hence, the summary remedy under section 212 of the Insolvency Act 1986 may be invoked against delinquent directors and others regardless of when the misfeasance, misconduct or misappropriation occurred.

### Fraudulent trading under section 213 of the Insolvency Act 1986

Section 213 of the Insolvency Act 1986 continues the previous law in relation to fraudulent trading. It re-enacts section 630 of the Companies Act 1985

---

1 *Derek Randall Enterprises Ltd (in liquidation ) v Randall* [1991] BCLC 379, [1990] BCC 749.
2 *Atwool v Merryweather* (1867) LR 5 Eq 464n; *Attorney-General's Reference (No 2)* [1984] 1 QB 624.
3 *Salomon v A Salomon & Co Ltd* [1897] AC 22; *Multinational Gas & Petrochemical Co v Multinational Gas & Petrochemical Services Ltd* [1983] Ch 258; *Rolled Steel Products (Holdings) Ltd v British Steel Corp* [1982] Ch 478, upheld in this point [1986] Ch 246; and *Brady v Brady* [1988] 2 All ER 617.
4 *Walker v Wimborne* (1976) 50 ALJR 446; *Re Horsley & Weight Ltd* [1982] Ch 442; *Nicholson v Permakraft (NZ) Ltd* [1985] 1 NZLR 242; and *Kinsela & Anr. v Russell Kinsela Pty Ltd* (1986) 10 ACLR 395.
5 See *Flitcroft's Case* (1882) 21 Ch D 519.
6 *Gluckstein v Barnes* [1900] AC 240.
7 *Liqr of Bankers and General Insurance Co Ltd v Lithauer* 1924 SLT 775.
8 *Liqrs of City of Glasgow Bank v Mackinnon* (1882) 9 R 535.

(formerly section 332 of the Companies Act 1948) with the exception that an action may no longer be brought by a contributory or a creditor[1].

In terms of the section, if in the course of the winding up of a company it appears that any business of the company has been carried on with the intent to defraud creditors of the company or creditors of any other person, or for any fraudulent purposes, the court may on the application of the liquidator of the company, declare that any persons who were knowingly parties to the carrying on of the business in such manner are to be liable to make such contributions (if any) to the company's assets as the court thinks proper. The restriction that only the liquidator may bring the action makes the section in line with the provisions relating to 'wrongful trading' which also may only be brought by the liquidator.

This section, and its statutory predecessors, apply not only to directors, but to 'any persons who are knowingly parties to the carrying on of the business'. Accordingly, not only officers of the company are liable, but any person who is party to the carrying on of the business. The class would include for example a creditor who accepts money which he knows has been procured by carrying on the business with intent to defraud creditors for the very purpose of making the payment[2], although it is not clear whether the creditor needs to have given some prior encouragement to the fraud or whether he could have acquiesced in it after the event. In setting up the liability under the section, the case law suggests the following:

(1)   What is required is to show a criminal intent, which is accordingly a subjective and not an objective test. It is accordingly necessary to show 'actual dishonesty involving, according to current notions of fair trading amongst commercial men, real moral blame'[3]. There can either be intent to defraud or reckless indifference whether or not the creditors were defrauded[4].

(2)   The onus of proving that the person charged has been guilty of dishonesty is upon the person who alleges it[5].

(3)   One transaction alone may be sufficient to set up liability, eg the acceptance of a deposit or the purchase price for goods in advance, knowing that the goods cannot be supplied and the deposit or price will not be repaid[6]. The mere giving or receipt of preference over other creditors will not necessarily constitute fraudulent trading[7].

(4)   In order to be party to the trading in question, the company itself must have been party to the fraud[8] and the individual took some active part. It is not enough that he failed to prevent it or failed to advise against it[9].

(5)   There is constructive intent to defraud established if credit is obtained at a time when the person knows that there is no good reason for thinking

1   Insolvency Act 1985, Sch 6, para 6.
2   *Re Gerald Cooper Chemicals Ltd* [1978] Ch 262.
3   *Re Patrick and Lyon* [1933] Ch 786; *R v Cox, R v Hodges* [1983] BCLC 169; *R v Lockwood* [1986] Crim LR 244.
4   *Hardie v Hanson* (1960) 105 CLR 451, H Ct of Australia; *Rossleigh v Carlaw* 1986 SLT 204.
5   *Re Patrick and Lyon* [1933] Ch 796 at 790.
6   *Re Gerald Cooper*, supra; *R v Lockwood*, supra.
7   *Re Sarflax* [1979] Ch 592; *R v Grantham* [1984] QB 675; *Rossleigh v Carlaw* 1986 SLT 204.
8   *Re Augustus Barnett* [1986] BCLC 170.
9   *Re Maidstone Builders* [1971] 1 WLR 1085.

that funds will become available to pay the debt when it becomes due or shortly thereafter. It is unnecessary to establish knowledge that funds will never become available[1].

(6)   Persons guilty of the conduct described above are criminally liable[2] as well as being civilly liable. 'Shadow directors' are also liable, as they are also for 'wrongful trading'. This expression is defined in both section 22(5) of the Company Directors Disqualification Act 1986 and section 741(2) of the Companies Act 1985 to mean a person in accordance with whose directions or instructions the directors of a company are accustomed to act (excluding a person who gives advice in a professional capacity). It obviously covers the case where a board is really taking directions from some outside controller. It could cover a holding company[3], or even a bank if the company invariably takes its instructions from its bank.

The case of *R v Grantham* mentioned in (5) above somewhat lowered the hitherto very tight definition of 'fraudulent' in this context, by holding that the dishonest intent (which has to be proved for a prosecution case to succeed) does not have to extend to an intention to deprive a creditor of his property permanently and that dishonesty may be inferred if credit is taken or lengthened in circumstances where there is no reasonable prospect of the debts being paid as they fall due, or shortly thereafter. That important case, although a criminal case, indicates that the courts were already moving in the direction of 'wrongful trading'.

### Section 213 action is compensatory and punitive

Where an action is brought under section 213 of the Insolvency Act 1986 for fraudulent trading, the court is entitled to make a compensatory order for the amount of loss incurred by the company as a result of the fraudulent trading from the date of the fraudulent trading and to extract a penalty from the person involved. In the English case of *Re a Company (No 001418 of 1988)*[4], Judge Bromley QC laid down the principles in terms of which relief would be granted under section 213 and how liability should be measured. He stated:

'The question now arises as to the form of relief. Having been helpfully taken through the authorities by Mr Hollington the following principles are in my view relevant on this application by a liquidator.

(i)   The declaration should specify responsibility for a definite sum and not be in general terms as, for example, to creditors whose debts were incurred after commencement of the fraudulent trading (see *Re William C Leitch Bros Ltd* [1932] 2 Ch 71 at 77–79, [1932] All ER Rep 892 at 895–896 per Maugham J).

(ii)   The provision being applied is in the nature of a punitive provision (see *Re William C Leitch Bros Ltd* [1932] 2 Ch 71 at 80, [1932] All ER Rep 892 at 896). It follows that the

---

1   *R v Grantham*, supra.
2   Companies Act 1985, s 458.
3   This is the nearest that the law has got to detraction from the limited liability of a company to open up the concept of 'group liability' as proposed in the EEC Ninth Directive on Company Law. The Cork Committee thought the matter of 'group liability' too complex for them, but one requiring urgent attention.
4   [1991] BCLC 197.

declared sum may be or contain a punitive element as well as a compensatory element (see *Re Cyona Distributors Ltd* [1967] 1 All ER 281 at 284, [1967] Ch 889 at 902 per Lord Denning MR).

(iii)   The usual order on an application by a liquidator is that the sum for which the person concerned is declared to be personally liable ought to be dealt with as part of the general assets in the liquidation (see in *Re William C Leitch Bros Ltd (No 2)* [1933] Ch 261, [1932] All ER Rep 897, per Eve J approved by Lord Denning MR in *Re Cyona Distributors Ltd* [1967] 1 All ER 281 at 284, [1967] Ch 889 at 902).

(iv)   So far as the sum for which the person in question is declared to be responsible is compensatory then in my judgment it is more appropriate under this particular provision to adopt the approach of Maugham J in the first *Leitch* case, [1931] 2 Ch 71 at 80, [1932] All ER Rep 892 at 896, i e to limit the sum to the amount of the debts of the creditor proved to have been defrauded by the fraudulent trading. Mr Hollington urged me to adopt the formulation of Knox J in *Re Produce Marketing Consortium Ltd (No 2)* [1989] BCLC 520 at 553 where he said:

> '*Prima facie* the appropriate amount that a director is declared to be liable to contribute is the amount by which the company's assets can be discerned to have been depleted by the director's conduct which caused the discretion under [s 214(1)] to arise.'

That is a reference to the Insolvency Act 1986. The preceding section, s 213 of the 1986 Act, is the re-enactment of s 630 of the Companies Act 1985, with which I am concerned. Knox J was however concerned with a different statutory provision and it is, I think, preferable to found myself on a direct nexus with the statutory language before me, particularly in the light of Maugham J's observations to which I have referred. (I add that there may not be a difference of principle and I am in no way dissenting from what Knox J said.) Where the context is fraudulent trading with intent to defraud creditors, there is a clear logic in asking what the creditors have lost as a result of the fraudulent trading. I agree with Mr Hollington that an adequate measure of the maximum compensatory element (I emphasise maximum) is the amount of the trading loss during the period of fraudulent trading. I differ from him in that I exclude the amount of extraordinary items for the year ended 31 March 1986, namely the loss on the sale of the freehold property, £4,136, and the loss on the sale of fixtures and fittings, £12,152. I see no nexus to establish these losses as the consequence of fraudulent trading or any evidence that those losses would have been different on a sale at any other time than, in fact, March to July 1985.

. . .

'I am satisfied that there are elements in this case which point to a need for a considerable punitive element, thus: firstly, the first defendant well knew from the years of the bank's concern expressed to him and the accounts that he was provided that he was trading dangerously. There were large excesses of current liabilities over the current assets which did not come down, and there were serious cash-flow difficulties. Secondly, the fraudulent trading continued for a long period after 31 July 1984 for some 22 months drawing more creditors into the net. Thirdly, the directors' remuneration was high in relation to a company in such a long-continued parlous financial state. Fourthly, the change of name and the reverse at the least must have been appreciated to be confusing to creditors, whether or not it was intended to lead to that conclusion. Fifthly, the company continued to pay throughout for the caravan as I have indicated [this was a private asset financed by the company].'

## Wrongful trading

Section 214 of the Insolvency Act 1986 (re-enacting section 15 of the Insolvency Act 1985), which came into force on 28 April 1986, created the legal concept of 'wrongful trading'. It applies only to directors and shadow directors[1], whereas fraudulent trading applies to a larger class of persons (see page 185). A similar concept was already established in several European countries, and this provision was introduced in large measure as a result of the anticipated need to conform with the draft EEC Bankruptcy Convention.

The Cork Committee had put forward its own draft definition of 'wrongful trading'[2], the essential part of which read: '. . . at any time when the company is insolvent or unable to pay its debts as they fall due it incurs further debts or other liabilities to other persons without a reasonable prospect of meeting them in full'.

The above definition, which is echoed in the case of *R v Grantham, supra*, was not adopted by Parliament, and is wider in its scope than that of section 214.

For the section to apply the following two conditions must be met:

(1)   the company must have gone into insolvent liquidation (ie liquidation at a time when its assets are insufficient for the payment of its debts and other liabilities and the expenses of winding up[3]); and

(2)   at some time before the commencement of the winding-up of the company, the person to be held liable was a director or a shadow director, and either knew or ought to have concluded that there was no reasonable prospect that the company would avoid going into insolvent liquidation[4].

Where these conditions are met the court may, on the application of the liquidator, declare that the director in question is liable to make a contribution to the company's assets as the court thinks proper.

There is a defence to the liability in section 214(3), in terms of which the declaration that the director shall make a contribution shall not apply where the court is satisfied that after the date of the actual or constructive knowledge there was no reasonable prospect that the company would avoid going into insolvent liquidation, the director took *every* step with a view to minimising the potential loss to the company's creditors that he ought to have taken (assuming him to have known that there was no reasonable prospect that the company would avoid going into insolvent liquidation). The onus of proof of 'having taken all the necessary steps' is accordingly placed on the director.

For the purpose of determining the fact which a director of a company ought to have known or ascertained, and the conclusions which he ought to have reached and the steps which he ought to have taken, the test is:

What would a reasonably diligent person have done, having both –

(a)   the general knowledge, skill and experience that may reasonably be expected of a person carrying out the same functions as are carried out by that director in relation to the company, and

(b)   the general knowledge, skill and experience that that director has?[5]

---

1  Insolvency Act 1986, s 214(1), (2) and (7).
2  Report, para 1806.
3  Insolvency Act 1986, s 214(6).
4  Ibid, s 214(2)(b) and (c).
5  Ibid, s 214(4).

## Differences between 'wrongful trading' and 'fraudulent trading'

There would appear to be the following key distinctions between wrongful trading and fraudulent trading apart from the fact that only directors and shadow directors may be liable for wrongful trading:

(1) in the case of fraudulent trading the onus of proof is on the person alleging fraud whereas in the case of wrongful trading once the conditions establishing liability are set up, the onus is on the director to prove that he was sufficiently diligent to avoid loss to creditors;
(2) in the case of fraudulent trading a positive act is required to establish liability whereas in the case of wrongful trading acts of omission may be sufficient;
(3) for the purpose of establishing fraudulent trading there would need to be actual knowledge that the company was unable to pay its debts, whereas with wrongful trading it is sufficient that the director ought to have known this; and
(4) going by the case of *R v Grantham*, fraudulent trading involves usually failure to have proper regard to the interests of future creditors (i e those extending credit to the company) whereas wrongful trading involves a failure to have regard to the interests of creditors as a class.

## 'Wrongful trading' and negligence

The concept of 'wrongful trading' extends the usual ambit of a director's liability for negligence. Previously the emphasis had been on the need for honesty and conscientiousness rather than a particular degree of professional skill, diligence or competence (see pages 181–182). There are two tests:

(1) What would a reasonably diligent person having the general knowledge, skill and experience reasonably to be expected of any person carrying out the same functions (a) have concluded about the prospects of the company avoiding insolvent liquidation; and (b) have done to minimise loss?

This is an objective test and looks to the job that the director is doing rather than to the particular skills of the director himself. Accordingly if a cost accountant is over-promoted to the job of finance director, he will not be able to argue that given his training and background he could not be reasonably expected to have the skills necessary to run a finance department. Section 214(5) of the Insolvency Act 1986 makes a further refinement. The director is first assumed to have the general knowledge, skill and experience that may reasonably be expected of a person carrying out 'the same functions' as are carried out by that director[1]. He is also however assumed to have these attributes in relation to functions entrusted to him by the company but which he does not carry out[2]. Hence if the finance director is responsible for the 'treasury' function in a company, it will not be open to him to say he did not understand anything about foreign exchange fluctuations and left it all to his treasurer.

---

1 Ibid, s 214(4)(a).
2 Ibid, s 214(5).

The objective test, having been thus established, is then applied both in determining whether the director ought to have known that there was no reasonable prospect that the company would avoid going into insolvent liquidation, and in determining what steps a reasonably diligent person would have taken[1]. In relation to deciding whether there is any reasonable prospect of the company avoiding going into insolvent liquidation the courts have not yet had to lay down guidelines as to what each director is supposed to know. Previously he was not thought obliged to attend all board meetings (see page 181) but this may now have to be revised in the light of this potentially higher duty.

(2)   What was 'the general knowledge, skill and experience' that the director had?

This is a subjective test and is in line with the previous law on negligence. It should be noted, however, that because the subjective test is in addition to the objective test, the director will be judged by the subjective test, if his skill, knowledge and experience is higher than that which could be reasonably expected from a person carrying out the same functions.

**Aspects of wrongful trading**

In relation to determining whether there is no reasonable prospect that the company would avoid going into 'insolvent liquidation', a company goes into 'insolvent liquidation' at a time when its assets are insufficient for the payment of its debts and other liabilities and the expenses of the winding up[2]. ('Insolvent liquidation' on the ingenious definition would not however cover a creditors' or compulsory winding up, where it turns out at the end of the day that there is a surplus of assets because of course in that event (eg Rolls-Royce Ltd) the creditors recover their debts, or where creditors had time-barred debts[3].) The inclusion of the 'expenses of the winding up' in the definition probably means that the director has to look not only to the state of the balance sheet when the company is trading to see if the company is solvent, but also to whether if it was forced into a winding up, there would be a surplus after taking into account the distress element in the realising of assets and the winding-up expenses. The test is probably therefore on a prospective 'balance sheet' rather than a 'liquidity' basis. This matter is still not resolved by the courts, and it may be that the courts decide that 'going into insolvent liquidation' means that assets are to be valued on a 'going concern' basis and not on a 'break-up' basis[4]. The authors think that on a 'break-up' basis is correct. The image the directors are meant to have in stark relief *is* a 'break-up' and the question is whether creditors would lose; if so urgent action is required. It is also not clear how contingent liabilities are to be valued. (For the different approaches to valuation including contingent liabilities, see pages 84–87.)

Although the implications of section 214 appear stringent, it is obviously

---

1  Insolvency Act 1986, s 214(4).
2  Ibid, s 214(6).
3  See Re Joshua Shaw and Sons Ltd [1989] BCLC 362.
4  See Re a Company [1986] BCLC 261, where Nourse J decided that in relation to 'inability to pay debts', one should look to whether money would be available at the time the debts became due (ie liquidity basis).

directed only at pronounced cases, namely, where there is 'no reasonable prospect' that the company would avoid going into insolvent liquidation. That does not mean that it was 'likely' that the company would go into insolvent liquidation. It only covers a situation where it would be unreasonable to say that there was any prospect of the company avoiding insolvent liquidation. Optimistic trading, or company doctors going in with a reasonable hope that they might turn round a company would seem not to be covered. It is thus much more directed at a situation where directors pay out to themselves large fees, or run up credit, when the company is obviously going into liquidation, or recklessly overtrade. There is however a practical problem with venture capital firms when only two in ten survive, and they are known from the outset as likely to go under. It may be objected that directors of venture capital firms are therefore unnecessarily inhibited, with the consequent discouragement of this type of important 'seedcorn' investment. The objection is unsound because directors of venture capital firms are not any more at risk than other directors, provided they insist that the firms are kept sufficiently capitalised, so that it is the 'venture capital' that is put at risk, not creditors' money.

The duty of directors is to cut the potential loss to the company's creditors. This goes against recent decisions of the courts denying the possibility that directors owe duties of any kind to creditors[1]. The measure of liability of the directors is also not the usual liability measured by loss to the creditors. It is 'such contribution' (if any) to the company's assets as the court thinks proper[2]. The Act is silent as to the criteria the courts should apply in deciding the measure of contribution (if any) which directors should make. The new formula gives the court wide discretion. It is drafted in an open fashion and does not, for example, say whether the financial means of the director are to be taken into account. The same formula is now used in relation to a contribution to be made by a director in the case of fraudulent trading[3]. (Previously a director was 'personally responsible, without any limitation of liability, for all or any of the debts or other liabilities of the company.')[4]

*Re Produce Marketing Consortium Ltd (No 2)*

Since the introduction of 'wrongful trading' by section 214 of the Insolvency Act 1986, the courts have had to deal with remarkably few cases. The reason for this may be that the section is having a deterrent effect both on directors and banks who are potentially liable as 'shadow directors'. The leading and first case was *Re Produce Marketing Consortium Ltd (No 2)*[5], which was heard in the Chancery Division of the High Court by Knox J over nine days in February and March 1989. Too much reliance perhaps should not be placed in one case, but Knox J took the opportunity to elaborate on certain of the propositions mentioned above which are extractable from the wording of section 214 itself. He laid down guidelines in the following areas:

---

1 *Multinational Gas and Petrochemical Co v Multinational Gas and Petrochemical Services Ltd* [1983] Ch 258; see *Winkworth v Edward Baron Development Co Ltd* [1986] 1 WLR 1512 at 1516, per Lord Templeman.
2 Insolvency Act 1986, s 214(1).
3 Ibid, s 213(2).
4 Companies Act 1948, s 333.
5 [1989] BCLC 520.

*Standard by which director's conduct to be judged*

Knox J stated (*supra* at 550), that the test to be applied in judging a director was by the standards of what can reasonably be expected of a person fulfilling his functions, and showing reasonable diligence in doing so. In this connection the requirement to have regard to the functions to be carried out by the director in question, in relation to the company in question, involved having regard to the particular company and its business. Accordingly the general knowledge, skill and experience postulated will be less extensive in a small company in a modest way of business, with simple accounting procedures and equipment, than it would be in a large company with sophisticated procedures. He then laid down what should be the minimum standards. He stated:

'Nevertheless, certain minimum standards are to be assumed to be attained.

Notably there is an obligation laid on companies to cause accounting records to be kept which are such as to disclose with reasonable accuracy at any time the financial position of the company at that time: see the Companies Act 1985, s 221(1) and (2)(a). In addition directors are required to prepare a profit and loss account for each financial year and a balance sheet as at the end of it: Companies Act 1985, s 227(1) and (3). Directors are also required, in respect of each financial year, to lay before the company in general meeting copies of the accounts of the company for that year and to deliver to the registrar of companies a copy of those accounts, in the case of a private company, within 10 months after the end of the relevant accounting reference period (see the Companies Act 1985, ss 241(1) and (3) and 242(1) and (2)).

As I have already mentioned, the liquidator gave evidence that the accounting records of PMC were adequate for the purposes of its business. The preparation of accounts was woefully late, more especially in relation to those dealing with the year ending 30 September 1985 which should have been laid and delivered by the end of July 1986.

The knowledge to be imputed in testing whether or not directors knew or ought to have concluded that there was no reasonable prospect of the company avoiding insolvent liquidation is not limited to the documentary material actually available at the given time. This appears from s 214(4) which includes a reference to facts which a director of a company ought not only to know but those which he ought to ascertain, a word which does not appear in sub-s (2)(b). In my judgment this indicates that there is to be included by way of factual information not only what was actually there but what, given reasonable diligence and appropriate level of general knowledge, skill and experience, was ascertainable. This leads me to the conclusion in this case that I should assume, for the purposes of applying the test in s 214(2), that the financial results for the year ending 30 September 1985 were known at the end of July 1986 at least to the extent of the size of the deficiency of assets over liabilities.'

*Amount the court would order to be contributed*

Knox J held that the amount to be contributed was primarily compensatory and not penal. He stated:

'On the nature of that discretion there were conflicting submissions made to me. Counsel for the first respondent submitted that the court's discretion is entirely at large, and he pointed to no less than three sets of words indicating the existence of a wide discretion: the court *may* declare that the person is to be liable to make *such* contribution (*if any*) to the company's assets as the court thinks *proper*. He also submitted that the provision is both compensatory and penal in character. He referred me to *Re William C Leitch Bros Ltd* [1932] 2 Ch 71 at 79, [1932] All ER Rep 892 at 896 where Maugham J said of s 275 of the Companies Act 1929:

'I am inclined to the view that s 275 is in the nature of a punitive provision, and that where the Court makes such a declaration in relation to 'all or any of the debts or other liabilities of the company', it is in the discretion of the Court to make an order without limiting the order to the amount of the debts of those creditors proved to have been defrauded by the acts of the director in question, though no doubt the order would in general be so limited.'

However, counsel for the first respondent also submitted that the amount which the court concluded had been lost as a result of the wrongful trading should provide a ceiling for the figure which the court declared should be contributed to the company's assets, which is of course the exact opposite of what Maugham J said in that regard. He also relied on the provisions of s 214(3) which prevent the exercise of the discretion under sub-s (1) in any case where, to put it briefly, the director has done everything possible to minimise loss to creditors, and he suggested that it would be inequitable for a director who has just failed to escape scot-free under the provision because he had only done nearly but not quite everything to that end to be treated on a par with a director who had done nothing to minimise loss to creditors.

Counsel for the liquidator . . . submitted that s 214 of the 1986 Act gave a purely civil remedy, unlike the predecessors of s 213 of that Act, such as s 275 of the Companies Act 1929 and s 332 of the Companies Act 1948 which combined the civil and criminal. More significantly for my purpose she submitted that s 214 was compensatory rather than penal. What is ordered to be contributed goes to increase the company's assets for the benefit of the general body of creditors. On that basis she submitted that the proper measure was the reduction in the net assets which could be identified as caused by the wrongful activities of the persons ordered to contribute. This jurisdiction, it was submitted, is an enhanced version of the right which any company would have to sue its directors for breach of duty, enhanced in the sense that the standard of knowledge, skill and experience required is made more objective.

On this analysis, once the circumstances required for the exercise of discretion under s 214(1) are shown to exist, she submitted that the situation was analogous to that obtaining where a tort such as negligence was shown to have been committed in that *quantum* was a matter of causation and not culpability. The discretion given to the court was to enable allowance to be made for questions of causation and also to avoid unjust results such as unwarranted windfalls for creditors. Thus in *West Mercia Safetywear Ltd (in liq) v Dodd* [1988] BCLC 250 at 253, Dillon LJ said of s 333 of the Companies Act 1948:

'The section in question, however, s 333 of the Companies Act 1948, provides that the court may order the delinquent director to repay or restore the money, with interest at such rate as the court thinks fit, or to contribute such sum to the assets of the company by way of compensation in respect of the misapplication as the court thinks fit. The court has a discretion over the matter of relief, and it is permissible for the delinquent director to submit that the wind should be tempered because, for instance, full repayment would produce a windfall to third parties, or, alternatively, because it would involve money going round in a circle or passing through the hands of someone else whose position is equally tainted.'

In my judgment the jurisdiction under s 214 is primarily compensatory rather than penal. *Prima facie* the appropriate amount that a director is declared to be liable to contribute is the amount by which the company's assets can be discerned to have been depleted by the director's conduct which caused the discretion under sub-s (1) to arise. But Parliament has indeed chosen very wide words of discretion and it would be undesirable to seek to spell out limits on that discretion, more especially since this is, so far as counsel were aware, the first case to come to judgment under this section. The fact that there was no fraudulent intent is not of itself a reason for fixing the amount at a nominal or low figure, for that would amount to frustrating what I discern as Parliament's intention in adding s 214 to s 213 in the 1986 Act, but I am not persuaded that it is right to ignore that fact totally.'

*Interest*

Knox J held that he was entitled to allow interest to be ordered to be contributed on the director's contribution from the commencement of the winding-up.

## Penal element in Scotland

As will be noted from what was said on page 186, in relation to fraudulent trading, and above in relation to wrongful trading, the English courts have allowed there to be a penal element in the financial order made against directors for fraudulent trading, and in the case of *Re Produce Marketing Consortium (No 2)*[1], have not discountenanced a penal element. It is not clear which approach the Scottish courts would take. In the case of section 212(3) of the Insolvency Act 1986 in relation to misfeasance the court may only order compensation. In relation to fraudulent trading in terms of section 213 of the Insolvency Act 1986:

'The court on the application of the liquidator may declare that any persons who are knowingly parties to the carrying on of the business . . . are to be liable to make such contributions (if any) to the company's assets as the court thinks proper.'

The payment provision is the same for wrongful trading under section 214(1) of the Insolvency Act 1986. Both these provisions are different from the previous section 630 of the Companies Act 1985 which provided that:

'The court, on the application of the official receiver, or the liquidator or any creditor or contributory of the company, may, if it thinks proper to do so, declare that any persons who are knowingly parties to the carrying on of the business in the manner above-mentioned are to be personally responsible, without any limitation of liability, for all or any of the debts or other liabilities of the company as the court may direct.'

The above provision sets an upper limit of liability as the debts of the company. A second difference is that the director is to be made liable for the debts; not to make a contribution to the assets of the company. It is not clear in section 630(2) whether the director would be guaranteeing the debts of the company and have a right of subrogation against the company or would have no right of subrogation. A further approach is given in sections 216 and 217 of the Insolvency Act 1986, which provide that a person is personally responsible for all the relevant debts of a company if at any time he is involved in the management of the company and it is trading under a restricted name. Section 217(2) states that where a person is personally responsible, he is jointly and severally liable in respect of those debts with the company and any other person who, whether under that section or otherwise, was so liable. Accordingly under that provision the director would be guaranteeing the debts only and would have a right of relief against any assets of the company. Accordingly he would effectively be underwriting the deficit of the company. A further complication is that section 215(5) provides that sections 213 and 214 are to have effect notwithstanding that the person concerned may be criminally liable in respect of matters on the ground of which the declaration under these sections is to be made. Accordingly a criminal fine is not ruled

---

1 [1989] BCLC 520.

out. What Judge Bromley QC seemed to say in *Re a Company (No 001418 of 1988)*[1], was that there was now no upper limit on the sum which the court could order a director to pay. The starting point was compensation of which the ceiling was the loss of the company as a result of the fraudulent trading, but there was no limit in theory to the punitive element. It is thought that that approach is misconceived. It is thought that the upper limit of liability of the director should be his being liable without relief for all the debts of the company from the date of the fraudulent trading whether induced by the fraudulent trading or not. It is thought that it is not the role of the civil court to impose a liability of a punitive nature in addition to that maximum limit. It is also thought that given that the wrongful trading provision is in the same terms and that there is an express provision that there may also be a criminal liability, that a punitive approach would be incorrect for wrongful trading. What is thought to be the correct approach, is for the court to take a view as to what the upper limit should be and then to order a contribution based on the degree of culpability and the extent, where knowable, that debts of the company have been induced by the fraudulent trading. It is thought that a civil court would be acting *ultra vires* of its jurisdiction if it was imposing a criminal penalty as normally understood.

## Relief in terms of section 727 of the Companies Act 1985

Section 727 of the Companies Act 1985 is a protective section for directors and other officers of a company. It provides that in any proceedings against, *inter alia*, a director for negligence, default, breach of duty or breach of trust, if a director who is or may be liable has, in the opinion of the court, acted honestly and reasonably, and if, having regard to all the circumstances of the case, including those connected with his appointment, he ought fairly to be excused, the court may wholly or partly relieve him from his liability, with the court having a discretion in the matter, and being able to impose terms. It is not enough to prove that a director acted reasonably and honestly. It is necessary, in addition, to prove that he ought fairly to be excused[2]. It has been held that the section applies only to actions brought by or on behalf of the company against its directors for breach of duty and not to acts related to third parties[3]. Section 727 of the Companies Act 1985 may be raised as a defence to an action brought under section 212 of the Insolvency Act 1986[4]. In the English case of *Re Produce Marketing Consortium Ltd*[5], it was held that a section 727 defence was not available against an action for wrongful trading under section 214 of the Insolvency Act 1986. In a subsequent English case of *Re D K G Contractors Ltd*[6], the court was prepared to entertain a section 727 defence to an action under section 214 of the Insolvency Act 1986, but held on the facts that the respondents had not acted reasonably and therefore ought not to be

---

1 [1991] BCLC 197.
2 *National Trustee Co of Australasia v General Finance, etc Co* [1905] AC 373; *Re Smith, Smith v Thompson* (1902) 71 LJ Ch 411; *Re Turner Barker v Ivimey* [1897] 1 Ch 536; *Re Second Dulwich 745 Starr-Bowkett Building Society* (1899) 68 LJ Ch 196; *Re Grindey, Clews v Grindey* [1898] 2 Ch 593; *Perrins v Bellamy* [1899] 1 Ch 797; *Re Lord de Clifford* [1900] 2 Ch 707.
3 *Customs & Excise Commrs v Hedon Alpha Ltd* [1981] QB 818, CA.
4 See *Re Claridges' Patent Asphalte* [1921] 1 Ch 543, where directors acted upon an opinion of counsel that the act was *intra vires*; and *Farquhar v McCall*. 10 April 1991, Oban Sh Ct, unreported.
5 [1989] 3 All ER 1.
6 [1990] BCC 903.

excused. It is thought that the provisions of section 727 should not excuse liability under section 214 of the Insolvency Act 1986. It is thought that sections 214(2) and 214(3) provide the only statutory excuse, ie in terms of section 214(2) that the person did not know or ought not to have concluded that there was no reasonable prospect that the company would avoid going into insolvent liquidation, or in terms of section 214(3) that the person took every step with a view to minimising the potential loss to the company's creditors. It is difficult to see how Parliament could countenance a second excuse having set up a specific excuse tailored for the circumstances of that particular type of action. In relation to an action under section 213 of the Insolvency Act 1986, it is thought that section 727 of the Companies Act 1985 would not *a fortiori* be available.

## Disqualification of directors

The Company Directors Disqualification Act 1986 builds on the previous law relating to director disqualification consolidated in sections 295–302 of, and Schedule 12 to, the Companies Act 1985, which set out the legal framework for making and registering disqualification orders, and set out the grounds on which a disqualification order should be made under the law then in force. The previous provisions relating to the disqualification of directors by reference to association with insolvent companies have been repealed and tighter provisions introduced.

Under the new law there are *six* grounds for disqualifying a person as a director. In terms of sections 2, 3, 4 and 5 of the Company Directors Disqualification Act 1986 a person may be disqualified for one of four criminal or apparently criminal activities (see paragraph 7.14). Fifthly, he may also be disqualified where the court has declared a director liable to make a contribution for fraudulent trading under section 213 of the Insolvency Act 1986, or wrongful trading under section 214 of the Insolvency Act 1986. The sixth ground and most usual is when the court is satisfied that he is 'unfit' to take part in the management of a company.

A disqualification order after a declaration of liability for 'fraudulent trading' or 'wrongful trading' under sections 213 and 214 can be made by the court itself or on the application of any person,[1] but in relation to 'unfitness' it must be brought by the Secretary of State for Trade and Industry, if he thinks it is expedient in the public interest.

There are two distinct procedures leading to an application by the Secretary of State for the disqualification on the grounds of 'unfitness':

(a)   a report by a liquidator, administrator, or administrative receiver under section 6 leading to an application; and
(b)   an inspector's report after a Department of Trade and Industry investigation leading to an application.

## Procedure for disqualification for unfitness under section 6

The procedure prior to a court hearing an application for a disqualification order under section 6 is two-stage:

---

1 Company Directors Disqualification Act 1986, s 10(1).

*First stage – report by office-holders*

First the office-holders of a company (i e liquidators, administrative receivers and administrators) have a statutory duty in terms of section 7(3) of the Company Directors Disqualification Act 1986 to report to the Secretary of State any person who is, or has been, a director of a company which has at any time become insolvent (whether while he was a director or subsequently) where it appears to the office-holders that the person's conduct as a director of that company (and conduct in relation to any other company may be taken into account) makes him unfit to be concerned in the management of a company. In this context director will include a 'shadow director', as defined by section 22(5) of the Company Directors Disqualification Act 1986 and section 741(2) of the Companies Act 1985, which is construed widely to include management consultants actively engaged in the running of a company[1]. Where it is alleged that the person concerned is a shadow director there should be a fairly arguable case that the individual exercised a degree of control over the company's affairs as to indicate that he was acting as more than just a professional adviser[2]. Conduct has to relate to matters connected with the insolvency of that company[3]. Reports must be made on prescribed forms[4]. In terms of section 6(2) of the Company Directors Disqualification Act the company is said 'to have become insolvent' only if an administrative receiver is appointed, or an administration order made, or the company goes into liquidation and its assets cannot meet its liabilities including winding-up expenses.

*Second stage – application by Secretary of State*

The second stage is that, if it appears to the Secretary of State that it is expedient in the public interest that a disqualification order should be made, he may make an application to the court for an order. He may not, except with the leave of the court, apply after the end of the period of two years beginning with the day on which the company of which the person accused is or has been a director became insolvent[5].

It is thought that the courts have power to disqualify a director in respect of a foreign company that is being wound up in Scotland and that in proceedings against the director of a Scottish company his conduct in relation to foreign companies of which he was also a director may be taken into consideration[6].

The court may waive some of the normal constraints attendant upon a disqualification order and allow the person subject to the order to remain as a director of a particular company that has not featured in the disqualification proceedings on giving suitable undertakings as to his future behaviour and the

1 *Re Tasbian Ltd (No 3)* [1991] BCC 435.
2 *Official Receiver v Nixon*, (1992) Financial Times, 6 March.
3 Company Directors Disqualification Act 1986, s 6(2).
4 Form D1(Scot) for liquidators, D2(Scot) for administrative receivers, and D5(Scot) for administrators in terms of r 2(2) of the Insolvent Companies (Reports on the Conduct of Directors) (No 2) (Scotland) Rules 1986. In all cases where the company has gone into insolvent liquidation, the liquidators, administrative receivers and administrators must make a report in terms of r 2(3) on Forms D3(Scot), D4(Scot) and D6(Scot) respectively – see ibid, r 2(3). The Department of Trade and Industry has issued Guidance Notes on the completion and return of the statutory reports.
5 Companies Directors Disqualification Act 1986, s 7(1) and (2).
6 *Re Eurostem Maritime Limited & Ors* [1987] PCC 190.

future administration of that named company. In the case of *Re Chartmore Ltd*[1], Harman J accepted an undertaking that board meetings in future would be held monthly and would be attended by a representative of the company's auditors. This would be for a trial period of one year with liberty for there to be an application for an extension of that period.

Provided applications are lodged with the court within the two-year period, it does not matter if the warrant for service is granted or service is effected after the expiry of the two-year period[2]. For the purposes of the time limit the company 'becomes insolvent' at the first occurrence of insolvent liquidation, administration, or administrative receivership. The occurrence of one of these régimes after the other, such as liquidation following administrative receivership, does not start running again for the purposes of the time limit[3]. As regards the exercise by the court of its discretion to allow an extension of the two-year period, the Court of Appeal has indicated that the court will grant leave to commence disqualification proceedings out of time provided there is an arguable case for disqualification, an adequate explanation for the delay in commencing proceedings and there is no prejudice to the director who is the subject of those proceedings[4].

## Procedure for disqualification for unfitness under section 8

In addition to and parallel to information being received from office holders of companies, the Secretary of State has power under the Companies Act 1985[5] to appoint inspectors to investigate the affairs of a company in a number of situations (eg on the application of the company itself or a section of its members)[6] if the court so orders[7], or of his own accord (if it appears to him that there are circumstances suggesting fraud or irregularity)[8] and has powers to require production to him of books or papers relating to a company and to ask for an explanation of them to be given. The Financial Services Act 1986[9] extends these powers of investigation to include (a) the affairs of a unit trust scheme or a collective investment scheme, and (b) possible contraventions of the insider dealing legislation[10]. If it appears to the Secretary of State from a report made to him, or from information or documents obtained by him under certain of these parallel powers, that it is expedient in the public interest that a disqualification order should be made against that person[11] he may apply under section 8 for a court order against a director or former director of any company.

Applications for disqualification under section 8 of the Company Directors Disqualification Act 1986 appear to be comparatively rare in comparison to

---

1 [1990] BCLC 673.
2 *Secretary of State for Trade and Industry v Josolyne* 1990 SCLR 32, 1990 SLT (Sh Ct) 48.
3 *Official Receiver v Nixon* (1990) Times, 16 February, CA affirming *Re Tasbian Ltd* [1989] BCLC 720.
4 *Official Receiver v Nixon*, Financial Times, 6 March 1992; see also *Re Cedac Ltd* [1990] BCC 555 and *Secretary of State for Trade and Industry v Langridge* [1991] BCLC 543, [1991] BCC 148 CA.
5 Companies Act 1985, ss 431–441.
6 Ibid, s 431.
7 Ibid, s 432(1).
8 Ibid, s 432(2).
9 Financial Services Act 1986, ss 94 and 176.
10 Company Securities (Insider Dealing) Act 1985.
11 Company Directors Disqualification Act 1986, s 8.

applications under section 6 of that Act. In the case of *Re Samuel Sherman plc*[1] Paul Barker QC, sitting as a High Court judge, said that that case was the first to be presented under section 8 of the Company Directors Disqualification Act, in which the test 'whether it was expedient in the public interest', following a report by inspectors fell into two distinct disqualification categories. The director persistently failed to comply with a range of statutory duties, which were of an administrative kind, and did not denote dishonesty. He also speculated wildly (and beyond the company's constitutional capacity) with the surplus cash received by the company from the sale of its assets; thereby turning a surplus of £300,000 into one of £26,000. The disqualification in that case was for 5 years. The fact that the respondent had not been dishonest, that he had not concealed any information, that he had himself lost a valuable investment and that he had co-operated with the DTI could not in the opinion of the court save him from disqualification. On the issue of the length of the disqualification period, the judge adopted the division of the 15 year maximum period which Dillon LJ had adopted in *Re Sevenoaks Stationers (Retail) Ltd*[2]. The respondent should have gone into the middle bracket. Little or no disqualification 'would give a signal that directors of public companies could readily avoid disqualification despite breaches of statutory provisions designed to inform and protect the investing public'. In fact the court placed him at the top of the most lenient category.

### Activities constituting unfitness under sections 6 and 8 of the Company Directors Disqualification Act 1986

In the case of applications brought under section 6 of the Company Directors Disqualification Act 1986 by the Secretary of State, following on the report of an office-holder of a company, the court is under a statutory duty to disqualify the unfit director, if it is satisfied that his conduct makes him unfit to be concerned in the management of a company[3]. In the case of an application brought by the Secretary of State following on reports by inspectors, the disqualification is not mandatory. The court has a discretion whether to disqualify or not[4].

Where the disqualification is mandatory, this means only that the court must disqualify him from acting *without leave of the court*, so that the court imposing the disqualification is entitled at the same time to grant leave, either generally or subject to restrictions, e g to specified companies or for a specified time. The director's conduct in relation to other companies, whether or not they themselves have become insolvent, may be taken into account but there must be some misconduct in relation to the insolvent company before section 6 applies[5].

In determining whether a person is unfit under the section 6 and section 8 procedures the court must have regard to the matters mentioned in Schedule 1 to the Company Directors Disqualification Act 1986[6]. These matters may be summarised as follows:

---

1 [1991] BCC 699.
2 [1991] Ch 164 at 174, [1990] BCC 765 at 771, [1991] BCLC 325 at 328 (see page 202).
3 Company Directors Disqualification Act 1986, s 6(1).
4 *Re Bath Glass Ltd* (1988) 4 BCC 130, [1988] BCLC 329.
5 Company Directors Disqualification Act 1986, s 8(2).
6 Ibid, s 9(1).

(1) any misfeasance or breach of a fiduciary duty or other duty owed by the director to the company;
(2) any misapplication of assets or conduct making him accountable to the company;
(3) his part in any improper transfer;
(4) his part in any failure by the company to keep proper records and registers and to file annual returns, etc.;
(5) the director's part in any failure to prepare annual accounts and directors' and auditor's reports;
(6) the extent of the director's responsibility for the causes of the company becoming insolvent;
(7) the extent of the director's responsibility for any failure by the company to supply any goods or services which have been paid for (in whole or in part);
(8) the extent of the director's responsibility for the company entering into any transaction which is at an 'undervalue' or which is voidable as a preference;
(9) the extent of the director's responsibility for any failure to summon a creditors' meeting in a creditor's voluntary winding up; and
(10) the director's failure to comply with certain procedural obligations imposed on directors in insolvency (eg the preparation of a statement of affairs).

All these criteria are to be looked to in the case of a company having become insolvent[1]. (When the company has not become insolvent the court only has to have regard to (1) to (5).) The list is not exhaustive since the court is to have regard to these matters 'in particular' and the list may be amended by order of the Secretary of State by statutory instrument, subject to annulment in pursuance of a resolution of either House of Parliament[2].

Most of what is set out in the Schedule is not new. It merely puts into a new statutory framework what previously were the sort of things that were taken into account in justifying a disqualification. The Guidance Notes available from the Department of Trade and Industry give a more detailed breakdown of how the insolvency practitioner should fill in his return to the Secretary of State. The guidelines also given an indication of the matters which will be of concern to the Secretary of State in deciding whether to bring disqualification proceedings. The following paragraph gives the tone:

'in forming a view of conduct which may be considered 'unfit,' office-holders are asked not to take a pedantic view of isolated technical failures, eg the occasional lapse in filing annual returns etc, but to form an objective view of the director's conduct. It is also stressed that the office-holder is required to consider matters of conduct on the basis of information acquired in the course of his normal duties and by reference to the books and records available to him and is not obliged to undertake investigations which he would not otherwise have considered it necessary to make. The conduct to be reported on may have arisen before the commencement date of 28th April 1986.'

A disqualification order under section 6, ie following a report by an office-holder, has a minimum period of two years and a maximum period of 15

---

1 Company Directors Disqualification Act 1986, s 9(1).
2 Ibid, s 9(4) and (5).

years[1]. A disqualification following an inspector's report has only a maximum penalty of a 15-year disqualification[2].

In cases which have been brought to court, a general picture is now clear of the type of situations in which a court will hold that a person is unfit to be a director. The level of blameworthiness that has to be established for there to be a finding that a person is unfit to be concerned in the management of a company has been stated in different ways by different judges. In *Re Bath Glass Ltd*[3], Peter Gibson J stated the test as follows:

'To reach a finding of unfitness the court must be satisfied that the director has been guilty of a serious failure or serious failures, whether deliberately or through incompetence, to perform those duties of directors which are attendant on the privilege of trading through companies with limited liability.'

Hoffman J suggested a somewhat higher degree of culpability. He said:

'There must, I think, be something about the case some conduct which if not really dishonest is at any rate in breach of standards of commercial morality, or some really gross incompetence which persuades the court that it would be a danger to the public if he were to be allowed to continue to be involved in the management of companies, before a disqualification order is made'[4].

Following that reasoning in that case Hoffmann J held that the fact that the unpaid debts include taxes does not in itself prove that there had been a sufficient breach of commercial morality to merit disqualification, and in *Re CU Fittings Ltd*[5] he held that the benefiting of ordinary creditors to a greater extent than the Crown was not necessarily a type of mismanagement which merited disqualification. A different view was taken by Vinelott J in *Re Stanford Services Ltd*[6], who made the point that the Crown is an involuntary creditor and that a director owes not merely a duty to keep a full and up to date record of tax deducted and collected but a duty to account for it and not use such tax to finance his business[7]. In the case of *Re Lo-line Electric Motors Ltd*[8], Browne-Wilkinson V-C, considered the non-payment of Crown debts as more culpable than non payment of other debts and the implication was that that rendered a person unfit to be a director. He stated:

'The debts owed by the companies included substantial Crown debts, ie sums for which the company was liable to the Inland Revenue or Customs and Excise in respect of PAYE, national insurance and value added tax. There is a slight difference of judicial approach to Crown debts. In *Re Dawson Print Group Ltd* [1987] BCLC 601 Hoffmann J, on the facts of that case, did not draw any distinction between a failure to pay Crown debts and the failure

---

1 Ibid, s 6(4).
2 Ibid, s 8(4).
3 (1988) 4 BCC 130.
4 *Re Dawson Print Group Ltd* (1987) BCC 322 at 324, cited with approval by Browne-Wilkinson V-C in *Re McNulty's Interchange Ltd* (1988) 4 BCC 533; see also *Re Douglas Construction Services Ltd* (1988) 4 BCC 553.
5 [1989] BCLC 556.
6 (1987) 3 BCC 326.
7 In *Re McNulty's Interchange Ltd* [1989] BCLC 709, 4 BCC 533, Browne-Wilkinson V-C did not regard it as improper that payment of Crown debts had been withheld where agreements had been reached with the Customs and Excise and the Inland Revenue for payment by instalments.
8 [1988] BCLC 698 at 704–705.

to pay other trading debts. However, in *Re Wedgecroft Ltd* (7 March 1986, unreported) Harman J treated crown debts as *"quasi-trust"* monies and the failure to pay them as being more morally culpable than failure to pay ordinary commercial debts. In *Re Stanford Services Ltd* [1987] BCLC 607 Vinelott J treated the failure to pay Crown debts as more serious than the failure to pay commercial debts. He described the Crown as an involuntary creditor and said (at 617): "the directors of a company ought to conduct its affairs in such a way that it can meet these liabilities when they fall due, not only because they are not monies earned by its trading activities, which the company is entitled to treat as part of its cash flow (entitled that is in that the persons with whom it deals expect the company to do so) but more importantly, because the directors ought not to use monies which the company is currently liable to pay over to the Crown to finance its current trading activities. If they do so, and if, in consequence, PAYE, national insurance contributions and VAT become overdue, and, in a winding-up, irrecoverable, the court may draw the inference that the directors were continuing to trade at a time when they ought to have known that the company was unable to meet its current and accruing liabilities, and were unjustifiably putting at risk monies which ought to have been paid over to the Crown as part of the public revenues to finance trading activities which might or might not produce a profit. It is, I think, misleading (or at least unhelpful) to ask whether a failure to pay debts of this character would be generally regarded as a breach of commercial morality. A director who allows such a situation to arise is either in breach of his duty to keep himself properly informed, with reasonable accuracy, as to the company's financial position . . . or is acting improperly in continuing to trade at the expense and jeopardy of monies which he ought not to use to finance the company's current trade."

I agree with those remarks and add this. Although the Crown debts are not strictly trust monies, the failure to pay them over does not only prejudice the Crown, as creditor, but in the case of PAYE and national insurance may also have a prejudicial effect on the company's employees. The use of monies obtained by compulsory deductions from wages for the financing of the company's business is to use monies which morally, if not legally, belong either to the employees or to the Crown without the consent of either. I consider the use of the monies which should have been paid to the Crown to finance contribution of a insolvent company's business more culpable than the failure to pay commercial debts.'

This approach has now been overturned in England by the Court of Appeal in the case of *Re Sevenoaks Stationers (Retail) Ltd*[1]. Giving the opinion of the court, Dillon LJ held that the non payment of Crown debts did not in itself indicate a higher degree of culpability than the non-payment of other debts. The test was to see what the significance of the non-payment of Crown debts was. He stated:

'I would see validity in this if it were correct, as the Vice-Chancellor apparently thought [in *Re Lo-Line Electric Motors Ltd*[2]], that failure to pay over to the Crown monies deducted from the wages of employees might have a prejudicial effect on the employees. On the hearing of this appeal, however, both sides have made enquiries, including enquiries from the Inland Revenue, to see what prejudice there may be to the employees, and no trace of any prejudice has been found. On the contrary the Revenue rightly accept that the burden of a failure by the employer as the Crown's appointed collector, to pay over to the Crown monies deducted from wages for PAYE or national insurance contributions must fall on the Crown and not on the employees. Therefore the employees are credited with what has been deducted from their wages even though what has been deducted has not been paid over to the Crown.

Moreover though the Crown had powers under the Social Security Act 1975 and previous such Acts to sue the directors personally for non remittance of national insurance

1 [1991] BCLC 325.
2 [1988] BCLC 698.

contributions deducted from wages of their company's employees, those powers were abolished by the Insolvency Act 1985, following an earlier public announcement by the Secretary of State for Trade that it had been decided as a matter of policy that no proceedings should be brought against directors for the recovery of such contribution.

As for VAT, no one suggests that a customer who pays VAT to a company as part of the price to him of goods sold or services rendered to him by the company has to pay VAT again to the Customs and Excise or is in any other way prejudiced by the failure of the company to account to the Customs and Excise for the VAT which the company has received. Moreover, for instance, a retailer (and the instance could apply equally to a manufacturer) sells goods to a customer and receives VAT in respect of the price, whether the price is quoted ex-VAT or inclusive of VAT, I find it very difficult to regard it as automatically more heinous on the part of the retailer not to account to the Customs and Excise for the VAT paid than it would be not to pay the supplier, who may be in a small way of business, in due time for the goods sold to the retailer's customer.

The Official Receiver cannot, in my judgment, automatically treat non payment of any Crown debt as evidence of unfitness of the directors. It is necessary to look more closely in each case to see what the significance, if any, of the non payment of the Crown debt is.'

In that case the Court of Appeal noted that there had been a deliberate decision to pay only those creditors who pressed for payment. The result was that companies had traded when they were insolvent and known to be in difficulties at the expense of those creditors who, like the Crown, had happened not to be pressing for payment. It held that such conduct on the part of a director could well be relied on as a ground for saying that the director was unfit to be concerned in the management of a company. What, however, was relevant in the Crown's position was not that the debt was a debt which arose from a compulsory deduction from the employees' wages or a compulsory payment of VAT, but that the Crown was now pressing for payment, and the director was taking unfair advantage of that forbearance on the part of the Crown, and, instead of providing adequate working capital was trading at the Crown's expense while the companies were in jeopardy. The court held it would be equally unfair to trade in that way and in such circumstances at the expense of creditors other than the Crown. It is thought by the authors that the opinion of Dillon LJ in *Re Sevenoaks Stationers*[1] is the correct approach.

In the case of *Re Sevenoaks Stationers (Retail) Ltd*[2], which was the first decision of the Court of Appeal on a disqualification under section 6 of the Company Directors Disqualification Act 1986, the court pronounced certain guidelines as to the applicable period of disqualification which should be imposed. In what might have been thought an obvious observation, the Court of Appeal affirmed that the potential 15 year disqualification period should be divided into three brackets, viz: (1) the top bracket of disqualification for a period over 10 years, which should be reserved for particularly serious cases. These may include cases where a director who has already had one period of disqualification imposed on him, is disqualified for a second period; (2) the minimum of 2–5 years' disqualification, which should be applied where, though disqualification is mandatory, the case is relatively, not very, serious; and (3) the middle bracket of disqualification for 6–10 years, which should apply for serious cases which do not merit the top bracket.

1 [1991] BCLC 325.
2 Supra; see also *Re Keypak Homecare Ltd* [1990] BCLC 440; *Re T & D Services (Timber Preservation and Damp Proofing Contractors) Ltd* [1990] BCC 592; and *Re Travel Mondial (UK) Ltd* [1991] BCLC 120.

## Other grounds for disqualification

Apart from the special provisions of section 10 of the Company Directors Disqualification Act 1986 which allow the court to make a disqualification order of its own motion or on the application of any person, where there has been wrongful or fraudulent trading, there are *four* other grounds on which the court may disqualify a person from being a director, which are listed in sections 2, 3, 4 and 5, of the Company Directors Disqualification Act 1986. They are: (1) conviction of an indictable offence, in connection with the promotion, formation, management or liquidation of a company, or with the receivership or management of a company's property; (2) persistent breaches of the companies legislation; (3) summary conviction under the companies legislation; and (4) fraud, fraudulent trading or breach of duty revealed in winding up. In those cases an application for a disqualification order may be made by the Secretary of State, or by the liquidator, or by any past or present member or creditor of any of the companies concerned. The grounds are essentially unchanged from the former reasons applicable prior to 28 April 1986, and the only ground of disqualification relevant in insolvency is the fourth ground, namely a disqualification order based on fraudulent trading. There is overlapping because a disqualification order may also be made on that ground under section 10 of the Company Directors Disqualification Act 1986. However, for section 10 to apply an order must first have been made declaring the person liable to contribute to the company's assets under section 213 of the Insolvency Act 1986.

## Main weakness of reforms

The weakness of the statutory reporting system and the liabilities which directors may incur is that it depends on the appointment of liquidators, administrators and administrative receivers to make the necessary investigations and report. If the company does not have sufficient funds to pay an office-holder, there will be no automatic vetting, only spot-checking by the Department of Trade and Industry. Paradoxically under the system the more ruthless directors are at stripping their companies bare, leaving nothing for creditors, the less likely they are to be caught.

## Criminal liabilities of directors outlined above

In addition to the civil liabilities outlined in this chapter and their openness to public examination proceedings, directors are also subject to a criminal code. For example, contravention of a disqualification order risks conviction of up to two years in prison or a fine or both[1]. There is also a quasi-criminal penalty in section 15 of the Company Directors Disqualification Act 1986 in that a person breaching a disqualification order becomes personally liable for all the debts of a company incurred while acting in breach of the order whether or not his actings had anything to do with their being run up. Further offences and

---

1 Company Directors Disqualification Act 1986, s 13.

their penalties in relation to insolvency may be found in Schedule 11 to the Insolvency Act 1986[1]. As at the date of publication there have been approaching 1,500 disqualification orders in England and Wales under the 1986 legislation, and about 50 orders in Scotland. All the Scottish orders have been under section 6 of the Company Directors Disqualification Act 1986 and all have been unopposed.

### Use of prohibited name

Section 216 of the Insolvency Act 1986 prohibits, except with the leave of the court, former directors of companies which have gone into insolvent liquidation from being directors of or concerned in, for five years from the liquidation, of another company with the same or similar name. They are liable to imprisonment for breach, and under section 217 liable for the debts of the subsequent company. This strikes at a formerly common abuse[2].

In the case of *Re Bonus Breaks Ltd*[3], a director (whose previous company had become insolvent) was given leave by the court to act as a director of a new company with a similar name to the unsuccessful predecessor. Assurances, however, were required from the director that the capital base of the new company would be maintained and that there would be no purchase or redemption of the company's shares for the next two years unless the transaction was approved by an independent director.

Persons have been convicted under this section for using the name 'Ardtalla Yacht Services Limited' without permission of the court, where the liquidated company had been called 'Ardtalla Yachts Limited'[4].

---

1 A comprehensive list of offences and penalties to which directors are subject generally is to be found in *Directors and their Liabilities*, published by the Institute of Directors.
2 See page 179 for a description of this abuse. See also Part 4, Chap 13 of the Insolvency (Scotland) Rules for details of legal practice.
3 [1991] BCC 546.
4 *Farquhar v McCall*, 10 April 1991, Oban Sheriff Court unreported.

Chapter 8

# Effect of corporate insolvency on diligence

## Introduction

Diligence is a collective name traditionally given in Scotland to an assortment of legal procedures. It is perhaps better defined as any judicial process whereby a creditor freezes ('litigiosity') or seizes ('nexus') assets of a debtor. Litigiosity merely stops the debtor from disposing of the assets. Nexus gives the creditor a real right ('judicial security'). There are *four* main types of diligence which creditors may use against a company. These are:

(1) *arrestment*;
(2) *inhibition*;
(3) *poinding*; and
(4) *adjudication*.

In addition to these four main types of diligence there are three other types, namely, real adjudication, maills and duties and real poinding ('poinding of the ground'). The last three types of diligence are uncommon in modern practice. They are dealt with briefly at page 212. The general nature of the four main types of diligence is as follows:

### (1) *Arrestment*

Arrestment is the diligence appropriate to attach financial obligations owed to the debtor by a third party; and corporeal moveables (ie physical assets) belonging to the debtor which are in the hands of the third party. In relation to the arrestment, the arresting creditor is known as the 'arrester', the third party as the 'arrestee' and the debtor as 'the common debtor'.[1] Arrestment to enforce payment of a decree is known as arrestment in execution. Arrestment to keep frozen some asset of the defender so that the asset may be realised to satisfy the decree which the pursuer hopes he is going to obtain is known as 'arrestment on the dependence'. The effect of an arrestment is to prevent the arrestee from paying over the sum attached to the common debtor. If he does so, he is liable to the arrester for the loss caused thereby. The arrestment freezes the assets, ie introduces 'litigiosity'. It gives the arrester no title to the assets which have been arrested. The arresting creditor completes his diligence (realises the assets subject to the arrestment) by bringing an action of 'furthcoming' against the arrestee and the common debtor in order to obtain 'a decree effectually transferring from the common debtor to the arresting creditor the obligation which was originally prestable to the former

---

1 Wilson on *Debt* (2nd edn, 1992), Chap. 16.

by the arrestee'[1]. In this way the arrester obtains payment of the debt owed by the arrestee to the common debtor.

In addition to arrestment so defined, which is intended as diligence, foreigners may be made subject to the jurisdiction of the Scottish courts by the arrestment of their assets in the hands of third parties in Scotland. This is known as arrestment to found jurisdiction (*ad fundandam juridictionem*).

## (2) Inhibition

An 'inhibition' is 'a writ passing under the signet, prohibiting the debtor from alienating any part of his estate, and from contracting debt by means of which it may be carried off, to the prejudice of the creditor inhibitor; and interdicting third parties from taking conveyancing of the heritage'[2]. It affects only the heritable estate of the debtor. It is not a complete diligence and its effect is merely prohibitory and preventive. It may be in execution of a decree, or on the dependence of an action.

Where a debtor has granted a heritable security and another creditor has inhibited, on the sale of the security subjects, the heritable creditor is entitled to be paid in full from the proceeds and the inhibiting creditor is entitled to the balance in preference to creditors whose debts were contracted after the date of the inhibition but not in preference to other creditors whose debts were contracted before the date of the inhibition[3]. Although in principle an inhibition is a protective diligence only and does not divest the debtor of any of his property, on the debtor's liquidation, the inhibitor is entitled to receive the same dividend from the heritable property as he would have received if no debts affecting it had been created after the date of the inhibition. This is achieved by a complicated process, which in effect results in the inhibitor being compensated for any shortfall in his dividend at the expense of posterior creditors[4].

## (3) Poinding

Poinding is the form of diligence appropriate to attach corporeal moveables belonging to the debtor himself which are in the custody or control of the debtor himself. It can also be used where corporeal moveables belonging to

1 *Lucas's Trs v Campbell and Scott* (1894) 21 R 1096 at 1103, per Lord Kinnear.
2 Bell, *Prin*, 2306.
3 For a full discussion, see Maher & Cusine, *The Law and Practice of Diligence*, Chaps 4 and 9; Wilson on *Debt* (2nd edn), Chaps 19 and 23, and cases referred to in these works.
4 Bell, *Comm*, ii, 413; see also *Baird & Brown v Stirrat's Tr* (1872) 10 M 414 at 419 where Lord President Inglis said that: 'The rule contemplates an inhibiting creditor, creditors whose debts were contracted prior to the inhibition, and creditors whose debts were contracted subsequent to the inhibition. All those creditors adjudge within a year and a day of one another, so that it does not matter which is the leading adjudication. In respect of their adjudications they all rank *pari passu*. But the inhibiting creditor has a preference over those whose debts were contracted subsequent to the inhibition. The prior creditors are to be neither hurt nor benefited by the inhibition. In these circumstances the clear and equitable rule of ranking was established, that the inhibitor's preference must be secured to him entirely at the expense of the subsequent creditors, while creditors whose debts were contracted prior to the inhibition draw just what they would have done had the whole creditors been ranked *pari passu*.' See *Graham Stewart*, p 567, for the proposition that liquidation acts like sequestration.

the debtor are in the possession of the creditor[1]. 'The essence of poinding is that the goods poinded may be taken to the market cross and sold'[2]. The effect of poinding is to lay a nexus on the goods and create a security over them in favour of the creditor[3].

### (4) Adjudication

Adjudication is the appropriate diligence to attach heritable property of the debtor. The subjects of the diligence are land and heritable rights. The procedure is by an action which can be raised only in the Court of Session.

### The effects of insolvency on diligence

In the absence of a provision to the contrary, an advantage at the expense of the general body of creditors might be secured by a creditor enforcing his debt by diligence against funds or assets belonging to the debtor. Any inequalities which might otherwise arise from the use of diligence are eliminated in *three* ways:

(1)  by the equalisation of some forms of diligence (arrestments, poindings and adjudications) outside liquidation;
(2)  by the equalisation or reduction of these forms of diligence in the event of liquidation; and
(3)  by the suspension of diligence during liquidation.

(In addition, where there is an application for an administration order, or an administration order, diligence may not be commenced or proceeded with in terms of sections 10(1)(c) and 11(3)(d) of the Insolvency Act 1986 except with the leave of the court. A voluntary arrangement under Part I of the Insolvency Act 1986, because it is binding, could entail a creditor being obliged to lift diligence.)

# (1)  EQUALISATION OF DILIGENCE OUTSIDE LIQUIDATION

Scots law is unusual among legal systems in creating rules for the *pari passu* ranking of creditors on the proceeds of diligence outside liquidation. These rules were designed to discourage a race of diligence among creditors, which might precipitate or aggravate the debtor's insolvency and lead to greater inequalities among the unsecured creditors. Independently of liquidation, provision is made for the *pari passu* ranking of creditors on the proceeds of adjudications for debt, arrestments and poindings.

In the case of the two most common forms of diligence, ie arrestments and poindings, equalisation depends on 'apparent insolvency'. 'All arrestments

---

1  *Lochead v Graham* (1883) 11 R 201.
2  *Trowsdale's Tr v Forcett Ry Co* (1870) 9 M 88 at 95, per Lord Neaves.
3  *Stephenson v Dobbins* (1852) 14 D 510.

and poindings which have been executed within 60 days prior to the constitution of the apparent insolvency of the debtor, or within four months
thereafter, shall be ranked *pari passu* as if they had all been executed on the
same date'[1]. The rule about equalisation of diligences outwith liquidation
applies equally to sequestration (a full discussion is to be found in *Clark v
Hinde, Milne & Co*[2]). Moreover, any creditor producing in that period a decree
for payment or liquid grounds of debt is entitled to rank as if he had executed
an arrestment or a poinding[3]. The same law applies to the arrestment of
ships, but not to the arrestment of earnings and maintenance arrestment[4].
There is a similar provision in principle although different in detail in relation
to the equalisation of adjudications for debt under the Diligence Act 1661
(c 34), and the Adjudication Act 1672 (c 45). The equalisation of adjudications
is unrelated to apparent insolvency and operates only in favour of creditors
actually adjudging before or within a year and a day after an effectual adjudication, not in favour of creditors who merely hold decrees or liquid grounds of
debt.

   'Apparent insolvency' is constituted if the company gives written notice to
its creditors that it has ceased to pay its debts in the ordinary course of
business; or if it grants a trust deed[5]. It is thought by the authors that an
administration order must be equivalent to a written notice to the company's
creditors that it has ceased to pay its debts in the ordinary course of business.
'Trust deed' does not seem to apply to voluntary arrangements under Part I of
the Insolvency Act 1986[6].

## (2) EQUALISATION OR REDUCTION OF PRIOR DILIGENCE ON LIQUIDATION

The justification for reducing or equalising diligences effected within a short
period prior to liquidation is simply stated in the Bills of Exchange (Scotland)
Act 1772[7], which, with reference to the diligences of arrestment and
poinding, proceeded on the narrative that:

'the personal estates of such debtors as become insolvent are generally carried off by the
diligences of arrestment and poinding, executed by a few creditors, who, from the nearness
of their residence to, and connection with such debtors, get the earliest notice of their
insolvency, to the great prejudice of creditors more remote and unconnected, and to the
disappointment of that equality which ought to take place in the distribution of estates of
insolvent debtors among their creditors.'

### (1) Equalisation of arrestments and poindings

The equalisation of arrestments and poindings arises independently of winding up. However, the commencement of a winding-up during the period of

1 Bankruptcy (Scotland) Act 1985, Sch 7, para 24(1); see also Gretton 'Multiple Notour Bankruptcy'
   28 JLSS 18.
2 (1884) 12 R 347 at 353, *per* Lord Shand.
3 Bankruptcy (Scotland) Act 1985, Sch 7, para 24(3).
4 *Harvey v MacAdie* (1888) 4 ShCt Rep 254; *Munro v Smith* 1968 SLT (ShCt) 26; Bankruptcy
   (Scotland) Act 1985, Sch 7, para 24(8).
5 Bankruptcy (Scotland) Act 1985, s 7(1)(b) and (c)(i).
6 Ibid, ss 5(2)(c) and 73(1).
7 12 Geo 3, c 72.

equalisation nevertheless has important consequences for the equalisation process. In terms of section 37(1) of the Bankruptcy (Scotland) Act 1985[1]:

'the commencement of winding up . . . shall have the effect in relation to diligence done (whether before or after the commencement of winding up) in respect of any part of the company's estate of –
(a) a decree of adjudication of the heritable estate of the company for payment of its debts which has been duly recorded in the register of inhibitions and adjudications on that date; and
(b) an arrestment in execution and decree of furthcoming, and arrestment in execution and warrant sale, and a completed poinding,
in favour of the creditors according to their respective entitlements.'

Section 37(4) of the Bankruptcy (Scotland) Act 1985[2] provides that:

'No arrestment or poinding of the estate of the company . . . executed
(a) within the period of 60 days before the commencement of winding up and whether or not subsisting at that date; or
(b) on or after the commencement of winding up,
shall be effectual to create a preference for the arrester; and the estate so arrested or poinded, or the proceeds of sale thereof, shall be handed over to the liquidator.'

Equalisation of arrestments and poindings arises independently of liquidation, but a winding up commenced during the period of equalisation has consequences for the equalisation process. If the winding up is the first constitution of 'apparent insolvency', then arrestments and poindings are cut down within 60 days of the liquidation because any arrestment or poinding executed within the period of 60 days preceding the winding up is ineffectual to secure a preference. A similar result is achieved where there has been an antecedent constitution of 'apparent insolvency' within the period of four months preceding the commencement of winding up, because the winding up has in terms of section 37(1) of the Bankruptcy (Scotland) Act 1985 the effect of a completed diligence in favour of creditors according to their respective entitlements. This effectively ranks their entitlements *pari passu* with any arrestment or poinding executed on or after the sixtieth day before the earlier constitution of 'apparent insolvency'[3].

Section 185(3) provides that where a company is being wound up by the court – and that would include a voluntary winding up converted into a compulsory one – the date of the commencement is to be the date of the order. If the first constitution of 'apparent insolvency' on a converted winding up is the winding-up resolution and the order is more than four months and 60 days thereafter the order will not be effective to equalise with diligence effected prior to the resolution.

## (2) Equalisation of inhibitions

Inhibitions, although different from arrestments and poindings in that they do not attach to a specific asset, do give the inhibiting creditor a preference over those whose debts were contracted subsequent to the inhibition. In order to establish this equalisation, there has been a change in the law by section 37(2) of the Bankruptcy (Scotland) Act 1985, applied by section 185(1) of the Insolvency Act 1986, which enacts:

1 As applied to windings up in Scotland by Insolvency Act 1986, s 185.
2 As applied to liquidations by Insolvency Act 1986, s 185(1).
3 For an illustration of this effect, see *Stewart v Jarvie* 1938 SC 309.

'No inhibition on the estate of the company which takes effect within the period of 60 days before the commencement of winding up shall be effectual to create a preference for the inhibitor and any relevant right of challenge shall, at the commencement of winding up, vest in the liquidator, as shall any right of the inhibitor to receive payment for the discharge of the inhibition:–
Provided that this subsection shall neither entitle the liquidator to receive any payment made to the inhibitor before the commencement of winding up nor affect the validity of anything done before that date in consideration for such payment.'

## (3) Effect of administration orders on equalisation of diligences

From the presentation of a petition for an administration order, no diligences may be commenced or continued[1]. There is provision for the administrator to sell, with the permission of the court, property which is subject to a security other than a floating charge[2]. This the authors interpret to mean that the security remains in place and no further legal steps may be taken by way of diligence whether by commencement or continuation. The authors do not interpret this to mean that a diligence is lifted. (There is no provision for diligences to be reactivated at the end of an administration order.) There would appear, however, to be perhaps an undesirable mischief created as a result. Because diligences are only struck at within 60 days of commencement of winding up, an administration order has the effect of depriving ordinary creditors of one means of striking at diligences within the 60 days by seeking a winding up. Because, however, it is thought that an administration order constitutes 'apparent insolvency', diligences will effectively be reduced if made within 60 days before the apparent insolvency provided the commencement of the winding up is within four months after the 'administration order'[3]. If an administration lasts more than four months, those creditors who have not arrested, or produced a decree or liquid grounds of debt, will be disadvantaged.

It is not thought that a creditor could ask the court to discharge an administration order under section 27(1) of the Insolvency Act 1986 on the grounds that the company's affairs were being managed by the administrator in a manner which was unfairly prejudicial to the interests of the creditor (unless delay is causing the four months to run unnecessarily), or that any actual or proposed act or omission of the administrator was or would be so prejudicial. That section is concerned with an act of the administrator. What the ordinary creditor is aggrieved at is the administration order itself. It is suggested that one possible, but by no means certain, route would be as follows:

In terms of section 8(1)(b) the court will only grant an administration order if it considers that the making of the order would be likely to achieve one or more of the justifying purposes of an administration order. It is thought that if the court is making an administration order for the purpose of

'(a)  the survival of the company, and the whole or any part of its undertaking, as a going concern;
 (b)  the approval of a voluntary arrangement under Part I;

1 Insolvency Act 1986, s 10(1)(c).
2 Ibid, s 15(2); see pages 116–120 for the criteria the courts apply.
3 The proposition that 'administration' constitutes 'apparent insolvency' is disputed by Professor Wilson – see *Wilson on Debt* (2nd edn), p 282. This is thought incorrect. An administration order is granted only if the company is or is likely to be unable to pay its debts; all the company's correspondence must state this, and it must be advertised publicly to creditors in terms of r 2.3(2) of the Insolvency (Scotland) Rules 1986.

(c)    the sanctioning under section 425 of the Companies Act of a com-
       promise or arrangement between the company and any such persons as
       are mentioned in that section,'

the court would not refuse an administration order on the ground that the four
months could run to the prejudice of the creditors without the benefit of an
arrestment. These justifying purposes do not envisage a winding up. However, if the justifying purpose is 'a more advantageous realisation of the
company's assets than would be effected on a winding up' (which the authors
have read to mean that winding up is nevertheless envisaged), it is suggested
that 'advantageous' could be read to mean not just that more money is realised
for creditors, but that the balance of interests in the winding up is not upset.
In particular, a public policy consideration in the four-month rule should not
lightly be discarded. Accordingly, it is suggested that the creditor who has
legitimate fears about the running of the four months could object at the stage
of the hearing of the petition for the administration order. He would have to
argue that he had a legal right to object which is not expressly written into the
Insolvency Act 1986.

## (3)    SUSPENSION OF DILIGENCE ON WINDING UP

Arrestments and poindings are ineffectual within 60 days of the commencement of liquidation or after the commencement of liquidation[1]. Adjudications
are now also ineffectual after the commencement of winding up[2]. Another
type of action – 'poinding of the ground' – is a diligence open to a creditor
holding a *debitum fundi*, such as a superior or a heritable creditor. It enables
the creditor to attach moveables on the heritable property affected by the
diligence. The underlying principle is that the creditor is merely giving effect
to a pre-existing right arising by virtue of his *debitum fundi* and accordingly no
competition of diligence can arise between creditors poinding the ground,
since they have priority according to the dates of their respective infeftments.
This type of action is now restricted by statute. In terms of section 37(6) of the
Bankruptcy (Scotland) Act 1985, 'no poinding of the ground in respect of the
estate of the company . . . executed within the period of 60 days before the
commencement of winding up or on or after that date shall be effectual in a
question with the liquidator, except for the interest on the debt of a secured
creditor, being interest for the current half yearly term and arrears of interest
for one year immediately before the commencement of that term'. In contrast
an action of maills and duties is available to a secured creditor whose security
includes an assignation of rents during a winding up. The creditor becomes
vested in the landlord's rights and accordingly may recover rents. A standard
security contains no assignation of rents but, under the Conveyancing and
Feudal Reform (Scotland) Act 1970, the creditor has, on default by the
debtor, a right to enter into possession of the security subjects and receive or
recover the rent. It may seem anomalous that whereas an action of maills and
duties is now unaffected by a liquidation, a poinding of the ground is affected.
However, an action of maills and duties, which puts a heritable creditor in the

---

1 Bankruptcy (Scotland) Act 1985, s 37(4) as applied to liquidations by Insolvency Act 1986, s 185(1).
2 Ibid, s 37(8) as applied to liquidations by Insolvency Act 1986, s 185(1).

position of the landlord in relation to the tenants, has a natural connection with the company's heritable property, whereas the remedy of poinding of the ground is directed not at the company's heritable property but at moveables on the property. Adjudications within a year and a day of the first adjudication are equalised[1]. In terms of section 37(1) of the Bankruptcy (Scotland) Act 1985: 'winding up has the effect of – (a) a decree of adjudication of the heritable estate of the company for payment of its debts which has been duly recorded in the Register of Inhibitions and Adjudications on that date; . . . in favour of the creditors according to their respective entitlements.' This means that although adjudication is competent during liquidation, any adjudication within a year before or a year after liquidation is effectively cut down. This does not apply to 'real adjudications' by which a creditor who already holds real security over heritable property enforces it.

### Effectually executed diligence in receivership and winding up

*(A)    Effectually executed diligence in receivership*

All persons who have effectually executed diligence on any part of the property of a company which is subject to the charge by which a receiver is appointed have priority to the holder of the floating charge[2]. The expression 'effectually executed diligence' has been the subject of some discussion[3].

*Arrestments*

An arrestment followed by a decree of furthcoming is an effectually executed diligence[4]. The commencement of winding up has the effect of being a completed diligence, and gives guidance to interpretation. Section 37(1) of the Bankruptcy (Scotland) Act 1985 states that commencement of winding up will have the effect: '. . . of (b) an arrestment in execution and decree of furthcoming, an arrestment in execution and warrant of sale, and a completed poinding.'

The statute envisages that an arrestment is not completed without a decree of furthcoming, or in the case of a ship, a warrant of sale. This is totally in line with the decision of the First Division in *Lord Advocate v Royal Bank of Scotland*[5], in which Lord President Emslie stated:

'The accurate description of an arrestment, however, is that it is merely an "inchoate" diligence[6], a "step" of diligence or an "inchoate or begun" diligence[7]. It has never been held otherwise and is succinctly described in *Lucas's Trustees v Campbell & Scott*[8] by Lord Kinnear – a master in this field of law – in these terms: "An arrestment and furthcoming is

---

1 Diligence Act 1661; Adjudications Act 1672.
2 Insolvency Act 1986, s 60(1)(b).
3 See cases cited in next footnote and *Armour and Mycroft, Petrs* 1983 SLT 453; Sim 1984 SLT (News) 25; Gretton, 1983 SLT (News) 145; JADH, 1983 SLT (News) 177; Wilson on *Debt*, p 202.
4 *Lord Advocate v Royal Bank of Scotland Ltd* 1977 SC 155; see also *Gordon Anderson Plant Ltd* 1977 SLT 7; *Cumbernauld Development Corpn v Mustone Ltd* 1983 SLT (Sh Ct) 55; and *Forth and Clyde Construction v Trinity Timber and Plywood Co* 1984 SLT 94.
5 1977 SC 155 at 169.
6 Stair, III, i, 42.
7 Ersk, III, vi, 11 and 15.
8 (1894) 21 R 1096.

an adjudication preceded by an attachment and the essential part of the diligence is the adjudication"[1]. It is accordingly part but not the essential part of a diligence consisting of arrestment and furthcoming.'

The conclusion, however, that the arrestment is totally defeated – ie the arrester gains no possible advantage in the competition – by a subsequent effectually executed diligence seems an unfounded further deduction. In the case of *Iona Hotels Ltd (In Receivership) Petitioners*[2], the First Division of the Court of Session addressed the case where a floating charge had been granted over the assets of a company after an arrestment had been laid on a debt. In the case of *Lord Advocate v Royal Bank of Scotland*[3] the arrestment had been after the creation of the floating charge. In the *Iona Hotels Ltd* case, applying the analogy of a fixed security the court held that property which is the subject of an assignation in security remains the property of the company subject to the rights of the assignee. Litigiosity which results from the arrestment restricts the power of a common debtor to affect his own property by his subsequent voluntary act, but it does not render that act worthless for all purposes. The rights of the assignee of a subsequent assignation in security are subject to the rights of the arrester whose advantage cannot be defeated by that security. But the extent of that advantage will depend on the outcome of the process in which the arrestment is used. If the action fails the arrestment falls and there is no longer any restriction on the rights of the assignee, and the fixed security will be effective in regard to any balance which may remain after any successful claim by the arrester has been satisfied. The same approach was appropriate in the case of a posterior floating charge. This was not in conflict with any of the provisions of the statute. The property to which the floating charge attaches is subject to the rights of an arrester whose arrestment was prior to the date of registration of the floating charge. The extent of those rights may be such as to render the floating charge worthless on crystallisation in regard to the property held by the arrestee, but they may not. The receiver must await the outcome of the process until the debt arrested for has been satisfied. What remains at that stage will be for him to collect because it is, as it all along had been, property of the company to which the floating charge had attached.

The court in the *Iona Hotels* case recognised that it would be anomalous if a debtor company which granted a bond and floating charge in favour of its creditor should be in a better position in regard to prior arrestments than a debtor which granted an assignation in security. It was not possible to distinguish between these two forms of security for the purpose of the competing security situation. This tackled the problem of circularity where a bare arrestment ranks before a subsequent intimation of an assignation in security but on the *Lord Advocate v Royal Bank of Scotland*[3] case behind a floating charge, but an assignation in security being a fixed security ranked ahead of a floating charge. The court, however, did not seem to examine whether the crystallisation of a floating charge was the critical fact, or the registration itself of the floating charge. Lord Hope stated:

'Against this background one must ask oneself why it should be that a debtor who grants a bond and floating charge in favour of his creditor should be in any better position in regard to prior arrestments than a debtor who grants an assignation in security. In principle I do

1 At 1103.
2 1991 SLT 11.
3 1977 SC 155.

not find it possible to distinguish between these two forms of security for present purposes. Both can be seen to be voluntary acts of the debtor at the date of granting of the relevant deed. The assignation in security is completed by intimation, which can be taken to be the equivalent of registration in the case of a floating charge: see s 410 of the Companies Act 1985. The assignation is of course a fixed security over the moveables to which it relates, whereas the floating charge does not acquire this character until the receiver is appointed. But on the appointment of a receiver the holder of a floating charge enjoys all the protection in relation to any item of attached property that the holder of a fixed security over that item would enjoy under the general law: *Forth & Clyde Construction Co Ltd v Trinity Timber & Plywood Co Ltd* 1984 SLT at p 96 per Lord President Emslie. The analogy is clearly seen in the case of a book debt. In regard to that kind of moveable property the only form of fixed security which is available under the general law is an assignation in security which has been duly intimated. Section 53(7) of the Insolvency Act 1986 provides that the attachment which takes place when the receiver is appointed under a floating charge has effect as if the charge were a fixed security over the property to which it has attached, so its effect in regard to book debts is the same as if they had been the subject of duly intimated assignation in security. No doubt there is this difference, that in contrast to the holder of a fixed security the rights of the holder of the floating charge are incomplete until the receiver has been appointed, because it is only then that the attachment can take place. But I think that this point merely serves to emphasise that the holder of a duly registered floating charge should not be in a better position in regard to prior arrestments than the assignee in security of the common debtor whose assignation has been intimated to the arrestee. In both cases the voluntary act of the common debtor has been completed, in the one case by registration which makes public the creation of the floating charge and in the other by intimation to complete the security. It seems to me to be clear in principle that the arrestment should prevail in both cases, since the litigiosity extends to any voluntary deed of the common debtor which is posterior to the arrestment.'

It is very difficult to see why Lord Hope considered that the arrestment has to be prior to the date of registration of the floating charge. The correct date, it is thought, should be the date of crystallisation of the floating charge when the assignation takes place. If the crystallisation takes place prior to the arrestment, the debt which is being purportedly arrested no longer may be competently arrested. However, until crystallisation, the floating charge floats. There may by registration of the floating charge be intimation of a future assignation; but until such an actual assignation by crystallisation the company may still assign its debts, and they are accordingly arrestable.

The *Lord Advocate v Royal Bank of Scotland*[1] case and *The Iona Hotels Ltd* case[2] leave the law in this area in an unsettled state. If arrestments not followed by a furthcoming, are completely trumped by the crystallisation of a floating charge, this has the benefit that if a receiver is appointed after the arrestment he will not be compelled to liquidate the company within 60 days of the arrestment being executed in order to have the arrestment cut down under the provisions for equalisation of diligence in terms of section 37 of the Bankruptcy (Scotland) Act 1985, as applied to liquidations by section 185(1)(a) of the Insolvency Act 1986. On the other hand following the *Iona Hotels Ltd* case[2] liquidations may unnecessarily be prematurely instituted.

## Poindings

The Bankruptcy (Scotland) Act 1985 only talks about a 'completed poinding'. It has been an open question for a century whether a poinding is held to

1  1977 SC 155.
2  1991 SLT 11.

be 'effectually executed' at (a) the date of execution of the poinding (when the officer 'adjudges' the goods to belong to the poinding creditor), or (b) only when the report of the sale is lodged, or there is delivery of the goods to the creditor[1].

It is not clear as a result of the *Iona Hotels Ltd* case (supra) whether a poinding also has to be executed prior to the registration of a floating charge to give the poinder a claim to the property to which the holder of the floating charge would have to be subject, or whether there might also need to be a completed poinding.

## Inhibitions

An inhibition is neither a 'completed diligence' nor an 'effectually executed diligence', and where a creditor refuses to lift it the receiver may apply to the court to have it lifted under section 61 of the Insolvency Act 1986[2]. A liquidator may sell heritable property, and this is not challengeable on the ground of any prior inhibition (reserving any effect of such inhibition on ranking) in a winding up by the court[3]. The liquidator in a voluntary winding up does not have this statutory power and would have to apply to the court for it under section 112 of the Insolvency Act 1986.

In the case of *Armour v Mycroft*[4], an inhibition had been registered against a company after it had granted a floating charge but before receivers were appointed. Following the appointment of joint receivers it was agreed between the joint receivers and the inhibitors that the inhibitors would grant a partial discharge of their inhibition, releasing heritable property which the receivers had sold to a third party, provided that the proceeds of sale would be consigned into court pending a determination by the court as to the relative entitlements of the floating charge holders and the inhibitors. Though the inhibitors initially argued that the inhibition represented an effectually executed diligence on the company's property, they eventually conceded that point and argued instead that an order should be made by the court that the inhibitor's debt should be met out of the proceeds of sale, either before payment to the floating charge holders or after payment but before payment to the company. The court held that the inhibitors should be paid after the debt of the floating charge holders had been met but before any payment was made to the company. That decision failed to recognise that at common law an inhibition itself would confer no priority on the inhibitors in respect of the proceeds of sale. Unfortunately in a subsequent case, *Taymech Ltd v Rush & Tompkins Ltd*[5] when a similar situation was dealt with by Lord Coulsfield it was not suggested by the counsel for the pursuers that a receivership might not prevail against the inhibitions and there was no indication that it was even possible that such an argument might be considered at a later stage in the proceedings. Also there was no suggestion that the inhibitions might be of any

1 Support for the latter view is found in *Tullis v Whyte*, 18 June 1817, FC; *Samson v McCubbin* (1822) 1 S 407; *S Yuile Ltd v Gibson* 1952 SLT (Sh Ct) 22. The former view appears to receive recognition in *New Glenduffhill Coal Co Ltd v Muir and Co* (1882) 10 R 372; *Galbraith v Campbell's Trs* (1885) 22 SLR 602; *Bendy Bros Ltd v McAlister* (1910) 26 Sh Ct Rep 152.
2 Formerly s 477 of the Companies Act 1985. See Wilson on *Debt* (2nd edn), p 117. As to whether an inhibition is an effectually executed diligence, see *Armour and Mycroft, Petrs* 1983 SLT 453.
3 Bankruptcy (Scotland) Act 1985, s 31(2) as conferred on liquidators by Insolvency Act 1986, s 169(2).
4 1983 SLT 453.
5 1990 SCLR 789n, 1990 SLT 681.

value to the pursuers in any competition with other creditors apart from those by whom the receiver had been appointed. Accordingly Lord Coulsfield recalled the inhibitions, but included a condition in the interlocutor to the effect of preserving any priority that the pursuers might have against the company.

*Adjudications*

The same problems arising out of *Lord Advocate v The Royal Bank of Scotland* case[1] and *Iona Hotels Ltd* case[2] arise in the case of adjudications. The first question would be whether a notice of litigiosity registered in connection with an adjudication could compete with a floating charge. The second problem would usually arise, in that the notice of litigiosity is invariably registered after the creation of the floating charge and so would only affect future advances secured by the floating charge. A third problem is caused by the terms of section 60(1) of the Insolvency Act 1986, which requires a receiver to rank a voluntary heritable security prior to an effectually executed diligence, which the authors read to include an effectually executed adjudication, irrespective of the times of infeftment and even although under the general law of ranking, the adjudication would have priority over the security. By this provision, floating charges distort the ranking of heritable securities and adjudications in a competition between them, although the competition has nothing to do with the floating charges. This would seem to require statutory amendment. A further problem is that under the ordinary common law, a duly registered inhibition gives the inhibitor a preference over a subsequently registered adjudication for debt when the debt enforced by the adjudication was 'contracted' after the registration of the inhibition. If an inhibition can never be ranked before a floating charge, but an adjudication can be so ranked, it follows that in a ranking by a receiver the adjudication will have priority over the inhibition in violation of the ordinary common law[3].

*(B)   Effectually executed diligence in winding up*

Although arrestments or poindings executed within 60 days before the commencement of winding up are ineffectual to create a preference for the arrester or poinder[4], this has been interpreted by the court in the case of arrestments only to apply to arrestments that were actually subsisting at the date of commencement of winding up and therefore had no application where the arrestment had been superseded by payment and was no longer subsisting at that date[5]. Accordingly, an arrestment followed by a furthcoming (ie an effectually executed diligence) would seem not to be reducible by a winding up. It is thought that the law would be the same in relation to poindings followed by a sale (ie an unequivocally completed poinding).

In terms of section 37(4) of the Bankruptcy (Scotland) Act 1985, as applied to liquidations by section 185(1) of the Insolvency Act 1986:

---

1  1977 SC 155.
2  1991 SLT 11.
3  See Scottish Law Commission Discussion Paper No 78 'Adjudications for Debt and Related Matters' (November, 1988, p 173).
4  Bankruptcy (Scotland) Act 1985, s 37(4) as applied to liquidations by Insolvency Act 1986, s 185(1).
5  *Johnston v Cluny Estates Trs* 1957 SLT 293.

'No arrestment or poinding of the estate of the debtor (including any estate vesting in the permanent trustee under section 32(6) of that Act) executed –

(a) within the period of 60 days before the date of sequestration and whether or not subsisting at that date; or

(b) on or after the date of sequestration,

shall be effectual to create a preference for the arrester or poinder; and the estate so arrested or poinded, or the proceeds of sale thereof, shall be handed over to the permanent trustee'.

It had been held, before the passing of the Bankruptcy (Scotland) Act 1985, in the case of *Johnston v Cluny Estates Trs*[1], that the provisions concerning the effect of sequestration on diligence contained in section 327(1)(a) of the Companies Act 1948 did not apply to funds arrested within 60 days of a sequestration if during that time the arrestment had been withdrawn or superseded by payment. The Scottish Law Commission in their *Report on Bankruptcy and Related Aspects of Insolvency and Liquidation*[2] proposed a provision as follows:

'No arrestment or poinding of the estate of the debtor (including any estate vesting in the permanent trustee under section 31(5) of this Act [the Bill of the Scottish Law Commission]) executed within the period of 60 days before the date of sequestration or after that date, and no inhibition taking effect within that period, shall be effectual to create a preference for the arrester, poinder or inhibitor; and the benefit of any such arrestment or poinding executed within that period or after that date, or inhibition taking effect within that period, shall vest in the permanent trustee.'

The last statement in that clause of the Bill, would have entailed that any benefit gained by an arrester or poinder would have gone into the estate of the bankrupt. If 'the benefit of any such arrestment or poinding' were read to mean the sale proceeds of any article poinded or arrested in the hands of the poinder or arrester, or any money paid over to an arrester, in the hands of an arrester, the perceived mischief of the case of *Johnston v Cluny Estates Trs*[3] would have been met. The mischief is that although subsisting arrestments or poindings are cut down, depriving the arresters or poinders of any benefit, the arresters or poinders would be benefited if the goods were sold and the proceeds handed over to them on the authority of the bankrupt, or the bankrupt had paid the arrester the sum claimed or instructed one of his debtors to pay the arrester. The clause proposed by the Scottish Law Commission would have produced an anomaly, in that unless payments could otherwise be struck down as 'unfair preferences', any benefit induced by an arrestment or poinding within the 60 day period would vest in the company; and this would put the arrester or poinder in a worse position than if the payments had been forthcoming without that type of legal pressure. Section 37(4) of the Bankruptcy (Scotland) Act takes the proposal of the Scottish Law Commission further. Because 'the estate so arrested or poinded, or the proceeds of sale thereof, shall be handed over to the permanent trustee' this would seem to attach a *vitium reale* to the proceeds of sale. But non-connected third parties seem to be required to hand over the proceeds of sale to the

1 1957 SLT 293.
2 (Scot Law Com No 68).
3 1957 SLT 293.

permanent trustee (the liquidator). It is thought that in terms of section 37(4) of the Bankruptcy (Scotland) Act 1985, even if read alone, an effectually executed diligence, whether an arrestment followed by a furthcoming or poinding followed by a sale would be reducible in a winding up, provided the diligence was within the 60 days. The reason would be that the furthcoming legally flowed from the arrestment and was dependent on the arrestment and the sale flowed legally from and was dependent on the poinding. This result is, in any event, entailed by the terms of section 37(1)(a) of that Act. Section 37(4), however (unlike the proposed provision suggested by the Scottish Law Commission), poses a separate problem as regards interpretation for cases where an arrestment has been only followed by payment by the debtor or by an instruction by the debtor to one of his debtors to pay the arrester. In addition to the anomalous consequences flowing from the provisions in relation to arrestments and poindings in section 37(4) of the Bankruptcy (Scotland) Act 1985 as described above, there is an express provision that the 'proceeds of a sale must be handed over to the permanent trustee. This the authors read to cover both a judicial sale dependent on a poinding and a situation where the owner of the poinded goods, namely the debtor, authorises the poinder to sell the goods and take the proceeds. However where there is an arrestment of a debt (as opposed to the arrestment of corporeal moveables in the hands of a third party), there is a real problem as to the inter-pretation of section 37(4) of the Bankruptcy (Scotland) Act 1985. On a very broad reading, the expression 'the estate so arrested . . . shall be handed over to the permanent trustee', could mean money paid to an arrester by the debtor of a company on the instruction of the company or by the company itself to persuade the arrester to lift the arrestment. It is thought, however, by the authors that where debts are arrested, one could not properly describe money paid to the arrester by a debtor of the company or by the company to lift the arrestments as 'the estate so arrested'. Neither could money paid over ever be classed as 'proceeds of sale'. If that interpretation is right, the problem raised in the case of *Johnston v Cluny Estates Trs*[1], is not met.

There is accordingly an incentive to creditors of any company to arrest the debts of a company whose creditworthiness is suspect, on the basis that debts paid even within the 60 days period, the payment of which has been induced by the arrestment, would not be clawed back under section 37(4) of the Bankruptcy (Scotland) Act 1985 as applied to liquidations. The provisions of section 37(4) of the Bankruptcy (Scotland) Act 1985 are ambiguous and create anomalies. They probably do not achieve their intended purpose in relation to meeting the problem in the case of *Johnston v Cluny Estates Trs*[1] and are likely to create confusion in this area of corporate insolvency.

## Diligence outwith statutory periods

Diligence outwith the statutory 60 days from winding up creates a preference even if not completed, but is ineffective against a receiver[2].

---

1 1957 SLT 293.
2 *Commercial Aluminium Windows Ltd v Cumbernauld Development Corpn* 1987 SLT (ShCt) 91.

# Chapter 9

# Trusts

## Trust prevails on insolvency

The right of a beneficiary of a trust against the trustee is anomalous in nature, in that it has features of both a real right and a personal right[1]. On the liquidation or sequestration of the trustee it is the features akin to a real right that are important. In the leading case, *Heritable Reversionary Co Ltd v Millar*[2], it was held that the right of a beneficiary under a trust prevailed on the trustee's sequestration against his trustee in sequestration and his personal creditors. Ostensibly the decision turns upon the meaning of the word 'property' in section 102 of the Bankruptcy Act 1856 (now represented by section 31 of the Bankruptcy (Scotland) Act 1985), which provided that the 'property' of a bankrupt should vest in his trustee. Lord Watson said:

'That which, in legal as well as conventional language, is described as a man's property is estate, whether heritable or moveable, in which he has a beneficial interest which the law allows him to dispose of. It does not include estate in which he has no beneficial interest, and which he cannot dispose of without committing a fraud.[3]'

This reasoning is equally applicable on both a creditors' voluntary winding-up of a company and a winding-up by the court. In the former case, section 107 of the Insolvency Act 1986 provides that 'the company's property in a voluntary winding up shall on the winding up be applied in satisfaction of the company's liabilities *pari passu*'. In the latter case, section 143(2) of the Insolvency Act 1986 provides that the functions of the liquidation are 'to secure that the assets of the company are got in, realised and distributed to the company's creditors'; while the word 'assets' is used instead of 'property' Lord Watson's reasoning clearly applies[4]. Before the decision in *Heritable Reversionary Co Ltd v Millar* it had been held that the right of a beneficiary under a

---

1 This topic is dealt with more fully in Chapters 1 and 9 of Wilson and Duncan on *Trusts, Trustees and Executors*. The former chapter, in particular, provides an extremely valuable historical discussion of the rights of the parties to a trust. See also Trusts, Rights of the Beneficiaries against Trustees and Trust Property in *Stair Memorial Encylopaedia*, vol 24, paras 49–52.

2 (1891) 18 R 1166; revsd on appeal (1892) 19 R (HL) 43. See also *Forbes' Trs v Macleod* (1898) 25 R 1012; *Hinkelbein v Craig* (1905) 13 SLT 84; *Turnbull v Liqr of Scottish County Investment Co Ltd* 1939 SC 5.

3 (1892) 19 R (HL) 43 at 49–50.

4 In *Turnbull v Liqr of Scottish County Investments Co Ltd* supra and *Gibson v Hunter Home Designs Ltd* 1976 SC 23, it was assumed without argument that the same reasoning applied on a winding up by the court. For the purposes of the insolvency legislation, 'property' is defined in s 436 of the Insolvency Act 1986 as including 'money, goods, things in action [incorporeal moveables, ie debts, shares and the like], land and every description of property wherever situated and also obligations and every description of interest whether present or future or vested or contingent, arising out of, or

trust prevailed against the diligence of the trustee's personal creditors[1]. It had also been held that the right prevailed against the alienation of trust property in breach of trust as long as the person acquiring it either has given less than full value for the property or has acquired it with actual or constructive knowledge of the trust[2]. If the trustees transact as such, there will obviously be knowledge of the trust[3]. Nevertheless the beneficiary's right does not prevail against a person who acquires trust property in good faith, without knowledge of the trust, and who gives full value[4]. It is in this respect that the rights of a beneficiary are in the last resort personal rather than real. This does not, however, affect the beneficiary's rights on winding up.

The rationale for the rule regarding an ordinary acquirer in good faith and for full value is that any other rule would impose an unacceptable degree of uncertainty on purchasers of property, who could never be certain whether the property acquired was subject to a latent trust[5]. An alternative formulation is that of Lord Watson in *Heritable Reversionary Co Ltd v Millar*:

'It must be kept in view that the validity of a right acquired in such circumstances by a *bona fide* onerous disponee for value does not rest upon the recognition of any power in the trustee which he can lawfully exercise, because breach of trust duty and wilful fraud can never be in themselves lawful, but upon the well-known principle that a true owner who chooses to conceal his right from the public and to clothe his trustee with all the *indicia* of ownership is thereby barred from challenging rights acquired by innocent third parties for onerous considerations under contracts with his fraudulent trustee.[6]'

These reasons do not, however, apply to the generality of creditors who are the persons in whose interests a winding up takes place. The general creditors are not persons who have purchased property subject to the trust, and have not, as a general rule, acquired rights on the faith of the trustees, apparent ownership. Lord Watson further stated:

'It is also necessary to keep in view that the rule of personal bar which must protect transactions with the trustee from challenge by the [beneficiary] only applies to transactions which affect and create an interest in the trust-estate. Personal creditors of the trustee who neither stipulate for nor obtain any conveyance to that estate do not, in the sense of law,

incidental to, property'. Although this definition is very wide, it does not appear to add to the notion of property at common law, and the statement of principle by Lord Watson in *Heritable Reversionary Co Ltd v Millar* (1892) 19 R (HL) 43 at 49–50 is still relevant. Any other view would cause difficulty in the application of various sections of the Insolvency Act 1986 notably sections 107 (distribution of company's property in voluntary winding up) and 127 (avoidance of dispositions of company's property after commencement of winding up) and Sch 1, paras 1, 2, 3, 12 and 16 (powers of administrator) and Sch 4, para 6 (power of liquidator to sell company's property).

1 At p 225 *infra*.
2 *Redfearn v Somervail* (1813) 1 Dow 50; 1 Pat App 707; *Taylor v Forbes* (1830) 4 W and S 444; *Macgowan v Robb* (1864) 2 M 943.
3 See Halliday, *Conveyancing Law and Practice*, vol 1, ss 1–24.
4 Referred to as a *bona fide* onerous disponee; *Heritable Reversionary Co Ltd v Millar* (1892) 19 R (HL) 43 at 47, per Lord Watson. 'Good faith' means simply that the acquirer should not have actual or constructive knowledge of the trust. See *Redfearn v Somervail, supra; Burns v Lawrie's Trs* (1840) 2 D 1348; *Thomson v Clydesdale Bank* (1893) 20 R (HL) 29. It is essential that the person acquiring the property should have a real right, duly completed by the legal procedures appropriate to the type of property in question, in order that his right may prevail against the trust.
5 *Redfearn v Somervail,* (1813) 1 Dow 50 at 72, per Lord Eldon and in the Court of Session at 3 Scots Revised Reports (HL) at 16 per Lord Hermand. Where the purchaser of the trust property does not give full value, it is obvious that no equity arises in his favour.
6 (1892) 19 R (HL) 43 at 47. See also Lord Craig at 3 Scots Revised Reports (HL) at 16.

transact on the faith of its being a property of the trustee. As Lord McLaren observed[1]. . . . "Creditors in general do not give credit to a bankrupt in reliance upon any supposed presumptions that property standing in his name is his private property. Unless they are going to advance money on heritable security they know nothing of his title-deeds and trust only to his personal credit." Accordingly, the contraction of debts by the trustee whilst the trust is latent creates no *nexus* [attachment] over the trust-estate in favour of personal creditors. If they proceeded to attach the trust-estate on the footing of its belonging to their debtor, the beneficiary could defeat their diligence by appearing to vindicate his right. An adjudging creditor gives no new consideration for the interest in the estate which he secures by the process of adjudication, and, in my opinion, he can be in no better position in a question with the *cestui que* trust [beneficiary] than if he had obtained a conveyance without value from the trustee.[2]'

The rule laid down in *Heritable Reversionary Co Ltd v Millar*,[3] that the rights of a beneficiary under a trust prevail on the insolvency of the trustee against his personal creditors, applies whether or not the trust is latent, that is, whether or not the trust appears on the face of the deed or other document which constitutes the trustee's title to the property in question. In *Heritable Reversionary Co*, the trustee's title to the heritable properties in question was absolute and unqualified and accordingly the trust was latent[4]. The beneficiary's rights were still preferred to the claim of the trustee's sequestrated estate. A case where the trust appeared on the face of the trustee's title would plainly be *a fortiori*.

### Administration; voluntary arrangements

Under section 14 of the Insolvency Act 1986 an administrator is entitled: 'to do all such things as may be necessary for the management of the affairs, business and property of the company'. The specific powers conferred by Schedule 1 similarly refer to the 'property' of the company as that word is used in particular in relation to taking possession of, collecting and getting the company's property (para 1), selling the company's property (para 2), granting security over the company's property (para 3) and realising the company's property (para 12). The administrator's general duties, specified in section 17, involve taking into his custody or under his control 'all the property to which the company is or appears to be entitled', and managing 'the affairs, business and property of the company'. In these repeated references to the 'property' of the company that expression must be given the sense referred to in *Heritable Reversionary Co Ltd v Millar*[5]. Consequently an administrator is in exactly the same position in relation to a trust as a liquidator.

This result will not usually be affected by sections 10 and 11 of the Insolvency Act 1986[6]. Sections 10(1)(b) and 11(3)(c) prohibit the enforcement without consent of the administrator or leave of the court of any security over the property of a company in respect of which a petition for an administration

---

1  (1891) 18 R 1166 at 1175.
2  (1892) 19 R (HL) 43 at 47.
3  (1892) 19 R (HL) 43.
4  Ibid at 46, per Lord Watson.
5  *Supra*. The definition of 'property' in section 436 of the Insolvency Act 1986 is again relevant: see note 4 on p 220, *supra*.
6  See generally chapter 4.

order has been presented or an administration order has been made. The only cases where these provisions will have an effect on a trust are where the trust is used as a pure form of security[1]. In most cases where a trust is used in a commercial agreement it involves part implement of a contract of sale of debts, or possibly other assets, and thus does not involve a 'security' in the sense of the companies legislation[2]. Section 11(3)(d) of the Insolvency Act 1986 prohibits other proceedings, execution (diligence) or other legal process against a company in administration or its property without the consent of the administrator or leave of the court. It has been held that the expressions 'other proceedings' and 'other legal process' must be construed *ejusdem generis* with the other provisions of section 11(3)[3], and it seems that this provision will not prevent the enforcement of a trust directly against trust property, as long as court proceedings or diligence against the company itself are not involved. If an administration order is made in respect of the trustee, the beneficiary will often be able to enforce the trust by using a power of attorney or a power to appoint a fresh trustee[4]. Alternatively an application can be made for the appointment of a judicial factor, but in that case section 11(3)(d) will apply as the company must, as trustee, be called as a respondent[4].

Part 1 of the Insolvency Act 1986 does not specify that a voluntary arrangement made thereunder must only deal with the 'property' or 'assets' of the company. Nevertheless, section 1(1) refers to a proposal to the company and to its creditors 'for a composition in satisfaction of its debts or a scheme of arrangement of its affairs'. It is thought that these words only authorise a composition or scheme which affects the property of the company, in the sense defined by Lord Watson, and the creditors of the company, who are thought not to include the beneficiaries under a trust. It is also thought that trust property is not 'property of the company [which is] subject to a security' in terms of section 15 of the 1986 Act unless the trust is in reality a security in the sense discussed in chapter 10.

## Floating charges and receivers

The effect of the grant of a floating charge or the appointment of a receiver on property held in trust by a company has not been judicially considered[5]. The result of these two events is determined by the nature of a floating charge. The crucial feature of such a charge is that it does not attach to any property of the company until either winding up[6] or the appointment of a receiver of the property subject to the charge[7]; until then it lies dormant, and does not prevent the company from dealing with the property subject to the charge. If the company alienates property before crystallisation of the charge, that property simply drops out of the charge. Not only outright alienation is permitted; lesser

---

1 See chapter 10 on the nature of a security.
2 *Re George Inglefield Ltd* [1933] Ch 1, discussed further at pages 253–254; see also *Armour v Thyssen Edelstahlwerke AG* 1990 SLT 991.
3 *Air Ecosse Ltd v Civil Aviation Authority* 1987 SLT 752; see generally, pp 116–120.
4 See pp 243–244, *infra*.
5 In *Tay Valley Joinery Ltd v C F Financial Services Ltd* 1987 SLT 207 it was argued that a latent trust had been created which did not prevail against the receiver, on the authority of *Burns v Lawrie's Trs* (1840) 2 D 1348, as he was an assignee for full value in good faith and neither he nor the floating charge holder had knowledge of the trust. This argument was rejected on the ground that the special case did not disclose adequate facts for any such argument.
6 Companies Act 1985, s 463.
7 Insolvency Act 1986, ss 53(7), 54(6).

rights, such as leases and rights in security, may be created over the property subject to the charge prior to crystallisation[1]. In exactly the same way, property subject to the charge can be subjected to a trust, and there seems to be no reason that the trust should not prevail; the floating charge holder expects, because of the nature of his security, that items of the company's property will be alienated, and a trust is simply a means of achieving that. Even if a latent trust has been created before the creation of the floating charge, it is thought that that trust should still prevail. The floating charge does not of itself create real rights over specific items of property, and it assumes that in future property may be alienated by the company. Thus the holder cannot be said to transact on the faith of a specific item of trust property's being or remaining the property of the company[2]. Consequently the floating charge holder is, in relation to trust property, in the same position as the general creditors, rather than the acquirer for value of a specific item of property.

When a receiver is appointed, the floating charge attaches to 'the property subject to the charge'. On the commencement of the winding up of a company that has granted a floating charge, the charge attaches to 'the property then comprised in the company's property and undertaking'[3]. In the expressions quoted, it seems clear that the word 'property' must have the same meaning as that explained by Lord Watson in *Heritable Reversionary Co Ltd v Millar*[4], with the result that property that has been rendered subject to a trust is excluded from the attachment of the floating charge. In virtually all cases involving receivership or winding up the company will be insolvent, and the meaning accorded by Lord Watson is appropriate in any insolvency regime. Moreover, if the floating charge attached to trust property, the result would be a circular series of priorities. The trust prevails over the creditors of the company, including preferential creditors and creditors who have done diligence. Those categories of creditor, however, prevail over the floating chargeholder[5]. It is thought that this result cannot be correct, and that in the legislation governing floating charges 'property' is used in the sense explained by Lord Watson. In addition, the floating chargeholder knows when he takes the charge that property may drop out of it as a result of alienation. The creation of a trust is merely one form of alienation. Thus there is no reason to regard his equity, and that of the receiver who represents him, as in any way preferable to that of the beneficiary of the trust, who has merely taken property which everyone concerned contemplated could be alienated. Moreover, the floating chargeholder cannot be said to have transacted on the faith of any item of property remaining the property of the trustee.

After the receiver has been appointed, the security created through attachment of the floating charge will obviously prevail over any trust that the company may subsequently try to create. The principle *assignatus utitur jure auctoris* applies[6].

---

1 This is subject to an exception if the creation of security rights is prohibited by the instrument creating the charge in terms of s 464 of the Companies Act 1985; this is a very frequent stipulation.
2 Compare Lord Watson in *Heritable Reversionary Co Ltd v Millar* (1892) 19 R (HL) 43 at 47.
3 Insolvency Act 1986, ss 53(7), 54(6); see chapter 5; Companies Act 1985, s 463(1).
4 (1892) 19 R (HL) 43 at 49–50; see p 220 *supra*.
5 See p 220, *supra* (trust and creditors) and p 225, *infra* (trust and diligence); Companies Act 1985, s 463(3) as amended and Insolvency Act 1986, ss 60(1)(e) and 175 (preferential creditors); Companies Act 1985, s 463(1)(a) and Insolvency Act 1986, s 60(1)(b) (creditors who have done diligence).
6 The transferee of a right can acquire no higher right than the person who transfers the right to him has. See *Scottish Widows' Fund v Buist* (1876) 3 R 1078.

## Diligence

The rules on the use of diligence in relation to a trust are consistent with those on insolvency. Private creditors of the trustee may not do any form of diligence against the trust estate[1]. The general rule is that arresters, inhibitors and adjudgers take the estate of the common debtor *tantum et tale* as it stands vested in him, and if the common debtor holds property as a trustee the diligence of his personal creditors will not affect that property[2]. Creditors of the trustee *qua* trustee may, however, do diligence against the trust estate; the primary remedy of a creditor of a trust is to obtain payment out of the trust estate[3]. Creditors of the beneficiary of a trust may do diligence against his beneficial interest in the trust estate; normally arrestment will be appropriate, but if the beneficiary's interest is heritable inhibition must be used[4]. Creditors of one of a number of beneficiaries cannot, however, attach the trust estate beyond the amount specifically destined to their debtor[4].

## Constitution of trust

If an alleged trust is to receive effect on the insolvency of the trustee, it is essential that it should have been properly constituted. The detailed requirements for the constitution of a trust are beyond the scope of this work[5]. Nevertheless, certain matters that may assume significance in the context of insolvency should be mentioned. The traditional form of trust is constituted by (1) the declaration of certain trust purposes by the truster, (2) the acceptance of those purposes by the trustee and (3) the transfer of property by either the truster or a third party to the trustee to be held for the purposes of the trust[6]. The transfer of property to the trustees must be effected in such a way as to confer real rights on them; otherwise the property will not be subjected to the trust and on the insolvency of the trustee it will be the donor or seller of the property who can claim it, not the beneficiary. The procedure necessary to confer real rights will of course vary according to the type of property concerned; generally speaking, recording in the General Register of Sasines (or registration in the Land Register) is required for heritage, assignation followed by intimation to the debtor for incorporeal moveables and delivery for corporeal moveables, except in the anomalous case of sale of goods where mere intention to transfer will suffice[7]. In addition, it should be borne in mind that, where property is held on an apparently absolute title taken with the

---

1 For arresters, see *Mackenzie v Watson* (1678) Mor 10188; *Brugh v Forbes* (1715) Mor 10213; Bell Comm, i.33; Graham Stewart on *Diligence*, pp 67–68. For adjudgers, see *Livingston and Shaw v Lord Forrester and Creditors of Grange* (1644) Mor 10200; *Preston v Earl of Dundonald's Creditors* (1805) Mor 'Personal and Real', App No. 2; Graham Stewart on *Diligence*, p 620. Inhibition is clearly *a fortiori* of adjudication.

2 Erskine, 3.6.16; *Mackenzie v Watson, supra.*

3 *Stewart v Forbes* (1888) 15 R 383. If such a creditor cannot obtain payment from the trust estate, he has a personal right of action against the trustee, unless it has been agreed, expressly or by implication, that only the trust estate is to be liable. For a fuller discussion of trustee's personal liabilities, see *Wilson and Duncan*, chap 26, especially pp 394–396; *Stair Memorial Encyclopaedia*, vol 24, para 225.

4 Graham Stewart on *Diligence*, pp 61–62.

5 See *Wilson and Duncan*, pp 21–31.

6 *Camille and Henry Dreyfus Foundation Inc v Inland Revenue* 1955 SLT 335 at 337, per Lord Normand.

7 Sale of Goods Act 1979, ss 17, 18. The detailed rules regarding the transfer of real rights to trustees are discussed in *Wilson and Duncan*, pp 33–39.

consent of the truster, a trust of that property can be proved only by the writ of the alleged trustee or by a reference to his oath[1]. The writ required to prove a trust can be informal, and need not refer expressly to the trust; it is enough that a trust can fairly be implied from its terms. Once the existence of the trust can be established by writ or oath, its terms and purposes can be proved parole.

Certain particular types of trust require special mention because of their importance in a commercial context. These are bare trusts, constructive trusts arising out of a fiduciary relationship, trusts implied where a fiduciary acquires property with funds derived from the person for whom he acts, and trusts where the truster declares himself a trustee.

## Bare trusts

In a commercial context the most usual example of the traditional trust will be a nominee holding, or bare trust, under which the trustee simply holds property for the behoof of a beneficiary, who may or may not be the truster. In such a case, the trust property will in the last resort be under the control of the beneficiary, who can call for it to be transferred into his own name at any time[2], even if the trustee is insolvent. The declaration of trust in such cases will generally be simple in nature; it is essential, however, that the requirements of the Blank Bonds and Trusts Act 1696 should be satisfied.

## Constructive trusts[3]

Constructive trusts are implied by law in two main sets of circumstances. The first is where a non-trustee acquires property from a trustee in breach of trust and either in the knowledge that it has been transferred to him in breach of trust or without giving full value for the property so transferred[4]. In such cases the transferee from the trust holds the property so transferred on a constructive trust for the beneficiaries of the original trust. The second case where a constructive trust arises is where a fiduciary acquires a benefit in consequence of his fiduciary position or from any breach of his fiduciary duties[5]. The latter type of constructive trust is of importance in a commercial context. Fiduciaries include, in addition to trustees, company directors[6], certain partners[7], agents[8] and persons to whom confidential information is imparted[9]. Every fiduciary is under a duty not to place himself in a position where his personal interest and his duty to look after the affairs of the person to whom

---

1 The authority for this rule is the Blank Bonds and Trusts Act 1696. See *Wilson and Duncan*, pp 50–61, and Walkers on *Evidence*, pp 122–123, for a detailed account of the law.
2 *Miller's Trs v Miller* (1890) 18 R 301.
3 See *Wilson and Duncan*, pp 77–80.
4 See footnote 2 on p 221.
5 The law relating to fiduciaries and constructive trusts arising therefrom is discussed in the *Stair Memorial Encyclopaedia*, vol 24, paras 170–188 on Trusts, Fiduciary Duties of Trustees and Others. The law relating to fiduciaries and their duties has developed from the law on trustees' duties of good faith; the trustee is the archetypal fiduciary.
6 *Aberdeen Ry Co v Blaikie Bros* (1854) 16 D 470, 1 Macq 461; *Regal (Hastings) Ltd v Gulliver* [1967] 2 AC 134n. See also chapter 7.
7 Partnership Act 1890, ss 26, 30; *McNiven v Peffers* (1868) 7 M 181; *Roxburgh Dinardo's JF v Dinardo* 1992 GWD 6–322.
8 See *Lothian v Jenolite Ltd* 1969 SC 111; *Boardman v Phipps* [1967] 2 AC 46.
9 *Boardman, supra*; *Seager v Copydex Ltd* [1967] 1 WLR 923; [1969] WLR 809.

the fiduciary duty is owed may possibly conflict[1]. If a fiduciary acts in breach of that duty, any profit or advantage or benefit that he receives as a result of the breach is held by him as a constructive trustee for the beneficiary of the fiduciary duty. That means that the rights of the beneficiary will prevail even on the fiduciary's insolvency. The breach of fiduciary duty is automatic; no inquiry is generally allowed as to the fairness of the transaction. An example of a transaction involving a breach of fiduciary duty which gives rise to a constructive trust is the purchase of trust estate by a trustee acting in his private capacity[2]; in such a case both the property purchased by the trustee and any proceeds following the resale of such property, including any profits accruing to the trustee, will be held on constructive trust for the purposes for which the trustee held the property so purchased[3]. Likewise, when a trustee or other fiduciary defeats the legitimate expectations of those to whom he stands in a fiduciary relationship, he will be a constructive trustee of the benefit so acquired. Examples include a trustee's obtaining a renewal of a lease to a trust in his own name[4], and a company director's diverting to himself contracts which the company might reasonably have expected to obtain[5]. The taking of unauthorised remuneration by a fiduciary such as an agent[6] and the use of confidential information acquired in a fiduciary capacity for the fiduciary's own purposes[7] will similarly give rise to a constructive trust.

A trust will not be implied in the absence of a pre-existing fiduciary relationship. In particular a trust will not be inferred from a mere personal obligation[8].

### Implied trusts: fiduciary relationships

The existence of a fiduciary relationship is also significant in that, where a fiduciary acquires property with funds derived from the person for whom he acts as fiduciary, it will readily be implied that he holds such property on trust for that person. Thus an agent who acquires property with funds provided by

---

1 *Aberdeen Ry Co v Blaikie Bros, supra.*
2 See *Magistrates of Aberdeen v University of Aberdeen* (1876) 3 R 1087; affd. (1877) 4 R (HL) 48; *Johnston v MacFarlane* 1987 SLT 593; *Elias v Black* (1856) 18 D 1225; *Wright v Morgan* [1926] AC 788, PC. In England it has been held that the purchase of property held for fiduciary purposes by an agent is not an automatic breach of fiduciary duty, but that an inquiry into the fairness of the transaction should be allowed: *Spencer v Topham* (1856) 22 Beav 573. This does not appear to accord with the Scottish authorities: cf *Elias v Black, supra; Aberdeen Ry Co v Blaikie Bros., supra.*
3 Cf. *Inglis v Inglis* 1983 SC 8; 1983 SLT 437. The sale to the trustee will also be reducible at the instance of a beneficiary.
4 *Keech v Sandford* (1726) Sel Cas Ch 61; *McNiven v Peffers, supra.*
5 *Cook v Deeks* [1916] 1 AC 554, PC; *Regal (Hastings) Ltd v Gulliver* (1942) [1967] 2 AC 143n. Considerable case law exists on this point; reference should be made to the standard works on company law.
6 See *Brown v IRC* 1964 SC (HL) 180; *Stair Memorial Encyclopaedia,* vol 24, para 183.
7 *Boardman v Phipps* [1967] 2 AC 46; see also *Stair Memorial Encyclopaedia,* vol 24, paras 184–185. In certain English cases involving the receipt of secret commissions by agents and directors, it has been held that the sum received by the agent or director was not held on constructive trust for the principal or company; *Metropolitan Bank v Heiron* (1880) 5 Ex D 319, CA; *Lister & Co v Stubbs* (1890) 45 Ch D 1, CA, *Powell and Thomas v Evan James & Co* [1905] 1 KB 11, CA. It is thought that those cases do not represent the law of Scotland, and that a constructive trust would be held to arise, as in any other case of breach of fiduciary duty; see *Stair Memorial Encyclopaedia,* vol 24, para 188.
8 See *Bank of Scotland v Liqrs of Hutchison Main & Co Ltd* 1914 SC (HL) 1 at 8, per Lord Kinnear and at 17, per Lord Shaw of Dunfermline; *Gibson v Hunter Home Designs Ltd* 1976 SC 23 at 27–28, per Lord President Emslie, and at 31, per Lord Cameron; *National Bank of Scotland Glasgow Nominees Ltd v Adamson* 1932 SLT 492. See pp 229–230 *infra.*

his principal[1] will normally hold that property on trust for the principal[2]. The same point applies in relation to company directors, whose relationship to the company is essentially that of principal and agent[3]. Even if funds are provided by a third party, such as a bank, if the loan is arranged in connection with the principal's business, it is likely that property acquired with such funds will be held on trust for the principal[4]. The question of whether parties are in fact in the relationship of principal and agent must be determined objectively, according to the commercial realities of the situation; the fact that a party is described as an agent for another, or as an independent principal, is not conclusive[5]. It should nonetheless be noted that the requirements for proof of a trust still apply, if the fiduciary has acquired the property on an apparently absolute title with the consent of the person for whom he acts[6]. Thus in cases where an agent or director is instructed to hold property, it is important that a written acknowledgement of trust should be obtained. The position is different if no instruction is given to the agent or director to take title in his own name; in that event there is no consent on the part of the principal, or company, and the Act of 1696 does not apply.

### Declaration of self as trustee

In the traditional form of Scottish trust, property was transferred to the trustees by the truster, or on occasion by a third party after the trust had been constituted by the truster. It is now clear, however, in view of the decision in *Allan's Trustees v Lord Advocate*[7], that it is competent for a truster to declare himself trustee of his own property, as long as the trust is intimated to the beneficiary, or to someone acting on his behalf. In that case Lord Reid stated:

'I think that we can now accept the position, as a reasonable development of the law, that a person can make himself a trustee of his own property, provided that he also does something equivalent to delivery or transfer of the trust fund. I reject the argument . . . that mere proved intention to make a trust coupled with the execution of a declaration of trust can suffice. If that were so it would be easy to execute such a declaration, keep it in reserve, use it in case of bankruptcy to defeat the claims of creditors, but, if all went well and the trustee desired to regain control of the fund, simply suppress the declaration of trust'.[8]

---

1 The original situation in *Heritable Reversionary Co v Millar, supra*: see (1892) 19 R (HL) 43 at 46.
2 See *Wilson and Duncan*, pp 11–12.
3 See *Aberdeen Ry Co v Blaikie Bros, supra*.
4 See *Bank of Scotland v Liqrs of Hutchison, Main & Co Ltd* 1914 SC (HL) 1 at 15, per Lord Shaw of Dunfermline.
5 *Michelin Tyre Co Ltd v Macfarlane (Glasgow) Ltd (in Liquidation)* 1917 2 SLT 205, where criteria for distinguishing agency are discussed by Lord Dunedin at 212.
6 See pp 225–226 *supra*; *Wilson and Duncan*, pp 56–58; cf. Bennett Miller on *Partnership*, pp 382–387.
7 1971 SC (HL) 45.
8 *Allan's Trs* 1971 SC (HL) 45 at 54, per Lord Reid. The practice appears to have originated in the commercial field, where a partner or employee took title to property in his own name but in trust for his employer or the partnership of which he was a member. *Heritable Reversionary Co Ltd v Millar, supra* can be regarded as an example of the former type of case, although the disposition to the employee trustee was clearly made in anticipation of the declaration of trust; *Hinkelbein v Craig* (1905) 13 SLT 84 is an example of the latter type of case. Other early authorities are collected in Lord Reid's speech in *Allan's Trs* at 53–54. Of these, the dissenting judgment of Lord Kyllachy in *Cameron's Tr v Cameron* 1907 SC 407 deserves notice.

It was held in *Allan's Trustees* that intimation to the beneficiaries was equivalent to delivery of the trust fund, and brought the trust into operation, and further[1] that intimation to one beneficiary out of several was sufficient, because it was the equivalent of delivery of the trust property, to bring the whole trust into operation[2].

*Allan's Trustees* has been followed in a number of cases[3]. As the more recent of these cases illustrate, the possibility of a truster's declaring himself trustee of his own property is of considerable commercial importance, principally because it provides a simple and informal method of obtaining security for the performance of contractual obligations. It is probably fair to say that the implications of this device are only starting to be worked out, and consequently it is thought appropriate to deal with this area of the law in some detail.

The requirements for declaring oneself a trustee were summarised by the Lord President in *Clark Taylor & Co Ltd v Quality Site Development (Edinburgh) Ltd*[4] in the following terms:

'In order to complete the successful constitution of a trust recognised as such by our law, where the truster and trustee are the same person, there must be in existence an asset, be it corporeal or incorporeal or even a right to future *acquirenda* [property coming into the estate in future], there must be a dedication of the asset or right to defined trust purposes; there must be a beneficiary or beneficiaries with defined rights in the trust estate, and there must also be delivery of the trust deed or subject of the trust or a sufficient and satisfactory equivalent to delivery, so as to achieve irrevocable divestiture of the truster and investiture of the trustee in the trust estate'.

The two features which cause the greatest difficulty in practice are the declaration of trust (the 'dedication of the asset or right to defined trust purposes') and the equivalent of delivery.

# DECLARATION OF TRUST

## Trust and contract

A declaration of trust must be sharply distinguished from a contract creating merely personal rights. The distinction is made clearly in the leading case, *Bank of Scotland v Liquidators of Hutchison Main & Co Ltd*[5]. In that case it was agreed between the bank and the company in liquidation that the bank would surrender a security held by it over certain of the company's assets and that the company would obtain a debenture from one of its debtors and assign it to the bank in lieu of the surrendered security. At the date of the company's liquidation, the agreement had been implemented except for the assignation of the debenture in favour of the bank. It was argued for the bank that the

---

1 Lord Guest dissenting.
2 See Lord Reid in *Allan's Trs, supra* at 55–56.
3 *Clark's Trs v Lord Advocate* 1972 SC 177; *Kerr's Trs v Lord Advocate* 1974 SC 115; *Export Credit Guarantee Department v Turner* 1979 SC 286; *Clark Taylor & Co Ltd v Quality Site Development (Edinburgh) Ltd* 1981 SC 111; and *Tay Valley Joinery Ltd v C F Financial Services Ltd* 1987 SLT 207.
4 1981 SC 111 at 118; the facts of the case are discussed below at pp 230–231.
5 1914 SC (HL) 1.

debenture was held by the company in trust for the bank; *Heritable Reversionary Co Ltd v Millar* was relied upon in support. That claim was rejected by the House of Lords. Lord Kinnear, distinguishing the trust in *Heritable Reversionary Co Ltd v Millar*, said:

'The trust so established was declared in express terms, and directly affected the constitution of the real right. It is a very different thing to say that a personal obligation to give the benefit of a specific fund to a particular creditor creates a trust which attaches to the fund and excludes it from the estate for distribution.[1]'

Lord Kinnear went on to refer to Lord Westbury's dictum in *Fleeming v Howden*[2] that 'an obligation to do an act with respect to property creates a trust', and expressed the view that it must be confined to obligations which affect the real right, and should not be extended to personal obligations[3].

### Clark Taylor

In *Clark Taylor & Co Ltd v Quality Site Development (Edinburgh) Ltd*[4], an attempt was made to set up a trust in favour of a supplier of goods over the proceeds of resale of those goods. The contract of sale between the supplier and the purchaser of a quantity of bricks contained the following clause (condition 11(b)):

'In the event of the buyer reselling or otherwise disposing of the goods or any part thereof before the property therein has passed to him by virtue of clause 11(a) hereof, then the buyer will, until payment in full to the seller of the price of goods, hold in trust for the seller all his rights under such contract of resale or any other contract in pursuance of which the goods or any part thereof are disposed of or any contract by which property comprising the said goods or any part thereof is or is to be disposed of and any money or other consideration received by him thereunder.'

The bricks were used by the purchaser in carrying out building works and the purchaser received payments under the building contracts, which were paid into its current bank account. Payments received under the building contracts were in all cases greater than the price of the bricks used in the contracts. The

---

1 *Bank of Scotland v Liqrs of Hutchison Main & Co Ltd, supra* at 7.
2 1868 6 M (HL) 113 at 121.
3 Lord Shaw of Dunfermline at 17 stated that the dictum did not represent the law of Scotland; it involved 'an invasion into the well-settled principle that a contractual obligation with regard to property, which has not effectually and actually brought about either a security upon it or a conveyance of it, is not *per se* the foundation of a trust or of a declarator of trust'. While that statement emphasises that a mere contractual obligation will not give rise to a trust, it must not be taken as detracting from the principle, established definitively in *Allan's Trs v Lord Advocate, supra*, that a trust may be created by a truster's declaring himself trustee and carrying out an equivalent of delivery. In any event, it is hard to see how a contractual obligation can of itself bring about a security, or, outside the anomalous case of sale of goods, a conveyance of property. Further criticism of Lord Westbury is found in the speech of Lord Watson in *Heritable Reversionary Co Ltd v Millar* (1892) 19 R (HL) 43 at 49. It should be noted that English law is in this respect radically different from Scots Law, and English authorities cannot be relied upon. In particular, English law will frequently imply an equitable assignment, giving rise to rights analogous to those under a trust, in circumstances where purely personal contractual obligations would arise in Scots law. See also *Gibson v Hunter House Designs Ltd* 1976 SC 23 at 27–28, per Lord President Emslie and at 31, per Lord Cameron; *National Bank of Scotland Glasgow Nominees Ltd v Adamson* 1932 SC 492.
4 1981 SC 111.

purchaser of the bricks went into liquidation while the price of the bricks was still outstanding to the supplier, and it was argued by the supplier that a trust had been constituted over the sums received under the building contracts. This argument was rejected as follows:

'Condition 11(b) cannot be read as containing any declaration of trust by the Company [the purchaser]. It is, rather, a condition which imposes upon the Company a contractual obligation to hold certain alleged "trust" subjects in "trust", in accordance with its precise terms. It cannot, therefore, by itself, in the context of the Contract as a whole, demonstrate that a trust was ever created in terms of the obligation. But there are more formidable objections than this to the submission of the first parties [the supplier]. Even if we assume, contrary to the opinion we have expressed, that condition 11(b) could fairly be read as containing a purported acceptance by the [Company] of an alleged trust over their own property, corporeal and incorporeal, the question is whether there can be identified any true trust in accordance with the law of Scotland. The alleged trust is to hold "for the seller" all the rights and all the moneys to come under all contracts not yet entered into in which any of the bricks sold are used, until the price of the bricks has been paid in full. It is at once obvious that the value of the alleged "trust" subjects might be (and as it proved in the event to be) infinitely greater than the price to which the first parties were entitled under the Contract with the [Company]. Yet according to the submission for the [first parties] all had ceased to be part of the [Company's] own estate and could not be released from the fetters of the trust unless and until such time as the [Company's] debt was paid, in full, presumably out of funds which were not burdened by any trust. What is really significant here is, of course, that in the so-called trust no beneficial interest whatever in the subjects thereof is or was conferred upon the alleged beneficiaries, the first parties. All they were entitled to receive was the price of the bricks. It is not provided that they should be entitled to have recourse to any part of the "trust" fund for this purpose. Properly construed, what condition 11(b) purports to do is to secure the freezing of the defined subjects, regardless of their value, under an alleged trust which gives no beneficial interest therein to the supposed "beneficiary" until they receive the price of the bricks which they sold to the [Company]. In our opinion the essential ingredients of a trust are entirely lacking and condition 11(b) can be seen for what it really is – as no more than an attempt, under the guise of an alleged trust, to keep valuable assets of the [Company] out of the hands of its other creditors, at least until the [suppliers] have themselves received payment in full of the price of the bricks sold to the [Company]. Before leaving this submission we ought to say two things. The first is that, even if the [purchaser] had on receipt of the various interim payments gone through the exercise of executing and intimating declarations of "trust" in the exact terms of condition 11(b) in relation to these payments, the essential ingredients of a trust would still be absent and the position of the first parties could not have been strengthened thereby. The second is that if a condition such as condition 11(b), designed only to freeze assets of a debtor and to keep them out of other creditors' hands until a particular creditor's debt is paid in full, were to be regarded as constituting a proper trust in accordance with the law of Scotland, and were to be adopted widely by sellers of goods, the damage which would be done to the objectives of the law of bankruptcy and of liquidation would be incalculable. Other interesting complications can easily be figured, and a person creating more than one such 'trust' in favour of his creditors could readily find himself in trouble under the criminal law.[1]'

## Tay Valley

In *Tay Valley Joinery Ltd v C F Financial Services Ltd*[2] the validity of a trust in an invoice discounting agreement, a type of debt factoring agreement, was

---

1 At 115–116 per Lord President Emslie.
2 1987 SLT 207.

considered[1]. The agreement involved the sale of the present and future book debts of a trading company (which were referred to in the agreement as 'receivables') to a factoring company. In a factoring or invoice discounting agreement, the factoring company makes payment to the trader for book debts shortly after they arise; the point of such an agreement is to assist the trading company's cash flow. This leaves the factoring company exposed, because unless it takes a formal assignation and intimates it to the trading company's debtors it has no real right to the debts. Thus if the trading company becomes insolvent, it is the receiver or liquidator, not the factoring company, who will be entitled to recover them. To avoid this, it is usual to create a trust over the outstanding book debts in favour of the factoring company, and this can most easily be achieved by the trading company's declaring itself a trustee[2].

The factoring agreement in *Tay Valley* was governed by English law. It provided that the purchase of receivables should be complete and that the right to receivables should vest in the factoring company upon such receivables coming into existence. It further provided that the trading company would (1) record the sale of receivables to the factoring company in its books, (2) notify the factoring company on special forms of receivables arising from time to time, (3) note on customers' accounts that they were held on trust for the factoring company (although this was not observed in practice), (4) as trustee for the factoring company keep remittances received in payment of any receivables separate from other moneys and pay those into a separate account, and (5) send the factoring company each month an aged analysis of receivables. It was agreed in the special case that, under English law, the invoice discounting agreement effected an equitable assignment to the factoring company of those book debts the proper law of which was English law, in consequence of which the trading company held those book debts for the factoring company under a constructive trust[3].

The court held that the invoice discounting agreement was effective as a declaration of trust in Scotland. Lord Robertson[4] held that the terms of the agreement, in the light of the practice followed by the parties, were sufficient for a trust to be inferred. Lord Dunpark, who discussed this question most fully[5], held that the agreement must be construed in accordance with English law, under which it constituted a declaration of trust; this construction was supported by the two references to a trust in the agreement[6] which, while they did not amount by themselves to a declaration of trust, clearly assumed that a trust had been created. Lord McDonald[7] held that a trust could be established from (a) the requirements that the trading company note on customers' accounts that they were held on trust for the finance company and (b) the fact that a note was made on copies of the trading company's consolidated

---

1 In an invoice discounting agreement intimation to the trading company's debtors is avoided, whereas in the more traditional type of factoring agreement such intimation is effected.
2 Halliday, *Conveyancing Law and Practice*, vol I, para 8.41.
3 The result would have been different if Scots law had been the proper law of the invoice discounting agreement; in that event, without an actual declaration of trust over specific assets (on which see pp 229–230, 233–235), only personal rights would have been created, and there would have been no trust.
4 At 212L–213G.
5 At 214H–215L.
6 See clauses (3) and (4) above.
7 At 219B–D.

monthly statements that the debts contained therein had been assigned to the factoring company.

## Requirements of effective declaration of trust: underlying commercial reality

As will be clear from the cases discussed so far, it is difficult to lay down any definitive rules for determining what amounts to an effective declaration of trust as against an agreement creating merely personal rights. The wording used by the alleged truster is clearly important. In an agreement whose construction is governed by Scots law, there must be a clear declaration that specific subjects are held on trust, or will when they come into existence be held on trust, for another person[1]. Such a declaration is not enough by itself, however. It is also essential to determine whether the alleged deed of trust is a genuine declaration of trust. For this purpose it is essential to consider the practical working of the supposed trust; a declaration of trust is not a mere form of words, but represents an underlying commercial or economic reality. If the wording used, purportedly creating a trust, does not conform to the underlying reality of a trust, it will be treated as a nullity. This can be clearly seen in the passage quoted above from *Clark Taylor & Co Ltd v Quality Site Development (Edinburgh) Ltd*[2] where it was held that the alleged trust was merely a device to keep valuable assets of the company out of the hands of its creditors. In that case the contractual entitlement of the supplier was to receive the price of the bricks sold, but the alleged trust, which was designed to create a security for the fulfilment of the purchaser's obligations under the contract for the sale of the bricks, extended to the whole of the rights enjoyed by the purchaser under the building contracts in which the bricks were used. The underlying commercial reality of the contract was the sale of the bricks, but the supplier attempted to create a trust security for the price over much more valuable rights under another, distinct contract. In these circumstances it was clear that the purported trust and the security created thereby had no connection with the commercial reality of the contract under which it bore to arise. The declaration of trust was accordingly treated as not being genuine.

*Tay Valley* also involved the use of a trust to create a form of security for the performance of contractual obligations; under the invoice discounting agreement the factoring company was ultimately entitled to payment of the receivables, and the trust was designed to secure that obligation. In this case, however, the amount over which the trust subsisted was precisely the factoring company's entitlement, and the trust could be regarded as involving

---

1 As a matter of practical drafting, the expression 'in trust for' should always be used, but expressions such as 'for behoof of' may, if the context supports the construction, be held equivalent. The use of agreements governed by other legal systems should be avoided. These are drafted against a different legal background; in particular, English agreements are drafted in the light of rules relating to equitable assignments which have no equivalent in Scots law. This means that agreement must be reached as to the construction of the agreement in the foreign legal system, or evidence must be led of foreign law. In any event, it is not clear that Scots law should, as a matter of policy, allow a foreign deed to affect real or trust rights in property which throughout the transaction remains in Scotland where that deed can be understood only by reference to foreign law; if a deed is to affect Scottish property which does not move out of Scotland, it should at least be comprehensible to a Scots lawyer.
2 1981 SC 111 at 115–116.

the part implement of the contract for sale of the receivables[1]. Thus the trust corresponded to the underlying commercial reality and there was no question of its being anything other than genuine.

The consequences of according validity to a trust-security which does not represent the underlying commercial reality can be seen from *Clark Taylor & Co Ltd v Quality Site Development (Edinburgh) Ltd*[2]. If the trust in that case had been held valid, the supplier of the bricks would have effectively frozen a major source, perhaps the only source, of the purchaser's income. This would have an obvious impact on the purchaser's cash resources; in many cases it would disable him from paying his other debts. Moreover, if one supplier is allowed to impose such a trust-security, others will obviously attempt to do so over the same funds. In *Clark Taylor*, for example, suppliers of sand, gravel and the like might have tried to impose trusts identical to the brick supplier's. The subjects of these purported trusts would necessarily be the same as the subjects of the brick supplier's trust, namely, the rights under the building contract of the purchaser in the supply contracts. If the brick supplier's trust is valid, however, the purchaser's rights under the building contract have passed out of its estate and have become part of the brick supplier's estate, and thus the purchaser would be disabled from creating any subsequent trusts. In these circumstances the court concluded in *Clark Taylor*[2] that 'a person creating more than one such "trust" in favour of his creditors could readily find himself in trouble under the criminal law'[3].

### Declaration of trust must affect specific property

A declaration of trust must take effect in relation to specific property, and it must be ensured that the wording of the declaration is appropriate to cover any particular property that is claimed to be subject to the trust. This is illustrated by *Export Credits Guarantee Department v Turner*[4], where the Export Credits Guarantee Department entered into a number of agreements with a company whereby they guaranteed advances to the company made by its bank against invoices for goods exported by the company. Under one of the agreements known as the recourse agreement, it was declared that: 'all sums received by the [company] or any person on its behalf in respect of any transaction which is the subject of a Guaranteed Advance shall . . . be received and held in trust by the [company] for the [Department] until the [company] has made repayment to the Bank or has paid to the [Department] the amount of any demand made'. The company became insolvent and went into liquidation. At that time certain debts which were the subject of guaranteed advances made by the bank to the company were outstanding, and those debts were subsequently paid to the liquidator. The Department claimed that those debts had been subject to the trust constituted by the recourse agree-

---

1 See p 242, *infra*. The fact that the trust involved part implement of a contract of sale meant that it did not constitute a charge or security for the purposes of the statutory provisions governing the registration of charges: *Re George Inglefield Ltd* [1933] Ch 1.
2 1981 SC 111 at 116.
3 In a number of English and Australian cases, the concept of the underlying commercial reality has been used to determine whether or not a trust subsists: *Foley v Hill* 2 HL Cas 28 (bank who mixes money deposited with his own is debtor, not trustee); *South Australian Insurance Co v Randell* (1869) LR 3 PC 101 (mixing of corn by miller incompatible with ownership of farmers); *Re Nevill* (1871) LR 6 Ch App 397 (parties' actings inconsistent with fiduciary relationship); *Re Bond Worth Ltd* [1980] Ch 228 (terms of contract of sale incompatible with trust).
4 1979 SC 286.

ment and were thus held for its behoof. This claim was rejected by the Second Division. The main ground of decision was that debts could not be included in the subjects of trust, since the declaration of trust referred only to 'sums received' and not to 'debts'[1]. In *Tay Valley*, on the other hand, the trust was constituted over 'receivables', which were defined in the factoring agreement as meaning:

'all the book debts, invoice debts, accounts, notes, bills, acceptances and/or other forms of obligations owed by or owing to the [trading company] which are in existence at the date of commencement of this Agreement or which come into existence during the currency of this Agreement in respect of contracts entered into by the [trading company] for the sale of goods or the provision of services in the ordinary course of business.'

It is essential that the trust subjects should be defined as fully as possible but not so widely that the trust goes beyond the underlying commercial purpose of the contract.

# EQUIVALENTS OF DELIVERY

## Intimation to beneficiaries

In *Allan's Trustees v Lord Advocate*[2] it was held that intimation to the beneficiaries was equivalent to delivery of the trust fund and brought the trust into operation, and further[3] that intimation to one beneficiary out of several was sufficient, because it was the equivalent of delivery of the trust property, to bring the whole trust into operation[4]. It has subsequently been held that intimation to an agent for the beneficiaries will suffice as an equivalent of delivery, even if the agent is also acting for the truster[5]. Intimation to the beneficiary or his agent is thus a sufficient overt act to give rise to the 'irrevocable divestiture of the truster and investiture of the trustee in the trust estate'[6] and at the same time to create the rights enjoyed by the beneficiary of a trust.

## Trust property must exist before intimation

When intimation is effected, however, it is essential that there should be in existence specific property which is to be rendered subject to the trust. In

---

1 *Export Credits Guarantee Department v Turner supra* at 294. The reference to 'sums recovered' seems to be an error. The Lord Justice-Clerk went on to say that '"debts" could not become part of the trust subjects unless the company has divested themselves of them and they could only do so by assignation [intimated] to the debtors.' This is clearly incorrect: see *Tay Valley*, at 212G–I per Lord Robertson, at 215G–K per Lord Dunpark and at 219G–J per Lord McDonald. Assignation followed by intimation would transfer the full real rights in a debt from cedent to assignee. A declaration of trust followed by intimation to the beneficiary, as in *Allan's Trs v Lord Advocate* does not transfer full real rights to the beneficiary, but only the quasi-real rights of a beneficiary under a trust (see above, at pp 220–222, 228–229). The function of intimation in the two cases is thus quite different. See also Lord Dunpark at 1979 SC 286 at 290.
2 1971 SC (HL) 45.
3 Lord Guest dissenting.
4 Lord Reid at 55–56.
5 *Clark's Trs v Lord Advocate* 1972 SC 177. The agent must have a right or duty to act on behalf of the beneficiaries: *Kerr's Trs v Lord Advocate* 1974 SC 115 at 127, per Lord Kissen and at 132 per Lord Fraser.
6 *Clark Taylor & Co Ltd v Quality Site Development (Edinburgh) Ltd* 1981 SC 111 at 118.

*Kerr's Trustees v Lord Advocate*[1] a truster purported to declare herself trustee of certain policies of assurance by intimating the trust to agents for the beneficiaries, but she did so before the policies had been taken out. It was held that a trust had not been validly created. Lord Fraser, after referring to the speech of Lord Reid in *Allan's Trustees*[2], expressed the rationale of the decision as follows[3]:

'What we are looking for . . . is something equivalent to delivery or transfer of a trust fund, and I cannot see how there can be such an equivalent until after the trust fund has come into existence.[4]'

In *Kerr's Trustees* it was further held that intimation, to be effective, must follow the declaration of trust. Lord Fraser stated[5]:

'It appears to me that anything said by an intended settlor to an intended beneficiary before the settlor has executed a declaration of trust cannot be more than an expression of intention and the intention could be changed at any time before the declaration is executed. The only exception would be where there is some contractual obligation by the settlor towards the beneficiary'.

It thus appears that, if a prospective truster agrees with a prospective beneficiary that he will set up a trust, then intimates to the prospective beneficiary that certain assets will be subject to the trust, and finally executes a declaration of trust, that will suffice. Lord Fraser went on to discuss the practical difficulties that would arise if intimation could precede the declaration of trust in cases where there is no antecedent contract: in particular, if the terms of the intimation differed from those of the declaration, or if the declaration only followed the intimation after a long interval, considerable doubts would arise as to the validity of the alleged trust. *Kerr's Trustees*[6] further makes it clear that the information given by way of intimation must be sufficient to specify the property held in trust[7].

### Intimation distinguished from acceptance of contractual obligation

In *Clark Taylor & Co Ltd v Quality Site Development (Edinburgh) Ltd*[8] it was argued on behalf of the supplier that the terms of the contract were sufficient to impose on the purchaser an obligation to create a trust of moneys received

1 1974 SC 115.
2 1971 SC (HL) 45 at 54.
3 1974 SC 115 at 129; see also Lord Kissen at 126.
4 In *Allan's Trs* the policy of assurance did not in fact come into existence until after the intimation (see 1971 SC (HL) 45 at 47–48) but this point was not argued.
5 At 130.
6 Lord Kissen at 127; Lord Fraser at 131.
7 In *Tay Valley Joinery Ltd v C F Financial Services Ltd supra* Lord Dunpark indicated at 215H–I that some trust property (debts in that case) must exist when the declaration of trust is executed, because there must be at that time some property to which the beneficial right may be transferred to a beneficiary by delivery or its equivalent. It is thought that this dictum was made *per incuriam*, and that 'executed' should read 'intimated'. That would bring the *dictum* into line with *Kerr's Trs supra*; in any event, it is difficult to see why a prospective trustee cannot execute a declaration of trust purposes, then obtain trust property, and finally intimate to the beneficiaries that that property is held for those purposes. In such a case the trust would come into existence on intimation.
8 1981 SC 111. See above at pp 230–231.

under the building contracts for behoof of the supplier, and that that contractual obligation was a continuing intimation that as soon as any such moneys reached the hands of the purchaser they would be held in trust in implement of that obligation. This continuing intimation was said to be a sufficient equivalent of delivery. The argument was rejected[1], on the ground that the alleged equivalent of delivery was not intimation of action taken in relation to existing assets or rights for behoof of the beneficiary; it was merely the acceptance of an obligation to hold in trust certain moneys that might be received in future. A contractual obligation to constitute a trust does not by its own vigour have the effect of constituting a trust in favour of one of the contracting parties; there must be 'some overt extraneous and ostensible act which involves acceptance of the trust and marks definitely the character of the trustee's possession'.[2] The court nevertheless stated[3] that intimation to the beneficiary or his agent was not the only equivalent to delivery of the subjects. Delivery of the trust deed will suffice, although that is essentially a form of intimation, but it appears that in appropriate cases other equivalents will be admitted.

### Intimation in relation to debts and acquirenda

The court also indicated in *Clark Taylor*[4] that the property subjected to a trust could be a right to *acquirenda*, that is, a right to items of property which the truster may acquire in future. It is clear that rights of this nature may be the subject of an ordinary assignation either absolutely or in security[5], and accordingly there seems no reason that they should not be the subject of a trust. Nevertheless, while an assignation of *acquirenda* will be effective as between cedent and assignee, intimation to the debtor is still required to create real rights which will prevail against third parties. For intimation to take place, the identity of the debtor must be known. That means that a distinction must be drawn between cases where a debt exists, even though it is not payable until a future date, or is contingent (the classic case of the *spes successionis*[6]), or is uncertain in amount, and cases where no debt yet exists; in the latter case no debtor exists to whom intimation can be made, and accordingly no real rights in the debt can be transferred to an assignee. Consequently an assignation of, for example, all debts which may in future become due to the cedent from his trade customers will only create personal rights between cedent and assignee. Real rights in relation to any particular debt will pass to the assignee only after intimation has been made to the customer who owes the debt, and for that purpose it is essential to know who the customer is. It is

1 At 118–119.
2 Following Lord Kyllachy in *Cameron's Trs v Cameron* 1907 SC 407 at 415. See also *Gibson v Hunter Home Designs Ltd* 1976 SC 23.
3 1981 SC 111 at 118.
4 At 117–118.
5 *Browne's Tr v Anderson* 1901 4 F 305; Gloag and Irvine, *Rights in Security*, pp 441–443. See McBryde, *Contract*, 17–106.
6 The authorities are discussed in the passages cited in the preceding footnote. The expression *spes successionis* is normally used to describe a contingent right to succeed to the estate of a deceased person, but, at least in the last century, it was also used to describe the right of the heir (at law and *in mobilibus*) of a person who was still alive and the right of the spouse and children of such a person to legal rights; the reason for treating the latter two types of right as a *spes* is that they would prevail unless defeated by a testamentary writing. A *spes successionis* cannot be arrested.

thought that the creation of trust rights is limited in a similar way. If a truster declares himself trustee for, say, a factoring company of future debts from trade customers, that may give rise to a personal right in the factoring company (if the wording of the declaration is appropriate), but no real rights will pass until a debt has actually become due from a specific customer and the truster intimates to the factoring company that the debt is held for the purposes of the trust. This appears to be in accordance with the approach of the Inner House in *Kerr's Trusteees v Lord Advocate*[1], where it was held that a trust cannot be created over property that does not yet exist. A trust can, however, be created over a future or contingent debt; in such cases the debt exists, even though it may never be payable, or may not be payable until a future date. Nor is it essential that the debt or other incorporeal moveable that is made subject to the trust should be capable of precise quantification or valuation. Thus a claim to damages against a particular person can be the subject of both an assignation and a trust.

In *Tay Valley Joinery Ltd v C F Financial Services Ltd*[2] the trading company was required by the invoice discounting agreement to notify book debts to the factoring company on special forms. Each form included a schedule which listed the receivables that had arisen since the last form had been prepared. Such forms were prepared and sent every few days, and on receipt the factoring company gave credit to the trading company for the receivables specified in the schedule. The sending of each form was held to amount to sufficient intimation that a trust had been created over the debts specified in the schedule to the form[3]. It is thought that a factoring agreement must incorporate an arrangement of this nature if its trust provisions are to be valid, in view of the considerations discussed in the last paragraph.

In *Export Credits Guarantee Department v Turner*[4] it was argued that intimation was effected when the recourse agreement, which contained the alleged trust, was delivered to the Department, or alternatively when trust property came into existence following such delivery. Both of these contentions were rejected[5] on the ground that intimation cannot be effected until there is a trust fund. If, however, a procedure similar to that in *Tay Valley* had been followed, there can be little doubt that the trust in favour of the Department would have been effective, on the assumption that the recourse agreement had been properly worded.

## Use of trusts in commercial agreements

The validity of a trust in a commercial agreement is likely to depend on two main factors, whether the trust truly represents the underlying commercial reality of the agreement, and whether an appropriate equivalent of delivery has been effected in relation to any particular asset. The most common case where a trust will represent the underlying commercial reality is likely to be where the trust is used to provide interim security for the performance of a contractual obligation, as in *Tay Valley*. It is essential, however, that the rights of the beneficiary under the trust should not extend to any greater assets

1 1974 SC 115. See pp 235–236.
2 1987 SLT 207; discussed above at pp 231–233.
3 Lord Robertson at 213F–G; Lord Dunpark at 216A–217A; Lord McDonald at 219E–K.
4 1979 SC 286; discussed above at pp 234–235.
5 See 1979 SC 286 at 294–295.

than do his contractual rights. Such a trust can be regarded as a form of part-implement of the contract, and appears unobjectionable from a policy standpoint.

It is also possible to use a trust to create a simple and informal type of security, in a manner similar to an ex facie absolute assignation. The owner of an asset, such as shares in a company, executes a declaration of trust in favour of the person who is to take the security, the trust being expressed in absolute terms, so that the truster becomes a bare trustee. At the same time a back letter similar to the type used for an ex facie absolute assignation[1] is executed; this should state that the beneficial interest of the beneficiary under the trust is truly enjoyed in security and should specify the terms of the security. Formal intimation of the trust should then be made to the beneficiary[2]. In the case of incorporeal property, the same result[3] can be reached by an ex facie absolute assignation. Nevertheless, there appears to be a considerable demand in commercial circles for a more informal type of security which does not involve intimation to the debtor; this can be seen in the practice followed by banks of taking a so-called 'pledge' of shares, the certificates for which are deposited with the bank along with an executed transfer, which in theory can be registered if insolvency threatens[4].

The use of a trust to create a security in the manner suggested is in accordance with the underlying commercial reality of the transaction as long as the back letter is framed appropriately. This should provide expressly that the lender beneficiary is entitled to call upon the trustee to denude in his favour (a right which would be implied anyway). It should further provide that, if the trustee is called upon to denude, the lender beneficiary will at once sell the trust subjects, will use the proceeds to satisfy his debt, and will account for the balance to the trustee. An arrangement of this nature goes no further by way of security than the trust that was upheld in *Tay Valley*, and there seems no reason to deny its validity. Where a trust of this sort may fail to represent the underlying commercial reality, however, is where the subjects selected are of a fluctuating nature, such as stock-in-trade; in such cases the trust is likely in any event to amount to an attempt to create a floating charge by means other than those specified in section 462 of the Companies Act 1985. It is thought that a trust may be used to create a security over heritable property, notwithstanding the terms of section 9(3) of the Conveyancing and Feudal Reform (Scotland) Act 1970, which provides that a grant of any right in an interest in land for the purpose of securing any debt by way of a heritable security shall be capable of being effected only if it is embodied in a standard security; a trust does not involve a heritable security, as defined in section 9(8). Care should in all cases be taken to ensure that a trust-security granted by a company does not require registration under section 410 of the Companies Act 1985[5]. It must also be ensured that the creation of further

---

1 Styles of back letter are found in Halliday, *Conveyancing Law and Practice*, vol I, chap 7; those paras 7–77 and 7–83 are especially useful, although they will need minor modification for a trust-security.
2 It may be possible to incorporate the intimation into the back letter.
3 Without the risk of the *bona fide* onerous assignee, whose rights prevail over a latent trust.
4 This device obviously creates no form of security in Scots law until the transfer is registered, or unless the shares are bearer securities. See *Halliday*, paras 7–76 et seq.
5 In *Tay Valley* the trust over the book debts did not require registration because it involved part-implement of a contract rather than a security; see *Re George Inglefield Ltd* [1933] Ch 1, and chapter 10.

securities is not prohibited or restricted by any prior security; such pro-
hibitions or restrictions, imposed under section 464 of the Companies Act
1985, are common in floating charges[1].

Attempts are made from time to time to create securities over Scottish
property by means of an English equitable charge, which is a type of security
analogous to a trust[2]. Apart from floating charges[3], these are ineffective, since
it is clearly established that the creation of security rights over property
situated in Scotland is governed by Scots law[4]. An English declaration of trust
followed by intimation sufficient to satisfy the requirements of Scots law will
be effective in Scotland, as *Tay Valley* makes clear. It is nevertheless unsafe to
rely on English forms of deed in this area of law; in English law equitable
interests (which are similar to the interests of a beneficiary under a trust) are
implied in a wide variety of transactions, and English deeds tend to be based
on the assumption that such inferences will be drawn. It would plainly be
quite unsatisfactory if the beneficial title to Scottish property depended upon
inferences drawn from a foreign deed in accordance with the rules of a foreign
legal system. For this reason it is thought that English equitable interests
other than express trusts followed by intimation to the beneficiary should not
be recognised as affecting Scottish property.

**Securitisation agreements**

Trusts may also be used in connection with the securitisation of debts, a form
of financing that has become fairly common in recent years in England and is
starting to spread to Scotland. The details of a securitisation agreement are
beyond the scope of the present work, but it is proposed to indicate how trusts
are used in such agreements to avoid the risk of insolvency.

Typically, a securitisation will involve selling the benefit of a large number
of relatively small debts, usually arising out of hire-purchase contracts or
loans secured over heritable property, to noteholders, and using the proceeds
of sale to finance further lending. The original creditor in the debts which are
sold is usually a hire-purchase or other consumer finance company. It sells the
debts for their market value to a trustee company[5], specially set up for the
securitisation, and as instalments of the debts are paid to it it passes these on to
the trustee company. The trustee company in turn sells and communicates
the benefit of the debts to the company which issues the notes to the public. It
does this in two ways. First, at the start of the transaction the trustee company
declares a trust over the debts and payments due to it from the finance
company, in favour of the note-issuing company; that provides protection
against the possible insolvency of the trustee company. Second as instalments
of the hire-purchase or other debts are paid by the finance company to the
trustee company, the trustee company passes these on to the note-issuing
company. The note-issuing company uses such payments to meet interest and
capital repayments due on the notes.

1 In the case of a factoring or invoice discounting agreement the trust will normally involve
part-implement of the contract for sale of the debts, and in such a case the consent of any prior
floating charge holder will not be required; see chapter 10.
2 In part this seems to reflect the desire of the commercial community for a simple and informal type
of security of general application.
3 English floating charges are recognised in Scotland by virtue of the Companies Act 1985, s 462(1).
4 *Mitchell v Burnet and Mouat* (1746) Mor 4468; *Inglis v Robertson and Baxter* (1898) 25 R (HL) 70.
5 In order to avoid stamp duty the sale will usually be completed offshore.

For such an arrangement to be financially viable, it is essential that the notes issued to the public should receive a high credit rating, and for that to be obtained it is important that the debts should be protected against the insolvency of the intermediaries. The trust declared by the trustee company is designed to achieve that result, but the more substantial risk of insolvency is that of the original finance company. Consequently it is usual for the finance company to declare a trust over the debts due to it from its customers. Conventional terminology uses the expression 'receivables' to cover both these debts and the payments made in respect of the debts[1]. When the finance company offers to sell a quantity of receivables to the trustee company, and the offer is accepted, one of the terms of the resulting contract is that the finance company declares a bare trust over those receivables (which must be specified in detail) in favour of the trustee company. That trust is then intimated to the trustee company as beneficiary, the intimation once again referring to the specific receivables that are to be subject to the trust[2]. Thereafter the debts owed to the finance company are owed to the trustee company. When a payment is made to the finance company in respect of one of those debts, it is received by the finance company as a trustee, and held for the purposes of the trust in favour of the trustee company[3].

The declaration of trust made by the trustee company in favour of the note-issuing company should relate not only to payments received from the finance company but also to the whole beneficial interest of the trustee company in the trust declared by the finance company. In this way the total entitlement of the trustee company is held on trust for the note-issuing company, and the risk of the trustee company's insolvency is avoided. The trust declared by the trustee company must be intimated to the note-issuing company[4]. If the trust declared by the finance company is a single trust, over all the receivables sold by that company, it is probably sufficient that the trustee company makes a single intimation to the note-issuing company that the beneficial interest under the finance company's trust is held on trust for the note-issuing company. Nevertheless, it is safer if a fresh intimation is made by the trustee company to the note-issuing company following each sale of receivables by the finance company to the trustee company; the intimation should refer to the trustee company's entire beneficial interest in the specific

1 Debts and payments are distinct items of property, and it is important that the expression 'receivables' should be defined in such a way as to cover both.
2 In conventional practice, it is usual to have the trust declared and intimated offshore, where the completion meeting takes place. Normally the trust is intimated verbally, and the trustee company provides a written acknowledgment, in order to avoid any risk of stamp duty. It is thought that verbal intimation of a trust will be adequate, on the basis of the speeches in *Allan Trs v Lord Advocate* 1971 SC (HL) 45 and the opinions of the Second Division in *Kerr's Trs v Lord Advocate* 1974 SC 115, but that a written acknowledgment is desirable to provide evidence that intimation has been made: see *Donaldson v Ord* 1855 17 D 1053 at 1061–1070, per LJC Hope. In spite of the usual practice, it is thought by the authors that no stamp duty is payable on either an intimation or an acknowledgment of intimation in any event, and that the only duty is the fixed duty of 50p on the declaration of trust (if that is made in or brought to the United Kingdom).
3 In practice such payments received from the finance company's debtors will be paid into a trust account for behoof of the trustee company set up for the purposes of the securitisation. That procedure is not necessary, however, to impress the trust on the payments received by the finance company.
4 This is so even if the trust declared by the trustee company is subject to English law (because both Scottish and English debts are involved in the securitisation), as it is essential that the trust is properly impressed on the beneficial interest in the trust declared by the finance company over Scottish receivables (which will usually be a Scottish trust).

debts that have been sold[1]. When a payment is made by the finance company to the trustee company there is no need for any further intimation, as the payment amounts to actual delivery of property (cash) to the trustee (the trustee company); intimation is only necessary as an equivalent of delivery where there is no actual delivery.

## Nature of beneficiary's interest in securitisation trusts

The trusts created for the purposes of a securitisation transaction involve a part-implement of the sale of receivables, and as such do not constitute a charge or security for the purposes of registration in the register of charges of either the finance company or the trustee company[2]. It is thought that this characterisation, as part-implement of a sale rather than a security, applies generally[3], with the result that any negative pledge that has been granted by either the finance company or the trustee company will strike at the securitisation trusts[4]. Likewise, if either company is placed in administration, the trusts will not be regarded as a security for the purposes of sections 10(1)(b) and 11(3)(b) of the Insolvency Act 1986[5]. It is immaterial that the finance company grants a trust over heritably secured debts, as a trust over heritable property does not contravene section 9(3) of the Conveyancing and Feudal Reform (Scotland) Act 1970[6].

The ability to use trusts to protect the noteholders in a securitisation against the insolvency of the finance company or the trustee company is nevertheless limited in one significant respect. If the contract between the finance company and its debtor ceases to oblige the debtor to make payments, as where goods are repossessed under a hire-purchase contract or where a standard security is called up, the trust created by the finance company will not apply to the proceeds of sale of the goods or security subjects. The contract for the resale of the goods or land in question will inevitably be created after the declaration of trust and relative intimation, and thus sums payable under the contract of resale cannot be the subject of that trust. A fresh trust can be created over such sums, but if the finance company is insolvent it will have no incentive to do so; the liquidator, administrator or receiver is likely to repudiate any personal liability to create such a trust and thus restrict the trustee company to a claim against the insolvency for breach of contract. The only means of avoiding this difficulty is by creating a floating charge over the finance company's rights in the subjects that it may have a right to repossess, and in any entitlement it may have in the proceeds of sale of those subjects. Thus in the case of a finance company which lets vehicles on hire purchase, a floating charge would be taken over that company's interest in the vehicles and its interest in any contract for the sale of those vehicles following repossession. Any such floating charge would require registration; it cannot be regarded as part-implement of a contract for sale of the debts.

---

1 As with the declaration of trust by the finance company, it is normal to use a verbal intimation followed by a written acknowledgment. See footnote 2 on p 241.
2 Under the Companies Act 1985, ss 410–424, to be replaced by the Companies Act 1989, ss 92–107; see *Re George Inglefield Ltd* [1933] Ch 1, discussed at pp 253–254 above.
3 See *Armour v Thyssen Edelstahlwerke AG* 1990 SLT 891, discussed at pp 250–252.
4 See pp 255–256.
5 See p 255.
6 See p 239.

## Enforcement of trust rights

The general rights of the beneficiary in a trust to enforce it against the trustee were described in *Inland Revenue v Clark's Trs*[1] in the following terms:

'When counsel was asked to state what rights of action a beneficiary has by our law to protect his interest in the trust estate, he was obliged to admit that these rights of action were a right to interdict the trustee from committing any breach of trust, and a right of personal action, for example a declarator or an action of accounting against the trustees, to compel them to administer the trust according to its terms. There is also a personal action for damages against the trustees for breach of trust, and it is open for the beneficiary, by suitable procedure in this court, to bring about a change of administration of the trust either by a transfer of the administration to new trustees or by transfer of the administration to a judicial factor. But there is no action by which a beneficiary as such can in any way vindicate for himself any of the trust property. . . . It is no exception from, but rather a confirmation of, this proposition, that a beneficiary may compel trustees to give the use of their names or to grant an assignation of their claim against a third party'[2].

Where the trustee is insolvent, a personal action for damages will obviously be of no assistance. An action for accounting may be of help if trust property can be traced in the hands of the trustee or elsewhere[3]. If the liquidator, administrator or receiver of an insolvent trustee attempts to interfere with trust property in such a way as to defeat the beneficiary's rights, an interdict against breach of trust will be appropriate. That is a competent course against an administrator, notwithstanding section 11(3)(d) of the Insolvency Act 1986, as only the administrator, and not the company, need be called as a defender. Likewise, interdict may be obtained against a liquidator without consent, notwithstanding section 130(2) of the same Act. Thus if the liquidator of a finance company that had entered into a securitisation agreement attempted to renegotiate hire-purchase contracts that had been made subject to a trust, the beneficiary in that trust could obtain interdict against such actings[4].

## Change in administration of trust

In appropriate cases, as Lord President Normand indicates in *Clark's Trs*[5], a beneficiary can change the administration of a trust. On the insolvency of a trustee, its liquidator, administrator or receiver is unlikely to be interested in continuing the administration of the trust, as the benefit will enure to the beneficiary, not the insolvency. Thus a change in administration is likely to be the beneficiary's most effective remedy. If no specific provision is made in the trust documents, the most appropriate course of action is the appointment of a

1 1939 SC 11.
2 Lord President Normand at 22; see also Lord Moncrieff at 26.
3 See pp 245–247.
4 Such interference, to be actionable, need not be with the actual rights of the beneficiary; it is sufficient that a liquidator or administrator of the trustee acts in such a way as to defeat or diminish the reasonable expectations of the beneficiary. On reasonable expectations, see *Inglis v Inglis* 1983 SC 8; *McNiven v Peffers* 1868 7 M 181; *Keech v Sandford* (1726) Sel Cas Ch 61; *Cook v Deeks* [1916] 1 AC 554; and *Boardman v Phipps* [1967] 2 AC 46.
5 1939 SC 11.

judicial factor[1]. This is achieved by the presentation of a petition to the court[2]. The petition should normally ask for the appointment of an *interim* judicial factor to deal with the position prior to the making of a final appointment. With most forms of commercial agreement involving trusts, notably factoring and securitisation agreements, there will be a constant inflow of funds into the trust, and immediate action will be needed to deal with these. In addition, in securitisation agreements, in particular, it is critical that the flow of funds from debtors through the finance and trustee companies to the note-issuing company should be maintained in order that the latter company can make payments of interest and capital to the noteholders; the note-issuing company will have no other source of income. The petition should also seek powers that will be necessary to enable the judicial factor to administer the trust properly. With a factoring or securitisation agreement, those powers must include power to enforce all of the trustee's rights and powers in respect of the debtors, to collect and if necessary sue for all receivables due from debtors, and to pay all sums collected to the beneficiary of the trust, after deduction of expenses. The factor should also be empowered to appoint agents to assist him in the performance of his duties.

It will usually be more satisfactory to include in the trust documents a specific power, exercisable by the beneficiary, to change the administration of the trust. One possibility is a simple power to appoint a new trustee in the event of the insolvency of the original trustee. It is commoner, however, to make use of a power of attorney granted by the trustee, exercisable on the trustee's insolvency[3]. Such a power must be contained expressly in the trust documents. It should entitle the attorney (as mandatory for the trustee) to administer the trust in place of the original trustee. The attorney should be expressly authorised to exercise the whole rights and powers of the original trustee, including any discretions exercisable by it. Power to collect and sue for debts or other trust property should also be conferred, and a power to appoint agents will probably be of assistance.

Another useful provision in the trust documents is a power, exercisable by the beneficiary, to call on the trustee to make over the whole rights that are subject to the trust. That is an example of the general principle that a beneficiary who is absolutely entitled to trust property (the beneficiary of a bare trust) and *sui juris* can call on the trustee to denude in his favour[4]. It should further be provided that the right of the beneficiary to call for a transfer of the trust funds is exercisable notwithstanding the insolvency of the trustee, and that in that event an assignation or other transfer of the trust property in favour of the beneficiary may be exercised by an attorney or other mandatory on behalf of the trustee[5]. Such a power merely involves the beneficiary's fundamental right to compel the trustee to denude, and it

---

1 On judicial factors, see generally Walker *Judicial Factors* (1974) and *Stair Memorial Encyclopaedia*, vol 24, paras 237 *et seq*.

2 When an administrator has been appointed, it will be necessary to obtain his consent or the leave of the court, as section 11(3)(d) will apply; likewise, with a liquidator, section 130(2) requires leave of the court; the company, as trustee, must be called as a respondent in the petition for appointment of a judicial factor. It is thought that there will be no difficulty in obtaining the leave of the court in such cases, even if the administrator will not give consent: see *Re Atlantic Computer Systems plc* [1992] 2 WLR 367, especially at 374–375, 381 and 395c–f. See further chapter 4.

3 On powers of attorney in insolvency, see Chapter 12.

4 *Miller's Trs v Miller* 1890 18 R 301; *Yuill's Trs v Thomson* 1902 4 F 815; *Stair Memorial Encyclopaedia*, vol 24, para 72; *Wilson and Duncan*, pp 140 *et seq*.

5 On the validity of such provisions, see Chapter 12.

provides a convenient method of superseding the trustee's administration in the event of its insolvency. Following an assignation or other transfer executed by the attorney, the beneficiary must take all necessary steps to complete its real rights. Thus, if an assignation of debts is involved, the beneficiary must intimate the assignation to each of the debtors.

### Administration of trust by liquidator, administrator or receiver

In certain cases the liquidator, administrator or receiver or a company that acts as a trustee may continue the administration of the trust, even though it does not benefit the insolvency. In such a case the person administering the trust is subject to the rights and duties of a trustee, and may be liable for breach of trust if he fails to administer the trust properly. In England it has been held that in such cases the liquidator or other insolvency practitioner is entitled to payment of his expenses and reasonable remuneration out of the trust funds[1]. It is thought that the result in Scotland would be the same. So far as expenses and outlays are concerned, the liquidator would be in the position of a *negotiorum gestor*[2]. The right to reasonable remuneration was founded on the equitable nature of trust rights, and that is a feature of Scottish trusts[3].

### Tracing of trust property

While the rights of a beneficiary against trust property on the trustee's insolvency are clearly established[4], practical difficulties often arise in determining what is trust property. There is obviously no problem if trust property is in the name of the trustee and if its state has not been altered. The trustee may, however, have used trust property to acquire other property, which may or may not be in his own name, or he may have mixed the trust property with his own, for example, by paying both his own funds and trust funds into a common bank account in his name. He may have granted real rights over the trust property in favour of a third party. Such cases are governed by two general principles. The first is that the rights of the beneficiary will continue to affect trust property in the hands of the trustee, or any person who acquires such property from the trustee, as long as it remains identifiable as trust property. The application of this principle is generally referred to as the tracing of the trust property. This first principle, however, is subject to the second, which is that the rights of the beneficiary will be defeated if trust property has found its way to a transferee who gives full value and takes in good faith without notice of the trust[5]. It is thought that the test for the identifiability of trust property should be a practical one: as long as it is possible to discover a fund or an item of property in the hands of the trustee or an acquirer from the trustee which contains trust property or was bought using trust property, or represents the proceeds of trust property, that item will be identifiable as trust property[6]. As long as this test is satisfied, it does

---

1 *Re Berkeley Applegate (Investment Consultants) Ltd* [1989] BCLC 28.
2 See Gloag on *Contract*, pp 334–335.
3 The word 'equitable' is here used in the Scottish sense, and not in the technical sense that it has acquired in English law.
4 See pp 220 *et seq*.
5 *Redfearn v Somervail* (1813) 1 Dow 50; 1 Pat App 707. See above at p 221.
6 No test has been laid down judicially, but a practical approach has clearly been followed in the cases discussed below. See Bell, *Comm*, I, 216.

not matter what the nature of the transaction was. Nor does it matter how many transactions may have affected the trust property[1].

### Inmixing of trust funds with trustee's own money

It frequently occurs in practice that an insolvent trustee has inmixed trust funds with his own money, usually in a bank account operated by him. The general rule in such cases is that: 'the court will, if it can, disentangle the account and separate the trust funds from the private monies, and award the former specifically to the beneficiaries[2].' If the trustee makes payments out of the account for his own purposes, the presumption is that these are made from his private money, and that what is left, or as much of that as is necessary, remains subject to the trust[3]. In such cases the rule in *Clayton's Case*[4] does not apply to trust funds that have been inmixed with a trustee's own funds. It is also established that the onus of proving which part of a mixed fund is the trustee's lies on him. 'If a man mixes trust funds with his own, the whole will be treated as the trust property, except so far as he may be able to distinguish what is his own.'[5] The result is different, however, when the trustee's bank account is overdrawn and trust money paid into it. In such cases, if the bank has no notice of the trust and applies the payments to reduce the trustee's overdraft, the trust money paid into the account will become the property of the bank and the beneficiaries' rights will be defeated[6]. In cases where the bank uses trust money to reduce the trustee's overdraft in ignorance of the trust, it is in the position of a transferee of trust money in good faith and for value, and thus its rights prevail against those of the trust beneficiaries. If, by contrast, the trustee's account is at credit, the bank does not give value, and thus its rights do not prevail against the trust. Consequently in such cases the beneficiaries are entitled to trace the trust money into the trustee's bank account. The same result follows if the bank knows of the trust, as it then lacks good faith[7].

Trust money may be inmixed with the funds of persons other than the trustee. In the only reported Scottish case on this area of the law, *Magistrates*

---

1 See *Newton's Exrx v Meiklejohn's JF* 1959 SLT 71, where the pledging of shares by a stockbroker under a general letter of hypothecation was held not to be sufficient to destroy the identity of those shares as trust property.

2 *Smith v Liqr of James Birrell Ltd* 1968 SLT 174 at 175, per Lord Fraser; see also *Macadam v Martin's Tr* (1872) 11 M 33; *Jopp v Johnston's Tr* (1904) 6 F 1028. The leading English cases on this problem are *Re Hallett's Estate* (1879) 13 ChD 696 and *Sinclair v Brougham* [1914] AC 398. English law differs markedly from Scots law in this area, however; in England distinct rights to trace property are recognised at law and in equity, and many of the cases turn on somewhat narrow distinctions that have not become part of Scots law.

3 *Jopp v Johnston's Tr* above, where *Re Hallett's Estate*, above, was followed.

4 1 Mer 572, discussed in Gloag on *Contract* at pp 713–715 and McBryde on *Contract* at paras 22–26 and 22–27.

5 *Frith v Cartland* (1865) 2 H and M 417 at 420–421, per Wood V.-C, cited with approval by Jessel MR in *Re Hallett's Estate*, above, at 719; and by Lord Justice-Clerk Macdonald in *Jopp v Johnston's Tr* above, at 1035.

6 *Hofford v Gowans* 1909 1 SLT 153. It is necessary that the bank should actually apply the money to reduce the overdraft if the beneficiaries' rights are to be defeated. This explains why the opposite result was reached in *Smith v Liqr of James Birrell Ltd*, above, where the bank did not consolidate the trustee's two accounts, one of which was overdrawn.

7 *Taylor v Forbes* (1830) 4 W & S 444.

*of Edinburgh v McLaren*,[1] the funds of two trusts were inmixed and administered together. It was held that the combined fund should be divided rateably between the trusts, according to the amounts derived from each. In making the division, income and capital were divided separately in such a way as to reflect the different periods during which the property of each trust had been part of the common fund. This result appears just, and is certainly preferable to the application of the rule in *Clayton's Case*, which may have very arbitrary consequences. When trust money is inmixed with the funds of a third party who acts in good faith, without knowledge of the trust, but does not give full value it is thought that the result should be the same as with the inmixing of the funds of two trusts. In such cases, if the third party removes more than his share from the mixed fund, the beneficiaries of the trust are entitled to recover the excess from him, since he has not given value for the money removed[2].

## Property derived from trust property

A trustee may use trust property held by him, either by itself or together with his own property, to acquire other property. In all such cases the property so acquired will be subject to the trust, and the beneficiaries will be entitled to claim it in the event of the trustee's insolvency[3]. It is essential, however, that the property should remain identifiable as trust property, in the manner discussed above[4]. If a third party who either knows of the trust or does not give full value acquires property using trust funds, the result is the same; the rights of such persons do not prevail against the trust.

If a trustee or third party acquires property using both his own funds and trust funds, it is thought that any increase in the value of the property so acquired should be shared rateably by the acquirer and the trust so long as the acquirer is acting honestly. If, on the other hand, the trustee commits a wilful breach of trust, or the third party knows that he is dealing with trust property, it is thought that any increase in value should accrue to the trust. In such cases there is a deliberate breach of trust, or deliberate acquiescence in a breach of trust, and it seems inequitable that the party guilty of such breach or acquiescence should profit in any way from his actions. Furthermore, if a third party takes title to trust property or deals with it in knowledge of the trust, he will take that property, or anything representing it, as a constructive trustee; the beneficiaries will thus be entitled to enforce the trust against him, and to claim any profits arising from the use of the trust property in exactly the same way as against the original trustee[5].

1 (1881) 8 R (HL) 140.
2 In so far as the English decision in *Re Diplock* [1948] Ch 465 goes beyond this proposition, it does not appear to be in accordance with Scots law.
3 *Jopp v Johnston's Tr* (1904) 6 F 1028, where money was withdrawn from a bank account that included both trust funds and the trustee's own funds and was placed on deposit receipt in the trustee's name.
4 See pp 245–246.
5 In England those who intermeddle with trust property are distinguished from those who act as agents for the trust within the scope of their authority as such agents; the latter are generally not held liable as constructive trustees: *Barnes v Addy* (1874) LR 9 Ch App 244; *Mara v Browne* [1896] 1 Ch 199; *Williams-Ashman v Price and Williams* [1942] Ch 219; *Carl Zeiss Stiftung v Herbert Smith & Co* (No 2) [1969] 2 Ch 276. If such a rule represents the law of Scotland, it is thought that it should not apply where an agent deals with or takes control of property in the knowledge that a breach of trust is being committed; in such cases the agent is actively and knowingly taking part in a breach of trust.

### Enforcement of creditors' rights against trustee[1]

A trustee who enters into a contractual obligation with a third party to the trust is generally personally liable on such an obligation[2]. It is possible for a trustee to contract in such a way that the trust estate only is bound, but that requires the agreement, express or clearly implied, of the other contracting party[3]. Even if the trustee is unable to meet his obligations from his own resources, a creditor who has contracted with the trustee in his capacity of trustee may claim payment from the funds of the trust[4]. That is so whether or not the creditor was aware of the existence of the trust; what matters is whether the trustee in fact contracted on behalf of the trust. It follows that, in the event of the trustee's insolvency, the creditors who contracted with the trustee on behalf of the trust may take steps to secure the administration of the trust so that they may be paid out of the trust assets. To this end, it will not usually be appropriate to appoint a liquidator to the trustee, as that will not segregate the trust funds from the trustee's own property[5]. Instead, it will generally be preferable to have a judicial factor appointed on the trust estate. The factor's duty is then to ingather the trust property and to pay the creditors of the trust and thereafter the beneficiaries.

Creditors of the trust are invariably entitled to payment out of trust funds in preference to beneficiaries of the trust, unless the creditor's claim involved a breach of trust by the trustee and (1) the creditor was aware of that breach of trust or (2) the creditor did not give full value for his debt[6]. The beneficiary's right is only to the balance of the trust funds after all debts properly constituted by the trustee have been paid. Consequently, if it appears likely that a trustee will make the whole of the trust property over to the beneficiaries without first paying all creditors of the trust, those creditors may obtain an interdict against the transfer to the beneficiaries. A trustee has a right to reimbursement out of the trust estate in respect of debts that he has properly contracted on behalf of the trust[7]. Moreover, in security of his right to reimbursement a trustee has a lien over trust property[8], and may in some circumstances have a right of general retention[9]. It follows that a trustee should not make over trust funds to a beneficiary unless he has made full provision for the debts of the trust. If he fails to make provision for the debts of the trust, his personal liability on such debts remains. If his own estate is not sufficient to meet those debts, the transfer to the beneficiary will constitute a gratuitious alienation[10], on the basis that there is no obligation to transfer funds to the beneficiary until the debts of the trust have been paid.

1 See generally *Stair Memorial Encyclopaedia*, vol 24, para 225; *Wilson and Duncan*, pp 394 *et seq*.
2 *Cullen v Baillie* 1856 8 D 511.
3 *Cullen v Baillie, supra; Lumsden v Buchanan* 1865 3 M (HL) 89 at 95 per Lord Cranworth.
4 *Cunnigham v Montgomerie* 1879 6 R 1333.
5 If the creditor has a prospect of recovering funds from the trustee's own estate, the appointment of a liquidator will be appropriate, but corporate trustees generally have no significant assets apart from the trust funds under their charge.
6 See p 221 above.
7 See generally *Wilson and Duncan*, pp 400 *et seq*; *Stair Memorial Encyclopaedia*, vol 24, paras 232 *et seq*.
8 Gloag & Irvine, *Rights in Security*, pp 403–405.
9 *Gloag & Irvine*, pp 330–340.
10 See chapter 15.

# Chapter 10

# The nature of a security

## Introduction

In common with other systems based on Roman law, Scots law has taken a restrictive approach to the creation of real securities. Three general categories of real security[1] existed at common law. Over land and heritable rights generally, the ex facie absolute disposition, normally accompanied by a back letter indicating the terms of the security, was the usual form, although two other forms, the bond and disposition in security and bond of cash credit, were both available[2]. Over corporeal moveable property (goods), the only form of security was the pledge[3]. Over incorporeal moveable property (debts, shares, policies of assurance and contractual rights generally), the only form of security was an assignation in security; the terms of the security might be set out on the face of the assignation or in a separate back letter[4]. In each case, security rights could be created only by delivery of possession or its equivalent. In the case of heritable securities, this was achieved by recording in the Register of Sasines. In the case of pledge, delivery of the goods, or of a document of title representing the goods, to the security holder was essential; the only exception occurred if the security holder already had possession, in which case retention served as the equivalent of delivery. In the case of assignation in security, intimation to the debtor formed the equivalent of delivery.

The common law has been modified by statute in two important respects. First, the old forms of heritable security were replaced in 1970 by the standard security[5]. Recording in the Register of Sasines (or, since 1979[6], registration in the Land Register) is still necessary, however, to create real security rights which will prevail on the insolvency of the owner of the property. Second, the

---

1 In a real security rights are created in favour of the security holder over items of property. That should be contrasted with personal security, or caution, which takes the form of a guarantee. A real security is enforceable over the property notwithstanding the insolvency of its owner (subject, in the case of petitions, for the appointment of an administrator and administration orders, to Insolvency Act 1986, ss 10(1)(b) or 11(3)(c)). A guarantee, by contrast, merely gives a personal right of action against the guarantor (unless it is backed by a real security), and on his insolvency the creditor can only rank for a dividend.

2 See Halliday, *Conveyancing Law and Practice*, vol 3, chs 32–34; Gloag and Irvine, *Rights in Security*, chs 2–6.

3 *Gloag and Irvine*, ch 7; Carey Miller, *Corporeal Moveables in Scots Law*, paras 11.04–11.14.

4 *Gloag and Irvine*, chs 13–16.

5 Conveyancing and Feudal Reform (Scotland) Act 1970, ss 9–31; see *Halliday*, chs 36–40, 42.

6 Land Registration (Scotland) Act 1979.

floating charge was introduced in 1961[1]. It is ineffective without registration in the company's register of charges[2].

Apart from the foregoing general categories of security, rights of retention and lien are recognised, founded on ownership or possession or on the principle of mutuality of contractual obligations[3]. Finally, there exist a number of highly specific securities in the nature of a hypothec (a security without delivery of possession or its equivalent), namely the landlord's and superior's hypothecs and a variety of securities over ships and aircraft[4]; these form exceptions of a limited nature to the rule that delivery or its equivalent is necessary to constitute a security.

The importance of identifying whether a right purportedly created by parties is of the nature of a real security is that, if it does not fit into one of the recognised categories of security, it will be ineffective on the insolvency of the granter. In particular, apart from the limited number of hypothecs and the floating charge, if delivery or retention of possession of the security subjects or an equivalent of delivery does not occur, any right of the nature of a security will be ineffective. Further, any attempt to achieve the result of a real security by means of a mere personal contract will not be recognised.

### Nature of a security: right accessory to creditor's primary right to sue for debt

Perhaps the most satisfactory description of a security in Scottish legal literature is that of Gloag and Irvine[5]:

'. . . any right which a creditor may hold for ensuring the payment or satisfaction of his debt, distinct from, and in addition to, his right of action and execution against the debtor under the latter's personal obligation. A creditor, in other words, who holds a right in security, has at his disposal some means of realising payments or exacting performance of the obligation due to him, distinct from, and in addition to, the means which are at the disposal of the debtor's general creditors, who have relied solely on the debtor's personal credit. Whatever the special form of the right in security may be, its effect is in all cases to put the party entitled to it in a position of advantage, and to render his power of realising payment of his debt more sure. . . . Further, a right of this kind is always necessarily accessory in its nature, being constituted for the merely subsidiary purpose of enabling the person entitled to it to make sure of receiving a certain sum which is due to him, if not otherwise, then at all events by means of the right in question'.

The critical feature of this description is the accessory nature of a security right; it is a right additional to the primary right to sue for payment of the debt.

### Qualifications

Gloag and Irvine's description of a right in security must now be regarded as qualified by the decision of the House of Lords in *Armour v Thyssen*

---

1 Companies (Floating Charges) (Scotland) Act 1961. The law is now contained in sections 462–466 of the Companies Act 1985. See ch 5.
2 See p 138 *supra*.
3 See *Gloag and Irvine*, chs 10 and 11; Gloag on *Contract*, pp 623–644.
4 See *Gloag and Irvine*, pp 406–437 (landlord's and superior's hypothecs), 291–302, 437–439 (securities over ships).
5 *Rights in Security*, pp 1–2.

*Edelstahlwerke AG*[1]. Lord Keith[2] drew attention to the following passage in Gloag and Irvine's introduction to their chapter on securities over moveables:

'It is proposed in this and the succeeding chapters to consider by what method a party in possession of [corporeal moveable] property may convey or transfer it in security; that is, by what methods he may, while retaining the ownership in, or at least the ultimate right to, the subject, confer on a particular creditor a right over it, which will enable that creditor to vindicate that subordinate right in a question with the general creditors of his author, with particular creditors attaching the subject by diligence, or with a third party to whom it may have been transferred.'[3]

He continued:

'Can it be said that Carron [the purchasers of goods under an "all sums" retention of title clause] somehow attempted to create a security over the goods in favour of the appellants [the sellers of the goods]? In order that it might do so it would require to have both the ownership and the possession, actual or constructive, of the goods. The essence of a right in security is that the debtor retains at least what Gloag and Irvine call the ultimate right to the goods. Can it be said that Carron obtained anything which gave it the capacity to retain an ultimate right to the goods? That could be so only if the contract of sale gave it the property in the goods, but the contract of sale said that the property in the goods was not to pass until all debts due to the appellants had been paid. We are now very far removed from the situation where a party in possession of corporeal moveables is seeking to create a subordinate right in favour of a condition while retaining the ultimate right to himself . . . Carron had no interest of any kind whatever in any particular goods. Carron was never in a position to confer upon the appellants any subordinate right over the [goods], nor did it ever seek to do so'[4].

In a later passage in his speech, Lord Keith stated:

'In all cases where a right in security is conferred the debtor retains an ultimate right over the subject matter in question. The creditor, having realised out of that subject matter a sufficient sum to meet the debt, is obliged to account to the debtor for any surplus'[5].

**Ultimate right over subject matter**

The main criterion in Lord Keith's analysis of the nature of a security is that the person granting the security should have an 'ultimate right' over the subject matter of the security. It is not wholly clear from the speech itself what the exact nature of such an 'ultimate right' should be. It is nevertheless thought that the right in question must be either a real right to the security subjects or an absolute personal right, that is, a personal right which is not qualified by any contingency.

In *Armour v Thyssen Edelstahlwerke AG*[6] the purchasers had agreed to buy a quantity of steel, but the contract provided that property in the steel would not pass until all debts due by the purchasers to the sellers had been paid. The purchasers' right to property in the steel was accordingly contingent upon

1 1990 SLT 891; the decision in that case is discussed at pp 262–263 below.
2 At 894F-H.
3 Ch 7; the passage occurs at p 187.
4 At 894I-L.
5 At 895C.
6 1990 SLT 891.

their payment of all debts to the sellers, and it was held that the purchasers were unable to create a security. On the other hand, the passage from Gloag and Irvine, *Rights in Security*[1] quoted by Lord Keith clearly differentiates between ownership, or a full real right, and the 'ultimate right' to the security subjects, which must therefore be something less than a full real right[2]. Likewise rights of retention founded on *ex facie* absolute ownership of property[3] involve the creation of a security right in favour of the actual owner of the property by a person, usually a purchaser or the beneficiary of a trust, who has a merely personal right, or at least a right less than a full real right, to the property. The problem with the view that an absolute personal right to property is necessary in order to create a security over it is that it is competent to assign a contingent debt, for example a term assurance policy, in security; likewise a *spes successionis* can be assigned absolutely or in security[4]. While a *spes successionis* can be regarded as a form of property right, the right of the holder of a life assurance policy as against the issuing company is a right arising under a personal contract, just as Carron's right to the goods in *Armour* was a right, albeit contingent, under a personal contract. The contingency in *Armour* was under the control of Carron, in that by making payment of all sums due to Thyssen they could obtain ownership, but continued payment of premiums is likewise a condition for the validity and enforceability of a life policy. It is in any event difficult to see as a matter of principle why a contingent right should not form the subject of a security, either by assignation or by retention.

### Earlier Scottish cases

In earlier Scottish cases under what is now section 62(4) of the Sale of Goods Act 1979[5] the approach taken by the court was to consider the substance of the transaction to determine whether it was intended to operate by way of security. The general approach was summarised by Lord Moncrieff in *Robertson v Hall's Tr*:

'The form of the contract is not conclusive. The reality of the transaction must be inquired into; and if, contrary to the form of the contract, and even the declaration of the parties, it appears from the whole circumstances that a true sale was not intended, it will be held that the property has not passed and that no effectual security has been acquired'[6].

It is thought that such a substantive approach should be applied in all cases where the question of whether a transaction is truly a security is in issue. Nevertheless, under section 62(4) a formal approach is clearly impossible, as

---

1 *Gloag and Irvine*, p 187; see p 251 above. It does not appear from the passage referred to that Gloag and Irvine intended that the 'ultimate right' to the security subjects should be the criterion of what amounts to a security; the concept does not even appear in the general discussion of the nature of a security in chapter 1 of their work.

2 Lord Keith does, however, suggest at 894 I that in order to create a security a person must have both ownership and possession of goods; that seems inconsistent with the other examples discussed in this paragraph.

3 *Gloag and Irvine*, pp 330–340.

4 *Browne's Tr v Anderson* 1901 4 F 305.

5 Formerly section 61(4) of the Sale of Goods Act 1893. The statutory context (see head (6) on p 256) has coloured these decisions to a considerable extent.

6 (1896) 24 R 120 at 134. See also *Hepburn v Law* 1914 SC 918 at 921; *Newbigging v Morton* 1930 SC 273; and *Scottish Transit Trust v Scottish Land Cultivators* 1955 SC 254.

the subsection applies only to transactions in the form of a contract of sale, and the reference in the subsection to the way the transaction is intended to operate invites a substantive approach.

In *Gavin's Tr v Fraser*[1], a contractor sold his plant to the timber merchant for whom he was working, at its fair value, and it was agreed that the contractor might buy back the plant within a year for the same price with interest at 6 per cent. The contractor gave no personal obligation to repay the price, but merely had an option to repurchase. It was held that the agreement was in fact a contract of sale, and was not intended to operate by way of security. The critical point was that there was no personal obligation to be secured by any intended security arrangement[2]. In other words, an obligation in security must be accessory to a principal obligation; if an obligation stands alone, it cannot be a security.

The approach of the House of Lords in *Armour v Thyssen Edelstahlwerke AG*[3] suggests that in future a more formal and less substantive approach is likely to be taken to the question of whether a particular right is truly a right in security. In this connection the classic English description of a security is likely to be of assistance. In *Re George Inglefield Ltd*[4]. Romer LJ differentiated a transaction of sale and a transaction of mortgage or charge (in Scottish terminology a security) in the following terms:

'In a transaction of sale the vendor is not entitled to get back the subject-matter of the sale by returning to the purchaser the money that has passed between them. In the case of a mortgage or charge, the mortgagor is entitled, until he has been foreclosed, to get back the subject-matter of the mortgage or charge by returning to the mortgagee the money that has passed between them. The second essential difference is that if the mortgagee realises the subject-matter of the mortgage for a sum more than sufficient to repay him, with interest and the costs, the money that has passed between him and the mortgagor he has to account to the mortgagor for the surplus. If the purchaser sells the subject-matter of the purchase, and realises a profit, of course he has not got to account to the vendor for the profit. Thirdly, if the mortgagee realises the mortgage property for a sum that is insufficient to repay him the money that he has paid to the mortgagor, together with interest and costs, then the mortgagee is entitled to recover from the mortgagor the balance of the money, either because there is a covenant by the mortgagor to repay the money advanced by the mortgagee or because of the existence of the simple contract debt which is created by the mere fact of the advance having been made. If the purchaser were to resell the purchased property at a price which was insufficient to recoup him the money that he paid to the vendor, of course he would not be entitled to recover the balance from the vendor'[5].

The critical features of a security, according to this description, are first that the granter of a security is entitled to recover the subject matter by paying his debt to the security holder and second that, if the security subjects are realised by the security holder, he is entitled to recover his full debt, but only that sum, regardless of the amount realised by the sale of the security subjects. Those features look to the practical operation of a right to discover whether it is a security, rather than to any underlying concept of what a security is. Nevertheless, while it cannot be regarded as a comprehensive description of a

1 1920 SC 674.
2 See Lord President Clyde at 634; Lord Mackenzie at 688–689.
3 1990 SLT 891.
4 [1933] Ch 1.
5 At 27–28.

security right, Romer LJ's opinion provides workable criteria for distinguishing a security, and is likely to be helpful in practice.

As the decision in *Re George Inglefield Ltd*[1] makes clear, if a right involves part implement of a contract of sale it will not constitute a security. In that case a furnishing company which carried on a considerable hire-purchase business had gone into creditors' voluntary liquidation. To finance its lending the furnishing company had entered into agreements with a discount company in terms of which the discount company purchased goods not on hire-purchase together with the benefit of the relative hire-purchase agreements. The furnishing company executed assignments of all such goods and hire-purchase agreements in favour of the discount company, but these were not intimated to the hirers of the goods[2]. It was claimed by the liquidator that the assignments were mortgages or charges of book debts which were void against the creditors of the furnishing company for want of registration. The Court of Appeal held that the agreements were for an out-and-out sale of the goods and the benefit of the hire-purchase contracts, and that the assignments, even though unintimated, were only the part-implement of that sale. The furnishing company had no right to the return of the property assigned, and was entitled to a definite sum (albeit calculated in accordance with a formula) which did not vary according to how much the discount company realised from the contracts assigned or from the resale of the goods which formed the subject matter of those contracts.

### Significance of characterisation as security

Characterisation of a right as a security rather than some other form of transaction such as a sale is important in a number of respects. These are enumerated below. For the most part the substantive law which governs the enumerated areas falls outwith the scope of the present work; references are given to the principal writings on each subject, to which reference should be made for the detailed law.

(1) A security right must fit into one of the categories of security recognised in Scots law. Otherwise it will be wholly invalid[3].

(2) Certain categories of security must be registered under sections 410 to 424 of the Companies Act 1985; otherwise they will be void against a liquidator and creditors of the company. If, however, a right does not amount to a security, it will not require registration. Sections 410 to 424 of the 1985 Act are due to be replaced by new provisions enacted by sections 97 to 107 of the Companies Act 1989; these will form sections 395 to 420 of the 1985 Act as amended, and will constitute a uniform scheme of registration for all companies registered under the Companies

---

1 At n 4 *supra*.
2 In Scotland assignation of goods is not competent, but the basic principle in the case still applies.
3 See pp 249–250. The classic work on rights in security is Gloag and Irvine, *Rights in Security*. For more up to date treatments of particular subjects, see the other works cited in the footnotes on pp 249–250, and also: Wilson, *Debt* (2nd edn, 1991) chs 7–9; Gloag and Henderson, *Introduction to the Law of Scotland* (9th edn, 1987) ch 20; Carey Miller, *Corporeal Moveables in Scots Law*, ch 11; Gordon, *Scottish Land Law*, ch 20; McBryde, *Contract*, paras 14–33 to 14–48 (retention and lien) and 22–44 to 22–88 (compensation and balancing of accounts on insolvency); Gloag on *Contract*, pp 623–644 (retention, lien, compensation, balancing of accounts on insolvency).

Acts throughout Great Britain[1]. In practice the most important categories of security are charges on land wherever situated (standard securities in Scotland), securities over book debts[2], securities over patents, trademarks and copyrights and associated licences, securities over ships and aircraft and floating charges. Under the new provisions in the 1989 Act there will be added a charge on goods or any interest in goods other than a charge under which the chargee is entitled to possession either of the goods or of a document of title to them[3]. It is thought that that provision will not affect practice in Scotland, where only securities over ships and aircraft will be registrable. The only general form of security over corporeal moveables recognised by Scots law, other than securities arising by operation of law, is pledge; it is established by *Armour v Thyssen Edelstahlwerke AG*[4] that a right of retention of title is not a security.

Section 395(2) of the 1985 Act as amended by the 1989 Act makes it clear that security interests arising by operation of law are not registrable. That is thought to cover rights of retention and lien and the landlord's and superior's and maritime hypothecs.

(3) In terms of section 9(3) of the Conveyancing and Feudal Reform (Scotland) Act 1970, a grant of any right over an interest in land for the purpose of securing any debt by way of heritable security may be effected only by means of a standard security. If a right is not granted for security purposes, the restriction does not apply[5], as in a securitisation agreement. 'Heritable security' is defined in section 9(8)(a) as any security capable of being constituted over an interest in land by disposition or assignation of that interest in security and of being recorded in the Register of Sasines. Thus rights under a trust over land or heritably secured debts will not be affected by section 9(3).

(4) It is common for floating charges to contain a prohibition on the grant without the consent of the security holder of further securities other than those arising by operation of law; such provisions, commonly known as negative pledges, are authorised in floating charges by section 464(1) of the Companies Act 1985. If a right is not a security, it is not struck at by a negative pledge. It should be noted that, under section 464(2), a fixed security arising by operation of law has priority over a floating charge, notwithstanding a negative pledge; that applies to rights of retention and lien and the landlord's and superior's and maritime hypothecs. A negative pledge is registrable under section 417(3)(c) of the Companies Act 1985. It is likely that this will continue to be the case when the 1989 provisions come into force, although section 415(2)(a) of the amended

1 See *Palmer's Company Law*, ch 49, and ch 46 so far as relevant to Scotland.
2 For definition of a book debt, see *Palmer's Company Law*, para 46–06; and *Alexander v Alexander* (1896) 23 R 724; *Tailby v Official Receiver* (1888) 13 App Cas 523; *Dawson v Isle* [1906] 1 Ch 633; *Re George Inglefield Ltd* [1933] Ch 1; *Re Kent and Sussex Sawmills Ltd* [1947] Ch 177; *Independent Automatic Sales Ltd v Knowles & Foster* [1962] 1 WLR 974; *Siebe Gorman & Co Ltd v Barclays Bank Ltd* [1979] 2 Lloyds Rep 142; *Carreras Rothmans Ltd v Freeman Matthews Treasure Ltd* [1985] Ch 207 (moneys in trust account not book debts); *Re Keenan Brothers Ltd* [1986] BCLC 242; *Re Brightlife Ltd* [1986] 3 All ER 673 (cash at bank not book debt).
3 See s 396(1), as amended.
4 *Supra*.
5 On the authority of *Re George Inglefield Ltd supra*, and *Armour v Thyssen Edelstahlwerke AG, supra*. See pp 239, 242.

form of the 1985 Act merely permits negative pledges to be included among the prescribed particulars[1].

(5)  On the presentation of a petition for an administration order, no steps may be taken to enforce any security over the company's property without the leave of the court in terms of section 10(1)(b) of the Insolvency Act 1986. When an administration order has been made and for as long as it is in force, under section 11(3)(b) of the Act no steps may be taken to enforce any security over the company's property except with the consent of the administrator or leave of the court. Under sections 15 and 16, an administrator has extensive powers to deal with property of the company over which a security subsists[2].

(6)  In terms of section 62(4) of the Sale of Goods Act 1979, the provisions of the Act do not apply to a transaction in the form of a contract of sale which is intended to operate by way of pledge or other security[3]. It is essential that the transaction should have the form of a contract of sale. Otherwise the critical question is whether the transaction is intended to operate by way of security. The courts have generally adopted a substantive rather than formal approach[4]. A sale with a *pactum de retrovendendo* (an agreement to transfer the subjects back to the seller for an agreed price) has been held not to be intended to operate as a security, but in circumstances where there was no principal debt to be secured by the agreement[5]; in other circumstances such an agreement might amount to a substantive security[6]. If the transaction is intended to operate by way of security, the result is that the 1979 Act does not apply and the sale is governed by the common law; consequently, in accordance with the common law rule, property passes on delivery, unless it is agreed that it should pass at a later time[7]. The transaction nevertheless remains a valid security, as long as property passes in accordance with the common law rule.

## Attempts to create preference by contract

Perhaps the most fundamental principle governing a Scottish insolvency is that the creditors rank equally in the assets that are available for distribution among them. The only creditors who receive a preference are those who have

---

1  Negative pledges undertaken by English companies are not at present registrable, although in practice they are often registered. As to notice of such provisions in respect of English companies, compare *Palmer's Company Law*, para 45–08, and Gore-Browne, *Companies*, para 18–14. The present English position causes difficulty in relation to securities created by English companies over Scottish property.
2  See Chapter 4 above.
3  See Carey Miller, *Corporeal Moveables in Scots Law*, paras 11.10 and 11.11; Gloag and Henderson, *Introduction to the Law of Scotland* (9th edn, 1987), para 17.12. An extensive case law exists on the subsection, although the cases generally turn on their own facts and the interpretation of s 62(4), and there is little by way of statements of general principle. See *Robertson v Hall's Tr* (1896) 24 R 120; *Jones & Co's Tr v Allan* (1901) 4 F 374; *Hepburn v Law* 1914 SC 918; *Gavin's Tr v Fraser* 1920 SC 674; *Newbigging v Morton* 1930 SC 273; *Scottish Transit Trust v Scottish Land Cultivators* 1955 SC 254; *G & C Finance Corpn v Brown* 1961 SLT 408; *Ladbroke Leasing (South West) Ltd v Reekie Plant Ltd* 1983 SLT 155.
4  *Robertson v Hall's Tr, supra*; *Scottish Transit Trust v Scottish Land Cultivators, supra*. See pp 252–253.
5  *Gavin's Tr v Fraser, supra*. See p 253.
6  Cf. *Scottish Transit Trust v Scottish Land Cultivators, supra*.
7  See Gloag and Irvine, pp 188–189; *Stair*, 1.xiii, 14; Bell, *Comm*, ii.11; Bell, *Prin*, § 1363.

properly constituted securities of a form recognised by the law, those who have done diligence and those whose debts receive a statutory preference under section 386 of and Schedule 6 to the Insolvency Act 1986[1]. In relation to securities, the only form of security recognised by Scots law that involves purely personal rights is the guarantee or cautionary obligation[2], where a third party incurs a personal accessory obligation. All other forms of security involve real, or trust, rights in particular items of property or, in the case of the floating charge, in a fluctuating fund of property. All such forms of security fall into nominate categories, and each has its own requirements for effective constitution, typically involving delivery, intimation or registration. On occasion attempts are made to confer the benefits of a real security through purely personal contractual arrangements. Such arrangements do not include the proper procedures for creation of any nominate security or form of diligence. Moreover, a mere contract is inherently incapable of creating anything more than personal rights[3]. Consequently any attempt to create rights similar to those of a real security, or of a trust, by merely contractual arrangements will be unsuccessful.

Typically such attempts involve an agreement which purports to vary the ranking which one of the parties will receive in the insolvency of the other. There is generally no objection to one party's agreeing not to enforce his debt until the ordinary creditors of the other have been paid in full[4], but any attempt to obtain a preference will be struck down by the courts unless it amounts to a form of security or diligence recognised by the law and properly carried into effect.

In *Farmers' Mart Ltd v Milne*[5] the pursuers, a firm of auctioneers and valuers, employed the defender to act as their manager. A clause in his contract of employment provided that all fees that the defender might earn from any appointment as factor or trustee on an estate should be pooled with all fees and commissions earned by the pursuers on such estate and the proceeds divided equally between the parties. The defender had in fact acted as a trustee in sequestration and a trustee for creditors[6], and the action related *inter alia* to his fees for these. It was held by the House of Lords that the agreement was illegal and accordingly unenforceable, in that it violated the fundamental principle of bankruptcy law providing for the equal distribution of assets among creditors. The objection to the pooling arrangement was described by Lord Dunedin as follows:

'If the defender acted as a trustee in a sequestration he would in terms of this agreement be bound to put the fees that he got as remuneration as trustee into a pool with any fees which they, the pursuers, got for employment which he gave them as trustee, and then in the

1 See chapter 13; certain categories of postponed debt also exist.
2 See *Gloag and Irvine*, pp 642–669; *Gloag and Henderson*, ch 21. It is possible to create a real third party security, as where one person grants a standard security in respect of the obligations of another; in such a case the granter of the security and the principal obligant stand in the relationship of cautioner and principal obligant, and are subject to the detailed rules relating to cautionary obligations. While a trust can be used as a security (see chapter 9), the rights of the beneficiary share important features with real rights, and cannot, in the context of insolvency be classified as purely personal.
3 See *Bank of Scotland v Liqrs of Hutchison Main & Co Ltd* 1914 SC (HL) 1; *Gibson v Hunter Home Designs Ltd* 1976 SC 23.
4 See pp 295–296 on the subordination of debt.
5 1914 SC (HL) 84.
6 See 1914 SC 129 at 130.

division there would not be absolutely equal division of those pooled fees, but before anything else the pursuers, if they were creditors on the estate on which he was a trustee, would receive such an allowance over and above the dividends which they would get in common with ordinary creditors as would give them 20s. in the £'[1].

Lord Atkinson considered the material clause to be:

'a device between the pursuers and the defender, in fraud of the bankruptcy laws, to secure to the pursuers a larger dividend than the other creditors in that estate are receiving. . . . In consideration that [the pursuers] would consent to the defender acting as trustee in certain bankruptcy matters in which they were creditors, he would allow part of his remuneration, which was paid out of the assets, to be applied in part to secure to the [pursuers] a larger dividend than the other creditors in those bankruptcy matters were receiving'[2].

In *British Eagle International Air Lines Ltd v Compagnie Nationale Air France*[3] various airline operators, including the plaintiffs (who were in liquidation) and the defendants, were parties to a clearing house arrangement set up by the International Air Transport Association for the monthly settlement of debits and credits which arose when members performed services for one another. The clearing house arrangement involved complex rules which prevented individual airlines from making claims against one another. It was held by the House of Lords, with Lords Morris and Simon dissenting, that the arrangements were contrary to public policy and unenforceable in that they contravened the principle[4] that the property of a company should be applied in satisfaction of its liabilities *pari passu*. Lord Cross expressed the reasoning of the majority as follows:

'It is true that if the respondents [the airline] are right the "clearing house" creditors will be treated as though they were creditors with valid charges on some of the book debts of British Eagle. But the parties to the "clearing house" arrangements did not intend to give one another charges on some of each other's future book debts. The documents were not drawn so as to create charges but simply so as to set up by simple contract a method of settling each other's mutual indebtedness at monthly intervals. Moreover, if the documents had purported to create such charges, the charges would have been unenforceable against the liquidator for want of registration under section 95 of the Companies Act 1948. The "clearing house" creditors are clearly not secured creditors. They are claiming nevertheless that they ought not to be treated in the liquidation as ordinary unsecured creditors but that they have achieved by the medium of the "clearing house" agreement a position analogous to that of secured creditors without the need for the creation and registration of charges on the book debts in question. The respondents argue that the position which, according to them, the clearing house creditors have achieved, though it may be anomalous and unfair to the general body of unsecured creditors, is not forbidden by any provision in the Companies Act, and that the power of the court to go behind agreements, the results of which are repugnant to our insolvency legislation, is confined to cases in which the parties' dominant purpose was to evade its operation. I cannot accept this argument . . . What the respondents are saying here is that the parties to the "clearing house" arrangements by agreeing that simple contract debts are to be satisfied in a particular way have succeeded in "contracting out" of the provisions contained in section 302 for the payment of unsecured debts "*pari passu*". In such a context it is to my mind

1 At 85.
2 At 88.
3 [1975] 1 WLR 758.
4 Stated in relation to voluntary winding up in s 302 of the Companies Act 1948, now the Insolvency Act 1986, s 107.

irrelevant that the parties to the "clearing house" arrangements had good business reasons for entering into them and did not direct their minds to the question how the arrangements might be affected by the insolvency of one or more of the parties. Such a "contracting out" must, to my mind, be contrary to public policy. The question is, in essence, whether what was called in argument the "mini liquidation" flowing from the clearing house arrangements is to yield to or to prevail over the general liquidation. I cannot doubt that on principle the rules of the general liquidation should prevail. I would therefore hold that notwithstanding the clearing house arrangements British Eagle on its liquidation became entitled to recover payment of the sums payable to it by other airlines for services rendered by it during that period and that airlines which had rendered services to it during that period became on the liquidation entitled to prove for the sums payable to them'[1].

The minority dissented on the ground that the insolvent company's claim against Air France was never part of its property; its property was limited to its entitlement under the clearing house arrangement[2]. While a provision designed to alter the contractual rights of the parties in the event of insolvency[3] would be invalid, there was nothing in the clearing house arrangements that brought about any change on insolvency.

In applying the principle that the ranking of creditors cannot be altered by contract, it must be borne in mind that Scots law allows wide rights of retention on insolvency[4], and contractual arrangements which do no more than reflect those rights will not offend against the basic principle. Thus the result in *Ex p Mackay*[5], the case principally relied on by the House of Lords in *British Eagle*, would probably have been different in Scotland. In that case one party sold a patent to another in exchange for payment of royalties. The second lent a sum to the first, and in consideration of the loan it was agreed that he would retain half of the royalties. It was further agreed that, in the event that the first party became bankrupt, the second could retain the whole of the royalties. The provision dealing with bankruptcy was held void. In Scotland, however, in the event of the insolvency of the first party owing money to the second, the second would have been entitled to retain all sums due by him to the first to the extent of the sum owed by the first. The contractual provision went no further than the common law.

In corporate banking arrangements, it is usual to find cross-guarantees from all of the companies in a group together with a contractual right of retention on the part of the bank in respect of any sums owed by the bank to companies in the group. Such arrangements do not contravene the principle that a preference cannot be conferred by contract, as the rights of retention involved go no further than the common law right of balancing accounts on insolvency as applied in a situation where companies have guaranteed one another's debts[6]. Contractual rights of retention will usually cover future and

1 [1975] 1 WLR 758 at 780 and 781.
2 See Lord Morris at 765, 769–771.
3 As in *Ex p Mackay* (1873) 8 Ch App 643.
4 See chapter 14 and Wilson on *Debt* (2nd edn, 1991) para 13.10.
5 *Supra.*
6 The principle that a bank may at any time, on giving notice, consolidate the accounts of one customer is also relevant. Because of the wide rights of retention which arise on insolvency in Scots law, the dictum of Millett J in *Re Charge Card Services Ltd* [1987] Ch 150, to the effect that in England a debtor cannot create a charge over funds in his own hands is not relevant in Scotland. In Scotland, a debtor is able to exercise a right of retention over such money at least in the event of the insolvency of his creditor, and the question of other rights in security is irrelevant.

   In the context of banking and clearing house arrangements, the exceptions to the general rules regarding retention in bankruptcy which are discussed in *Mycroft, Petitioner* 1983 SLT 352, will

contingent debts, such as those arising under performance bonds, cautionary obligations and rights of relief. These are taken into account when the ordinary common law rules relating to the balancing of accounts in insolvency are applied[1]; each such right is valued at the time of the insolvency, and the resulting value is taken into the accounting between the parties. Consequently contractual rights of retention should provide for the valuation of future and contingent rights on insolvency in such a way that they do not go beyond the common law. If they do exceed the common law right they may be struck down on the basis that the equal ranking of creditors is altered[2].

Trust rights, if properly constituted, will not be treated as an attempt to secure a preference by personal contract alone[3]. This accords with the basic treatment of such rights on insolvency; property held on trust does not fall under the insolvency[4].

It should be noted that Part VII (sections 154–191) of the Companies Act 1989 makes detailed provision for the recognition of the rules of certain investment exchanges and clearing houses, even where these differ from the usual rules governing the distribution of assets on insolvency. These provisions effectively override the effect of the *British Eagle* decision in relation to the insolvency of persons participating in recognised investment exchanges and clearing houses, and are designed to safeguard the operation of the financial markets concerned.

---

rarely be relevant. These relate to funds held on deposit, funds held for a person to whom the holder stands in a fiduciary relationship and funds appropriated to a specific purpose. The contract of deposit involves the delivery of property for safe custody only, and does not apply to the ordinary relationship of debtor and creditor which governs relations between banker and customer; it will apply only when valuables are handed to a banker for safe keeping. Where an account is appropriated for a special purpose, notably in the case of a trust account, it will not be available for the bank's general right of retention on insolvency.

1 In relation to future and contingent debts, see *Borthwick v Scottish Widows' Fund* (1864) 2 M 595, and *Gloag and Irvine*, pp 314–320. In the case of contingencies such as performance bonds, the bank may be able to obtain insurance to lessen the future risk.

2 The principal advantage of a bank's making specific contractual provision for retention rather than relying on the common law is that the rights of retention can be combined with cross-guarantees. That improves the bank's position significantly in a group insolvency.

3 *Carreras Rothmans Ltd v Freeman Matthews Treasure Ltd* [1985] Ch 207.

4 See Chapter 9.

# Chapter 11

# Retention of title

## Introduction

When goods are sold and the seller gives credit to the purchaser, an obvious means of protecting against the seller's insolvency is to stipulate that property in the goods will not pass until the price has been paid; that device has been in use for many years[1]. At common law, although it was presumed that property passed on delivery, a condition suspensive of the passing of property was recognised[2], and thus the parties were apparently free between themselves to determine when property should pass, at least after delivery. Under the Sale of Goods Act 1979[3], where there is a contract for the sale of specific or ascertained goods, parties are free to determine the time at which property is to be transferred to the buyer, which may be before or after delivery of the goods[4]. Further, where there is a contract for the sale of specific goods, or where goods are subsequently appropriated to the contract, the seller may by contract reserve the right of disposal of the goods until certain conditions are fulfilled, and in that event property in the goods will not pass until the conditions are fulfilled[5]. Both of these provisions clearly authorise retention of title to goods by a seller until such time as the price is paid in full, and the validity of clauses retaining title in that way was recognised in a number of cases[6].

In certain cases attempts were made by suppliers of goods to retain property in the goods until all sums due by the purchaser to the seller had been paid. Such a provision prevents the passing of property until every debt due by the purchaser to the supplier has been paid, whatever the source of the debt may have been. Initially clauses of retention of title of that nature were held invalid by the Scottish courts on the basis that they were attempts to create a security over corporeal moveable property without possession of the security subjects; subject to a small number of specific exceptions, it is impossible to create a security right over corporeal moveable property in Scots law unless possession

---

1 See *Stair*, I.xiv.4–5, Erskine, *Inst*, III.iii.11; Bell, *Comm*, 1.258; M P Brown on *Sale*, p 43; *Murdoch & Co Ltd v Greig* (1889) 16 R 396.
2 Ibid.
3 S 17(1).
4 For the common law, see *Gloag and Irvine*, pp 188–189; *Stair* I.xiii.14; Bell, *Comm*, II.11; Bell, *Prin*, § 1363; *Pattison's Tr v Liston* (1893) 20 R 806.
5 Sale of Goods Act 1979, s 19(1).
6 *Michelin Tyre Co Ltd v Macfarlane (Glasgow) Ltd (in Liquidation)* 1917 2 SLT 205 (a contract of sale and return); *Archivent Sales and Development Ltd v Strathclyde Regional Council* 1985 SLT 154; *Glen v Gilbey Vintners Ltd* 1986 SLT 553. Such clauses merely suspend the time for performance of one party's obligation under the contract of sale, to transfer property, until such time as the other party's principal obligation, to pay the price, is itself performed; cf. *Johnston v Robertson* (1861) 23 D 646 at 656, per LJ-C Inglis; *Turnbull v McLean & Co* (1874) 1 R 730 at 738, per LJ-C Moncrieff.

of the property is given to or retained by the holder of the security[1]. When the matter reached the House of Lords, however, in *Armour v Thyssen Edelstahlwerke AG*[2] it was held that such clauses were valid.

## The decision in *Armour v Thyssen Edelstahlwerke AG*[2]

In *Armour v Thyssen Edelstahlwerke AG*[2] the retention of title clause under consideration was a very elaborate German provision, the first part of which was translated as follows:

'All goods delivered by us remain our property (goods remaining in our ownership) until all debts owed to us, including any balances existing at relevant times – due to us on any legal grounds – are settled. This also holds good if payments are made for the purpose of settlement of specially designated claims. Debts owed to companies, being members of our combine, are deemed to be such debts.'

There followed a series of sub-clauses which dealt with the consequences of the processing of the goods, the combination of the goods with other goods and the resale of the goods; these sub-clauses provided for co-ownership of products and the assignation of claims to the proceeds of sale in ways that are allowed by the German Civil Code but are not in accordance with the rules of Scots law relating to accession and specification (in respect of ownership of products) and the requirements of a valid assignation. The validity of the first part of the retention of title clause, quoted above, was the only question in issue by the time the case reached the House of Lords. That provision had been held ineffective in the Court of Session[3], but its decision was reversed in the House of Lords. The critical reasoning in the speech of Lord Keith is as follows:

'In the present case the appellants, the owners of the steel strip, transferred possession of it to Carron under what was unquestionably a contract of sale. There was no question of the appellants creating a right of security. They were not in the position of debtors seeking to give a right of security to a creditor. They were themselves creditors of Carron for the price of the steel strip and it may be for other debts also. Carron obtained possession of the steel strip upon delivery, subject to a condition that it should not obtain the property until it had paid all debts due to the appellants. Can it be said that Carron somehow attempted to create a security over the goods in favour of the appellants? In order that it might do so it would require to have both the ownership and the possession, actual or constructive, of the goods. The essence of a right in security is that the debtor retains at least what *Gloag and Irvine* call the ultimate right to the goods. Can it be said that Carron obtained anything which gave it the capacity to retain an ultimate right to the goods? That could be so only if the contract of sale gave it the property in the goods, but the contract of sale said that the property in the goods was not to pass until all debts due to the appellants had been paid. We are here very far removed from the situation where a party in possession of corporeal moveables is seeking to create a subordinate right in favour of a creditor while retaining the ultimate right to himself. It is true that by entering into the contract of sale Carron agreed that it should

---

1 *Emerald Stainless Steel Ltd v South Side Distribution Ltd* 1982 SC 61; *Deutz Engines Ltd v Terex Ltd* 1984 SLT 273; *Hammer und Sohne v HWT Realisations Ltd* 1985 SLT (Sh Ct) 21; *Tramp Oil and Marine Ltd v Captain Ros*, January 1986, unreported; *Armour v Thyssen Edelstahlwerke AG* 1986 SLT 452 (Lord Mayfield); 1989 SLT 182 (Second Division). These cases, and the reasoning underlying them are discussed in detail in the first edition of this work; essentially, the retention clause amounted to security in respect of all debts other than the price of the particular goods.
2 1990 SLT 891.
3 See footnote 1 above.

receive possession of the goods on delivery but should not acquire the property until all debts due to the appellants had been paid, and thus agreed that the appellants would in effect have security over the goods after they had come into Carron's possession. But at that stage Carron had no interest of any kind whatever in any particular goods. Carron was never in a position to confer upon the appellants any subordinate right over the steel strip, nor did it ever seek to do so.

Section 17 of the Sale of Goods Act 1979 provides:

"(1) Where there is a contract for the sale of specific or ascertained goods the property in them is transferred to the buyer at such time as the parties to the contract intend it to be transferred. (2) For the purpose of ascertaining the intention of the parties regard shall be had to the terms of the contract, the conduct of the parties and the circumstances of the case."

In the present case the parties in the contract of sale clearly express their intention that the property in the steel strip should not pass to Carron until all debts due by it to the appellants had been paid. In my opinion there are no grounds for refusing to give effect to that intention.

Further, section 19(1) of the same Act provides:

"Where there is a contract for the sale of specific goods or where goods are subsequently appropriated to the contract, the seller may, by the terms of the contract or appropriation, reserve the right of disposal of the goods until certain conditions are fulfilled; and in such a case, notwithstanding the delivery of the goods to the buyer, or to a carrier or other bailee or custodier for the purpose of transmission to the buyer, the property in the goods does not pass to the buyer until the conditions imposed by the seller are fulfilled."

Here the appellants, by the terms of the contract of sale, have in effect reserved the right of disposal of the steel strip until fulfilment of the condition that all debts due to them by Carron have been paid. By virtue of this enactment, that has the effect that the property in the goods did not pass to Carron until that condition had been fulfilled. Counsel for Carron argued that the word "conditions" in section 19(1) must be read as excluding any condition which has the effect of creating a right of security over the goods. I am, however, unable to regard a provision reserving title to the seller until payment of all debts due to him by the buyer as amounting to the creation by the buyer of a right of security in favour of the seller. Such a provision does in a sense give the seller security for the unpaid debts of the buyer. But it does so by way of a legitimate retention of title, not by virtue of any right over his own property conferred by the buyer"[1].

It therefore appears that sections 17 and 19 of the Sale of Goods Act apply directly to a clause which reserves ownership until all debts owed by the purchaser to the seller have been paid. The argument which found favour in the Scottish courts was rejected because the 'all debts' clause was not characterised as a security, but was rather considered a legitimate use of the contractual freedom conferred by sections 17 and 19[2]. That meant that 'all sums' retention of title provisions were valid. It further indicates that a clause which retains property in goods until all sums due to the seller or to other companies in the seller's group[3] have been paid will be valid. If a retention of title is not a security because the purchaser never obtains the right of ownership or 'ultimate right' to the goods that is necessary to constitute a security, such a clause cannot be a security either. In neither case does the

---

1 1990 SLT 391 at 894H–395B. See also Lord Jauncey at 895K–896G.
2 See pp 250–252.
3 Or, if adequately defined, associated in any other way with the seller.

purchaser ever obtain either property in the goods or the ultimate right to the goods[1].

### Seller's remedies on insolvency of purchaser

Lord Keith further considered the question of the seller's remedies in the event of the insolvency of the purchaser at a time when debts remain outstanding from the purchaser to the seller. On this point he stated:

'In all cases where a right of security is conferred the debtor retains an ultimate right over the subject matter in question. The creditor, having realised out of that subject matter a sufficient sum to meet the debt, is obliged to account to the debtor for any surplus. Where, however, the seller of goods retains title until some condition has been satisfied, and on failure of such satisfaction repossesses them, then he is not obliged to account to the buyer for any part of the value of the goods. Where the condition is to the effect that the price of the goods shall have been paid and it has not been paid, then in the situation where the market price of the goods has risen, so that they are worth more than the contract price, the extra value belongs to the unpaid seller. That is clearly the position where the condition relates to payment of the price of the actual goods, and goes to show that the retention of title provision is not one creating a right of security forming an exception to the general rule requiring possession by the creditor. The same is true, in my opinion, where the provision covers not only the price of the very goods which are the subject of the particular contract of sale, but also debts due to the seller under other contracts.'[2]

The result of this reasoning seems to be that a seller who has the benefit of an all sums retention of title clause may repossess the whole of the goods supplied by him to the extent that property has not passed to the purchaser. That appears to be so even if the value of those goods is greater than the sum outstanding from the purchaser. In that case there will be an obligation on the seller to account to the purchaser for the difference between the value of the goods repossessed and the debt outstanding on insolvency from the purchaser to the seller. The basis for such an obligation is presumably the *condictio causa data causa non secuta*[3].

A similar problem may arise in a case where property is retained merely until payment of the price of the goods, but part of the price is paid before repossession. That situation was considered by the Court of Appeal in England in *Clough Mill Ltd v Martin*[4]; Robert Goff LJ discussed it as follows:

'The difficulty with the present condition is that the retention of title applies to material, delivered and retained by the buyer, until payment in full for all the material delivered under the contract has been received by the seller. The effect is therefore that the seller may retain his title in material still held by the buyer, even if part of that material has been paid for. Furthermore, if in such circumstances the seller decides to exercise his rights and resell the material, questions can arise as to (1) whether account must be taken of the part payment already received in deciding how much the seller should be entitled to sell, and (2)

---

1 Such clauses have been common in German contracts, and an example is found in the contract between Thyssen and Carron. The evidence of German law at first instance in *Armour v Thyssen Edelstahlwerke AG* indicated that such clauses are now regarded as of doubtful validity in Germany, and that even 'all sums' clauses are coming under challenge. The matter is discussed in the full version of Lord Mayfield's opinion, issued on 4 February 1986.
2 1990 SLT 891 at 895C–E.
3 See Gloag on *Contract*, pp 57–60. The basis of the *condictio* is failure of consideration.
4 [1985] 1 WLR 111.

whether, if he does resell, he is accountable to the buyer either in respect of the part payment already received, or in respect of any profit made on the resale by reason of a rise in the market value of the material.

Let me highlight these problems by taking a hypothetical example. Suppose that the seller agrees to sell 1,000 tons of material to the buyer at £10 a ton. He delivers 500 tons. Of those 500 tons, only 250 tons are paid for by the buyer: so £2,500 have been paid, and another £2,500 are due and outstanding. The buyer becomes insolvent, and is unable further to perform the contract. The seller accepts the repudiation. Of the 500 tons delivered, 300 tons are still at the buyer's premises, unsold and unused, now worth £4,000 instead of £3,000 as they were at the time of the contract of sale. Can the seller resell the whole 300 tons? And, if he can and does so, does he have to account to the buyer for that part of the price already paid which cannot be appropriated to the 200 tons already used by the buyer in manufacture and so must be appropriated to part of the 300 tons, i e £500? And must the seller account to the buyer for the profit element of £1,000 obtainable on the resale, no doubt allowing for any expenses of the sale?

Now, if the contract was still subsisting, instead of having been determined by the seller's acceptance of the buyer's repudiation, it would be perfectly possible to conclude, on the basis of an implied term in the contract, that the seller could only resell so much of the material as was necessary to pay the outstanding part of the purchase price, the rest to remain available to the buyer for the purposes of the contract, and that if, contrary to that term, the seller were to sell more than was necessary to pay off the balance of the price, he must account for the surplus to the buyer. On that basis, any part payment would be taken into account, and there would be no question of the seller retaining any profits obtained on a resale. But, if the contract has been determined, such term could not be given effect to, unless it were to be held, on a true construction of the contract, that the term survived the determination of the contract upon the seller's accepting the buyer's repudiation, for which I can see no basis as a matter of construction. So the situation would simply be that the property in the 300 tons belonged to the seller who could exercise his rights as owner uninhibited by any contractual restrictions. He could therefore sell the material for his own account; though he would, I consider, be bound to repay any part of the purchase price already paid by the buyer which must be appropriated to the goods so sold, because such sum would be recoverable by the buyer on the ground of failure of consideration.

There is another possible solution to this problem. This is that the seller should be held to retain the title to the material as trustee, upon trust to sell the goods and apply the proceeds of sale, first in discharge of the outstanding balance of the purchase price, and then as to any surplus upon trust for the buyer. On that basis the seller, in my hypothetical example, would on selling the 300 tons hold the balance realised on the resale over and above the outstanding purchase price on trust for the buyer.

To me, the answer to these questions lies in giving effect to the condition in accordance with its terms, and on that approach I can discern no intention to create a trust. The condition provides that the plaintiff retains his ownership in the material. He therefore remains owner; but, during the subsistence of the contract, he can only exercise his power as owner consistently with the terms, express and implied, of the contract. On that basis in my judgment, he can during the subsistence of the contract only resell such amount of the material as is needed to discharge the balance of the outstanding purchase price; and if he sells more, he is accountable to the buyer for the surplus. However, once the contract has been determined, as it will be if the buyer repudiates the contract and the seller accepts the repudiation, the seller will have his rights as owner (including, of course, his right to sell the goods) uninhibited by any contractual restrictions; though any part of the purchase price received by him and attributable to the material so resold will be recoverable by the buyer on the ground of failure of consideration, subject to any set-off arising from a cross-claim by the plaintiff for damages for the buyer's repudiation.'[1]

1 At 117–118.

The foregoing views appear generally consonant with Scots law. The concept of a failure of consideration corresponds generally to the *condictio causa data causa non secuta*. The case for a trust would be considerably weaker in Scots law, on the basis that there appeared to be no intimation to the alleged beneficiary or other equivalent of delivery of the supposed trust fund.

### Practical consequences[1]

The main practical advantage of an all sums retention of title clause is that it is not necessary to determine whether the purchaser has made payment for each consignment of goods supplied. It is sufficient that the seller can establish in relation to any particular item supplied by him that, since the date of supply, there has always been a sum outstanding from the purchaser. That will usually be easier. Indeed, where goods are supplied at short intervals on a period of credit, used by the buyer, that is significantly longer than the intervals between supplies, sums will always be due by the buyer to the seller and property in goods will never pass until they have been used in manufacture or resold[2]. That result is somewhat anomalous, as it may mean that goods supplied will remain the seller's property even though the buyer never exceeds the allowed period of credit.

An all sums clause may provide that property will not pass until all debts due by the purchaser to the seller, at any time and from time to time, and whether before or after the date of the particular contract of sale, have been paid. It is thought that that was the intended effect of the clause under consideration in *Armour v Thyssen Edelstahlwerke AG*[3] although the wording of the clause is not wholly clear. In some cases, however, as a matter of construction the clause may mean that property will pass when all debts due to the seller by the purchaser at the date of the contract, including the price of the goods supplied under the contract, have been paid.

### Ancillary provisions in retention of title clauses

If an all sums retention of title clause is to be effective, it is desirable that certain ancillary provisions should be added. The most important of these is a power to rescind the contract of sale in the event that payment for any goods supplied is not made within the period of credit or in the event of the buyer's insolvency even if payment of the price has been made. Failure to make payment timeously is not generally a ground for rescission unless an ultimatum has been given making time of payment of the essence of the contract[4]. Likewise, insolvency by itself is not a ground for rescission (although consequential failure to perform may be)[5]. If the analysis in *Clough Mill Ltd v Martin*[6] of the rights arising on repossession is followed, it is important that the contract should be rescinded, but if there is no express term allowing rescission an ultimatum procedure must be used, which entails considerable delay and uncertainty. Accordingly, an express power to rescind in the event

---

1 See p 269.
2 See pp 270–275.
3 1990 SLT 891.
4 Gloag on *Contract*, 617–618. See also *Rodger (Builders) Ltd v Fawdry* 1950 SC 483.
5 Gloag on *Contract*, p 601.
6 [1985] 1 WLR 111.

of a failure to make timeous payment for any goods supplied is desirable. Such a provision will not help, however, in cases where it cannot readily be proved that the buyer has exceeded his period of credit in respect of particular goods, and to deal with such cases a power to rescind in the event of the buyer's insolvency[1] as advisable.

It is also desirable to include an express power to repossess goods supplied in the event of recission of the contract of sale. Such a power can be useful in an application for *interim* interdict, and may be worded in such a way as to give the seller a clear right to go on to the buyer's premises in order to search for and remove the goods.

## Severance

In the law relating to restrictive covenants in restraint of trade[2], it is recognised that in some cases it is possible to sever the invalid part of a covenant from the valid part and to uphold the latter[3]. There seems no reason why the same principle should not apply to any retention of title clause which is partly valid and partly invalid; an example would be a German clause which contained provisions which purported to alter the Scottish rules on specification and accession[4], or to nullify the effect of section 25 of the Sale of Goods Act 1979[5]. If severance is to be effected, however, it is essential that it should be possible to separate physically the valid and invalid parts of the clause and to delete the invalid part without altering the meaning of the valid part. In addition, the provisions of the clause must not be so closely interconnected that the sense of the clause is destroyed by the excision of the offending provisions. In particular, if the deletion of the offending part alters the meaning of the remainder in any way, severance will not be permitted. In the restraint of trade cases, it is a general rule that the courts will not countenance the rewriting of a restrictive covenant[6], and if the meaning of the remaining sections of the clause is altered in any way, that is taken to amount to a rewriting.

In *Emerald Stainless Steel Ltd v South Side Distribution Ltd*[7] it was argued that the contractual term under consideration could be severed, with the earlier part receiving effect. This argument was rejected by Lord Ross[8], on the ground that the condition must be read as a whole and could not be broken down in that way. In *Deutz Engines Ltd v Terex Ltd*[9] severance was also argued. Lord Ross did not find it necessary to decide the question, because even if severance was effected, the clause was objectionable, according to the law as then understood, as an 'all-sums' clause. The only reported case where

---

1 'Insolvency' should be defined in the contract, to cover at least insolvent winding up, administration and receivership. The grounds for apparent insolvency contained in the Bankruptcy (Scotland) Act 1985, s 7 might also be added to the definition.
2 On which, see Gloag on *Contract*, pp 569–577; Walker on *Contracts*, paras 12.24 to 1243, and McBryde on *Contract*, paras 25–55 to 25–109.
3 See esp *Gloag*, p 574; *Walker*, para 12.42; *McBryde*, para 25–101; *Mulvein v Murray* 1908 SC 528.
4 See p 275.
5 See pp 270–271.
6 See *Walker*, para 12.43; and *Dumbarton Steam Boat Co v MacFarlane* (1899) 1 F 993.
7 1982 SC 61.
8 At 64.
9 1984 SLT 273, discussed above.

severance has been permitted is *Glen v Gilbey Vintners Ltd*[1]. The clause there, so far as material, provided as follows:

'(a) Unless otherwise agreed in writing between the Company and the Purchaser, property and title in Goods shall not pass to the Purchaser until the whole price therefor (each contract for the sale or supply of Goods being treated as a separate contract) has been received by the Company; and
(b) Unless the Seller removes his claim to the property and title in the Goods by giving written notice to the Buyer the property and title shall not pass to the Purchaser until all sums due by the Purchaser to the Company on any account whatsoever has been received by the Company; and in each case until the price or other sums due as the case may be has or have been received by the Company, the Purchaser shall hold such Goods in trust for the Company and shall not dispose of them save as Agent for the Company.
Sub-clauses (a) and (b) above shall be construed and receive effect as a separate Clause and accordingly in the event of either of them being for any reason whatsoever unenforceable according to its terms, the other shall remain in full force and effect.'

It was argued for the receivers of the purchaser that the clause was self-contradictory in that it purported both to reserve title in the seller and to impose a trust on the goods in the buyer's hands for behoof of the seller. This argument was rejected by Lord Clyde on the basis that the expression 'in trust for' was not to be construed as creating a strict relationship of trustee and beneficiary but rather an agency relationship. Lord Clyde further held that, although the seller admitted that sub-clause (b) was invalid as an 'all-sums' clause, that provision could be severed from sub-clause (a), which involved simple retention of title. Lord Clyde said[2]:

'In my view this is a clear case where severance of what is recognised to be invalid can be made so as to preserve what is valid. The two provisions are set out separately from each other and there is an express provision whereby if the one is found to be unenforceable the other shall remain in full force and effect. Counsel for the [receivers] founded on the passage which immediately follows the two paragraphs. He argued that even if para (b) was deleted this passage would still stand in its entirety and accordingly the defect which was sought to be removed by a separation of para (b) still remained. On this approach, the passage in question would still refer to the price or other sums due as the case may be having been received by the company. In my view however if a separation is made then it is necessary to restrict the scope of the passage in question to such parts as apply to para (a). Such a restriction can be made without violence to the language or the grammar of the passage. The objectionable parts of the clause can then be wholly severed so as to leave a clear and enforceable provision.'

Lord Clyde went on to distinguish the case from other cases where the good and bad parts of the clause were so woven together as to make separation impossible.

### Identification of goods and payments

When a clause of retention of title is applied following insolvency, practical problems can arise in identifying which articles in the insolvent company's possession have and have not been paid for. The issues involved are generally factual in nature but certain legal principles are relevant. In the case of a clause

1 1986 SLT 553.
2 At 555.

which only retains title until the price of the particular goods has been paid, it is important to consider whether the individual articles sold to the insolvent company can be identified, either through a serial number or through elements in their description. If they can be, it is a relatively straightforward accounting exercise to discover which articles have been paid for. In this connection, however, it is important to bear in mind the rules relating to the appropriation of payments[1]. The general rule is that the debtor, in this case the buyer, is entitled to appropriate payments to any particular debt owed by him to the seller. If, as is frequent, he fails to do so, the seller may appropriate the payment to any debt he pleases. If there is an account current, as will frequently be the case where credit is supplied by a seller to a buyer over a substantial period[2], if no ascription is made the rule in *Clayton's Case*[3] applies, and payments are ascribed to the items in the account in chronological order.

If the articles in the insolvent company's possession cannot be individually identified, it must be discovered whether the company operated a regular stock control system. The commonest system is FIFO (first in first out), but in the case of heavy items, such as steel plates, which are regularly stacked on top of one another LIFO (last in first out) may be used. If there is evidence of the regular use of such a system, it should be possible for the seller to establish, at least on a balance of probabilities, which of the goods in store have not been paid for and hence remain his property. On occasion, however, no stock control system is used and it is simply impossible to discover which individual articles have and have not been paid for. Such cases may raise difficult questions of balance of proof, but normally the burden of proving ownership is on the seller.

If the clause retains title until all sums owed by the purchaser to the seller have been paid, the first question is to identify when any particular item of property was supplied. That involves identifying the particular item of property, either by reference to a serial number or some other identifying mark or by reference to a regular stock control system. Once it has been discovered when an item of property was supplied, the next step is to examine the state of indebtedness between seller and purchaser during the intervening period. If the whole indebtedness of the purchaser to the seller was paid at any time during that period the retention of title will not operate; if it was never paid in full the retention will operate. If the retention applies to the whole debts owed by the purchaser to the seller's group, the investigation of the purchaser's indebtedness must be widened accordingly. In many cases, however, the purchaser's indebtedness will have subsisted continuously for a very long time. In such cases it may appear on a balance of probabilities that the goods in question are likely to have been supplied during the period of continuous indebtedness. In that event the seller will be able to prove his continuing ownership fairly readily. Such cases are likely to be frequent where goods are supplied at short intervals on a longer period of credit. Thus if supplies are made every week on 30 days' credit, and the purchaser makes use of the period of credit, it is inevitable that indebtedness will always be outstanding, even if the period of credit is never exceeded.

In most cases a seller who attempts to reclaim goods from an insolvent purchaser must, because he is pursuer in the resulting action, overcome the

<hr>

1 Discussed in detail in *Gloag*, pp 711–715; *Walker*, para 31.34; *McBryde*, paras 22–26 to 22–29.
2 See *Thomas Montgomery & Sons v Gallacher* 1982 SLT 138.
3 (1816) 1 Mer 572.

burden of proving on a balance of probabilities that he is the owner of the particular goods in question.

### Subsales

Where a retention of title clause is effective, the buyer may want to resell goods subject to the clause to his own customers. In some cases, express authority to sell is given[1]. In most cases the seller will be aware of the nature of the buyer's trade and that the buyer is likely to resell the goods in the course of that trade, and in such cases authority to resell the goods will almost certainly be implied; to withhold such authority would effectively destroy the whole purpose of the contract of sale containing the retention clause. Consideration of such implied terms will not usually be necessary, however, in view of the terms of section 25 of the Sale of Goods Act 1979. Section 25(1) provides as follows:

'Where a person having bought or agreed to buy goods obtains, with the consent of the seller, possession of the goods or the documents of title to the goods, the delivery or transfer by that person . . . of the goods or documents of title, under any sale, pledge, or other disposition thereof to any person receiving the same in good faith and without notice of any lien or other right of the original seller in respect of the goods, has the same effect as if the person making the delivery or transfer were a mercantile agent in possession of the goods or documents of title with the consent of the owner.'

The leading case in Scotland on section 25 is *Thomas Graham and Sons Ltd v Glenrothes Development Corporation*[2], where the Lord President stated the requirements of what is now section 25(1) in the following terms[3]:

'The first requirement of that subsection is that a person, having bought or agreed to buy goods, obtains, with the consent of the seller, possession of the goods. This requirement is admittedly satisfied in the present case . . .
The second requirement of the subsection is the delivery or transfer by that person . . . of the goods under any sale of other disposition thereof to any person receiving the same in good faith and without notice or any right of the original seller in respect of the goods . . .
The main attack, however, upon the relevancy of the defenders' averments was that they have not satisfied by averment the requirement of delivery or transfer by [the original buyer] under a sale or other disposition to the defenders [the buyers under the contract of resale]. But in my opinion, although with some hesitation, I consider that there is just enough in the averment . . . that, when the lorries arrived at the site, employees of the [original buyers] took delivery of the materials by unloading them and thereafter placed them on the defenders' site.'

The Lord President went on[4] to state that the effect of the subsection is that the buyer under the original contract will have the ostensible authority of a mercantile agent to pass the property in the goods. The effects of section 25(1) in the context of retention of title were considered in *Archivent Sales and*

---

1 As in *Emerald Stainless Ltd v South Side Distribution Ltd* 1982 SC 61, where the power was restricted to sales in good faith and for full value in the normal course of the buyer's trading. Such restrictions do not oust s 25 of the Sale of Goods Act, which is designed essentially for the protection of third-party purchasers.
2 1967 SC 284.
3 At 293.
4 At 294.

*Development Ltd v Strathclyde Regional Council*[1] where a contract for the sale of ventilators to the main contractor acting under a building contract contained a simple retention of title clause. The building contract[2] contained a clause (cl 14(1)) in the following terms: 'Where the value of any materials or goods has . . . been included in any interim Certificate under which the Contractor has received payment, such materials and goods shall become the property of the employer.' The ventilators in question had undoubtedly been included in an interim certificate, and the question arose of whether property had passed to the employers under the building contract, thereby defeating the rights of the original supplier. Lord Mayfield[3] considered the requirements of section 25(1), as discussed in *Thomas Graham & Sons Ltd v Glenrothes Development Corporation*[4]. It was not disputed that the employer under the building contract acted in good faith and without notice of any right in the original seller in respect of the goods, as it was unaware of the provisions in the contract of sale which reserved title. The main contractor had on the evidence obtained possession of the ventilators[5]. Finally, delivery to the employers under the building contract took place when the ventilators, after they had been incorporated into the building, had been measured on the site by the employer's surveyor and not rejected. In these circumstances, Lord Mayfield held that the requirements of section 25(1) had been satisfied, with the result that property had been passed to the employer.

Section 25(1) is likely to be of fairly general application in cases where goods subject to a retention of title clause have been resold. It is clearly impossible for a seller and purchaser to contract out of the subsection in such a way as to bind a sub-purchaser. It is important, however that the specific requirements of the subsection, as discussed by the Lord President in *Thomas Graham & Sons Ltd*, should be satisfied. A possible difficulty is that, as the use of retention of title clauses becomes virtually universal, the requirement that the sub-purchaser should be in good faith will not be satisfied, because he knows that there is at least a substantial possibility that the goods are subject to a retention of title clause. It is suggested that the courts should not be anxious to construe the subsection in this way, for obvious practical reasons. In any event, as suggested above, it should be possible to imply authority to resell even before the passing of property in the great majority of contracts of sale incorporating retention of title clauses, and that would avoid any difficulty caused by the wording of section 25(1).

## Accession and specification: fixtures

Goods subject to a retention of title clause will frequently be combined with other goods to create a new product. When a minor article is added to a major one in such a way as to form part of it, as when a plate is welded to a ship under repair, the process is known as accession. When a wholly new article is created, as when a great diversity of components are combined to build a ship,

---

1 1985 SLT 154.
2 In the JCT Standard Form, Local Authorities Ed. with Quantities (1963 ed.) (July 1977 revision).
3 At 156–157.
4 Above.
5 Factors Act 1889 s 1(2) which provides that a person shall be deemed to be in possession of goods or documents of title to goods where the goods or documents are in his actual custody, was founded upon for this purpose.

the process is known as specification[1]. In such cases the question arises as to whether the owner of the goods that have been used can maintain his property in the goods, or whether property in the goods passes, either to the owner of the major component in the case of accession, or to the manufacturer in the case of specification. The rule followed in Scots law in cases of specification has been stated as follows[2]:

'Where the new species can be again reduced to the mass or matter of which it was made, the law considers the former subject as still existing: therefore the new species continues to belong to the proprietor of that former subject, which still exists, though under another form; as in the case of plate made of bullion. But where the new species cannot be so reduced, there is no room for that *fictio juris*; as in wine, which, because it cannot be again turned into the grapes of which it was made, becomes the property, not of the owner of the grapes, but of the maker of the wine'[3].

With accession to moveables, the rule is similar except that ownership of the component passes to the owner of the major article to which it is attached. An example of the application of these rules is found in *International Banking Corporation v Ferguson, Shaw & Sons*[4], where oil was used in the manufacture of lard; because it was impossible to restore the oil to its original state, property passed to the manufacturer of the lard[5].

Accession (but not specification) also operates when moveable articles are attached to land or buildings. Components of a building, such as bricks or joists or windows, become part of the building; that applies even to components such as doors which can be removed without damage[6]. The same applies to articles such as pipes and cables which are buried in land; although a wayleave or other servitude right may be reserved, that does not amount to ownership[7]. Other moveable objects may pass to the owner of the heritage as fixtures; these are articles which are necessary to the land and building but are so fixed to it as to become part of the heritage[8]. In determining whether an article has become a fixture, it is not only the degree of physical attachment that is relevant[9]; the factors that are relevant have been described as follows:

'The question whether a particular thing has become a fixture, that is, has become a part of the soil, or of some building attached to the soil, has not to be solved by the mere consideration whether it is, as a matter of fact affixed to the soil or building. That consideration, as well as the degree or extent of its attachment, is to be taken together with other elements. These elements are: whether it can be removed *integre, salve et commode*, i e

1  The law on these topics is discussed in Stair, *Inst*, II i,39–41; Erskine, *Inst*, II, i,15–16; Bell, *Comm*, I, 276–278; and Bell, *Prin*, §§ 1296–1298.
2  Erskine, *Inst*, II, i,16.
3  Specification is equitable in nature, and it is essential that the manufacturer should have been in good faith if it is to obtain its advantages: *McDonald v Provan Ltd* 1960 SLT 231. This is not likely to be a problem in retention of title cases.
4  1910 SC 182; see also *Oliver & Boyd v Marr Typefounding Co Ltd* (1901) 9 SLT 170.
5  The owners of the oil were found entitled to its value.
6  Stair, *Inst*, II, i,40; Erskine, *Inst*, II, i,16–17; Bell, *Comm*, I, 752 *et seq.*; Bell, *Prin*, § 1473.
7  *Crichton v Turnbull* 1946 SC 52.
8  The leading case on fixtures is *Brand's Trs v Brand's Trs* (1876) 3 R (HL) 16, where the question of whether an article of moveable property has been attached to land in such a way as to become a fixture is distinguished from the right that a limited owner such as a tenant may in exceptional circumstances have to remove the article. The latter question is unlikely to be relevant in retention of title cases.
9  *Scottish Discount Co Ltd v Blin* 1986 SLT 123.

without the destruction of itself as a separate thing, or of the soil or building to which it is attached; whether its annexation was of a permanent or *quasi*-permanent character; whether the building to which it was attached was specially adapted for its use; how far the use and enjoyment of the soil or building would be affected by its removal; the intention of the party attaching it. Intention, however, in this question means intention discoverable from the nature of the article and of the building, and the manner in which it is affixed, not intention proved by extrinsic evidence'[1].

The question of whether an article has become a fixture is the subject of a large number of judicial decisions; the principal cases will be found from the works undernoted[2].

In cases involving accession or specification, a party who contributes materials or labour but loses or fails to obtain a right of property may have a remedy in recompense; reference should be made to the standard works on this subject[3].

The foregoing principles have important consequences for retention of title. It is generally considered impossible to contract out of the rules described above, as they involve methods of original acquisition of property which follow automatically if the particular requirements occur and are independent of the intention of the parties concerned. If goods are sold subject to a valid retention clause but are used to manufacture a new product, in such a way that they cannot be restored to their original state, property in the goods will pass to the manufacturer as a result of specification or accession. Similarly, if the goods are used in the construction of a building, or are attached to a building in such a way that they become a fixture, property will pass to the owner of the building. Thus a retention clause applying to goods which are intended for use in manufacturing or construction is severely limited in its effectiveness, as it will not help the seller once the goods cannot be returned to their original state, or once they have become part of heritable property. This is of great practical importance, and difficult factual problems arise in determining whether goods can be restored to their original state on removal from a manufactured object, or whether goods have become a fixture.

Specification has been considered in two reported retention of title cases. In *Zahnrad Fabrik Passau GmbH v Terex Ltd*[4], axles and transmissions had been sold by the pursuers to the defenders and incorporated into finished or partly-finished earth-moving vehicles. It was averred that the axles had been attached to the main frame, painted and filled with oil. These averments were held irrelevant, in that they did not specify the mode of attachment to the main frame, and it was not averred that the axles could not be removed, or what damage or detriment would result if they could be removed. It was averred that the transmissions had been attached to the vehicles and painted and that alterations had been made in the pipes and plates attached to the

1 *Green's Encyclopaedia of the Laws of Scotland*, vol 7, para 362, approved in *Scottish Discount Co Ltd v Blin*. See also *Howie's Trs v McLay* (1902) 5 F 214, per Lord President Kinross.
2 Article by Professor Gloag in *Green's Encyclopaedia of the Laws of Scotland*, vol 7, paras 361–385; Gloag and Henderson, *Introduction to the Law of Scotland* (9th edn), pp 623–624. The most recent case in the Inner House, in which the general principles of the law are reviewed, is *Scottish Discount Co Ltd v Blin* (above).
3 Gloag on *Contract*, pp 319 *et seq.*; *Gloag and Henderson*, pp 161–164; Scot Law Com, Memo, No 28: *Corporeal Moveables, Mixing, Union and Creation*. The last-mentioned work is a useful discussion of accession and specification in general.
4 1986 SLT 84.

transmissions. These averments were also held irrelevant; they did not indicate that the transmissions could not be removed from the vehicles without suffering damage. In reaching these conclusions, Lord Davidson stated the test that he applied as follows[1]:

'I think that the appropriate test is not what is the diminution in the market value of the item once it has been separated from the vehicle, but rather what is the diminution, if any, in its efficiency as an axle or transmission.'

In *Armour v Thyssen Edelstahlwerke AG*[2] steel strip was supplied to manufacturers of sinks. It was not contested that property in finished sinks, where the steel had been formed into shape, had passed by specification. The question arose, however, whether property had passed when the steel, which was supplied in long coils, had been cut into short lengths. Evidence was led that the cut steel was not readily saleable, and that it could not be re-welded to a saleable size and form. Melting down was not practicable because it caused a change in the composition of the material. Lord Mayfield concluded that specification operated, on the ground that once the steel was cut it was in a different form, and could not be returned to its original form. Lord Mayfield was influenced by the fact that when the steel was cut it was saleable only in a different market; he held that the evidence on this matter was a recognition by the steel trade that the steel was in fact in a different form and thus in a manufacturing sense a new species. His decision on this point was reversed by the Second Division[3] although it did not affect their dismissal of the reclaiming motion. The Second Division held that the steel had not become a new species by being cut into strips.

It cannot be claimed that the rules on specification and accession are particularly satisfactory. They are derived from Roman law[4], and are perhaps better suited to an age of primitive technology. Even in such conditions, however, they suggest a rather imperfect compromise. It is not easy to see, for example, why a metal founder should be denied ownership when a woodworker is allowed it. The inadequacy of the rules is even more apparent when they are applied to modern manufacturing processes. When, for example, a vehicle is manufactured, components such as engines, gearboxes and wheels are usually bought by the manufacturer from outside suppliers. These are then built into the vehicle on the assembly line, but in such a way that they can be fairly easily removed; this is essential if repairs and replacements are to be possible during the working life of the vehicle. According to the established tests, such components are capable of being restored to substantially their original condition, and thus should remain the property of the supplier. If a component is removed, however, it will only have a second-hand value, and in some cases may even be almost unsaleable. In such circumstances, the usual practice is that the receiver or liquidator of the manufacturer agrees to make partial payment to the supplier and the supplier agrees that property should

---

1 At 88.
2 1986 SLT 452.
3 1989 SLT 182 at 188k–l, per LJ-C Ross and at 190i–j per Lord McDonald. The matter was not argued in the House of Lords.
4 They are in fact the compromise that was reached in the *Digest* between the competing views of the Proculeians and the Sabinians; the former favoured the manufacturer and the latter the owner of the materials.

pass to the manufacturer, who alone can use the component effectively. A possible solution, although it is not one favourable to suppliers of goods, is to shift the emphasis in the basic test away from the question of whether the goods can be restored to their original state towards the question of whether the goods have retained substantially their original value; in other words, the economic status of the goods would be substituted for their physical status. This would allow the supplier to recover his goods in cases where they were as valuable to him as to the manufacturer, but not in cases where the goods have, through incorporation in the product, become much more valuable to the manufacturer than to the supplier. Nevertheless, this approach has been rejected by Lord Davidson and by the Second Division; it would undoubtedly represent a shift in the established law and can hardly be conceived without legislation.

In certain German clauses[1], it is provided that, if the goods sold are used in the manufacture of a new product, the seller is to become part-owner of the product. Specific provision for joint ownership in such circumstances is made in paragraph 947(1) of the German Civil Code, and without such legislative provision it is difficult to see how such rights could be made effective. It seems clear that a Scottish retention of title clause could not effectually incorporate such a provision; an agreement to that effect would not amount to a sale of the product, at least under the Sale of Goods Act,. since there is no money consideration for the transfer of property in the product[2], and except in the case of sales under the Act the transfer of property in goods must generally be effected by delivery or its equivalent. The nearest that Scots law has come to such a concept is the decision in *Wylie & Lochhead v Mitchell*[3]. In that case, a manufacturer agreed to construct a hearse for a firm of undertakers to a design provided by them, the materials being supplied partly by each party. It was held that the parties became joint proprietors of the hearse, in proportion to the value of their contributions. The case is an unusual one, and it is significant that the contract was for the construction of the new article. There seems to be no justification for extending similar reasoning to sale of goods. The underlying commercial reality of a contract of sale of goods is that the seller passes property in goods to the buyer who is in turn obliged to pay the seller the price. If the contract of sale provided that the seller was to be entitled to a species of joint property in the manufactured product, the value of that right would usually be more than the price as it would include a share of the manufacturer's profit. That does not seem to accord with the commercial reality of sale. Moreover, practical difficulties would arise in realising the product, especially in cases where components from a large number of suppliers are combined to form one product. Calculating the value of the various part-owners' interests would be equally difficult, especially where some components are and others are not capable of removal.

### Commixtion and confusion

Bulk goods such as grain or liquids such as whisky may be mixed in a store with other similar products, in such a way that the constituents cannot be separated. This is referred to as commixtion in the case of solids and confusion

---

1 As in *Armour v Thyssen Edelstahlwerke AG* and *Zahnrad Fabrik Passau GmbH v Terex Ltd, supra.*
2 Cf Sale of Goods Act 1979, s 2(1).
3 (1878) 8 M 552.

in the case of liquids. In such cases, the owners of the constituents become *pro indiviso* proprietors of the new product, their shares being in proportion to the quantity and value of their contribution[1]. If the articles can be separated, property is not affected. Normally it is relatively simple to deal with cases where the various constituents are inseparable, as long as the combined product is still in existence. Problems can arise, however, when part or all of the combined product is drawn off and new ingredients are added, as happens in a grain store. In such cases the supplier faces difficulties of identification. Essentially he has to prove that some of his component is likely, on a balance of probabilities, to remain in the store, and thereafter he must prove the proportion that his component bears to the others in store. In appropriate cases, it may be possible to achieve this by means of the FIFO (first in first out) principle. This would apply, for example, to a grain store where grain was introduced at the top and drawn off at the bottom. Where, on the other hand, grain was introduced and drawn off at the top, the LIFO (last in first out) principle would be more appropriate. In either case, the supplier will be heavily dependent on the buyer's records relating to the store, and if these are inadequate the seller is likely to fail.

In cases where the goods are capable of physical separation, with the result that *pro indiviso* property does not arise, the problems of identification discussed at pages 268–270 will be relevant.

**Trusts**

Purported retention of title clauses frequently attempt to make use of the machinery of a trust[2]. There is no point in using a trust in relation to the goods themselves, because retention of title, as long as it is in appropriate terms, will suffice to protect the seller's position[3]. Attempts may be made, however, to create trust rights in favour of the seller over either the proceeds of sale of the goods or the products into which the goods have been incorporated. A clause designed to create a trust over proceeds of sale was discussed at length in *Clark Taylor & Co Ltd v Quality Site Development (Edinburgh) Ltd*, where its validity was decisively rejected. In view of the reasoning in that case, it appears extremely unlikely that valid trusts can be created over either proceeds of sale or manufactured products. The practical difficulties that would arise if such trusts were accorded recognition are fully discussed in the Lord President's opinion, and because of these difficulties there are excellent reasons for simply holding that there is no underlying commercial reality of a trust in such cases. Apart from this consideration, the formal requirements for a person's declaring himself a trustee of his own property are likely to be difficult to satisfy in such cases, and this will normally form an additional reason for refusing validity. In the two later cases, *Emerald Stainless Steel Ltd v South Side*

---

1 Erskine, II, i,17; Bell, *Prin,* § 1298.
2 As in *Clark Taylor & Co Ltd v Quality Site Development (Edinburgh) Ltd* 1981 SC 111, *Emerald Stainless Steel Ltd v South Side Distribution Ltd* 1982 SC 61, and *Deutz Engines Ltd v Terex Ltd* 1984 SLT 273.
3 This did not prevent the sellers in *Emerald Stainless Steel* and *Deutz* from trying to incorporate trust provisions into their retention of title clauses; the clauses in these cases display a fundamental misunderstanding of what retention of title is designed to achieve.

*Distribution Ltd* and *Deutz Engines Ltd v Terex Ltd, Clark Taylor* was treated as effectively precluding the use of trusts in retention of title clauses[1].

## Agency

A manufacturer or wholesaler who wants to distribute his goods to the public is not restricted to selling his goods to retailers who in turn resell them to the public. If he prefers, he can proceed by way of agency rather than sale. This enables him to retain the ownership of the goods until they reach the ultimate customer, with the result that he can reclaim them in the event of the agent's insolvency. Moreover, when goods are sold by an agent on his principal's behalf, the principal and agent may agree that the proceeds belong to the principal, not the agent, or are to be paid into a trust account for the principal[2]. The contract concluded by the agent is the principal's contract, and thus the price is *prima facie* the principal's. Moreover, agency is a fiduciary relationship[3], and thus it is quite consistent with the agent's holding assets on trust for the principal; in some cases a constructive trust would be implied[3].

Agency nevertheless has disadvantages for the principal. Because the principal is a party to the contract with the consumer, he is liable on any warranties as to the quality or fitness for purpose of the goods. Further, if the agency relationship is genuine, it is likely in practice that the manufacturer or wholesaler will be much more closely concerned with the distribution of his goods and relations with consumers than if he sells through retail distributors, using ordinary contracts of sale. That may be something that he wants to avoid.

It is essential to ensure that an alleged agency is genuine, and not a disguise for what is truly a contract of sale. The criteria for distinguishing agency from sale are discussed by Lord Dunedin in *Michelin Tyre Co Ltd v Macfarlane (Glasgow) Ltd (in Liquidation)*[4]. If the sums owed or paid by the ultimate customer to the alleged agent and by the alleged agent to the alleged principal appear in reality to be retail and wholesale prices respectively, it is likely that

1 The court's approach in *Clark Taylor* is in complete contrast to the treatment of retention of title clauses in the leading English case, *Aluminium Industrie Vaasen BV v Romalpa Aluminium Ltd* [1976] 1 WLR 676, where it was held that an 'all-sums' clause created a fiduciary relationship (a relationship analogous to a trust) between the parties, which conferred upon the sellers equitable rights in the proceeds of sale of the goods supplied. The difference of approach is not surprising; the two systems are perhaps at their furthest apart in the law of moveable property, and English principles of equity frequently imply fiduciary relationships in situations where Scots law would not. What is surprising is that the *Romalpa* decision, and indeed subsequent English cases involving fiduciary relationships and rights in equity, such as *Borden (UK) Ltd v Scottish Timber Products Ltd* [1981] 1 Ch 25, have been extensively cited in argument in Scottish cases; it is perhaps notable that none of those cases has been founded upon to any significant extent in Scottish judicial decisions. Scots law has its own distinctive approach to problems involving moveable property, and it has no need to invoke decisions which turn on highly technical concepts of English equity. It is most disappointing that the Government has seen fit to appoint an English lawyer, however eminent he may be in his own field, to review the law of securities over moveables in both jurisdictions. Indeed, especially in the field of retention of title, there is much to be said for review of the law on a European basis, since retention clauses drafted under the legal systems of other member-states of the European Communities are frequently encountered in practice. The European Commission had the matter under review for a time, but it is understood that its work has now been suspended.
2 The agent will usually be entitled to deduct commission.
3 See *Stair Memorial Encyclopaedia*, vol 24, paras 170–188.
4 1917 2 SLT 205 at 212.

the relationship is sale, not agency. In particular, if an alleged agent appears to take the chance of profit and to bear the risk of loss on the goods, the relationship is likely to be sale; an agent is normally paid by commission, either fixed or related to the price for which the goods are sold.

## Retention of title in the conflict of laws

### Lex situs governs real rights

Retention of title clauses are extremely common in contracts which involve the sale of goods by a seller in one jurisdiction to a buyer in another. In such cases, the question arises of which legal system is to determine the validity of the clause. The answer is, it is thought, quite straightforward. A retention of title clause purports to retain property in goods in the seller. The question in issue in any dispute about retention of title is whether the seller has been successful in retaining property, or whether property has in fact passed to the purchaser. Scots law has adopted the general rule that property rights, and indeed real rights for all sorts, in both moveable and immoveable (heritable) property, are governed by the lex situs (the law of the jurisdiction where the item of the property in question is situated for the time being). The reason for adopting this rule is that property rights, and real rights of every sort, affect third parties; a real right is good against the whole world. The persons most immediately affected by real rights in a particular item of property are those in the jurisdiction where it is situated, and from a practical standpoint the only sensible rule is that rights in any given item of property should be governed by the law of the jurisdiction where it is situated.

The leading Scottish case is *Inglis v Robertson and Baxter*[1], which involved an attempted hypothecation of whisky which was said to have been created by the handing over of delivery warrants. The alleged hypothecation was effected by one Englishman in favour of another Englishman, but the whisky was situated in a warehouse in Glasgow. Creditors of the alleged hypothecator subsequently arrested the whisky. Lord Watson held that the validity of the alleged hypothecation must be governed by Scots law. He said[2]:

'The present question does not arise between two Englishmen, nor does it arise in relation to mercantile transactions which can reasonably be characterised as English. The *situs* of the goods was in Scotland. The Scottish creditors who claim their proceeds did not make any English contract; and in order to attach them they made use of the execution which the law of Scotland permits for converting their personal claim against the owner into a real charge upon the goods themselves. It would, in my opinion, be contrary to the elementary principles of international law, and so far as I know, without authority, to hold that the right of a Scottish creditor when so perfected can be defeated by a transaction between his debtor and the citizen of a foreign country which would be according to the law of that country, but is not according to the law of Scotland, sufficient to create a real right in the goods.'

Lord Watson then referred to the question of whether the party who received the alleged hypothecation had a real right in the goods and continued:

1 (1897) 24 R 759; (1898) 25 R (HL) 70.
2 At 73.

'That is a question which I have no hesitation in holding must, in the circumstances of this case, be solved by reference to the law of Scotland. The whisky was in Scotland, and was there held in actual possession by a custodier for [the alleged hypothecator] as the true owner. That state of the title could not, so far as Scotland was concerned, be altered or overcome by a foreign transaction of pledge which had not, according to the rules of Scottish law, the effect of vesting the property of the whisky, or, in other words, a *jus in re*, in the pledgee.'

It is further clear that the general rule that the *lex situs* governs real rights extends to security rights over moveable property; this was expressly held in the old case of *Mitchell v Burnet and Mouat*[1] and reaffirmed in the judgment of Lord Keith in *Carse v Coppen*[2]; the applicability of the *lex situs* did not arise on the approach taken by the Lord President, with whom Lord Russell agreed, and Lord Carmont, both of whom held that a Scottish company had no power to grant a floating charge, even over English assets[3].

*Application of lex situs to sale of goods: governs real rights*

International contracts of sale of goods normally display one particular feature, namely that the goods move from one jurisdiction to another under the contract of sale. Thus, if a manufacturer in France sells to a customer in Scotland, the goods will usually be situated in France at the time when the contract is concluded and in Scotland after the contract has been performed. The approach generally followed by the Scottish courts is that the legal system which should govern systems of proprietary right in the goods is that of the country where the goods are to end up. It is respectfully suggested that this is the only sensible solution. First, the parties' expectations throughout the transaction are that the goods will be delivered to and held in that jurisdiction. Consequently that is the jurisdiction where the goods are likely to be situated when any question of proprietary right arises. Second, the rationale of the choice of law rules relating to property rights, and especially those relating to securities and their validity, is largely the protection of those transacting with the possessor of goods; such persons may deal with the goods themselves, as in the case of sub-purchasers or pledgees, or may want to do diligence or its foreign equivalents in relation to the goods. Persons who transact with the possessor of the goods are likely to be in the jurisdiction where the goods are situated, or at least to regard that jurisdiction as the one with which the goods are connected. Where, under a contract of sale, goods are delivered to premises in a particular jurisdiction with a view to being resold or worked upon on those premises, it is obvious that that jurisdiction is the one to which third parties transacting with the possessor will look. In the third place, in many cases considerable practical problems will arise if rules belonging to the legal system of one jurisdiction are applied to property situated in another jurisdiction. The rules of property law are generally highly specific to one legal system. Moreover, property law is normally conceived as an integrated system, where the rules are tailored to fit in with one another. Rules of this sort cannot readily be grafted on to another system. For example, the English system of equitable rights cannot readily be inserted among the rules of Scots

---

1 (1746) Mor 4468.
2 1958 SC 233 at 245–246.
3 See also Anton on *Private International Law* (2nd edn) pp 611–626.

property law and the elaborate German rules on co-ownership which correspond broadly to the Scots law of accession and specification cannot readily be integrated with the general conceptions and principles of Scots law. It is accordingly essential that one legal system should govern all real rights in any particular item of property. The only practical system for this purpose is the *lex situs* for the time being, and in an international sale, after delivery of the goods, the *situs* is clearly the jurisdiction where the goods have ended up. It is thought that the exact nature of the contract of sale, whether cif, fob, ex works or whatever, should not affect the question of the *lex situs* as long as the parties understand, as will nearly always be the case, that the goods are to end up in a particular jurisdiction; it is in that jurisdiction that the retention of title clause will have practical effect, and it is third parties in that jurisdiction who are most likely to be affected by it. Similarly, it should not matter in which country delivery is actually effected. The *situs* of the goods when they leave the seller's premises, and any intermediate *situs* that they acquire in the course of delivery, do not seem relevant to the choice of law for two reasons; first, the location of the goods in those *situs* is only transitory, and, second, third parties who seek to acquire rights in the goods are much less likely to be situated in these intermediate jurisdictions. It would be possible to apply a rule that the validity of an attempt to retain title depends on the *lex situs* of the goods from time to time, but such a mechanical application of the *lex situs* could lead to arbitrary, and even bizarre, results. If, for example, a liquidator in Scotland wished to defeat an 'all-sums' retention of title which was valid under Scots law, he could move the goods to a warehouse in France to invoke the local law, which is hostile to such provisions. Moreover, the ownership of goods could change repeatedly in the course of a journey. These results do not appear desirable[1], and they can be avoided by adoption of the rule discussed in the last paragraph. The one exception to this, however, may be where there is no understanding between buyer and seller as to where the goods will end up[2]; in that case there is probably no alternative to the mechanical application of the *lex situs* from time to time.

*Proper law of the contract of sale: affects personal rights*

The other legal system that may have a bearing on retention of title clauses is the proper law of the contract containing the clause, but the scope of the proper law is strictly limited[3]. The application of the proper law is confined to the personal rights and obligations of the parties to the contract, that is, to the rights and obligations that bind the parties to the contract themselves but not

1 Although the first could be defeated by the application of public policy, and the second is more objectionable in theory than practice, as questions relating to real rights in the goods will hardly ever arise before they have reached the purchaser's premises.
2 Although this will be highly unusual, since a seller will nearly always know where buyers from him carry on business, and will in any event see the shipping documents before the goods are despatched.
3 For discussion of the meaning and application of the proper law, see Anton, *op cit*, pp 262–274. Where there is a choice of law clause in the contract, that will normally determine the proper law, although there are signs that the Scottish courts are prepared to disregard the parties' apparent choice if it appears to conflict with the true nature of the contract. If there is no choice of law clause, the proper law will be the system with which the contract appears to have its closest connection, in the light of its terms and all the surrounding circumstances. Generally speaking the place of performance is given primacy, but other elements may overrule that.

outsiders. In particular, the proper law of the contract will determine the extent and interpretation of the parties' personal rights[1]. It will not govern the acquisition and transference of property, because that involves real rights and obligations, which are binding on third parties to the contract. Thus a third party may attempt to acquire the goods sold, or to do diligence against those goods; whether he can do either of those things depends on property rights in the goods, and those property rights are governed, as explained above, by the *lex situs*[2].

Apart from the above considerations, there are practical reasons for not applying the proper law of the contract to determine the validity of retention of title clauses. If unlimited scope were given to the parties to choose the proper law, it would be relatively easy to select a legal system which encourages retention of title. In practice, the choice of the proper law is rarely if ever discussed by parties, and the normal practice is that the seller imposes his legal system on the transaction. Thus a seller in France could choose a system such as German law in order to allow retention of title. The courts would probably have little difficulty in striking down a choice of legal system that had no genuine bearing on the contract, on public policy grounds. The second practical problem is more serious, however. Application of the proper law would mean that sellers resident in countries such as Scotland, England and Germany, where a favourable attitude has been taken to retention of title clauses, would obtain an advantage over sellers resident in countries such as France and Italy, where a much more restrictive attitude has been taken. That problem does not arise, however, if the *lex situs* governs the question of validity.

### Cases on choice of law

In *Emerald Stainless Steel Ltd v South Side Distribution Ltd*[3] and *Deutz Engines Ltd v Terex Ltd*[4], the contract of sale under consideration contained choice of law clauses which declared that the contract was to be governed by English law. In each case, Lord Ross found it unnecessary to determine whether English law was relevant because it was not averred in the pleadings, and he was accordingly bound to assume that it was the same as Scots law. The earliest case in which choice of law was a live issue was the decision of Sheriff Jardine in *Hammer und Sohne v HWT Realisations Ltd*[5]. Sheriff Jardine was prepared to concede that West German law was the proper law of the contract in that case, but held that the proper law was not the correct way to approach the question in issue. He pointed out[6] that the correct inquiry is not what law governs the contract but what law governs the particular question raised in the

---

1 This is subject, however, to the two important limitations laid down in *Hamlyn & Co v Talisker Distillery* (1894) R (HL) 21 at 22–23, per the Lord Chancellor and at 25–26, per Lord Watson, namely that questions relating to the remedy sought are governed by the law of the forum and that Scots law will not apply rules of the proper law that are contrary to its own fundamental policy: see below, pp 283–284.
2 Apart from the clear authorities on the application of the *lex situs*, it is obviously unreasonable that the legal system chosen by the parties to a contract of sale should affect the rights that third parties may acquire in the subjects of sale.
3 1982 SC 61.
4 1984 SLT 273.
5 1985 SLT (Sh Ct) 21.
6 At 23.

instant proceedings. The present case involved an order for delivery sought in a Scottish court in respect of goods situated in Scotland. The question at issue was whether a security had been created over those goods and, on the authority of *Mitchell v Burnet and Mouat*[1], Sheriff Jardine held that the *lex situs* governed the creation of securities over moveables, and accordingly that Scots law governed the question at issue.

Sheriff Jardine referred to *Hamlyn & Co v Talisker Distillery*[2], a leading case on the application of the proper law to questions of contractual right. In that case, the House of Lords held that questions of the construction of a contract are governed by its proper law[3], but admitted two important exceptions, namely questions relating to the remedy sought, which are governed by the law of the forum where the question is determined, and matters where recognition of the rule of the proper law would be contrary to the fundamental policy of Scots law. Sheriff Jardine held that the principle of Scots law that a security over moveables cannot generally be created without possession is such a fundamental principle and cannot be overcome by the application of the proper law of the contract.

In *Zahnrad Fabrik Passau GmbH v Terex Ltd*[4] goods were supplied by a German company to a Scottish company under the supplier's standard form of contract, which included a German choice of law clause and a German retention of title clause. It was argued for the Scottish company and its receivers that the validity of the retention of title clause must be tested against Scots law alone and not German law. This argument was rejected by Lord Davidson (although this part of his judgment was not necessary for his decision, and is accordingly *obiter*). He dealt with the matter as follows[5]:

'If . . . the parties to a contract are entitled to agree when property is to pass, then I think it is wrong to regard the *lex situs* as being an inflexible corpus of law . . . In a contract regulating the rights and obligations *hinc inde* of two contracting parties, *prima facie* I see no reason why they should not incorporate into the contract one or more provisions of a foreign legal system. If the contracting parties choose to do that, then the condition relied upon may be open to challenge on, among others, the ground that it is opposed to a fundamental principle of the law of Scotland.'

On this basis, he allowed the averments of German law to go to proof.

It is significant that Lord Davidson left open the possibility that the Scots rules governing the validity of retention clauses (which in this case were the rules relating to accession and specification) were so fundamental that any contrary foreign rule would be disregarded by Scots law. Nevertheless it is thought that any suggestion that the proper law of a contract can govern the creation of security and other property rights is not correct.

In *Armour v Thyssen Edelsahlwerke AG*[6] the question of choice of law arose at first instance, although the matter was not pursued on appeal by the sellers on the basis that the evidence of German law had been inadequate for their argument. The contract of sale by a German supplier to a Scottish customer included a German choice of law clause and a very elaborate German retention

1 (1746) Mor 4468.
2 (1894) 21 R (HL) 21.
3 See the Lord Chancellor at 22–23 and Lord Watson at 25–26.
4 1986 SLT 84.
5 At 88–89.
6 1986 SLT 452.

of title clause. Lord Mayfield held that the validity of the clause was governed exclusively by Scots law. He referred[1] to *Inglis v Robertson and Baxter*, and held that that case was clear authority that the *lex situs* governs the creation of real rights in corporeal moveables. He stated[2]:

'In my view . . . there is clear authority that the *lex situs* governs the creation of real rights in corporeal moveables. I consider it is also clear that whether or not a security has been created (or the effectiveness or otherwise) has to be determined by the law of the place where the goods are actually located. In my view that is supported by *Mitchell v Burnet and Mouat*. Accordingly, it is my further view that if a security has been created then Scots law governs.'

Lord Mayfield went on to consider the decisions of Lord Ross in *Emerald Stainless Steel* and *Deutz* and concluded that both those cases and the instant case raised questions about security rights, governed by the *lex situs*.

Lord Mayfield subsequently considered *Hamlyn & Co v Talisker Distillery*[3], and on the basis of the statements of principle in that case advanced a further reason for rejecting the application of the proper law on the basis of the then prevalent view that an 'all sums' retention of title clause was an attempt to create a security without possession. He pointed out[4] that the purpose of the rule that security over moveables cannot be created without possession is the protection of creditors. He regarded that as a fundamental principle of Scots law which must prevail against the proper law of any contract.

Although it was not necessary for his decision, Lord Mayfield went on to consider the evidence of German law that was led in the case at some length. He concluded that none of the three experts who gave evidence had complete confidence in his position, and that accordingly the averments of German law made by the defenders had not been proved. The case illustrates the extreme difficulty of proving foreign law in a field such as retention of title, and it may be that attempts to invoke foreign law fail simply because of the difficulty of adducing sufficient evidence. A further argument for the seller deserves notice. It was maintained that German law was the proper law of the contract and therefore governed its construction. Under German law, it was said, conditions of business might be applied to the extent that they were valid, even if they were in part invalid or ineffective; and consequently German law would treat the elaborate 'all-sums' retention of title clause in the parties' contract as a clause of simple retention if that was all that Scots law, as the *lex situs*, would recognise[5]. Lord Mayfield did not require to deal with the substance of this issue because of his finding that the averments of German law had not been proved. It seems, however, that the seller's argument cannot be correct, on the basis of the two exceptions recognised in *Hamlyn & Co v Talisker Distillery*[6]. In the first place, it is clear that the application of the alleged rule of German law founded on by the seller would involve the rewriting of the retention of title clause, and not the mere interpretation of its wording. The opening part of the clause provided that: 'All goods delivered by us remain our property . . . until all debts owed to us . . . are settled'. It is

1 At 455.
2 At 456.
3 (1894) 21 R (HL) 21.
4 1986 SLT 452 at 457.
5 See 455F–I, 457G–H.
6 Above.

plain that that wording cannot be turned into a clause of simple retention by mere deletion. In any event, turning such wording into a simple retention clause would fundamentally alter the import of the clause. For these reasons, the rewriting involved would go well past the Scots rules allowing severance. That, it is submitted, would be contrary to a fundamental principle of Scots law, which has steadfastly set itself against the remaking of contracts. In the second place, the remaking or rewriting of a contractual provision, as against its mere interpretation, should not be governed by the proper law. It is rather a question of remedy and that, as *Hamlyn* makes clear, is a matter for the law of the forum[1].

## Procedural considerations

It remains to notice certain procedural matters that may be encountered in practice. As has been mentioned, goods subject to a valid retention clause may be recovered by the seller by virtue of his right of ownership; if court proceedings are required they will usually take the form of an action for delivery, or declarator and delivery. This is often combined with a conclusion for *interim* interdict, to prevent the receiver or liquidator or buyer from selling or disposing of goods in the buyer's possession. Motions for *interim* interdict are usually disposed of, if the retention clause appears *prima facie* valid, by the receiver or liquidators' granting an undertaking that (1) he will keep a detailed record, including serial numbers, if any, of all products obtained from the seller that are used or sold by him, and (2) he will account to the seller for the contract price of any article so used or sold in the event that the clause is eventually held to be (a) valid and (b) applicable to such article. The receiver's or liquidator's liability will be a debt of the receivership or liquidation, and thus payable in full. If such an undertaking is not given, *interim* interdict will normally be granted or refused according to the court's view of the validity of the retention clause in the particular instances of the case; the balance of convenience is rarely, if ever, the determining factor. Nevertheless, Lord Jauncey commented on the balance of convenience in *Goodyear Tyre and Rubber Co (Great Britain) Ltd v Hunter*[2]. In that case, Goodyear tyres had been supplied to the insolvent defenders both by the pursuers and by independent wholesalers. The tyres had no serial numbers, and it was doubtful if tyres supplied by the pursuers could be identified, as all the stock had been inmixed. Moreover, attempts were being or would be made to sell the shares in the insolvent defenders or their business, but if *interim* interdict were granted the defenders would be forced to cease trading. Further, if the trustee in sequestration or liquidator of the defenders sold tyres in which the property had not passed from the pursuers, they would remain liable in damages to the pursuers for the value of the tyres, or to account to the pursuers for their value. In these circumstances Lord Jauncey expressed the view that any prejudice suffered by the defenders if interdict were granted would probably be far greater than any prejudice suffered by the pursuers in the event of a refusal.

1 An argument broadly similar to that in *Armour*, but based on English principles relating to severance, was rejected by Lord Jauncey, in *Goodyear Tyre and Rubber Co (Great Britain) Ltd v Hunter* (20 August 1986, unreported), on the ground that the 'all moneys' provision in the retention clause was simply not capable of severance.
2 Above.

He would accordingly have refused *interim* interdict on the balance of convenience alone had he not done so on the merits.

Care must be taken to ensure that a retention of title clause does not amount in reality to a floating charge; if it does, it is likely to be void either as not being in the form prescribed by section 462 of the Companies Act 1985 or as not being registered under section 410 of that Act.

# Chapter 12

# Mandates and powers of attorney

## Nature of rights

Mandate is the term traditionally used in Scots law for the relationship of agency where the agent, or mandatory, is not remunerated as such. In modern commercial practice such a relationship usually arises as an ancillary part of a wider agreement, designed to aid the enforcement of the parties' rights and obligations. A power of attorney[1] is simply a written mandate, usually specifying the powers of the attorney, or mandatory, in considerable detail. The legal position of the attorney is exactly the same as that of a mandatory.

## Mandate given in interests of mandatory

Where a mandate is given for the purposes of the mandatory, rather than the mandant, it is irrevocable without the mandatory's consent[2]. It may, further, amount to an assignation, as where the mandatory is empowered to collect for his own purposes funds due to the mandant[3]. In such a case the mandate by itself will confer only personal rights on the mandatory, albeit of an irrevocable nature; in order to obtain a real right the mandatory must still intimate the assignation to the mandant's debtor. Both a cheque, at least if granted for the payee's own purposes[4], and a bill of exchange operate as a mandate and assignation[5]. Presentation to the bank on which the cheque or bill is drawn operates as intimation to the debtor, completing the payee's real right in the funds assigned, to the extent that funds are available to meet the cheque or bill[6].

---

1 The expression is English in origin, but has been used in Scotland for many years. In older cases and textbooks 'factory' is often used as a synonym.
2 Bell, *Prin*, 1.228; *Premier Briquette Co v Gray* 1922 SC 329. Such a mandate is sometimes known as a procuratory *in rem suam*.
3 *Carter v McIntosh* (1862) 24 D 925, especially at 933, per LJ-C Inglis.
4 It is thought that it is not essential that the cheque should be given for value, but that it will suffice if it is given for the payee's own purposes: cf. *British Linen Co Bank v Carruthers* (1883) 10 R 923, where the criterion adopted is whether the cheque amounts to a procuratory *in rem suam*, for which value is not essential. For a further discussion of this issue, see McBryde *Contract*, paras 17–64 to 17–72; the distinction between an ordinary mandate and a mandate for the mandatory's own purposes should be borne in mind in considering this issue, as it is only the latter that can amount to an assignation.
5 *British Linen Co v Carruthers, supra*.
6 Bills of Exchange Act 1882, s 53(2), re-enacting the common law, as amended by the Law Reform (Miscellaneous Provisions) (Scotland) Act 1985, s 11. Section 75A of the 1882 Act, introduced by s 11 of the 1985 Act, has the effect of making the assignation of a cheque subject to the resolutive condition that the drawer does not countermand payment; if he does, the bank is treated as having no funds available to meet the cheque.

A mandate not given in the mandatory's interests, but merely to serve the purposes of the mandant, is revocable by the mandant at any time[1].

### Effect of insolvency on mandate

If the mandate is not given in the mandatory's interests, it is treated as revoked by the insolvency of the mandant or the mandatory[2]. If it is given in the mandatory's interests, the effect of the mandant's insolvency varies according to the nature of the rights that the mandate is designed to enforce. If it is designed to facilitate the enforcement of real rights or trust rights or rights in security it will survive the mandant's insolvency, and can be enforced if necessary against the liquidator, administrator or receiver of the mandant. The critical point in such a case is that the rights that are to be enforced using the mandate are rights which prevail against the insolvency of the mandant[3], and any procedure designed to enforce such rights will likewise prevail against the insolvency. If, on the other hand, the mandate is designed merely to facilitate the enforcement of personal rights that the mandatory has against the mandant, it will fall on the mandant's insolvency. If the rule were otherwise, the result would be that the mandatory was able to secure a preference in the mandant's insolvency in respect of purely personal rights, rather than ranking in the insolvency like all other personal creditors. That would contravene the fundamental principle of the law of insolvency that, apart from securities, diligence and statutory preferences, all personal creditors rank equally[4].

### Mandates to enforce real and trust rights and rights in security

In *Broughton v Stewart & Co*[5], one merchant had consigned goods to another firm of merchants as commission agents, and on the faith of those consignments the commission agents had made considerable advances to the consigner. As commission agents the consignees had a mandate to sell the goods, which remained the property of the consigner. They also enjoyed a factor's lien over those goods in security of the advances, that they had made[6]. The consigner was sequestrated, and the trustee in his sequestration attempted to interdict the commission agents from selling any of the goods. Interdict was refused, on the basis that, after advances had been made on the faith of the security conferred by the lien, the mandate to sell became a mandate for the mandatory's own interests, designed to enforce his lien. The lien was a security right that prevailed against the sequestration, and the mandate accordingly survived along with the lien. Lord Meadowbank, who delivered the opinion of the court, said:

'The mandate of a factor to sell is an ordinary mandate, revocable at pleasure; but if the consignee, on the faith of his lien, makes advances, he becomes *praepositus in rem suam* [a mandatory in his own interest] under the factory [mandate] to sell. He is entitled to say, "Though I have a mandate revocable at pleasure, you must indemnify me *instanter* of any advances, or relieve me of the security I have come under for you." If the trustee had said,

---

1 Erskine, *Inst*, III.iii.32, 40.
2 Bell, *Comm*, 5th edn, i.488–496.
3 For trust rights, see chapter 9.
4 See pp 256–260.
5 17 December 1814, F.C.
6 See Gloag and Irvine, *Rights in Security*, pp 363 *et seq*.

"There is money to relieve you, and I recall the order to sell," he was entitled to do so, but it is only in that way that the mandate can be revoked, because *res non sunt integrae*. After advances are made, it is not enough to say that the lien over the goods is sufficient to secure the consignee; that is not the way in which the mercantile world goes on; the mandate becomes irrevocable, unless immediate means are taken to relieve the factor of his advances, and I have no doubt that such is the practice; for what man would engage in the business of a mercantile agent on other terms, or what can he do for all the bills he grants on the faith of the lien, unless he can bring the lien to market?'

In *Struthers v Commercial Bank of Scotland*[1] a bank letter of credit granted by Sir W Forbes and Company was drawn in favour of Craig, payable on or after 7 July. On 2 July it was indorsed in favour of the Commercial Bank by Craig's agent, full value less discount being given in exchange. It was presented for payment on 6 July, 7 July being a Sunday, and payment was refused, on the basis that Craig's estates were then in the process of being sequestrated; sequestration was awarded later the same day. In a competition between the trustee in sequestration and the Commercial Bank it was held that the Commercial Bank, as indorsee, was entitled to payment. Lord Fullerton, with whom the Lord President agreed, stated:

'A letter of credit of this kind is an order to honour the draft of the party to whom it is granted, and an authority to such party to draw. But it is perfectly understood in practice, that the power can only be exercised by the person with the document in his possession. The letter of credit . . . is given to the Commercial Bank indorsed; and they pay the amount minus the discount . . . I think that, by putting the letter of credit into the hands of the Commercial Bank for value, there was a mandate by Craig to the Commercial Bank to draw the money. And it was an effectual mandate, because no one could draw the money without being possessed of the letter of credit . . . If it were an ordinary gratuitous mandate to a third party, the mandant might put an end to it when he chose, and his creditors could compel him to do so. But it was not so. It was a mandate to draw for the mandatory's own behoof, he having in the meantime made the advance. He was mandatory *in rem suam*, and it is not in the power either of the bankrupt or of his creditors to revoke such a mandate. . . . Whenever a mandatory has contracted an obligation on the faith of the mandate, it cannot be recalled'[2].

The critical point is that the letter of credit was for practical purposes equivalent to a negotiable instrument, and that the power in it could be only exercised by a person with the letter in his possession. Thus, once value had been given for it, possession of the document conferred a real right to the sum payable under the letter of credit[3], and the mandate in favour of the Commercial Bank to claim payment from Sir W Forbes and Company was designed to permit enforcement of that real right.

## Mandates to enforce purely personal rights

The case mentioned above should be contrasted with the case where a mandate is designed only to assist in the enforcement of personal rights. In such a case, it is a fundamental principle that a mandate cannot be used to alter the ranking of the personal creditors. Consequently any mandate which would have that effect will be revoked by the insolvency of the mandant.

1 (1842) 4 D 460.
2 At 468. See also Erskine, *Inst*, iii.40.
3 See *Gloag and Irvine*, pp 577–578.

In *McKenzie v Campbell*[1] Fraser, who had been charged with forgery, asked the defender, a law agent, to act for him in connection with the charge, and sent him a sum of money with authority to use it for the purposes of the defence to the charge. Shortly thereafter Fraser was sequestrated, but the defender continued to make use of the money for the purposes of the defence. The trustee in sequestration brought an action of accounting to recover the money, and was successful. On sequestration, the defender's employment as law agent was terminated, and the mandate, which was only designed to facilitate the performance of those services, was revoked with the employment. While the reasoning of the First Division is based on the fact that the mandate in favour of the solicitor was not granted for his purposes, and was therefore revocable on that account alone, it is clear that the result would have been the same if the mandate was for the solicitor's purposes but was only designed to assist enforcement of a personal right. Thus the Lord Ordinary (Kincairney) refers[2] to the relevance of the distinction between cases such as those under consideration where the money remained the property of the bankrupt and cases where it had become the property of the solicitor, and Lord McLaren makes a similar point in his opinion[3].

1 (1894) 21 R 904.
2 At 907.
3 At 911.

# Chapter 13

# Proof and ranking of claims

## Proof and admissibility of claims

Creditors in a liquidation may prove in respect of all debts of the company or claims against the company. The claims may be present or future, contingent, certain or uncertain, liquid or illiquid.

The creditor must submit his claim to the liquidator using a statutory style of form[1] (no oath required), and producing an account or voucher (according to the nature of the debt claimed) which constitutes prima facie evidence of the debt[2]. The liquidator may dispense with this requirement in respect of any debt or class of debt[3]. The liquidator, in order to satisfy himself as to the validity or amount of a claim submitted by a creditor, may require the creditor to produce further evidence, or require any other person who he believes can produce relevant evidence, to produce such evidence[4]. In order to vote at a meeting of the creditors, a claim must be submitted at or before the meeting[5]. In order to receive a dividend out of the assets of the company in respect of any accounting period, the claim must be submitted not later than eight weeks before the end of the accounting period[5].

In a compulsory liquidation, in terms of section 153 of the Insolvency Act 1986: 'The court may fix a time or times within which creditors are to prove their debt or claims or to be excluded from the benefit of any distribution made before those debts are proved'. This rule would appear to be procedural and is subordinated to the general principle of *pari passu* treatment of all creditors applied by section 107 of the Insolvency Act 1986 to voluntary windings up, and by rule 4.66(4) of the Insolvency (Scotland) Rules 1986 to compulsory windings up. Accordingly the creditor is entitled to prove late and have payments made to him in respect of dividends in which he has not participated. In terms of section 52(9) of the Bankruptcy (Scotland) Act 1985[6]:

'Where a creditor submits a claim to the liquidator later than 8 weeks before the end of an accounting period but more than 8 weeks before the end of a subsequent accounting period in respect of which, after making allowance for contingencies, funds are available for the payment of a dividend, the liquidator shall, if he accepts the claim in whole or in part, pay to the creditor –

1 Form 4.7 (Scot), as amended by Insolvency (Scotland) Amendment Rules 1987. See Appendix I.
2 Insolvency (Scotland) Rules 1986, r 4.15(1).
3 Ibid, r 4.15(2).
4 Bankruptcy (Scotland) Act 1985, s 48(5) as applied to liquidations by Insolvency (Scotland) Rules 1986, r 4.16(1).
5 Ibid, r 4.15(1).
6 As applied to liquidations by Insolvency (Scotland) Rules 1986, r 4.68(1).

(a)   the same dividend or dividends as has or have been paid to creditors of the same class in respect of any accounting period or periods; and

(b)   whatever dividend may be payable to him in respect of the said subsequent accounting period:

Provided that paragraph (a) above shall be without prejudice to any dividend which has already been paid.'

The effect of the above provision is to allow proving late, but not to allow any disturbance of dividends already paid. It would be difficult in practice to reclaim dividends already paid. A creditor must accordingly at the very latest submit his claim at least eight weeks before the end of the final accounting period, and then he runs the risk that there may not be sufficient funds to pay him the dividends in which he has not participated.

The presentation of a petition for liquidation or the concurrence in such a petition, or the submission of a claim in the liquidation interrupts prescription and bars the effect of any enactment or rule of law relating to the limitation of actions in any part of the United Kingdom[1]. A debt or any other liability arising out of a market contract which is the subject of default proceedings by an investment exchange or clearing house recognised under the Financial Services Act 1986 may not be claimed until the completion of those proceedings[2].

## Valuation of claims

### (1)   *Amount which may be claimed generally*

A creditor is entitled to claim the accumulated sum of principal and any interest which is due on the debt as at the date of the commencement of the winding up[3].

### (2)   *Discounts*

In calculating the amount of his claim, a creditor must deduct any discount (other than any discount for payment in cash) which is allowable by contract or course of dealing between the creditor and the company or by the usage of trade[4].

### (3)   *Future debts*

In terms of paragraph 1(2) of Schedule 1 to the Bankruptcy (Scotland) Act 1985[5]:

'If a debt does not depend on a contingency but would not be payable but for the liquidation until after the date of commencement of winding up, the amount of the claim

---

1 Bankruptcy (Scotland) Act 1985, ss 8(5), 22(8), 73(5), as applied by the Insolvency (Scotland) Rules 1986, r 4.76.

2 Companies Act 1989, s 159(4).

3 Bankruptcy (Scotland) Act 1985, Sch 1, para 1(1) as applied to liquidations by Insolvency (Scotland) Rules 1986, r 4.16(1).

4 Bankruptcy (Scotland) Act 1985, Sch 1, para 1(3) as applied to liquidations by Insolvency (Scotland) Rules 1986, r 4.16(1).

5 As applied to liquidations by Insolvency (Scotland) Rules 1986, r 4.16(1).

shall be calculated as if the debt were payable on the date of commencement of winding up but subject to the deduction of interest at whichever is the greater of –
(a)  the prescribed rate at the date of commencement of the winding up; and
(b)  the rate applicable to that date apart from the liquidation –
from the said date until the date for payment of the debt.'

What the above provision aims at is a 'discounting' of a future debt to give it its 'net present value'. The provision, however, does not result in 'net present value' being arrived at. The 'net present value' is meant to be that sum which, if interest were payable thereon from the present until the date when the future debt is due, would, together with the accumulated interest, equal the future debt (e g if the sum were put in the bank the future debt could be met by the banked sum with accumulated interest).

What the provision achieves is a very perverse result. If, for example, a debt of £1,000 was due to a bank five years from the date of winding up and overdraft interest was 20 per cent, the bank would have to deduct five times 20 per cent of £1,000 from the £1,000. This would result in the bank not being able to claim anything for its future debt.

### (4)  Contingent debts

A creditor is not entitled to vote or claim for a contingent debt. However, he may apply to the liquidator or, if there is no liquidator, to the court to put a value on debt in so far as it is contingent[1]. The value which the liquidator or the court puts on the contingent debt is then the sum which the creditor is entitled to claim and no more. Where the debt subject to the contingency is an annuity, a cautioner for its payment is liable only for the value so determined. That is not the position, however, of cautioners in respect of debts other than annuities. Any interested person may appeal to the court against a valuation of a contingent debt and the court may affirm or vary that valuation[2].

### (5)  Secured debts

The term 'security' is widely defined by section 248(b) of the Insolvency Act 1986 and includes 'any security (whether heritable or moveable), any floating charge and any right of lien or preference and any right of retention (other than a right of compensation or set off)'. Inhibitions, arrestments in security and a right of retention over the future proceeds of insurance policies have been held to come within the meaning of that expression[3].

In calculating the amount of his claim, a secured creditor must deduct the value of any security as estimated by him. He is, however, entitled to surrender the security. The liquidator may, at any time after the expiry of 12 weeks from the date of commencement of winding up, require a secured creditor, at the expense of the company's assets, to discharge the security or convey or assign to the liquidator on payment to the creditor of the value specified by the creditor; and the amount in respect of which the creditor shall

---

1 Bankruptcy (Scotland) Act 1985, Sch 1, para 3 as applied to liquidations by Insolvency (Scotland) Rules 1986, r 4.16(1).
2 Bankruptcy (Scotland) Act 1985, Sch 1, para 3(3) as applied to liquidations by Insolvency (Scotland) Rules 1986, r 4.16(1).
3 *Goudy*, p 187.

then be entitled to claim shall be any balance of his debt remaining after receipt of such payment[1]. Where a creditor realises his security, he must deduct the amount realised (less the expenses of realisation) from the amount of his claim[2]. Where a liquidator requires a secured creditor to discharge a security, the creditor may not make a further claim specifying a different value for the security[3].

In terms of section 56 of the Bankruptcy (Scotland) Act 1913 a creditor for voting purposes had to put a specified value on the obligation of any co-obligant who was liable to relief to the company and on any security which he held from an obligant liable in relief to the company or from whom the company had a right of relief. This provision is repealed.

### (6) Co-obligant/Rule against double ranking

Where there is a co-obligant with the company and a creditor proceeds in the first instance against that co-obligant and secures payment of his debt, the co-obligant is subrogated to the creditor's claim and will obtain a ranking in place of the creditor[4]. The co-obligant who has paid the debt may require and obtain at his own expense from the creditor an assignation of the debt on payment of the debt and thereafter may in respect of that debt submit a claim, and vote and draw a dividend[5]. Where there is a co-obligant to the company, and the creditor assents to a composition, the co-obligant is not freed or discharged from liability for the debt as a result[6]. If, however, a creditor draws a dividend from the liquidation and then obtains payment of the deficiency from a co-obligant, the co-obligant cannot rank in the liquidation because of the rule against double ranking[7].

A special problem arises where the co-obligant holds a security over any of the company's assets. The creditor may choose to claim in the first instance either against the co-obligant or against the company. At common law, if the creditor adopted the latter course, the loss to the company's assets would be considerably greater, since the co-obligant would not be required to account for his security. To avoid this mischief, it is provided by section 60(2) of the Bankruptcy (Scotland) Act 1985[8] that:

'Where
(a)  a creditor has had a claim accepted in whole or in part; and
(b)  a co-obligant holds a security over any part of the company's estate, the co-obligant shall account to the liquidator so as to put the company in the same position as if the co-obligant had paid the debt to the creditor and thereafter had had his claim accepted in whole or in part in the liquidation after deduction of the value of the security.'

---

1 Bankruptcy (Scotland) Act 1985, Sch 1, para 5(2) as applied to liquidations by Insolvency (Scotland) Rules 1986, r 4.16(1).
2 Bankruptcy (Scotland) Act 1985, Sch 1, para 5(3) as applied to liquidations by Insolvency (Scotland) Rules 1986, r 4.16(1).
3 Insolvency (Scotland) Rules 1986, r 4.15(4).
4 Gloag and Irvine, *Rights in Security*, pp 831–832.
5 Bankruptcy (Scotland) Act 1985, s 60(3) as applied to liquidations by Insolvency (Scotland) Rules 1986, r 4.16(1).
6 Bankruptcy (Scotland) Act 1985, s 60(1) as applied to liquidations by Insolvency (Scotland) Rules 1986, r 4.16(1).
7 Bell, *Comm*, ii, 420; *Mackinnon v Monkhouse* (1881) 9 R 393.
8 As applied to liquidations by Insolvency (Scotland) Rules 1986, r 4.16(1).

(7)  *Foreign currency claims*

A creditor may state the amount of his claim in a currency other than sterling where:

(a)    his claim is constituted by decree or other order made by a court ordering the company to pay to the creditor a sum expressed in a currency other than sterling, or

(b)    where it is not so constituted, his claim arises from a contract or bill of exchange in terms of which payment is or may be required to be made by the company to the creditor in a currency other than sterling.

Where a claim is stated in currency other than sterling, the rule is that it shall be converted into sterling at the rate of exchange for that other currency at the mean of the buying and selling spot rates prevailing in the London market at the close of business on the date of commencement of winding up[1]. This means that a creditor may suffer loss as a result of movements in exchange rates. The creditor does not have a claim for that loss. It does not rank *pari passu* with creditors claiming post-liquidation interest[2]. However, there are suggestions in the judgments in the case of *Re Lines Bros*[3], that in the case of a liquidation which turns out to be solvent, if a foreign currency creditor has been paid less than his full contractual foreign currency debt, it is the duty of the liquidator to make good the shortfall before he pays anything to the shareholders. He has in effect a postponed ranking. Although such a debt is not now classed as 'postponed', it is thought that it would rank now after 'postponed' debts prior to payment to shareholders.

**Adjudication of claims**

(1)  *Voting at meetings*

At the commencement of every meeting of creditors (other than a statutory meeting) the liquidator must accept or reject the claim of each creditor for the purpose of voting at that meeting[4].

(2)  *Adjudication for dividend payment*

The liquidator must accept or reject every claim submitted to him at least four weeks before the end of every accounting period, if funds are going to be available for payment of a dividend[5]. If the claim is rejected, the liquidator must forthwith notify the creditor giving reasons for the rejection. In the case of both acceptance and rejection, the liquidator must record in the sederunt book his decision on the claim specifying:

(1)    the amount of the claim accepted by him,

---

1  Ibid, r 4.17.
2  *Re Lines Bros Ltd (In Liquidation)* [1983] Ch 1, [1982] 2 All ER 183.
3  *Supra.*
4  Bankruptcy (Scotland) Act 1985, s 49(1) as applied to liquidations by Insolvency (Scotland) Rules 1986, r 4.16(1).
5  Bankruptcy (Scotland) Act 1985, s 49(2) as applied to liquidations by Insolvency (Scotland) Rules 1986, r 4.16(1).

(2)  the category of debt, and the value of any security, as decided by him, and
(3)  if he is rejecting the claim, his reasons therefor[1].

The adjudication for voting purposes does not affect the adjudication made for the purpose of entitlement to a dividend. This is because it may be impracticable at the stage of a meeting to determine whether or not the debt truly subsists.

### (3)  Appeal from adjudication

The company, or any creditor, may, if dissatisfied with the acceptance or rejection of any claim, appeal to the court in relation to the amount of the claim accepted, the categorisation of the debt, the valuing of a security, and in relation to reasons given for the rejection of a claim[2]. If the acceptance or rejection is in relation to voting, the appeal to the court must be within two weeks of the acceptance or rejection, and where the acceptance or rejection is in relation to dividend, the appeal must be not later than two weeks before the end of the accounting period[2]. If the deadline is missed, it is suggested that recourse should be had to the court's power to cure defects (see page 72).

# APPLICATION OF ASSETS IN WINDING UP

## (1)  Pari passu principle

The assets of a company in voluntary liquidation are to be applied to the discharge of its liabilities. In terms of section 107 of the Insolvency Act 1986, a company's debts, subject to the provisions relating to preferential debts, must be paid *pari passu*. Preferential debts must also be paid *pari passu*[3]. By statutory instrument the *pari passu* principle has also been applied in Scotland to debts in a compulsory winding up[4]. A provision in a contract under which, in the event of a winding up, the company's assets are not to be distributed *pari passu* among creditors will be void in England, but not always in Scotland (see Chapter 4)[5].

## (2)  Subordinated debt

Just as the *pari passu* principle is invoked to avoid a creditor gaining an advantage in a liquidation, it also entails that a creditor is not entitled to subordinate his debt in England. Subordinated debt is allowed in several countries and the Cork Committee[6] recommended that such an option be enforceable in Britain. This was not accepted. It is considered however that a

---

1 Bankruptcy (Scotland) Act 1985, s 49(4) and (5) as applied to liquidations by Insolvency (Scotland) Rules 1986, r 4.16(1).
2 Bankruptcy (Scotland) Act 1985, s 49(6) as applied to liquidations by Insolvency (Scotland) Rules 1986, r 4.16(1).
3 Insolvency Act 1986, s 175(2)(a).
4 Insolvency (Scotland) Rules 1986, r 4.66(4).
5 *British Eagle International Airlines Ltd v CIE Nationale Air France* [1975] 2 All ER 390; *Carreras Rothmans Ltd v Freeman Matthews Treasure Ltd (in Liquidation)* [1985] 1 All ER 155, [1984] BCLC 420.
6 Report of the Review Committee on Insolvency Law and Practice Cmnd 8558 paras 1448–1449.

term of a contract which made the payment of a debt subject to the contingency that other debts were paid would be enforceable in Scotland (see Chapter 14).

## Order of priority in liquidations

In terms of rule 4.66(1) of the Insolvency (Scotland) Rules 1986:

'The funds of the company's assets shall be distributed by the liquidator to meet the following expenses and debts in the order in which they are mentioned:
(a)  the expenses of the liquidation;
(b)  any preferential debts within the meaning of section 386 (excluding any interest which has been accrued thereon to the date of commencement of the winding up within the meaning of section 129);
(c)  ordinary debts, that is to say a debt which is neither a secured debt nor a debt mentioned in any other subparagraph of this paragraph;
(d)  interest at the official rate on –
     (i) the preferential debts, and
     (ii) the ordinary debts,
     between the said date of commencement of the winding up and the date of payment of the debt; and
(e)  any postponed debt.'

## Secured debts

In terms of rule 4.66(6), the order of priority must not affect the right of a secured creditor which is preferable to the rights of the liquidator. Accordingly secured creditors may redeem their securities without reference to the liquidator, or the liquidator may require them to discharge the security by payment to him of the value of the security[1] (see page 292). A problem arises in the case of a receiver being appointed after the commencement of the winding up. It has been noted (see pages 23, 158, 161) that, following the ruling in *Manley, Petitioner*[2], a holder of a floating charge may appoint a receiver after the commencement of winding up and the receiver takes precedence over the liquidator. This means that the receiver is liable for the payment of the secured and preferential creditors of the company. This would give preferential creditors an interest in having a receiver appointed and the receiver would have a statutory duty to pay the preferential creditors and then the holder of the floating charge. There is an unfortunate failure in the legislation to deal with the expenses of the liquidation, where a receiver is appointed after winding up (see page 158). The preferential creditors have priority in a winding up to the holder of the floating charge[3].

## Expenses of the liquidation

The court has a discretion in the event of the assets of a company being insufficient to satisfy the liabilities to make an order as to the payment out of the assets of the company of the expenses incurred in the winding up in such

1  Bankruptcy (Scotland) Act 1985, Sch 1, para 5(2) as applied to liquidations by Insolvency (Scotland) Rules 1986, r 4.16(1).
2  1985 SLT 42.
3  Insolvency Act 1986, s 175(2).

order of priority as the court thinks just[1]. (By rule 4.66(1) of the Insolvency (Scotland) Rules 1986 as amended, expenses of a voluntary arrangement in force prior to a petition for winding up appear to rank immediately after the expenses of the liquidation. This is anomalous since the expenses of a prior insolvency procedure should rank before the expenses of the liquidation.) Subject to the court's discretion, there is a legal order of priority. The expenses of the liquidation have the following order of priority:

(a)   any outlays properly chargeable or incurred by the provisional liquidator in carrying out his functions in the liquidation, except those outlays specifically mentioned below;
(b)   the cost, or proportionate cost, of any caution provided by a provisional liquidator, liquidator or special manager;
(c)   the remuneration of the provisional liquidator (if any);
(d)   the expenses of the petitioner in the liquidation, and of any person appearing in the liquidation whose expenses are allowed by the court;
(e)   the remuneration of the special manager (if any);
(f)   any allowance made by the liquidator for the cost of the preparation of a statement of affairs;
(g)   the remuneration or emoluments of any person who has been employed by the liquidator to perform any services for the company, as required by law;
(h)   the remuneration of the liquidator determined in accordance with the rules relating thereto; and
(i)   the amount of any corporation tax on chargeable gains accruing on the realisation of any asset of the company (without regard to whether the realisation is effected by the liquidator, a secured creditor or otherwise)[2].

If there are no assets the liquidator is not entitled to receive any remuneration (unless an outside party is underwriting the costs of the liquidation) and he is personally liable for legal expenses incurred in the liquidation. He may be personally liable for other expenses of the liquidation, if any contracting party has insisted on a personal guarantee from the liquidator.

### Preferential debts

Section 386 of and Schedule 6 to the Insolvency Act 1986 (which consolidates provisions in Schedule 4 to the Insolvency Act 1985) makes major changes to the previous categories of preferential debts in a liquidation and receivership. The main changes are as follows:

(1)   direct taxes to the Inland Revenue are no longer preferential debts;
(2)   local rates are no longer preferential debts;
(3)   debts due to the Customs and Excise are for a more limited period.

### Debts to Inland Revenue

The only preferential debts to the Inland Revenue are sums due at the *relevant* date from the company on account of deductions of income tax from

---

1   Ibid, ss 112 and 156.
2   Insolvency (Scotland) Rules 1986, r 4.67(1), as amended by paragraph 32 of the Schedule to the Insolvency (Scotland) Amendment Rules 1987.

emoluments paid to employees and payments made to sub-contractors. The deductions are (i) those which the company was liable to make under section 203 of the Income and Corporation Taxes Act 1988 (PAYE) during the period of 12 months next before the relevant date, less the amount of the repayments of income tax which the company was liable to make during that period and (ii) sums due from the company in respect of deductions required to be made by it under section 559 of that Act (sub-contractors in the construction industry)[1]. For the purposes of the provision the *relevant* date is defined by section 387(3) of the Insolvency Act 1986 as being, in the case of a company ordered to be wound up compulsorily, the date of the first appointment of a provisional liquidator, or, if none was appointed, the date of the winding-up order, and in the case of creditors' windings up the date of the passing of the resolution for winding up. If there had been an administration order immediately prior to the winding up by the court, the relevant date is the date of the making of the administration order.

### Debts due to Customs and Excise

Preference is given to any value added tax due, at the *relevant* (for 'relevant' see supra) date, from the company and having become due within six months next before that date. Where tax falls partly within and partly outside the requisite six-month period, it is taken to be such part of the tax due for the whole of that accounting reference period as is proportionate to the part of the period falling within the six months[2]. The amount of any car tax due, at the *relevant* date, from the company and having become due within the 12 months next before that date is also given priority[3]. Similarly any amount due by way of general betting or bingo duty, or under section 12(1) or section 14 of or Schedule 2 to the Betting and Gaming Duties Act 1981 is also given priority. These sums must be due from the company at the *relevant* date and have become due within the 12 months next before that date[4].

### Social security contributions

Preference is given to amounts due on the relevant date from the company on account of Class 1 or Class 2 contributions under the Social Security Contributions and Benefits Act 1992 or the Social Security (Northern Ireland) Act 1975 and which became due from the company in the 12 months next before the *relevant* date. All sums which, on the relevant date, have been assessed on and are due from the company on account of Class 4 contributions under either of these Acts of 1975 are included, being sums which are due to the Commissioners of Inland Revenue (rather than to the Secretary of State or a Northern Ireland department), and are assessed on the company up to 5 April next before the relevant date, provided they do not exceed, in the whole, any one year's assessment[5].

---

1 Insolvency Act 1986, Sch 6, paras 1 and 2.
2 Ibid, Sch 6, para 3.
3 Ibid, Sch 6, para 4.
4 Ibid, Sch 6, para 5.
5 Ibid, Sch 6, paras 6 and 7.

## Contributions to occupational pension schemes

Preference is given to any sum which is owed by the company and is a sum to which Schedule 3 to the Social Security Pensions Act 1975 applies (contributions to occupational pension schemes and state scheme premiums)[1].

## Remuneration of employees

Preference is given to the wages or salary (whether payable for time or for piece work or earned wholly or partly by way of commission) of any person who is or has been an employee of the company in respect of services rendered to the company in respect of the whole or any part of the period of four months next before the *relevant* (for 'relevant' see page 298) date provided they do not exceed an amount which may be prescribed by regulations made by the Secretary of State[2]. Any remuneration payable by the company to a person in respect of a period of holiday or of absence from work through sickness or any other good cause is deemed to be wages or (as the case may be) salary in respect of services rendered to the company in that period, and includes any sums which, if they had been paid, would have been treated for the purposes of the enactments relating to social security as earnings in respect of that period[3]. Similarly the following payments are also deemed to be wages or salary:

(a)   a guarantee payment under section 12(1) of the Employment Protection (Consolidation) Act 1978 (employee without work to do for a day or part of a day);
(b)   remuneration on suspension on medical grounds under section 19 of the Employment Protection (Consolidation) Act 1978;
(c)   any payment for time off under sections 27(3) (trade union dues), 31(3) (looking for work, etc.) or 31A(4) (antenatal care) of the Employment Protection (Consolidation) Act 1978; or
(d)   remuneration under a protective award made by an industrial tribunal under section 101 of the Employment Protection Act 1975 (redundancy dismissal with compensation)[4].

## Accrued holiday remuneration

Preference is given to any sums owed by the company by way of accrued holiday remuneration in respect of any period of employment before the relevant date (for 'relevant' see page 298) to a person whose employment by the company has been terminated, whether before, on or after that date. Where a person's employment has been terminated by or in consequence of his employer going into liquidation or (his employer being a company not in liquidation) by or in consequence of the appointment of a receiver under section 53(6) or 54(5) of the Insolvency Act 1986, holiday remuneration is deemed to have accrued to that person in respect of any period of employment if, by virtue of his contract of employment or any enactment, that remunera-

---

1 Ibid, Sch 6, para 8.
2 Ibid, Sch 6, paras 9 and 13.
3 Ibid, Sch 6, para 15.
4 Ibid, Sch 6, para 13(2).

tion would have accrued in respect of that period if his employment had continued until he became entitled to be allowed the holiday[1].

### Payments by persons advancing money to the company for wages, etc.

Where third parties have advanced money to the company for the purpose of the payment of wages or accrued holiday remuneration, which, if they had not been paid, would have been given priority as above, the persons who have advanced the moneys have priority for these advances[2]. A banker may obtain the maximum benefit under this provision by opening a separate 'wages account' out of which advances are made for the payment of wages. The money must not only be advanced 'for the purpose of paying the wages' but the money so advanced must have actually paid the wages, so reducing the employee's priority claims[3]. In addition, if loans are made by the bank to the company and these are secured, the bank may, on realising the security, appropriate the proceeds to paying off first the non-preferential part of the company's indebtedness, so that its preferential rights can be exercised in full in respect of any balance outstanding[4]. The bank faces a difficulty by the operation of the rule in *Clayton's Case*[5] to the effect that any credit received must first be applied in discharging the earliest debit on the account which may have the effect of reducing its potential preferential claim. A further difficulty arises where a bank lends money on the 'wages account' but at the same time, by some arrangement, money is lodged in another account by the company[6]. Briefly, it has been held that where there were two interdependent accounts of which one was a wages account, and the bank would not have met the wages account unless the other account was maintained in sufficient credit to cover the wages account, the bank never did in fact make advances to meet wages; the company, when it drew on its wages account, was really drawing its own moneys standing to the credit of the other account[7]. However, a preference has been held to be obtained for sums transferred to the wages account by debiting an overdrawn current account[8].

### Payments under Reserve Forces (Safeguard of Employment) Act 1985

Preference is given to any amount which is ordered (whether before or after the *relevant* date) (for 'relevant' see page 298) to be paid by the company under the Reserve Forces (Safeguard of Employment) Act 1985, and is so ordered in respect of a default made by the company at that date in the discharge of its obligations under that Act, provided that the amount does not exceed such amount as may be prescribed by regulation by the Secretary of State[9]. The

---

1 Insolvency Act 1986, Sch 6, paras 10 and 14.
2 Ibid, Sch 6, para 11.
3 *Re E J Morel (1934) Ltd* [1962] Ch 21; *Re Yeovil Glove Co Ltd* [1965] Ch 148, CA.
4 *Re William Hall (Contractors) Ltd* [1967] 1 WLR 948.
5 *Devaynes v Noble* (1816) 1 Mer 572.
6 For a discussion, see Greene and Fletcher, *Law and Practice of Receivership in Scotland* (2nd edn, 1992) paras 9.22–9.28.
7 *Re E J Morel (1934) Ltd* [1962] Ch 21.
8 *Re James R Rutherford & Sons Ltd* [1964] 3 All ER 137.
9 Insolvency Act 1986, Sch 6, para 12. The prescribed amount at the date of publication of this book is £800 in terms of the Insolvency Proceedings (Monetary Limits) Order 1986 (SI 1986/1996).

same provisions in relation to wages and accrued holiday remuneration apply in relation to such orders.

## Levies on coal and steel production

Preference is also given to debts comprising any sums due at the relevant date[1] from the company in respect of:

(1) the levies on the production of coal and steel referred to in Articles 49 and 50 of the ECSC Treaty, or

(2) any surcharge for delay in payment of the levies[2].

## Ordinary debts

Ordinary debts are defined by rule 4.66(1) of the Insolvency (Scotland) Rules 1986 as amended by Article 31 of the Schedule to the Insolvency (Scotland) Amendment Rules 1987 as all debts of a company which are neither (1) the expenses of the liquidation and of the administration of any preceding voluntary arrangement; (2) preferential debts; (3) interest on preferential debts and ordinary debts between the date of commencement of the winding up and the payment of the debt; or (4) a postponed debt. They are usually the largest category of debt, but frequently receive no dividend.

## Interest on claims

Where there is a surplus remaining after payment of the debts of a company proved in a winding up, the surplus is by statute now applied to paying interest on those debts in respect of the periods during which they have been outstanding since the company went into liquidation[3]. In relation to this post-liquidation interest there is no ranking, and the preferred and ordinary creditors rank equally (section 189(3) of the Insolvency Act 1986). The rate of interest payable shall be the greater of the rate of interest specified in the debt contract or that prescribed under the Insolvency Rules[4]. The current 'official rate' is 15 per cent[5].

## Postponed debt

Before the current legislation a claim which a loser on a foreign currency conversion debt might have (see page 294) was treated as a 'postponed' debt. Now rule 4.66(2) of the Insolvency (Scotland) Rules 1986 gives a statutory category of postponed debt. In terms of that rule, a postponed debt is also a creditor's right to any alienation which has been reduced or restored to the company's assets under section 242 of the Insolvency Act 1986 or to the proceeds of sale of such an alienation. This definition will apply where a gratuitous alienation has been reduced and the proceeds of the reduction are

---

1 For 'relevant' see the Insolvency Act 1986, s 387(3), and p 298.

2 Provided for in Article 50(3) of that Treaty and Article 6 of Decision 3/52 of the High Authority of the Coal and Steel Community; Insolvency Act 1986, Sch 6, para 15A (added by the Insolvency (ECSC Levy Debts) Regulations 1987, SI 1987/2093); the regulations implement EC Commission Recommendation 86/198 (OJ L144, 29.8.56, p 40)).

3 Ibid, s 189(2).

4 Ibid, s 189(4) and (5).

5 Insolvency (Scotland) Rules 1986, r 4.66(2)(b).

sufficient to pay the ordinary creditors in full; the alienee then ranks as a postponed creditor for any part of the proceeds of the reduction that is left. The statutory category will precede the creditor claiming a foreign currency loss.

In terms of section 178 of the Companies Act 1985, an obligation by a company to redeem or repurchase its shares, provided it is enforceable prior to winding up and the company could lawfully have made a distribution equal in value during the period between enforceability and winding up, is a debt on the company but postponed to all other debts including shareholders with prior rights.

A final type of debt which is dealt with by statute in so far as it is after a 'postponed' debt is a debt owed by the company as a dividend to the shareholders. It may be taken into account in adjusting the rights of contributories in terms of section 74(2)(f) of the Insolvency Act 1986.

Chapter 14

# Debt subordination agreements

## Introduction

In recent years there has been an increasing demand for a legal structure which allows companies to issue subordinated debt. In its simplest form subordinated debt is a transaction by which the lender of money to the company has his claim for repayment of the money subordinated to that of the other creditors. They have to be paid in full before he is entitled to any dividend out of the assets of the company. A second type of subordination is where one creditor agrees that he shall not be entitled to claim his full *pro rata* entitlement in the liquidation until one or more of the ordinary creditors in the liquidation have had their claims met beyond what would be otherwise their *pro rata* entitlement. Although these concepts are simple their legal implications are complicated. Different legal devices and structures have been used in different jurisdictions to create enforceable legal instruments. They have been widely used in particular in relation to company buy-outs, intermediate financing arrangements and the issue of so-called 'junk' bonds in takeovers. The issues involved such as third party enforcement, the *pari passu* rules, and the *British Eagle* case[1] have been the subject of much legal discussion in books and legal articles[2].

Most debt subordination instruments as used in England, the United States and the Commonwealth are cumbersome and complex structures which do not always achieve with certainty their objectives.

It is proposed in this chapter:

(1)  to look at the objectives of debt subordination instruments;
(2)  to examine in the context of English law the type of debt subordination instruments most commonly used; and
(3)  to examine the Scottish law in relation to debt subordination and to discuss the legal instruments which are effective under Scottish law to achieve the objectives of debt subordination.

## Objectives of debt subordination instruments

Although it is possible legally to bind a creditor of a solvent company in such a way that his debt is not paid before the payment of another debt, (which might

1  *British Eagle International Airlines Ltd v Compagnie Nationale Air France* [1975] 1 WLR 758.
2  See especially, B Johnston, 'Debt Subordination: the Australian Perspective' [1987] Australian Business Law Review 80; P R Wood, *Law and Practice of International Finance* (1980), p 403; D H Calligar, 'Subordination Agreements' (1961) 70 Yale Law Journal 376; and B Johnston, 'Contractual Debt Subordination and Legislative Reform' [1991] The Journal of Business Law 225.

be called 'complete subordination'), subordination is usually only contracted to operate in the event of the bankruptcy or liquidation of the debtor. Where ordinary creditors, whether as a class or individually, lend to a company, the company's creditworthiness as far as they are concerned is significantly improved if money is lent to the company which is not to be paid in the event of the liquidation of the company before the ordinary creditors. This is because subordinated debt of that category is available to meet the claims of these creditors in the same way as share capital and reserves ie equity. Indeed for certain regulatory purposes subordinated debt is treated as share capital. In for example the *Report of July 1988 of the Basle Committee on Banking Regulations and Supervisory Practices on International Convergence of Capital Measurement and Capital Standards*, the banks concerned were required by 1992 to maintain capital of 8 per cent of their assets and exposures. For this purpose capital was divided into two tiers comprising core capital (such as equity and disclosed reserves) and supplementary capital which could include certain categories of subordinated debt. Perpetual subordinated debt issues having the characteristics of equity and subordinated term debt having a maturity of more than five years could be included subject to detailed qualifications and limits. In this type of situation the subordinated debt especially if it is perpetual debt is intended to be the equivalent of permanent capital.

Just as regulators may insist on capital ratios in which they include subordinated debt as capital, to ensure the creditworthiness of companies regulated for the benefit of ordinary creditors, especially depositors, so also private organisations lending large sums to companies where effectively they become in practice by far the largest creditor, often insist that the holding company or owners or backers of the company provide finance at the same time which is to be subordinated to ordinary creditors. The main beneficiary of such an arrangement is the financing organisation. Although this purpose may also be achieved by the holding company or owner putting in equity into the company, the equity solution is not always the preferable solution. That may be for a variety of reasons including the following:

(1)  dividends may be subject to a withholding tax whereas interest may not;
(2)  capital duty may be payable on the issue of shares whereas not payable on the issue of loan capital, although this is no longer the case in the United Kingdom;
(3)  a company may repay debt (which is acting as *de facto* capital) without triggering the possible need to reduce its share capital;
(4)  the subordination agreement may be structured in such a way that the creditor receives a better financial result in the event of the liquidation of the company than if the holding company put the money in as equity; and
(5)  the subordinated creditor may be given a favourable rate of interest to compensate him for his debt being locked into the company which would not be the case if share capital had to be issued.

### English law and debt subordination instruments

The chief legal difficulty with debt subordination arises on the insolvency of the debtor company. In terms of the Insolvency Act 1986 all distributions from a company upon the winding up of the company must be made *pari passu* amongst ordinary creditors[1]. The problem is that the *pari passu* rule is mandatory and it appears not possible validly to contract out of the rule.

In *British Eagle International Airlines Ltd v Compagnie Nationale Air France*, Lord Cross said:

'. . . What the respondents are saying here is that the parties . . . by agreeing that simple contract debts are to be satisfied in a particular way have succeeded in "contracting out" of [the *pari passu* provisions] for the payment of unsecured debts *pari passu* . . . [S]uch "contracting out" must, to my mind, be contrary to public policy . . . I cannot doubt that on principle the rules of general liquidation should prevail.'[2]

The proposition that the statutory rules of *pari passu* distribution were mandatory and that creditors could not contract out was taken further in *Carreras Rothmans Ltd v Freeman Matthews Treasure Ltd*[3] in which Peter Gibson J summarised the principle in the *British Eagle* case as follows:

'. . . Where the effect of a contract is that an asset which is actually owned by a company at the commencement of its liquidation would be dealt with in a way other than in accordance with [the *pari passu* provisions], then to that extent the contract as a matter of public policy is avoided, whether or not the contract is entered into for consideration and for bona fide commercial reasons and whether or not the contractual provision affecting the asset is expressed to take effect only on insolvency.'

There have been several attempts to distinguish the *British Eagle* case[4]. In particular in Australia in the Victoria Supreme Court in the case of *Horne v Chester & Fein Property Developments Pty Ltd*[5], Southwell J tried to distinguish the *British Eagle* case in relation to a debt subordination agreement and gave a detailed review of the authorities. In that case the creditors of the company that had gone into liquidation had previously agreed to defer their claims to the claims of another creditor. Southwell J stated in trying to distinguish the House of Lords' decision in the *British Eagle* case:

'. . . "The policy of the insolvency laws" . . . as it appears to me, was never intended to alter the rights and obligations of parties freely entering into a contract, unless the performance of the contract would upon insolvency adversely affect the rights of strangers to the contract . . . [T]he principle [of the *British Eagle* case] is, I believe, that in insolvency law, the whole of the debtor's estate should be available for distribution to all creditors, and no one creditor or group of creditors can lawfully contract in such a manner as to defeat other creditors not parties to the contract . . . When so examined, it may readily be seen that *British Eagle* is distinguishable from the present case, in which, as I have earlier said, the performance of the agreement between the three parties can in no way affect the entitlement of creditors not a party to that agreement.'[6]

---

1 See page 295; Insolvency Act 1986, s 107 and Insolvency Rules 1986, r 4.181; and, in Scotland, Insolvency (Scotland) Rules 1986, r 4.66(4).
2 [1975] 1 WLR 758 at 780–781; see also *National Westminster Bank Ltd v Halesowen Pressworks & Assemblies Ltd* [1972] AC 785 discussed at p 326.
3 [1985] 1 All ER 155.
4 See Johnston, 'Debt Subordination: the Australian Perspective' [1987] Australian Business Law Review 80 at 102 ff.; R B Grantham, 'Legal Imperialism and Debt Subordination' [1989] New Zealand Law Journal 224; *Re Malborough Concrete Constructions Pty Ltd* [1977] Qd R 37; and *Re Industrial Welding Co Pty Ltd and the Companies Act* (1978) 3 ACLR 754.
5 (1987) 5 ACLC 245.
6 *Supra* at 245, 248 and 250.

R M Goode has said:

'. . . Southwell J in [the *Horne* case] . . . distinguished the [*British Eagle* case and the House of Lords' decision in *National Westminster Bank Ltd v Halesowen Presswork & Assemblies Ltd*] on the ground that they involved cases in which an agreement excluded the statutory rules which would have operated to the prejudice of other creditors. This is true of *British Eagle* but certainly not of *Halesowen* where other creditors would not in any way have been prejudiced by an agreement to exclude set-off. In any event, both decisions were firmly based on public policy, not on prejudice to other creditors. Australian courts are not, of course, bound by decisions of the House of Lords, and the decision in *Horne* has the great merit of allowing sensible priority agreements between creditors which in policy terms are quite unobjectionable and may well be accepted in practice by many liquidators. English courts, however, will almost certainly consider that priority agreements are governed by the same principles as agreements excluding set-off and that they are bound by the House of Lords' decisions to rule that such agreements must be disregarded by a trustee or liquidator in distributing the assets.'

The narrow view as to the strictures entailed by *British Eagle* enunciated in the *Horne* case has not been widely accepted in England[1].

In order to get round the problems perceived to be raised in the *British Eagle* case, English legal practitioners have used a variety of structures in framing debt subordination agreements.

The two most usual instruments used are:

(1)   Contractual or 'contingent debt' subordination agreements; and
(2)   subordination trusts.

### Contractual or 'contingent debt' subordination agreements

In a contingent debt subordination agreement, the subordinated debt is set up in such a way that the subordinated creditor has only a contingent or conditional right to repayment of the debt. This conditionality can apply either from the date of lending or more usually in the event of the insolvency or liquidation of the borrower. The debt is contingent or conditional in so far that the subordinated debt is either not to be repaid until the other creditors have been repaid in full, or the amount that is to be recovered by the subordinated creditor is stipulated to be only the amount that shareholders themselves would receive in a winding up. Under this scheme, a contingent or conditional debt will be admissible to proof in the winding up of the debtor company, but will only prove for a nominal or nil value.

An example of such a clause might be:

'(1)   If the debtor becomes subject to any liquidation, dissolution or similar insolvency proceedings or to any assignment for the benefit of its creditors or any other distribution of its assets, the junior debt will be repayable only on condition that the senior debt has been or is capable of being paid in full. Accordingly in any such event the junior debt will be reduced to such amount down to zero as is necessary to ensure that the debtor is able to pay the senior debt in full.
(2)   The reduction of the junior debt will be applied first to costs and expenses, secondly to interest, and thirdly to principal of the junior debt.[2]'

---

1 See R M Goode, *Legal Problems of Credit and Security* (2nd edn, 1988), p 96.
2 See P Wood: 'The Law of Subordinated Debt', p 12 for this example.

Other methods provide that in the liquidation or dissolution proceedings, the subordinated debt is contingent on the debtor being solvent and that accordingly the subordinated debt is not payable except in so far that the debtor could pay it and still be solvent after the payment. It is stated that the debtor is solvent only if the company is able to pay its provable debts as they fall due disregarding any debts which are subordinated. The subordinated debt, as a contingent debt, will be admissible to proof in the winding up of the debtor company, but will have only a nominal or nil value. That is because, the company being in liquidation, it is expected that the subordinated creditor will receive no dividend. If it is given a nominal value that is to reflect the market value of the subordinated debt on the basis of there being a gamble that something in the end of the day might be received. If as sometimes happens there is supervening solvency (ie repayment of ordinary creditors) the procedure in England is for the contingent claim to be amended to the face value of the subordinated debt with the subordinated creditor then entitled to prove for the full amount of the subordinated debt[1].

## Subordination trusts

In England, especially where there is a complex refinancing package in relation to a company, it is often desired that the benefit of the subordination of the subordinated creditor is not extended to the body of creditors, ie all are not paid *pro rata* and in full before the subordinated creditor is entitled to a dividend. Usually the object is to structure the deal in such a way that another creditor obtains a distinct advantage in an insolvency over the body of ordinary creditors. Because of the *pari passu* rule, the highest right which an ordinary creditor could have in the liquidation is to a dividend as an ordinary creditor. Accordingly if the object of the deal is to give the contractually preferred creditor the benefit of the subordinated creditor's dividend, it is sometimes contracted between the subordinated creditor and a preferred creditor that the subordinated creditor shall pay over all dividends received to the preferred creditor. This of course is not a real subordination (any more than the contingent debt structure was a real subordination) but it achieves, where it is effective, a result by which the preferred creditor is contractually entitled to obtain from the subordinated creditor all the subordinated creditor's dividends before the subordinated creditor is entitled to any payment. The weakness of this arrangement is that it is dependent on a contractual right of the preferred creditor against the subordinated creditor. It would obviously

---

1 See B H McPherson *The Law of Company Liquidation* (2nd edn, 1980), p 330 where McPherson states:

'The timing for estimating the value of a contingent claim is the date of the winding up. If the liquidator is uncertain as to how its value should be estimated the proper course is either for him to place a nominal value on the claim or for the creditor himself to make an estimate in his proof and then to have the matter determined by the court. If the contingency happens during the winding up [as it may in a debt subordination], the creditor is entitled to prove for the actual amount; if the proof has already been lodged, he will be permitted to withdraw and amend accordingly, though not so as to disturb dividends already paid [such as dividends already paid to the senior creditors]. The effect is not to convert the claim into a debt for the purposes of proof: it remains a contingent claim, but the happening of the contingency is treated as admissible evidence of the actual value at the time winding up commenced.'

break down if the subordinated creditor was insolvent. In order to overcome this perceived risk the commonest structure is that the subordinated creditor agrees to hold dividends, proceeds and other payments on the subordinated debt received by the subordinated creditor on trust for the preferred creditor as property of the preferred creditor and in satisfaction of the preferred creditor's debt until the preferred creditor is paid in full. This type of device, although providing a legal structure which meets the objective of subordination, has a practical weakness. Trusts, as the Maxwell pension funds have shown in stark relief, may have their funds misappropriated if the trust is held by unscrupulous or negligent persons. Where a company is veering to insolvency, there is a risk that the funds intentionally or negligently may be treated as funds of the company and thereby lost.

A recent case to consider debt subordination trusts was *Re British & Commonwealth Holdings plc (No 3)*[1]. In that case there was a summons for directions by administrators who proposed a scheme of arrangement under section 425 of the Companies Act 1985 to enable them to make an interim distribution of the proceeds of assets realised in the administration. The company had issued convertible subordinated unsecured loan stock ('CULS'). In terms of the issue of the loan stock contained in a trust deed, the debt of the holders of the loan stock was subordinated to the claims of all other creditors in the event of a winding up. The administrators sought directions as to whether they could exclude the subordinated creditors from the scheme, and the trustee representing them from voting at the meeting to approve the scheme. The administrators argued that because there was an estimated deficiency for creditors whose debts were not subordinated, the subordinated creditors had no interest in the company and accordingly no right to vote at a meeting convened to consider the scheme. The trustee for the subordinated creditors did not concede that the proceeds of realisation would inevitably be insufficient to meet the claims of the scheme creditors, and submitted that unless and until there was a winding up the trustee was a creditor and had the same rights as any other creditor. Alternatively, the trustee argued that the holders of CULS would not be subordinated creditors in relation to any entitlement interest on any surplus once the scheme creditors were paid in full.

In the course of his judgment Vinelott J detailed the main provisions of the scheme as follows:

'I must first say a little more about the terms of the trust deed. Clause 2 contains a covenant to pay to the trustee the principal moneys and premium (if any) owing on the CULS on 31 December 2000 and in the meantime interest at 7¾ per cent by half yearly payments. It also provides that payments to the holders of stock in respect of principal premium or interest are to be taken in satisfaction of the covenant with the trustee. That provision is, of course, permissive only and does not give the holders any right to call for payment.

Clause 5, which provides for subordination, I must read in full:

"(A) In the event of the winding up of the company the claims of the stockholders will be subordinated in right of payment to the claims of all other creditors of the company (other than subordinated creditors) and any amounts payable to and received by the trustee in respect of the stock will be received by the trustee on trust to apply the same:

(i) first, in payment or satisfaction of the costs, charges, expenses and liabilities incurred by and any unpaid remuneration of, the trustee;

---

1 [1992] BCC 58.

    (ii)    secondly, in payment of the claims of other creditors of the company (not being creditors who are, or are trustees for, subordinated creditors) to the extent that such claims are admitted to proof in the winding up and are not satisfied out of the other resources of the company; and

    (iii)    thirdly, as to the balance (if any) in or towards payment of the amounts owing on or in respect of the stock.

(B)    The trust secondly mentioned in subcl. (A) of this clause may be performed by the trustee paying over to the liquidator for the time being in the winding up of the company (the 'liquidator') the amounts received by the trustee as aforesaid (less any amounts thereof applied in the implementation of the trust first mentioned in subcl. (a) of this clause) on terms that the liquidator shall distribute the same accordingly and the receipt of the liquidator for the same shall be a good discharge to the trustee for the performance by it of the trust secondly mentioned in subcl. (A) of this clause.

(C)    The trustee shall be entitled and it is hereby authorised to call for and to accept as conclusive evidence thereof a certificate from the liquidator as to:

    (i)    the amount of the claims of the other creditors referred to in subcl. (A)(ii) of this clause (except as therein mentioned); and

    (ii)    the persons entitled thereto and their respective entitlements.

(D)    The trustee is entitled (to the exclusion of the stockholders) to take proceedings for the winding up of the company in the event of the stock becoming immediately due and repayable to recover amounts owing in respect of the stock but no other remedy shall be available to the trustee or the stockholders to recover such amounts."

Clause 10 gives the trustee power to determine that the CULS are immediately due and payable with accrued interest in specified events which include default in payment of principal and interest, the making of an order or the passing of a resolution for the winding up of the company or a subsidiary or the making of an administration order in relation to the company or a subsidiary. Notice has been duly given of a determination by the trustee.

Clause 12 provides that:

"The trustee shall (subject always to the provisions of cl. 5(A)) apply all monies received by it under these presents in respect of the stock at any time after the stock shall have become immediately due and repayable . . ."

—first, in paying its costs, charges, expenses and liabilities, and as to the residue towards payment of arrears of interest and then the principal and any premium due in respect of the stock. It is also provided that any payment to the stockholders is to be made *pari passu* in proportion to the amounts owing to them respectively.

Lastly clause 32 provides that:

"Each of the stockholders shall be entitled to sue for the performance and observance of the provisions of these presents so far as his stock is concerned save where the trustee has and exercises a discretion herein."'

He then concluded that the only way in which the sums due in respect of CULS could be enforced was by the presentation of a winding-up petition. He said further that the terms of the document of trust gave rise to issues of considerable complexity. He wondered whether, notwithstanding the decision of the House of Lords in *British Eagle International Airlines Ltd v Compagnie Nationale Air France* [1975] 1 WLR 758, clause 5(A) took effect as a contract by the trustee on behalf of the holders of CULS not to claim any payment towards satisfaction of the CULS until the other creditors had been paid in full, or whether clause 5(1) operated by imposing a trust on any payment received in the winding up of the company. He said the resolution of this difficult and complex question might take years of court time to resolve. He held, however, that the effect of clause 5(A)(ii) was subordination. He stated:

'The effect of clause 5(A)(ii) in my judgment is to subordinate the holders of CULS *to the claims* of other creditors, including claims to interest prior to winding up and admitted to proof or under section 189(2) in respect of claims admitted to proof; it would otherwise conflict with the opening words of clause 5(A) which provides that the claims of the holders of CULS are to be subordinated to "*the claims* of all other creditors of the company (other than subordinated creditors)".'

Finally he held that if the subordinated creditors had had an interest in the company and to the extent that their interest was affected in a way which did not affect the other creditors, then *prima facie* they would have constituted a separate class. In so far as they had no interest in the assets of the company (and the case had been argued on the footing that 'they do not stand to receive a share of the assets') and equally to the extent that any interest they may have had was unaffected by the scheme, then whether considered as a single or as a separate class, they had no right to object to it.

Although he resolved certain questions, Vinelott J could not, given the present state of English law, give a certain immediate ruling on the subordination device used in that case; which was 'state of the art'.

### Proposed reform of the English law on debt subordination

Because the devices described are complex, cumbersome and do not always achieve the type of debt subordination aimed for, the United Kingdom Review Committee on Insolvency Law and Practice advocated reform. They stated in 1982:

'. . . all unsecured debts must be paid *pari passu*. . . . It is therefore not open to a creditor to advance money on terms that the debt will be subordinated to other claims in the event of the borrower's insolvency . . . We can see no reason why a creditor who wishes to do so should not be permitted to subordinate his claim to those of all other creditors, or all other creditors except those of like degree. In this case the sophisticated conveyancing devices which have to be adopted to enable subordinated debt to be included will not be necessary. We therefore recommend the inclusion of an appropriate proviso to [the *pari passu* provisions] to allow effect to be given to subordination agreements.[1]'

Despite the recommendation that a provision similar to section 510(a) of the United States Bankruptcy Code of 1978 (which expressly makes subordination agreements enforceable) be introduced in England and Wales, this proposal was not adopted.

### Application of *pari passu* rule in Scotland

In Scotland a simple agreement between a creditor and a debtor company by which the creditor agrees that his debt will be subordinated to ordinary creditors' claims is legally valid. An undertaking to the debtor company that a secured creditor's debt will be subordinated to other secured creditors, is called by Bell 'preference by exclusion'. Bell states:

'Rights of exclusion have in themselves no character of a Real Right, but operate merely in the way of Prohibition or Exclusion against claims which otherwise would be entitled to a preference. . . . In consequence of a personal exception pleadable against a creditor, or against a class of creditors as competitors with others; or in consequence of a consent granted by one creditor to the preference of another – the order of preference, as it would stand according to the natural import and effect of the rival securities, may be altered.

1 *Report of the United Kingdom Review Committee on Insolvency Law and Practice* (1982) Cmnd 8558, paras 1448, 1449.

Exceptions pleadable to actions differ from objections in this, that the latter are in the nature of negations to the action; the former, positive allegiances which, admitting the action to be otherwise good, exclude, or as our authors express it, elide the action. In actions of competition, as ranking and sale, sequestration, or multiple poinding which are each a congeries of all the reciprocal actions necessary for determining on the rights and preferences of the competitors, effect is given to the several exceptions by which, on the one hand, the general body of creditors exclude a particular creditor, or by which individual creditors exclude each other . . .

2.    Sometimes the creditor related to the debtor, or particularly interested in him, gives an express consent to his having a preference over the consenter. This has the effect of a personal exception to exclude the consenter from entering into competition against the person in whose favour he has yielded his rights; but that right as against other creditors remains unimpaired, unless insofar as necessarily implied in the preference to which consent has been given. . . .

4.    The effect of personal exceptions can be available only to those entitled to take benefit by them, but not so as to injure in other respects the right of the creditor against whom they operate. . . .'[1]

This 'preference by exclusion' or 'negative pledge', operates also in relation to ordinary creditors subordinating their claims over unsecured estate to other ordinary creditors, although the cases do not refer to the term expressly. The leading Scottish cases on the subordination of an ordinary unsecured debt to claims of ordinary creditors are *Fair v Hunter*[2] and *MacKinnon's Trustees v Dunlop*[3]. In *MacKinnon's Trustees v Dunlop*, Lord President Dunedin categorised the status of this type of subordinated debt in Scots law and approved *Fair v Hunter*. He stated:

'Counsel for the respondents in a very able argument particularly appealed to the case of *Fair v Hunter*, in which it was held that an obligation to pay "as soon as I have it in my power" was a proper debt. Well, all depends on what one means by proper debt. The truth is, there are three forms of obligations in such matters. There is the form of an ordinary debt which you are bound to pay the moment that you are sued upon it. It is not suggested that there is such a debt here. Then, on the other hand, there is a form of *quasi*-obligation which is truly no obligation at all, which simply says, "I promise to pay if I like to pay"; and I agree with the learned counsel that the obligation here is not of that kind. But there is the third and intermediate case of which I think *Fair v Hunter* was an instance, in which a debtor may be bound in the sense that the obligation is good against him and yet it cannot come into competition with his ordinary and proper creditors, and that is just where the respondents' case fails, because there is no proper *jus crediti* which will destroy the father's power of disposal.

    The circumstances in *Fair's* case were that Mr Hunter had a son through whom Fair had lost money, and the father was very anxious to make up to Fair the money which his son had lost. He was not in a condition at the time to do so. He had not any ready money, his money being locked up in Australia, and he was a member of a firm of Writers to the Signet in Edinburgh under a contract of copartnery by which he had become bound not to enter into any obligation, and he therefore did not wish to transgress the terms of his own copartnery. He entered into negotiations with Fair, and they came to an agreement by which Fair remitted a certain considerable portion of the son's debt, and the father gave an obligation that he would pay the rest when he could. And the father wrote a letter in which he said: "I shall be most happy to pay to you, with interest, as soon as I have it in my power, by remittances from Australia or otherwise." (24 D at 5). The father died, and an executor was appointed who proceeded to realise the estate, and the action was brought by Fair for

---

1  Bell *Comm*, ii p 132.
2  (1861) 24 D 1 (2nd Division).
3  1913 SC 232.

constitution of the debt against the father's executor. The learned Judges held that it was a debt which could be constituted against the executry. But I think they clearly held that it was a debt of what I may call the intermediate kind, because the Lord Ordinary (Lord Kinloch), after giving his views, in which he said that this was not a mere promise which was no promise at all, namely, to pay if he chose, says this; "Whether or not the pursuer shall be entitled to rank on the executry funds in competition with other creditors of the deceased, is not as the Lord Ordinary thinks, now the question. Those creditors are not here. No question is or can be raised in this process with them. It will be for the pursuer to consider, when he has got his decree, what he will do with it; and for other creditors of the deceased, and for the defender, to consider what effect is due to it, as respects any ranking on the estate of the deceased."'

### In Scotland subordinated debt is not a 'contingent' debt

In light of the dicta of Lord Dunedin in *MacKinnon's Trustees* it is clear that the type of subordinated debt referred to in *Fair v Hunter* is a 'preference by exclusion'. It does not rank as an ordinary debt and compete with ordinary creditors[1]. What a creditor is saying is that 'my debt shall be subordinated to that of other creditors'. The Scottish position is therefore essentially that as enunciated by Southwell J in *Horne v Chester & Fein Property Developments Pty Ltd*[2]. It is therefore a true subordinated debt. The English device of structuring such a subordinated debt as a 'contingent' debt is rather irrational. When claims are valued in a bankruptcy or liquidation, it is irrational to value for the purposes of the bankruptcy or liquidation, a debt as having a nil or nominal value, (if it is otherwise a valid and payable debt) merely because the funds in the bankruptcy or liquidation are very unlikely to be sufficient to meet it. After all ordinary debts are not given a nil or nominal value on the basis that the secured creditors and preferential creditors are likely to exhaust the funds. Similarly postponed debts are valued at their face value. The internal availability of funds in a liquidation sufficient to meet a class of subordinated debts, is not a real contingency such as to make those debts 'contingent' debts. In Scotland there may be a serious risk if a subordinated debt agreement is constituted as a contingent debt arrangement. Liquidations leading to 'supervening solvency', are not uncommon viz. the liquidation of Rolls Royce. It is not certain that if a subordinated debt agreement were constituted as a contingent debt agreement in Scotland it would be simple to amend the valuation of the contingent debt at the later stage. Accordingly it is suggested that where the intention is to set up a subordinated debt agreement by which one creditor agrees to be subordinated to the general body of creditors, a clause along the following lines is agreed between the debtor company and the subordinated creditor:

'If the debtor company becomes subject to any liquidation, dissolution, rehabilitation or insolvency proceeding or to any arrangement or composition for the benefit of its creditors or any other distribution of its assets, or any analogous event occurs, the subordinated creditor will rank subordinate to and after the prior payment of ordinary debts.'

### Subordination in Scotland by assignations in security

Although in England, where the subordinated creditor wishes to give the preferred creditor the benefit of any dividend to which he may be entitled in a

1 Gloag on *Contract* (2nd edn, 1929), p 56.
2 (1987) 5 ACLC 245.

liquidation, a trust mechanism is sometimes used, this, as has been noted, has drawbacks. Although it is possible, where there is a trust, for there to be an independent trustee appointed (the international stock exchange in London requires the appointment of a trustee for domestic debt issues), there is no statutory requirement for a trustee. Accordingly trust monies may become intermingled with non-trust monies or misappropriated if the recipient of the dividends is also acting as trustee for a third party creditor. Secondly the courts in certain civilian countries have not received the trust or recognised equivalent instrument. Under certain régimes the trustee has been treated as the sole owner. Hence the beneficial ownership by the beneficiaries is simply not recognised and the beneficiaries are treated as having only a contractual right against the trustee, ie the beneficiary is treated as if he were in a creditor–debtor relationship with the trustee. Accordingly the beneficiaries are exposed to the insolvency of the trustee because other creditors of the trustee will have claims on the purported trust assets. This exposure has been partially overcome recently, but the situation is unsafe. The Hague Convention on the Law Applicable to Trusts and on their Recognition, implemented in Britain by the Recognition of Trusts Act 1987, meets the problem in relation to trusts in countries which are a party to the Convention. In terms of Article 8, in the contracting states the validity of a voluntary written trust, its construction, effects and administration will be governed by the governing law of the trust. This may be expressly chosen by the settlor. A trust created in accordance with that law is to be recognised as a trust in terms of Article 11. A third problem in relation to the trust device in Scotland is that there is not a developed law of 'equitable estates' as in England[1].

The most appropriate type of legal structure which is available in Scotland to achieve the purpose of having the preferred creditor receive the dividends of the subordinated creditor is a structure by which the subordinated creditor assigns his future dividends to the preferred creditor as security for an obligation undertaken by him in terms of which he is obliged to pay a sum equal to his dividends received to the preferred creditor. Such an agreement would usually limit the obligation to the extent of any shortfall on the preferred creditor's debt. The undertaking would also be limited to the amount of any dividends actually payable to the subordinated creditor. Finally it is advisable that the preferred creditor is given an irrevocable power of attorney by the subordinated creditor to lodge claims on behalf of the subordinated creditor in the event of the liquidation of the company. Only by that device can the preferred creditor force the subordinated creditor to lodge claims and hence make dividends payable which can be assigned in advance in security of the sums which may become payable. In Scotland it is open to a person in advance to assign future or contingent debts[2]. It is essential in Scotland that the assignation by the subordinated creditor to the preferred creditor of these future debts is intimated to the debtor company. This is best achieved by making the debtor company a party to the debt subordination agreement which includes the assignation in security. The following is the format for a common type of debt subordination agreement whereby a bank agrees to lend money to the subsidiary of a holding company, provided the holding company also puts money in as debt which is subordinated to the loan

1 See *Stair Memorial Encyclopaedia*: 'Trusts', vol 24, para 7 *et seq.*
2 *Flowerdew v Buchan* (1835) 13 S 615; *Carter v McIntosh* (1862) 24 D 925; *Allan & Son v Brown & Lightbody* (1890) 6 Sh Ct Rep 278; and Wilson on *Debt* (2nd edn) p 284.

of the bank, entitling the bank to any dividends payable to the subordinated creditor in the event of the liquidation of its subsidiary.

That debts 'assigned in security' by a company are not affected by its insolvency and are not attachable by others has recently been affirmed in England[1].

DEBT SUBORDINATION AGREEMENT between:

AB (Of the First Part), a company incorporated under the Companies Acts and having its registered office at _____ (hereinafter referred to as 'the Holding Company') and

CD (Of the Second Part) a company incorporated under the Companies Acts having its registered office at _____, a subsidiary of AB (hereinafter referred to as 'the Subsidiary') and

L Bank (Of the Third Part) a company incorporated under the Companies Acts and having its registered office at _____ (hereinafter referred to as 'the Lending Bank').

Whereas:
  (i)   The Holding Company and Lending Bank have agreed between themselves and with the Subsidiary that the Holding Company shall extend a loan ('the Loan') and the Lending Bank shall extend a loan facility ('the Facility') to the Subsidiary;

  (ii)  the Holding Company, the Lending Bank and the Subsidiary are agreed that the Lending Bank shall extend the Facility to the Subsidiary on condition that as between the Holding Company and the Lending Bank the Loan shall be subordinated (only so far as legally sufficient to effect the legal consequences of the subordination measures stipulated in paragraph (iii)) in any claim for sums payable under it against the Subsidiary in the event of the liquidation of the Subsidiary to sums payable to the Lending Bank in terms of the Facility;

  (iii) the Holding Company has agreed with the Lending Bank and the Subsidiary in order to effect the subordination referred to in (ii) above to undertake in the event of the liquidation of the Subsidiary to pay to the Lending Bank a sum equivalent to the amount of all sums due and payable to the Holding Company as a dividend in the liquidation of the Subsidiary to the extent of the difference between any dividends due and payable to the Lending Bank and the amount of any sums outstanding to the Lending Bank owed in terms of the Facility immediately before payment of said dividends (hereinafter referred to as 'the Undertaking');

  (iv)  the Holding Company is prepared to assign to the Lending Bank in security of the Undertaking any dividends payable to it in the event of the liquidation of the Subsidiary to the extent of the Undertaking; and

---

1 *Re Atlantic Computer Systems* [1991] BCLC 606 at 629.

(v)   the Holding Company has agreed to grant the Lending Bank a Power of Attorney on its behalf to lodge all claims in the liquidation of the Subsidiary for repayment of the Loan.

IT IS ACCORDINGLY AGREED AS FOLLOWS:

1.   The Holding Company and the Lending Bank have agreed with each other and with the Subsidiary and hereby agree that the Holding Company shall lend the Subsidiary the Loan of £X as fixed 7% 10-year loan stock and the Lending Bank shall extend to the Subsidiary the Facility in terms of which the Subsidiary may borrow sums from time to time over a period of 10 years not exceeding in aggregate £X.

2.   The Holding Company has agreed with the Lending Bank and the Subsidiary to undertake and hereby undertakes to pay to the Lending Bank in the event of the liquidation of the Subsidiary a sum equivalent to the amount of any dividends due and payable to the Holding Company out of the assets of the Subsidiary to the extent of the difference between dividends due and payable in the said liquidation to the Lending Bank and the amount of sums due and payable by the Subsidiary to the Lending Bank in terms of the Facility immediately before payment of said dividends if any ('the Undertaking').

3.   The Holding Company has agreed and hereby agrees with the Lending Bank and the Subsidiary to assign and hereby assigns to the Lending Bank in security of sums to be owed to the Lending Bank in terms of the Undertaking all dividends due and payable to the Holding Company from the Subsidiary in the event of the liquidation of the Subsidiary to the extent of the liability of the Holding Company in terms of the Undertaking.

4.   The Holding Company has agreed to grant and hereby grants the Lending Bank its Power of Attorney on its behalf to lodge claims in and prove in any liquidation of the Subsidiary for all sums owed under the Loan. The conditions of the Power of Attorney are contained in the First Schedule to this Debt Subordination Agreement.

IN RESPECT WHEREOF

# Chapter 15

# Set-off

## Introduction

It is not within the scope of this work to give a detailed analysis of the general working of set-off. Good descriptions are to be found in Gloag on *Contract*, pages 626, 644–654; Wilson on *Debt*, Chapter 13 and McBryde on *Contract*, pages 531–540. An analysis will be attempted of the peculiar problems of set-off in insolvency. Like many other aspects of insolvency law, the courts have not always interpreted set-off in a clear and consistent manner.

### Definition of set-off

Although set-off or 'compensation' existed at common law[1], the law of set-off is for most purposes contained in the Compensation Act 1592. The effect of set-off is that one debt extinguishes another. The essential features of set-off under the Compensation Act are as follows:

(1)  *Liquid debts only*

Debts must be both liquid or capable of immediate liquidation. A debt is liquid when it is actually due and the amount ascertained, unless the counterclaim can immediately be made liquid[2]. The dispute of a claim makes it illiquid, while an admission of a claim may make it liquid[3].

(2)  *Debts due at the same time*

Both debts must be due at the same time. A debt which is presently due may not be set off against a future debt or a contingent debt[4].

(3)  *Concursus debiti et crediti*

Each party must be debtor and creditor in the same capacity. A sum due to the defender as an executor may not be set off against a sum due to him personally[5].

---

1  See McBryde on *Contract*, para 22–24.
2  *Munro v MacDonald's Exrs* (1866) 4 M 687; *Niven v Clyde Fasteners Ltd* 1986 SLT 344.
3  *Hamilton v Wright* (1839) 2 D 86; *Thoms v Thoms* (1868) 6 M 704; *Scottish NERy Co v Napier* (1859) 21 D 700.
4  Bell, *Comm*, ii, 122; *Paul and Thain v Royal Bank* (1869) 7 M 361.
5  *Stuart v Stuart* (1869) 7 M 366.

## (4)   *Set-off must be pled*

Set-off does not operate *ipso jure*. Set-off must be both pled and sustained by judgment before it has effect, unless there is an agreement to set off[1]. If set-off is allowed, it has a retrospective effect with the result that interest may not be due on a debt after the date of concursus, even if one of the debts at that time was illiquid[2]. Not only must set-off be pled, it must be pled before decree is passed against a debtor.

## (5)   *Debts of the same nature*

The debts must be of the same nature. A money debt can be pleaded against a money debt. A demand for delivery of goods may be set off against a claim for similar goods, but a money debt may not be set off against a claim for delivery of goods[3]. If money is deposited and appropriated to a particular purpose, it cannot be set off against a separate debt due by the depositor[4].

## Balancing of accounts in bankruptcy

The statutory rules about set-off do not apply to insolvency. Rather the ordinary common law rules about set-off are widened so that:

## (1)   *Liquid and illiquid claims*

When one of the parties is insolvent, an illiquid claim may be set-off against a liquid claim[5].

## (2)   *Debts not of the same nature*

When one of the parties is insolvent, set-off may be pleaded by the debtor to an insolvent company although the two claims are not of the same nature. For example a claim for debt may be set off against a claim for delivery of goods[6].

## (3)   *Debts due at different times*

The party who is sued on a claim which he admits to being payable may put forward in defence claims which are not yet due which involve only a contingent liability or which are disputed and require to be established by proof[7].

---

1 *Cowan v Gowans* (1878) 5 R 581.
2 *Inch v Lee* (1903) 11 SLT 374.
3 Bell, *Comm*, ii, 122.
4 *Mycroft Petr* 1983 SLT 342.
5 Bell, *Comm*, ii, 122; *Scott's Tr v Scott* (1887) 14 R 1043 at 1051, per Lord President Inglis; *Clydesdale Bank Ltd v Gardiner* (1906) 14 SLT 121.
6 Bell, *Comm*, ii, 122.
7 Ibid; *Mill v Paul* (1825) 4 S 219; *Hannay & Sons, Tr v Armstrong Bros* (1875) 2 R 399; *Borthwick v Scottish Widows Fund* (1864) 2 M 595.

## (4)    *Concursus debiti et crediti*

The debtor and the creditor must be in the same capacity[1].

### Bankruptcy, liquidation, receivership, administration

### (1)    *Bankruptcy and liquidation*

The case law in relation to the 'balancing of accounts in bankruptcy', which is the name given by Bell to the equitable right of retention or species of set-off available on insolvency, was developed in relation to the bankruptcy of individuals. Similar rules have been applied in the liquidation of companies[2]. The key fact which triggers the equitable right is the insolvency of the debtor. Liquidation, sequestration or a trust deed for creditors are equivalent to 'bankruptcy[3]'.

Attempts have been made to extend the equitable right of retention to cases of 'near insolvency' but there would seem to be need of averments that the company is in financial difficulties and facing insolvency[4]. The Scottish law in this field is not statutory (whether this is an equitable right of retention or species of set-off available on insolvency is important where there is an international dimension to the insolvency)[5]. Most jurisdictions have some form of set-off in this sort of situation. The jurisdictions in favour of insolvency set-off are the United States jurisdictions (except perhaps Louisiana), most, if not all, of the English-based jurisdictions, including Australia, New Zealand, Canada (including Quebec, where set-off is allowed by virtue of the Federal bankruptcy legislation which is overriding), Bahamas, Bermuda, the Cayman Islands, Hong Kong, India, Pakistan, Singapore, Zambia. Set-off on insolvency is also allowed in the Germanic and Scandinavian jurisdictions; in particular it is allowed in Austria (KO Article 19), Germany, Finland, Denmark, Japan, Korea, Netherlands, Norway, Sri Lanka and Switzerland. It has been allowed in Italy since 1942 and, it is also allowed in Panama. China has enacted a bankruptcy law relating to enterprises which includes an insolvency set-off clause in terms of Article 33, although this is of limited application. Jurisdictions not allowing this species of set-off are France, Belgium, Egypt, Greece, Luxembourg, Spain, Chile, Brazil, Argentina, Columbia and South Africa[6]. It is important to note that none of the provisions in these jurisdictions whether under statute or at common law is totally equivalent. They are also subject to constant change. The Scottish courts will recognise set-off in certain insolvency situations where there is an international element (see page 399). This list should not be relied on except to give an initial impression. Liquidators must carefully check the position with a relevant jurisdiction before any decision whether to allow or disallow set-off is made.

---

1 *Cauvin v Robertson* (1773) Mor 2581; *Taylor's Tr v Paul* (1888) 15 R 313.
2 *Atlantic Engine Co (1920) Ltd v Lord Advocate* 1955 SLT 17.
3 *G and A (Hotels) Ltd v THB Marketing Services Ltd* 1983 SLT 497; *Liquidators of Highland Engineering Ltd v Thomson* 1972 SC 87.
4 *Busby Spinning Co Ltd v BMK Ltd* 1988 SLT 246.
5 See p 399.
6 See Philip Wood, *English and International Set-off* 1989.

In the case of *G & A (Hotels) Ltd v T H B Marketing Services Ltd*[1], it was suggested by Lord Cowie, relying on *dicta* of Lord Fraser in the case of *Liquidators of Highland Engineering Ltd v Thomson*[2] that the right of retention was available in any liquidation and it was not necessary to aver that there was insolvency. Lord Cowie stated:

'This submission was based on the statement in Gloag on *Contract* at p 626 which is in the following terms: "The rule that a demand for a liquid debt is not relevantly met by a defence founded on an illiquid or unascertained claim does not hold where the pursuer is bankrupt or where it is averred that he is insolvent". Counsel for the pursuers founded strongly on the words "where it is averred that he is insolvent", and argued that unless that was done, the exception did not apply, and the general rule must be enforced. I must confess that I was impressed by this argument since it seemed to me that it was for the defenders to bring themselves within the exception if they were going to found on it. Moreover it was explained to me by counsel for the pursuers that there was no question in the present case of the pursuers not being able to pay their debts in full. In these circumstances had it not been for an observation by Lord Fraser in the case of *Liquidators of Highland Engineering Ltd v Thomson* 1972 SC 87 at p 91, I would have been inclined to give effect to this argument by counsel for the pursuers. The observation of Lord Fraser to which I refer comes in a passage where he is dealing with the general rule that retention or set-off cannot be pleaded unless both debts are liquid, but is pointing out that the general rule does not hold as to the balancing of accounts in bankruptcy. He then goes on: "In the present case the respondents are debtors in a liquid debt, while their claim for remuneration is still illiquid, but as the matter arises in a liquidation (which for present purposes, I think is equivalent to bankruptcy) no difficulty arises on that account".

In my opinion what Lord Fraser is saying in that passage, is that for the purposes of the exception to the general rule governing liquid and illiquid debts a liquidation is the equivalent of bankruptcy. If that is right then provided it is clear that the first pursuers are in liquidation it is not in my opinion necessary to aver that they are insolvent. It is perhaps of interest to note that in that case as in the present, Lord Fraser was informed that the company, although in members' voluntary liquidation, had an estimated surplus. I am not of course bound by the authority of Lord Fraser even assuming that I have interpreted his words correctly, but I would be slow to dissent from a judge of such eminence in the field of company law, and accordingly I have come to the conclusion that it is not necessary to make the specific averment of insolvency which counsel for the pursuers says the defenders must make to bring themselves within the exception, and I accordingly reject this submission also.'

It is thought that Lord Cowie did not properly understand the *dicta* of Lord Fraser. In the case of the *Liquidators of Highland Engineering v Thomson*[3] there indeed was a members' voluntary winding-up. Howeover there had been a petition for compulsory winding up and the company had been put into provisional compulsory winding up on a creditor's petition ie provisional insolvent winding up. The provisional liquidator was claiming the right of retention in relation to sums owed to him as remuneration as provisional liquidator. The winding-up order as sought was eventually refused, but the set-off period was the period of the provisional compulsory winding-up. Indeed the company was still in provisional winding up when Lord Fraser held that set-off was open. It was only after allowing set-off that he moved on to deal with whether he should grant the petition. Accordingly it is thought

1 *Supra.*
2 *Supra.*
3 *Supra.*

that when he stated 'a liquidation (which for present purposes, I think is equivalent to bankruptcy)' he was referring to the specific circumstances of that case. It is thought that Gloag is right and that there has to be insolvency. The widening of the rules of set-off occurs in many countries, but only in the event of insolvency (see page 318). Of course it may emerge that there is a supervening solvency, but the general principle would be that there had to be some form of finding of insolvency to start with. In the case of a provisional compulsory winding up, the Lord Ordinary would have had to be satisfied that there was a *prima facie* case on the creditor's petition for the compulsory winding-up order. Not only is there no previous suggestion in the authorities that there could be balancing of accounts in a non-insolvent liquidation, but Gloag states that it has to be averred that there is insolvency. Because the rights of retention in the balancing of accounts in bankruptcy are open both to the trustee and creditors, the extending of these rights to voluntary liquidations would open the way to persons voluntarily reconstructing companies in order to obtain the wider rights of retention if it suited them. It is not clear that these arguments were put to Lord Cowie. He says that Lord Fraser was informed that the company, although in members' voluntary liquidation, had an estimated surplus. This suggests that a clear picture was not given to Lord Cowie in argument because a members' voluntary liquidation requires an estimated surplus. It is hoped that in the near future the Inner House will clarify the position in relation to these cases.

## (2)   *Receivership*

In relation to receivership, it was suggested by Lord Ross in the case of *Taylor, Petitioner*[1] that the rules of insolvency do not apply in receivership. He stated:

'In these circumstances, it does not appear to me . . . that receivership is so similar to bankruptcy or liquidation that the principles of law applicable to insolvency should be applied. Furthermore I am not satisfied that compensation should be disallowed for reasons of equity or public policy. The normal rules of compensation are plain (Gloag on *Contract* (2nd edn), pp 644–645). I see no ground for introducing into the law any fresh exception based on alleged public policy. There may well be reasons for certain exceptions in the case of bankruptcy or insolvency, but I see no ground for extending them to cases of receivership. As already pointed out, receivership is different to liquidation or bankruptcy, and there is no reason why the same rules should apply to these different situations.'[1]

However, in the subsequent case of *McPhail v Cunninghame District Council; William Louden & Son Ltd v Cunninghame District Council*[2], Lord Kincraig accepted that the wider rules of set-off were available if the company was insolvent. He stated:

'It is no objection to the right of set-off that the defenders' claim arises under a different contract from that out of which the debt to the pursuer arises. See Gloag on *Contract*, p 626. Here the defenders allege that the company was insolvent on 26 February 1975 and the principle stated in Gloag therefore applies.'

1  1982 SLT 171 at 172.
2  1985 SLT 149 at 152.

The principle quoted in Gloag was that enunciated by Lord McLaren in *Ross v Ross*[1], where he stated:

'The doctrine [of retention] has received much extension in cases of bankruptcy and insolvency, where it is practically settled that anyone who has a claim against an insolvent estate is entitled to keep back money which he owes to the estate, and cannot be compelled to pay in full while he only receives a dividend.'

Receivership does not itself entail insolvency. In terms of certain debentures, a receiver may be appointed if certain capital ratios are breached or where events of default not connected with solvency occur. Accordingly, receivership itself may not be relied on to invoke the wider rules of set-off. However it is suggested that they may be invoked if insolvency accompanies the receivership.

### (3) *Administrations*

It has not yet been judicially determined whether administration *per se* amounts to insolvency. In terms of section 245(5) of the Insolvency Act 1986, administration is defined as the onset of insolvency. An administration order is granted in terms of section 8(1) of the Insolvency Act 1986 only if the court is satisfied that a company is or is likely to become unable to pay its debts. If a trust deed for creditors is equivalent to 'bankruptcy', it is suggested that a voluntary arrangement involving remission of debts would also entail insolvency. If administration is just meant to be a more efficient method of gathering in assets prior to liquidation it will involve insolvency. It is thought therefore that, except in very exceptional circumstances, an administration order will be equivalent to insolvency.

### Debts prior to and post-insolvency

Although presently payable debts may be set off against unascertained and contingent debts, the obligations must exist at the date of insolvency. The presently payable debt may not be set off against an obligation incurred after the date of the insolvency. In *Asphaltic Limestone Co v Corporation of Glasgow*[2], the company, at the date of its liquidation, had two separate contracts with the corporation. One of these the liquidator declined to carry out. The other he implemented, and thereby acquired a claim for the contract price. The contention of the corporation that they were entitled to retain that price in security of their claim of damages for breach of the other contract was repelled on the ground that the damages were due by the company and the price was due to the liquidator, and that there could be no retention or compensation between a debt due before bankruptcy and a debt arising thereafter. Lord McLaren observed that the argument of the corporation in favour of set-off was:

'founded on a complete misapprehension of the principle of retention in cases of bankruptcy or insolvency. In such cases, if the insolvent estate has a liquid claim against a solvent debtor, who again has a liquid claim against the insolvent estate, the principle of

1  (1885) 22 R 461 at 465.
2  1907 SC 463.

compensation is applied exactly as it would be if both parties were solvent. But if the claim of the solvent party is not liquid, e g, if the work has been done, but the time of payment has not arrived, then by an equitable extension of the principle of compensation he is allowed to retain the money which he owes against his claim on the insolvent estate, so that he may not suffer the injustice of having to pay his debt in full while only receiving a dividend on his own claim. But this principle of bankruptcy law presupposes reciprocal obligations which are both existing at the time of the declaration of insolvency, although only one of them is, it may be, immediately exigible. It has no application to the case of a new obligation arising after bankruptcy or declaration of insolvency when the rights of the parties are irrevocably fixed.'

The situation in *Asphaltic Limestone Co Ltd* was reasonably straight-forward. There was clearly a wholly new post-liquidation obligation on behalf of Glasgow Corporation to the company in liquidation. It will often be difficult to determine, where a claim arises after liquidation, whether the claim arose from obligations existing prior to the liquidation. For example, in the case of *Myles J Callaghan Ltd (in Receivership) v City of Glasgow District Council*[1], Lord Prosser held that a claim by a contractor for return of plant, which could be claimed only at the end of a contract which terminated after liquidation, could be set off against a claim by the employer for breach of contract occasioned by the contractor's going into receivership prior to liquidation. The use by the employer of the contractor's property was subject to rights vesting in the owners pending the date for return. Accordingly the claim for return, although it only became exigible after liquidation, had existed in the requisite sense prior to liquidation.

Lord McLaren in *Asphaltic Limestone Co* referred to 'declaration of insolvency'. It is not clear what precisely a 'declaration of insolvency' is. In England in *Eros Films Ltd*[2] the court held that the giving of notice of a meeting for a creditors' voluntary winding up was analogous to the filing, by an individual, of a declaration of inability to pay debts. It is thought that 'apparent insolvency' as defined by section 7 of the Bankruptcy (Scotland) Act 1985 would constitute a declaration of insolvency.

### Debts incurred after insolvency

A debt which arises after insolvency may be set off against another debt which also arises after insolvency[3].

### Peculiar problems on receivership

*Forth and Clyde Case*

The effect of the crystallisation of a floating charge on debts owed to a company was clarified in the case of *Forth and Clyde Construction Co Ltd v Trinity Timber & Plywood Co Ltd*[4] by the First Division of the Scottish appeal court. The court examined the meaning of sections 13(7) and 31(1) of the

1 1988 SLT 227.
2 [1963] Ch 565.
3 *Liqrs of Highland Engineering v Thomson* 1972 SC 87.
4 1984 SLT 94.

Companies (Floating Charges and Receivers) (Scotland) Act 1972[1] which read:

'13. – . . . (7) On the appointment of a receiver under this section, the floating charge by virtue of which he was appointed shall, subject to sections 106A and 322 of the Act of 1948, attach to the property then subject to the charge; and such attachment shall have effect as if the charge were a fixed security over the property to which it has attached.'

'31. – (1) In this Act, unless the context otherwise requires, the following expressions shall have the following meanings respectively assigned to them, that is to say – "Act of 1948" means the Companies Act 1948; . . . "fixed security", in relation to any property of a company, means any security, other than a floating charge or a charge having the nature of a floating charge, which on the winding up of the company in Scotland would be treated as an effective security over that property, and (without prejudice to that generality) includes a security over that property, being a heritable security within the meaning of section 9(8) of the Conveyancing and Feudal Reform (Scotland) Act 1970; "floating charge" has the meaning assigned to it by section 1 of this Act; . . . "receiver" means a receiver of such part of the property of the company as is subject to the floating charge by virtue of which he has been appointed under section 11 of this Act.'

The court held that the only type of 'effective security' in relation to book debts was an assignation in security, duly intimated to the debtor. Lord Emslie stated:

'It is, of course, the case that the Act has not expressly provided that book debts shall be regarded as having been assigned in security to the holder of the floating charge on the date upon which it attaches to them but the language of s 13(7) makes it quite clear that the attachment is to have effect "as if" such an assignation in security had been granted and intimated by the company. From the date of the appointment of a receiver, the company, no doubt, retains the title to demand payment of the debt but no longer for its own behoof. The interest in the recovery of the debt is that of the holder of the floating charge, and a receiver who seeks recovery in the name of the company does so in order to secure the application of the recovered sum towards satisfaction of the company's debt due to the creditor in the floating charge.'

*Set-off to be pled against an assignee*

When a debt is assigned, the debtor may plead against the assignee a debt owed by the cedent provided that there was *concursus debiti et crediti* before the assignation was completed by intimation[2]. If however a debt is assigned, and the assignation intimated before the counter debt arises, there is no set-off. According to Bell, 'the right to compensate passes against assignees if once vested against the cedent by a proper concourse before assignation. But if a debt be assigned, and the assignation intimated before the counter debt arises, the concourse is prevented, and there is no compensation'[3]. Thus if a debtor has a claim against a company, and the company has assigned a counterclaim to a third party, then the debtor may plead set-off against the assignee provided that the right of set-off existed prior to the assignation duly intimated. Where a debtor acquires debts by purchase from other parties after the insolvency of a company, these debts may not be set off against any claims

---

1 1988 SLT 227.
2 Bell, *Comm*, ii, 131; *Shiells v Fergusson, Davidson & Co* (1876) 4 R 250; *Taylor, Petr*, 1982 SLT 172 at 177, per Lord Ross.
3 Bell, *Comm*, i, 138.

against the debtor assigned to a third party prior to insolvency, because the acquired debts would be post-insolvency debts.

### Implications of Forth and Clyde case for set-off

Given that a receiver is to be treated, following the decision in the *Forth and Clyde* case[1], as if he were an assignee of any debts due to a company, and given that the ordinary principles of set-off entail that the receiver, as assignee, is subject to all pre-existing pleas of set-off pleadable against the cedent (the company) but is not subject to any such pleas manufactured by post-receivership purchase of creditors' claims against the company, it might be thought that the law was clear. Provided that receivership could be shown to be accompanied by insolvency[2] no problem would arise.

### Difficulties in case law in relation to set-off in receivership

The problem in the case law arises especially out of three cases, *McPhail v Lothian Regional Council*[3] ('the *Lothian Region* case'), *Taylor, Petitioner*[4], ('the *Typesetting* case') and *Myles J Callaghan Ltd (in Receivership) v City of Glasgow District Council*[5] ('the *Myles Callaghan* case'). The first two cases were decided before the decision in the *Forth and Clyde* case and in particular before that case explained how the fixed security enforced by a receiver could be reconciled with the retention by a company of legal title to its assets such as its book debts. In the *Lothian Region* case, a debt owed to a company, which had granted an all-assets floating charge, was owed by a debtor who was, at the date of attachment, also a creditor of the company. When the receiver of the company raised an action against the debtor in his own name for payment of the debt, it was argued: (1) that the debt should be set off against the debtor's counterclaim as creditor; and (2) that the receiver could have no title to sue in his own name for what was due to the company.

Lord Grieve dealt with the set-off argument on the basis that whether the receiver had a right to receive the charged debt free of a plea of set-off depended on whether the receiver took action in his own name or in that of the company. If he took action in his own name, set-off would not be available because mutuality would not exist, whereas if he took action in the name of the company, set-off could be pled. This distinction is now irrelevant in the light of the analysis given in the *Forth and Clyde* case of how a debt due to a company becomes, on crystallisation, due to the company for behoof of the floating charge creditor.

In the *Typesetting* case, Lord Ross proceeded on the basis that a receiver could not be treated as having the rights of an assignee of a company debt unless and until he obtained an actual assignation of the debt. On that basis, he decided that a debtor owing a charged debt could defeat a receiver's claim thereto by purchasing from other creditors a claim against the company in receivership and setting that claim off against the charged debt. Lord Ross

1 *Forth and Clyde Construction Co Ltd v Trinity Timber and Plywood Co Ltd* 1984 SLT 94.
2 See pp 320–321.
3 1981 SC 119.
4 1982 SLT 172.
5 1988 SLT 227.

also stated, as referred to above, that receivership was different from liquidation or bankruptcy and rejected the idea that the rules relating to the balancing of accounts in bankruptcy should apply.

In the *Myles Callaghan* case, Lord Prosser: (1) followed Lord Ross by agreeing that the company should sue in its own name for a debt after crystallisation of a floating charge[1]; (2) held that, although the attachment of a floating charge 'has effect as if the charge was a fixed security over the property to which it has attached', this did not imply that one must imagine some actual assignation with all the effects that that assignation would have upon title. The statutory provision was concerned with the effect of a security as a security. Title remained in the company (as it would not on assignation and intimation) but all the security effects of an assignation in security were to be regarded as available to the receiver; (3) held that the receiver, having acquired the company's interest in a *jus crediti* (right to payment of a debt) for security purposes, did not acquire any right when suing in the company's name to deny the ordinary defences available to third parties against the company.

In the case of *McPhail v Cunninghame District Council* and *William Louden & Son Ltd v Cunninghame District Council* ('the *Louden* case')[2], which preceded the *Forth and Clyde* case, Lord Kincraig took the view that the appointment of a receiver operated as an intimated assignation of the company's right to recover a debt due to the company and this right was subject to all the defences which could be pled against the cedent, i e the company, and if the company could be met successfully with a plea of set-off, the receiver's right must also be subject to the same set-off.

### Effect of differences in case law

The different approaches taken by Lord Kincraig and Lord Prosser in the *Louden* and *Myles Callaghan* cases have no real difference in effect, as was acknowledged by Lord Prosser[3]. The Scottish Law Commission, in their Consultative Memorandum No 72 on 'Floating Charges and Receivers' in October 1986, prior to Lord Prosser's judgment in the *Myles Callaghan* case, took the view that the route followed by Lord Kincraig in the *Louden* case was the correct approach, namely that the receiver was to be treated as an assignee subject to all pre-existing pleas of set-off pleadable against the cedent (the company). The Scottish Law Commission, however, suggested that the rule arrived at by Lord Kincraig and Lord Prosser be put into statutory form because of confusion in the past. Their working party suggested the following formulation:

'The powers of a receiver to take possession of and realise the property of a company attached by a floating charge shall have effect subject to any rights of compensation or retention which have arisen prior to the attachment of the floating charge, but shall prevail over any such rights which may arise after such attachment.'

---

1 It is thought by the authors that a receiver may sue either in his own name under para 1 of Sch 2 or in the name of the company under para 5. The wording of para 1 seems conclusively to indicate this, as debts owed to the company are clearly its incorporeal moveable property. For this purpose no distinction can be drawn between actions to recover property and actions to recover debts.
2 1985 SLT 149.
3 *Myles J Callaghan Ltd (in Receivership) v City of Glasgow District Council* 1988 SLT 227.

This formulation puts into statutory form the effect of Lord Prosser's and Lord Kincraig's judgments in so far as set-off is available against a receiver. However, it entails that rights which arise after the attachment of a floating charge may not be pled against debts owed to a company prior to the attachment of the floating charge.

It is thought that the Scottish Law Commission is correct in following Lord Kincraig in the *Louden* case where he held that receivership accompanied by insolvency opened the door to the general rules about the balancing of accounts in bankruptcy.

### Set-off excluded by agreement

It is thought that in Scotland a party may by agreement exclude his right to claim a right of retention in the balancing of accounts in bankruptcy, as well as a right of compensation generally[1]. By contrast in England, set-off in insolvency, although procedural in the sense that it is part of the process of proof and requires the taking of an account, has been held to be mandatory by the House of Lords[2]. In England the parties may not exclude the statutory provisions by contract and these override any prior agreement between the parties to keep the accounts separate. These statutory provisions in England are considered to regulate matters of public interest in the orderly administration of insolvent estates and are not purely a source of private rights enacted for the benefit of individual debtors of the estate having cross-claims against it. The ruling in the *Halesowen* case prevents pre-bankruptcy waiving by creditors of their rights and would appear to render unenforceable agreements thereby to subordinate unsecured debt on insolvency (see chapter 14). In contrast in Scotland the right of retention has to be pled. It is therefore a private right and it is open to the parties to agree not to enforce such a right in the event of insolvency.

### Proof of the claim giving rise to the right in the insolvency

It is thought that because in Scotland the right of retention has to be pled and is, as it were, a defence to the action of a company for debt, the claim giving rise to the right does not have to be lodged in the liquidation. This has important implications. Generally in a liquidation a creditor is entitled to claim only the accumulated sum of principal and any interest which is due on the debt as at the date of the commencement of the winding up[3], although where there is a surplus remaining after payment of the debts of a company proved in a winding up, the surplus is by statute now applied to paying interest on those debts in respect of the periods during which they have been outstanding since the company went into liquidation[4]. This means that interest running on any debt from the date of the commencement of the winding up is subordinated to all claims apart from those of shareholders in terms of section 189 of the Insolvency Act 1986. Because, however, the defence of set-off may fail if the debt being pled is a post-insolvency debt

---

1 See McBryde *Contract*, p 540.
2 *National Westminster Bank Ltd v Halesowen Presswork & Assemblies Ltd* [1972] AC 785.
3 Bankruptcy (Scotland) Act 1985, Sch 1, para 1(1) as applied to liquidations by Insolvency (Scotland) Rules 1986, r 4.16(1).
4 Insolvency Act 1986, s 189(2).

being claimed against a pre-insolvency debt[1], it is important that the creditor also has a claim lodged in the liquidation. Although there is a provision in terms of section 52(9) of the Bankruptcy (Scotland) Act 1985 (as applied to liquidations by Insolvency (Scotland) Rules 1986, r 4.68(1)), for the late lodging of claims, this is not allowed to upset dividends already paid out (see pages 290–291). It is suggested, therefore, where there is any doubt as to whether the plea of a right of retention will succeed, there should also be a claim lodged in the liquidation. Because however, it is thought, the two could not be run simultaneously, the claim should be a contingent claim subject to the plea of the right of retention not being upheld. The liquidator will then be forced into a position of making a full provision for the claim so that there will be funds to meet its entitled *pro rata* payment, in the event that the contingent claim is upvalued on the plea of retention not succeeding.

*Secured creditors and preferential creditors*

A secured creditor is in a different position. He does not need to enter the liquidation process at all, but may merely enforce his security. If he proves in the liquidation he is entitled to the principal plus interest to the date of payment[2]. If he proves in the liquidation he ranks only for non-secured debt (see pages 292–293). In England because set-off on insolvency is mandatory on debts proved in a liquidation, the secured creditor opens himself to a plea of set-off if he proves for the secured debt in the liquidation[3]. It is thought that in England if a secured debtor with also unsecured debt proves both debts in a liquidation, he runs the risk, given the mandatory set-off rules, that the liquidator could have set-off against the secured debt unsecured debt of the company leaving the creditor to rank for his unsecured debt. In terms of rule 4.66(6) of the Insolvency (Scotland) Rules 1986, the order of priority in a liquidation must not affect the right of a secured creditor which is preferable to the rights of the liquidator. The secured creditors may redeem their securities without reference to the liquidator or the liquidator may require them to discharge their securities by payment to them of the value of their securities[4]. It is thought that, because the secured element in the debt, is not even classed as a claim, it will not be open to the liquidator to plead the right of retention against the secured debt to the prejudice of the secured creditor. It is thought that this argument would not apply in relation to a creditor who was both a preferential creditor and an ordinary creditor. In terms of section 248(b) of the Insolvency Act 1986 a 'security is widely defined to include 'any security (whether heritable or moveable), any floating charge and any right of lien or preference and any right of retention (other than a right of compensation or set-off)'. It may be argued that preference here would include a preferential creditor. However it is difficult to see how the rights of a preferential creditor could be superior to the rights of a liquidator for his remuneration in the same way as a secured creditor having a lien or a standard security, had superior rights. It is also not a 'preference over property', and thought therefore not relevant. In the English case of *Re Unit 2 Windows Ltd*[5], which

1 In the case of *Myles J Callaghan Ltd (in receivership) v City of Glasgow District Council* 1988 SLT 227 on slightly different facts that type of situation could have arisen.
2 *National Commercial Bank of Scotland v Liquidators of Telford Grier McKay & Co* 1969 SC 181.
3 *Re Norman Holding Co Ltd* [1990] 3 All ER 757.
4 Bankruptcy (Scotland) Act 1985, Sch 1, para 5(2) as applied to liquidations by Insolvency (Scotland) Rules 1986, r 4.16(1).
5 [1986] BCLC 31.

preceded the Insolvency Act 1986, the court addressed itself to this sort of problem under the English legislation. Walton J admitted that the case raised an austere point of law. He referred to a 'fasciculus' of sections in the Companies Act which were not all that helpful. He thought that there was almost nothing to go on and held that set-off should be apportioned rateably between preferential debts and non-preferential debts. It is thought that that case is not helpful. Walton J acknowledged that his solution was a novel solution. He did not follow a previous case of *Re E J Morel (1934) Ltd*[1], in which Buckley J took a different and, it is thought, correct approach. He stated:

'On the one hand, counsel for the liquidator says that when the statutory set-off has been carried out, all the components have lost their identity, and the resulting balance cannot be said to consist either wholly or to any ascertainable extent of a debt which qualifies for preference, unless the credit which is to be set off against the debt is less than the debt in respect of advances for wages, in which case manifestly some part of the advance for wages must remain unsatisfied. He says that in those circumstances the person who is claiming preference cannot establish his claim to preference, because he cannot identify the character of any part of the resulting balance. In my view, the right solution for this problem is to treat the balance which results from the set-off as being non-preferential except to the extent that it can be demonstrated that the credit is insufficient to discharge the preferential claim in full. The result of a set-off is to give the creditor payment in full of his claim to the extent of the set-off, and in that way he is better off than creditors who merely have to rely on their right to prove and get a dividend. If he obtains, by set-off, payment in full, it seems reasonable that that payment in full should be treated as being in respect of that part of his debt which would rank first in priority. Moreover, the fact that if the preferential claim exceeds the amount of the credit to be set-off against it, there would be some part of the preferential claim which demonstrably had not been paid off, and could still claim preference, is a circumstance that seems to demonstrate that my method of approaching the solution is the right one.'

Because in a 'balancing of accounts in bankruptcy' the accounts of the different parties are run together and set-off may be pled against any other debt, it is thought by the authors that a trustee in bankruptcy or liquidator could plead in defence to a claim which happened to carry the preferential status, any counter debt.

## Subordinated debt

A separate question arises where the liquidator owes subordinated debt, ie the subordinated creditor is not entitled to payment except from a surplus after ordinary creditors have been paid in full. The question is whether the subordinated creditor is entitled to set off his subordinated claim against an ordinary claim or, if he is in liquidation, a preferential claim. Although it is thought that an ordinary creditor can set off his claim against a preferential claim or an ordinary claim and may choose to set off first against the preferential claim, a subordinated creditor is in a different position. He is not entitled to participate in the assets of a company until all debts preferential and ordinary are paid off. The position seems to the authors to be analogous to that of a contributory who is also a creditor of the company. In the leading case of *Cowan v Gowans*[2], the Inner House reviewed the English cases, which are still the main authorities, and held that set-off was not admissible in that type of relationship. It stated:

1 [1961] 1 All ER 796, [1962] Ch 21.
2 (1878) 5 R 581.

'The name of Mr Gowans appears in the list of contributories made up by the liquidator as owner of 720 shares. The total amount of the calls payable on these shares is £7,200. . . . Mr Gowans objects to be put on the list of contributories on the ground that he is a creditor of the company for work done under his contract to a larger amount than the calls said to be due. In other words, he pleads compensation, founding upon the debts due by the company to him for the purpose of extinguishing the debt due by him for calls to the company. Now, one thing is clear, that if the claim of compensation be sustained the effect will be that Mr Gowans will receive payment in full of a part of his claim corresponding to the amount of calls due by him, and will thus secure a preference over the other creditors of the company. . . . I think it would be strange if in a procedure, which has for its object the *pari passu* ranking of creditors, one creditor, because he also happens to be a contributory, should secure a preference over the other creditors of the company. Of course this question depends on the provisions of the Companies Acts, 1862 and 1867, and I am glad to be spared the necessity of examining these Acts in detail, because they have been made the subject of decision by the Court of Chancery in England in two cases. The first of these judgments was pronounced in a case of *Grissell* ([1866] 1 Ch App 528) by Lord Chelmsford with the assistance of the Lords Justice of Appeal, and the second in a case of *Black & Co* ([1872] 8 Ch App 254) by Lord Selborne with the same assistance. I will take the liberty of reading a passage from the opinion of Lord Selborne in the latter case, which is directly applicable here, and expresses exactly the view I take of the circumstances which have arisen. He says, – "The different sections of the Act," ie the Act of 1862 "those which define the liability of limited companies, the 7th, 8th, 23d and 38th, those which deal with the administration of assets, the 98th 101st and 133d, those which give the power to make calls, not in the ordinary way, but specially for the purposes of this Act, the 102d and 133d, all have in view the payment *pari passu* and equally of the debts due to the creditors, and the liquidator who receives the calls necessarily receives them as a statutory trustee for the equal and rateable payment of all the creditors. The result of this contention, that one particular creditor may pay himself in full by retaining his own calls and not paying them, would in effect be to give him a preference, and to exonerate him from his obligation as a shareholder to contribute towards the payment of the debts of the other creditors. That appears to me to be utterly opposed to the whole principle of the law of set-off, and to all the provisions of the Act which bear on this subject" (8 Ch App 262). We find there not only the result of the consideration of the statutes by these Judges, but also a principle or reason on which the rule is founded, and which is perfectly satisfactory to my mind.'

It is thought that a subordinated creditor is in the same position as a shareholder. The shareholders claim to an entitlement from the company's assets is conditional on all the creditors being paid. Hence the claim of a contributory is in a different class to that of the creditors. It is very important when deciding whether a subordinated claim can be set off against an ordinary claim to examine the exact structure of the debt subordination agreement (see chapter 14). If the debt subordination agreement is structured so that the subordinated debt is claimable only after ordinary debts have all been collected and ordinary creditors paid off, then the subordinated creditor would be entitled to no set-off against an ordinary claim. If however the claim is exigible as soon as the debtor has paid ordinary creditors, it may be argued that the subordinated creditor could then set off his subordinated claim against any debt due by him to the debtor company still owing after sufficient of his ordinary debt has been paid to render the company sufficiently in funds to meet ordinary claims. In exercising that limited right of set off, the subordinated creditor who was also a debtor of the company could thereby improve his position as against the other subordinated creditors.

## Letters of set-off

The balancing of accounts in bankruptcy or liquidation allows one party to set off or balance claims against another party on the insolvency of the other party. A banker therefore could combine the accounts of a customer in order to effect the balancing in the bankruptcy[1], except where money is deposited and appropriated to a particular purpose[2]. Organisations extending credit, especially banks, often seek to rely on more than a bilateral right of retention between the organisation and its debtor. They will often try to set up letters of set-off whereby a sum due by one customer to the organisation can be retained against a sum due to the organisation by another customer. The latter feature does not appear to be objectionable. Nevertheless, the security conferred by letters of set-off amounts to a floating charge, unless a fixed sum is deposited with the organisation by the granter of the security. The criterion for determining whether a security is a floating charge is whether property can be taken out of the security without specific action on the part of the security holder, such as a partial discharge or retrocession; if it can, the security is a floating charge. With letters of set-off, the customer whose account is in credit normally decides whether money is to be withdrawn; the bank must comply with his instructions. It follows that the funds which constitute the security subjects can be withdrawn from the security without the consent of the security holder. Three consequences flow from the fact that the letters of set-off constitute a floating charge: first, such a security can only be created by a company; second, it must be registered under sections 410 to 424 of the Companies Act 1985; and, third, the bank's security will only rank on insolvency as a floating charge, after the preferential creditors.

### Letters of set-off containing equitable charge

Banks sometimes have lending agreements with customers which talk of a bank's 'lien' on a customer's credit balance. In England it has been held that 'a debtor cannot sensibly be said to have a lien on his own indebtedness to his creditor'[3]. By that token he would not be able to grant an equitable charge over his indebtedness to his creditor, but could give such a charge to a third party. These principles were explicitly or by implication brought out in the case of *Re Charge Card Services Ltd*[4]. The facts of the *Charge Card* case were as follows:

> Charge Card Services Ltd (the Company) entered into an invoice discounting agreement by which it agreed to factor its receivables to Commercial Credit Services Ltd (the Factor). Under clause 3(a) of the agreement the Factor could require the Company to repurchase any receivable in stated events, such as the debtor's dispute of liability, and under 3(c) the Company guaranteed payment by every debtor and agreed to indemnify the Factor against loss resulting from a debtor's failure to pay. Clause 4 provided that the purchase price payable by the Factor for any receivable was to be the gross amount payable by the debtor less any discount allowable to him unless the Factor's discount charge was calculated in the manner prescribed by standard condition 3. Under clause 6 the Factor's obligation to pay was made subject to the right of debits and rights of

1 Bell, *Comm*, II, 122.
2 *Mycroft Petr* 1983 SLT 342.
3 *National Westminster Bank Ltd v Halesowen Presswork and Assemblies Ltd* [1971] 1 QB 1 at 46C per Buckley LJ.
4 [1986] 3 All ER 289.

retention provided by standard condition 3. Standard condition 3(A) required the Factor to maintain a current account to which would be credited sums including the purchase price of each receivable before deducting the discounting charge and debited sums including certain contingent liabilities of the company under the agreement and the discounting charge. By standard condition 3(B) the Factor was to remit to the company or its order any balance for the time being standing to the credit of the current account less any amount which the factor in its absolute discretion decided to retain as security for claims against the Company, any risk of any non-payment by a debtor and any amount prospectively chargeable to the Company as a debit under standard condition 3(A). Clause 10 (when read with clause 11) provided that if the Company went into liquidation the Factor could terminate the agreement and require the Company to repurchase any outstanding receivables previously purchased by the Factor. The repurchase price was not an item falling to be debited to the current account under standard 3(a).

The Company went into insolvent liquidation and contended that the Factor's right of retention under standard condition 3(B) was taken as security for rights of set-off and constituted a charge on book debts which was void against the liquidator for want of registration under the Companies Act.

It was held that the amount payable by the Factor for a receivable was not the purchase price as such but the balance standing to the credit of the Company's account after the relevant debits had been made and subject to the right of retention. Accordingly it was a case of accounting, not one of set-off, for there were no mutual but independent obligations capable of set-off. The question was merely a right of payment of a single balance remaining after the exercise of the right of retention. The consequence was that the right of retention was not a charge on money due to the Company. The reason was because the amount that was due was arrived at after the deduction of the sum retained so that there was no relevant property capable of forming the subject matter of the charge.

As to the question of the Factor's right to terminate the agreement and require the Company to repurchase the outstanding receivables, that was not a case for debit to the current account. It constituted a true set-off. It was not able to be characterised as a charge because it was not possible for a charge to be given in favour of a debtor over his own indebtedness. In the course of the arguments it had been conceded that a debt could not be assigned back to the debtor by way of a mortgage, for that type of assignment would operate as a release of the debt. The same applied to an equitable charge. The court, however, affirmed that there was no objection to granting that type of equitable charge; it could not however be structured in that way. The court stated:

'The objection to a charge in these circumstances is not the process by which it is created, but to the result. A debt is a chose in action; it is the right to sue the debtor. This can be assigned or made available to a third party, but not to the debtor, who cannot sue himself. Once any assignment or appropriation to the debtor becomes unconditional, the debt is wholly or partially released. The debtor cannot, and does not need to, resort to the creditor's claim against him in order to obtain the benefit of his security; his own liability to the creditor is automatically discharged or reduced.'

It is thought that the principle enunciated in that case that a debtor cannot give any form of security over his indebtednes to his creditor is also the law of Scotland, but that the other principles relating to an equitable charge do not have any bearing on any Scottish form of security.

### Letters of set-off containing an 'assignation in security'

One method by which a debtor may give his creditor rights against debts owed to the debtor by third parties is to grant the creditor an 'assignation in security' of debts owed to the debtor by third parties. This means that the creditor could claim these assigned debts directly from the debtors without reference to the debtor himself. It is necessary in that type of arrangement that the debtors of the debtor have intimated to them that assignation is taking place. This can be done by notice from the debtor to these debtors, or by the debtors being made to sign the agreement containing the letters of set-off. Such a situation was considered in the case *Gallemos Ltd (in receivership) v Barratt Falkirk Ltd*[1]. In that case a company in receivership raised an action for payment against a construction company in respect of goods and services supplied. The pursuers had received goods and services from an associated company of the defenders. The defenders asserted that certain acknowledgment of order forms in respect of the goods and services supplied by their associated company to the pursuers constituted valid assignations in security to the associated company of the defenders' debts to the pursuers. On the forms the associated company reserved the right 'to *contra* any monies overdue by the pursuers against debts due to the pursuers *inter alia* the defenders, if payment was not made within 60 days. The court held that the assignation had to be in words that could be construed as effecting an immediate transference of rights from the debtor to the assignee, and the transfer became complete when intimation of the transfer was made to the debtor who then knew that the assignee had become creditor in the place of the assignor. It was vital that the document intimated to the debtor should inform the debtor of the extent of the right transferred to the assignee, because there could be no transfer of an undefined right, because the assignor's debtor must know the extent of his obligation to the assignee.

It is important if 'an assignation in security' is contained in so-called letters of set off that those handling the paperwork know what is happening. Otherwise a valid device may be undermined by actings.

### Letters of set-off containing guarantees

If it is not open to a party (not being a company) to give a floating charge over its receivables, and it is not desired that the party's debts are assigned to the creditor in security for his debt, there is another method of avoiding the difficulties. In place of the form of letters of set-off containing an English style equitable charge (not enforceable over debts situated in Scotland) or there being assignations in security, the credit extending organisation could take a guarantee from each of the third parties providing security, in respect of debts due to the credit organisation by all persons on whose behalf the security is to be provided. The arrangement becomes a multipartite personal guarantee of

---

1  1990 SLT 98.

a sort which is quite frequently used in Scotland. Under this arrangement each of the guarantors grants the bank or credit organisation a conventional right of retention in respect of all sums owing by the bank to the guarantor; that right of retention could be contained in the same document as the guarantee (usually the letters of set-off). The consequence of such an arrangement can be seen by considering guarantees and rights of retention granted by two associated companies. If both companies become insolvent, one owing money to the bank but the other having a credit balance in its account, the bank can demand payment from the second company under the guarantee. Thereafter the bank can exercise its right of retention in respect of the sums due by it to the second company; for this purpose it probably does not matter whether the right of retention is conventional or merely the common law right of balancing accounts in bankruptcy. The fact that the sum due under the guarantee is not payable until after insolvency (that being when the demand is made) does not matter. In *Asphaltic Limestone Co v Glasgow Corporation*[1], Lord McLaren, discussing the common law right of balancing accounts in bankruptcy, said[2]:

'But this principle of bankruptcy law presupposes reciprocal obligations which are both existing at the time of the declaration of insolvency, although only one of them is, it may be, immediately exigible.'

This means that it does not matter whether the obligations can be enforced before insolvency; what matters is whether they have been created before insolvency (see page 322). It is thought by the authors that a similar principle would apply where the right of retention on insolvency was conventional.

### Set-off and performance bonds

In some cases the obligation owed to or by a bank is not a money debt but a contingent liability. A common example would be where a performance bond has been granted. It is thought that a guarantee combined with a right of retention will be equally effective in such cases. Although the bank's obligation to pay money may be instantly due, but the obligation owed to the bank contingent, the bank is entitled to retain the debt due by it in security of its contingent claim. It is a straightforward application of the principle of balancing accounts in bankruptcy[3]. Exactly the same result would occur where the right of retention is a conventional right designed to operate on insolvency and it cannot make any difference that the liability owed to the bank arises under a guarantee as long as the liability was created before insolvency. The same rule applies when the obligation of the customer is to pay a money debt instantly due but the obligation owed by the institution is contingent. This is clear from the decision in *Borthwick v Scottish Widows' Fund*[4]. In that case, a bankrupt had effected three life assurance policies with the defenders, and was also indebted to the defenders in a substantial sum. It was held that the defenders, as debtors in the sums in the policies, were entitled to withhold payment of those sums so long as a debt of equal amount was due to them by the bankrupt.

1 1907 SC 463.
2 At 474.
3 See Gloag & Irvine on *Rights in Security*, pp 314–315.
4 [1864] 2 M 595.

The case proceeded on the principle of balancing accounts in bankruptcy, and, although the decision was reached by a majority of five to two, must be unimpeachable authority for the proposition that a contingent debt may be retained against a liquid debt in cases of insolvency[1].

### Foreign currency debts

A right of retention is, in essence, a right to refuse to pay a debt or fulfil some other sort of obligation until the creditor performs an obligation due by him to the debtor. The obligation of either party can be an obligation to deliver goods, or to grant a disposition of land, or to do many other things apart from pay money. Consequently there can be no reason for refusing legal or conventional rights of retention when one obligation is to pay sterling and the other is to pay a foreign currency. The English case of *Re Dynamics Corporation of America*[2], suggests that the date for the conversion of the foreign currency debt should be the date of the winding up. It is thought that that case has no application to Scotland if set off is pled. As noted on page 294 the Scottish rule in the case of a creditor claiming in a foreign currency is that:

'A creditor may state the amount of his claim in a currency other than sterling where:
(a) his claim is constituted by decree or other order made by a court ordering the company to pay the creditor a sum expressed in a currency other than sterling, or
(b) where it is not so constituted, his claim arises from a contract or bill of exchange in terms of which payment is or may be required to be made by the company to the creditor in a currency other than sterling.
(2) Where a claim is stated in currency other than sterling for the purpose of the preceding paragraph, it shall be converted into sterling at the rate of exchange for that other currency at the mean of the buying and selling spot rates prevailing in the London market at the close of business on the date of commencement of winding-up.[3]'

It is thought that the Scottish courts would apply the conversion rate as in the case of a claim but not have the date of the commencement of the winding up as the date of the establishment of the debt or the conversion date, unless a claim is lodged (see page 326). It is thought that where compensation is pled, interest does not run after the date when the compensation is effected and compensation is effected *retro*[4]. However in the case of the balancing of accounts in bankruptcy it is thought that the object of the equitable right is so that the retainer of the debt does not lose out against the claim from the insolvent estate. Because the debt of the insolvent estate keeps carrying interest, it would not be equitable for the claim of the person having the equitable right to be frozen as at the date of the commencement of the winding-up or the winding-up order if interest carried on being paid on the counter-debt. Bell states[5]: 'Thus, the settlement of mutual debts may be referred to two distinct principles: The one is virtual payment in extinction; the other, retention till counter performance.' It is thought that counter performance

---

1 In the case all the other six judges of the Court of Session declined in consequence of being policy holders of the defender. It is also so treated in Gloag and Irvine on *Rights in Security*, pp 318–319.
2 [1976] 2 All ER 669.
3 Insolvency (Scotland) Rules 1986, r 4.17.
4 *Inch v Lee* 1903 11 SLT 374.
5 Bell, *Comm*, II, 124.

must mean the paying of the debt in full plus interest until payment. This is all the more so in the present financial markets, where debt instruments may be structured so that a very high interest rate may be payable to compensate for a poor deal on principal. Hence the person exercising the right of retention can hold out for principal, interest until payment and conversion at that date. He is, of course, sometimes advised also to lodge a contingent claim on a different basis (see page 327).

## Set-off and the Crown

In relation to the balancing of accounts in bankruptcy and set-off generally, a party is not allowed by statute to claim set-off or retention in any proceedings brought by the Crown without leave of the court, unless the subject-matter of the counterclaim relates to the government department on whose behalf the proceedings are brought. By the same token, however, in any proceedings against a government department, the Crown may not take a plea of set-off or retention, without the leave of the court, if the subject-matter of the counterclaim does not relate to that department[1]. This is procedural because leave is normally given. Set-off is not open in a Crown claim for taxes, penalties, etc[2].

## Calls in liquidation

In a liquidation, a contributory may not set off amounts due by the company to him against calls unless all the creditors have been paid in full[3].

---

1 Crown Proceedings Act 1947, s 50; *Atlantic Engine Co (1920) Ltd v Lord Advocate* 1955 SLT 17; *Laing v Lord Advocate* 1973 SLT (Notes) 81; *Smith v Lord Advocate (No 2)* 1981 SLT 19.
2 Crown Proceedings Act 1947, s 50.
3 Companies Act 1985, s 552; *Cowan v Gowans* (1878) 5 R 581; *Property Investment Co of Scotland v Aikman* (1891) 28 SLR 955; *Property Investment Co of Scotland v National Bank* (1891) 28 SLR 884.

# Chapter 16

# Challengeable transactions

## Introduction

The Insolvency Act 1986 and accompanying reforms significantly change the Scottish law relating to challengeable transactions in liquidation. First, the Insolvency Act 1986 (which consolidated provisions in the Companies Act 1985 introduced on 1 April 1986 by the Bankruptcy (Scotland) Act 1985) replaced the provisions in the Bankruptcy Act 1621[1] and the Bankruptcy Act 1696[2] which made challengeable 'gratuitous alienations' and 'fraudulent preferences' on bankruptcy. Secondly, section 617 of the Companies Act 1985[3], which allowed challenges to floating charges created within 12 months of the commencement of a winding-up, was replaced by section 245 of the Insolvency Act 1986 which strengthened the former rules and abolishes the previous provision contained in section 617(3) of the Companies Act 1985, under which, in Scotland, a floating charge was only reducible under the Companies Acts. (This followed the recommendation of the Scottish Law Commission contained in its report on bankruptcy and related aspects of insolvency and liquidation[4]). Thirdly, there is a major new enactment introduced by section 244 of the Insolvency Act 1986 under which 'extortionate credit transactions' may be reduced on an application to the court by an administrator or a liquidator, with the onus being on the provider of the credit to prove that the transaction was not extortionate.

There are now accordingly *four* major categories of transactions which may be challenged in a liquidation;

(A) *Gratuitous alienations*;
(B) *Unfair preferences*;
(C) *Floating charges*; and
(D) *Extortionate credit transactions*.

## (A) GRATUITOUS ALIENATIONS

### Common law

The Scottish common law has long recognised that there is always a risk that a debtor, appreciating that his affairs are becoming embarrassed and that he

1 (c 18).
2 (c 5).
3 Derived from the Companies Act 1948, s 322, the Companies (Floating Charges and Receivers) (Scotland) Act 1972, s 8.
4 Scot Law Comm No 68.

may be insolvent, may seek to put his assets out of the reach of his creditors by transferring them to other persons, particularly to friends and relations. Accordingly, the common law allows challenge of a gift by an insolvent donor on the ground that such a gift amounts to a fraud upon his creditors. Indeed the common law allows a successful challenge of a voluntary alienation by a debtor, irrespective of proof of intention to defraud, where it can be shown that:

(1)   the debtor was insolvent at the time of the challenge and was either insolvent at the time of the alienation or was made insolvent by it; and
(2)   the alienation was made without onerous consideration; and
(3)   the alienation was to the prejudice of the challenging creditor.

The common law challenge may be made by any creditor, whether his debt was contracted before or after the alienation[1]. Insolvency in the context of the common law challenge means the debtor's absolute insolvency, in the sense that his overall liabilities are greater than his assets. Such insolvency is difficult for a creditor to establish in any event, but it is especially difficult in relation to a point of time in the past. The common law, therefore, was strengthened by the Bankruptcy Act 1621. Both the common law rules relating to gratuitous alienations as well as the 1621 Act apply to companies (including limited liability companies) as well as to individuals. This was unequivocally stated by the First Division of the Court of Session in the case of *Bank of Scotland v Pacific Shelf (Sixty-Two) Ltd*[2] affirming the case of *Abram Steamship Co Ltd v Abram*[3]. Lord Brand, delivering the opinion of the court, stated

'We have no doubt that the petitioners have the rights of creditors at common law.
   The common law conferred upon creditors the right to challenge certain actions by their debtors. There is no reason in principle why, after 1856, this right should not, in the absence of statutory provision to the contrary, have been available against debtors who happen to be limited companies. We are in complete agreement with the opinion of the Lord Ordinary that this right has survived successive statutory enactments regulating the affairs of limited companies. As my Lord in the chair pointed out it would not have been difficult in the course of the debate, to restrict the common law rights of creditors in clear language, if that had been the intention of the legislature. In our opinion those rights could only be abrogated by clear statutory provision of necessary implication. We were not referred to any such statutory provision and the implications point in the opposite direction.'

In terms of section 242(7) of the Insolvency Act 1986 a liquidator and an administrator are expressly stated to have the same common law rights as a creditor to challenge an alienation of a company made for no consideration or no adequate consideration. The granting of a floating charge may be challenged as a gratuitous alienation at common law as well as under section 245 of the Insolvency Act 1986[4].

The law contained in the 1621 Act (although it is repealed) still applies to all transactions entered into before 1 April 1986. Such transactions may only be set aside as gratuitous alienations to the extent that they could have been set

1  *Goudy*, p 33 and cases cited there. See in particular *Wink v Speirs* (1867) 6 M 77 at 79, per Lord Justice Clerk Patton.
2  1988 SCLR 487, 1988 SLT 690.
3  1925 SLT 243.
4  See the Insolvency Act 1986, s 9(3)(b)(iv) as renumbered by the Companies Act 1989, Sch 16, para 3(2).

aside under the 1621 Act[1]. For some time, therefore, that Act will remain of some significance.

## Bankruptcy Act 1621 ('the Act')

The Act provides that when a debtor makes an alienation to 'any conjunct or confident person without true just and necessary causes and without a just price truly paid, the same being done after the contracting of lawful debts from true creditors', the latter may challenge the gift.

'Conjunct and confident persons' are described in the preamble to the Act as 'wives, children, kinsmen, allies and other confident and interposed persons'. Case law has interpreted the expression 'conjunct persons' to include those who are closely related to the debtor, such as a spouse, parent, children, brothers, sisters, uncles and sons-in-law. It has also been held to include those in a confidential relationship with the debtor, such as business partners, clerks, servants, etc. There is no rule to the same effect in the common law, but Bell suggests that 'where the connection between the parties has been very close and intimate, the Court has raised a presumption to the effect of throwing the *onus probandi* of solvency on the holder of the deed[2].

The Act has been interpreted in such a way that, if it can be established that the debtor was insolvent at the date of the challenge, it is presumed (a) that he was also insolvent at the date of the alienation and (b) that the alienation was made without onerous consideration. It is not wholly clear whether, if the debtor was insolvent at the date of the alienation, the gift will be set aside where it can be shown that its effect was to render the debtor insolvent[3]. If, however, it is established that the debtor was or became solvent after the date of the alienation, the right of challenge disappears.

The Act provides that the person making the challenge may be 'any true creditor'. This has been construed to mean only creditors whose debts were contracted before the alienation. Challenge under the Act is therefore in this respect more restricted than under the common law. The liquidator may make the challenge whether representing prior creditors or not.

The words 'true, just and necessary causes', although in terms conjunctive, have always been construed disjunctively[4]. Accordingly a challenge under the Act can be defeated where it can be shown that the alienation was made for a 'true' or 'just' cause even if strict necessity is absent. The cause must be 'existing and operating at the date of the deed'[5]. It is not a condition of any challenge under the common law or under the Act that the alienation was entirely gratuitous. It suffices that there was a materially inadequate consideration in money or in money's worth. Where there is a material inadequacy, the transaction is held to be gratutitous to the extent of the inadequacy and may be reduced[6]. Although the Act declares the alienations, dispositions, etc, to which it refers 'to have been from the beginning and to be in all times coming null and of no avail force nor effect', it nevertheless extends pro-

---

1 Insolvency Act 1986, Sch 11, para 9(1).
2 Bell *Comm*, ii, 184, citing *Crs of Marshall v His children* (1709) Mor 48 Note; *Inglis v Boswell* (1676) Mor 11567; *McChristian v Monteith* (1709) Mor 4931.
3 Contrast *McLay v McQueen* (1899) 1 F 804 with *Abram Steamship Co v Abram* 1925 SLT 243, OH.
4 Bell, *Comm*, ii, 176, citing *Grant v Grant of Tullifour* (1748) Mor 949 at 952.
5 *Horne v Hay* (1847) 9 D 651 at 665, per Lord Justice-Clerk Hope.
6 *Glencairn v Brisbane* (1677) Mor 1011; *Miller's Tr v Shield* (1862) 24 D 821; *Gorrie's Tr v Gorrie* (1890) 17 R 1051; *Tennant v Miller* (1897) 4 SLT 318; *Abram Steamship Co v Abram, supra*.

tection to 'any of His Majesty's good subjects (no way partakers of the said frauds) having purchased one of the said bankrupt's lands or goods by true bargains'. Accordingly a third party, receiving the subject matter of the alienation for value and in good faith, is protected. The donee, however, is liable to make good to the bankrupt's creditors the price he receives.

Challenges at common law and under statute to prior transactions of a company are excluded in terms of section 165 of the Companies Act 1989 in relation to a market contract to which a recognised investment exchange or recognised clearing house is a party or which is entered into under its default rules, or in relation to a disposition of property pursuant to such a market contract. Where margin is provided under a market contract which is thus excluded, the protection extends to the provision of the margin, to any contract effected by the exchange or clearing house for the purpose of realising the property provided as margin, and to a disposition of property in accordance with the rules of the exchange or clearing house as to the application of such property.

## Effect of challenge

The effect of a successful challenge is that the subject of the alienation becomes an asset of the debtor's estate and may be attached by the diligence of any creditor[1]. The challenging creditor is not entitled to delivery of the asset.

## Alienations

The Act applies to 'all alienations, dispositions, assignations, and translations, whatsoever made by the debtor of any of his lands, teinds, reversions, actions, debts, or goods whatsoever'. The subjects of the alienation must be able to be attached by the diligence of the creditors[2]. The following would be included: the granting of a bill[3] or a promissory note[4], the assignation of a life interest or insurance policy, a lease[5], the discharge of a claim[6], a decree allowed to pass in absence[7], the abandonment of an action[8]. It applies to the delivery of goods[9]. The conveyance may be direct or indirect[10]. Accordingly a conveyance from the seller to the conjunct or confident person, the price being paid by the insolvent, is an alienation[11]. Cash payments are not alienations under the Act[12] whereas under the common law they are[13].

## Gratuitous alienations under the Insolvency Act 1986

In terms of section 242(1) of the Insolvency Act 1986 certain alienations are challengeable in the case of a winding up by either the liquidator, or any

---

1 *Cook v Sinclair and Co* (1896) 23 R 925.
2 Bell, *Comm*, ii, 178–179.
3 Ibid, ii, 177.
4 *Thomas v Thomson* (1865) 3 M 1160.
5 *Gorrie's Tr v Gorrie* (1890) 17 R 1051.
6 *Laing v Cheyne* (1832) 10 S 200.
7 McKenzie, *Works*, II, p 8.
8 *Wilson v Drummond's Reps* (1853) 16 D 275.
9 *NB Ry Co v White* (1882) 20 SLR 129.
10 Bell, *Comm*, ii, 174.
11 *Ross v Hutton* (1830) 8 S 916; *Bolden v Ferguson* (1863) 1 M 552.
12 *Gilmour Shaw and Co's Tr v Learmonth* 1972 SC 136.
13 *Dobie v Mitchell* (1854) 17 D 97; *Main v Fleming's Trs* (1881) 8 R 880.

creditor who is a creditor by virtue of a debt incurred on or before the date of the commencement of the winding up. Where an administration order is in force, an alienation is challengeable by the administrator but not by the creditors[1]. Alienations prior to 1 April 1986 and thereafter may be challenged under the Insolvency Act 1986[2]. The transitional provisions in paragraphs 4 and 9 of Schedule 11 to the Insolvency Act 1986 suggest that the only ground under the Insolvency Act 1986 is that contained in section 242 and that it does not matter whether the liquidation or administration commenced prior to 1 April 1986 or thereafter. Section 242 of the Insolvency Act 1986 concerns itself with companies and is accordingly much clearer than challenges under the Bankruptcy Act 1621, the enactment of which preceded the institution of sequestration, let alone windings up or administrations. The question of who was a confident or conjunct person in relation to a company was never totally clear and had to be inferred by analogy from that of a personal debtor. This is now clarified. The expression 'associate' as defined by the Bankruptcy (Scotland) Act 1985, s 74, as amended by Regulation 11 of the Bankruptcy (Scotland) Regulations 1985, replaces the old expression 'conjunct and confident' person (see pages 242–243 *infra*).

### Ground of challenge and onus of proof

A challenge may be brought under section 242(1) of the Insolvency Act 1986 by a pre-liquidation creditor, liquidator or administrator, on the grounds that an alienation has favoured some person. The court must grant a decree of reduction or for such restoration of property to the company's assets or other such redress as may seem appropriate.[3]

If reduction is competent in the situation, it has been held by the Second Division of the Inner House in the case of *Alexander Short's Tr v Tai Lee Chung*[4], that reduction must be granted. This means that if heritable property has been alienated for less than the full value, the heritable property is returned to the company and the person to whom the property was gratuitously alienated ranks as a 'postponed creditor' for the consideration which was given. That would normally mean that the postponed creditor got nothing. This remedy is different to the English remedy under section 238(3), in terms of which the court makes an order restoring the position to what it would have been if the company had not entered into the transaction. This discrepancy between the English and the Scottish approach to these transactions at undervalue, or gratuitous alienations, may lead to problems when these orders are being enforced in the different jurisdictions under section 426 of the Insolvency Act 1986. It is thought that the Second Division took the correct, although restrictive view, in their interpretation of section 34 of the Bankruptcy (Scotland) Act 1985 which is the counterpart to section 242 of the Insolvency Act 1986 for sequestration purposes. The court stated:

'The starting point in a case of this nature for interpretation of section 34(4) is that the original alienation has been avoided and the transaction has been vitiated. This is not a good starting-point for an argument which is based solely on equity. It is in our opinion

1 Insolvency Act 1986, s 242(1)(b).
2 Ibid, s 242(2)(a).
3 Ibid, s 242(4).
4 1991 SCLR 629.

clear from a reading of section 34(4) that the general purpose is to provide that as far as possible any property which has been improperly alienated should be restored to the debtor's estate. In the case of a disposition of heritable property this can easily be done by reduction of that disposition. We consider that the reference to 'other redress as may be appropriate' is not intended to give the court a general discretion to decide a case on equitable principles but is designed to enable the court to make an appropriate order in a case where reduction or restoration of the property is not a remedy which is available. As reduction is available in this case, we consider that it is the proper remedy and for this reason we would refuse the reclaiming motion.'

The Scottish law in this area under statute seems intended to penalise the recipient of a gratuitous alienation. If restoration of the status quo was what was sought, it is difficult to see why the legislature would have prescribed in terms of section 51(3)(c) of the Bankruptcy (Scotland) Act 1985 and rule 4.66(2)(a) of the Insolvency (Scotland) Rules 1986 that a creditor's right to any alienation which has been reduced or restored to the company's assets under section 242 of the Insolvency Act 1986 or to the proceeds of sale of such an alienation, is to be classed as a 'postponed debt'.

As with the construction of sections 123(2) and 214(6), a question arises under section 242(4)(a) whether the test to be applied in relation to the valuation of a company's assets is a test based on valuation as a 'going concern' or, on a 'break up' basis (see pages 84–88 and 190–191). It is thought by the authors that the 'going concern' test will be applied. Even although there is a legal presumption of insolvency, to be rebutted by the person granting the alienation, any benefit of the doubt is given to the donor trying to establish his solvency. Bell states[1]:

'It has been held sufficient if the debtor had at the time of the deed a *visible* estate, although *ex eventu*, he should prove insolvent. The subsequent depression of the funds, or the fall of markets for land or goods, will therefore afford a good answer on the question of insolvency, where, on a fair reckoning of the estate as at the date of the deed, the debtor was solvent. This retrospective reckoning is to be favourably viewed where the challenge is at a distant time'.

In England, by contrast, the test is whether the company is 'unable to pay its debts' within the terms of section 123 of the Insolvency Act 1986, and hence is both a 'balance sheet' test and a 'liquidity or cash flow' test.

It is thought that in Scotland a person may seek a declarator that there has been a gratuitous alienation, and not have it preceded by an action of reduction[2]. It is thought that the court may look behind a series of transactions to see whether collectively they may be struck at as a gratuitous alienation and come within the terms of section 242 of the Insolvency Act 1986[2]. It is thought by the authors that although that proposition has been decided where transactions were being challenged at common law, the same would apply to a series of transactions being challenged under section 242 of the Insolvency Act 1986[2]. The court however shall not grant such a decree if the person seeking to uphold the alienation establishes:

(1) that immediately, or at any other time, after the alienation, the company's assets were greater than its liabilities, or

1 Bell, *Comm*, ii, 186.
2 *Mycroft v Boyle* 1987 SCLR 621.

(2)    that the alienation was made for adequate consideration, or
(c)    that the alienation –
  (i)    was a birthday, Christmas or other conventional gift; or
  (ii)   was a gift made, for a charitable purpose to a person who is not an associate of the company,
which, having regard to all the circumstances, it was reasonable for the company to make[1].

As in the 1621 Act, the rights of any person who acquires in good faith and for value from or through the transferee in the alienation are not prejudiced[1].

### Types of alienation struck at

All types of alienation are now struck at if they are for no consideration or no adequate consideration including payments in cash, even if there was a prior obligation[2]. Because an alienation in implementation of a prior obligation is deemed in terms of section 242(6) of the Insolvency Act 1986 to be one for which there was no consideration or no adequate consideration to the extent that the prior obligation was undertaken for no consideration or no adequate consideration, this means that rights to claim on the company's property such as under guarantees etc. are ineffectual because they are liable to be frustrated to the extent that the guarantee is quashed by the gratuitous alienation provision. It does seem strange that the company is still entitled to make a birthday, Christmas or other conventional gift, which would appear to be more appropriate in the case of personal debtors. However, this is qualified by what would be reasonable having regard to all the circumstances. It may also be struck at as *ultra vires* of the company.

### Time limits

There are no time limits at common law or under the Bankruptcy Act 1621. Section 242(3) of the Insolvency Act 1986 now sets time limits. In terms of that section, an alienation may be struck at if it becomes effectual, where an 'associate' of the company is favoured, within five years of the commencement of the winding up of the company, or within five years of an administration order being made. In all other cases the alienation must become effectual in favouring the 'non-associate' of the company within two years before the commencement of the winding up or the administration order[3]. Section 242(3) accordingly brings alienations to 'non-associates' within the scope of statutory challenge, whereas previously such alienations could only be challenged under the common law. The time limits apply to challenges applying the former law[4].

### Definition of 'associate'

'Associate' is defined in terms of section 74 of the Bankruptcy (Scotland) Act 1985 as amended by regulation 11 of the Bankruptcy (Scotland) Regulations

1 Insolvency Act 1986, s 242(4).
2 Ibid, s 242(6).
3 Ibid, s 242(3).
4 Ibid, s 242(2).

1985. It may be that further regulations will extend the categories of persons who are the associates of a company. However, at present 'associates' of a company appear to be confined to the following categories of persons.

### (1) *Other companies*

A company is an associate of another company – if one person has control of both, or where a person has control of one company and persons who are associates of that person, or the person and persons who are his associates, have control of the other[1]. Alternatively, companies are associated if a group of two or more persons has control of each company, and the groups either consist of the same persons or could be regarded as consisting of the same persons, by treating (in one or more cases) a member of either group as replaced by a person of whom he is an associate[2].

Individuals are associated if the 'associate' is the individual's husband or wife or is a relative, or the husband or wife of a relative of the individual or if the individual's husband or wife, and a relative of an individual includes the individual's brother, sister, uncle, aunt, nephew, niece, lineal ancestor or lineal descendant, treating any relationship of the half blood as a relationship of the whole blood and the step-child or adopted child of any person as his child and an illegitimate child as the legitimate child of his mother and reputed father. Husband or wife includes a former husband or wife and a reputed husband or wife[3].

### (2) *Employers*

A person is an associate of any person whom he employs or by whom he is employed; and any director or other officer of a company is to be treated as employed by that company[4].

### (3) *Controllers*

A company is an associate of another person if that person has control of it or if that person and his associates have control[5]. In deciding whether a person shall be taken to have control of a company, a person is deemed to have control of the company if (a) the directors of the company or of another company which has control of it (or any of them) are accustomed to act in accordance with his directions or instructions; or (b) he is entitled to exercise, or control the exercise of, one-third or more of the voting power at any general meeting of the company or of another company which has control of it; and where two or more persons together satisfy either of these conditions, they are taken to have control of the company[6].

There would seem to be an omission in the Regulations inasmuch as

---

1 Bankruptcy (Scotland) Act 1985, s 74(5A) as inserted by Bankruptcy (Scotland) Regulations 1985, reg 11(3).
2 Bankruptcy (Scotland) Act 1985, s 74(5A)(b) as inserted by Bankruptcy (Scotland) Regulations 1985, reg 11(3).
3 Bankruptcy (Scotland) Act 1985, s 74(2), (3) and (4).
4 Ibid, s 74(5).
5 Ibid, s 74(5B).
6 Ibid, s 74(5C) as inserted by Bankruptcy (Scotland) Regulations 1985, reg 11(3).

relatives as defined by the Bankruptcy (Scotland) Act 1985 of shareholders do not seem to be classed as 'associates' of companies or relatives of directors of companies. These would seem to be the most obvious people who would be made recipients of gratuitous alienations. This may be rectified by future legislation.

## (B) UNFAIR PREFERENCES

### Common law

An 'unfair preference' (formerly described as a 'fraudulent preference') may be challenged at common law. Essentially a creditor may challenge voluntary transactions by which, after the insolvency of a debtor, another creditor receives a preference, or in the words of Bell a debtor 'after his funds have become inadequate to the payment of all his debts, intentionally, and in contemplation of his failing, confers on favourite creditors a preference over the rest[1]'. The challenge can be at the instance of any creditor[2] or the liquidator or administrator[3]. The courts have readily permitted the awareness of the debtor of his insolvency to be inferred from circumstances. Knowledge of the debtor's insolvency or collusion on the part of the preferred creditor need not be established[4]. Conversely, the creditor's knowledge of the debtor's absolute insolvency does not transform the payment of the debt into an unfair preference where the payment would not otherwise be so regarded[5].

### Bankruptcy Act 1696

Although the Bankruptcy Act 1696 has been repealed, preferences which have been effected before 1 April 1986 may only be set aside, as in the case of gratuitous alienations, to the extent that they could have been set aside under the law in force immediately before that day[6]. Legal time limits applying to the Bankruptcy Act 1696 mean that it will not be applied any longer, but an understanding of the Act elucidates the new law.

The Bankruptcy Act 1696 provided:

'All and whatsoever voluntary dispositions, assignations, or other deeds which shall be found to be made or granted directly or indirectly, by the aforesaid debtor or bankrupt either at or after his becoming bankrupt or in the space of 60 days before in favour of his creditors, either for their satisfaction or further security, in preference to other creditors, to be void and null.'

The reference to 'becoming bankrupt' is a reference to the old concept of notour bankruptcy, replaced now by apparent insolvency (see pages 208–220). The period of 60 days was increased to six months in terms of section 115(3) of the Companies Act 1947. Accordingly, any fraudulent preference

---

1 Bell, *Comm*, ii, 226.
2 *Goudy*, p 42.
3 Insolvency Act 1986, s 243(6).
4 *McCowan v Wright* (1853) 15 D 494; see also *Whatmough's Tr v British Linen Bank* 1932 SC 525 and 1934 SC (HL) 51.
5 *Nordic Travel Ltd v Scotprint Ltd* 1980 SLT 189 at 198, per Lord President Emslie.
6 Insolvency Act 1986, Sch 11, para 9(1).

within six months of notour bankruptcy could be reduced. A company could be rendered notour bankrupt to the effect of permitting the reduction of preferences struck at by the 1696 Act[1].

Under the common law and the 1696 statute, challenge was excluded in the case of (i) *nova debita* (transactions where the bankrupt and another party have undertaken reciprocal obligations); (ii) cash payments of debts actually due; and (iii) transactions in the course of ordinary trade or business.[2] Such transactions and payments are completely protected unless they form part of a collusive arrangement to create a preference. The rational basis of these exceptions was stated by Lord President Inglis in *Anderson's Trustee v Flemming*.[3]

'It would be a very unfortunate thing for the trade of this country if such exception did not exist; because if the Act of 1696 were allowed to extend to all the ordinary transactions of traders, not contemplating bankruptcy, and not aware of their being insolvent, it would disturb their business relations to a most calamitous extent. A man may go on trading in the honest belief of his own solvency, and that even up to the date of bankruptcy, and his ordinary transactions will not be held to fall under the operation of this statute. The law is fixed, both in expediency and equity, that they shall not be so.'

## Unfair preferences under section 243 of the Insolvency Act 1986

Unlike section 242, which makes major changes to the Bankruptcy Act 1621, section 243 follows in large part the Bankruptcy Act 1696. The same provisions apply in relation to *nova debita*[4] with the added clarification that the performance of the reciprocal obligations need not take place at the same time. Similarly transactions in the ordinary course of business or trade are exempt[5]. Cash payments for debts which have become payable are also exempt[6].

In the case of *Nicoll v Steel Press (Supplies) Ltd*[7] the court held that in relation to *nova debita* reciprocity meant full consideration for any new transaction. It stated:

'Having considered the foregoing contentions of the parties we are not persuaded by the argument for the defenders that the passage cited from Bell and Goudy proceeds on the basis of broad equivalence between the contributions of debtor and creditor in transactions to be excepted from the general rule against unfair preferences. It appears to us that paragraph 3 of Goudy, read short from page 90 to the top of page 91, gives its overall sense quite clearly as follows:

"A *novum debitum* strictly signifies an obligation undertaken by the bankrupt in respect of some present consideration received . . . the implement of such obligations within the days of bankruptcy is protected from the operation of the statute on the ground that the bankrupt does not thereby give a preference by way of satisfaction or further security but simply gives the specific subject which he bargained to give, and in respect of which an

1 *Clark v Hinde, Milne & Co* (1884) 12 R 347.
2 See *Nordic Travel, supra*; *Horsburgh v Ramsay & Co* (1885) 12 R 117; *Walkraft Paint Co Ltd* 1964 SLT 103 and 104; *Whatmough's Tr, supra* which qualify the classic statements of the law in important ways.
3 (1871) 9 M 718 at 722.
4 Insolvency Act 1986, s 243(2)(c).
5 Ibid, s 243(2)(a).
6 Ibid, s 243(2)(b).
7 1992 SCLR 332.

equivalent has accrued to his estate . . . Moreover . . . the parties do not *quoad hoc* stand in any prior relation of debtor and creditor. The consideration given to the bankrupt must be a real one and fair value.'

We consider that the passage from Bell is to be read in a similar sense. The principle behind both passages, as we see it, is that the consideration given to the debtor in the transaction cannot be less than full value to qualify for the exception. Strict equivalence is essential in that the debtor's estate must not be diminished as a result of the transaction. . . .

Further, we doubt whether reduction of prior indebtedness could ever qualify as a valid consideration in a *novum debitum*. That appears to be the effect of the second-last sentence of the passage from Goudy quoted above. Such consideration clearly arises from indebtedness previously incurred which is precisely the area struck at by the law of preferential repayment of creditors. In reality, it is an old debt disguised as a new consideration.'

## Arrestments

The Scottish Law Commission highlighted a complication where the debtor has taken action within the period of challenge to fulfil an obligation which he has already assumed and gave the example of a case where, following an arrestment placed by a creditor, the debtor arranges to pay the debt by means of a mandate granted to the arrestee. Although in one sense such a payment is a voluntary payment, since the debtor could have allowed the arrestment to proceed to a furthcoming, there could be an alternative view that he was merely anticipating the inevitable. It was not clear from the authorities whether such a payment would be protected either as a cash payment or as being made involuntarily[1]. Following the Law Commission's recommendations, there is now a statutory exemption to challenge as an unfair preference where the transaction consists of:

'the granting of a mandate by a company authorising an arrestee to pay over the arrested funds or part thereof to the arrester where –
 (i)   there has been a decree for payment or a warrant for summary diligence, and
 (ii)  the decree or warrant has been preceded by an arrestment on the dependence of the action or followed by an arrestment in execution[2]'.

## Protection of third parties

Again following the recommendation of the Scottish Law Commission as in the case of gratuitous alienations, the rights of innocent third parties are now expressly protected where the third party has acquired a right or interest in good faith and for value from or through the creditor in whose favour a preference has been created, although the preferred creditor will of course have to account[3].

## Persons entitled to challenge unfair preferences

Unfair preferences may be challenged by any creditor who is a creditor by virtue of a debt incurred on or before the date of commencement of winding up, or by the liquidator[4]. In the case of an administration order, the admini-

1 Scot Law Com No 68 at 12.39.
2 Insolvency Act 1986, s 243(2)(d).
3 Ibid, s 243(5).
4 Ibid, s 243(4)(a).

strator only may make the challenge[1]. This follows the scheme in relation to the persons who may challenge a gratuitous alienation under section 242 of the Insolvency Act 1986.

## Challengeable period

The period covered by a challenge is now restricted to six months prior to the commencement of winding up or administration order. The provisions previously existing by which a company could be made notour bankrupt for this purpose have been replaced by section 243(1) of the Insolvency Act.

## Types of transactions struck at

The type of transactions which a company may enter into which create a preference in favour of a creditor to the prejudice of the general body of creditors is only limited by human deviousness. The following types of transaction have been held to be unfair preferences:

- the return of moveables bought but not paid for under an arrangement made in view of the buyer's insolvency[2];
- the discharge of a right[3];
- the abandonment of a competent defence[4];
- the allowance of a decree by default[5]; and
- the granting of a delivery order for moveables[6].

# (C)   FLOATING CHARGES

## Common law

For the avoidance of doubt, section 613(3) of the Companies Act 1985 (first introduced by section 8 of the Companies (Floating Charges and Receivers) (Scotland) Act 1972) provided that where a company was being wound up in Scotland, a floating charge over all or any part of its property was not to be held an alienation or preference avoidable by statute (other than by that provision) or at common law on the ground of insolvency or notour bankruptcy. That provision has now been repealed. The previous doubt now resurfaces, and it is now an open question whether floating charges may be struck at under common law or under the provisions as to gratuitous alienations and unfair preferences under the Insolvency Act 1986. It is suggested that floating charges may now be reduced as gratuitous alienations or unfair preferences in terms of sections 242 and 243 of the Insolvency Act 1986 and at common law. Challenges under sections 242 and 243 are different in result to a challenge under section 245 of the Act. The different results as described later show why

---

1 Ibid, s 243(4)(b).
2 *Watson & Sons Ltd v Veritys Ltd* (1908) 24 Sh Ct Rep 148.
3 *Keith v Maxwell* (1795) Mor 1163.
4 *Wilson v Drummond's Reps* (1853) 16 D 275.
5 *Lauries' Tr v Beveridge* (1867) 6 M 85.
6 *Wright v Mitchell* (1871) 9 M 516; *Price & Pierce Ltd v Bank of Scotland* 1910 SC 1095, 1912 SC (HL) 19; for a fuller list and for further analysis of cash payments, transactions in the ordinary course of business and *nova debita*, see Wilson on *Debt*, pp 239–240.

these should be seen as parallel challenges. The scheme of the Insolvency Act 1986 allows overlapping challenges in terms of different sections of that Act.

## Avoidance of certain floating charges under section 245 of the Insolvency Act 1986

In relation to floating charges created after 29 December 1986 they may be reduced in terms of section 245. In relation to those created before 29 December 1986 they are only reducible to the extent that they would have been reducible under the law previously in force[1]. Unlike the new provisions in relation to gratuitous alienations and unfair preferences, which were introduced on 1 April 1986 by the Bankruptcy (Scotland) Act 1985 amending the Companies Act 1985, this provision only came into force on 29 December 1986. Accordingly, the previous law applies to all floating charges created prior to 29 December 1986.

### Floating charges created before 29 December 1986

Section 617 of the Companies Act 1985 provides that, where a floating charge has been created within 12 months of the commencement of a winding up, then unless it is proved that the company was solvent immediately after the creation of the charge it shall be invalid except to the amount of any cash paid to the company at the time of or subsequent to the creation of, and in consideration for, the charge, together with interest.

### New provisions under section 245 of the Insolvency Act 1986

Section 245 of the Insolvency Act 1986 changes the law in several important aspects:

(1) *Categories of floating charge holders*

Section 245 divides floating charge holders into two categories:
  (i) connected persons; and
  (ii) any other persons.
A 'connected person' is a person who is a director or shadow director of the company (ie a person in accordance with whose directions or instructions the directors are accustomed to act), or an associate of such person, or an associate of the company, 'associate' being as defined by section 435 of the Insolvency Act 1986[2]. This definition is wider than the definition contained in section 74 of the Bankruptcy (Scotland) Act 1985 as amended by regulation 11 of the Bankruptcy (Scotland) Regulations 1985. The key difference is that a 'connected person' is held to be a director or shadow director or an 'associate' of such a director or shadow director. The definition which applies to gratuitous alienations does not at present cover 'associates' of directors or shadow directors. The definition of 'associate' in section 435 of the Insolvency Act 1986 is similar to, although wider than, that contained in the Bankruptcy

---

1 Insolvency Act 1986, Sch 11, para 9.
2 Ibid, s 249.

(Scotland) Act 1985, s 74 as amended by regulation 11 of the Bankruptcy (Scotland) Regulations 1985. This seems unnecessarily complicated and means that the precise definition must be consulted in any case arising.

## (2) Time limits

In the case of floating charges created in favour of unconnected persons, they are challengeable if created within 12 months of the commencement of winding up, where a company goes into liquidation, and within 12 months of the presentation of a petition for an administration order where there is an administration order[1]. In the case of persons connected with the company, the time limit is a period of two years ending with the presentation of the petition for an administration order, or the commencement of winding up.

## (3) Defence to challenge

In the case of persons not connected with the company, the floating charge may be challenged only if, at the time of the creating of the floating charge, the company was unable to pay its debts in terms of section 123 of the Insolvency Act 1986, or became unable to pay its debts within the meaning of that section in consequence of the transaction under which the charge is created[2].

A company is deemed unable to pay its debts if it is proved to the satisfaction of the court that the value of the company's assets is less than the amount of its liabilities, taking into account its contingent and prospective liabilities[3] (see pages 84–88, 190–191 and 341). Secondly, a company is deemed unable to pay its debts in terms of section 123 if a demand notice for over £750 has not been paid after three weeks, or the induciae of a charge, decree or extract has expired without payment[4]. In the case of connected persons this defence is not open. There is a technicality in so far as a floating charge is created between the presentation of a petition for an administration order and the making of an administration order[5]. The defence that the company was able to pay its debts is not open, even to an unconnected person if the floating charge has been granted between the presentation of a petition for an administration order and the granting of the administration order[6].

## (4) Challenge to a floating charge

A successful challenge to a floating charge has the effect of invalidating the security created by the floating charge except to the extent of the aggregate of –

(a)  the value of so much of the consideration for the creation of the charge as consists of money paid, or goods or services supplied, to the company at the same time as, or after, the creation of the charge;

(b)  the value of so much of that consideration as consists of the discharge or

---

1 Ibid, s 245(3) and (5).
2 Ibid, s 245(4).
3 Ibid, s 123(2).
4 Ibid, s 123(1)(a) and (b).
5 Ibid, s 245(3)(c).
6 Ibid, s 245(3)(c) and (4).

reduction, at the same time as, or after, the creation of the charge, of any debt of the company; and

(c)    the amount of such interest (if any) as is payable on the foregoing amount in pursuance of any agreement under which the money was paid for the goods or services supplied[1].

In other words, the floating charge is invalidated except to the extent of new money granted in return for the floating charge or company debt reduced as a result of the granting of the floating charge, or interest on either of these. The floating charge is not allowed merely to secure debt already in place without new considerations being given.

As an extra safeguard, in the case of goods or services supplied, if an unrealistic price is set on them, the value of any goods or services supplied by way of a consideration for a floating charge is now by statute the amount in money which at the time of their supply could reasonably have been expected to be obtained for supplying them in the ordinary course of business and on the same terms (apart from the consideration) as those on which they were supplied to the company[2]. In deciding whether cash payments qualify for the exception, it is necessary to look at the substance to see whether the payments were truly made for the benefit of the company or were indirectly to give a preference to an existing creditor[3].

## (5)    Effect of challenge to a floating charge

A floating charge is only avoided (without reduction) in the course of an administration or a winding up under section 245 of the Insolvency Act 1986. The floating charge holder is then not entitled to rely on his security in an administration or a winding up to the extent that the security is invalidated in terms of section 245 of the Insolvency Act 1986 as described above. If however prior to the winding up or the administration, a receiver has been appointed under a floating charge and money ingathered for payment to the debenture holder, neither is the appointment of the receiver invalid nor the payment of sums towards the debenture holder reduced, if subsequently it is held that the floating charge is invalid. There also seems no reason why in the course of a winding up a receiver may not be appointed over assets secured by that part of the floating charge which is not invalidated. The effects described above differ radically from the effects of gratuitous alienations and unfair preferences which are struck at. In *Mace Builders (Glasgow) Ltd v Lunn*[4], Scott J compares the differing effects of a challenge under section 320 of the Companies Act 1948[5] with that of a floating charge avoided under section 322 of the Companies Act 1948[6]. He states:

'. . . I have no difficulty in accepting counsel for the plaintiff's submission as to the effect of section 320 on a mortgage. The purpose of section 320 is to enable to be avoided transactions which constitute fraudulent preferences. If a mortgage is granted by way of a

1    Insolvency Act 1986, s 245(2).
2    Ibid, s 245(6).
3    *Libertas-Kommerz GmbH* 1978 SLT 222.
4    [1986] Ch 459; affd [1987] Ch 191, CA.
5    Companies Act 1985, s 615, now revised in Insolvency Act 1986, s 243.
6    Subsequently Companies Act 1985, s 617, now revised extensively in Insolvency Act 1986, s 245.

fraudulent preference, it is not only the charge which is tainted but the whole contents of the mortgagee's powers and remedies and the mortgagor's covenants for payment of principal and interest are as much a part of the fraudulent preference as the charge itself. The purpose of the fraudulent preference is to enable the creditor to obtain repayment with priority over the other creditors. It must follow that the avoidance of the transaction which constitutes the fraudulent preference will include the avoidance of the act whereby the creditor's debt is repaid.

'It is to be noted that section 320 in terms incorporates the law of bankruptcy. Fraudulent preference in bankruptcy is dealt with by section 44 of the Bankruptcy Act 1914. Subsection (1) of that section provides for the avoidance of transactions of fraudulent preference. Subsection (2) provides that: "this section shall not affect the rights of any person taking title in good faith and for valuable consideration through or under a creditor of the bankrupt'.

'Accordingly, on the avoidance of a transaction under section 320, the position of purchasers who have dealt with the preferred creditor before the commencement of the bankruptcy is protected. Section 322 does not have any similar saving for the rights of the purchasers. If the effect of section 322 is, as counsel for the defendant contends, simply to avoid the charge in the winding-up, there is no need for any such saving. The validity of the pre-winding up transactions of the debenture holder or of a receiver appointed by the debenture holder are not affected by section 322.

'[The] subsection[1] reads: "where a company is being wound up, a floating charge . . . shall be invalid". This is language which focuses attention on the course of the winding up and which avoids the charge in and for the purpose of the winding up.

'Counsel for the plaintiff's analogy with section 320 is not, in my view, an apt one. Section 320 incorporates the law of bankruptcy, and declares that transactions of fraudulent preference shall "be invalid accordingly". Section 322 has no analogous content. Further, the legislative intention under section 320 is to avoid transactions of fraudulent preference. It is inherent in that intention that transactions which pre-date the commencement of the winding up or bankruptcy will have to be set aside. But I can discern in section 322 no legislative intention beyond an intention that in the circumstances specified in the section, the debenture holder should not be permitted in the winding up to have the benefit of the security. That intention does not, in order to be satisfied, require more than that the charge cannot be relied on in the winding up.'

The differing effects support the contention that different grounds of challenge are open against floating charges, the most root and branch being that it is an unfair preference or gratuitous alienation. It could also be challenged as an extortionate credit transaction under section 244 of the Insolvency Act 1986 as described in the following sections.

### English cases of *Re M C Bacon Ltd* and *Re M C Bacon (No 2) Ltd*

Decisions of Millett J in *Re M C Bacon Ltd*[2] and *Re M C Bacon Ltd (No 2)*[3], have been treated by certain authorities as of significance in relation to the granting of securities by insolvent companies to their banks. The facts of the case were briefly as follows: M C Bacon Limited ('the company') went into creditors' voluntary liquidation on 24 August 1987 with an estimated deficiency as regards unsecured creditors of £329,435. At the date of liquidation the company's overdraft at the National Westminster Bank ('the Bank') stood at £235,530. The overdraft was secured by a fixed and floating charge dated

---

1 Companies Act 1948, s 322(1).
2 1990 BCC 78; [1990] BCLC 324.
3 [1990] 3 WLR 646; [1990] BCLC 607; [1991] Ch 127.

20 May 1987. On 4 September 1987 the bank demanded payment and on the same date it appointed an administrative receiver. Mr Ian Clark ('the liquidator') was appointed liquidator of the company at a meeting of creditors on 7 September 1987, thereby replacing a liquidator who had been appointed on 24 August 1987. On 28 September 1987 he issued an application seeking (1) to have the bank's security set aside, (a) under section 239 of the Insolvency Act 1986 as a voidable preference or (b) under section 238 of the Insolvency Act 1986 as a transaction at an undervalue; and (2) a declaration under section 214 of the Insolvency Act 1986 that the bank was liable to make a substantial contribution to the company's assets on the ground that for the last few months of the company's life it had been a shadow director of the company and had thereby rendered itself responsible for what was alleged to have been wrongful trading by the company. An application by the bank to strike out the proceedings failed before Knox J, and the trial began before Millet J on 23 October 1989. It lasted for seventeen days. On the twelfth day of the trial and after nearly six days of oral evidence the liquidator abandoned the wrongful trading claim. The bank led no evidence. On 30 November 1989 Millet J dismissed the proceedings on the basis that the transaction did not amount to a preference under section 239 of the Insolvency Act 1986 and that the creation of the security over the company's assets did not come within section 238(4)(b) of the Insolvency Act 1986 since it did not diminish or deplete the value of the assets. He also ordered the liquidator to pay the costs personally. Subsequently the liquidator unsuccessfully sought an order that the liquidator should be reimbursed so far as possible for the bank's costs which he had been ordered to pay and for his own costs out of the assets subject only to the bank's floating charge, as 'expenses incurred in the winding up' within the meaning of section 115 of the Insolvency Act 1986 and 'expenses of the winding up' within section 175(2)(a) of that Act. In the course of his judgments after these hearings Millet J held:

(1)   Because in terms of section 239(5) an order striking at a preference in England and Wales, may not be made unless the company which gave the preference was influenced in deciding to give it by a desire to create a preference, it was incumbent upon the party seeking to have a prior transaction set aside as a voidable preference to establish that the debtor company 'positively wished' to improve the creditor's position in the event of its own insolvent liquidation. Section 239(5) did not require that this motive should have been a dominant factor influencing the decision to enter into the transaction, nor even that it should have had any special force in 'tipping the scales' nor have been a '*sine qua non*'. All that was required by the subsection was that the requisite desire should have 'influenced' the decision; which is hardly an exacting requirement, if all that has to be shown is that this was one of the factors which operated on the minds of those who made the decision.

(2)   The relevant time at which the requisite desire had to be shown to have been operative was the time when the decision was taken to grant the preference, rather than the actual date of the transaction.

(3)   Because in terms of section 238(4)(b) for there to be a transaction at undervalue in England and Wales, the company has to enter into a transaction with a person for a consideration the value of which . . . is significantly less than the value . . . of the consideration provided by the company, the creation of a security over a company's assets was not caught by that subsection since it did not diminish or deplete the value of the assets.

(4)   Any sums recovered from a creditor who has been wrongly preferred

enures for the benefit of the general body of creditors, not for the benefit of the company or the holder of a floating charge. It does not become part of the company's assets but is received by the liquidator impressed with a trust in favour of those creditors among whom he has to distribute the assets of the company. *Re Yagerphone Ltd*[1] was still the law in England and Wales notwithstanding section 239(3) of the Insolvency Act 1986 which empowers the court on finding a voidable preference proved to make such order as it thinks fit for 'restoring the position to what it would have been if the company had not given that preference', and section 241(1)(c) which empowers the court to 'release or discharge . . . any security given by the company'. Those powers were not intended to be exercised so as to enable a debenture holder to obtain the benefit of the proceedings brought by the liquidator.

It has been suggested by certain authorities that the decisions of Millet have important implications. For example, Professor Ian F Fletcher in discussing the first judgment[2] states:

'This decision will be welcomed by companies and by banks and by other institutional lenders alike, for it ensures that, provided the company is motivated only by proper commercial considerations, it is possible for a company in economic difficulties to seek financial assistance, and to effect a security in exchange for the injection of fresh funds into the company, without the risk that the lender's security will be subsequently rendered voidable in the event of the company's insolvency. This surely accords with common sense, and with commercial expediency, and is also consistent with the traditional concept of what should amount to an impeachable preference, namely a debtor's conscious attempt in contemplation of the onset of insolvency to place certain creditors – typically friends, relatives or associates – in an advantageous position vis-à-vis the general body of creditors. Such conduct is readily distinguishable from the orthodox commercial practice of a prudent lender taking a standard form of registrable security in the context of providing the funds for the company's continued effort to trade through a period of crisis.'

It is thought by the authors that the Scottish courts should take a very guarded approach to the findings in *Re M C Bacon Ltd*[3] for a number of reasons. First the authors can see no reason why a floating charge granted in the circumstances of that case would not be caught by the provisions of section 245 of the Insolvency Act 1986. Though new money was granted, the floating charge was mainly to secure old money and hence would have been invalid to that extent in terms of section 245(2) of the Insolvency Act 1986. The company certainly was insolvent within twelve months of the date of the creation of the floating charge, and hence would be caught by section 245(3)(b) of the Insolvency Act 1986. It may even have been caught by section 245(3)(a) of that Act if the bank had been found to be a 'shadow director' and hence a 'connected' person in terms of section 249 of that Act. This ground of challenge does not seem to have been pled in that case. Secondly, it is thought that in Scotland the granting of a security would be caught by the gratuitous alienation provision of section 242(4)(b) when read with section 242(6) of the Insolvency Act 1986. Even where a company is solvent, secured debt is more

---

1 [1935] Ch 392.
2 [1991] The Journal of Business Law at p 74; see *Barclays Bank plc v Homan* (1992) Independent, 1 September, where Hoffmann J accepted that a 'subjective intention' to prefer was necessary if s 239 of the Insolvency Act 1986 were invoked in an English administration, but refused an injunction preventing ancillary US examiner applying to US court for recovery under paragraph 541 of US Bankruptcy Code in terms of which no intention was necessary.
3 1990 BCC 78, [1990] BCLC 324.

valuable than unsecured debt. For there to be adequate consideration, with a solvent company there would have to be a premium to reflect the upgrading in the value of a debt in translating it from an unsecured to a secured debt. The less creditworthy a company becomes, the greater is the premium in value of its secured debt over its unsecured debt. If a company in any circumstances grants a floating charge over its whole business and undertaking, it is giving up the right to grant other persons a first charge; which is an economic asset of a company. Thirdly in Scotland there is no equivalent provision of section 239(5) of the Insolvency Act 1986. 'Desire' is not necessary in terms of the Scottish section 243 of the Insolvency Act 1986 to create a preference. A transaction is struck at, which creates a preference, unless it falls within the exceptions.

It is difficult to see how the transaction mentioned in *Re M C Bacon Ltd*[1], could come within the Scottish excepting provisions. It is not a payment in cash for a debt which has become payable in terms of section 243(2)(b) of the Insolvency Act 1986. It is not a transaction whereby the parties undertake reciprocal obligations in terms of section 243(2)(c) because there was not strict equivalence in value of the obligations as required in Scotland[2]. It is finally difficult to see how the transaction could be classed as 'a transaction in the ordinary course of trade or business' and be covered by section 243(2)(a) of the Insolvency Act 1986. Although the type of transaction mentioned in *Re MC Bacon Ltd* may happen often in the business world, it is not 'in the ordinary course' of trade or business. It is an extraordinary transaction if but for it, the ordinary course of business or trade ceases[3]. In relation to Millet J's finding that property made over to a company following an order under section 239 of the Insolvency Act 1986 does not form part of the assets of the company and accordingly would not be attached by a floating charge, see pages 140–142.

## (D)  EXTORTIONATE CREDIT TRANSACTIONS

In terms of section 244 of the Insolvency Act 1986 an administrator or a liquidator may seek a court order in relation to transactions under which credit has been extended to a company within the period of three years ending with the day on which the administration order was made or the commencement of the liquidation.

### Definition of 'extortionate'

In terms of section 244(3) of the Insolvency Act 1986 'a transaction is extortionate if, having regard to the risk accepted by the person providing the credit –

    (a) the terms of it are or were such as to require grossly exorbitant payments to be made (whether unconditionally or in certain contingencies) in respect of the provision of the credit, or

    (b) it otherwise grossly contravened ordinary principles of fair dealing.'

1 *Supra.*
2 See *Peter Nicoll v Steel Press (Supplies) Ltd* 1992 SCLR 332.
3 See *Bob Gray (Access) Ltd* 1987 SCLR 720 and cases cited there.

The definition is largely modelled on the provisions in sections 137–139 of the Consumer Credit Act 1974 which allowed the re-opening of extortionate creditor bargains in cases falling within the ambit of that Act.

The test of 'grossly exorbitant' in relation to the payments will be a question of fact and circumstance. There is a presumption in terms of section 244(3) that a transaction is extortionate, unless the contrary is proved. The power which the liquidator or administrator has to strike at a credit transaction under section 244 is in addition to his right to strike at the transaction as a gratuitous alienation under section 242 of the Insolvency Act 1986.

### Remedies under section 244 of the Insolvency Act 1986

An order under section 244 may contain one or more of the following provisions:

(a)  a provision setting aside the whole or part of any obligation created by the transaction;

(b)  a provision otherwise varying the terms of the transaction or varying the terms on which any security for the purposes of the transaction is held;

(c)  a provision requiring any person who is or was a party to the transaction to pay to the office holder any sums paid to that person, by virtue of the transaction, by the company;

(d)  a provision requiring any person to surrender to the office holder any property held by him as security for the purposes of the transaction;

(e)  a provision directing accounts to be taken between any persons.

# Chapter 17

# Accounting law and practice

## Introduction

Although the Companies Acts have laid down detailed rules about the preparation, auditing and publication of accounts of companies registered under the Companies Acts (sections 221 to 262 of the Companies Act 1985, as amended by sections 1 to 23 of the Companies Act 1989), there had until the recent reforms been little detailed legislation in relation to the accounting and reporting of insolvent companies in Scotland. The recent legislation filled this gap although to a certain extent it merely makes mandatory what was accounting convention or 'best practice' prior to 29 December 1986.

## Statement of affairs

The main reform in the legislation was the introduction of a 'statement of affairs' of the company, which is a statement giving a detailed breakdown of all the assets and liabilities of the company as far as ascertainable. A prescribed form of the statement of affairs is set out in the Insolvency (Scotland) Rules 1986 for liquidations, administrations and receiverships. The style is set out in Appendix III[1]. The only difference in the forms relates to whether it is an administration, receivership or liquidation. Where there is a 'voluntary arrangement' the Rules list particulars to go into a statement of affairs but no form is prescribed[2].

Administrators and receivers in Scotland are now under a statutory duty to require those connected with the company[3] to complete a statement of affairs[4]. Liquidators, in cases where the court has made a winding-up order, have a discretion whether to require those connected with the company to complete a statement of affairs[5]. In the case of a creditors' voluntary winding up, the directors of the company are under a statutory duty to make out a statement of affairs of the company and have that statement laid before the creditors' meeting[6]. It must then be sent to the liquidator[7]. Similarly where a members' voluntary winding up is converted into a creditors' voluntary winding up, the liquidator is under a statutory duty to make out a statement of

---

1 The form in liquidations is Form 4.4(Scot); in administrations it is Form 2.6(Scot); and in receiverships it is Form 5(Scot).
2 r 1.5.
3 See page 361.
4 Insolvency Act 1986, ss 22 and 66.
5 Ibid, s 131.
6 Ibid, s 99(1) and (2).
7 Insolvency (Scotland) Rules 1986, Sch 1, para 4.

affairs in the prescribed form and lay the statement before the creditors' meeting[1]. When the directors are proposing a 'voluntary arrangement' under Part 1 of the Insolvency Act 1986, they must deliver a statement of affairs to the 'nominee' within seven days of the delivery of the proposal or such other time as he allows[2]. The statement must include all the details on the statutory forms used by administrators, liquidators and receivers since rule 1.5 follows the format. In addition there must be included (a) particulars of debts owed by or to it by persons connected to it, (b) details of members and shareholdings, and (c) any other relevant particulars[2]. Similarly if the proposal is by the liquidator or administrator but he is not the nominee, a statement of affairs, as in the case of a directors' proposal, must be submitted to the nominee[3].

In the case of a members' voluntary winding up, there is no statutory scope for a statement of affairs. Rather the directors make a statutory declaration of the company's solvency, ie that they have formed the opinion that the company will be able to pay its debts in full, together with interest at the full rate (ie the higher of the contracted rate or judicial rate), within a period of not more than 12 months from the date of the commencement of the winding up[4]. The declaration must be in the prescribed form[5].

## Function and format of statement of affairs

### (1) *Function*

The function of the statement of affairs is:

(a) to get as detailed a picture of the company's financial position as possible with the accounting format specially tailored to the accounting questions which arise on insolvency; and

(b) to provide the 'base accounts' which can be used to measure progress or movement in the liquidation, administration, receivership or voluntary arrangement.

### (2) *Format*

The first page of the statement of affairs is a balance sheet detailing the total assets and liabilities of the company. It gives figures of the projected surplus/deficiency, based on estimated realisable values of assets less liabilities, available for distribution to the various categories of creditors, ie to:

(1) preferential creditors;
(2) floating charge holders;
(3) unsecured creditors; and
(4) shareholders.

---

1 Insolvency Act 1986, s 95(3); and rule 4.8, as applied to members' voluntary windings up by Sch 2 to the Rules.
2 r 1.5.
3 Insolvency Act 1986, s 2(3) and rule 1.12(5).
4 Insolvency Act 1986, s 89(1).
5 Form 4.25(Scot).

The totals of assets and liabilities are backed up by 'lists'. Lists A and B give respectively 'assets which are not secured' and 'assets which are secured'. Lists C, D, E, F and G are lists of liabilities according to ranking and type of liability, as follows:

Preferential creditors – List C
Holders of floating charges – List D
Trade accounts – List E ⎫
Bills payable – List F ⎬ Unsecured creditors
Contingent liabilities – List G ⎭

List A of 'assets not specifically secured' has schedules I, II, III, IV and V giving details of:

Schedule I – marketable securities;
Schedule II – bills of exchange, promissory notes, etc;
Schedule III – trade debtors;
Schedule IV – loans and advances; and
Schedule V – unpaid calls.

The format of the statement of affairs must be followed 'with such variations as circumstances require'.[1] This is an important provision because the format is not comprehensive, as will be discussed later in this chapter.

## Compilation and distribution of statement of affairs

The Insolvency Act 1986 and the Insolvency (Scotland) Rules 1986 make provisions for the distribution of the statement of affairs by the:

(a)   administrator;
(b)   receiver;
(c)   liquidator; and
(d)   nominee in the case of proposed voluntary arrangements.

The provisions are similar but not the same. They are as follows:

(1)   *Administrator*

Where an administration order has been made, the administrator is under a statutory duty to require a statement of affairs to be compiled[2]. The procedure is for the administrator to serve a 'notice requiring submission of administration statement of affairs' on certain persons connected with the company outlined in the statute (see page 361). The notice has to be in a prescribed form[3]. The persons required to compile the statement have 21 days beginning on the day after they get the notice[4]. The persons making up the statement may be

---

1 Insolvency (Scotland) Rules 1986, r 7.30.
2 Insolvency Act 1986, s 22(1).
3 Form 2.5(Scot).
4 Insolvency Act 1986, s 22(4).

paid by the administrator out of his receipts[1]. The administrator is under a statutory obligation within three months of the administration, unless the period is extended by the court, to send a statement of his proposals to the Registrar of Companies and to all creditors, and to lay a copy before a meeting of the creditors[2]. The statement of the proposals must have attached a copy or summary of the statement of affairs with the administrator's comments, if any[3].

## (2) Receiver

A receiver is also under a statutory duty to require a statement of affairs[4]. This he must do as soon as he is appointed[5]. As in the case of an administrator, the persons who are required to produce a statement of affairs (see page 361) must do so within 21 days from the day after the notice of requirement of a statement of affairs is given to them by the receiver[6]. The form of notice of requirement to give a statement of affairs is Form 3.1 (Scot). As in the case of an administrator, the persons compiling the statement may be paid by the receiver, as expenses of the receivership, the reasonable costs of compiling the report[7]. The receiver is under a statutory duty within three months of his appointment to send to the registrar, to the holder of the floating charge, to any trustees for secured creditors and the creditors themselves, a report giving the background to the receivership and the amounts likely to be available for payment to preferential creditors and other creditors[8]. The receiver is also under a statutory duty to send a copy of the report to all unsecured creditors or to publish a notice stating an address to which unsecured creditors of the company should write for copies of the report to be sent to them free of charge[9]. A report must also be laid before a meeting of the company's unsecured creditors on not less than 14 days' notice[9]. Though the statement of affairs does not have to be sent to the various persons mentioned above, the receiver is under a statutory duty to include in the report a summary of the statement of affairs and his comments on it[10]. Section 67(6) of the Insolvency Act 1986 makes it clear that the receiver does not have to include in his report information which might seriously prejudice the carrying out of the receivership. This would include matters under negotiation with third parties and indicate why the statement of affairs itself would be too sensitive for publication. When the company is collecting in debts, it does not want to have to publish what the receiver thinks is the likely realisable value of the book debts.

## (3) Liquidations

Where in the course of a members' voluntary winding up, the liquidator is of the opinion that the company will be unable to pay its debts in full, the

---

1 Insolvency (Scotland) Rules 1986, r 2.6(1).
2 Insolvency Act 1986, s 23(1).
3 Insolvency (Scotland) Rules 1986, r 2.7(d).
4 Insolvency Act 1986, s 66(1).
5 Ibid, s 66(1).
6 Ibid, s 66(4).
7 Insolvency (Scotland) Rules 1986, r 3.3(1).
8 Insolvency Act 1986, s 67(1).
9 Ibid, s 67(2).
10 Ibid, s 67(5).

liquidator is under a statutory obligation to compile a statement of affairs[1]. The statement of affairs shall be in a prescribed form[2]. In the case of a creditors' voluntary winding up, the directors of the company are under a statutory obligation to make out a statement of affairs[3]. The statement of affairs shall be in a prescribed form[4]. In the case of a winding up by the court, the liquidator may require a statement of affairs from persons connected (see paragraph 5) with the company[5]. The procedure, as in receiverships and administrations, is for a notice to be served on the persons who are to draw up the statement of affairs. The notice has to be in a prescribed form[6]. Persons being required to draw up the statement of affairs have 21 days from the day after the serving of the notice to make up the statement of affairs[7].

In the case of a creditors' voluntary winding up the liquidator is under a statutory duty to send a copy of the statement of affairs or a summary of it to all creditors and contributories within 28 days of the first meeting following the resolution for winding up of the company (Schedule 1, paragraph 6 of the Insolvency (Scotland) Rules 1986)[8]. In the case of a winding up by the court, where there has been a statement of affairs, the liquidator has a discretion whether to send out a copy of the statement of affairs or summary to creditors and contributories[8].

In addition, the liquidator, if required by the liquidation committee, shall send a written report to every member of the committee setting out the position generally as regards the progress of the winding up and matters arising in connection with it, to which the liquidator considers the committee's attention should be drawn[9].

## (4)   Voluntary arrangements

Where the directors are making a proposal under section 1 of the Insolvency Act 1986 and make up a statement of affairs under rule 1.5, the nominee must give a report to the court within 28 days of getting notice of the proposal (subject to extension by the court)[10]. This report must have lodged with it a copy or summary of the statement of affairs[11]. If the report is in favour of the proposal being considered, the nominee is duty bound to summon a meeting of the company and its creditors on at least 14 days' notice (not more than 28)[12] to consider the proposal[13]. The notice shall include a copy of the statement of affairs, or if he thinks fit, a summary of it, which must include a list of the creditors and the amount of their debts[14].

Where an administrator or liquidator is making a proposal but is not the

---

1 Insolvency Act 1986, s 95(3).
2 Form 4.4(Scot).
3 Insolvency Act 1986, s 99(1).
4 Form 4.4(Scot).
5 Insolvency Act 1986, s 131(1).
6 Form 4.3(Scot).
7 Insolvency Act 1986, s 131(4).
8 Insolvency (Scotland) Rules 1986, r 4.10 as amended by Article 12 of Schedule to Insolvency (Scotland) Amendment Rules 1987.
9 Insolvency (Scotland) Rules 1986, r 4.56(1).
10 Insolvency Act 1986, s 2(2).
11 Insolvency (Scotland) Rules 1986, r 1.7(1).
12 Ibid, r 1.9(1).
13 Insolvency Act 1986, s 3(1).
14 Insolvency (Scotland) Rules 1986, r 1.9(2).

nominee, there is the same duty described above on a nominee, as there is when directors are making the proposal, about reporting to the court and summoning a meeting of the company and the creditors, with the same need to lodge with the court a copy or summary of the statement of affairs and attach a copy or summary of the statement of affairs and attach a copy or summary to the notice of the meeting[1].

Where an administrator or liquidator is intending to make a proposal and is the nominee, he must call a meeting of the company and its creditors on at least 14 days' notice to consider the proposal[2], and as above include a copy or summary of the statement of affairs[3].

### Persons to compile statement of affairs

Where an administrator requires a statement of affairs in terms of section 22(1), a receiver requires a statement of affairs in terms of section 66(1) and a liquidator requires it in terms of section 131(1) of the Insolvency Act 1986, they may require the information from various people connected with the company. They can ask all of them or some of them. The people who may be required are:

(a) current or former officers of the company (ie directors, managers or secretaries)[4];
(b) anyone who has taken part in the formation of the company within one year before the administration order, appointment of receiver or appointment of provisional liquidator (if no provisional liquidator the date of the winding-up order)[4];
(c) persons who are current employees of the company or who have been employees within the last year who, the administrator, receiver or liquidator is of the opinion, are capable of giving the requisite information[4];
(d) persons who have been directors, managers, secretary or employees of any company who is a director, manager or secretary of the company, or has been a director, manager or secretary of the company within a year[4].

These statements of affairs must be verified by affidavit by the persons required to submit them[5]. The administrator, receiver or liquidator respectively may release any person from any requirement if they think fit[6].

### Abstract of receipts and payments

The Insolvency (Scotland) Rules lay down a prescribed form on which administrators, receivers and liquidators have to report what money they have received and what money they have paid out during the course of their administrations, receiverships and liquidations, in accordance with their

1 Insolvency Act 1986, ss 2(3) and 3(2), and r 1.12(6).
2 Ibid, s 3(2), and r 1.11(1).
3 Insolvency (Scotland) Rules 1986, r 1.11(2).
4 Insolvency Act 1986, ss 22(3), 66(3) and 131(3).
5 Ibid, ss 22(2), 66(2) and 131(2).
6 Ibid, ss 22(5), 66(5), and 131(5).

reporting duties set out in paragraph 7[1]. The forms for administrators and receivers are the same and require details of receipts and payments and totals from the previous abstract carried forward and added to the receipts and payments within the period to which the current abstract relates. The form for liquidators has a similar style in relation to receipts and payments but also has a section setting out an 'Analysis of Balance' which breaks down the balance of receipts over payments in the hands of the liquidator into:

(1) cash in the hands of the liquidator;
(2) balances on current account or deposit receipt; and
(3) investments made by the liquidator.

There is also a section headed 'Progress Report'. This merely sets out in brief the estimated assets and liabilities at the date of the commencement of the winding up in accordance with the statement of affairs, setting down the assets and inserting figures for secured creditors, debenture holders, preferential claims and services, and leads to the sum which should be available for unsecured creditors. There is then a third section which requires the following:

(a) total amount of the capital paid up at the commencement of the winding up;
(b) a description with relevant estimated financial figures of changes in the projected financial state of affairs of the company from that originally projected in the statement of affairs;
(c) a description and estimated value of outstanding unrealised assets of the company;
(d) causes which might delay the termination of the winding up; and
(e) the period which the liquidator projects that he will need to complete the winding up.

The reason for the 'Analysis of Balance' and 'Progress Report' (it is not a new style – formerly Form 92(Scot)) in the case of liquidations is to give the creditors and contributories a running report of the likely dividend, if any, they are going to get in accord with their particular claim. This progress report is not really necessary in the case of administrations and receiverships. Administrations and receiverships are not directed primarily to liquidating the company's assets and giving dividends to creditors and contributories. If that becomes necessary in the course of an administration or receivership, the company will go into liquidation and the fuller form of abstract of receipts and payments will be made by the liquidator.
Where there is a supervisor of a voluntary arrangement no style of abstract is prescribed although the style of the return is prescribed[2]. The accounting date is the date of the supervisor's appointment or of the end day of his last abstract[3]. Most abstracts will be quite simple but where a complicated scheme is involved detail should be given of the scheme so that it is clear from the abstract whether the scheme is working.

1 Administrations – Form 2.9(Scot); receiverships – Form 3.2(Scot); and liquidations – Form 4.5(Scot).
2 Form 1.3(Scot).
3 Insolvency (Scotland) Rules 1986, r 1.21(3).

## Reporting requirements in relation to abstracts

Administrators, receivers, liquidators and supervisors of voluntary arrangements have slightly different reporting requirements. They are as follows:

### (1) *Administrators*

The administrator is under a statutory duty to send to the court, to the Registrar of Companies, and to each member of the creditors' committee, an abstract of receipts and payments as referred to above[1]. The abstract must be sent within two months from the end of the six months after the date of his appointment and within two months of every subsequent period of six months. He must also send an abstract within two months after he ceases to act as an administrator[2].

### (2) *Receivers*

The receiver is under a statutory duty to send an abstract of his receipts and payments[3] to the Registrar of Companies, the holder of a floating charge by virtue of which he was appointed, and the members of the creditors' committee if there is one[4]. The receiver must send the abstract within two months from the end of 12 months after his appointment and thereafter at 12-monthly intervals. He must also send an abstract within two months after he ceases to act as a receiver[4].

### (3) *Liquidators*

The liquidator is under a statutory duty to send to the Registrar of Companies a statement if the winding up of a company is not concluded within one year after its commencement[5]. The first statement must be sent not more than 30 days after the end of that year, and subsequent statements must be sent not more than 30 days after the end of each accounting period after that year[6]. The statute lays down that the report must not only give particulars in relation to the proceedings in the liquidation but also the position of the liquidation. The prescribed form includes an abstract or statement as well as a progress report. Hence the need for the expanded Form 4.5(Scot) in comparison to the ones for administrations and receiverships with shorter forms.

### (4) *Supervisors of voluntary arrangements*

Where there is a supervisor of a voluntary arrangement he shall send, every 12 months, an abstract of receipts and payments to the court, the Registrar of Companies, the company, those creditors bound by the arrangement and, when the company is not in liquidation, to the company's auditors[7].

1 Insolvency (Scotland) Rules 1986, r 2.17.
2 Insolvency (Scotland) Rules 1986, r 2.17(1).
3 Form 3.2(Scot).
4 Insolvency (Scotland) Rules 1986, r 3.9(1).
5 Insolvency Act 1986, s 192(1).
6 Insolvency (Scotland) Rules 1986, r 4.11, as amended by the Insolvency (Scotland) Amendment Rules 1987, Schedule, art 13.
7 Insolvency (Scotland) Rules 1986, r 1.21(2).

## Annual accounts

### (1) Receivers

In addition to his duty to prepare an abstract of his receipts and payments, the receiver has a duty, as the company's agent, to keep sufficient accounting records to enable the company to comply with section 221 of the Companies Act 1985, as amended by section 2 of the Companies Act 1989, in relation to accounting, i e sufficient to disclose with reasonable accuracy, at any time, the financial position of the company at that time[1].

### (2) Administrators

Though the question has not been tested in Scotland, it is thought that administrators are under the same duty as receivers in relation to the keeping of accounting records for the following reasons:

(1)  an administration order cannot be pronounced when a company has gone into liquidation[2];
(2)  no resolution may be passed or order made for the winding up of the company during the period beginning with the presentation of a petition for an administration order and ending with the making of an order or dismissal of the petition[3];
(3)  an administrator may remove a director, but until he is removed the director remains in office[4];
(4)  on the making of an administration order, any petition for the winding up of the company shall be dismissed and any administrative receiver of the company shall vacate office[5];
(5)  the administrator is deemed to act as the agent of the company[6].

These reasons for the purposes of the accounting provisions of the Companies Acts suggest that an administrator is in an analogous position to a receiver. He, as deemed agent of the company, will be under a duty to keep accounting records. (There is a provision in the Insolvency (Scotland) Rules 1986 that the requirement of a receiver to send abstracts of his receipts and payments is 'without prejudice to the receiver's duty to render proper accounts required otherwise'[7]. This is probably a reference to the generally accepted accounting duties of a receiver in terms of section 221 of the Companies Act 1985, as amended by section 2 of the Companies Act 1989. Surprisingly, there is no direct reference to this in relation to administrators.)

---

1 *Smith Ltd v Middleton* [1979] 3 All ER 942.
2 Insolvency Act 1986, s 8(4).
3 Ibid, s 10(1).
4 Ibid, s 14(2).
5 Ibid, s 11(1).
6 Ibid, s 14(5).
7 Insolvency (Scotland) Rules 1986, r 3.9(4).

## Final accounts

### (1)   *Voluntary windings up*

Only in the case of liquidations can one properly talk about a 'final account'. In the case of a receivership and an administration, there is no final account, merely the last account after they cease to act[1]. In the case of a members' voluntary winding up and a creditors' voluntary winding up the liquidator is under a statutory duty to make up an account of the winding up, showing how it has been conducted and how the company's property has been disposed of[2]. In the case of a members' voluntary winding up, he must then call a general meeting of the company for the purpose of laying before it the account, and giving an explanation of it[3]. Similarly in the case of a creditors' voluntary winding up, he must then call a general meeting of the company and a meeting of the creditors for the purpose of laying the account before the meeting and giving an explanation of it[4]. Within one week of the meeting/meetings, the liquidator is under an obligation to send to the Registrar of Companies a copy of the account. He must also make a return of the holding of the meeting/ meetings and of their dates[5]. There is a prescribed form for the liquidator's statement of account in members' and creditors' voluntary windings up, namely Form 4.26(Scot) (see Appendix VII). The statement of account in voluntary windings up briefly gives a statement of receipts taken in by the liquidator less his outgoings giving 'net realisations'. There is then a flow chart showing how the net realisations have been distributed in order of: (a) expenses of solicitor to liquidator, (b) other legal expenses, (c) liquidator's remuneration, (d) other liquidation expenses, (e) payments to debenture holders, (f) payments to preferential creditors, (g) payments to unsecured creditors (dividends in the £), (h) returns to contributories with a division according to the type of shares.

### (2)   *Winding up by the court*

In a winding up by the court, the liquidator must submit a final liquidator's statement of receipts and payments but this is still in the form of previous statements, namely Form 4.5(Scot). The final return should be sent immediately the assets have been fully realised and distributed, notwithstanding that six months may not have elapsed since the previous return (returns have to be at six-monthly intervals)[6]. The Form 4.26(Scot) for voluntary windings up is a more extensive form than Form 4.5(Scot) for windings up by the court when it is serving as a final return. (The format of Form 4.5(Scot) makes no mention of distributions to contributories.) It is suggested that a schedule is attached to the liquidator's statement of receipts and payments in a final return to give a breakdown of the receipts, a breakdown of the statement of assets and liabilities and finally a breakdown of payments running through the items in the order that they are found in a

---

1 Insolvency (Scotland) Rules 1986, rr 2.17(1) and 3.9(1).
2 Insolvency Act 1986, ss 94(1) and 106(1).
3 Ibid, s 94(1).
4 Ibid, s 106(1).
5 Ibid, ss 94(3) and 106(3).
6 r 4.11 as amended by the Insolvency (Scotland) Amendment Rules 1987, Schedule, art 13.

statement of account in a voluntary winding up. Obviously, where there is no payment to contributories, the final section of the account can be omitted.

(3) *Supervisor of voluntary arrangement*

In terms of rule 1.23 the supervisor must send to the members, creditors who are bound by the scheme and the Registrar of Companies, a copy of a report by him, summarising all receipts and payments made by him in pursuance of the arrangement, and explaining any difference in the actual implementation of it as compared with the proposal approved by the creditors' and company meetings. The report to the Registrar goes with Form 1.4(Scot).

## Reports under Company Directors Disqualification Act 1986

Liquidators, administrators and receivers are under a duty to make a report to the Secretary of State if it appears to them that a person who has been a director of the company which has become insolvent has conducted himself in a way which renders him unfit to be concerned in the management of a company[1]. The matters which are relevant in considering whether a director is unfit are listed in Part II of Schedule I to the Company Directors Disqualification Act 1986. From an accounting point of view, the key parts are:

(1) paragraph 6 of Schedule 1: 'the extent of the directors' responsibility for the causes of the company becoming insolvent';
(2) paragraph 7 of Schedule 1: 'the extent of the directors' responsibility for any failure by the company to supply any goods or services which have been paid for (in whole or in part).'

The liquidator, administrator or receiver must form a view as to the accounting information which was available and should have been available to directors and whether that should have put them on the alert. In determining whether a company was insolvent, the company is now deemed to be unable to pay its debts if it is proved to the satisfaction of the court that the value of the company's assets is less than the amount of its liabilities, taking into account its contingent and prospective liabilities.

## General accounting matters in insolvency accounts

There are no accounting conventions in Scotland which specifically govern the preparation of insolvency accounts which are not now implicit in the legally prescribed forms, although if the business continues to trade other conventions will be applicable to the trading accounts. There are also no Standard Statements of Accounting Practice (SSAPs). The following paragraphs give one or two points of practical guidance.

(1) *Assets – realisable value*

In the 'statement of affairs', which is now the fundamental accounting document in insolvency, the figures which are being asked for are the sums

---

1 Company Directors Disqualification Act 1986, s 7(3).

which the various assets are estimated to produce. To highlight how this concept differs from a normal annual account, a separate column is given in list A for 'book values'. Apart from liquid assets like bills of exchange, promissory notes, stocks and shares and short-term loans, the estimated realisable value of assets is likely to differ from book value. Normally stock is put in at cost and 'work in progress' is listed at cost. This means that in a company healthily trading, its stock and work in progress has a book value less than the market value of those items. The liquidator will have to look very carefully to whether the 'distress' element of an insolvency sale is going to reduce the value of these items or whether there is a sufficient market for there to be no 'distress element'.

In relation to heritable property, book value is normally historical cost. A liquidator should take appropriate steps to ascertain the present value of heritable property which might require him to commission an independent valuer's report. In relation to vehicles, they are probably being written down over five years and the book value may not reflect current market value. Plant and machinery is much more difficult to value and valuation will depend on the type of machinery. If the machinery is specialised for a particular trade which is now redundant, there could be no market at all for the machinery.

## (2)   Patents, trade marks

Patents, trade marks and other intellectual property may not have a book value in the last set of accounts. Trade marks and patents are dependent for their value on there being a demand for the goods for which they are patents or trade marks. If the market for these goods collapses (which often happens on insolvency), then the company has properly not ascribed them any book value. Great care should be taken not to dissipate the value of trade marks. The services of a trade mark agent should be taken for valuation purposes and guidance.

## (3)   Goodwill

As in the case of patents and trade marks, the last accounts will not normally have a figure for goodwill. Secondly, liquidation often leads to the dissipation of goodwill. However, this is not necessarily the case if parts of the business can be salvaged. Sometimes the goodwill is attached to a heritable property, in which case the goodwill will be valued under the estimated realisable value of the heritable property.

## (4)   Going concern

Assets will normally fetch more in the market place if they are sold as part of a going concern. Accordingly, the statement of affairs should list any part of the business which is likely to be able to be sold as a going concern. A trading account should be attached, as well as a balance sheet listing the assets of the going concern. This balance sheet could include the goodwill asset.

## (5)   Contingent liabilities

In normal accounts, a potential liability only has to be classed as a 'contingent liability' if it is considered that there is a realistic possibility of the liability crystallising within the foreseeable future. In a liquidation account, however, it is important to list all liabilities, however contingent, with a detailed analysis of them.

## (6)   *Deficiency account*

The statement of affairs in an insolvent company is bound to show a deficiency. A deficiency account attempts to explain in financial terms how the deficiency has arisen under heads such as (a) the amount by which the assets have been written down for the purposes of the statement of affairs; (b) the liabilities arising as a result of the insolvency; and (c) the trading loss since the last accounts.

# Chapter 18

# Creditors' committees

## Introduction

Under the Insolvency Act 1986, there is now provision for the establishment of creditors' committees in all three legal régimes on insolvency, namely administrations[1], receiverships[2] and liquidations[3]. In the case of administrations and receiverships, the committee of creditors is to be known as 'the creditors' committee'[4]. In liquidations the committee of creditors is to be known as 'the liquidation committee'.[5] Creditors' committees in administrations and receiverships perform almost exactly the same functions. In liquidations, the liquidation committee has a larger role and one significantly enhanced to that which it had previously, although the reforms have not gone as far as the Cork Committee recommended[6]. It is proposed to treat the creditors' committees in administrations and receiverships together, and then to deal with the liquidation committee.

## Creditors' committees in receiverships and administrations

### (1)  *Establishment and membership*

An administrator is required within three months of the making of the administration order (or such longer period as the court may allow) to summon a meeting of the company's creditors to decide whether to approve the administrator's proposals[7]. At this meeting, if (and only if) the meeting approves (with or without modifications) the proposals, the creditors may establish a creditors' committee[8]. Similarly, a receiver must within three months (or such longer period as the court may allow) after his appointment summon a meeting of the company's unsecured creditors in order to give them a report on the receivership[9]. That meeting of creditors may, if it thinks fit, establish a creditors' committee[10]. The committee must consist of at least three and not more than five creditors of the company elected at the meeting. Any creditor

---

1 Insolvency Act 1986, s 26(1).
2 Ibid, s 68(1).
3 Ibid, ss 101 and 142(1).
4 Ibid, ss 26(1) and 68(1).
5 Ibid, ss 101(1) and 142(1).
6 Report of the Review Committee on Insolvency Law and Practice (Cmnd 8558) at Chap 19.
7 Insolvency Act 1986, s 23.
8 Ibid, s 26.
9 Ibid, s 67(2).
10 Ibid, s 68(1).

of the company who has lodged a claim is eligible to be a member of the committee, so long as his claim has not been rejected for the purpose of his entitlement to vote[1]. A body corporate or a partnership may be a member of the committee, but it cannot act as such otherwise than by a representative appointed[2]. The creditors' committee comes into existence when the administrator or receiver issues a certificate of due constitution[3]. If the chairman of the meeting which resolves to establish the committee is not the administrator or receiver, he must forthwith give notice of the resolution to the administrator or receiver and inform him of the names and addresses of the persons elected to be members of the committee[4]. No person may act as a member of the committee unless and until he has agreed to do so, and the administrator's or receiver's certificate of the committee's due constitution must not be issued until at least the minimum number of persons has agreed to act. The receiver or administrator then issues a certificate[5] which he must send to the Registrar of Companies[6]. Any change in the establishment of the committee must be reported by the receiver or administrator to the Registrar of Companies[7].

## (2)  *Expenses of creditors' committees*

The administrator or receiver must defray any reasonable travelling expenses directly incurred by members of the creditors' committee or their representatives in respect of their attendance at the committee's meetings, or otherwise on the committee's business as an expense of the administration or receivership[8]. This does not apply to any meeting of the committee held within three months of a previous meeting[9].

## (3)  *Duties, powers and functions of creditors' committee*

The creditors' committee in relation to the administrator or receiver acts in such a manner as may be agreed from time to time with the administrator or receiver[10]. In addition, the creditors' committee in an administration must assist the administrator in discharging his functions[11]. In contrast, the creditors' committee in a receivership has no duty to assist the receiver, because their interests are usually not the same, but rather are under a legal duty to represent to the receiver the view of the unsecured creditors[12]. The creditors' committees may require the administrator or receiver to attend before them at any reasonable time on seven days' notice and require the administrator or receiver to furnish them with such information relating to the carrying out of his functions as they may reasonably require[13]. The committee in an

---

1 Insolvency (Scotland) Rules 1986, rr 2.15(1) and 3.4(2).
2 Ibid, rr 2.15(1) and 3.4(3).
3 Ibid, rr 2.15(1), 3.6(1) and 4.42(1).
4 Ibid, rr 2.15(1), 3.6(1), 4.42(2).
5 Form 4.20(Scot).
6 Insolvency (Scotland) Rules 1986, rr 2.15(1), 3.6(1) and 4.42(5).
7 Ibid, rr 2.15(1), 3.6(1) and 4.42(6).
8 Ibid, rr 2.15(1), 3.6(1) and (4) and 4.57(1).
9 Ibid, rr 2.15(1), 3.6(1) and 4.57(2).
10 Ibid, rr 2.15(4) and 3.5.
11 Ibid, r 2.15(4).
12 Ibid, r 3.5.
13 Insolvency Act 1986, ss 26(2) and 68(2).

administration is given the specific power on a vacancy occurring in the office of administrator in the absence of any continuing administrator to apply to the court to fill the vacancy[1]. The administrator or receiver must call a first meeting of the committee to take place within three months of his appointment or of the committee's establishment, whichever is the later, and after that he is under an obligation to call a meeting of the creditors' committee if he is requested by a creditor member of the committee; the meeting must then be held within 21 days of the request being received by the administrator or receiver[2].

## Liquidation committee

### (1) Establishment and membership

At the first meeting of creditors, the creditors may establish a liquidation committee[3]. In addition, in a compulsory winding up only, the liquidator may at any time, if he thinks fit, summon a general meeting of the company's creditors and contributors for the purpose of determining whether such a committee should be established, and if it is so determined, of establishing it[4]. He must also summon a meeting if he is requested in accordance with the Rules to do so by one-tenth in value of the company's creditors[5]. The liquidation committee in an insolvent liquidation consists of at least three and not more than five creditors of the company, elected by the meeting of creditors[6]. As in administrations and receiverships, the liquidation committee is constituted when the liquidator issues a certificate of its due constitution. The chairman of the meeting which resolved to establish the committee, if he is not the liquidator, must give notice of the resolution to the liquidator, and inform him of the names and addresses of the persons elected to be members of the committee[7]. The certificate must be sent by the liquidator to the Registrar of Companies[8].

### (2) Expenses of members of the liquidation committee

Members of the liquidation committee are entitled to reasonable travelling expenses as an expense of the liquidation, unless the previous meeting was held less than three months before[9]. The members of the liquidation committee occupy a fiduciary position in relation to the company and no conflict of interest should arise between their interests and their duty if this can be helped[10]. This is reinforced by the Insolvency (Scotland) Rules 1986 which contain detailed provision relating to dealings by committee members. Briefly a member of a committee is prohibited from receiving out of the company's assets any payment for services given or goods supplied in connection with the

---

1 Ibid, s 13(3).
2 Insolvency (Scotland) Rules 1986, rr 2.15(1), 3.6(1) and 4.45.
3 Insolvency Act 1986, ss 101 and 142.
4 Ibid, s 142(2).
5 Ibid, s 142(3).
6 Insolvency (Scotland) Rules 1986, r 4.41(1).
7 Ibid, r 4.42(2).
8 Ibid, r 4.42(5); Form 4.20 (Scot).
9 Insolvency (Scotland) Rules 1986, r 4.57.
10 Re F T Hawkins & Co Ltd [1952] Ch 881.

liquidation, or obtaining any profit from the liquidation, or acquiring any part of the company's assets[1]. This however is allowed (i) with the prior leave of the court, or (ii) if he does so as a matter of urgency, or (iii) by performance of a contract in force before the date on which the company went into liquidation, if the committee member obtains the court's leave for the transaction, having applied for leave without undue delay[2]. Alternatively, he may enter into a transaction with the prior sanction of the liquidation committee, where it is satisfied (after full disclosure of the circumstances) that the transaction will be on normal commercial terms[3].

### (3)   *Powers of liquidation committee*

The sanction of the committee or the court is necessary in a compulsory winding up, but not a creditors' voluntary winding up, to empower a liquidator to engage in legal proceedings[4]. Similarly in a compulsory winding up, but not a creditors' winding up, the sanction of the liquidation committee or the court is necessary to enable a liquidator to carry on the business of the company for its beneficial winding up[5]. In addition, the sanction of the liquidation committee or the court is necessary for the liquidator to distribute the estate, shorten the accounting period, pay a class of creditors in full, make compromises and arrangements with creditors or compromises with debtors (see 'extraordinary powers of liquidators', chapter 3).

### (4)   *Relationship of liquidator to liquidation committee*

The liquidator is under an obligation to report to the liquidation committee such matters as appear to him, or they have indicated are, of interest to them. In the latter case, the liquidator need not comply if:

(1)   the request is frivolous or unreasonable;
(2)   the cost of compliance is out of proportion to the importance of the information;
(3)   there are insufficient assets[6].

The liquidation committee meets when the liquidator decides, subject to two conditions:

(a)   the first meeting must be held within three months of the committee's establishment or the liquidator's appointment, whichever is later;
(b)   thereafter, meetings must be called if requested by a creditor member of the committee (the meeting to be held within 21 days of the request being received), and be set for a specified date if the committee has previously so resolved, with meetings held on seven days' notice[7].

The liquidator must report to the liquidation committee in writing as directed

---

1 Insolvency (Scotland) Rules 1986, r 4.58(2).
2 Ibid, r 4.58(3).
3 Ibid, r 4.58(3)(c); see *Re Gallard* [1896] 1 QB 68.
4 Insolvency Act 1986, ss 165 and 167 and Sch 4, para 4.
5 Ibid, ss 165 and 167 and Sch 4, para 5.
6 Insolvency (Scotland) Rules 1986, r 4.44.
7 Ibid, r 4.45.

by it (but not more often than once in any period of two months), setting out the position as regards the progress of the winding up and matters arising out of it[1].

## Meetings of creditors' committee and liquidation committee

The chairman of meetings is to be the administrator, receiver or liquidator or a person nominated by him to act[2]. If he is acting through a nominee, the nominee must be a person who is qualified to act as an insolvency practitioner in relation to the company, or an employee of the administrator, receiver, or liquidator, or his firm, who is experienced in insolvency matters[3]. A meeting of the committee is duly constituted if due notice of it has been given to all the members and at least two members are present or represented[4]. A member of the creditors' committee or liquidation committee may be represented by another person duly authorised by him for that purpose, provided that the person acting as a committee member's representative must hold a mandate entitling him to act (either generally, or specially) signed by or on behalf of the committee member[5]. A member of the creditors' or liquidation committee may resign by notice in writing delivered to the administrator, receiver or liquidator[6]. Membership of the creditors' or liquidation committee is automatically terminated if the member becomes bankrupt, does not attend three consecutive meetings of the committee (unless at the third of those meetings it is resolved that this rule should not apply), or the creditor ceases to be or is found never to have been a creditor[7]. A member of the committee may be removed by resolution at a meeting of the creditors[8].

## Liquidation committee where winding up follows administration

If a creditors' committee has been established in an administration, and a liquidation follows on from the administration, the creditors' committee continues and is deemed to be a liquidation committee[9].

---

1 Ibid, r 4.56.
2 Ibid, rr 2.15(1), 3.6(1) and r 4.46(1).
3 Ibid, rr 2.15(1), 3.6(1) and 4.46(2).
4 Ibid, rr 2.15(1), 3.6(1) and 4.47.
5 Ibid, rr 2.15(1), 3.6(1) and 4.48(1) and (2), as amended by the Insolvency (Scotland) Amendment Rules 1987, Schedule, art 24.
6 Insolvency (Scotland) Rules 1986, rr 2.15(1), 3.6(1) and 4.49.
7 Ibid, rr 2.15(1), 3.6(1) and 4.50.
8 Ibid, rr 2.15(1), 3.6(1) and 4.51.
9 Ibid, r 4.61(1).

# Chapter 19

# Miscellaneous aspects of corporate insolvency law

## Meetings

The Insolvency (Scotland) Rules 1986 lay down detailed provisions in relation to meetings held in insolvency proceedings, other than meetings of creditors' committees in administrations or receiverships or of the liquidation committee. 'Insolvency proceedings' is defined to mean any proceedings in relation to voluntary arrangements, administrations, receiverships and windings up[1]. There is therefore now in place a general code for the conduct of meetings. In addition, given the special nature of the proceedings, where a voluntary arrangement is being considered, and where an administrator's proposals are being considered, there are special provisions[2].

Most of the above-mentioned rules are of a procedural nature and should be consulted by those convening meetings, or attending meetings. However, the provisions are dealt with briefly from a legal point of view.

### (1)  *Summoning of meetings*

In fixing the date, time and place for a meeting, the person summoning the meeting ('the convenor') must have regard to the convenience of the persons who are to attend, and meetings in all cases must be summoned for commencement between 10 am and 4 pm on a business day, unless the court otherwise directs[3]. The convenor must give not less than 21 days' notice of the date, time and place of the meeting to every person known to him as being entitled to attend the meeting except where the meeting is one of creditors to consider a directors' proposal for voluntary arrangement, or a meeting of creditors summoned to consider an administrator's proposals, or a meeting of unsecured creditors in receivership, under section 67(2) of the Insolvency Act 1986, or a meeting of creditors or contributories under section 138(3) or (4) of the Insolvency Act 1986, when the requisite notice is 14 days[4]. The notice must have accompanying it a proxy form[5]. The statutory style of proxy form is Appendix V.

---

1 Insolvency (Scotland) Rules 1986, r 0.21.
2 Ibid, Pt I, chap 5 and Pt II, chap 3.
3 Ibid, r 7.2. A 'business day' is defined by r 0.2(1) to be any day other than a Saturday or Sunday, Christmas Day, Good Friday or a day which is a bank holiday in any part of Great Britain (ie bank holidays in Scotland and England, but not in Northern Ireland).
4 Ibid, r 7.3(1) and (2), as amended by the Insolvency (Scotland) Amendment Rules 1987, Schedule, art 35.
5 Insolvency (Scotland) Rules 1986, r 7.3(5).

## (2)  Quorum

The requisite quorum in a creditors' meeting is at least one creditor, and in the case of a meeting of contributories, at least two contributories, or all the contributories, if their number does not exceed two[1]. A quorum may be constituted by a proxy vote[2].

## (3)  Entitlement to vote

At a creditors' meeting, a creditor is entitled to vote at any meeting if he has submitted his claim to 'the responsible insolvency practitioner', which is defined to mean in relation to any insolvency proceedings the person acting as supervisor of a voluntary arrangement, the administrator, the receiver or liquidator or provisional liquidator[3]. In relation to members of the company or contributories at their meetings, votes are according to the rights attaching to shares in accordance with the articles of association of the company[4]. In the case of a meeting of members of the company in a voluntary arrangement, even if no voting rights attach to his member's share, a member is entitled to vote either for or against the proposal or any modification of it[5].

## (4)  Chairman of meetings

The chairman at any meeting of creditors in insolvency proceedings other than a meeting of creditors summoned under section 98 of the Insolvency Act 1986 must be the responsible insolvency practitioner, or a person nominated by him in writing, and if a person is nominated he must, except at a meeting of creditors summoned under section 95 of the Insolvency Act 1986, be either qualified to act as an insolvency practitioner or an employee of the firm of the insolvency practitioner who is experienced in insolvency matters[6]. The same provision applies to meetings of contributories in a liquidation[7].

## (5)  Resolutions

At any meeting of creditors, contributories or members of a company, a resolution is passed when a majority in value of those voting, in person or by proxy, has voted in favour of it[8]. However, as previously referred to at page 167, there is an important exception in the case of a voluntary arrangement. At a creditors' meeting for any resolution to pass, approving any proposal or modification, there must be at least three-quarters in value of the creditors present or represented and voting, in person or by proxy, in favour of the resolution[9]. In the case of a resolution for the appointment of a liquidator, where there is more than one candidate the person with a majority in value of

---

1 Ibid, r 7.7(1).
2 Ibid, r 7.7(2).
3 Ibid, rr 0.2(1) and 7.9(2).
4 Ibid, r 7.10(1).
5 Ibid, r 7.10(2).
6 Ibid, r 7.5(2).
7 Ibid, r 7.5(3).
8 Ibid, r 7.12(1).
9 Ibid, r 7.12(2).

the votes is appointed, with progressive elimination of candidates until one candidate has a clear majority where there are several candidates[1].

## (6) *Voluntary arrangements*

Where meetings of creditors and contributories are summoned under section 3 of the Insolvency Act 1986 to consider a proposal for a voluntary arrangement, the meetings of creditors and contributories must be held on the same day and in the same place but the creditors' meeting must be fixed for a time in advance of the company meeting[2]. The convenor may require directors of the company to attend or other officers of the company, past and present[3]. On the day on which the meetings are held, they may from time to time be adjourned, or may be held together if the chairman thinks that appropriate for the purpose of obtaining simultaneous agreement of the meetings to the proposal[4]. If the requisite majority is not obtained, the chairman may adjourn the meetings, and must adjourn the meetings if that is resolved[5]. If there are subsequent adjournments, the final adjournment may not be later than 14 days after the date on which the meetings were originally held, and if following any final adjournment of the meetings the proposal is not agreed by both meetings, it is deemed to be rejected[6].

## (7) *Administrations*

The administrator must give at least 14 days' notice to any directors or officers that he requires them to attend a meeting of creditors summoned under section 23(1) of the Insolvency Act 1986 to consider his proposals[7]. If at the meeting there is not the requisite majority for approval of the administrator's proposals (with modifications, if any), the chairman may, and must if a resolution is passed to that effect, adjourn the meeting for not more than 14 days[8].

## Proxies and corporate representatives

A proxy may be given generally for all meetings in insolvency proceedings or for a particular meeting or class of meetings[9]. Forms of proxy must be sent out with every notice summoning a meeting of creditors or contributories[10]. A proxy must be in the form sent out with the notice summoning the meeting or in a form substantially to the same effect[11]. A form of proxy must be filled out and signed by the principal, or by some person acting under his authority. Where it is signed by someone other than the principal, the nature of his

---

1 Insolvency (Scotland) Rules 1986, r 7.12(3).
2 Ibid, r 1.14(2).
3 Ibid, r 1.15.
4 Ibid, r 1.16(1).
5 Ibid, r 1.16(2).
6 Ibid, r 1.16(6).
7 Ibid, r 2.10(1).
8 Ibid, r 2.10(2).
9 Ibid, r 7.14(2).
10 Ibid, r 7.15(1).
11 Ibid, r 7.15(3).

authority must be stated on the form[1]. A proxy given for a particular meeting may be used at any adjournment of the meeting[2]. The proxy may be lodged at or before the meeting at which it is to be used[3]. Where the responsible insolvency practitioner holds proxies to be used by him as chairman of the meeting and some other person then acts as chairman, the other person may use the insolvency practitioner's proxies as if he were himself proxy-holder[4]. Where a proxy directs a proxy-holder to vote for or against a resolution for the nomination or appointment of a person to be the responsible insolvency practitioner, the proxy-holder may, unless the proxy states otherwise, vote for or against (as he thinks fit) any resolution for the nomination or appointment of that person jointly with another or others[5]. A proxy-holder may propose any resolution which, if proposed by another, would be a resolution in favour of which he would be entitled to vote by virtue of the proxy[6]. Where a proxy gives specific directions as to voting, this does not, unless the proxy states otherwise, preclude the proxy-holder from voting at his discretion on resolutions put to the meeting which are not dealt with in the proxy[7]. The insolvency practitioner must retain all proxies in the sederunt book[8]. Creditors, members and contributories have a right to inspect proxies used at their respective meetings, and to take copies on paying the appropriate fee. The creditors are defined in the case of a company in liquidation as those creditors whose claims have been accepted in whole or in part, and in any other case, persons who have submitted in writing a claim to be creditors of the company concerned[9]. In neither case is a creditor included whose claim has been wholly rejected for purposes of voting, dividend or otherwise[9]. The rule allowing inspection is also available to the directors[10]. Any person attending a meeting is entitled to inspect proxies and claims, either immediately before or during the meeting, and whether they are to be used at the meeting or not[11]. A proxy-holder must not vote in favour of any resolution which would directly or indirectly place him, or any associate of his, in a position to receive any remuneration out of the insolvency state unless the proxy specifically directs him to vote in that way[12]. Where a person is authorised under section 375 of the Companies Act 1985 to represent a corporation at a meeting of creditors or contributories, he must produce to the chairman of the meeting a copy of the resolution from which he derives his authority[13]. The copy must be executed in accordance with what is now section 36B of the Companies Act 1985 as added by section 130(3) of the Companies Act 1989, but substituted by the Law Reform (Miscellaneous Provisions) (Scotland) Act 1990, or be certified by the secretary or a director of

1 Ibid, r 7.15(4).
2 Ibid, r 7.16(1).
3 Ibid, r 7.16(2).
4 Ibid, r 7.16(3).
5 Ibid, r 7.16(4) (inserted by the Insolvency (Scotland) Amendment Rules 1987, Schedule, art 43.
6 Insolvency (Scotland) Rules 1986, r 7.16(5) (inserted by the Insolvency (Scotland) Amendment Rules 1987, Schedule, art 43.
7 Insolvency (Scotland) Rules 1986, r 7.16(6) (inserted by the Insolvency (Scotland) Amendment Rules 1987, Schedule, art 43.
8 Insolvency (Scotland) Rules 1986, r 7.17(3).
9 Ibid, r 7.18.
10 Ibid, r 7.18(3).
11 Ibid, r 7.18(4) (amended by Insolvency (Scotland) Amendment Rules 1987, Schedule, art 44.
12 Insolvency (Scotland) Rules 1986, r 7.19.
13 Ibid, r 7.20(1).

the corporation to be a true copy in terms of rule 7.20(2) of the Insolvency (Scotland) Rules 1986.

## Winding up of insurance companies

### Separate régime of insurance companies

Insurance companies are treated in a different legal way from other companies. The legislation governing them in Scotland is largely covered by the Insurance Companies Act 1982 and the Insurance Companies Winding Up (Scotland) Rules 1986. As a result of the need to conform with an EEC Directive No 73/239, 23 July 1973, and EEC Directive No 79/267, 5 March 1979, insurance companies including life assurance companies must maintain solvency margins at least as high as the Community margin of solvency which is uniform throughout the European Community[1]. The other key feature in relation to insurance companies is that where the company carries on ordinary long-term business or industrial assurance business, the company must maintain an account in respect of that business and the receipts of that business must be entered in the account maintained for that business and form a separate insurance fund with an appropriate name[2]. The fund maintained by an insurance company in respect of its long-term business must be applicable only for the purposes of that business, and may not be transferred so as to be available for other purposes of the company except where the transfer constitutes reimbursement of expenditure borne by other assets (in the same or the last preceding financial year) in discharging liabilities wholly or partly attributable to long-term business[3]. It is not open to the company to grant a floating charge over these assets and they may not be attached by way of diligence[4]. Insurance companies may not be wound up voluntarily[5]. In contrast to other companies, where an insurance company carries on long-term business the liquidator must, unless the court otherwise orders, carry on the long-term business of the company with a view to its being transferred as a going concern to another insurance company[6]. When an insurance company which carries on long-term business is in winding up, its businesses are separated. The assets of the company which are available for meeting the liabilities of the company attributable to its long-term business are to be applied in discharge of those liabilities as though those assets and those liabilities were the assets and liabilities of a separate company[7]. The assets of the company available for meeting the liabilities of the company attributable to its other business are applied in discharge of those liabilities as though those assets and those liabilities were the assets and liabilities of a separate company[8].

1 Insurance Companies Act 1982, s 32(3).
2 Ibid, s 28(1).
3 Ibid, s 29(1).
4 Ibid, s 29(5).
5 Ibid, s 55(2).
6 Ibid, s 56(2).
7 Insurance Companies (Winding Up) (Scotland) Rules 1986, r 5(2).
8 Ibid, r 5(3).

## Remuneration of liquidators

The basis of remuneration which a liquidator may claim may be calculated by reference to the value of the company's estate; but there has to be taken into account (a) the work which, having regard to that value, was reasonably undertaken by the liquidator; and (b) the extent of his responsibilities in administering the company's assets[1]. The liquidator may at any time before the end of an accounting period submit to the liquidation committee (if any) an interim claim in respect of that period for the outlays reasonably incurred by him, and for his remuneration; and the liquidation committee may make an interim determination in relation to the amount of the outlays and remuneration payable to the liquidator. Where they do so, the committee must take into account that interim determination when making their final determination[2]. If the liquidator considers that the remuneration fixed by the remuneration committee is insufficient, he may request that it be increased by a resolution of the creditors[3]. If the liquidator is still not satisfied, he may apply to the court for an order increasing the amount or rates. The liquidation committee may be heard at the hearing of the application or, if there is no such committee, the court may order that notice of the application be sent to one or more creditors, who may nominate one or more of their number to appear or be represented[4]. Any remuneration fixed by the liquidation committee or by resolution of creditors may be challenged on application by creditors representing 25 per cent or more in value of the creditors on the basis that the liquidator's remuneration is excessive[5].

1 Bankruptcy (Scotland) Act 1985, s 53 as applied to liquidators by Insolvency (Scotland) Rules 1986, r 4.32(1).
2 Insolvency (Scotland) Rules 1986, r 4.32(2).
3 Ibid, r 4.33.
4 Ibid, r 4.34.
5 Ibid, r 4.35.

# Chapter 20

# Corporate insolvency – international dimensions

## Introduction

Where corporate insolvencies have an international dimension, such as where a Scottish company in winding up seeks to have its orders enforced in another country, or the equivalent of the liquidator of a company under a winding up régime in a separate jurisdiction wishes to have his court order enforced in Scotland, these problems are settled by the Scots rules of private international law. Although the Treaty of Union 1707 united the kingdoms of England and Scotland 'into one kingdom by the name of Great Britain' (Union with England Act 1706, Art I), this did not mean that questions of private international law would no longer arise between England and Scotland. On the contrary the Treaty of Union ensured that they would arise. Accordingly for the purposes of Scots private international law England remains a foreign country. Lord Chancellor Campbell stated in the case of *Stuart v Moore*[1]:

'As to judicial jurisdiction, Scotland and England, although politically under the same Crown, and under the supreme sway of one united legislature, are to be considered as independent countries, unconnected with one another. This case is of a judicial nature . . . and it is to be treated as if it had occurred in the reign of Queen Elizabeth.'

Similarly the Isle of Man, the Channel Islands and Northern Ireland are treated as foreign countries for the purposes of Scots private international law. That is of course true with the law of Ireland itself as with all other countries[2]. This separate system of international law has been consistently recognised in England. In the case of *Queensland Mercantile and Agency Co, ex p Australasian Investment Co*[3] Lindley LJ stated:

'are we to say that the Scotch court is wrong because it takes a different view of the application of international law than that which we should take? I think not. This part of the international law as recognised by the Scotch law becomes part of the Scotch law; and, to my mind, this court at all events is not at liberty to review international law so far as it becomes part of the Scotch law, and which Scotch lawyers say is Scotch law.'

Accordingly Scots private international law must be proved as a question of fact by evidence in the English courts when questions arise, as must English private international law in the Scottish courts. The Scottish courts may also

---

1 (1861) 4 Macq 1.
2 *Faulkner v Hill* 1941 JC 20.
3 [1892] 1 Ch 219 at 226.

refuse to follow English principles in the field of private international law, where these principles are regarded as unsound in Scotland[1].

Although Scotland has a very different tradition in the field of private international law from England[2], the infrequency of cases in Scotland in comparison to England, and the growing uniformity of commercial law has meant that the Scottish courts have looked increasingly to English authority for guidance when questions arise. For example in the case of *Inland Revenue v Highland Engineering Ltd*[3] Lord Grieve stated:

'So far, I have considered the question apart from any authority which bears upon it, there being no Scottish authority that does. There are, however, two English authorities which do and I am happy to think that both support the view which I have taken regarding the suggested qualification of s 399 by s 444 (the Companies Act 1948). Had they not done so I would have felt constrained to reconsider my own opinon because it is clearly desirable that the construction of statutes which affect the United Kingdom should be the same both north and south of the border, particularly statutes such as the Companies Act.'

In fact in recent years the Scottish courts have turned more and more to English authorities for guidance and for understanding how this field of law was developing. In fact, in the words of Anton[4]:

'It would be unrealistic to suppose that the House of Lords would sanction one solution in England and another in Scotland.'

This inter-United Kingdom drive to a uniform approach, has been further reinforced not only by the increasing internationalisation of commerce and the need for corresponding uniformity of approach, but also by Brussels inducing legislation. The review of the insolvency laws themselves under Sir Kenneth Cork in the reports in 1976 and 1982[5] were produced under the assumption that it would soon be necessary for the United Kingdom to implement a projected EC wide draft Bankruptcy Convention. The motivation for the project of a European Bankruptcy Convention derived from a requirement imposed on the member states of the Community by Article 220 of the Treaty of Rome. In terms of the fourth paragraph of that Article there was an obligation on the member states to conclude a convention to secure, for the benefit of nationals, 'the simplification of formalities governing the reciprocal recognition and enforcement of judgments of courts or tribunals'. At an early stage, it was decided to separate the field of insolvency from the rest of the area of civil and commercial judgments covered by the remit in Article 220(4). The non-insolvency field became the subject of a separate convention which was concluded and came into force in February 1973. This Convention on Jurisdiction and Enforcement of Judgments in Civil and Commercial Matters ('the Brussels Convention') was incorporated into United Kingdom law by the Civil Jurisdiction and Judgments Act 1982. Although the Brussels Convention attempts formally to exclude insolvency matters, the dividing line between what is an insolvency matter and what is not is important in the determining of the scope of the Brussels Convention.

---

1 *McElroy v McAllister* 1949 SC 110 at 133.
2 See Anton *Private International Law* (2nd edn, 1990) pp 9–16.
3 1975 SLT 203 at 205.
4 *Anton*, p 14.
5 Cmnd 6602, and Cmnd 8558.

The draft Bankruptcy Convention proved too difficult and complex for agreement of the member states to be reached. The project has therefore been discontinued, without ever having been formally or publicly renounced[1]. Because of the discontinuance of the draft EC Bankruptcy Convention, there is now only a half finished structure in place in relation to the reciprocal enforcement of civil decrees in corporate insolvencies amongst the member states of the European Community and within the United Kingdom itself. Any matters falling within the area covered by the Civil Jurisdiction and Judgments Act 1982 must be decided in accordance with that Act. Similarly matters within the United Kingdom have to be determined by the Insolvency Act 1986 but also in accordance with the Civil Jurisdiction and Judgments Act 1982. It is accordingly proposed that this chapter shall be divided into three parts:

> PART I    describes generally the problems of international corporate cross-border insolvencies in Scots law;
> PART II   describes the scope and application of the Civil Jurisdiction and Judgments Act 1982 in cross-border corporate insolvency matters; and
> PART III  describes enforcement of court orders within the United Kingdom in corporate insolvency cases.

# I. INSOLVENCIES WITH INTERNATIONAL DIMENSIONS

### Jurisdiction of Scottish courts to wind up companies

The Court of Session has jurisdiction to wind up any company registered in Scotland[2]. Where the amount of a company's share capital paid up or credited as paid up does not exceed £120,000, the sheriff court of the sheriffdom in which the company's registered office is situated has concurrent jurisdiction with the Court of Session to wind up the company[3]. For the purposes of the Insolvency Act, the expression 'registered office' means the place which has longest been the company's registered office during the 6 months immediately preceding the presentation of the petition for winding up[4]. Formerly it was a matter of judicial construction that companies could not be wound up under the Scottish bankruptcy legislation[5]. The Bankruptcy (Scotland) Act 1985 states that the estate belonging to 'a body corporate or an unincorporated body' may be sequestrated, but provides that it shall not be competent to sequestrate the estate of:

'(a)   the company registered under the Companies Act 1985 or under the former Companies Act (within the meaning of that Act); or

---

1 For a short history of its progress, see Ian F Fletcher, *The Law of Insolvency* pp 619–623.
2 Insolvency Act 1986, s 120.
3 Ibid, s 120(3).
4 Ibid, s 120(4).
5 *Standard Property Investments Co Ltd v Dunblane Hydropathic Co Ltd* (1884) 12 R 328.

(b)   an entity in respect of which an enactment provides, expressly or by implication, that sequestration is incompetent.'[1]

The Bankruptcy (Scotland) Act 1985 is silent about foreign corporations, but the reasoning in the *Dunblane Hydropathic* case[2] would suggest that a court might well infer that sequestration was not competent in relation to foreign or other companies which may be wound up under the Insolvency Act 1986 as unregistered companies. Although sequestration is not apparently competent in relation to corporations, as an alternative to liquidation, the court may appoint a judicial factor[3]. It is thought that the court could appoint a judicial factor in the case of a foreign company, and it is perhaps sometimes a desirable option especially if there is a winding up already in place in another country. Although jurisdiction in personal insolvencies is clearly spelt out in section 6 of the Bankruptcy (Scotland) Act 1985 the jurisdiction of the Scottish courts to wind up foreign companies is not made clear. Section 221 of the Insolvency Act 1986 does not expressly refer to foreign companies. Section 225 of the Insolvency Act 1986 refers to 'a company incorporated outside Great Britain . . . may be wound up as an unregistered company'. The matter is further complicated by the fact that Part V of the Insolvency Act 1986 is not exhaustive. It is necessary in terms of the Civil Jurisdiction and Judgments Act 1982 to have regard to where a company has its 'seat' and whether it is solvent under the jurisdiction of the place of its 'seat' in determining whether it falls under that Act[4]. This matter is discussed in Part II of this chapter.

### Scottish companies

The Court of Session and sheriff courts have jurisdiction to wind up companies registered in Scotland[5]. Similarly the High Court and county courts have jurisdiction to wind up companies registered in England and Wales[6]. It is irrelevant where the registered address of a company is situated[7]. In the case of unregistered United Kingdom companies, those companies are deemed to be registered in those parts of the United Kingdom where they have their principal places of business[8]. If the company has a principal place of business situated in both England and Wales, and Scotland it is deemed to be registered in both countries and may be wound up in either country[9]. The Court of Session has no jurisdiction to wind up companies registered in Northern Ireland.
    The jurisdiction of the Scottish courts to wind up a company registered in Scotland is not in any way qualified by the nationality of its shareholders, the place where its business may be conducted or where its assets are situated. Lord Carmont in the case of *Carse v Coppen* stated[10]:

1 Bankruptcy (Scotland) Act 1985, s 6(2).
2 (1884) 12 R 328.
3 *Fraser* 1971 SLT 146 and *McGuinness v Black (No 2)* 1990 SLT 461.
4 Civil Jurisdiction and Judgments Act 1982, s 43 and Sch 1, arts 1(2) and 16(2).
5 Insolvency Act 1986, s 120.
6 Ibid, s 117.
7 *Re Baby Moon (United Kingdom)* [1985] CLY 327; [1985] PCC 103.
8 Insolvency Act 1986, s 221(2) and (3).
9 Ibid, s 221(3).
10 1951 SC 233 at 243–244.

'A company's domicile is created by registration; it is, so to say, born in Scotland and, however widespread its activities and contacts with other legal systems in the days of its vigour, to Scotland it must come to be laid to rest when its days are done, and according to Scots law should its affairs be wound up.'

For winding up purposes most other EC countries look beyond the place of incorporation to determine the 'nationality' of a company. The court looks at the *siège rélle*, the place where decisions are taken and orders given, the place of its central management. In Scotland and England the courts will not refuse to wind up under Scottish or English law even if all the business and assets of a company and its management are not in Scotland or England, and even if the liquidation in Scotland was not recognised in the country where the assets and business were[1]. The Civil Jurisdiction and Judgments Act 1982 does not affect the jurisdiction of the Scottish courts to wind up Scottish companies[2].

It is usual that a liquidator appointed by the Scottish court should reside within the jurisdiction and applications to appoint persons resident outwith Scotland have been refused[3]. However, it is not an inviolable rule that the liquidator in a Scottish winding up must reside in Scotland. As Lord President Robertson stated in the case of *The Barberton Development Syndicate*[4]:

'I am not disposed to hold it incompetent to appoint a liquidator ouside of our jurisdiction. But for manifest reasons it is preferable to have an officer within our jurisdiction, and residing at or near to the registered office, which is the headquarters of the company.'

This opinion of Lord President Robertson was affirmed in the case of *The Liquidators of Bruce Peebles and Co Ltd v Shiells*[5] by Lord President Dunedin.

The position about the appointment of liquidators, who do not need to be resident in Scotland, is in contrast to the position of interim and permanent trustees in bankruptcy, who must reside within the jurisdiction of the Court of Session[6]. The creation of 'insolvency practitioners' under the Insolvency Act 1986 would suggest that there is less desirability now for the liquidator to reside in Scotland. The main reason for the desirability of residing in Scotland was convenience. It may now be thought a restriction on the free movement of services under the Treaty of Rome if the Court of Session, for no good reasons, were to insist that liquidators be resident in Scotland. It is thought that Anton is incorrect in *Private International Law*[7] where he states that a liquidator appointed by the Scottish court must reside within the jurisdiction.

---

1 *Smyth & Co v The Salem (Oregon) Capital Flour Mills Co Ltd* (1887) 14 R 441; and *A-G v Jewish Colonisation Association* [1900] 2 QB 556; [1901] 1 QB 123, CA.
2 See the Civil Jurisdiction and Judgments Act 1982, s 43.
3 *Brightwen & Co v City of Glasgow Bank* (1878) 6 R 244; *The Barberton Development Syndicate* (1898) 25 R 654; *Skinner (Hannan's Development and Finance Corpn Ltd)* (1899) 6 SLT 388 (where a liquidator was removed from office as being in England and outwith the jurisdiction).
4 *Supra*.
5 1908 SC 692.
6 Bankruptcy (Scotland) Act 1985, ss 2(2) and 24(2).
7 At page 722.

## Foreign companies

Foreign companies come under the definition of 'unregistered companies'. Section 220 of the Insolvency Act 1986 defines the expression 'unregistered company' to include 'any association and any company' with the following exceptions:

'(a)   a railway company incorporated by Act of Parliament,
 (b)   a company registered in any part of the United Kingdom under the Joint Stock Companies Acts or under legislation (past or present) relating to companies in Great Britain.'

This definition comprehends a large range of foreign types of company. It does not comprehend certain international organisations. Municipal courts are not competent to adjudicate upon or to enforce their rights arising from transactions entered into by independent sovereign states on the international law planes. International organisations created by treaty are created by an exercise of the royal prerogative and an organisation created by an exercise of the royal prerogative is not a corporation in terms of the Companies Acts unless it has been incorporated into law by Parliament[1].

## Grounds for winding up a foreign company

Section 221(5) of the Insolvency Act 1986 lays down the circumstances in which an unregistered company may be wound up. It states:

'(5)   The circumstances in which an unregistered company may be wound up are as follows –
 (a)   if the company is dissolved, or has ceased to carry on business, or is carrying on business only for the purpose of winding up its affairs;
 (b)   if the company is unable to pay its debts;
 (c)   if the Court is of the opinion that it is just and equitable that the company should be wound up.'

The following examples show the type of situation where a winding-up order has been made of a foreign company:

## Example 1

In the case of *Marshall, Petitioner*[2], a petition was presented to the First Division of the Court of Session by the Reverend Theodore Marshall, 19 Coates Gardens, Edinburgh and other creditors of the Fidelity Loan and Trust Company under the 199th section of the Companies Act, 1862[3], praying the court, after intimation and service, 'to order that the said Fidelity Loan and Trust Company be wound up by the court. The Fidelity Loan and Trust Company was a company incorporated under the laws of the State of Iowa, United States of America, and had its principal place of business at Sioux

---

1 *JH Rayner (Mincing Lane) Ltd v Department of Trade and Industry* [1990] 2 AC 418.
2 (1895) 22 R 697.
3 The terms of s 199(3) are the same as the Insolvency Act 1986, s 221(5).

City, Iowa. It also carried on business in England and Scotland; its principal place of business in the United Kingdom was at 63 Castle Street, Edinburgh. It was not registered in the United Kingdom.

The business conducted at the Edinburgh branch office consisted in the borrowing of money on debentures of the company secured by mortgages on real estate in the United States, deposited with and held by the Honourable Francis J Moncreiff, CA, Robert Strathern, WS, and John P Wright, WS, all of Edinburgh, as trustees under an agreement and deed of trust entered into between them and the company in October and November 1889.

It was provided that the Agreement should be construed and interpreted, and the rights of parties determined by the law of Scotland. The company became unable to meet its liabilities, and was obliged to to suspend payment. It ceased to carry on business, and receivers were in the course of being appointed over the assets of the company by the United States courts. The chief assets of the company in Scotland were mortgages lodged to secure the due payment of debentures and, in addition, the company held various bonds, stocks and other assets although these were pledged to a large extent in security of advances made to the company in America.

In that case the Court of Session, in granting the prayer of the petition, expressed the view that the proceedings in Scotland should be ancillary to those in the United States which was the proper domicile of the company.

**Example 2**

In the case of *Inland Revenue v Highland Engineering Ltd*[1] a petition was presented by the Lord Advocate for and on behalf of the Commissioners of Inland Revenue for the compulsory winding up of a company called Industrial Estates (New Zealand) Limited. The petitioner averred that Highland Engineering Ltd (which was in members' voluntary liquidation) was indebted to Industrial Estates (New Zealand) Ltd to the sum of £12,223 and that that debt was the company's only remaining asset. He also averred that Highland Engineering Ltd, was indebted to the Inland Revenue in the sum of £7,969.91 as income tax. Highland Engineering Ltd denied that they were indebted to the company. The petitioner and the respondents agreed that the company was an unregistered company, that it had been struck off the New Zealand Register of Companies in 1973, and that it was now a dissolved company. The respondents pleaded that the court had no jurisdiction to wind up the company, because in order to comply with section 399(5)(a) of the Companies Act 1948[2], an unregistered company must not only have been dissolved, but must also have carried on business in Great Britain. The petitioner had not averred that Industrial Estates (New Zealand) Ltd had carried on business in Great Britain. The prayer of the petition should therefore not be granted.

Lord Grieve held that the requirements necessary for a winding up order had been met in as much as the company was unregistered and had been dissolved. Since it was not suggested that the company had assets in any country other than Scotland and all the interested parties were in Scotland, the winding-up petition was granted.

---

1 1975 SLT 203.
2 Now Insolvency Act 1986, s 221(5).

## Example 3

In the case of *Compania Merabello San Nicholas SA*[1] referred to and quoted with approval by Lord Grieve in *Inland Revenue v Highland Engineering Ltd*[2], a Spanish company, Fertilisantes made a claim for breach of a contract of carriage in respect of a cargo carried to Spain by a 'one ship company' which had been incorporated in Panama. At all material times the company's ship had been insured with a mutual insurance club called 'Oceanus'. Neither the company nor Oceanus had met the petitioners' judgment claim and the only known asset of the company was its right against Oceanus. The English court made a winding-up order, the consequence of which was that the right of the company against Oceanus automatically vested in the petitioners in accordance with the Third Parties (Rights against Insurers) Act 1930. In his judgment Megarry J[3] stated:

'I would accordingly attempt to summarise the essentials of the relevant law relating to the existence of jurisdiction to make a winding up order in normal cases in respect of a foreign company as follows.
(1)  There is no need to establish that the company ever had a place of business here.
(2)  There is no need to establish that the company ever carried on business here, unless perhaps the petition is based upon the company carrying on or having carried on business.
(3)  A proper connection with the jurisdiction must be established by sufficient evidence to show
     (a)  that the company has some asset or assets within the jurisdiction, and
     (b)  that there are one or more persons concerned in the proper distribution of the assets over whom the jurisdiction is exercisable.
(4)  It suffices if the assets of the company within the jurisdiction are of any nature; they need not be "commercial" assets, or assets which indicate that the company formerly carried on business here.
(5)  The assets need not be assets which will be distributable to creditors by the liquidator in the winding up: it suffices if by the making of the winding up order they will be of benefit to the creditor or creditors in some other way.
(6)  If it is shown that there is no reasonable possibility of benefit accruing to creditors from making the winding up order, the jurisdiction is excluded.'

### Jurisdictional problems caused by section 221 of the Insolvency Act 1986

Section 221 of the Insolvency Act 1986 has raised problems of jurisdiction under English law. It is thought that Scottish law arrives at the same answer as in England by the 'exercise of a discretion once jurisdiction is established by the statutory criteria'; as opposed to in England having first the statutory criteria for jurisdiction followed by further jurisdictional criteria. Briefly section 221 sets down certain statutory circumstances in which a foreign company may be wound up. These are very wide. In the case of *Banque des Marchands de Moscou (Koupetschesky) v Kindersley*[4] the Master of the Rolls

---

1  [1973] Ch 75.
2  1975 SLT 203.
3  Applied in *International Westminster Bank v Okeanos* [1987] 3 All ER 137, sub nom *Re a Company (No 00359 of 1987)* [1988] Ch 210.
4  [1951] Ch 112.

Lord Evershed doubted that the statutory criteria for establishing jurisdiction were sufficient to establish jurisdiction. He stated:

'As a matter of principle, our courts would not assume, and Parliament should not be taken to have intended to confer, jurisdiction over matters which naturally and properly lie within the competence of the courts of other countries. There must be assets here to administer and persons subject, or at least submitting, to the jurisdiction who are concerned or interested in the property distribution of the assets. And when these conditions are present the exercise of the jurisdiction remains discretionary. Prima facie if the local law of the dissolved foreign corporation provided for the due administration of all the property and assets of the corporation wherever situate among the persons properly entitled to participate therein, the case would not be one for the interference by the machinery of the English courts. In the present case there are substantial assets standing in the name of the bank or its liquidator, and there are persons within the jurisdiction having claims to participate in the distribution of those assets. At the same time, by reason of the total extinction in Russia of the bank and the absence of any machinery under Russian law for the due distribution of the assets among the persons regarded as properly having claims upon them, there would be, unless the machinery of winding up under the Companies Act is available, no means of any kind existing for the administration of the English assets.'

In the case of *Re Lloyd Generale Italiano*[1] Pearson J had held that the English court had no jurisdiction to wind up an Italian company that had carried on business through an agent in England and did not have a branch office or any assets in England. In the judgment in *Banque des Marchands de Moscou (Koupetschesky) v Kindersley*[2] the Master of the Rolls Lord Evershed stated that he regarded the case of in *Re Lloyd Generale Italiano* as only authority for the proposition that there had to be assets in England, not for the view that proof of the existence of a 'place' of business in England, whether established or otherwise, was a condition to the existence of jurisdiction in the English court. The views in *Banque des Marchands de Moscou (Koupetchesky) v Kindersley* have been generally approved including in Scotland[3].

These cases would suggest that it is necessary that there be assets in England to establish jurisdiction (irrespective of the statutory criteria having been met). This test, however, has apparently been reduced in two recent cases. In the case of *Re Eloc Electro-Optieck and Communicatie BV*[4], Nourse J held that the English court had jurisdiction to wind up a Dutch company which had no assets within the English jurisdiction. In that case the Dutch company had traded in England but never had a place of business there. The petitioners were two employees whom the Dutch company dismissed. They recovered judgment against the company. The Dutch company ceased operating. On the hearing of the petition the Dutch company was not represented but in a reserve judgment it was held that the court had jurisdiction to wind it up. Nourse J referred to Megarry J's summary of the essentials in a normal case and to the fact that the petitioners had applied to the Department of Employment for payment out of the redundancy fund but that under the statutory provisions no payment could be made until the company was wound

1 [1885] 29 Ch D 219.
2 [1951] Ch 112
3 *Tong Aik (Far East) Ltd v Eastern Minerals and Trading (1959) Ltd* (1965) 2 MLJ 149 (a Singapore case); *Re Kailis Groote Eylandt Fisheries Pty Ltd* (1977) 2 ACLR 574 (a South Australian case); *IRC v Highland Engineering Ltd* 1975 SLT 203 and *Re Irish Shipping Ltd* [1985] HKLR 437 (a Hong Kong case).
4 [1982] Ch 43.

up. He held that there was a reasonable possibility of benefit accruing to the petitioner from the making of a winding-up order. He stated:

'The benefit would consist of assets coming into the hands of the petitioners not from the company but from an outside source which can only be tapped if an order is made. In the light of that consideration and of the facts, first, that the company did carry on business in England and Wales, secondly, that it employed the petitioners in that business, and, thirdly, that the potential source of assets is directly related to that employment, there is, in my judgment, sufficient to found the jurisdiction of the court. To put it another way, it would, in my judgment, be a lamentable state of affairs if the court's jurisdiction was excluded by the mere technicality that the assets, in respect of which the reasonable possibility of benefit accruing to the petitioners derived, belonged not to the company but to an outside source. I think that support for this view is to be found in the fourth and fifth essentials in Megarry J's summary [1973] Ch 75, 92: . . . .' [and then he cites those essentials and continues] 'That shows, first, that the assets can be of any nature and, secondly, that the consequential benefit accruing to a creditor or creditors need not be channelled through the hands of the liquidator. To my mind that confirms that the ownership of the assets by the company is not a matter of crucial importance. I must again observe that Megarry J's summary of the essentials was directed to normal cases.'[1]

The second case apparently reducing the non statutory jurisdictional criteria in England is the case of *Re a Company (No 00359 of 1987)*[2]. In that case the business of a Liberian company Okeanos was managed in England by an associated company. The Liberian company contracted in 1984 for the building of a bulk carrier. About $13.5m of the total price of $18m was provided by the petitioner, an English bank, in return for a first secured mortgage on the vessel and the assignment to the petitioner of all the vessel's earnings. The company undertook that for the duration of the facility there would be no change in the ownership and control of the company and that the vessel would be kept fully insured. The vessel was delivered to the company in January 1985 and the company drew on the whole of the facility. In 1986 the company was in financial difficulties and in September defaulted in the interest payment. On 17 November the petitioner declared the whole of the company's indebtedness to be due in accordance with the provisions of the loan agreement. The petitioner obtained judgment for the amount of the debt in January 1987 and on 3 February presented a petition for the winding up of the company. On the question of whether the court had jurisdiction to wind up the company under section 221 of the Insolvency Act 1986, it was held that, since the company was unable to pay its debts and its only known asset was substantially less than its liabilities, the condition for the making of a winding-up order contained in section 221(5)(b) of the Insolvency Act 1986 was fulfilled. It was not necessary for the making of a winding-up order against a foreign company that the court be shown that the company had assets within the jurisdiction. A sufficiently close connection with the jurisdiction had to be established. Peter Gibson J stated, referring to the *Eloc* case[3]:

---

1 Approved in *Re a Company (No 00359 of 1987)* [1988] Ch 210 at 223–224.
2 [1988] Ch 210 (sub nom *International Westminster Bank plc v Okeanos Maritime Corpn* [1987] BCLC 450, noted [1989] Lloyd's MCLQ 20).
3 [1982] Ch 43.

'In the circumstances, I am prepared consistently with the *Eloc* case [1982] Ch 43 to hold that the presence of assets in this country is not an essential condition for the court to have jurisdiction in relation to the winding up of a foreign company. In my judgment, provided a sufficient connection with the jurisdiction is shown, and there is a reasonable possibility of benefit for the creditors from the winding up, the court has jurisdiction to wind up the foreign company.'

It is thought in contrast that in Scotland provided the statutory criteria are met, the court will have jurisdiction. In the case of *Inland Revenue v Highland Engineering Ltd*[1] Lord Grieve did not require proof of the existence of assets in Scotland to found jurisdiction, or any benefit to creditors. In narrow terms he stated:

'It follows that, in my judgment, the requirements necessary for a winding up order being issued are met on averment, the company being unregistered and admittedly being dissolved.'

In accepting the argument on behalf of the petitioners by David Hope, Advocate, he accepted a test for the discretionary exercise of the jurisdiction which is for all intents and purposes equivalent to the English test for the establishment of the jursidiction once the statutory criteria are met. He stated:

'In my judgment having regard to the fact that it is not suggested that the company has assets in any country other than Scotland, and particularly not in New Zealand; that it is alleged that the company has an asset in Scotland, and that all persons concerned with the distribution of the company's assets, if any, are situated in Scotland, I should exercise my discretion in favour of the petitioners and grant the prayer of the petition; . . .'

## Oversea companies

An 'oversea company' in terms of section 744 of the Companies Act 1985 is defined as:

'(a)   a company incorporated elsewhere than in Great Britain which, after commencement of this Act establishes a place of business in Great Britain, and

(b)   a company so incorporated which has, before that commencement, established a place of business and continues to have an established place of business in Great Britain at that commencement;'

Also in terms of that section 'place of business' includes a share transfer or share registration office. A company has an established place of business in Great Britain if it has a specified or identifiable place at which it carries on business[2]. In the case of *Lord Advocate v Huron and Erie Loan and Savings Co*[3] Lord Dunedin held that a Canadian company did not have a place of business in Scotland although it carried out business in Scotland by touting for loans and in order to tout properly had agents operating in Scotland.

---

1 1975 SLT 203.
2 *Banque des Marchands de Moscou (Koupetschesky) v Kindersley* [1951] Ch 112 at 126, 132, per Evershed MR.
3 1911 SC 612 at 616.

In the case of 'oversea companies' the Court of Session will always have jurisdiction to wind up if the place of business is in Scotland.

## Recognition of foreign liquidations

Windings up in England and Wales, or Northern Ireland, will always be recognised by the Scottish courts. Section 426(1) of the Insolvency Act 1986 provides:

'An order made by a court in any part of the United Kingdom in the exercise of jursidiction in relation to insolvency law shall be enforced in any other part of the United Kingdom as if it were made by a court exercising the corresponding jurisdiction in that other part'[1].

The obligation on the courts having jursidiction in relation to insolvency law in any part of the United Kingdom to recognise a liquidation by a court in another part of the United Kingdom extends to the assisting of other courts having corresponding jurisdiction to the courts of the Channel Islands, the Isle of Man and any other country or territory designated for the purpose by the Secretary of State by order made by statutory instrument[2].

## Foreign companies: place of incorporation as basis for winding up

Since it is for the personal law of a company to indicate the person or persons who are entitled to act on its behalf, the title of a liquidator appointed in accordance with the law of the place of incorporation will be recognised in Scotland[3]. In the case of *Dairen Kisen Kabushiki Kaisha v Shiang Kee*[4] a company incorporated under the laws of, and resident in, the Republic of China, and having one of its branches at Hong Kong where there were valuable assets belonging to it, was dissolved in China by decree of a Chinese court in accordance with the law of China. With reference to the dissolved Chinese company, Lord Romer stated:

'The position therefore, is this. The company has ceased to exist by an act of the country by whose acts and under whose law it was made a juristic entity, and must, accordingly be treated as non-existent by all courts administering English law . . .'.

In fact the recognition by the court of a liquidator appointed under the law of the place of incorporation is almost without exception[5].

1 See *Scottish Pacific Coast Mining Co Ltd v Walker* (1886) 13 R 816 and [1886] WN 63 for example of procedure under previous legislation. In those cases a Scottish order was enforced in England in relation to proceedings in California. Section 426(1) applies to corporate and personal insolvency.
2 Insolvency Act 1986, s 426(4); the countries which have been designated are Anguilla, Australia, The Bahamas, Bermuda, Botswana, Canada, Cayman Islands, Falkland Islands, Gibraltar, Guernsey, Hong Kong, Republic of Ireland, Montserrat, New Zealand, St. Helena, Turks and Caicos Islands, Tuvalu and Virgin Islands; Co-operation of Insolvency Courts (Designation of Relevant Countries and Territories) Order 1986, SI 1986/2123; Insolvency Act 1986 (Guernsey) Order 1989 SI 1989/2409.
3 Anton *Private International Law* at p 724; *Stair Memorial Encyclopaedia*, vol 4, para 945 (Companies).
4 [1941] AC 373.
5 See *Baden, Delvaux and Lecuit v Société Générale pour Favoriser le Développment du Commerce et de L'Industrie en France SA* [1983] BCLC 325, where four foreign liquidations were recognised.

It is thought that in the case of foreign régimes analogous to liquidations, the same basis of recognition will be used[1].

## Multiple incorporation

A company formed under the Companies Act 1985 may only be domiciled in England and Wales or Scotland. However, it is possible in certain jurisdictions, especially federal states, that a corporation may be formally incorporated in more than one state within the federal unit. There are, however, legal systems which permit a corporation to be incorporated locally as well as in some other foreign jurisdiction.[2] While a United Kingdom company cannot reincorporate abroad, it may register in a foreign country in order to do business there[3]. The only exception to this under the Insolvency Act 1986 would seem to be in the case of a foreign company which had a principal place of business in England and Wales, and in Scotland. In terms of section 221(3):

'(3) For the purpose of determining a court's winding up jurisdiction, an unregistered company is deemed –
  (a) to be registered in England and Wales or Scotland, according as its principal place of business is situated in England and Wales or Scotland, or
  (b) if it has a principal place of business situated in both countries, to be registered in both countries;
  and the principal place of business situated in that part of Great Britain in which proceedings are being instituted is, for all purposes of the winding up, deemed to be the registered office of the company.'

This would seem not to preclude the possibility of a foreign company being deemed to be registered in both England and Wales, and in Scotland. This would allow a winding up in England and a winding up in Scotland. There is an exception to the above jurisdiction rule: if the company is solvent but a winding-up order is nevertheless sought, an English court, for example, would have no jurisdiction to make the order if the central management and control of the company is not exercised in England and the company has its seat in a state which is a party to the 1968 Brussels Convention. This is because, in those circumstances, the English court would not possess jurisdiction[4]. If the central management and control of the company were in Scotland or Northern Ireland but not in England the court in England would have jurisdiction if the company also had a principal place of business in Scotland or Northern Ireland and in England because the amended version of the 1968 Convention applicable in intra-United Kingdom cases, does not apply to the winding up even of solvent companies, unless again, the company has its seat

---

1 See *Schemmer v Property Resources Ltd* [1975] Ch 273 for a discussion of the basis of recognition of foreign receivers and the necessary nexus between the receivership and any foreign property claimed; *Marshall, Petr* (1895) 22 R 697 where Scottish liquidation is made ancillary to a receivership in Iowa. It was sufficient for the Scottish courts to recognise the Iowa receivership that the assets of the company were being administered by the Receivers appointed by the United States courts for the benefit of the debenture holders and other creditors.
2 For a discussion of the resolution of conflicts as to the content of the laws where there are two corporate domiciles. See Smart 'Corporate Domicile' (1990) *Journal of Business Law* 126.
3 *Tayside Floorcloth Co Ltd (Petrs)* 1923 SC 590.
4 See Civil Jurisdiction and Judgments Act 1982, ss 43(2)(b), 43(3)(b), 43(7)(a)–(b); Sch 1, arts 1(2), 16(2).

in a state which is a party to the 1968 Brussels Convention, in which case jurisdiction will not exist[1].

## Foreign liquidations: bases of recognition other than place of incorporation

Although the place of incorporation has prime place as a basis of recognition of a foreign liquidation, the Scottish and English courts seem to take a slightly different approach to the questions, although the law appears to be developing rapidly in England.

### No possibility of liquidation in the country of incorporation

The English courts have been reluctant to recognise liquidations except in the place of the incorporation of the company. An exception to this is where there is no likelihood of a liquidation in the country of incorporation. The thinking would appear to be that on the basis of 'comity' it is defensible only to recognise a liquidation conducted in the country of incorporation just as the English courts justify their own jurisdiction to make a liquidation order. Such concern is not shown where there is no likelihood of a liquidation in the country of incorporation[2].

### English and Commonwealth cases of recognition of liquidation not in place of incorporation

In the case of *Re Russo-Asiatic Bank*[3] decided in Hong Kong, a banking corporation established in Russia had branches in London, Shanghai and Hong Kong. The Hong Kong court denied effect to Soviet decrees dissolving the Russo-Asiatic Bank. Liquidations of the branch offices took place in London, Shanghai and Hong Kong, with a surplus resulting in the Hong Kong winding up. There was no liquidation in the place of incorporation. The liquidators in Shanghai applied for an order that they be given the surplus assets from the Hong Kong winding up. The London liquidator merely sought to represent the creditors in the English proceedings and to enter pleas in the Hong Kong winding up on behalf of those creditors. The Hong Kong court did not rule out recognition of the liquidations in London and Shanghai. Sir Henry Gollan CJ stated:

'But the rule that the liquidation in Hong Kong of a branch of a foreign company should be ancillary to a liquidation in the country of its domicile can have no application in the circumstances of this case . . . as the liquidation proceedings in Hong Kong cannot be taken as ancillary to those in Russia, it follows that there is no court elsewhere which can . . . be regarded as the principal court to govern the liquidation.

There is no precedent to guide me in the exceptional circumstances of this case. But, it appears to me that, on principle, there is no reason why the London liquidator should not put in proofs on behalf of the creditors whom he represents, and I give him leave to do so.

---

1 See also Dicey & Morris, *The Conflict of Laws* (11 edn) pp 1145, 1146.
2 See *Dicey & Morris*, p 1151; *Re Azoff Don Commercial Bank* [1954] Ch 315; the passage in *Dicey & Morris* was cited with apparent approval in *Felixstowe Dock and Railway Co v United States Line Inc* [1989] QB 360 at 374–375.
3 [1930] HKLR 16.

So far as the claim of the Shanghai liquidators for payment to them of the surplus is concerned, I dismiss it'[1].

In *Re a Company (No 00359 of 1987)*[2], a Liberian one ship company had connections with England and Greece. Peter Gibson J, having determined that the English court had jurisdiction to make a winding-up order turned to consider whether there was any more appropriate foreign jurisdiction. He stated:

'It is also appropriate for the court to consider whether any other jurisdiction is more appropriate for the winding up of this admittedly insolvent company. In my judgment, there is none. Miss Heilborn accepts that Liberia is not a serious rival to this country for the purpose of jurisdiction. The Company seems to have had nothing to do with Liberia after its incorporation. But she suggested that Greece might be a more appropriate jurisdiction. I do not accept that. Apart from the fact that the vessel flies a Greek flag and that notices under the loan agreement and first preferred mortgage are required to be sent to the company care of Esperos in Greece I cannot see on what basis Greece would be a more appropriate jurisidiction to wind up the company. In my judgment, for the reasons I have given, the company has a much closer connection with this jurisdiction.'

## Scotland: bases of recognition of liquidations not in place of incorporation

There would appear to be no doubt that it is open to the Scottish courts to recognise a liquidation not in the place of the incorporation of the company. In the case of *Queensland Mercantile and Agency Co Ltd v Australasian Investment Co Ltd*[3], a Queensland company went into liquidation in Queensland and subsequently applied for and obtained a winding-up order in London where it had assets and creditors. The winding-up order there was ordered to be ancillary to the proceedings in Australia[4]. In the course of the ancillary winding up in England the English liquidator obtained an order for a stay of proceedings already under way in Scotland. The Scottish court gave effect to the order of the English High Court and recognised a liquidation other than under the law of the place of recognition. Lord President Inglis stated:

'The order which is sought to be enforced in the first petition before us is one issued by Mr Justice North in the liquidation of the Queensland Mercantile and Agency Co, Limited in England; and it has been contended by the respondents that that order ought not to be enforced, because the liquidation in which it was pronounced was not a statutory or valid liquidation. The company was in liquidation in Queensland before the application for the winding-up order was made in London; and that, it is said, precluded the possibility of any such English winding-up order being pronounced. I am in some doubt whether we ought to entertain that question, because we have before us an order of a competent court of jurisdiction, whose orders presumably, and upon the face of them, are to be enforced in this country; and I doubt whether it is right that we should enquire into the validity of these orders, unless there is something upon the face of them that shews that they are incompetent. But I think it right to say that I have no doubt whatever of the competency of the English liquidation, assuming the facts to be as stated – that is to say, that the Queensland company had a branch business in London, that they had assets there and

1 At 20–21.
2 [1988] Ch 210.
3 (1888) 15 R 935.
4 (1888) 58 LT 878 at 879.

creditors there, and shareholders in the country also. It has been contended that the effect of the liquidation is the same as that of a sequestration in making the administration of the estate of the company one and indivisible; but that I think is a mistake. In a sequestration under our statute of 1856 the entire estate of the bankrupt is transferred to the trustee wherever situated and his title is of a very effective and strong kind; it makes him for the benefit of the creditors the absolute and exclusive proprietor of that estate, fortified by every kind of title that a statute is capable of conferring upon him. And, therefore, in such a case as that, it is quite impossible to say that there can be a second sequestration either in the same country or in a different country from that in which the first has taken place; the whole estate is vested in one person, and it cannot, therefore, become *pro parte* vested in some other person by a subsequent proceeding. But a liquidation is followed by a very different state of affairs. The estate of the company is not transferred from the company to the liquidator, it remains vested in the company just as it was before the winding-up order, and the liquidator is a mere administrator of the affairs of the company. He can do nothing in the way of using action or diligence except in the name of the company; and the company never becomes dissolved, and never is completely divested of its estate until the liquidation has come to an end. It may, therefore very well be, that although there is a winding up in the colony which would enable the liquidator there to ingather the whole assets of the company, if he can reach them, it may aid him very much in the performance of that duty that there should be another liquidation in England or elsewhere where also the company has been carrying on business. There seems to me to be nothing incompatible in the co-existence of the two. Therefore the suggestion that the English liquidation is invalid and cannot possibly co-exist with the Queensland liquidation I think is out of the case'[1].

In the case of *The Governor and Company of the Bank of England*[2], the Bank of Credit and Commerce International SA ('BCCI') was incorporated in Luxembourg and had branches in England and Scotland. A winding-up order of the bank was made in Luxembourg on 3 January 1992. The High Court in England ordered an 'ancillary' winding up on 14 January 1992. Parallel with the proceedings in England were two requests by the High Court in England under section 426 of the Insolvency Act for assistance of the Scottish courts. In terms of the first petition which was brought to the English court in the name of The Governor and Company of the Bank of England, the High Court in England requested the Scottish courts to appoint provisional liquidators on the branch of BCCI in Scotland. This was granted. Simultaneously with the hearing of the winding-up order on 14 January 1992 in England, a request was made by the High Court in England for the Court of Session to appoint liquidators in Scotland on BCCI. This the Court of Session did on 15 January after the making of the English winding-up order. The Court of Session, accordingly, recognised the English 'ancillary' winding-up order and winding up proceedings in England. More problematic, however, is the status of the liquidators of BCCI in Scotland. (See discussion on page 409).

It is thought now that the English courts, given their experience in the BCCI case, will recognise liquidations although they are not in the place of incorporation. In contrast in *Re IIT*[3] Houlden JA, having recognised a Luxembourg liquidation, stated:

'Indeed, I do not think that any other jurisdiction would have had authority to appoint liquidators for IIT.'

---

1 *Queensland Mercantile and Agency Co Ltd v Australasian Investment Co Ltd* (1888) 15 R 935 at 939.
2 Court of Session: 1991 and 1992 unreported.
3 (1975) 58 DLR (3d) 55 at 58.

This comment by a Canadian judge is obiter and was made without the relevant English authorities being cited, let alone the recent BCCI case. In addition, the evidence before the court in Ontario did not suggest that IIT had carried on business within, or submitted to, the jurisdiction of a court in any other country. This comment, therefore, can be ignored, especially in the light of the developments in the BCCI case, in assessing the attitude of the Scottish and English courts in the recognition of liquidations in other countries where a company has not been incorporated.

### 'Ancillary' liquidations

As a general rule matters affecting the affairs of a corporation are usually determined by the law of the state where the company was incorporated. Because, however, the Scottish courts may wind up a company in Scotland which is also being wound up in the country of its incorporation, it is usual that the Scottish court will regard its own proceedings as ancillary to the main liquidation taking place in the state in which the company is incorporated. So for example in the case of *Marshall, Petitioner*,[1] where a company was in receivership in the State of Iowa where it was incorporated, but there were assets and affairs in Scotland, the Court of Session ordered that the Scottish liquidation be ancillary to the liquidation in the country in which the company was being wound up. In expressing the view that the Scottish liquidation should be 'ancillary' to the liquidation in Iowa, the court relied inter alia on the English authority of *Re Commercial Bank of South Australia*[2]. In that case a banking company, incorporated and carrying on business in Australia had a branch office in London but was not registered in England. The company, however, had English creditors, and assets in England. In granting a winding-up order Sir Ford North described how an ancillary winding up should operate. He stated:

'I think therefore, that the English creditors are entitled to have a winding up order made by this court. I do not think it would be right to insert any special directions in the order; this is not the proper time for giving such directions. But I will say this, that I think the winding up here will be ancillary to a winding up in Australia, and, if I have the control of the proceedings here, I will take care that there will be no conflict between the two courts, and I shall have regard to the interests of all the creditors and all the contributories, and shall endeavour to keep down the expenses of the winding up so far as is possible.'

In the subsequent case of *Re English, Scottish & Australian Chartered Bank*[3], Vaughan Williams J set out the much quoted basis of an ancillary winding up:

'One knows that where there is a liquidation of one concern the general principle is – ascertain what is the domicil of the company in liquidation; let the court of the country of domicil act as the principal court to govern the liquidation; and let the other courts act as ancillary, as far as they can, to the principal liquidation.'

An example of an ancillary winding up, which founded *inter alia* on the above mentioned English cases was *Re National Benefit Assurance Co*[4], in which a

1 (1895) 22 R 697.
2 [1886] 33 Ch D 174.
3 [1893] 3 Ch 385 at 394.
4 (1927) 3 DLR 289.

company incorporated in England had also carried on business in Canada. The Canadian liabilities were far less than the English. The company was in liquidation in England and a liquidator had also been appointed in an ancillary winding up in the Canadian province of Manitoba. The Court of Appeal in Manitoba held that, because the duties of the Canadian liquidator were ancillary to the English winding up proceedings, assets collected by the Canadian liquidator had to be handed over to the English liquidator after payment of preferred creditors in Canada and the costs of the liquidation. After that the majority of creditors were left to bring their claims in the liquidation in England. In its judgment the Manibota Court of Appeal stated:

'If, in the present liquidation, the Canadian assets were retained here it would only be for the purpose of paying the Canadian creditors *pari passu* with the English and other creditors. . . . As there can be no apprehension that the Canadian creditors will not have equal treatment with all other creditors, there is no reason why the assets in the hands of the Canadian liquidator should not now be remitted to the English liquidator, less amount required to pay Canadian preferred creditors, and other amounts either approved by the court or by the English liquidator, and costs of the liquidation.'

## Co-ordination of proceedings through ancillary windings up

The reason for a liquidation being made ancillary to another liquidation is to co-ordinate the insolvency proceedings, as well as to protect the assets in the ancillary jurisdiction or the rights of creditors there if the main liquidation law is in conflict with that in the local jurisdiction. A good example of the way this co-ordination works is found in the insolvency of the *Queensland Mercantile and Agency Co Ltd*[1]. The facts were as follows:

Queensland Mercantile and Agency Co Ltd (the Queensland company) was incorporated in Queensland where it acted as agent for the Australasian Investment Co ('AIC'), a company registered in Scotland. In October 1887 the Queensland company was ordered to be wound up in the courts in Queensland. In January 1888 a winding-up order in respect of the Queensland company was made in England and the winding up there was directed to be ancillary to the proceedings in Australia. In February 1887 AIC commenced proceedings against the Queensland company in Scotland prior to the orders of the Australian and English courts. It alleged that the Queensland company had misappropriated investments belonging to AIC. In the Scottish proceedings AIC arrested certain assets belonging to the Queensland company in Scotland and thereby became a secured creditor on the arrested funds. The question before the English courts was whether the English should issue a restraining order on AIC from proceeding with the Scottish action. North J stated:

'It is true that there is a liquidation of the company also going on in Queensland, where the head office of the company was situate. To a certain extent I treat the winding up here as ancillary to the winding up there, but not to such an extent as to make this court an agent for the courts in Queensland, and I must investigate the matter as far as I can here.'

1 *Re Queensland Mercantile and Agency Co Ltd* (1888) 58 LT 878; For subsequent proceedings see *Re Queensland Mercantile and Agency Co Ltd, ex p Australasian Investment Co* [1892] 2 Ch 536; *Queensland Mercantile and Agency Co Ltd v Australasian Investment Co* (1888) 15 R 935; see also *Barclays Bank plc v Homan* (1992) Independent, 1 September where Hoffmann J refused injunction in MCC case against examiner in proceedings in US under Bankruptcy Code ancillary to English administration from applying to US court for recovery of $30 million from Barclays as a preference, which would not have been recoverable under Insolvency Act 1986, s 239.

North J attempted to co-ordinate the two liquidations and the Scottish proceedings. He granted a stay of the Scottish proceedings and ordered that AIC's claim against the Queensland company was to be determined in Queensland, but with express reservation to AIC of the benefit of the arrestment.

Although a winding up may be described as 'ancillary', the amount of work undertaken by the court where the ancillary winding up is taking place may expand and dwarf the proceedings in the court where the main winding up is held.

## BCCI case

The proceedings in the English winding up of BCCI, as ordered on 14 January 1992, are likely to be a good example of the ancillary winding up dwarfing the main winding up.

### Order of priorities in an ancillary winding up

The general rule is that secured creditors, preferred creditors and the expenses of the ancillary winding up are paid prior to funds being paid over to the lead liquidator. It was noted in the Canadian case of *Re National Benefit Assurance Co*[1], that the Manitoba Court of Appeal ordered that assets in the hands of the Canadian liquidator should be remitted to the lead English liquidator 'less amount required to pay Canadian preferred creditors, and other amounts either approved by the court or by the English liquidator, and costs of the liquidation'. Also in the case of *Re Queensland Mercantile Agency Co Ltd*[2] North J expressly reserved to Australasian Investment Co Ltd the benefit of the security it had allegedly obtained by arresting assets in Scotland. In the case of *Carron Iron Co v Maclaren*[3], Lord St Leonards said that:

'Nor will the rule operate to destroy any priority to which, from the nature of his security, a creditor in Scotland or Ireland is entitled against the assets in either country according to the law of the country, although they may come to be distributed here.'

A similar ruling was made in *Re Standard Insurance Co Ltd*[4]. A New Zealand company was in liquidation in New Zealand but there was an ancillary winding up in Queensland and in each of the other Australian states. The court in Queensland held that when a winding up was proceeding in different jurisdictions, the principle which had to be applied was that, subject to priorities secured by the local law, all creditors of the company were as far as possible to be treated equally wherever they were and wherever their debts were contracted.

It will be seen from a reading of the above mentioned cases that, where there is a lead liquidation, an ancillary liquidation and perhaps a second ancillary liquidation, the distribution of the assets in the second ancillary liquidation will be according to priorities and securities of the *lex situs*. The assets are then transmitted, as in the *Queensland Mercantile* case to the first

1 (1927) 3 DLR 289.
2 (1888) 58 LT 878 at 879.
3 [1855] 5 HL Cas 416 at 455.
4 [1968] Qd R 118.

ancillary liquidation where they are subject to any priorities in the first ancillary liquidation before being transmitted to the lead liquidator.

## Set-off

The principle of set-off in Scots law is founded upon the Act of 1592[1], which provides that:

'Only debt de liquido ad liquidum instantile verefiet be wreit or aith of the partie before the geving of decreit be admittit be all Jugis withine this realme be way of exceptioun.'

The language suggests that the rule is one of procedure only. If so, it would be applied even in a Scottish liquidation with a foreign element. This does not mean that foreign rules of set-off may never be applied in Scotland. Under some systems of law the rules relating to set-off take effect by mere operation of the law and affect the substance of the obligation. If by applicable foreign law the obligation of one of the parties were so extinguished or reduced the fact would be noticed by the Scottish courts[2]. Similarly in England, whether there may be set off, or counterclaim has been regarded as a matter of procedure to be governed by English law[3]. The English courts, however, recognise the right of a Scottish debtor to plead set off if it is available under the Scots law of the debt. In the case of *Macfarlane v Norris*[4], the plaintiff in England had been appointed in a Scottish sequestration as trustee. In the English action the defendant pleaded a Scottish set off. The English court accepted that set off was generally in England a matter of procedure. However, Blackburn J was prepared to give effect to the Scots law of set off. He stated:

'The plaintiff sues as trustee of a trader in Scotland, who became bankrupt; and the question, what passed under the transfer of the bankrupt's goods and chattels to the trustee must be settled by the Scotch law, which must be averred on the pleadings. . . And I cannot read the averment at the end of the plea otherwise than as averring that the property of the bankrupt, under such circumstances, came to the trustee with a right to deduct cross claims; – in other words, that the transfer in the Scotch law is a transfer of a balance of account after allowing for mutual credits.'

Cockburn CJ also stated:

'It is true the pleader has adopted the form of the English plea of set off and mutual credit; but we must take the plea as substantially amounting to this; – here are mutual credits, the effect of which, by Scotch law, is the discharge of the debtor from all excepting the balance.'

## Discharge of debts under a foreign liquidation

Under Scottish law a foreign liquidation discharges only a company's liabilities as are properly governed by the law of the country in which the liquidation

---

1 c 143.
2 Anton, *Private International Law* (2nd edn, 1990), p 248.
3 *Meyer v Dresser* [1864] 16 CB (NS) 646.
4 [1862] 2 B & S 783; it is thought that the analysis in this case is not totally convincing unless the Scots rule is more than procedure.

takes place. They may not be discharged by a law of the country of the liquidation if that is not the proper law of the liability[1]. In 1724, for example, the Scottish court held that a debt in terms of an English bond was regulated by English law and hence discharged upon the defender's bankruptcy in England[2]. Alternatively if a creditor participates in a foreign liquidation he is precluded from taking any separate measures in Scotland to obtain a preference. In the case of *Rhones v Parish*[3], a merchant had been bankrupted under the law of Bremen. The creditors, including the respondents, then elected certain of their number as members of the Senate of Bremen as trustees. The respondents meanwhile arrested moveables in Scotland belonging to the bankrupt and also entered a proof in the proceedings in Bremen. The interlocutor of the Lord Ordinary which was adhered to by the whole court stated:

'the respondents having given their vote for the choice of trustees, or having proved their debts before the trustees, and made a demand for payment, is sufficient evidence of their having acceded to the trust right, which it seems by the law of Bremen is vested in certain members of the Senate, chosen by the creditors, and that accession precludes them from taking separate measures in this country in order to obtain a preference over the rest of the creditors'[4].

### Grounds for non-enforcement of orders made in foreign liquidations

Although a Scottish court may recognise a foreign liquidation, that does not necessarily entail that the Scottish court will enforce the order of a foreign liquidation court. Generally the courts in the United Kingdom will not render assistance to a foreign insolvency proceedings which offended against some over-riding principle of public policy[5]. It is not sufficient that the foreign law is different from that in Scotland[6].

The grounds for refusal to enforce a foreign judgment in a foreign liquidation are no different from the grounds for the non-enforcement of any other foreign judgment[7]. The main grounds can be summarised briefly as follows:

(1)   revenue law;
(2)   penal law;
(3)   fraud;
(4)   natural justice; and
(5)   reciprocity.

---

1   *Adams v National Bank of Greece* [1961] AC 255, HL.
2   *Rochead v Scot* (1724) Mor 4566.
3   (1776) Mor 4593 and App No (2) (foreign).
4   See also *Glover v Vasie* (1776) Mor 4562 and App No (3) (foreign) where a like determination was made with reference to an English bankruptcy. Vasie had received a dividend under an English commission but later arrested assets in Scotland. The court held that Vasie was barred from competing by arrestment with the English assignees; *Rose v M'Leod* (1825) 4 S 311.
5   *Re a debtor, ex p Viscount of the Royal Court of Jersey* [1981] Ch 384 at 402.
6   *Baden, Delvaux and Lecuit v Société Générale pour Favoriser le Développment du Commerce et de L'Industrie en France SA* [1983] BCLC 325; *Connal & Co v Loder* (1868) 6 M 1095.
7   For detailed discussion see Anton *Private International Law* (2nd edn, 1990) pp 99–106; Dicey & Morris *The Conflict of Laws* (11th edn) pp 92–115.

*Revenue law*

The United Kingdom courts and the Irish courts have firmly set themselves against the enforcement of foreign revenue claims. In the case of *Government of India v Taylor*[1], the House of Lords unanimously held that a claim by or on behalf of a foreign state to recover taxes was unenforceable in the English courts. Lord Keith of Avenholm observed that 'in no circumstances will the courts directly or indirectly enforce the revenue laws of another country'[2]. This approach had been taken by the Irish courts in the case of *Peter Buchanan Ltd v McVey*[3], concerning a Scottish company in liquidation in Scotland at the instance of the Scottish Revenue. The liquidator brought an action in Ireland to recover assets of the company. Because it was shown that after payment of the costs of the liquidation any money recovered would go to the Inland Revenue in Scotland, Kingsmill Moore J held that essentially the action was an action to enforce a revenue debt of the Inland Revenue in Scotland and could not be enforced by the Irish court. He stated:

'For the purpose of this case it is sufficient to say that when it appears to the court that the whole object of the suit is to collect tax for a foreign Revenue, and that this will be the sole result of a decision in favour of the plaintiff, then the Court is entitled to reject the claim by refusing jurisdiction.'

This case was upheld on appeal to the Supreme Court. The action was held to have the sole purpose of recovering taxes and was therefore not enforceable in Ireland. Maguire CJ observed, however:

'I agree that if the payment of a Revenue claim was only incidental and there had been other claims to be met, it would be difficult for our courts to refuse to lend assistance to bring assets of the company under the control of the liquidator.'

This approach of the Irish courts[4] is exactly the approach taken by the Scottish courts. The leading Scottish case of *Scottish National Orchestra Ltd v Thomson's Executors*[5] concerned a claim by the Swedish administrators of the estate of a person who had died domiciled in Sweden, but with assets in Scotland. The claim was *inter alia* for Swedish inheritance tax. Lord Robertson said that the administrators' claim would have failed if the only purpose had been to pay Swedish tax. However, after the tax had been paid, there were remaining assets which would be held for the beneficiaries in Sweden. Accordingly, as the enforcement of a foreign revenue debt, was not the sole purpose of the action, the claim of the Swedish administrators would be upheld.

---

1 [1955] AC 491.
2 At 510.
3 [1954] IR 89.
4 See the comments also of Lord Mackay of Clashfern in *Williams & Humbert Ltd v W & H Trademarks (Jersey) Ltd* [1986] AC 368 at 440, which approve the analysis of Maguire CJ.
5 1969 SLT 325; see also *Attorney-General of Canada v William Schulze & Co* (1901) 9 SLT 4.

*Penal law*

The Scottish courts will not uphold the criminal or penal law of a foreign country. It is not sufficient that there is a penal element[1].

*Fraud*

The Scottish courts will deny recognition to a foreign decree obtained by fraud. This is because under Scots law no judgment obtained by fraud could have any legal validity, and certainly not in any court of equity[2]. There is also some old authority for the proposition that foreign insolvency proceedings, even where they are conducted properly according to the foreign law, may in certain circumstances be a type of fraud upon the other creditors and should not be upheld if resorted to merely to undermine or preclude Scottish insolvency proceedings. In the case of *Geddes v Mowat*[3] a debtor was domiciled, resident and carried on business in Scotland. On 4 January 1820 a commission of bankruptcy was issued in England. A week later the debtor's estate was sequestrated in Scotland. The English commission was later found to be invalid and a new commission was issued. The second commission was based upon the original act of bankruptcy. The English assignees petitioned the Scottish court, on the basis that the sequestration had been superseded by the English commission. This claim was rejected by the Court of Session. The House of Lords also held that the English commission was a nullity and accordingly the sequestration had been the first in time. Lord Gifford suggested in his opinion that where a person resorts to a foreign insolvency proceedings in order to undermine the general body of creditors, this could be a 'fraud of the law of Scotland'. He stated[4]:

'There is another point to be observed upon; the bankrupt, as has already been stated, was a domiciled Scotsman . . . it is strongly to be suspected, that finding himself in difficulties in Scotland, and foreseeing a sequestration, he removed to England, in order to commit an act of bankruptcy, and upon that the English commission was founded; . . . and I think it might admit of a serious question, independently of the point of priority, whether this commission of bankruptcy in England, under these circumstances, might not be considered as having been issued in fraud of the law of Scotland; issued as it was against a party, native of Scotland, then resident in Scotland, domiciled in Scotland for years, going to England, in December, and on 4 January committing an act of bankruptcy.[5] . . .'

1 *Huntington v Attrill* [1893] AC 150 at 157 where Lord Watson states: 'A proceedings, in order to come within the scope of the rule, must be in the nature of a suit in favour of the state whose law has been infringed'; *Re IIT* (1975) 58 DLR (3d) 55 in which a Canadian court rejected the submission that a Luxembourg regulation was penal in nature on the grounds that, while it contained penal provisions, it was not penal in nature in the sense in which that term was interpreted in the conflict of laws; *Schemmer v Property Resources Ltd* [1975] Ch 273; *Larkins v NUM* [1985] IR 671; *Attorney-General of New Zealand v Ortiz* [1984] AC 1.
2 *Boe v Anderson* (1857) 20 D 11 at 32.
3 [1824] 1 Gl & J 414; 2 Shaw's App Cas 230.
4 At 423.
5 See also in England *Re Henry Hooman* (1895) 1 LT 46; *Jet Holdings Inc v Patel* [1990] QB 335; and *Adams v Cape Industries plc* [1990] 2 WLR 657; and *Foster v Taylor* (1871) 31 UCR 24.

*Natural justice*

A foreign judgment may be denied recognition if there has been a breach of the rules of natural justice[1]. It is not necessary that every creditor must have received notice of the liquidation and been able to lodge a claim if there has been no unfairness[2].

*Reciprocity*

There is some Commonwealth authority suggesting that courts sometimes consider whether recognition should be restricted in the case of a foreign insolvency where there is a lack of reciprocity[3]. In England, if anything, the courts seem to disregard the question of reciprocity, if perhaps on this fictional assumption that it exists[4].

# II. CIVIL JURISDICTION AND JUDGMENTS ACT 1982

## Introduction

The question of which judgments of the Scottish courts may or must be enforced in countries outside the United Kingdom and which judgments of countries outside the United Kingdom may or must be enforced by the Scottish courts is exceedingly complicated. Briefly until the Civil Jurisdiction and Judgments Act 1982 came into force on 1 January 1987, there was only direct reciprocal enforcement of judgments between the United Kingdom courts and foreign countries where there was a treaty for the reciprocal enforcement of judgments. These countries were said to be countries to which the Foreign Judgments (Reciprocal Enforcement) Act 1933 applied[5]. This enforcement régime depends on bilateral arrangements between the United Kingdom and foreign countries. In contrast, the Brussels Convention on Jurisdiction and the Enforcement of Judgments in Civil and Commercial Matters of 1968 ('the Brussels Convention'), as amended by the 1978 Convention on Accession of Denmark, Ireland and the United Kingdom thereto, is a multilateral, direct (or double) jurisdiction (and recognition and enforcement) convention. It goes beyond the merely bilateral plane of adoption between separate sovereign states and its provisions are not limited to control of conditions of recognition and enforcement of judgments on the basis of determined factors. From 1 January 1987 the Civil Jurisdiction and Judgments Act 1982[6] incorporates these conventions directly into United

1 *Det Norske Bjergnings og Dykkercompagni v M'Laren* (1885) 22 SLR 861; *Price v Dewhurst* (1837) 8 Sim 279; *Bergerem v Marsh* (1921) 91 LJKB 80, where a judgment based on *ex parte* proceedings with full notice was held to constitute a valid judgment in a Belgian insolvency; *Larkins v NUM* [1985] IR 671; *Bond Brewing Holding Ltd v Crawford* (1989) 92 ALR 154.
2 *Pattison v McVicar* (1886) 13 R 550; *Southgate v Montgomerie* (1837) 15 S 507; *Strike v Gleich* (1879) OB & F 50.
3 *Williams v Rice* (1926) 3 DLR 225 at 250–251.
4 *Employers' Liability Assurance Corpn v Sedgwick, Collins & Co* [1927] AC 95 in which the House of Lords treated as valid the liquidation of a company in Russia, although no provision had been made for English claims.
5 The Act currently applies to Austria, Belgium, Germany, France, Israel, Italy, Holland, Norway, India, Bangladesh, Pakistan, parts of Canada, Australian Capital Territory, Surinam, Tonga, Guernsey, Jersey and the Isle of Man.
6 Commencement (No 3) Order 1986, SI 1986/2044.

Kingdom law. Section 2(1) of the 1982 Act provides that the conventions shall have 'the force of law' in the United Kingdom and that judicial notice shall be taken of them. Section 2(2) of the 1982 Act also states that for 'convenience of reference', there are set out in Schedules 1, 2 and 3 respectively of the Act the English texts (being texts prepared from the authentic English texts referred to in articles 37 and 41 of the Accession Convention) of:

(1) the 1968 Convention as amended by Titles II and III of the Accession Convention;

(2) the 1971 Protocol as amended by Title IV of the Accession Convention; and

(3) Titles V and VI of the Accession Convention (transitional and final provisions).

The effect of these provisions in section 2 is that the conventions themselves are law in the United Kingdom, as supplemented by various rules laid down in other sections of the 1982 Act[1]. A further parallel convention to the Brussels Convention was signed at Lugano on 16 September 1988. This should eventually furnish a basis for recognition and enforcement of judgments between eighteen European states[2].

Accordingly to its overall spirit and purpose, requiring concentration and rationalisation of Contracting States' jurisdiction for the purpose of facilitating recognition and enforcement, the convention, where proceedings fall within its scope, is applicable by the court of its own motion; that is to say, its application is mandatory on the part of the court and does not depend upon having been pleaded by either party to the proceedings.

Proceedings in bankruptcy are expressly excluded from the scope of application of the convention under article 1, para 2(2).

### Certain corporate insolvency proceedings not excluded from the scope of the Brussels Convention

Article 1, para 2(2) excludes from the scope of the convention certain insolvency proceedings. It provides as follows:

Article 1, para 2   The Convention shall not apply to:
   (1) . . .'
   (2) bankruptcy, proceedings relating to the winding up of insolvent companies or other legal persons, judicial arrangements, compositions and analogous proceedings;

The text distinguishes between bankruptcy and the winding up of insolvent companies. The reason for the distinction is stated in the Schlosser Report. It states:

---

1 For the texts of the Accession Convention and the Original Convention as thereby amended, see OJ 1978 L304/1 and L304/77. The latter text is also published, together with an Explanatory Note, in the *Encyclopaedia of European Community Law*, vol BII. For another commentary upon the Convention, see Jenard, OJ 1979 C59/1; Schlosser, OJ 1979 C59/71; Fletcher, *Conflict of Laws in European Community Law* (1982), ch 4, and references therein cited, especially in nn 18 and 23; Lasok and Stone, *Conflict of Laws in the European Community* (1987), chaps 5–7; Hartley, *Civil Jurisdiction and Judgments* (1984); Collins, *The Civil Jurisdiction and Judgments Act 1982* (1983); Dashwood, Hacon and White, *A Guide to the Civil Jurisdiction and Judgments Convention* (1986); Kaye, *Civil Jurisdiction and Enforcement of Foreign Judgments* (1987); O'Malley and Layton, *European Civil Practice*; Fletcher, *The Law of Insolvency* (1990), which lists these references.
2 OJ 1988 L319/9.

'The Bankruptcy Acts do not apply to them (companies), but instead they are subject to the winding up procedure of the Companies Acts, even if they are not registered companies. Winding up is not a special bankruptcy procedure, but a legal concept which can take different forms and serves different purposes. A common feature of all winding up proceedings is a disposal of assets and the distribution of their proceeds among the persons entitled thereto with a view of bringing the company to an end. The start of winding up proceedings corresponds, therefore, to what is understood by "dissolution" on the continent. The dissolution of a company on the other hand is identical with the final result of a liquidation under continental legal systems.'

Accordingly to be excluded from the scope of the convention under the heading of 'proceedings relating to the winding up of insolvent companies or other legal persons', the proceedings must be concerned with a registered or unregistered company under Scots law, or with an entity which has legal personality under the laws of any Contracting State. Secondly, the entity must be insolvent. Accordingly, voluntary windings up appear not to be included. The most difficult question relates to the expression 'proceedings relating to winding up'. For example it is important to know whether 'relating to' winding up would cover proceedings taking place in the course of a winding up, other than merely those consisting in the application itself to wind up; for example, those in respect of a preference, or for misfeasance, or for fraudulent trading. It is also necessary to know whether 'proceedings' would cover a creditors' voluntary winding up, if the company is insolvent, or an application to the court under section 425 of the Companies Act 1985 to sanction a proposed scheme of compromise or arrangement, or administration proceedings or receivership. These are highly technical questions and it is not possible at present to answer them all in advance. The best guide as to how the European Court would interpret the scope of the Brussels Convention is to be found in the case of *Gourdain v Nadler*[1]. The case concerned a German manufacturer which set up a French subsidiary to market its products in France. The German company was wound up and the French subsidiary was in financial trouble. The Commercial Court of Paris declared that the necessary conditions existed for a winding up of the French company and appointed Gourdain as 'syndic'. Nadler, who was managing director of the German company was regarded by the French courts as *de facto* manager of the French company and was ordered by the Paris Commercial Court to contribute a sum towards the French company's debts under the French law of insolvency enabling the court to order a *de iure* or *de facto* manager of a company in winding up or similar proceedings to bear the liability for any loss if there was deficiency of assets unless the manager could prove that the company's business had been managed with requisite skill and diligence (the French equivalent of 'wrongful trading' under the Insolvency Act 1986). Gourdain sought enforcement of the Paris court's order against Nadler in the district court of Limburg in Germany under article 31 of the Brussels Convention. The German court granted the order for enforcement under article 31 but the Court of Appeal in Frankfurt set it aside, on the ground that the proceedings against Nadler in the Paris court, resulting in his being found personally liable for the company's debts, were proceedings relating to the winding up of an insolvency company within article 1, para 2(2) of the Brussels Convention and consequently were outside the scope of the application of the latter. Gourdain

---

1 Case: 133/78 [1979] ECR 733, [1979] 3 CMLR 180.

appealed against the finding to the Federal Supreme Court of Germany. That court requested a ruling from the European Court upon whether the Paris court's judgment was given in proceedings relating to winding up within the meaning of article 1, para 2(2) of the Brussels Convention or whether the judgment was in fact a decision given in a civil and commercial matter under article 1, para 1 and hence enforceable under the Brussels Convention.

The European Court declared that the reasons for the Convention not applying to bankruptcy and winding up proceedings was because of the profound differences between the laws of the Contracting States in relation to bankruptcy and winding up. The court held that in winding up and other proceedings mentioned in article 1, para 2(2) of the Brussels Convention, which 'involve the intervention of the courts' or which culminate 'at least in supervision by the courts', it is necessary if decisions relating to bankruptcy and winding up are to be excluded from the scope of the Judgments Convention, that such related proceedings 'must derive directly from the bankruptcy or winding up and be closely connected with' the proceedings. It held that the judgment ordering the *de facto* manager of a legal person to pay a certain sum into the assets of a company must be considered as given in the context of bankruptcy, proceedings relating to the winding up of insolvent companies or other legal persons. It would seem therefore that for proceedings to be excluded from the scope of the Convention there must be intervention or at least supervision by the national courts in relation to the main winding up proceedings. Hence it is thought that a creditors' voluntary winding up would not be excluded. Receivership would not be excluded because it would not be a court procedure in Scotland. Thirdly administration which had as its object the resuscitation of the company would not be excluded, but administration leading to a more orderly winding up would be included. The court, also, by placing limits on the type of proceedings, 'relating' to the winding up, to those which 'derive directly from' the winding up and are 'closely connected with' the winding up would seem to exclude from article 1, para 2(2) of the Convention the following proceedings:

proceedings taking place in the course of a winding up but not directly dependent on the existence of a winding up;

proceedings brought by a liquidator in order to enforce performance of a contractual obligation or payment of a debt owed to the company by a third party, the extent of which liability would have been just the same had the third party been sued by the company when the company was not in insolvent liquidation.

Actions which would be excluded from the scope of the Convention would be actions for wrongful trading and fraudulent trading, which are dependent on the winding up, but perhaps not misfeasance which is not dependent on a winding up.

Similarly questions which arise in the liquidation of a company which concern the company's corporate structure and the relationship between shareholders *inter se* and the relationships between them and the company would not be excluded for the purposes of the Brussels Convention. This was recently held in the case of *Powell Duffryn plc v Petereit*[1]. In that case the Court

---

1 Case: 214/89 (Judgment 10 March 1992) reported Times Law Reports 15 April 1992.

of Justice of the European Communities accepted jurisdiction for the purposes of the Brussels Convention in answering questions submitted to it by the Oberlandesgericht (Higher Regional Court) Koblenz, on the interpretation of article 17 of the Brussels Convention. Powell Duffryn, a company established under English law, had purchased shares in IBH Holding AG, a company governed by German law, in the context of an increase of the capital of the latter company in September 1979. In July 1980 Powell Duffryn had taken part in a meeting of IBH Holding during which shareholders unanimously adopted decisions amending the articles of association of IBH, in particular by inserting a clause according to which they agreed, for the purpose of disputes betwen themselves and the company, to submit those disputes to the court which normally had jurisdiction over the company. In 1983 IBH became bankrupt and Mr Petereit, acting as liquidator, brought an action before the Landgericht (Regional Court), Mainz, maintaining that Powell Duffryn had not fulfilled its obligations towards IBH Holding with regard to cash payments which it was obliged to make in accordance with increases in the capital of the company. He also claimed the repayment of dividends which, according to him, had been wrongly paid to Powell Duffryn. The Landgericht, Mainz, which was the court designated by the jurisdiction clause, rejected the claim of lack of jurisdiction raised by Powell Duffryn, which had argued that such a claim could not constitute an 'agreement' and that therefore it should have been sued in England, where it was domiciled.

The company appealed to the Oberlandesgericht, Koblenz which, took the view that the case raised a question of interpretation of article 17 of the Brussels Convention and stayed the proceedings and referred a number of questions to the European Court for a preliminary ruling. Article 17 of the Brussels Convention provided that if the parties, one of whom was domiciled in a contracting state, had agreed that the courts of a contracting state were to have jurisdiction to settle any disputes which might arise in connection with a particular legal relationship, those courts should have exclusive jurisdiction. In its judgment the European Court of Justice accepted jurisdiction for the purposes of the Brussels Convention, although the case had been brought by a liquidator of a bankrupt company. It also ruled:

(1)   A clause conferring jurisdiction on a court of a Contracting State for the purpose of disputes between a company and its shareholders, included in the articles of association of that company and adopted in accordance with the relevant provisions of national law and with the articles of association themselves, was an agreement conferring jurisdiction within the meaning of article 17 of the Brussels Convention.

(2)   The means of acquisition of the shares was irrelevant. The formal requirements laid down by article 17 were fulfilled in respect of all shareholders where the agreement conferring jurisdiction appeared in the articles of association of the company and where those articles had been lodged in a place to which the shareholder might have access or where they appeared in a public register.

(3)   The requirement that the application of an agreement conferring jurisdiction to be limited 'to disputes which might arise in connection with a particular legal relationship within the meaning of article 17' was satisfied if the clause conferring jurisdiction which appeared in the articles of association of a company could be interpreted as meaning that

it referred to disputes between the company and its shareholders as such.

(4)   It was for the national court to interpret a clause conferring jurisdiction which had been raised before it in order to determine disputes which fell within its scope.

The only Scottish case to date to touch on these difficult questions was the case of *Ferguson's Trustee v Ferguson*[1] which was an action by a Scottish trustee to interdict the bankrupt from dealing with and in particular selling certain immoveable property in Spain. It was held that there was no jurisdiction to restrain the bankrupt. The court held, and was upheld on appeal by Sheriff Principal Mowat, that article 16(1) of the Convention conferred exclusive jurisdiction on the Spanish courts. He stated:

'Turning to the 1982 Act, I accept the solicitor for the pursuer's submission that article 16(1) does not create an exclusive jurisdiction in all issues relating to heritage in the *forum rei sitae*. The question is whether this interdict raises questions relating to a right *in rem* . . . it seems to me that the pursuer is seeking to prevent the defender from exercising a right in rem by selling the property and is raising a question as to whether the defender has such a right. For these reasons, I consider that . . . the court had no jurisdiction in these proceedings.'

It is thought that the Scottish court erred in not raising the question of jurisdiction being excluded because the matter was a bankruptcy matter. It is thought that the interdict against a bankrupt selling heritage, only is obtainable when there is a sequestration. Otherwise a non-bankrupt is entitled to sell heritage.

## III.   ENFORCEMENT OF COURT ORDERS WITHIN THE UNITED KINGDOM

Section 426 of the Insolvency Act 1986 provides for co-operation between courts exercising jurisdiction in relation to insolvency. It applies chiefly to co-operation between courts within different countries in the United Kingdom, but also between courts in the United Kingdom and courts in the Channel Islands or the Isle of Man, or any other designated country or territory. The key provision is section 426(4) which provides that:

'The courts having jurisdiction in relation to insolvency law in any part of the United Kingdom shall assist the courts having the corresponding jurisdiction in any other part of the United Kingdom or any relevant country or territory.'[2]

Section 426(5) then details how a request for help may be implemented. It provides:

---

1   1990 SLT (ShCt) 73.
2   The Co-operation of Insolvency Courts (Designation of Relevant Countries and Territories) Order 1986, SI 1986/2123. The countries and territories so designated are: Anguilla, Australia, the Bahamas, Bermuda, Botswana, Canada, Cayman Islands, Falkland Islands, Gibraltar, Hong Kong, Republic of Ireland, Montserrat, New Zealand, St. Helena, Turks and Caicos Islands, Tuvalu, and the Virgin Islands.

'For the purposes of subsection (4) a request made to a court in any part of the United Kingdom by a court in any other part of the United Kingdom or in a relevant country or territory is authority for the court to which the request is made to apply, in relation to any matters specified in the request, the insolvency law which is applicable by either court in relation to comparable matters falling within its jurisdiction.

In exercising its discretion under this subsection, a court shall have regard in particular to the rules of private international law.'

An example of section 426 in operation is the case of *First Tokyo Index Trust Ltd, Petitioners*[1]. In that case the joint liquidators of the Scottish company First Tokyo Index Trust plc, a company in the Maxwell group of companies, petitioned the Court of Session for orders under sections 236, 237 and 426 of the Insolvency Act 1986. Section 236 concerns the private examination of the office holder of a company. Section 237 concerns the production of evidence. The petition requested the court to order a private examination of Kevin Maxwell, who was a director of the petitioners, and Larry Trachtenburg, who had been the secretary of the petitioners. The petition also asked the Court of Session to issue to the High Court of Justice in England a request for assistance to examine the respondents in private and for documents to be produced before the court in England. The respondents consented to the granting of the orders and the Court of Session made an order under section 236 for the respondents to be examined on oath in England. The Court of Session also ordered the respondents to produce property and documents, and issued a request to the High Court in England for assistance in the examination.

That case raises the question of how section 236 would be interpreted under Scottish law (see pages 64–70). Apart from that issue, it shows that the courts may ask each other for examinations of persons and for documentation to be produced before either court. Appendix IX gives a style for such a request to an English court. The case of *BCCI*[2] was a case where the English court asked the Court of Session to appoint certain persons as liquidators of BCCI in Scotland. The High Court in England had issued a winding-up order for the ancillary winding up of BCCI in England. This was after a winding-up order in Luxembourg. The Scottish court acceded to the request of the English court and appointed as joint liquidators of BCCI in Scotland one person resident in England and another resident in Scotland. No winding-up order was issued in Scotland. That case raises much more difficult problems than the case of *First Tokyo Index Trust Ltd*[3]. It suggests that under section 426 of the Insolvency Act 1986, the assisting court cannot only enforce an order of the requesting court, but may also give the requesting court almost a blank cheque by appointing liquidators, one of whom in that case was also a liquidator of BCCI in the English winding up. Because these liquidators are not appointed in a Scottish winding up, it is not clear what powers they would have in Scotland. Liquidators are normally considered the creatures of the insolvency legislation and not common law appointments. The appointment of a judicial factor of course is the common law approach (see page 383). Section 426(3) concerns the ingathering of property in different parts of the United Kingdom. It reads:

1 21 February 1992 unreported.
2 Court of Session 1991 and 1992 (unreported).
3 At note 1 *supra*.

'The Secretary of State, with the concurrence in relation to properties situated in England and Wales of the Lord Chancellor, may by order make provision for securing that a trustee or assignee under the insolvency law of any part of the United Kingdom has, with such modifications as may be specified in the order, the same rights in relation to any property situated in another part of the United Kingdom as he would have in the corresponding circumstances if he were a trustee or assignee under the insolvency law of that other part.'

That provision is specifically directed at the vesting of property in a trustee in a different part of the United Kingdom. Similarly, section 426(6) reads:

'Where a person who is a trustee or assignee under the insolvency law of any part of the United Kingdom claims property situated in any other part of the United Kingdom (whether by virtue of an order under Section (3) or otherwise), the submission of that claim to the Court exercising jurisdiction in relation to insolvency law in that other part shall be treated in the same manner as a request made by a court for the purpose of subsection (4).'

It is difficult, given the terms of section 426(3) and 426(6), to see how section 426(4) and 426(5) can be read to entitle an assisting court to appoint a liquidator in another jurisdiction without an ancillary winding up any more than the court could appoint a trustee in the other jurisdiction. Perhaps it would have been more felicitous if the Scottish courts had granted the liquidators in the English winding up powers to do anything in relation to assets and liabilities in Scotland as if they had been liquidators appointed in a Scottish winding up. It is thought that the order made by the Court of Session goes beyond the type of order intended under section 426(4) and 426(5) of the Insolvency Act 1986.

Section 426(1) relates to 'insolvency law' which is defined in section 426(10) to cover bankruptcy and the various insolvency régimes. It accordingly allows administrators and administrative receivers the equivalent access to the judicial co-operation machinery as liquidation. In the *Goodman International* case[1] an application was made by the examiner (the Irish equivalent of a reporter to the court, under the Irish equivalent to an administration under the Irish Companies (Amendment) Act 1990, set up by that Act) to the High Court of Ireland asking it to request the assistance of the High Court in England pursuant to section 426 of the Insolvency Act 1986 to recognise the Irish régime as equivalent to administration and to protect assets of the Goodman Group in England and Wales from creditor action with the same protection as the assets and companies in Ireland had under the Irish statute. The Republic of Ireland is a designated country pursuant to The Co-operation of Insolvency Courts (Designation of Relevant Countries and Territories) Order 1986. The reasoning behind this application was that unless the creditors of the companies were restrained from proceeding against the companies and their assets in England and Wales, it would be open to those creditors to obtain an advantage as regards creditors who were prevented from taking action in Ireland against the companies or their assets in Ireland by the provisions of section 5 of the Companies (Amendment) Act 1990 of Ireland (which section is similar in essence to section 11 of the Insolvency Act 1986). An order was duly granted by the High Court of England and actions by creditors were stayed.

1 Application to the Irish Courts – August 1990.

# Chapter 21

# Possible future developments

## Introduction

It was thought by the authors that it would be useful for the reader to have highlighted some of the legal developments likely in the foreseeable future in this field.

## Group trading

The EEC draft 9th Directive on the harmonisation of company law contemplates recognition of the group principle. All the members of the Cork Committee recognised the need for a change in this direction, but all appreciated the enormous complexities of the subject. The perceived mischief is where a subsidiary becomes insolvent and goes into liquidation, and the parent company declines all liability for its subsidiary's debts to external creditors, and indeed competes with them by submitting a proof in respect of its own loan. The result is that, out of the total funds realised by the liquidator for distribution among the creditors, a substantial proportion goes to the parent company. The problem is that an alteration in law would introduce a difference between types of shareholders as regards the fundamental principle of limited liability. An individual shareholder could limit his exposure in a commercial venture by entering into it through the medium of a limited company. If the group principle is adopted, a corporate shareholder might no longer have the same facility, or at least not to the same extent. The wrongful trading provisions in relation to 'shadow directors' is the nearest so far which company law in the United Kingdom gets to group liability.

The Cork Committee saw attractions in the law of the USA, where loans by a parent company to a subsidiary could be subordinated on insolvency to debts owed to outside creditors, if it was shown that the debt owed to the parent represented long-term working capital. Under United States law, the result is achieved by the court exercising an equitable jurisdiction to subordinate these claims. Without a change in the law, this would not be possible in Scotland because in terms of section 107 of the Insolvency Act 1986 (in relation to a creditors voluntary winding up) and in terms of rule 4.66(4) of the Insolvency (Scotland) Rules 1986 (relating to compulsory winding ups), the *pari passu* principle has been preserved.

## Security over moveable property

### (1) *The existing law and its difficulties*

The characteristic feature of the common law of Scotland is the restrictive effect produced by the requirement that a fixed security over corporeal moveable property in Scotland requires possession of the property by the creditor. It is customary to describe this possession in security as a pledge where it is created by agreement between the creditor and the debtor and as lien, or sometimes retention, where it is created by law. There are exceptions to the general rule in certain conventional and legal hypothecs (eg the hypothec of a landlord over the goods of his tenant) and the facilities for creating securities over stocks of agricultural merchandise, ships and aircraft, provided respectively by the Agricultural Credits (Scotland) Act 1929, the Merchant Shipping Act 1984, and the Mortgaging of Aircraft Order 1972. Retention of title in a contract of conditional sale or hire purchase may have the practical effect of a non-possessory security for payment of the price of goods, but it can only be employed in that context.

The restrictive effect of the common law is also apparent as regards the creation of a fixed security over incorporeal moveable property. In a typical case the debtor will grant an assignation to the creditor, and completion of the assignation will require that it be intimated to the debtor in the assigned obligation. The effect of intimation is to divest the assignor of the right to demand fulfilment of the obligation and to vest that right in the assignee. Intimation may be impracticable or impossible in certain circumstances, for example where the debtors and the assigned obligations are numerous (as in the case of book debts) or where the debts have yet to be incurred.

In the case of goods, the historical justification for delivery to the creditor was 'that commerce may be the more sure, and everyone may more easily know his condition with whom he contracts'[1]. However, modern commercial practices such as hire purchase and conditional sale have in many cases created a gap between the apparent and the actual ownership of goods, and it cannot be said today that credit is given on the faith of possession of moveable property. Nevertheless, it is important that those who want to acquire rights in at least valuable items of moveable property should be able to discover what security rights exist over the property. For this reason, if the traditional law is to be departed from, it is essential that a system of registration should be introduced, on lines similar to the existing system of registration of company securities but allowing for registration of all securities over moveables worth more than a specified sum.

The creation of such a system makes it all the more important that the permissible categories of security should be clearly defined. This is particularly relevant to the question of retention of title, in so far as that amounts to a security. As indicated in the chapter dealing with that topic[2], that rights of retention of title are not now confined to clauses of simple retention, and extend to 'all sums' and other wider forms of clauses. The same applies to the use of trusts to provide security in the context of sale of goods; once again, for the reasons advanced in *Clark Taylor & Co Ltd v Quality Site Development (Edinburgh) Ltd*[3] sellers cannot be given unrestricted freedom to create any rights they want. In both those instances, it is thought that the test of validity should be whether the alleged security right is truly in accordance with the underlying commercial reality of a contract of sale of goods.

1 Diamond Report.
2 Chap 11.
3 1982 SC 111.

## (2)   *Pressure for reform*

Recommendations were made by the Crowther Committee in 1971[1], in relation not only to consumer credit but also to the creation of an entirely new legal framework in connection with all loans secured over moveable property. The recommendations for the protection of the consumer were largely given effect to by the Consumer Credit Act 1974. As yet there is no indication when the government proposes to implement the committee's recommendations for the creation of a new system of security over moveable property. In 1986, a working party of the Scottish Law Commission under the chairmanship of Professor J M Halliday, CBE, issued a report and made the following recommendations.

(1)   A system should be introduced for creating security over moveable property based upon the establishment of a register of security interests with notice filing, i e registration by computer without the need for paperwork as at other registers.

(2)   There would be no requirement of possession of the security subjects by the creditor, except in the case of certain categories of transaction (e g transactions involving the creation of security interests in consumer goods, transactions where the security subjects are equipment and the amount of the secured loan does not exceed a prescribed amount, securities over subjects for which adequate statutory facilities involving special registers already exist, corporate securities, commercial paper and securities over assets not normally used in commercial transactions). Securities in the excluded sector would continue to be regulated by the existing law.

(3)   Within the sphere of its application, the scheme would be mandatory for the creation by agreement of a valid security except that it would remain competent to create security over corporeal moveables by way of pledge.

(4)   Rules would be provided under the scheme with regard to the form and content of a loan agreement and the requirements for the security to attach to the security subjects so as to be valid between the creditor and the debtor and for it to be 'perfected' so as to be valid also in questions with third parties.

(5)   Provision would be made for the establishment of a register of security interests and for filing of notice of the creation of a security, this being an essential element of perfection of a security under the scheme.

(6)   The extent and effect in law of a security under the scheme would be defined.

(7)   Provision would be made for regulating the priority of the security in question between the creditor and the third party.

(8)   Provision would also be made for the enforcement, transfer and discharge of the security.

Professor A L Diamond was asked to consider the law of security over property other than land in both Scotland and England on behalf of the minister for corporate and consumer affairs. This is an area where the divergence between Scots law and English law is at its widest, and it is unfortunate that the task of reviewing the law should be confined solely to an English lawyer. A consultative document was issued, which suggested tentative

---

1 Cmnd 4596, published in March 1971.

proposals for reform based largely upon the present law in the United States. It is too early to know what the outcome of these deliberations is, but it looks highly likely that the old Scottish law in relation to security over moveables, including book debts and acquirenda, will be changed by statute.

## Draft bankruptcy convention

All the contracting states of the EEC are bound to seek to harmonise their bankruptcy laws including winding up, in order that a Convention on bankruptcy may be acceded to. See chapter 20 at pages 381–382.

# APPENDIX I

The Insolvency Act 1986 Form 4.1 (Scot)

## Statutory Demand for Payment of Debt

Pursuant to section 123(1)(a) or section 222(1)(a) of the Insolvency Act 1986

### Warning

- This is an important document. This demand must be dealt with within 21 days of its service upon the company or a winding up order could be made in respect of the company

- Please read the demand and the notes carefully

- There are additional notes on the two following pages

## Demand

To _____

Address _____

_____

This demand is served by the creditor;

Name _____

Address _____

_____

_____

The creditor claims that the company owes

the sum of | £ _____ |

Full particulars of the debt/s claimed to be owed by the company are set out on page 2 of this demand.

**The creditor demands that the company pays the above sum or secures or compounds for it to the creditor's satisfaction**

Signature _____

Name _____
(BLOCK LETTERS)

Position with or relationship to creditor _____

_____ duly authorised

Address _____

_____

Tel. No. _____

Ref. _____

**N.B. The person making this demand must complete the whole of this page and Parts A and B on page 3.**

## Notes for Creditors

- This demand can only be used by the creditor to demand a sum exceeding £750.

- If the creditor is entitled to the debt by way of assignation, details of the original creditor and any intermediate assignees should be given in Part B on page 3.

- If the amount includes interest, details should be given including the grounds upon which interest is charged. The amount of interest must be shown separately.

- Any other charge payable from time to time may be claimed. The amount or rate of the charge must be identified and the grounds on which it is claimed must be stated.

- In either case the amount claimed must be limited to that which has accrued and is due at the date of the demand.

- If the signatory of the demand is a solicitor or other agent of the creditor the name of his/her firm should be given.

**Particulars of Debts.** (These particulars must include (a) the date or dates when the debt/s was/
were incurred, (b) the grounds of claim and (c) the amount due as at the date of this demand.)

**Notes for Creditor**

Please make sure
that you have read
the notes on page 1
before completing
this page.

**Note:**

If the space is
insufficient
continue on reverse
of page 3 and
clearly indicate on
this page that you
are doing so.

**Form 4.1 (Scot)**
**(contd)**

Part A

The person or persons to whom any communication regarding this demand should be addressed is/are

Name    _____
        (BLOCK LETTERS)

Address _____

        _____

Tel. No. _____

Reference _____

Part B

For completion if the creditor is entitled to the debt by way of assignation

|                    | Name | Date(s) of Assignation) |
|--------------------|------|-------------------------|
| Original creditor  |      |                         |
| Assignees          |      |                         |

**How to comply with a statutory demand**

If the company wishes to avoid a winding up petition being presented it must pay the sum shown on page 1 and of which particulars are set out on page 2 of this demand within the period of 21 days of its service upon the company.

Alternatively, the company may attempt to reach a settlement with the creditor. To do this the company should:

inform the person (or one of them, if more than one) named in Part A above immediately that it is willing and able to offer security for the debt to the creditor's satisfaction; or
inform the person (or one of them) named in Part A immediately that it is willing and able to compound for the debt to the creditor's satisfaction.

If the company disputes the demand in whole or in part it should;

contact the person (or one of them) named in Part A immediately.

**REMEMBER! The company has only 21 days from the date of service on it of this document before the creditor may present a winding up petition**

# APPENDIX II

Rule 4.15     The Insolvency Act 1986         Form 4.7 (Scot)

## Statement of Claim by Creditor

**Pursuant to Rule 4.15(2)(a) of the Insolvency (Scotland) Rules 1986**

---

**WARNING**

It is a criminal offence

● for a creditor to produce a statement of claim, account, voucher or other evidence which is false, unless he shows that he neither knew nor had reason to believe that it was false; or

● for a director or other officer of the company who knows or becomes aware that it is false to fail to report it to the liquidator within one month of acquiring such knowledge.

On conviction either the creditor or such director or other officer of the company may be liable to a fine and/or imprisonment.

---

*Notes*

(a) *Insert name of company*

(b) *Insert name and address of creditor*

(c) *Insert name and address, if applicable, of authorised person acting on behalf of the creditor*

(d) *Insert total amount as at the due date (see note (e) below) claimed in respect of all the debts, the particulars of which are set out overleaf.*

(e) *The due date in the case of a company*

   *(i) which is subject to a voluntary arrangement is the date of a creditors' meeting in the voluntary arrangement;*
   *(ii) which is in administration is the date of the administration order;*
   *(iii) which is in receivership is the date of appointment of the receiver; and*
   *(iv) which is in liquidation is the commencement of the winding up.*

*The date of commencement of the winding up is*

   *(i) in a voluntary winding up the date of the resolution by the company for winding up (section 86 or 98); and*
   *(ii) in a winding up by the court, the date of the presentation of the petition for winding up unless it is preceded by a resolution for voluntary winding up (section 129).*

(a) _____
_____

(b) _____

(c) _____
_____

I submit a claim of (d) £_____ in the liquidation of the above company and certify that the particulars of the debt or debts making up that claim, which are set out overleaf, are true, complete and accurate, to the best of my knowledge and belief.

Signed _____
   *Creditor/person acting on behalf of creditor*

Date _____

PARTICULARS OF EACH DEBT

*Notes*

*A separate set of particulars should be made
out in respect of each debt.*

*1. Describe briefly the debt, giving details of its nature,
the date when it was incurred and when payment
became due.*

   *Attach any documentary evidence of the debt, if
available.*

1. **Particulars of debt**

*2. Insert total amount of the debt, showing separately
the amount of principal and any interest which is
due on the debt as at the due date (see note (e)).
Interest may only be claimed if the creditor is entitled
to it. Show separately the V.A.T. on the debt and
indicate whether the V.A.T. is being claimed back
from H.M. Customs and Excise.*

2. **Amount of debt**

*3. Insert the nature and amount of any preference
under Schedule 6 to the Act claimed in respect of the
debt.*

3. **Preference claimed for debt**

*4. Specify and give details of the nature of any security
held in respect of the debt including –
(a) the subjects covered and the date when it was
given;
(b) the value of the security.*

   *Security is defined in section 248(b) of the
Insolvency Act 1986 as meaning "any security
(whether heritable or moveable), any floating charge
and any right of lien or preference and any right of
retention (other than a right of compensation or set
off)." For claims in administration procedure
security also includes a retention of title agreement,
hire purchase agreement, agreement for the hire of
goods for more than three months and a conditional
sale agreement (see Rules 2.11 and 2.12).*

*In liquidation only the creditor should state whether he
is surrendering or undertakes to surrender his security;
the liquidator may at any time after 12 weeks from the
date of commencement of the winding up (note (e))
require a creditor to discharge a security or to convey or
assign it to him on payment of the value specified by the
creditor.*

4. **Security for debt**

*5. In calculating the total amount of his claim in a
liquidation, a creditor shall deduct the value of any
security as estimated by him unless he surrenders it
(see note 4). This may apply in administration (see
Rule 2.11).*

5. **Total amount of the debt**

# APPENDIX III

Rules 4.7,
4.8

The Insolvency Act 1986                                    Form 4.4 (Scot)

## Statement of Affairs

**Pursuant to sections 95, 99 and 131 of the Insolvency Act 1986 and Rules 4.7 and 4.8 of the Insolvency (Scotland) Rules 1986**

Insert name of
the company

Statement as to affairs of

---

Affidavit

This affidavit must be sworn/affirmed before a Notary Public, Justice of the Peace or Commissioner for Oaths or other person duly authorised to administer oaths, when you have completed the rest of this form.

(a) Insert full name(s) and occupation(s) of deponent(s)

I/We (a) _____

_____

(b) Insert full address(es)

of (b) _____

do swear/affirm that the statement set out overleaf and the lists A to G annexed and signed as relative hereto are to the best of my/our knowledge and belief a full, true and complete statement as to the affairs of the above named company as at

(c) insert date of commencement of the winding up which is:
   (i) in a voluntary winding up the date of the resolution by the company for winding up (section 86); and
   (ii) in a winding up by the court, the date of the presentation of the petition for winding up unless it is preceded by a resolution for voluntary winding up under (i) (section 129), but in the case of a creditors' voluntary winding up, the date inserted should be the nearest practicable date before the date of the meeting of creditors under section 98.

(c) _____

Sworn/affirmed at _____

Date _____

Signature(s) of deponent(s) _____

_____

Before me _____
Person administering the oath or affirmation

**The person administering the oath or affirmation is particularly requested, before swearing the affidavit, to make sure that the full name, address and description of the Deponent(s) are stated, and to ensure that any crossings-out or other alterations in the printed form are initialled.**

## NOTE

This affidavit should be sworn/affirmed and the statement made out and submitted:

(1) in a winding up by the court by any person required to do so under section 131 of the Act by the Liquidator;

(2) in a members' voluntary winding up which becomes a creditors' voluntary winding up under sections 95 and 96, by the Liquidator under section 95; and

(3) in a creditors' voluntary winding up, by the directors.

**Rules 4.7**
**4.8**

STATEMENT as to affairs of the company as at _____

Please do not write in this margin

| | Estimated Realisable Values £ |
|---|---|
| | Please complete legibly, preferably in black type, or bold block lettering |
| **ASSETS** | |
| Assets not specifically secured (as per List "A" _____ | |
| Assets specifically secured (as per List "B") | |
| Estimated realisable value £ | |
| **Less:** Amount due to secured creditors | |
| Estimated surplus _____ | |
| Estimated Total Assets available for preferential creditors | |
| Holders of floating charges and unsecured creditors _____ | |
| **LIABILITIES** | |
| Preferential creditors (as per List "C") _____ | |
| Estimated balance of assets available for – holders of floating charges and unsecured creditors _____ | |
| Holders of floating charges (as per List "D") _____ | |
| Estimated surplus/deficiency as regards holders of floating charges _____ | |
| Unsecured Creditors £ | |
| Trade accounts (as per List "E") _____ | |
| Bills payable (as per List "F") _____ | |
| Contingent or other liabilities (as per List "G") _____ | |
| Total unsecured creditors _____ | |
| Estimated Surplus/Deficiency as regards creditors | |
| Issued and Called-up Capital _____ | |
| Estimated Surplus/Deficiency as regards members | |

These figures must be read subject to the following:–

[(a) There is not unpaid capital liable to be called up]†

[(b) The nominal amount of unpaid capital liable to be called up is £ _____ estimated to produce £ _____ which is/is not charged in favour of the holders of Floating Charges]†

† delete as appropriate

The estimates are subject to expenses of the Liquidation and to any surplus or deficiency on trading pending realisation of the Assets.

## Statement of affairs LIST 'A'

Assets not specifically secured

| Particulars of assets | Book value £ | Estimated to produce £ |
|---|---|---|
| Balance at bank ................ | ..................... | ..................... |
| Cash in hand ................... | ..................... | ..................... |
| Marketable securities (as per schedule I) ......... | ..................... | ..................... |
| Bills receivable (as per schedule II) ......... | ..................... | ..................... |
| Trade debtors (as per schedule III) ...... | ..................... | ..................... |
| Loans and advances (as per schedule IV) ...... | ..................... | ..................... |
| Unpaid calls (as per schedule V) ......... | ..................... | ..................... |
| Stock in trade_____ | | |
| _____ | | |
| _____ | ..................... | ..................... |
| Work in progress_____ | | |
| _____ | | |
| _____ | ..................... | ..................... |
| Heritable property ............ | ..................... | ..................... |
| Leasehold property ......... | ..................... | ..................... |
| Plant, machinery and vehicles ................... | ..................... | ..................... |
| Furniture and fittings, etc ... | ..................... | ..................... |
| Patents, trade marks, etc ... | ..................... | ..................... |
| Investments other than marketable securities ...... | ..................... | ..................... |
| Other properties ............... | ..................... | ..................... |
| Total | | |

Signed                                    Date

## SCHEDULE I TO LIST 'A'
## Statement of affairs

Marketable Securities

Names to be arranged in alphabetical order and numbered consecutively

| No | Name of organisation in which securities are held | Details of securities held | Book value £ | Estimated to produce £ |
|---|---|---|---|---|
|  |  |  |  |  |

Signed                                        Date

## SCHEDULE II TO LIST 'A'
## Statement of affairs

Bills of exchange, promissory notes, etc, available as assets

Names to be arranged in alphabetical order and numbered consecutively

| No | Name and Address of acceptor of bill or note | Amount of bill or note £ | Date when due | Estimated to produce £ | Particulars of any property held as security for payment of bill or note |
|----|----|----|----|----|----|
|    |    |    |    |    |    |

Signed                                    Date

Please do not
write in this
margin

Please complete
legibly, preferably
in black type, or
bold block lettering

## SCHEDULE III TO LIST 'A'
## Statement of affairs

### Trade debtors

Names to be arranged in alphabetical order and numbered consecutively

| No | Name and address of debtor | Particulars of any securities held for debt | Amount of debt £ | Estimated to produce £ |
|----|----------------------------|---------------------------------------------|------------------|------------------------|
|    |                            |                                             |                  |                        |

**Note:**
If the debtor to the company is also a creditor, but for a lesser amount than his indebtedness, the gross amount due to the company and the amount of the contra account should be shown in the third column and only the balance be inserted in the fourth column. No such claim should be included in List 'E'

Signed                                    Date

## SCHEDULE IV TO LIST 'A'
## Statement of affairs

### Loans and Advances

Names to be arranged in alphabetical order and numbered consecutively

| No | Name and Address of debtor | Particulars of any securities held for debt | Amount of debt £ | Estimated to produce £ |
|---|---|---|---|---|
|  |  |  |  |  |

Signed                                        Date

## SCHEDULE V TO LIST 'A'
# Statement of affairs

## Unpaid calls

Names to be arranged in alphabetical order and numbered consecutively

| No | No. in share register | Name and Address of shareholder | No. of shares held £ | Amount of call per share unpaid £ | Total amount due £ | Estimated to produce £ |
|----|----|----|----|----|----|----|
|  |  |  |  |  |  |  |

Signed _____     Date _____

## LIST 'B' (consisting of _____ pages)
## Statement of affairs

Assets specifically secured and creditors fully or partly
secured (not including debenture holders secured by a
floating charge)

| No | Particulars of assets specifically secured | Date when security granted | Name of creditor | Address and occupation |
|----|--------------------------------------------|----------------------------|------------------|------------------------|
|    |                                            |                            |                  |                        |

The names of the secured creditors are to be shown against the assets on which their claims are secured, numbered consecutively, and arranged in alphabetical order as far as possible.

| Consideration | Estimated value of assets specifically secured £ | Total amount due creditor £ | Balance of debt secured £ | Balance of debt unsecured carried to list E £ | Estimated surplus from security £ |
|---|---|---|---|---|---|
|  |  |  |  |  |  |
|  |  |  |  |  |  |

Signed                                        Date

Please do not
write in this
margin

Please complete
legibly, preferably
in black type, or
bold block lettering

# LIST 'C' (consisting of _____ pages)

## Statement of affairs

Preferential creditors for taxes, salaries, wages and otherwise

Names to be arranged in alphabetical order and numbered consecutively

| No | Name of creditor | Address |
|----|------------------|---------|
|    |                  |         |

| Nature of claim | Total amount of claim | Amount ranking as preferential | Balance not preferential carried to List 'E' |
|---|---|---|---|
| | | | |
| | | | |

Signed _____    Date _____

Please do not
write in this
margin

**LIST 'D'**

## Statement of affairs

List of holders of debentures secured by a floating charge

Names to be arranged in alphabetical order and numbered consecutively

Please complete
legibly, preferably
in black type, or
bold block lettering

| No | Name and address of holder | Amount £ | Description of assets over which security extends |
|----|----------------------------|----------|---------------------------------------------------|
|    |                            |          |                                                   |

Signed                                    Date

Please do not
write in this
margin

Please complete
legibly, preferably
in black type, or
bold block lettering

**Note**

\* When there is a contra
account against the
creditor less than his
claim against the
company, the balance
only should be inserted
under the heading
'Amount of the debt'

**LIST 'E' (consisting of _____ pages)**

## Statement of affairs

### Unsecured creditors – trade accounts

Identify separately on this list customers claiming amounts paid in advance of the
supply of goods and services

Names to be arranged in alphabetical order and numbered consecutively

| No | Name and address of creditor | Amount of the debt*<br>£ |
|---|---|---|
|  |  |  |

Signed      Date

## LIST 'F'
## Statement of affairs

Unsecured creditors – Bills payable, promissory notes, etc.

Names to be arranged in alphabetical order and numbered consecutively

**Note**

* The particulars of any
bills of exchange and
promissory notes held by
a holder should be
inserted immediately
below the name and
address of such creditor.

| No | Name and address of acceptor of bill or note | Name and address of holder* | Date when due | Amount of claim £ |
|----|----|----|----|----|
|    |    |    |    |    |

Signed                                    Date

# LIST 'G'
## Statement of affairs

Unsecured creditors – contingent liabilities

Names to be arranged in alphabetical order and numbered consecutively

| No | Name and address of creditor | Nature of liability | Amount of claim £ |
|----|------------------------------|---------------------|-------------------|
|    |                              |                     |                   |

Signed                                           Date

# APPENDIX IV

The Insolvency Act 1986                                    Form 4.5 (Scot)

**Liquidator's Statement of Receipts and Payments**

**Pursuant to section 192 of the Insolvency Act 1986 and Rule 4.11 of the Insolvency (Scotland) Rules 1986**

Name of Company _____

Nature of winding up (delete as appropriate):–

(*a*) Members' Voluntary     (*b*) Creditors' Voluntary     (*c*) By the Court

Date of commencement of winding up _____

Date to which last statement, if any, made up _____

Date to which this statement is made up _____

Name and address of liquidator _____

LIQUIDATOR'S STATEMENT OF ACCOUNTS for the period

from_____ to_____

|  | RECEIPTS | | | PAYMENTS | |
|---|---|---|---|---|---|
| *Nature of Receipts* | Amount £ | | *Nature of payments* | Amount £ | |
| Total receipts from last account | | | Total payments from last account | | |

## ANALYSIS OF BALANCE

at _____ 19 ____

| | £ | |
|---|---|---|
| Total Receipts, per Account ........................................ | | |
| Total Payments, per Account ....................................... | | |
| Balance................................................ | | |

Made up as follows:–
1. Cash in hands of Liquidator .....................................
2. Balances at Bank:
   On Current Account ...............................................
   On Deposit Receipt ..............................................
3. Investments made by Liquidator ............................

   Balance as above ...............................

## PROGRESS REPORT

A. Amount of the total estimated assets and liabilities at the date of the commencement of the winding up per Statement of Affairs

| | £ |
|---|---|
| Assets – | |
| *less:* Secured Creditors ................. | |
| Debenture Holders ................. | |
| *less:* Preferential claims and services | |
| Available for Unsecured Creditors | |
| Unsecured creditors ....................... | |

B. Total amount of the capital paid up at the commencement of the winding up.
C. General description and estimated value of:
   (i)  any material alterations to the amounts shown in (A) above
   (ii) outstanding unrealised assets.
D. Causes which delay the termination of the winding up.
E. Period within which the Liquidator expects to complete the winding up.

Signature of Liquidator _____

Date _____

**NOTES**
(1) Where practicable, receipts and payments should be individually listed, but trading and certain other recurring transactions may be suitably grouped or collated if these are numerous.
(2) Contra items such as cash lodged in bank on current account or on deposit receipt or withdrawn therefrom should be excluded from the receipts and payments.
(3) No balance should be shown on the Account. The balance and its analysis should be entered above.
(4) Where there have been no receipts or payments since the last Account, the Liquidator shall give a certificate to that effect.

# APPENDIX V

The Insolvency Act 1986                    Form 4.29 (Scot)

## Proxy

### Pursuant to Rules 7.14 and 7.15 of the Insolvency (Scotland) Rules 1986

(a) Insert name of the company
(b) Insert nature of insolvency proceedings

(a) _____

(b) _____

Name of Creditor/Member _____

Address _____

_____

(hereinafter called "the principal").

(c) Insert the name and address of the proxy-holder and of any alternatives. A proxy-holder must be an individual aged over 18.

Name of proxy-holder (c) 1. _____

Address _____

_____

whom failing 2. _____

_____

_____

whom failing 3. _____

_____

_____

I appoint the above person to be the principal's proxy-holder at

*Delete as appropriate

*[all meetings in the above Insolvency proceedings relating to the above company]

*[the meeting of *creditors/members of the above Company to be held on _____
or at any adjournment of that meeting].

## Voting Instructions

**The proxy-holder is authorised** to vote or abstain from voting in the name, and on behalf, of the principal in respect of any matter*/s, including resolution*/s, arising for determination at said meeting*/s and any adjournment*/s thereof and to propose any resolution*/s in the name of the principal, either

    (i)  in accordance with instructions given below or,

    (ii)  if no instructions are given, in accordance with his/her own discretion.

(d) Complete only if you wish to instruct the proxy-holder to vote for a specific person as liquidator

(d) 1. To *propose/support a resolution for the appointment of

_____

of _____

whom failing _____

as liquidator of the company.

(e) Delete if the proxy-holder is only to vote as directed in (1)

(e) [in the event of a person named in paragraph (1) withdrawing or being eliminated from any vote the proxy-holder may vote or abstain in any further ballot at *his/her discretion.]

(f) Set forth any voting instructions for the proxy-holder. If more room is required attach a separate sheet

2. (f) _____

_____

_____

_____

Signed _____ Date _____

Name in BLOCK LETTERS _____

Position of signatory in relation to the *creditor/or member or other authority for signing.

_____

_____

## Notes for the Principal and Proxy-holder

1. The chairman of the meeting who may be nominated as proxy-holder, will be the insolvency practitioner who is presently *liquidator/receiver/administrator/nominee under the voluntary arrangement or a director of the company.
2. All proxies must be in this form or a form substantially to the same effect with such variations as circumstances may require. (Rules 7.15(3) and 7.30).
3. To be valid the proxy must be lodged at or before the meeting at which it is to be used. (Rule 7.16(2)).
4. Where the chairman is nominated as proxy-holder he cannot decline the nomination. (Rule 7.14(4)).
5. The proxy-holder may vote for or against a resolution for the appointment of a named person to be liquidator jointly with another person, unless the proxy states otherwise. (Rule 7.16(4)).
6. The proxy-holder may propose any resolution in favour of which he could vote by virtue of this proxy. (Rule 7.16(5)).
7. The proxy-holder may vote at his discretion on any resolutions not dealt with in the proxy, unless the proxy states otherwise. (Rule 7.16(6)).
8. The proxy-holder may not vote in favour of any resolution which places him, or any associate of his, in a position to receive remuneration out of the insolvent estate unless the proxy specifically directs him so to vote. (Rule 7.19(1)).
9. Unless the proxy contains a statement to the contrary the proxy-holder has a mandate to act as representative of the principal on the creditors' or liquidation committee. (Rule 4.48).

# APPENDIX VI

**Rule 4.31**   **The Involvency Act 1986**   **Form 4.17 (Scot)**

**Notice of Final**
**Meeting of Creditors**   # R4.31

**Pursuant to sections 171(6) and 172(8) of the Insolvency Act 1986 and Rule 4.31(4) of the Insolvency (Scotland) Rules 1986**

**For official use**

To the Registrar of Companies

To the Court        Company number

Name of Company

(a) Insert name of company

(a) _____

I/We _____

of _____

_____

_____

_____

\* Delete whichever does not apply

(b) Insert date

the liquidator(s) of the above company give notice that the Final General Meeting of creditors under section *94/106/146 of the Insolvency Act *[was held]/[is deemed, in terms of Rule 4.31(5), to have been held] on (b)_____ and I/We attach a copy of the report which was laid before the meeting.
*No quorum was present at the meeting.
*The following resolutions were passed by the meeting:

_____

_____

_____

*I was/was not released as liquidator.

_____

Signed _____ Date _____

_____

Presenter's name, address and reference (if any)

**For Official use**
**Liquidation Section**       **Post Room**

440

# APPENDIX VII

Sections 94
106

The Involvency Act 1986

Form 4.26 (Scot)

**Return of Final
Meeting in a
Voluntary
Winding Up**

# S94/106

**Pursuant to sections 94 and 106 of the Insolvency Act 1986**

For official use

To the Registrar of Companies

Company number

Name of Company

(a) Insert name of
company

(a)

(b) Insert full name(s)
and address(es)

I/We (b)

give notice:

\* Delete as applicable

(c) Insert date

(d) The copy account
must be authenticated
by the written
signature(s) of the
liquidator(s)

1. that a general meeting of the company was duly \*[held on]/
[summoned for] (c)_____ pursuant to Section
\*[94]/[106] of the Insolvency of Act 1986, for the purpose of having an
account (of which a copy is attached (d)) laid before it showing how the
winding up of the company has been disposed of and \*[that the same
was done accordingly]/[no quorum was present at the meeting].

(e) Delete in members'
voluntary winding up

(e) 2. that a meeting of the creditors of the company was duly
\*[held on]/[summoned for]
(c) _____ pursuant to section 106 for the purpose
of having the said account laid before it showing how the winding up
of the company has been conducted and the property of the
company has been disposed of and \*[that the same was done
accordingly]/[no quorum was present at the meeting].

Signed _____ Date _____

Presenter's name,
address and
reference (if any)

**For Official use**
Liquidation Section | Post Room

441

**Sections 106**                                    **Form 4.26 (Scot) (contd.)**

# Liquidator's Statement of Account in a Voluntary Winding Up

Statement showing how winding up has been conducted and the property of the company has been disposed of.

Name of Company _____

From _____ (commencement of winding up) to _____
(close of winding up)

| | Statement of assets and liabilities | Receipts | | Payments |
|---|---|---|---|---|
| **Receipts** | | | | £ |
| Cash at Bank | | | Expenses of Solicitors to Liquidator | |
| Cash in hand | | | Other Legal Expenses | |
| Marketable Securities | | | | |
| Sundry Debtors | | | Liquidator's Remuneration | |
| Stock in Trade | | | | |
| Work in Progress | | | By whom fixed _____ | |
| Heritable Property | | | | |
| Leasehold Property | | | | |
| Plant and machinery | | | Auctioneer's and Valuer's Charges | |
| Furniture, Fittings, Utensils, etc | | | Expenses of Management and Maintenance of Assets of the Company | |
| Patents, Trademarks etc | | | Expenses of Notices in Gazette and Local Paper | |
| Investments other than Marketable Securities | | | Incidental Outlays | |
| Surplus from securities | | | | |
| Unpaid Calls at Commencement of Winding Up | | | Total Expenses and Outlays          £ | |
| Amount Received from Calls on Members/Contributories made in the Winding Up | | | (i) Debenture Holders:          £ | |
| Receipts per Trading Account | | | Payment of £ per £ debenture | |
| Other Property, viz: | | | Payment of £ per £ debenture | |
| | | | Payment of £ per £ debenture | |
| | | | (ii) Creditors:          £ | |
| | £ | | | |
| | | £ | *Preferential | |
| Less | | | *Unsecured | |
| | | | Dividends of    p in £  on £ | |
| Payments to Redeem Securities | | | (The estimate of amount expected to rank for dividend was £          ) | |
| Expenses of Diligence | | | | |
| Payments per Trading Account | | | (iii) Returns to Contributories:          £ | |
| | | | .... per £ ........ | |
| | | | .... † share | |
| Net realisations          £ | | | .... per £ ........ | |
| | | | .... † share | |
| | | | .... per £ ........ | |
| | | | .... † share | |

**Note**
   \* State number. Preferential creditors need not be separately shown if all creditors have been paid in full.          **Balance**
   † State nominal volume and class of share.

**Sections 94**                    **Form 4.26 (Scot) (contd.)**
           **106**

(1) Assets, including _____ shown in the statement of assets and liabilities and estimated to be of the value of £_____ have proved to be unreliable.

---

(2) State amount in respect of:

    (a) unclaimed dividends payable to creditors in the winding up.     £

    (b) other unclaimed dividends in the winding up.     £

    (c) moneys held by the company in respect of dividends or other sums due before the commencement of the winding up to any person as a member of the company.     £

(3) Add here any special remarks the Liquidators think desirable:

Dated _____

Signed (by the Liquidator(s)) _____

Names and addresses of Liquidators (IN BLOCK LETTERS) _____

_____

_____

# FORMS OF ADVERTISEMENT

## WINDING UP BY THE COURT

### First Order (with provisional liquidator)

[_____] LIMITED

Notice is hereby given that on _____ a petition was presented to (the Sheriff at Glasgow) by _____ Ltd. (*address*) craving the court, *inter alia*, that _____ Ltd, having its registered office at _____ Glasgow, be wound up by the Court and that an interim liquidator be appointed, and that in the meantime _____, C.A., (address), be appointed as provisional liquidator of the said company; in which petition the Sheriff at Glasgow by interlocutor dated _____ appointed all persons having an interest to lodge answers in the hands of the Sheriff Clerk, Glasgow, within 8 days after intimation, advertisement or service; and *eo die* appointed the said _____, C.A., to be provisional liquidator of the said company with the powers specified in Part II of Schedule 4 to the Insolvency Act 1986; of all of which notice is hereby given.

_____

Solicitors

_____

Glasgow

Agents for the Petitioners

### Winding up order with appointment of liquidator

[_____] (IN LIQUIDATION)

Notice is hereby given that by interlocutor of the Sheriff at Glasgow dated _____, C.A., (*address*) was appointed interim liquidator of _____ Ltd, having its registered office at _____ Glasgow; it is the intention of the interim liquidator to summon a meeting of creditors for the purpose of establishing a liquidation committee; of all of which intimation is hereby given.

_____

Solicitors

# CREDITORS' VOLUNTARY WINDING UP

## Meeting of creditors

[                              ] LIMITED (IN LIQUIDATION)

Notice is hereby given that a meeting of the creditors of _____ Ltd, having their registered office at _____ , Glasgow, will be held at _____ , at _____ a.m. on _____ , for the purposes of choosing a person to be liquidator of the company, and of determining whether to establish a liquidation committee in terms of section 101 of the Insolvency Act 1986. The attention of creditors is drawn to the following:

(1) A creditor is entitled to vote only if he has submitted his claim (Form 4.7 (Scot)) to the address mentioned below, and his claim has been accepted in whole or in part.

(2) A resolution at the meeting is passed if a majority in value of those voting vote in favour of it.

(3) Proxies may be lodged at or before the meeting at the offices of the responsible insolvency practitioner mentioned below, marked for the attention of Mr                      .

(4) Claims may be lodged by those who have not already done so at or before the meeting at the said offices.

(5) The provisions of Rules 4.15–4.17 (as amended by Schedule 1) and of Rule 7 of the Insolvency (Scotland) Rules 1986.

(6) A list of names and addresses of the company's creditors will be available for inspection, free of charge, at the offices of Messrs _____ , Chartered Accountants, (*address*), on the two business days prior to the said meeting.

If you are in any doubt as to any of these matters, you should consult your solicitor immediately.

Director

Dated this _____ day of _____ 19_____

## Appointment of liquidator

[                              ] LIMITED (IN LIQUIDATION)

Notice is hereby given that by resolution of the creditors dated _____ , C.A., (*address*), was appointed liquidator of _____ Ltd, having its registered office at _____ Glasgow, and a liquidation committee was established on that date.

_____

Solicitor

# FORMS OF REQUEST FOR ASSISTANCE UNDER SECTION 426 OF THE INSOLVENCY ACT 1986

| | |
|---|---|
| 1. Sender | The Deputy Principal Clerk of Session, Parliament House, Edinburgh, EH1 1RF[1]. |
| 2. Central authority of the requested state | The High Court of Justice, Strand, London. |
| 3. Person to whom the executed request is to be returned | The Deputy Principal Clerk of Session, Parliament House, Edinburgh, EH1 1RF. |
| 4. The undersigned applicant has the honour to submit the following request. | |
| 5. (a) Requesting judicial authority | The Court of Session, Parliament House, Edinburgh, EH1 1RF. |
| (b) To competent authority | The High Court of Justice, Royal Courts of Justice, London. |
| 6. Name and addresses of the parties and their representatives | (a) JL Undertaker, 1 Gravesend Quay, Glasgow, liquidator/administrator/administrative receiver of MT Shelfco Ltd., a company incorporated under the Companies Acts and having its registered office at 10 Clyde Street, Glasgow represented by Jaggers, Solicitors, Broomielaw, Glasgow and MJ Shelfco Ltd. |
| (b) Respondents | 1. First Director of MT Shelfco Ltd. 2. Second Director of MT Shelfco Ltd. 3. First Director of subsidiary of MT Shelfco Ltd. 4. Second Director of subsidiary of MT Shelfco Ltd. 5. Subsidiary of MT Shelfco Ltd. |
| (c) Other parties | The respondents have been represented as follows: The first respondents' solicitors are Messrs ————; The second respondents' solicitors are Messrs ————; The third respondents' solicitors are Messrs ————; The fourth respondents' solicitors are Messrs ———— and; The fifth respondents' solicitors are Messrs ————. |

[1] This form of request is equally competent in a Sheriff Court.

7. Nature and purpose of the proceedings and summary of the facts

The Petition seeks the granting of orders as follows:

(a) Under Section 236 of the Insolvency Act 1986. The Orders are sought for the purpose of investigating the conduct of the affairs of Shelfco Ltd and subsidiary of Shelfco Ltd, the circumstances of the lending, sale or disposal of the assets of the said companies and the disposal of the proceeds, with a view to recovering such monies as may be recoverable and otherwise pursuing such remedies as may appear appropriate.

(b) (Appropriate in the case of an administration) for an order, while an application for an administration order is pending in the Court of Session (Scotland) which has the effect of applying Section 10 of the Insolvency Act 1986 to MT Shelfco Ltd and the subsidiary of MT Shelfco and its subsidiary and their assets within the jurisdiction of the High Court of Justice, London, and in the event of the Court of Session (Scotland) granting an administration order under Section 8 of the Insolvency Act 1986, an order which has the effect of Section 11 of the Insolvency Act 1986 in relation to MT Shelfco and its subsidiary and their assets within the jurisdiction of the High Court of Justice, London.

8. Evidence to be obtained or other judicial act to be performed

The production to the court of the documents and property appended hereto; and the examination of the respondents on oath concerning the business, dealings, affairs and property of MT Shelfco Ltd and the subsidiary of MT Shelfco Ltd.

9. Identity and address of any person to be examined

The first four respondents.

10. Questions to be put to the persons to be examined or statement of the subject matter about which they are to be examined

The respondents are to be examined about the lending of securities owned by MT Shelfco Ltd or the subsidiary of MT Shelfco Ltd, their dealings with _____, the sale or disposal of their assets, and the disposal of the proceedings of such sales, all as are more fully specified in the Petition.

11. Documents or other property to be inspected

See 10 above.

12. Any requirement that the evidence be given on oath or affirmation and any special form to be used

See 8 above.

13. Special methods of procedure to be followed

In relation to an examination under Section 236 of the Insolvency Act 1986, the hearings at which the respondents are examined should take place in private; and a report of the proceedings should be transmitted, in sealed form together with any productions rendered, to the Deputy Principal Clerk of Session.

14. Request for notification of the time and place of the execution of the request and identity of any person to be notified

It is requested that such notification be given to Messrs Jaggers, Solicitors, Broomielaw, Glasgow, solicitors for the petitioners.

15. Request for attendance or participation of judicial personnel of the requesting authority at the execution of the letter of request

It is requested that the request should be executed as if the order made under Section 236 had been made by the High Court of Justice in England.
(Appropriate in the case of an administration.)
It is requested that the request should be executed as if the orders giving an effect equivalent to Sections 10 and 11 of the Insolvency Act 1986 had been the effect pursuant to an application for an administration order to the High Court of Justice in England, and the granting of such an order by the High Court of Justice in England.

16. Specification of privilege or duty to refuse to give evidence under the law of the State or origin

None.

17. The fees and costs incurred will be borne by:

_____WS, Edinburgh.

18. Date of Request

Date _____

19. Signature and seal of the requesting authority

All in terms of Section 426(5) of the Insolvency Act 1986.

# TIMETABLES AND FLOW-CHARTS

## (A)  COURT LIQUIDATION

| | Insolvency Act 1986 | Insolvency (Scotland) Rules 1986 |
|---|---|---|
| *PRELIMINARY* | | |
| *COMMENCEMENT OF WINDING UP* | | |
| 1.  A company may be *wound up by the court* if any of eight conditions is applicable. | s 122/123 | |
| 2.  There are four categories of *competent* petitioner for the winding up of a company. | s 124 | |
| 3.  The *commencement* of the liquidation is the *date* of the *presentation of the petition for winding up* unless a resolution was previously passed by the members of the company for its voluntary winding up when it is the date of passing of the resolution. | s 129 | |
| *PROVISIONAL LIQUIDATOR* | | |
| 4.  (i)  The court may appoint a *provisional liquidator* at any time before the winding-up order is made. The provisional liquidator shall carry out such functions as the court may confer on him. | s 135 | |
| (ii)  Application for a provisional liquidator's appointment can be made by any one of five categories of applicant. | | 4.1 |
| (iii)  The provisional liquidator must give notice of his appointment *forthwith* to; | | 4.2 |
| (a) Registrar of Companies, (b) the company, (c) any receiver. | | |
| The *court* shall give directions regarding the *advertisement* of his appointment. | | |
| (iv)  The provisional liquidator *must find caution* based on his *estimated value of the company's assets* at the date of his appointment, having regard to the estimated value of those assets disclosed in any statement of affairs (SI 1986/1995). | | 4.3 4.4 |
| (v)  The provisional liquidator's *remuneration* will be fixed by the court and his *appointment will be terminated* by the court either on his own application or on that of any of the persons entitled under rule 4.1 | | 4.5 4.6 |

| | Insolvency Act 1986 | Insolvency (Scotland) Rules 1986 |
|---|---|---|
| (vi) The provisional liquidator may require a *statement of affairs* to be made out by any of one of four categories of person. Such person *must be given notice* of this requirement. | s 131 | 4.8 |
| (vii) The *statement of affairs* must be inserted in the *Sederunt Book* which will be maintained by the relevant appointee throughout the life of the liquidation. | | 4.7 4.8 |
| 5. When a winding-up order is made, a copy must be forwarded *forthwith* to the *Registrar* by the company (or otherwise as the court orders). | s 130 | |

## INTERIM LIQUIDATOR

| | | |
|---|---|---|
| 6. (i) Where a winding-up order is made by the court, a liquidator shall be appointed who shall be known as the *interim liquidator* and who shall continue in office until another person becomes liquidator in his place. However, the court shall not make the appointment unless and until a statement has been lodged to the effect that the person to be appointed is an insolvency practitioner, duly qualified under the Act to be the liquidator, and that he consents to act. The court shall send a copy of the order to the Liquidator, whose appointment takes effect from the date of the order. | s 138(1) s 138(2) | 4.18(1) 4.18(2) 4.18(3) |
| (ii) The *interim liquidator* must *give notice of his appointment* to; | | 4.18(4) |
| (a) the *Registrar of Companies* within seven days | | |
| (b) the *creditors and contributories* within *28 days*, – or the court may direct him to advertise his appointment. | | |
| (iii) *Within that same 28-day period*, the interim liquidator shall summon *separate meetings of creditors and contributories* for a date not later than 42 days after the date of the winding-up order or such longer period as the court may allow; | s 138(3) | 4.12 7.2 |
| (a) choose a *liquidator* in place of the interim liquidator; | s 139 | 4.12(3) |
| (b) determine whether a *liquidation committee* should be established and who are to be the members of the committee if established; | s 142(1) | 4.12(3) |

| | Insolvency Act 1986 | Insolvency (Scotland) Rules 1986 |
|---|---|---|
| (c) *if no committee established*, specify the *terms of the liquidator's remuneration* or to defer consideration of that matter (no meeting of contributories is necessary if the company is unable to pay its debts)" and | | 4.12(3) |
| (d) consider the resolutions laid down in rule 4.12(3)(*d*) and (*e*) of the Insolvency (Scotland) Rules 1986. | | 4.12(3) |
| (iv) The meetings must be summoned at *not less than 14 days' notice* for | | 7.2 |
| commencement between 10.00 and | | 7.3 |
| 16.00 hours on a business day by | | 7.5 |
| *individual notice and* by *advertisement* in one or more local newspapers *unless* the court orders otherwise. | | 7.7 |
| (v) The *quorum* for these meetings is: | | 7.7 |
| (a) *creditors' meeting* – one creditor entitled to vote, in person or by proxy; | | |
| (b) *contributories' meeting* – at least two contributories. If the total number of contributories does not exceed two, then the total constitutes a quorum. | | |
| (vi) *Forms of proxy*: | | 7.14 |
| (a) must be sent with every notice calling a meeting of creditors/contributories; | | 7.15 |
| (b) must not have any name or description of any person inserted in it; | | |
| (c) must be retained in the Sederunt Book if used for voting at any meeting; | | 7.17 |
| (d) can be inspected by the creditors. | | 7.18 |
| (vii) A *certificate of posting* the notice must be prepared by the Interim Liquidator | | 7.23 |
| together with *a report of the meeting* – copies of these should be inserted in the Sederunt Book. | | 7.13 |
| (viii) Only a creditors' meeting need be summoned where a company is being wound up on grounds including its inability to pay its debts. | s 138(4) | |

*LIQUIDATOR*

| | | |
|---|---|---|
| 7. (i) If the meetings of creditors and contributories *do not appoint* or nominate a liquidator, the interim liquidator shall *report to the court* who will appoint a liquidator. However, the court *shall not make the appointment unless and until a* | s 138(5) | 4.18(1) |
| | | 4.18(2) |

| | Insolvency Act 1986 | Insolvency (Scotland) Rules 1986 |
|---|---|---|
| *statement* has been lodged to the effect that the person to be appointed is an insolvency practitioner, duly qualified under the Act to be the liquidator, and that he consents so to act. The court shall send a copy of the order to the liquidator whose appointment takes effect from the date of the order. | | |
| (ii) The liquidator shall then give notice of his appointment to the Registrar, creditors and contributories as in para 6(ii). | | 4.18(4) |
| 8. (i) If the meetings of creditors and contributories *nominate different persons* to be liquidator, the person nominated by the creditors shall be liquidator *unless* an objection is lodged in court. | s 139 | 4.19 |
| (ii) The chairman of the meeting shall certify the appointment of the liquidator *but not until* the person to be appointed has provided him with a statement as in para 7(i). | | 4.19(2) |
| (iii) The liquidator's appointment is, however, effective from the date of the passing of the resolution for his appointment. | | 4.19(3) |
| (iv) The liquidator shall give notice of his appointment to; | | 4.19(4) |
| (a) the *court forthwith*; | s 138(6) | |
| (b) the *Registrar* within seven days; | | |
| (c) the *creditors and contributories* within *28 days* (by newspaper advertisement). | | |

### LIQUIDATION COMMITTEE

| | Insolvency Act 1986 | Insolvency (Scotland) Rules 1986 |
|---|---|---|
| 9. (i) The first meetings in the liquidation may establish a *liquidation committee* to carry out such functions as are prescribed by the Act. | s 142 | |
| (ii) The committee shall consist of at *least three and not more than five* creditors. | | 4.41(1)(a) |
| (iii) *Any creditor* is *eligible* to be a member provided *certain criteria* are satisfied. | | 4.41(2)–(6) |
| (iv) The *liquidation committee cannot come into being* until the members have *consented to act* and the liquidator has issued a *certificate of constitution*. | | 4.42 |
| (v) The liquidator must *send the certificate* to the *Registrar* together with a *notice*. | | |
| (vi) A meeting of contributories *may* elect the liquidation committee *under certain circumstances*. | | 4.43 |

| | Insolvency Act 1986 | Insolvency (Scotland) Rules 1986 |
|---|---|---|
| (vii) If *no liquidation committee* established at the *first statutory meeting*, the liquidator *may* call other meetings for the purpose and *must* do so if requested by one-tenth in value of creditors. | s 142(2)(3) | |
| (viii) If no liquidation committee is established, its functions are vested in the court except to the extent that the rules otherwise provide. | s 142(5) | |

### *DURING LIQUIDATION:*
### *GENERAL PROVISIONS*

| | | |
|---|---|---|
| 10. As soon as possible after the making of the winding-up order, the court shall settle a list of contributories, *unless* it appears to the court that this can be dispensed with. | s 148 | |
| 11. The liquidator shall *take possession* of the company's assets, books, etc, and shall *make up and maintain an inventory* and valuation of the assets which he shall retain in the *Sederunt Book.* | | 4.22 |
| 12. When the company's premises have been vacated, the liquidator should change the situation of the *registered office* to his own address and *within 14 days* advise the Registrar (s 287(2), Companies Act 1985). | | |
| 13. The liquidator may exercise any of the *powers* contained in Parts I and II of Schedule 4 to the Act with the sanction of the court or the liquidation committee and those contained in Part III of said Schedule with or without such sanction. If the liquidator, in pursuance of his powers disposes of any assets to any person associated with the company or employs a solicitor to assist him in the carrying out of his functions, notice thereof must be given to the liquidation committee (if any). | s 167 | |
| 14. Until all assets have been distributed, the *liquidator* shall make up *accounts of his intromissions* in *respect of periods of 26 weeks,* the first period commencing with the date of the commencement of the winding up. | | 4.68<br>4.16(2) |
| 15. (i) *Creditor's claims* should be *submitted* either;<br>   (a) *at or before* the relevant creditors' meeting or, as the case may be,<br>   (b) not later than *eight weeks* before the end of the relevant accounting period.<br>   (ii) Claims must be submitted by a statement of claim in the prescribed form. | | 4.15 |

| | Insolvency Act 1986 | Insolvency (Scotland) Rules 1986 |
|---|---|---|
| (iii) The court *may* fix a closing time for claims to be proved, or excluded from the benefit of any distribution before these debts are proved. | s 153 | |
| 16. The expenses of the liquidation have first call on the funds of the company's assets, in the order of priority laid down in the Insolvency (Scotland) Rules 1986. | | 4.66(1)(a) 4.67 |
| 17. When the funds permit, the liquidator will pay *dividends* to the creditors in the following order: | | 4.66(1) |
| (1) secured creditors from the proceeds of their security, any shortfall being given an ordinary/preferential ranking; | | 4.66(6) |
| (2) preferential creditors; | s 386 | |
| (3) creditors having a valid floating charge; | s 175 | |
| (4) ordinary creditors; | | |
| (5) interest at official rate on | | |
| (a) preferential debts *and* (b) ordinary debts; | | |
| (6) any postponed debt. | | |
| 18. (i) *Before paying creditors* the liquidator shall adjudicate on every claim in respect of which he intends to pay a dividend in any accounting period. | | 4.16(1),(2) |
| (ii) The adjudication shall be made and issued not later than four weeks before the end of the period. | | |
| (iii) The liquidator *shall record in the Sederunt Book* his decision on each claim, specifying – | | |
| (a) the amount of the claim accepted by him; | | |
| (b) the category of debt and the value of any security, as decided by him; and | | |
| (c) his reasons for rejecting any claim. | | |
| 19. *Appeals* against these adjudications must be submitted to the court within *two weeks* and the liquidator shall record the sheriff's decision in the Sederunt Book. | | |
| 20. When paying the creditors, the liquidator may ask for a receipt to be completed and returned to him before or upon payment of the dividend, or he may pay by a cheque which has a form of receipt on the back of it. If he is able to pay all creditors as defined in para 17, any surplus will be distributed to members. | | |

*26-week Accounting Periods*

| | | |
|---|---|---|
| 21. As mentioned in para 14 above, the liquidator shall make up accounts of his intromissions in respect of periods of 26 weeks. | | 4.68 |

| | Insolvency<br>Act 1986 | Insolvency<br>(Scotland)<br>Rules<br>1986 |
|---|---|---|
| 22. *In any accounting period* the liquidator may:<br>   (i) pay a dividend to the creditors if there are<br>     sufficient funds and he has allowed for<br>     future contingencies; | | 4.68 |
|    (ii) pay any outlays incurred either by himself<br>     or by the provisional liquidator; and | | 4.68<br>4.67(1) |
|    (iii) pay any class of creditors in full with the<br>     sanction of the liquidation committee or<br>     the court. | s 167 | |
| 23. If the liquidator considers it would be<br>*inappropriate to pay* a dividend in any<br>accounting period, he may postpone to the<br>next accounting period with the consent of the<br>liquidation committee or if none the court. | | 4.68 |
| 24. The liquidator may *accelerate the payment of a<br>dividend* if he wishes and so shorten the<br>relevant accounting period accordingly. | | 4.68 |
| 25. Within *two weeks* after the end of an<br>accounting period, the liquidator shall submit<br>to the liquidation committee or, if none exists,<br>the court: | | 4.32(1)<br>4.68 |
|    (i) his account of intromissions for audit,<br>     together with a scheme of division; and | | |
|    (ii) a claim for his remuneration and outlays.<br>Where these papers are submitted to a<br>liquidation committee, copies should be sent<br>to the court. | | 4.32(1) |
| 26. The liquidator *may make an interim claim* to<br>the liquidation committee in respect of his<br>outlays and fees at any time before the end of<br>an accounting period.<br>   The liquidation committee may make an<br>interim determination and, where they do so,<br>they shall take into account that interim<br>determination when making their<br>determination at the end of the relevant<br>accounting period. | | 4.32(2) |
| 27. All accounts in respect of *legal services*<br>incurred by the liquidator must be submitted<br>to the *Auditor of Court* for taxation before<br>payment can be made, unless the court<br>authorises the liquidator to pay any such<br>account without taxation. | | 4.68 |
| 28. Within *six weeks after the end of an accounting<br>period*, the liquidation committee, or the court,<br>shall:<br>   (i) audit the accounts; and<br>   (ii) issue a determination fixing the amount of<br>     outlays and fees payable to the liquidator. | | 4.68 |
| 29. The liquidator *shall make the audited accounts*,<br>scheme of division and the determination<br>*available for inspection* by the creditors and the<br>company. | | 4.68 |

|  | Insolvency Act 1986 | Insolvency (Scotland) Rules 1986 |
|---|---|---|
| 30. If the liquidator considers the *remuneration* fixed by the liquidation committee to be *insufficient* he may request that it be increased by *resolution of the creditors*. |  | 4.33 |
| 31. If the liquidator is still dissatisfied he may apply to the *court* for an *order increasing the amount* and he must give at least *14 days' notice of* his application to the liquidation committee or if there is no liquidation committee to any creditor(s) as directed by the court. |  | 4.34 |
| 32. Any creditor(s) representing at least 25 per cent in value may appeal against the amount of the liquidator's remuneration on the grounds that it is excessive. |  | 4.35 |
| 33. The liquidator, the company or any creditor must lodge their appeal against the amount of the liquidator's remuneration within *eight weeks* after the end of an accounting period. |  | 4.68 |
| 34. The liquidator should pay the appropriate dividend to the creditors only on the expiry of the appeal period. |  | 4.68 |
| 35. The liquidator must *insert the audited accounts, scheme of division* and *determination* of his fees in the *Sederunt Book*. |  | 4.68 |
| 36. The liquidator shall report to the creditors within six weeks after the end of each accounting period and will include a summary of the statement of affairs, if appropriate. Alternatively, he may submit such a report to a meeting of creditors held within such period. |  | 4.10 |

## LIQUIDATION COMMITTEE

|  | Insolvency Act 1986 | Insolvency (Scotland) Rules 1986 |
|---|---|---|
| 37. *It is the duty of the liquidator* to *report to the members* all matters as appear to be of interest to them, although he can refuse a request for information on certain grounds. |  | 4.44 |
| 38. The *liquidation committee shall meet* when and where determined by the liquidator although the first meeting must be called within three months of the liquidator's appointment or the establishment of the committee, whichever is the later. |  | 4.45 |
| 39. The *chairman* at any meeting shall be the liquidator or his nominee and the quorum is two members present or represented. |  | 4.46 4.47 4.48 |
| 40. There are certain rules regarding the *resignation, removal or termination of membership* of members of the committee and the filling of any subsequent vacancy. |  | 4.49 4.50 4.51 4.52 4.53 |

| | Insolvency Act 1986 | Insolvency (Scotland) Rules 1986 |
|---|---|---|
| 41. There are also certain rules regarding voting rights and the passing of resolutions. It should be noted that a copy of every resolution must be retained in the Sederunt Book. | | 4.54 4.55 |
| 42. The liquidator shall send a *written report* to each member of the committee at least every six months but not more often than every two months (as directed by the committee). The committee are entitled to payment of reasonable expenses. | | 4.56 |
| 43. There are strict rules governing dealings by committee members and others. | | 4.58 |
| 44. If *all creditors have been paid in full* with interest, the liquidator issues a *certificate* to this effect and notifies the Registrar of Companies immediately. This certificate has an effect on the composition of the liquidation committee. | s 189 | 4.59 |

### INFORMATION

| | | |
|---|---|---|
| 45. The liquidator must send a statement of receipts and payments to the Registrar *within 30 days* of the expiration of the first year and at six-monthly intervals thereafter. | s 192 | 4.11 |
| 46. The liquidator is required to summon a meeting of creditors in each year during the liquidation. | | 4.13 |

### FINALISATION

### REMOVAL/RELEASE OF LIQUIDATOR

#### Prior to Completion of the Winding Up,

| | | |
|---|---|---|
| 47. A *liquidator may be removed* from office by a *general meeting of creditors* summoned in accordance with the rules. | s 172(2) s 174(4)(a) | 4.23 4.24 4.25(1) 4.27 |
| 48. Where the *meeting resolves against his release*, or he is removed by the court, the liquidator *must apply* to the Accountant of Court for his release. | s 172(2) s 174(4)(b) | 4.25(2) 4.25(3) 4.27 |
| 49. An application may be made to the court to have the liquidator removed. | s 172(2) | 4.25 4.26 |
| 50. A liquidator may resign his office on certain grounds, but he must call a meeting of creditors to accept his resignation. | s 172(6) s 174(4)(c) | 4.28 4.29 4.30 |

### EARLY DISSOLUTION

| | | |
|---|---|---|
| 51. If after a meeting or meetings under s 138 it appears to the liquidator that the *realisable assets* are *insufficient to cover* the *expenses of the winding up*, he may apply to the court for an order that the company be dissolved. | s 204 | 4.77 |

| | Insolvency Act 1986 | Insolvency (Scotland) Rules 1986 |
|---|---|---|
| A copy of the order must be forwarded to the *Registrar* within *14 days* of its date. | | |

## COMPLETION OF WINDING UP

| | Insolvency Act 1986 | Insolvency (Scotland) Rules 1986 |
|---|---|---|
| 52. When the *winding up has been completed*, the liquidator must summon a *final general meeting* of creditors to:<br>(a) receive his report of the winding up; and<br>(b) determine whether the liquidator should be released. | s 146 | |
| 53. The liquidator must: | | |
| (i) give *at least 28 days' notice* of the final meeting of creditors to all creditors whose claims have been accepted. | | 4.31 |
| (ii) within *seven days* of the meeting give notice to the court and to the Registrar that the final meeting has been held. A copy of the report laid before the meeting should accompany the notice. | s 205 | 4.77 |
| (iii) unless the liquidation lasted less than one year, the liquidator must also file final Forms 4.5 (Scot) and 4.6 (Scot). | s 192 | 4.11 |
| 54. The Registrar shall, on receipt of the notice mentioned in 53(ii) above, forthwith register it and at the expiry of three months from the date of registration the company shall be dissolved. | s 205(2) | |
| 55. It is considered that the *books and papers* of the company in a court liquidation may be disposed of by resolution of the liquidation committee or, if there is none, as directed by the court. | s 142(1)<br>s 142(5) | 4.54<br>4.55 |
| 56. After the winding up has been completed but before dissolution, the liquidator must send to the Accountant of Court in Edinburgh deposit receipts *(consignation receipts)* for any moneys lodged in an appropriate bank for all unclaimed dividends, unapplied or undistributable balances. | s 193 | |
| 57. The court may, on application of any person who appears to have an interest, defer the dissolution of the company for such period as the court thinks fit. | s 205(5) | |
| 58. If a deferment is granted, the court order in question must be sent to the Registrar of Companies within seven days. | s 205(6) | 4.77 |

# (B)   CREDITORS' VOLUNTARY LIQUIDATION

| | Insolvency Act 1986 | Insolvency (Scotland) Rules 1986 |
|---|---|---|
| *PRELIMINARY* | | |
| 1. The company will call *extraordinary general meeting* (s 369(1)(*b*), Companies Act 1985) with 14 days' notice to Pass an extraordinary resolution (s 378(1), Companies Act 1985) that the company cannot continue business by reason of its liabilities and that it is advisable to wind up. (The quorum for this meeting and all other general meetings, if not otherwise specified in the articles, is two persons present in person or by proxy.) Subject to passing the above resolution, the meeting may pass an ordinary resolution nominating a liquidator. | s 84(1)(c) | |
| 2. The company will also call a *meeting of creditors* with seven days' notice to be summoned for a day not later than the 14th day after the day on which there is to be held the company meeting at which the resolution for voluntary winding up is proposed. (The quorum for this meeting and all other creditors' meetings is one creditor entitled to vote who may be represented by proxy by any person.) | s 98(1)(a) s 98(1)(b) | 7.7 |
| 3. The notice of the creditors' meeting shall state *either*; | s 98(2) | |
| (a) the name and address of a person qualified to act as an insolvency practitioner in relation to the company who during the period before the day on which that meeting is to be held, will furnish creditors free of charge with such information concerning the company as they may reasonably require; or | | |
| (b) a place in the relevant locality where, on the two business days before the meeting day, a list of the names and addresses of the company's creditors will be available for inspection free of charge. | | |
| 4. Notice of the creditors' meeting must be *advertised* in the *Edinburgh Gazette* and in two local newspapers. | s 98(1)(c) | |
| 5. *A form of proxy*: | | 7.14 |
| (a) Must be sent with every notice calling a meeting of the company creditors. | | 7.15 |
| (b) Must not have any name or description of any person inserted in it. | | |
| (c) Must be retained in the Sederunt Book, if used for voting at any meeting. | | 7.17 |
| (d) Can be inspected by the creditors. | | 7.18 |

| | Insolvency Act 1986 | Insolvency (Scotland) Rules 1986 |
|---|---|---|
| 6. The directors must prepare a *statement of affairs* in the prescribed form, cause that statement to be laid before the creditors' meeting under s 98, and appoint one of their number to preside at that meeting. | s 99 | 4.7(2) |
| 7. A *certificate of posting* of the notice must be prepared by the responsible insolvency practitioner, together with a *report of the meeting* – copies of these to be inserted in the Sederunt Book. | | 7.23 <br> 7.13 |
| 8. Payment of initial expenses may be made as an expense of the liquidation. Where such payments are made before the commencement of the winding up, the director presiding at the creditors' meeting shall inform the meeting of their amount and the identity of the persons to whom they were made. | s 98 | 4.9 <br> 4.14A |
| 9. The creditors and the company at their respective meetings may nominate a *liquidator*. The liquidator shall be the person nominated by the creditors, or, where no person is so nominated, the person nominated by the company. Where different persons are nominated, any director, member or creditor may within seven days apply to the court for an order either directing that the person nominated by the company shall be liquidator, solely or jointly, or appointing some other person to be liquidator instead of the person nominated by the creditors. | s 100 | |
| 10. As mentioned in para 2 above, the company meeting can be held up to 14 days before the creditors' meeting. The *powers* of a liquidator nominated by the company in the period before the holding of the creditors' meeting are limited to collecting and protecting the assets. He may dispose of perishable goods or goods which will diminish in value unless they are sold immediately. The powers conferred on a liquidator under s 165 shall not be exercised except with the sanction of the court. | s 98(1)(a) <br><br> s 166(3) | |
| 11. The person who is appointed *liquidator* must give the chairman of the meeting a written statement that he is qualified to act as an insolvency practitioner in relation to the company and that he consents to act as liquidator. The chairman can then issue a *certificate of appointment*, although the appointment of the liquidator is effective from the date of the passing of the resolution for his appointment. | | 4.19(2) |

| | Insolvency Act 1986 | Insolvency (Scotland) Rules 1986 |
|---|---|---|
| 12. A printed copy of the extraordinary resolution passed by the members must be *filed with the Registrar of Companies* within 15 days of being passed, and the liquidator within 14 days must *file with the Registrar* notice of his appointment of Form 600. | s 84(3)<br><br><br><br>s 109(1) | |
| 13. Notice of passing of the extraordinary resolution for winding up must be *advertised in the Edinburgh Gazette* within 14 days and the liquidator must *advertise his appointment in the Edinburgh Gazette*, also within 14 days. | s 85(1)<br><br>s 109(1) | |
| 14. The liquidator must find *caution* based on his estimated value of the company's assets at the date of his appointment, having regard to the estimated value of those assets disclosed in the statement of affairs (SI 1986/1995). | | |
| 15. The liquidator shall give *notice of his appointment* to the creditors within 28 days of his appointment (by newspaper advertisement). | | 4.19.4(b) |
| 16. The liquidator shall, within 28 days of a meeting held under s 98, send to creditors and contributories of the company: | | |
|   (a)  a copy of summary of the statement of affairs; and | | |
|   (b)  a report on the proceedings at the meeting. | | 4.10 |
| 17. The *statement of affairs* referred to in para 6 above shall be sent by the directors to the liquidator when appointed, and the liquidator shall insert a copy of it in the Sederunt Book. | | 4.7(3)<br><br><br>4.7(4) |
| 18.  (i)  The creditors at the meeting held under s 98 or at any subsequent meeting may establish a *liquidation committee* to carry out such functions as are prescribed by the Act. | s 101 | |
|   (ii)  The committee shall consist of at *least three and not more than five* creditors. | | 4.41(1)(a) |
|   (iii)  *Any creditor* is *eligible* to be a member provided *certain criteria* are satisfied. | | 4.41(2)–(6) |
|   (iv)  The *liquidation committee cannot come into being* until the members have *consented to act* and the liquidator has issued a *certificate of constitution*. | | 4.42 |
|   (v)  The liquidator must *send the certificate* to the *Registrar* together with a *notice*. | | |

## DURING LIQUIDATION

## GENERAL

| | | |
|---|---|---|
| 19. The liquidator shall *take possession* of the company's assets, books, etc., and shall make up and maintain an *inventory and valuation* of the assets which he shall retain in the Sederunt Book. | | 4.22 |

| | Insolvency Act 1986 | Insolvency (Scotland) Rules 1986 |
|---|---|---|
| 20. When the company's premises have been vacated, the liquidator should change the situation of the *registered office* to his own address and within 14 days advise the Registrar (s 287(2), Companies Act 1985). | | |
| 21. The liquidator may exercise any of the *powers* contained in Part I of Schedule 4 to the Act with the sanction of the court or the liquidation committee and those contained in Parts II and III of said Schedule with or without such sanction. If the liquidator in pursuance of his powers disposes of any assets to any person associated with the company, notice thereof must be given to the liquidation committee (if any). | s 165 | |
| 22. (i) *Creditors' claims* should be submitted either: | | 4.15 |
|     (a) *at or before* the relevant creditors' meeting or, as the case may be, | | |
|     (b) not later than *eight weeks* before the end of the relevant accounting period. | | |
|   (ii) Claims must be submitted by a *statement of claim* in the prescribed form. | | |
| 23. The expenses of the liquidation have first call on the funds of the company's assets, in the order of priority laid down in the Insolvency (Scotland) Rules 1986. | | 4.66(1)(a)<br>4.67 |
| 24. When the funds permit, the liquidator will pay *dividends* to the creditors in the following order: | s 107 | 4.66(1) |
|   (1) secured creditors from the proceeds of their security, any shortfall being given an ordinary preferential ranking; | | 4.66(6) |
|   (2) preferential creditors; | | s 386 |
|   (3) creditors having a valid floating charge; | | s 175 |
|   (4) ordinary creditors; | | |
|   (5) Interest at official rate on | | |
|     (a) preferential debts *and* | | |
|     (b) ordinary debts; and | | |
|   (6) any postponed debts. | | |
| 25. (i) *Before paying creditors* the liquidator shall adjudicate on every claim in respect of which he intends to pay a dividend in any accounting period. | | 4.16(1)(2) |
|   (ii) The adjudication shall be made and issued not later than four weeks before the end of the period. | | |
|   (iii) The liquidator *shall record in the Sederunt Book* his decision on each claim, specifying: | | |
|     (a) the amount of the claim accepted by him; | | |
|     (b) the category of debt and the value of any security, as decided by him; and | | |

|  | Insolvency Act 1986 | Insolvency (Scotland) Rules 1986 |
|---|---|---|

(c)  his reasons for rejecting any claim.

26. *Appeals* against these adjudications must be submitted to the court within *two weeks*, and the liquidator shall record the sheriff's decision in the Sederunt Book.

27. When paying the creditors, the liquidator may ask for a receipt to be completed and returned to him before or upon payment of the dividend, or he may pay by a cheque which has a form of receipt on the back of it. If he is able to pay all creditors as defined in para 24, any surplus will be distributed to members.

*26-week Accounting Periods*

28. The liquidator shall make up accounts of his intromissions in respect of periods of 26 weeks, the first period commencing with the date of the commencement of the winding up. — 4.68

29. *In any accounting period* the liquidator may: — 4.68

   (i)  pay a dividend to the creditors if there are sufficient funds and he has allowed for future contingencies;

   (ii)  pay any outlays incurred by himself; and — 4.68 / 4.67(1)

   (iii)  pay any class of creditors in full with the sanction of the liquidation committee or the court. — s 165

30. If the liquidator considers it would be *inappropriate to pay* a dividend in any accounting period, he may postpone to the next accounting period with the consent of the liquidation committee or if none the court. — 4.68

31. The liquidator may *accelerate the payment of a dividend* if he wishes and so shorten the relevant accounting period accordingly. — 4.68

32. Within *two weeks* after the end of an accounting period, the liquidator shall submit to the liquidation committee or, if none exists, the court: — 4.32(1) / 4.68

   (i)  his account of intromissions for audit, together with a scheme of division; and

   (ii)  a claim for his remuneration and outlays. — 4.32(1)
Where these papers are submitted to a liquidation committee, copies should be sent to the court.

33. The liquidator *may make an interim claim* to the liquidation committee in respect of his outlays and fees at any time before the end of an accounting period. — 4.32(2)

    The liquidation committee may make an interim determination and, where they do so,

| | Insolvency Act 1986 | Insolvency (Scotland) Rules 1986 |
|---|---|---|
| they shall take into account that interim determination when making their determination at the end of the relevant accounting period. | | |
| 34. All accounts in respect of *legal services* incurred by the liquidator must be submitted to the *Auditor of Court* for taxation before payment can be made, unless the court authorises the liquidator to pay any such account without taxation. | | |
| 35. Within *six weeks after the end of an accounting period*, the liquidation committee, or the court, shall:<br>(i) audit the accounts; and<br>(ii) issue a determination fixing the amount of outlays and fees payable to the liquidator. | | 4.68 |
| 36. The liquidator *shall make the audited accounts*, scheme of division and the determination *available for inspection* by the creditors and the company. | | 4.68 |
| 37. If the liquidator considers the *remuneration* fixed by the liquidation committee to be *insufficient*, he may request that it be increased by *resolution of the creditors*. | | 4.33 |
| 38. If the liquidator is still dissatisfied he may apply to the *court* for an *order increasing the amount* and he must give at least *14 days' notice* of his application to the liquidation committee or if there is no liquidation committee to any creditor(s) as directed by the court. | | 4.34 |
| 39. Any creditor(s) representing at least 25 per cent in value may appeal against the amount of the liquidator's remuneration on the grounds that it is excessive. | | 4.35 |
| 40. The liquidator, the company or any creditor must lodge their appeal against the amount of the liquidator's remuneration within *eight weeks* after the end of an accounting period. | | 4.68 |
| 41. The liquidator should pay the appropriate dividend to the creditors only on the expiry of the appeal period. | | 4.68 |
| 42. The liquidator must *insert the audited accounts, scheme of division* and *determination* of his fees in the *Sederunt Book*. | | 4.68 |
| 43. The liquidator shall report to the creditors within six weeks after the end of each accounting period and will include a summary of the statement of affairs, if appropriate. Alternatively, he may submit such a report to a meeting of creditors held within such period. | | 4.10 |

|  | Insolvency Act 1986 | Insolvency (Scotland) Rules 1986 |
|---|---|---|
| **LIQUIDATION COMMITTEE** | | |
| 44. *It is the duty of the liquidator to report to the members* all matters as appear to be of interest to them, although he can refuse a request for information on certain grounds. | | 4.44 |
| 45. The *liquidation committee shall meet* when and where determined by the liquidator although the first meeting must be called within three months of the liquidator's appointment or the establishment of the committee, whichever is the later. | | 4.45 |
| 46. The *chairman* at any meeting shall be the liquidator or his nominee and the quorum is two members present or represented. | | 4.46<br>4.47<br>4.48 |
| 47. There are certain rules regarding the *resignation, removal or termination of membership* of members of the committee and the filling of any subsequent vacancy. | | 4.49<br>4.50<br>4.51<br>4.52<br>4.53 |
| 48. There are also certain rules regarding voting rights and the passing of resolutions. It should be noted that a copy of every resolution must be retained in the Sederunt Book. | | 4.54<br>4.55 |
| 49. The liquidator shall send a *written report* to each member of the committee at least every six months but not more often than every two months (as directed by the committee). The committee are entitled to payment of reasonable expenses. | | 4.56<br><br><br>4.57 |
| 50. There are strict rules governing dealings by committee members and others. | | 4.58 |
| 51. If *all creditors have been paid in full* with interest, the liquidator issues a *certificate* to this effect and notifies the Registrar of Companies immediately. This certificate has an effect on the composition of the liquidation committee. | s 189 | 4.59 |
| **INFORMATION** | | |
| 52. The liquidator must send a statement of receipts and payments to the Registrar *within 30 days* of the expiration of the first year and at six-monthly intervals thereafter. If the liquidation lasts for less than one year, Forms 4.5 (Scot) and 4.6 (Scot) are not required. | s 192 | 4.11 |
| 53. Within three months of the end of the first year from the date of liquidation and of every succeeding year, the liquidator must call a *general meeting of the company* and a *meeting of the creditors* with 21 days' notice and lay before each of the meetings an account of his acts and dealings and of the conduct of the winding up during the preceding year. (No advertisement is necessary.) | s 105 | 4.13(1)<br>7.2<br>7.3 |

| | Insolvency Act 1986 | Insolvency (Scotland) Rules 1986 |
|---|---|---|
| *FINALISATION* | | |
| *REMOVAL/RELEASE OF LIQUIDATION* | | |
| 54. A liquidator may be removed from office only by an order of the court or by a general meeting of the company summoned specially for that purpose. | s 171(2) | 4.23 4.24 4.25 4.26 |
| 55. A liquidator shall vacate office if he ceases to be qualified to act as an insolvency practitioner in relation to the company. | s 171(4) | |
| 56. A meeting for removal of a liquidator must be convened by the liquidator if requested to do so by not less than one-quarter in value of the creditors. The notice shall draw attention to s 173(2)(a) or (b) with respect to the liquidator's release. | s 171(2) | 4.23 |
| 57. A liquidator may resign on the grounds of: | s 171(5) | 4.28(3) |
| (a) ill health; | | |
| (b) intending to cease to be in practice as an insolvency practitioner; | | |
| (c) conflict of interest or change of personal circumstances which precludes or makes impractical the further discharge by him of the duties of the liquidator. | | |
| 58. A meeting of creditors must be called to receive his resignation. Notice thereof must draw attention to s 173(2)(c) and rule 4.29(4) with respect to the liquidator's release and shall be accompanied by a statement of his intromissions. The liquidator gives notice of his accepted resignation to the Registrar of Companies. | | 4.28(1) 4.28(2) 4.29 |
| 59. Where a final meeting has been held under s 106 (liquidator's report on completion of winding up), the liquidator whose report was considered at the meeting shall vacate office as soon as he has given notice to the Registrar of Companies that the meeting has been held and of the decisions (if any) of the meeting. | s 171(6) | |
| 60. A person who has ceased to be a liquidator shall have his release with effect from the following times: | s 173 | |
| (i) *After Removal by Meeting of Creditors* | | |
| (a) If no resolution against his release, the time at which notice is given to the Registrar of Companies that that person has ceased to hold office. | s 173(2)(a) | 4.25 |
| (b) If resolution against release, the liquidator must apply to the Accountant of Court for his discharge. | s 173(2)(b) | |

| | Insolvency Act 1986 | Insolvency (Scotland) Rules 1986 |
|---|---|---|
| When the Accountant of Court releases the former liquidator he shall issue a certificate of release to the new liquidator who shall send a copy of it to the court and to the Registrar of Companies. | | |
| (ii) *On Resignation* | s 173(2)(c) | 4.29(4) |
|   (a) If no resolution against release, from such date as the meeting convened to consider the resignation may determine. | | |
|   (b) If resolution against release, as outlined in para (i)(b) above. | | |
| (iii) *On Death* | | |
| Notice must be given to the liquidation committee or any member thereof and the Registrar of Companies. | | 4.36 (as amended) |
| (iv) *On Completion of Winding Up* | | |
|   (a) If at final meeting of creditors under s 106 no resolution against release – release from time he vacates office and gives notice to the Registrar of Companies. | | 4.31 |
|   (b) If at final meeting of creditors resolution against release, as outlined in para (i)(b) above. | | |

## COMPLETION OF WINDING UP

| | Insolvency Act 1986 | Insolvency (Scotland) Rules 1986 |
|---|---|---|
| 61. When the winding up has been completed, the liquidator must make up an *account* of the winding up. | s 106(1) | |
| 62. The liquidator must thereupon call a *general meeting of members* and a *meeting of creditors* to lay the account before them. These meetings must be called by advertisement in the *Edinburgh Gazette* and published at least a month before the meetings. (No other advertisement is necessary.)<br><br>These meetings need not be held on the same dates. | s 106(2) | |
| 63. Within one week of the date of the meetings (or of the later one if they are held on separate dates) the liquidator must file *with the Registrar of Companies on Forms 4.26 (Scot) and 4.26 (Scot)* a return of the holding of the meetings or that they were not held because no quorum was present. Unless the liquidation lasted for less than one year, the liquidator must also file final Forms 4.5 (Scot) and 4.6 (Scot). The liquidator vacates office as soon as he has sent the return to the Registrar of Companies. | s 106(3)<br><br>s 192 | 4.11 |

|  | Insolvency Act 1986 | Insolvency (Scotland) Rules 1986 |
|---|---|---|
| 64. When he receives the final account and returns, the Registrar of Companies will register them and at the expiry of three months from the date of registration the company shall be deemed to be *dissolved*. | s 201(2) | |
| 65. After the winding up has been completed but before the dissolution, the liquidator must send to the Accountant of Court in Edinburgh deposit receipts (*consignation receipts*) for any moneys lodged in an appropriate bank in respect of all unclaimed dividends, unapplied balances or undistributable balances. | s 193 | |
| 66. The court may, on application of any person who appears to have an interest, defer the dissolution of the company for such period as the court thinks fit. | s 201(3) | |
| 67. If a deferment is granted, the court order in question must be sent to the Registrar of Companies within seven days. | s 201(4) | |

# Index